Strategic Management Cases

THE SERIES IN MANAGEMENT

CARLAND/CARLAND *Small Business Management: Tools for Success*
CAVALERI/OBLOJ *Management Systems: A Global Perspective*
DAVIS/COSENZA *Business Research for Decision Making,* Third Edition
DUNCAN/GINTER/SWAYNE *Strategic Issues in Health Care Management*
DUNCAN/GINTER/SWAYNE *Strategic Management of Health Care Organizations*
FINLEY *Entrepreneurial Strategies: Text and Cases*
GRIGSBY/STAHL *Strategic Management Cases*
KEMPER/YEHUDAI *Experiencing Operations Management: A Walk-Through*
KIRKPATRICK *Supervision: A Situational Approach*
LANE/DISTEFANO *International Management Behavior,* Second Edition
MENDENHALL/ODDOU *Readings and Cases in International Human Resource Management*
MITCHELL *Human Resource Management: An Economic Approach*
NKOMO/FOTTLER/MCAFEE *Applications in Human Resource Management: Cases, Exercises, and Skill Builders,* Second Edition
PLUNKETT/ATTNER *Introduction to Management,* Fourth Edition
PUFFER *Managerial Insights from Literature*
PUNNETT *Experiencing International Management*
PUNNETT/RICKS *International Business*
ROBERTS/HUNT *Organizational Behavior*
SCARPELLO/LEDVINKA *Personnel/Human Resource Management: Environments and Functions*
STAHL/GRIGSBY *Strategic Management for Decision Making*
STAHL/GRIGSBY *Strategic Management: Formulation and Implementation*
STARLING *The Changing Environment of Business,* Third Edition
STEERS/UNGSON/MOWDAY *Managing Effective Organizations: An Introduction*
TATE/COX/HOY/STEWART/SCARPELLO *Small Business Management and Entrepreneurship*
TOSI *Organizational Behavior and Management: A Contingency Approach*

Strategic Management Cases

DAVID W. GRIGSBY
Clemson University

MICHAEL J. STAHL
University of Tennessee

WADSWORTH PUBLISHING COMPANY
Belmont, California
A Division of Wadsworth, Inc.

Assistant Editor: Marnie Pommett
Production Editor: Catherine D. Griffin
Manufacturing Coordinator: Marcia A. Locke
Interior Designer: Eve Mendelsohn Lehmann
Cover Designer: Catherine D. Griffin
Cover Calligraphy: Amy S. Veaner
Interior Illustrator: Chris Hayden
Typesetter: Pine Tree Composition, Inc.
Cover Printer: John P. Pow Company, Inc.
Printer/Binder: Arcata Graphics/Halliday

 This book is printed on acid-free, recycled paper.

Copyright © 1993 by Wadsworth, Inc. All rights reserved. No part of this book may be reproduced, stored in a retrieval system, or transcribed, in any form or by any means, electronic, mechanical, photocopying, recording, or otherwise, without the prior written permission of the publisher, Wadsworth Publishing Company, Belmont, California 94002.

Printed in the United States of America.

1 2 3 4 5 6 7 8 9 10—97 96 95 94 93

Library of Congress Cataloging-in-Publication Data

Grigsby, David W.
    Strategic management cases / David W. Grigsby, Michael J. Stahl.
      p. cm.
    Includes bibliographical references.
    ISBN 0-534-93134-0
    1. Strategic planning. 2. Decision-making. 3. Industrial management—Case studies. I. Stahl, Michael J. II. Title.
HD30.28.G755   1992
658.4′033—dc20   92-30048
                                                                           CIP

CONTENTS

PREFACE vii

CASE ANALYSIS GUIDE 2

Introduction **2**
Reading and Studying the Case **3**
Doing the Analysis **4**
    Organize the Case Facts **4**   *Start with Financial Analysis* **4**
    Focus Your Analysis **6**   *Make Recommendations* **7**
Class Discussions **8**
Oral Presentations **9**
Written Case Assignments **10**
Doing Additional Research **10**
Working in Teams **12**
Summary **12**
Appendix A: Case Analysis Outline **14**
Appendix B: Resources for Case Research **18**

CASES 38

Strategic Decision Makers

1. Carmike Cinemas, Inc. *Marilyn L. Taylor* **38**
2. Liz Claiborne, Inc. *David W. Grigsby* **54**
3. Pizza Delights *Jay Horne, Christine Perkins, Kim Goates, Peter Asp, Ken Sarris, John Leslie, and James J. Chrisman* **74**
4. The Utah Jazz Arena *Gary McKinnon, Gary Cornia, Robert Parsons, and Dale Wright* **102**
5. The Rise and Fall of Yugo America, Inc. *Carolyn Silliman and Jeffrey S. Harrison* **122**

Corporate-Level Strategy Formulation and Implementation

6. From Airline to Empire: United Airlines Under Richard Ferris *Gary E. Willard* **135**
7. NCNB, Inc. *Frank C. Barnes* **156**
8. Sonoco Products, Inc. *Myra Register, Lisa Scott, Sheryl West, and David W. Grigsby* **181**
9. Eastman Kodak Company: The Sterling Drug Acquisition *David W. Grigsby and Charles G. Carter* **206**

Business-Level Strategy Formulation and Implementation

10. Lincoln Electric Company, 1989 *Arthur D. Sharplin* **226**
11. Carnival Cruise Lines *Barbara-Jean Ross, Chekitan S. Dev, and Kathleen M. Dennison* **251**
12. Toys "R" Us, 1989 *Caron H. St. John* **268**
13. Delta Air Lines, Inc. *Michele Boren, Regina Bruce, Barron Green, Victor Khoo, Sexton Adams, and Adelaide Griffin* **281**
14. Sun Microsystems *William C. House and Walter E. Greene* **300**
15. WordPerfect Faces the Nineties *Charles Boyd* **313**
16. Lands' End, Inc. *Caron H. St. John* **334**
17. Harley-Davidson, Inc. *Scott Draper, A. Scott Dundon, Allen North, Ron Smith, Sexton Adams, and Adelaide Griffin* **352**
18. UNICRE, S. A. and the Credit Card Industry in Portugal *David W. Grigsby and Vitor E. Gonçalves* **378**

Corporate Social Responsibility in Strategic Decisions

19. Yeast West Bakery *Coral R. Snodgrass and Gerald S. Rosenfelder* **405**
20. Polaroid Corporation/Inner City, Inc. *John A. Seeger and Marie Rock* **425**

International Strategic Decisions

21. GM Allison Japan Ltd. *Richard T. Dailey* **444**
22. The Swatch *Arieh A. Ullmann* **462**
23. NEC Corporation's Entry into European Microcomputers *Michael Hergert and Robin Hergert* **483**
24. Maytag Corporation *Peter P. Schoderbek and Satish P. Deshpande* **516**
25. Caterpillar, Inc., in Latin America *Robert P. Vichas and Tomasz Mroczowkski* **536**

APPENDIX: fisCAL SOFTWARE 558

PREFACE

Strategic Management Cases is designed to provide students with the best means available for developing their decision-making skills. This edition contains twenty-five comprehensive, timely cases featuring a wide range of organizations that are undergoing strategic change. Twelve cases are entirely new, and the remaining thirteen were taken from among the best of those in *Strategic Management for Decision Making*. All cases feature actual organizations, with real people and real problems. They range in size from small businesses such as Yeast West Bakery to the industry giants United Airlines and Eastman Kodak. In order to provide a realistic appraisal of situations, the case writers have included a wealth of industry data. All of the cases have been "classroom tested," and most have been critically reviewed by members of the North American Case Research Association. The emphasis is on international strategic decisions: besides a special section containing five international strategy cases, many of the other cases involve important aspects of international competition. The combined result of these features is an appealing casebook that can be used in both undergraduate and graduate strategic management courses. It may be used with the paperback text *Strategic Management: Formulation and Implementation* (1992) by Stahl and Grigsby or with other texts or books of readings.

The cases are arranged in five groups, the first of which focuses on individuals who are strategic decision makers and the processes they use in formulating and implementing strategy. In "*Carmike Cinemas, Inc.*," the first case, extensive conversations with the company's president provide insights into the thinking of key strategists. "*Liz Claiborne, Inc.*" follows the progress of strategic decision making in this well-known fashion apparel company with its glamorous founder. The problems and opportunities involved in a business expansion decision are central to the next case, "*Pizza Delights.*" "*The Utah Jazz Arena*" illustrates the complexity of making strategic decisions when multiple constituencies must be considered. The final case in the first group, "*The Rise and Fall of Yugo America, Inc.*" chronicles one of the most-publicized business failures in recent years.

The second group features cases in corporate-level strategic decisions. Here the companies and the topics are familiar ones, especially to those who follow press accounts of mergers, takeovers, and acquisitions. The United Airlines case deals with that company's controversial diversification strategy. "*NCNB, Inc.*" highlights strategy in the fastest-growing banking firm in the United States. In a less well-known industry, "*Sonoco Products, Inc.*" illustrates the process of corporate adaptation to a changing environment. How a large corporation goes about implementing a major strategic decision is the focus of "*Eastman Kodak Company: The Sterling Drug Acquisition,*" the final case in this group.

The third and largest group of cases features business-level strategic decisions. "*Lincoln Electric Company, 1989,*" a perennial favorite in strategic management courses, appears in a recently updated version of the classic case. "*Carnival Cruise Lines,*" a new case, emphasizes strategic decision making in the fastest-growing segment of the travel industry. Another favorite in strategy courses, "*Toys 'R' Us, 1989*" yields insights into the remarkable strategies that led this firm to industry dominance. In "*Delta Air Lines, Inc.*" students can investigate the effects of deregulation on both the airline industry and one of its leading firms. A pair of new cases, "*Sun Microsystems*" and "*WordPerfect Faces the Nineties,*" provides contrasting perspectives on dealing with the problems associated with rapid growth in high-technology businesses. One of the multiple focuses of "*Lands' End, Inc.*" is strategy formulation in a highly saturated market. "*Harley-Davidson, Inc.*" chronicles the recent turnaround of this almost legendary American company, including its successful quality-enhancement strategy. Strategic response in a deregulated environment is the decision focus in the final case in this section, "*UNICRE, S.A. and the Credit Card Industry in Portugal.*"

Two special cases on social responsibility make up the fourth section. "*Yeast West Bakery*" requires students to make business decisions while taking into account the impact of the owner's values. The dual-focus aspects of profit making and societal response in a larger company are illustrated in "*Polaroid Corporation/Inner City, Inc.*"

Two new cases lead off the last section on international strategic decisions. "*GM Allison Japan Ltd.*" features the problems involved in developing and operating joint ventures abroad, and "*The Swatch*" deals with one company's successful response to structural changes affecting a global industry. The NEC case, which has been a favorite in strategy courses for several years, looks at competition in the European personal computer market as it developed in the 1980s. "*Maytag Corporation,*" another new case, concerns strategic responses to worldwide consolidation in the home appliances industry. The final case, "*Caterpillar, Inc., in Latin America,*" involves strategic decisions in the company's duel with Komatsu, Inc. of Japan for market dominance.

The comprehensive "*Case Analysis Guide*" preceding the cases introduces students to the case method and gives detailed advice on how to prepare for class discussions, oral reports, and written assignments. The guide contains an extensive outline that can serve as a checklist for a strategic audit when you are conducting detailed case analyses. A very comprehensive listing of outside resources is also provided for students and instructors who choose to conduct their own additional research.

To help students prepare financial analysis, sensitivity analysis, and comprehensive industry analysis, a financial software package containing data from eight of the cases and comparative industry statistics is available to accompany the casebook. The software, called *fisCAL,* was developed by the Halcyon Group and is the best financial analysis package available for use in strategic management courses. A guide for using the software is contained in a special appendix following the cases.

A complete instructor's manual also accompanies the casebook. It contains detailed teaching notes for each case arranged in a standardized format. Each teaching note contains a summary of the case; teaching suggestions for alternative ways of using the case; thought-provoking questions that can be used either as discussion starters or for testing; and detailed, step-by-step analysis, including financial analysis. Many of the case notes also contain updates on the companies and the situations featured in the case.

Whether used alone or with an accompanying text such as *Strategic Management: Formulation and Implementation,* we feel this casebook with its accompanying software can provide a very appealing incentive for you to study and develop strategic management skills. We hope that you enjoy using it.

David W. Grigsby
Michael J. Stahl

Strategic Management Cases

Case Analysis Guide

INTRODUCTION

If your strategic management course is like most, the instructor will make extensive use of case analysis. You will study business strategy cases, which are accounts of actual business situations, and be placed in the role of a top-level decision maker. By introducing a variety of situations, the case method provides a wide range of opportunities for you to apply the skills learned in this course and other business courses and to begin building confidence in your decision-making ability.

Although case study may be a new experience for you and therefore confusing at first, you will quickly see that it can increase your understanding of the complex world of strategic decision making and sharpen your analytical skills. Case study will also enhance your knowledge of the strategic conditions in different industries. Although there is no substitute for real-world management experience, case study is "the next best thing to being there."

This case study guide is offered to familiarize you with the expectations of you as a student. It will help guide you through your first cases and will show you how to prepare the analyses that will be required. The cases represent a broad range of strategic decisions, all taken from real life. There are large and small businesses; for-profit and not-for-profit organizations; and companies engaged in manufacturing, service industries, and distribution activities. There are successful organizations as well as organizations that are struggling. In some, the company and the names of managers have been disguised, but many of the organizations are ones that you will readily recognize. The majority deal with recent events, but there are also a few classic business strategy cases.

READING AND STUDYING THE CASE

Because you are expected not only to read cases as they are assigned, but to analyze them and develop sound, reasoned judgments that will lead to recommendations, the case method requires a level of preparation that often goes well beyond that required in a traditional lecture course. It is important, therefore, that you devote plenty of time to studying and analyzing each case.

To get the most out of a case, read it at least two times and, if possible, separate the two readings in time. On the first reading, go through the case rather quickly, without trying to take notes or underline. Read it as you would a magazine article or short story. Get a general idea of the situation the company is in—its industry, its position within the industry, and its competition. Note the date of the latest case information. Treat the tables and financial statements merely as illustrations rather than try to analyze them at this time.

Before your second reading, stop and think about the case. Ask yourself, "What are the central issues?" and "What do I need to try and uncover in my analysis?" All business strategy cases revolve around one or, at most, two or three major problems or decision points. The earlier you can identify these the better, as they will guide your analysis. During your second reading of the case, take notes on the case facts that are important for analysis.

There will undoubtedly be instances when you feel that you do not have all the information you need to make the best decision. The information provided in case reports is often incomplete by design. Just as real-world managers are often called on to make decisions without extensive information, this aspect of the case method is not unlike real experience. One of the most important steps toward becoming an effective strategic decision maker is knowing how to make the most of the limited amounts of information the environment provides.

The time frame for decisions is an important element in any case. That is, you should make decisions based only on information that was available to the managers at the time of the case date, although it may seem a bit artificial at times. You may even be required to ignore some information you may have about the company or its situation. For instance, if you are analyzing a 1986 case, your knowledge of the stock market crash of October 1987 should not affect your handling of the case. Although you are encouraged to do outside research, you should resist the temptation to second-guess the decision makers on the basis of information they could not have had.

Your professor may assign you or other class members the responsibility of updating a case by researching recent information on the company. Later information about the strategies that firms actually adopted and their subsequent outcomes often proves to be an interesting way to complete the study of a case. Appendix B of this guide contains information that can assist you in doing outside research on companies. A company's actual strategy should not be taken as the "right" answer, however, even if it proved to be a very profitable one for the company, as any number of other recommended strategies might also have been successful.

DOING THE ANALYSIS

ORGANIZE THE CASE FACTS

Cases sometimes present a bewildering number of names, titles, dates and other facts that are hard to keep straight. Before proceeding with an in-depth analysis of the case, make sure you have a sufficient grasp of the facts. Sometimes it may be necessary to construct a chronology to help you keep in mind the sequence of significant case events and their relationships. To keep names, organizational titles, and relationships in focus, you may need to sketch a rough organization chart if one is not provided in the case. Once you have an adequate grasp of the case facts and the central issues, you are ready to begin an in-depth analysis.

START WITH FINANCIAL ANALYSIS

"Number crunching" is nearly always the best way to begin a case analysis, as it gives you an objective assessment of the company's performance and can help identify problem areas for further analysis. Key financial ratios must be calculated so that you can get a reading on the company's financial performance and condition. Exhibit 1 provides a review of the most often used financial ratios (in case your ratio analysis skills are a bit rusty). Keep in mind that ratios should be interpreted only in light of the organization's situation, and remember that trends are always important. For that reason, two or more years of financial statements are usually included in the cases so that any trends in the ratios can be discerned. Industry averages with which to compare the key ratios are also helpful; if not contained in the case, these averages are available from a number of reporting services (see Appendix B).

Converting the financial statements to "common-size" ones is also helpful. The balance sheet is common-sized by setting total assets equal to 100 percent and then calculating each balance sheet account as a percentage of total assets. Income statements are common-sized by setting net sales equal to 100 percent and then calculating each item as a percentage of net sales. With common-size statements, relative relationships among the various accounts can readily be seen and trends noted over time. These relationships and trends can indicate other problems to be investigated. Common-size statement information is best used in combination with other information. For example, a steadily increasing cost of goods sold as a percentage of net sales may indicate waste, loss of efficiencies in production, increased raw materials prices that have not been passed on to buyers, or some combination of these factors.

Financial analysis can be one of the most time-consuming parts of your preparation. You can save yourself a lot of time if you do only those analyses

EXHIBIT 1 KEY FINANCIAL RATIOS

RATIO	FORMULA	EXPRESSED AS
PROFITABILITY RATIOS		
Return on investment	$\dfrac{\text{Net income after taxes}}{\text{Total assets}}$	percentage
Return on stockholders equity	$\dfrac{\text{Net income after taxes}}{\text{Total stockholder's equity}}$	percentage
Earnings per share	$\dfrac{\text{NIAT-preferred dividends}}{\text{No. common shares outstanding}}$	dollars
Gross profit margin	$\dfrac{\text{Sales}-\text{CGS}}{\text{Sales}}$	percentage
Operating profit margin	$\dfrac{\text{Net income before taxes and interest}}{\text{Sales}}$	percentage
Net profit margin	$\dfrac{\text{Net income after taxes}}{\text{Sales}}$	percentage
LIQUIDITY RATIOS		
Current ratio	$\dfrac{\text{Current assets}}{\text{Current liabilities}}$	decimal
Quick (acid-test) ratio	$\dfrac{\text{Current assest}-\text{inventories}}{\text{Current liabilities}}$	decimal
Inventories to net working capital	$\dfrac{\text{Inventories}}{\text{Current assets}-\text{current liabilities}}$	decimal
LEVERAGE RATIOS		
Debt to assets	$\dfrac{\text{Total debt}}{\text{Total assets}}$	percentage
Debt to equity	$\dfrac{\text{Total debt}}{\text{Total stockholders equity}}$	percentage
Long-term debt to equity	$\dfrac{\text{Long-term debt}}{\text{Total stockholders equity}}$	percentage
Times-interest earned	$\dfrac{\text{NI before taxes and interest}}{\text{Interest expenses}}$	decimal
Fixed-charge coverage	$\dfrac{\text{NI before taxes and interest} + \text{lease obligations}}{\text{Interest expenses} + \text{lease expenses}}$	decimal

(continued)

EXHIBIT 1 (continued)

RATIO	FORMULA	EXPRESSED AS
ACTIVITY RATIOS		
Total asset turnover	$\dfrac{\text{Sales}}{\text{Total assets}}$	decimal
Fixed asset turnover	$\dfrac{\text{Sales}}{\text{Fixed assets}}$	decimal
Net working capital turnover	$\dfrac{\text{Sales}}{\text{Current assets} - \text{Current liabilities}}$	decimal
Inventory turnover	$\dfrac{\text{Sales}}{\text{Average inventory of finished goods}}$	decimal
Collection period for receivables	$\dfrac{\text{Average accounts receivable}}{\text{Annual credit sales}/365}$	days
INVESTMENT RATIOS		
Price-earnings ratio	$\dfrac{\text{Market price per share}}{\text{EPS}}$	decimal
Dividend payout	$\dfrac{\text{Annual dividends per share}}{\text{EPS}}$	percentage
Common stock dividend yield	$\dfrac{\text{Annual dividends per share}}{\text{Market price per share}}$	percentage

that you need rather than using the same standard analyses for every case. Thus, you need to use your head at least as much as your calculator or computer spreadsheet. The focus should be on developing information to help you understand the company and to provide the basis for recommendations to solve its problems.

FOCUS YOUR ANALYSIS

Effective case analysis must include both an internal analysis of the firm and an external analysis of the firm's operating environment. Internal analysis is usually handled by taking a functional approach, first making sure you understand the organization's top management and its corporate- and business-level objectives and strategies, and then moving on to analyze each of the company's functional-level objectives and strategies. Part II of the Case Analysis Outline (Appendix A) contains a step-by step internal analysis plan.

External analysis can best be accomplished by breaking the environment down into sectors and analyzing the influence of each sector separately. Consider the possible effects of the economy, demographics, and social change. Analyze the regulatory environment, resource availability, and technological change. Above all, do a thorough analysis of the competitive environment. Part III of the Case Analysis Outline (Appendix A) lists some questions to consider in external analysis.

The analysis process can be very time consuming if one tries to analyze every aspect in detail. For that reason, you should let the key issues in each case indicate which aspects of the case you will treat in detail. The Case Analysis Outline (Appendix A) can help you through the analytical process. Keep in mind that it is intended as comprehensive resource rather than a structured checklist. You will probably want to emphasize different aspects of analysis for each individual case, as the focal points in each case are different.

MAKE RECOMMENDATIONS

The end result of your analyses will be your recommendations. These should be based solely on the findings of your analysis and should include supporting evidence for any judgmental elements included. Although real-world business decisions are often subject to intuitive processes, more analytical processes are always preferred unless the decision makers have a great deal of firsthand experience with the type of strategic problems encountered in the case. Therefore, a statement such as "My analysis shows the following..." is always better than "I believe the company should...."

Most professors prefer that you prepare a list of several feasible alternatives to the case problems. This process allows you to compare competing solutions from which you select your recommendations. In drafting the solution, implementation issues should not be ignored, especially financial ones. A recommendation is always strengthened considerably if you can show that the company has the resources to accomplish it and if you present well-laid-out implementation scheme including as much detail as facts allow. If you recommend a strategic change, include a timetable and budget for accomplishing the new strategy, assign specific managers the responsibility for carrying it out, and tell how the company should follow up to make sure the new strategy is successful.

Perhaps one of the hardest adjustments to make to the case method is the realization that there is no such thing as the "right" answer or even the "right" approach. After all the work you put in, there is a natural tendency to wonder, "Did I get it right?" Remember that strategic decision making is not an exact science. Just as two businesses that adopt completely different courses of action while competing in the same markets are often both successful, different approaches and solutions to the same case also are often both "right." (It is exactly that quality that makes strategic management a challenging and interesting field.) Although no single solution or approach is the only "right" one, there are always some decisions that are better than others and some ways to approach a decision situation that are superior to other approaches. As you develop and refine your case analysis skills, you will also increase your ability to identify the conditions under which different approaches and solutions may be successful. The important thing to remember in case analysis is to justify and support your recommendations with thorough analysis.

CLASS DISCUSSIONS

Instructors have a number of ways of handling case discussions in class. These range from structured discussion, in which specific questions about the case are asked and sometimes distributed in advance, to unstructured discussions, in which the students are given some latitude in identifying the important issues in the case and in presenting their analyses and recommendations. As most business strategy courses utilize the unstructured approach, and few students have encountered it before, we discuss it here.

A good case discussion can be a very rewarding class experience for everyone, but its success depends on good preparation by you and the right set of expectations. Keep the following points in mind:

1. Before class, reduce your analysis to two or three pages of notes. Your notes should include your list of the key issues in the case, a SWOT summary (identifying strengths, weaknesses, opportunities, and threats), key financial ratios, a list of two or three feasible alternatives, and your recommendations. Refer to these notes often during the discussion, and add any new ideas that come up.

2. One of the most important things to bring to class with you is an open mind. Once the discussion starts, you will undoubtedly find that there are nearly as many approaches to the case as there are class members. Although there is merit in standing by your convictions, keep in mind that most complicated management problems can best be approached by the refinement process, which requires decision makers to be open to a variety of views.

3. Make the classroom time count by not rehashing case facts. Assume that everyone is familiar with the facts and get right into identifying key issues and problems and analyzing them. Strive to reach the decision-making level of participation (see Exhibit 2).

4. Remember that you cannot test your ideas if you remain silent. In an active class, that may mean that you have to assert yourself to get the floor. Be careful not to equate "air time" with participation, however. Do not dominate the conversation, especially if you have little to add.

5. If a class discussion is going well, you will discover that the professor has done very little of the talking. His or her role in the discussion is to keep the flow of ideas coming, challenge opinions that are offered, insist on reasons behind your statements, and occasionally summarize the analysis.

> **EXHIBIT 2** FOUR LEVELS OF CASE DISCUSSION
>
> FACT SHARING
> The lowest level of discussion. The class simply goes over case facts without really analyzing them. Symptoms of underlying problems are discussed without uncovering the problems themselves.
>
> PROBLEM FINDING
> A step above fact sharing. The class goes through a structured analysis of the company. Strengths, weaknesses, opportunities, and threats are uncovered, and the problems underlying the symptoms are identified.
>
> PROBLEM SOLVING
> The third level of class discussion. Attention is directed to the problem areas, problems are prioritized, and recommended solutions are developed for each problem area.
>
> DECISION MAKING
> The highest level of class discussion. Organizational problems are seen as a whole. Solutions are merged into an overall strategic plan, and implementation considerations are included.

ORAL PRESENTATIONS

Students are sometimes assigned cases to present orally, usually in teams of three or four students. The degree of formality in the presentation is up to the professor, but regardless of the formality, preparation for the presentation and the actual conduct of the case in class will differ markedly from informal class discussion. Thorough preparation will naturally be important, as the entire presentation of issues, analysis, and decision may be up to you and the other members of your team. Here are some points to keep in mind if you are assigned an oral case presentation:

1. Make sure the audience knows the case facts. If the case has not been assigned to the rest of the class to read, the first part of the presentation will have to be devoted to factual material. Although this step is important, keep it brief to allow time for your analysis. Handing out fact sheets is a good way to move this step along quickly.

2. It often helps to identify a role for yourself. The role of outside analyst or consultant is usually preferable to the role of corporate official, as it allows you to speak more objectively.

3. Organization is important, and communicating the organization of your talk early in the presentation is a good idea. Identify the issues early in the presentation so you can focus on them throughout the analysis. Summarize at several points to remind the audience of where you are in the talk.

4. Visual aids can significantly improve a presentation, but they also can be overdone. Prepare a few good charts and graphs to help tell the story, but don't bury the audience in needless detail.

5. Make your recommendations as thorough as you can. Always include financial and staffing plans for the implementation of your recommendations and provide for evaluation and follow-up.

6. Take questions from the floor if allowed. They are a good way to demonstrate your knowledge of the case and depth of thinking. You should set up ground rules for questions at the beginning, however, so you won't be interrupted at unwanted times.

WRITTEN CASE ASSIGNMENTS

A written case analysis may be assigned, either as a structured paper in which you are asked to address specific issues or topics in the case, or as a comprehensive analysis. To prepare a written analysis, you should go through much the same preparation as for class discussions, but here your analysis would probably need to be more thorough.

The written format of your paper will vary according to the particular case and the wishes of your professor. If the assignment is a structured one, you may want to address the questions one by one and present your recommendations. If the unstructured approach is taken, you may need some suggestions as to how you should organize the contents of the paper. The outline in Exhibit 3 is offered as an example that applies to most business strategy cases in your textbook.

DOING ADDITIONAL RESEARCH

Case analysis sometimes requires research to find additional information about the firm or its industry in order to recommend a course of action. You may, for example, want to update the information in a case that is several years old or to investigate more thoroughly the firm's environment or competition. You may also use the library to develop your own business strategy case from secondary sources.

Fortunately, most college and university libraries and public libraries are well equipped to provide the necessary resources. The companies themselves also can be important source of current information, and many of them will willingly provide you with copies of their quarterly and annual reports as well as other information. Company sources should not be relied on exclusively, however, as information that is unfavorable to the company is unlikely to be obtained that way. Whatever your approach, Appendix B contains a listing of the most frequently used resources for case research.

> **EXHIBIT 3   SUGGESTED OUTLINE FOR WRITTEN CASES**
>
> I. Introduction. Give a brief statement of the purpose of the report and how the report is organized. You might also include some basic facts about the company as a way of introduction.
>
> II. Internal Analysis.
>   A. Present situation. Discuss the firm's present strategy. Describe its markets, products or services; its competitive orientation; and the scope of its activities. What is being attempted, and how? How well is it working?
>   B. Financial resources. Describe the financial condition of the company and assess its ability to meet the demands of its environment and to provide for future growth.
>   C. Strengths and weaknesses. Discuss the company's strong and weak points as uncovered in your analysis of the various functional areas.
>
> III. External Analysis.
>   A. General environment. Describe any feature of the economic, technological, regulatory, physical, and social environments that is relevant to the organization's future.
>   B. Operating environment. Describe the competitive environment. Who are the competitors? What are their strengths and weaknesses?
>   C. Opportunities and threats. Summarize all of the relevant issues uncovered by your external analysis.
>
> IV. Key Decisions. Identify the main points at issue in the case. What are the problems and decisions the company faces? What should be the focus of the recommendations?
>
> V. Alternatives. Describe each of the possible strategies the firm could adopt. Discuss each one and include its strong and weak points.
>
> VI. Recommended Decisions. Tell what you think the company should do. What should its strategy be? Justify your choice on the basis of analysis. Discuss implementation, evaluation, and follow-up. Include time estimates for implementation and financial staffing plans where appropriate.
>
> VII. Appendices, Tables, and Graphs.

Keep in mind that sometimes the cases use disguised company names and are therefore impossible to research directly. Also, most privately held companies do not make it a practice to share financial information with the public, as publicly held companies are required to do. This limitation can make it difficult to obtain the latest information on some companies, although you can usually obtain information about their industries. The major financial reporting services often report estimates of the sales, profits, and key ratios for private companies, and their estimates are considered quite accurate.

It is generally true that the larger the company is, the more information you will find. Most of the Fortune 500-size companies discussed in the cases are the subjects of many news articles, industry analyses, and trade reports and therefore make excellent subjects for secondary case research.

WORKING IN TEAMS

Just as strategic decisions in real businesses are often the products of teams of managers working together, professors frequently assign class members to teams for the preparation of case reports in order to provide a more realistic experience in the decision-making process. Teamwork may be a new experience for you and the other members of your team. The following points may make your team experience a more successful and satisfying one:

1. Determine the relative strengths and skills of team members and divide the work to take advantage of them. Breaking the analysis down into distinctive parts will avoid duplication of effort.

2. Meet often and work as a team. Remember that your performance on the assignment depends on each other. Make sure that meetings are scheduled when all members can attend and that meetings are planned ahead of time.

3. Use consensus processes and make decisions jointly. Make sure the final product is consistent throughout. Teams often make the mistake of presenting a final paper or presentation that is simply an accumulation of parts instead of a single analysis with a unified set of recommendations.

SUMMARY

This chapter presents a general framework for analyzing strategic management cases and developing case reports. These guidelines may seem long to you now, but as you become more familiar with the process, much of it will become automatic. The purpose is to get you started on the road to formulating effective strategic decisions and communicating the results of your analyses.

Case analysis, like any other valuable skill, takes time to develop and requires concentration and hard work. The rewards are plentiful, however. In addition, case analysis is very personal. Every successful decision maker eventually adopts a style that is his or her own. For that reason, you will probably find it necessary to modify the framework presented in this chapter to fit your own work habits and decision style. We suggest that you follow this guide closely until you feel comfortable with the process, and then use it only occasionally to review your own procedure and analyses.

APPENDIX A

Case Analysis Outline

I. The Present Situation
  A. Mission, objectives, strategies, policies
    1. Mission: What business(es) is the company in? Is the mission relatively stable or undergoing change?
    2. Objectives: What is the company trying to accomplish? Are corporate-level, business-level, and functional objectives consistent with the corporate mission and with each other? Are objectives written down, or must they be inferred from performance?
    3. Strategies: How is the company attempting to achieve its objectives? Are the strategies consistent with the mission and objectives? Are strategies coordinated, or do they appear to be developed piecemeal?
    4. Policies: Does the corporation have well-developed guidelines for carrying out its strategies? Do they seem to enhance or hinder goal accomplishment?
  B. Corporate performance
    1. Financial performance: Is the company's financial performance adequate? What is its net profit margin, its return on investment, and earnings per share? What are the trends in these overall measures of performance?
    2. Goals: How well is the organization meeting its objectives? Does present performance match expectations?
    3. Competitive stance: Is the company remaining competitive in its industry? Is it maintaining or enhancing its market share?

II. Internal Analysis—Strengths and Weaknesses
  A. Organizational structure and corporate culture
    1. Type: What type of organizational structure does the firm have: simple, functional, divisional, or matrix?

2. Centralization: Is decision making centralized at top management levels, or decentralized throughout the organization?
3. Culture: Is there a well-defined culture? Is the culture market oriented, product oriented, or technology oriented?
4. Consistency: Are the company's structure and culture consistent with the firm's objectives and strategies?

B. Top management and board of directors
1. The CEO: How would you rate the CEO in terms of knowledge, skills, and abilities? Is his/her overall management style autocratic or participative?
2. The board: Is the board of directors directly involved in the strategic management process, or is it a "rubber-stamp" board?
3. Top managers: How would you rate the overall capability of the top management team? Is there an adequate plan for executive succession and training for top management positions?

C. Financial management
1. Functional objectives and strategies: Does the company have clearly stated financial objectives and strategies? Are they consistent with the company's overall objectives?
2. Profitability: How is the company performing in terms of profitability ratios? How does this performance compare with past performance and industry averages? Does a common-sized income statement reveal any discrepancies in the components of net income?
3. Liquidity and cash management: How is the firm performing in terms of its liquidity ratios? Are cash-flow problems indicated? How do the ratios compare with past performance and industry averages?
4. Leverage and capital management: Is the firm's leverage appropriate, as evidenced by its leverage ratios? Is the amount of leverage in keeping with the industry and the company's strategies for expansion?
5. Asset management: Are inventories, fixed assets, and other resources being effectively managed as indicated by the activity ratios? How do these ratios compare with the firm's past performance and other firms in the industry?
6. Financial planning and control: What individuals are involved in the firm's financial planning? How often are budgets prepared? How closely are spending decisions monitored, and who has the authority to control financial resources? How sophisticated are the financial and asset management systems of the firm?

D. Operations management
1. Technical core: Does the technical core of the organization center around production, service, or merchandising?
2. Capacity: Is the productive capacity of the firm adequate for present needs and for future growth in operations?

3. Quality: Is the quality of the product or service adequate and in keeping with the company's goals? Are quality assurance systems in place and functioning properly?
4. Efficiency: Is operating efficiency adequate? Can it be improved?

E. Marketing management
1. Product: What is the company's present mix of products and/or services? At what stages in their product life cycles are they? Who are the firm's target customers? Is there a readily identifiable product-mission philosophy?
2. Price: Are prices competitive and in keeping with product quality and the target market? Is price determination demand based, competitive, or on a cost-plus basis?
3. Place: Is the distribution system adequate? Does the company maintain its own sales team or depend on outside firms? Is it an integrated part of the company or separately controlled? Are relations with the sales force and distributors good? Do compensation systems provide the right amount of incentives?
4. Promotion: How does the company advertise and promote its products or services? Is the promotion effort effective? Is promotion designed in-house or by outside firms?
5. Marketing information systems: How does the company identify new markets or target groups? Is the marketing department involved in the development of new products? How does the company exchange information with the distribution system?

F. Human resources management
1. Human resources planning: Is there an effective human resources planning effort? Are personnel requirements included in strategy formulation and facilities planning?
2. Obtaining personnel: Are adequate processes in place for obtaining qualified personnel? How are personnel recruited and selected?
3. Retaining and improving human resources: Are training programs effective? Are performance evaluation and improvement managed effectively? Are grievances handled well?
4. Compensation: Is the compensation system effective and fair? Is pay generally competitive or above competitive levels? Are fringe benefits high or low for the industry? Does the firm have a profit-sharing plan?
5. Labor relations: If the company is unionized, are relations with labor organizations congenial or combative?

G. Research and development
1. Organization: Is there one centralized R&D department, or is R&D decentralized?
2. Level of R&D effort: What percentage of the firm's resources are devoted to the R&D effort? How does this compare with competitors?

3. Control: How is the R&D effort controlled? Where in the organization is policy established for R&D?
    H. Management information systems
        1. Is a management information system in use at all levels—operational, middle management, and top management?
        2. Is the system adequate to meet information needs at each level?
        3. Does the organization use a centralized MIS or independent decentralized systems for various departments and functions?
        4. Is the MIS cost effective?
        5. Does the strategic management process make use of a decision support system (DSS) to aid in strategic analysis?

III. External Analysis—Opportunities and Threats
    A. Economic environment. What is forecast for the industry, and how are economic events likely to affect this firm? How would an inflationary period or a recession affect product demand?
    B. Technological environment. What innovations are likely to occur that will affect either products and services or production processes? Is the rate of change in technology increasing or slowing?
    C. Regulatory environment. Are there any present or expected government and/or industry regulations that present either threats or opportunities? Are there ongoing efforts to monitor or actively participate in the regulatory process?
    D. Physical environment. Can we expect any significant depletion of needed resources? Will there be any changes in the physical surroundings of the organization that might affect the accomplishment of its goals or present opportunities?
    E. Social/demographic environment. Are any important demographic changes in customers, suppliers, or the labor pool expected? Are tastes and preferences changing in a way that might affect this firm?
    F. Competitive environment. Who are the firm's competitors? What are their market shares? How effective are they? How likely is the entrance of new competition? Are there close substitutes for the company's products or services?

APPENDIX B

Resources for Case Research

■ COMPUTERIZED DATA BASES

CD/Corporate: U.S. Public Companies [formerly DATEXT]
Cambridge, Mass.: Lotus Development Corporation. Updated quarterly.
A menu-driven CD-ROM data base of financial and business information on nearly 12,000 U.S. publicly held companies, 50 industry groups, all Standard Industrial Classification (SIC) business groups, and top corporate executives. The information, which is primarily from the Disclosure II data base (Disclosure, Inc.), provides financial data and textual information extracted from Securities and Exchange Commission (SEC) filings of public companies. Material from six other sources provides selected Wall Street security analysts reports, abstracts and citations to journal articles, biographical information, and stock transaction information.

Corporate and Industry Research Reports (CIRR)
Wellesley Hills, Mass.: Silver Platter Information. Updated monthly.
A CD-ROM data base indexing research reports and periodicals published by Wall Street analysts and economists from major security and investment firms. Information can be searched by company, industry, or keyword terms.

InfoTrac
Belmont, Calif.: Information Access Company.
InfoTrac is a microcomputer-based index on CD-ROM. Information included in the InfoTrac data base comprises a general, comprehensive, research-oriented data source. It provides general interest topics, business information, and technical data as well as current data from the *New York Times* and the *Wall Street Journal*. InfoTrac can be searched by subject, personal name, corporate name, geographic place name, title or book, and other classifications. Book and movie reviews are also included.

Adapted from Siler, F. B., and M. L. Moon, *Reference Guide No. 3: Information on Companies and Industries* **(Clemson, S.C.: Clemson University Libraries, 1990).**

HANDBOOKS AND GUIDES

Business Researchers Handbook, 2nd ed.
Washington, D.C.: Washington Researchers. 1983.
A how-to guide to working with information requesters, getting the best research results, and putting together cogent research reports. Appendices include a listing of federal centers, a list of toll-free hotlines to call for business information, a listing of government offices that offer free market studies, a list of who has what in terms of company information, and federal sources of information on private and public companies.

Competitor Intelligence: How to Get It, How to Use It
By Leonard M. Fuld. New York: Wiley. 1985.
Provides a basic understanding of intelligence-gathering techniques and practices. It also provides an extensive listing of basic sources of intelligence such as federal, state, and local sources; corporate intelligence in print; sources for specific industries; statistical sources, directories, and associations; data bases for corporate intelligence; and sources of foreign intelligence.

Company Information: A Model Investigation, 2nd ed.
By Wendy Law-Yone. Washington, D.C.: Washington Researchers. 1983.
This model investigation of a closely held private company reveals the depth of information that can be uncovered in company research. It describes methodology, techniques, and sources for finding facts about a company's structure, marketing, finances, philosophies, and labor situation.

Finding Company Intelligence: A Case Study
By Howard John Endean, Jr. Washington, D.C.: Washington Researchers. 1984.
Provides a candid account of the complex task of piecing together a company profile. MCI Airsignal, a wholly owned subsidiary of MCI Communications Corporation, is used as a model for this investigation of a business enterprise. Biographical references are included.

GENERAL INFORMATION SOURCES

Business Information Sources, rev. ed.
By Lorna M. Daniells. Berkeley: University of California Press. 1985.
A basic, annotated guide to important reference sources such as indexes, directories, financial manuals, and statistical publications as well as selected books, periodicals, and reference works pertaining to specific companies and industries.

Encyclopedia of Business Information Sources, 8th rev. ed.
Detroit: Gale Research. 1990.
Lists books, periodicals, organizations, bibliographies, data bases, and other

sources of information on a wide variety of business-related topics. A good source to use for information on specific industries.

How to Find Information About Companies: The Corporate Intelligence Sourcebook, 7th ed.
Lorna M. Daniells, Elizabeth M. Williams, and Beth Gibber, eds. Washington, D.C.: Washington Researchers. 1988.
A guide to facts and figures about public and private companies, domestic or foreign. It also provides a list of annotated sources such as directories, investment services, indexes, and abstracts.

Business Information: How to Find It. How to Use It, 2nd ed.
By Michael R. Lavin. Phoenix: Oryx Press. 1991.
This text is organized into four parts. Part I introduces concepts important to business and discusses basic forms of published information, major sources of unpublished information, and basic finding tools. Part II provides sources of information on companies. Part III provides sources of information such as demographic data, statistics and industries, and general economic indicators. Part IV provides information on specific areas of business such as marketing information, business law sources, and tax law publications. Title and subject indexes are included.

Business Firms Master Index
Jennifer Mossman and Donna Wood, ed. Detroit: Gale Research. 1985.
A guide to sources of information about companies in the United States and Canada and foreign firms with offices in the U.S. Indexes specialized and general sources such as directories, dictionaries, encyclopedias, buying guides, and special issues of leading magazines.

Small Business Sourcebook
Detroit: Gale Research. Published biennially and updated between editions by supplements.
Part I provides profiles of 100 popular small businesses, describing sources and services for each particular business. Included are information sources such as associations, educational programs, reference works, sources of supply, statistical sources, trade periodicals, and consultants. Part II identifies general types of organizations and publications of interest to small business owners such as government agencies, associations, and venture capital firms.

Guide to U.S. Government Publications
J. L. Andriot, ed. McLean, Va.: Documents Index. Published annually with updating supplements issued quarterly.
An annotated guide to the important series of periodicals currently being published by various U.S. government agencies. Agency and title indexes are included. This is an excellent source for serial publications published by the Department of Commerce.

Source of State Information on Corporations
Washington, D.C.: Washington Researchers. 1984.
Describes documents that are available through nineteen state offices within all fifty states. Documents available from the state offices include financial statements, environmental impact studies, uniform commercial code documents, and reports of inspections and investigations of businesses.

DIRECTORIES

U.S. BUSINESSES

Million Dollar Directory
New York: Dun & Bradstreeet, Marketing Services Division. Published annually.
Lists businesses whose net worth is $500,000 or more. This source is composed of four volumes, one of which is a master index for all volumes containing an alphabetical listing of businesses, businesses listed geographically, and businesses grouped by industry classification. For each form it gives officers and directors, line of business, Standard Industrial Classification (SIC) codes, approximate sales, number of employees, stock exchange abbreviation, stock ticker symbol, division names and functions, principal bank, accounting firm, and other information.

Standard & Poor's Register of Corporations, Directors, and Executives
New York: Standard & Poor's. Published annually and includes supplements for U.S. and Canadian corporations and executives.
This register covers more than 37,000 corporations and over 405,000 corporate executives in all areas of U.S. business and industry. Volume I is an alphabetical listing of corporations and includes information such as principal directors and personnel, SIC codes, address and telephone number, sales volume, and number of employees for each company. Volume II contains biographical data. Volume III provides the four-digit codes for over 900 industries, groups companies by their SIC codes, and arranges companies geographically by state and city.

The Facts on File Directory of Major Public Corporations
Stanley R. Greenfield, ed. New York: Facts on File. Updated annually.
Contains key statistical and personnel data on 6,000 American public corporations. Includes the following information for each corporation: name, address, telephone number, SIC code, number of employees, corporate officers, selected financial information, and more. The following indexes are provided: directors by company, a geographical list of corporations, corporations by primary four-digit SIC code, and an alphabetical listing of all officers and directors.

Everybody's Business: An Almanac, the Irreverent Guide to Corporate America
Milton Moskowitz, Michael Katz, and Robert Levering, eds. San Francisco: Harper & Row. 1980.
A profile of about 317 large companies, including such information as address, history and background, sales, profits, number of employees, stock performance, and consumer brands.

Directory of American Research and Technology
Jaques Cattell Press, ed. New York: Bowker. Updated annually.
Alphabetical listing of public and private businesses in the United States performing research and development activities. This source includes 6,040 parent organizations with the 4,951 subsidiaries. Information given for each company includes name, address, telephone number, telex numbers, cable address, fields of research and development, and more. Includes a geographical, personnel, and subject classification index.

Directory of American Firms Operating in Foreign Countries
New York: Simon & Schuster. Updated annually.
Volume I lists over 4,000 American corporations controlling more than 16,000 foreign business enterprises. Gives name, address, officer in charge, products, services, and number of employees. Volumes II and III list businesses by country of operation, giving address, products, and home office in the U.S.

CORPORATE AFFILIATIONS

Directory of Corporate Affiliations
Skokie, Ill. National Register Publishing. Published annually with supplements issued as *Corporate Action*.
Section I is a cross-reference index for all subsidiaries, divisions, and affiliates. Section II lists over 4,000 major American parent companies, giving line of business; approximate sales; number of employees; ticker symbol; top officers; and subsidiaries, divisions, or affiliates. Includes a geographic and SIC index.

America's Corporate Families
Parsippany, N.J.: Dun's Marketing Services. Published annually. Also known as *The Billion Dollar Directory*.
Contains information on more than 8,000 U.S. parent companies and their 44,000 domestic divisions and subsidiaries. An essential tool for tracking nationwide corporate linkage and ownership. Companies are listed alphabetically, by ultimate parent, geographically, and by industry classification. A cross-reference of divisions and subsidiaries is included.

America's Corporate Families and International Affiliates
Parsippany, N.J.: Dun's Marketing Services. Published annually.
Section I lists companies alphabetically by U.S. ultimate parent and their Canadian and other foreign subsidiaries, alphabetically by Canadian ultimate parent and their U.S. subsidiaries, and alphabetically by foreign ultimate parent and their U.S. subsidiaries. Section II lists multinational businesses geo-

graphically. Section III lists multinational businesses by industry SIC. A subsidiary–to–ultimate parent cross-reference is provided.

INTERNATIONAL BUSINESSES

Principal International Businesses
New York: Dun & Bradstreet. Published annually. Subtitled "The World Marketing Directory."
Contains detailed data on 55,000 leading firms in 133 countries. Includes name, address, cable or telex number, sales volume, number of employees, SIC number, description of activities, name of chief executive, and more. The businesses are arranged alphabetically, geographically, and by industry classification.

The China Directory of Industry and Commerce and Economic Annual
New York: Van Nostrand Reinhold.
Lists 10,000 Chinese industrial and commercial enterprises, industry by industry, giving their name, address, major products and business lines, and other information. Also included is an economic annual providing information on trade with China; the general economic situation; the economic situations of municipalities, provinces, and autonomous regions; economic laws and regulations; and a chronicle of major events in China from 1978 to 1982.

Europe's 15,000 Largest Companies
London: Europe's Largest Companies.
Published annually.
This source pinpoints the profit makers and money losers; the largest companies by country and by industry; the largest banks, insurance companies by country and by industry; the largest banks, insurance companies, and advertising companies; and hotels and restaurants.

Canadian Trade Index
Toronto: Canadian Manufacturers' Association. Published annually.
A comprehensive directory listing over 13,000 Canadian manufacturing firms. The firms are listed alphabetically with address, telephone number, branch and sales offices, senior operating executive, parent and subsidiary companies, products, brand names, export contacts, Telex/TWX, and more. Also lists head offices and plants alphabetically by municipality and province and lists companies alphabetically by 10,000 product classifications.

The French Company Handbook
Paris: International Business Development, published with the *International Herald Tribune.*
A blue-chip guide for evaluating French companies. Gives key company profiles of French companies, industry evaluations, history and structure of the Paris Stock Market, and other information.

Japan Trade Directory
Tokyo: Japan External Trade Organization. Also known as *Nihon Boeki Shinkokai.* Updated periodically.

Provides information on about 2,200 Japanese companies and 10,000 products and services. Part I, Products and Services, contains alphabetical export and import indexes to companies listed in Part II. Part II, Prefectures and Companies, gives business and tourist information on each prefecture, including main products, crafts, industries, and tourists attractions, in an attractive color layout. In addition, detailed information is provided on each company operating within the prefecture. Part II also contains a listing of trade and industrial associations, an alphabetical company index, and a trade name index. Part III, Advertising, contains additional information on products and companies, along with photographs or illustrations of featured products.

How to Find Information About Japanese Companies and Industries
Washington, D.C. Washington Researchers. 1984.
Describes sources of information such as international organizations; Japanese government agencies; U.S. federal and state organizations in Japan; private sector organizations such as banks, accounting firms, and consultants that maintain offices in Japan; and sources of published information.

Directory of Foreign Manufacturers in the United States, 4th ed.
By Jeffrey S. Arpan and David Ricks. Atlanta: Georgia State University, College of Business Administration, Business Publications Division. 1990.
Contains a list of foreign manufacturers in the United States, giving the parent company, product, and SIC code. Includes the following indexes: U.S. companies by state location, parent companies by name, parent companies by country, and products by Standard Industrial Classification.

MINORITY BUSINESSES

National Directory of Minority and Women-Owned Business Firms
Oak Brook, Ill. Business Research Services. Published annually and supplemented by *Update*.
Lists 30,000 minority-owned business firms and 10,000 women-owned business firms. Each business listing is grouped first by SIC code and business description and then by geographic area.

MERCHANTS AND MANUFACTURERS

Thomas Register of American Manufacturers and Thomas Register Catalog File
New York: Thomas Publishing. Published annually with some volumes accompanied by supplements entitled "Important Addenda."
A comprehensive directory of American manufacturing firms. Volumes 1–12 list over 115,000 U.S. manufacturers by specific product or service. Volumes 13–14 list the companies alphabetically, giving address, branch offices, subsidiaries, production asset classification, and principal offers. Volumes 15–21 are "Catalogs and Companies."

Kelly's Manufacturers and Merchants Directory
Kingston upon Thames (U.K.): Kelly's Directories. Published annually.
Merchants, manufacturers, wholesalers, and firms are listed by trade and pro-

fession, brand and trade name, and alphabetically in this world directory. Other sections include Products and Services Showcase and International Exporters and Services.

Brandnames: Who Owns What
By Diane Waxer Frankenstein (in consultation with George Frankenstein). New York: Facts on File. 1986.
A guide to the corporation that ultimately owns each product. Divided into four sections: Section 1 is an alphabetical list of brand names arranged by product category. Section 2 is an alphabetical list of consumer companies giving a brief history, a description of all consumer brands, address, telephone number, chief officer, and more. Section 3 is an alphabetical list giving brand names, of the largest foreign consumer companies selling in the U.S. Section 4 is an index by company and brand name.

BUSINESS ASSOCIATIONS AND ORGANIZATIONS

Encyclopedia of Associations
Detroit: Gale Research. Published annually in four volumes.
Volumes I and II contain a listing of over 25,000 national and international associations arranged by broad classification. Gives the following information for each association: the name of the chief officer, a brief statement of activities, number of members, names of publications, and more. Volume III is a Names and Key Word index, and Volume IV is a Geographic and Executive index.

Business Organizations, Agencies and Publications Directory
Detroit: Gale Research. (Continues *Business Organizations and Agencies Directory.*) Updated annually.
A guide to trade, business, and commercial organizations, government agencies, stock exchanges, labor unions, chambers of commerce, diplomatic representation, trade and convention centers, trade fairs, publishers, data banks and computerized services, educational institutions, business libraries and information centers, and research centers.

National Directory of Addresses and Telephone Numbers
New York: Bantam Books. Updated annually.
Contains a listing of 150,000 hard-to-find business names, addresses, and telephone numbers. Includes special sections on accounting, advertising, banks, law firms, travel, and other categories and a classified listing of private and public corporations. All entries are listed alphabetically and by category.

The Directory of Directories
Detroit: Information Enterprises, distributed by Gale Research. Published biennially.
An annotated guide to business and industrial directories, professional and scientific rosters, and other lists and guides of various kinds.

BIOGRAPHICAL

Reference Book of Corporate Management
New York: Dun & Bradstreet. Published annually.
Contains biographical data on 200,00 principal officers and directors of more than 13,000 leading U.S. companies. Entries included the following data: name and title, year of birth, marital status, education, military service, and career information.

The Corporate 1000: A Directory of Who Runs the Top 1000 U.S. Corporations
Washington, D.C.: The Washington Monitor.
A guide to the men and women who direct and manage America's largest corporations. The individual companies are listed alphabetically with a brief business description and an approximation of sales or assets. Includes a name index, a company index, an index of companies by industry classification, and a geographical index.

Who's Who in America
Chicago: Marquis Who's in America. Published as part of *Who's Who in American History*. Published biennially.
Presents biographical data on prominent living Americans, including the most important business executives.

INDUSTRY INFORMATION

INDUSTRY INFORMATION SOURCES

Standard Industrial Classification Manual
Washington, D.C.: Office of Management and Budget. Available from the U.S. Government Printing Office. Some volumes accompanied by supplements.
The SIC manual is a guide to one of the most extensive classification systems in use in the United States. It divides U.S. industries by type of activity and assigns an industry code number that is determined by the product or service rendered. The entire field of economic activity (agriculture, forestry, construction, manufacturing, wholesale and retail trade, finance real estate, and so on) is covered. Classifies to a maximum of four digits. An alphabetical index is included.

Standard & Poor's Industry Surveys
New York: Standard & Poor's. Published quarterly.
Provides economic and investment analyses of 65 major industries divided into 34 surveys. Operating and financial data is given for leading companies (approximately 1,500) in each industry, allowing for comparison. For each survey a basic analysis giving an in-depth description of the industry's performance and forecasting short- and long-term prospects for sales and earnings is published yearly. Three "Current Analyses," which report on late developments and estimate results for the period immediately ahead, are also published annually.

INDUSTRY INFORMATION

Moody's Investors Industry Review
New York: Moody's Investors Service. Published biweekly. Also known as *Moody's Investors Fact Sheets Industry Review.*
Provides a ranked list of the leading companies in over 140 industry groups according to 12 key financial, operating, and investment criteria. Includes comparative financial statistics such as stock price range and earnings per share for the 5 or so leaders. About 4,000 companies are included in all.

U.S. Industrial Outlook
Washington, D.C.: Business and Defense Services Administration. Available from the U.S. Government Printing Office. Published annually.
Gives information on recent trends and outlook for about five years in over 200 individual industries. The short narratives with statistics usually contain discussions of changes in supply and demand for each industry, developments in domestic and overseas markets, price changes, employment trends, capital investment, and other measures.

Current Industrial Reports
Washington, D.C.: U.S. Department of Commerce, Bureau of the Census. Available from the U.S. Government Printing Office. Published monthly.
Gives current statistics on commodity production and shipments for approximately 5,000 products accounting for more than one-third of all U.S. manufacturing. The series includes monthly, quarterly, and semiquarterly reports. Publication schedules vary for individual industries. All monthly and quarterly series include annual summaries.

INDUSTRY FINANCIAL STATISTICS

Industry Norms and Key Business Ratios
New York: Dun & Bradstreet Credit Services. Subseries of *Dun's Financial Profiles.* Published annually.
Contains financial ratios for 125 retailing, wholesaling, manufacturing, and construction lines of business.

RMA Annual Statement Studies
Philadelphia: Robert Morris Associates. (Continues *Annual Statement Studies.*)
Gives financial and operating ratios for about 300 lines of business including manufacturers, wholesalers, retailers, services, and contractors. Contains six parts: Parts 1–4 cover balance sheet and profit and loss composites, with selected ratios, all by company size and groups; Part 5 contains additional profit and loss data; and Part 6 contains a finance industry supplement for small loan and sales finance ratios.

Almanac of Business and Industrial Financial Ratios
Englewood Cliffs, N.J.: Prentice-Hall. Published annually.
Gives financial and operating ratios for about 160 industries, including banks and financial industries as well as manufacturing, wholesaling, and retailing industries.

Quarterly Financial Report for Manufacturing, Mining, and Trade Corporations.
Washington, D.C.: U.S. Department of Commerce, Bureau of the Census. Available from the U.S. Government Printing Office.
Gives estimated statements of income and retained earnings, balance sheets, and related financial and operating ratios for all manufacturing, mining, and trade corporations. The statistical data are classified by industry and by asset size.

SPECIAL ISSUES GUIDES FOR INDUSTRY TRADE JOURNALS

Guides to Special Issues and Indexes of Periodicals, 3rd ed.
Miriam Uhlan, ed. New York: Special Libraries Association. 1985.
Designed to facilitate rapid location of specialized data published in consumer, trade, and technical periodicals. Also provides a classified listing of periodicals and a subject index of special issues. It gives details on over 1,200 periodicals that publish special features or indexes on a regular basis.

Special Issues Index: Specialized Contents on Business, Industrial, and Consumer Journals
Compiled by Robert Sicignano and Doris Prichard. Westport, Conn.: Greenwood Press. 1982.
An alphabetical list of over 1,300 periodicals, giving for each the names of the special issues (and dates) in four categories: buyer's guides/directories, statistical summaries, convention and show reports, and review/preview issues. A subject index is included.

Guide to Industry Special Issues.
Cambridge, Mass.: Ballinger Publishing. Published annually. Also known as *Harfax Guide to Industry Special Issues.*
Lists special issues and regular features of trade, business, and economic journals. The articles identified by this guide all contain marketing and financial statistics or directory information on 65 industries. Entries include articles showing market shares of particular products; production statistics for, or financial analysis of an industry; and lists of products or companies.

CORPORATE FINANCIAL INFORMATION

CORPORATE ANNUAL REPORTS AND 10-K REPORTS

Perhaps the most commonly cited source of information about a company is the annual report to stockholders. The annual report contains two basic types of information: an explanation of the company's operations during the prior year and developments that may affect operations in succeeding years and financial reports, usually in the four basic forms of income statement, balance sheet, statement of retained earnings, and statement of change in financial position.

Similar information is filed annually in 10-K reports to the Securities and

Exchange Commission. Submitted in standard form by all corporations, the 10-K report includes a narrative description of the business, management decisions and analysis, financial statements, legal proceedings, and several other categories of information.

Annual reports are readily available from the issuing corporation. Many annual and 10-K reports are available through subscription services such as Q-FILE, a microfiche collection from Q-DATA Corporation, St. Petersburg, Florida. Q-FILE provides annual reports, 10K reports, and proxy statements since 1983 for companies listed on the New York Stock Exchange.

Company Profile Resources
New York, N.Y.: R. R. Bowker.
This source consists of a printed catalog and company profiles on microfiche. It provides profiles of over 1,200 publicly owned corporations, private companies, government agencies, and educational institutions. The profiles contain directory information such as name of company, address, city and state, zip code, telephone number, industry code, date founded, number of employees, subsidiaries or parentage, sales and assets, date of fiscal year ended, and inclusion in the Fortune 500 list of major U.S. corporations. Indexes to the printed catalog include employer, industry, and geographic guide. The documents on microfiche contain information such as the annual report, the company's overview, product description, research activities, 10K annual report, 10Q quarterly report, career opportunity information, benefits, and a research analyst report.

Directory of Companies Required to File Annual Reports with the Securities and Exchange Commission
Washington, D.C.: U.S. Securities and Exchange Commission. Available from the U.S. Government Printing Office. Published annually.
Contains a listing of companies required to file annual reports under the Securities Act of 1934. Includes companies with securities listed on national securities exchanges as well as companies with securities traded over the counter. Companies are listed alphabetically and by industry group.

MOODY'S INVESTOR SERVICE

Moody's publishes a series of seven manuals that collectively provide information on more than 20,000 domestic and foreign corporations and over 15,000 municipal governments and government entities. Information includes company histories, financial performance, industry norms and trends, and comparative statistics. All seven Moody's manuals, which are listed below, are published annually and are kept up to date by frequent new reports.

Banking and Finance Manual
Industrial Manual
International Manual
Municipal Government Manual
OTC Industrial Manual

Public Utility Manual
Transportation Manual

In addition, Moody's publishes surveys and reviews that are issued frequently and on a regular basis:
Bond Review
Bond Survey
Dividend Record
Handbook of Common Stock
Investors Industry Review

CORPORATE/BUSINESS RANKINGS

Dun's Business Rankings
Parsippany, N.J.: Dun's Marketing Services. Published annually.
Ranks 7,500 top U.S. public and privately owned businesses by sales volume and by employee size within state and industry category. Separate sections rank public and private companies individually by number of employees and by sales. Other useful features include a numeric and alphabetical SIC code index; a stock ticker symbol cross-reference; a division cross-reference (alphabetical index); and Selected Business Executives, listed by function.

Ward's Business Directory of Largest U.S. Companies
Belmont, Calif.: Information Access Co. Published annually.
This directory is divided into three sections. In Section A, Part 1 ranks 8,000 public companies by sales within SIC industry classification and displays up to 30 fields of financial data taken from annual reports and 10-K reports. Part 2 ranks public and private companies according to sales volume within SIC industry classifications. Section B lists public and private companies in zip code order by states and cities. Section C lists companies in alphabetical order. A special feature includes "top 1,000" listings in several categories: most profitable U.S. corporations, publicly held companies ranked by sales volume, privately held companies ranked by sales volume, and others.

Ward's Business Directory of Major U.S. Private Companies
Belmont, Calif.: Information Access Co. Published annually.
Lists major U.S. private companies with sales ranging from $500,000 to $11 million per year. Section A ranks private companies according to annual sales within SIC industry classifications. Section B lists major U.S. private companies in zip code order by states and cities. Section C identifies companies alphabetically by company name. Section M is a master index of 100,000 companies listed in all three volumes of *Ward's Business Directory*. Special features include listings of U.S. companies with sales of $10 million, companies with 200–500 employees analysis of private companies by SIC industries, and analysis of private companies by state.

The 101 Best-Performing Companies in America
By Ronald N. Paul and James W. Taylor. Chicago: Probus Publishing. 1986.
Ranks the 101 best-performing companies by sales volume, labor productivity, capital productivity, number of employees, growth in stockholder equity, year-end stock price, and longevity. Also profiles the 101 companies, giving a brief business description, officers, and financial data for each.

Dow Jones–Irwin Business and Investment Almanac
Homewood, Ill.: Dow Jones–Irwin. Published annually.
Includes a section entitled Largest Companies, which provides rankings for U.S. and international industrial and service companies.

What's What in American Business: Facts and Figures on the Biggest and the Best
By George Kurian. Chicago: Probus Publishing. 1986.
Provides a comprehensive ranking of companies and industries in numerous categories.

The Almanac of American Employers: A Guide to America's 500 Most Successful Large Corporations
By Jack W. Plunkett. Chicago: Contemporary Books. 1985.
Companies from all parts of the United States and from all industry segments are profiled and ranked by salaries, benefits, financial stability, and advancement opportunities. Alphabetical, geographical, and industry indexes are included.

The 100 Best Companies to Work For in America
By Robert Levering, Milton Moskowitz, and Michael Katz. Reading, Mass. Addison-Wesley. 1984.
100 companies are rated in the following areas: pay, benefits, job security, chance to move up, and ambience. Also provides information on work environment, number of employees, headquarters, and location of headquarters and main employment centers for each company.

CORPORATE/BUSINESS PERFORMANCE STATISTICS

Value Line Investment Survey
New York: A. Bernhard. Published weekly.
Analyzes and reports on about 1,700 stocks in 80 industries. The statistics, charts, and brief explanatory text are reviewed and updated industry by industry on a rotating basis every thirteen weeks. Data includes a ten-year history on 23 key investment factors plus future estimates for the next three to five years. Quarterly sales, earnings, dividends, Value Line ratings, reviews of late developments, and future prospects also are reported. This service includes a weekly letter called "Selection & Opinion," which gives views on business, economic outlook, advice on investment policy, Value Line's stock price averages, and other information.

NEWSPAPERS AND NEWSPAPER INDEXES

National Newspaper Index
Belmont, Calif.: Information Access Company. Available on microfile.
Lists articles from the *New York Times,* the *Wall Street Journal,* the *Christian Science Monitor,* the *Los Angeles Times,* and the *Washington Post* from 1984 to the present.

Wall Street Journal Index
Wooster, Ohio: Newspaper Industry Center, MicroPhoto Division, Bell & Howell. Published monthly.
A monthly index, cumulated yearly, listing all articles published in the *Wall Street Journal.* Articles are organized by subject and then listed chronologically.

The Wall Street Journal
New York: Dow Jones. Published daily except Saturday and Sunday.
The leading U.S. daily financial newspaper, indispensable for business people. It includes business and financial news, numerous informative articles, company news and digest of earnings, commodity prices, stock market price quotations, P/E ratios, and sales for the NYSE, AMEX, OTC, CBOE, and so on. Dow Jones, Value Line, Standard & Poor's, and other averages are given as well.

Barron's National Business and Financial Weekly
Chicopee, Mass.: Dow Jones & Co.
Excellent articles on prospects for industries and individual companies, new regulations, and other business and financial topics of interest to investors. Includes weekly stock and bond prices for the NYSE, AMEX, OTC, CBOE and for mutual funds. Quotes current Dow Jones averages and other market indicators, basic economic and financial indicators, foreign exchange rates, and more.

Journal of Commerce and Commercial
New York: Journal of Commerce and Commercial Bulletin. Published daily, except Saturday and Sunday.
Contains general business and industrial news, but is especially important for its coverage of commodities, commerce, and shipping.

INDEXES AND ABSTRACTS

Predicast's F & S Index: United States
Cleveland, Ohio: Predicasts. Formerly *F & S Index of Corporations & Industries.* Published weekly with monthly, quarterly, and annual cumulations.
Best source for periodical information on specific companies or specific industries. Indexes the *Wall Street Journal* and the financial pages from the *New York Times.* Each issue has two sections: citations arranged alphabetically by company name and a section arranged numerically by SIC code number.

Business Periodicals Index
New York: H. W. Wilson Co. Published monthly with a cumulative annual edition.
A cumulative subject index to periodicals in the fields of accounting, advertising, banking and finance, general business, insurance, labor and management, marketing and purchasing, office management, public administration, taxation, and others. Entries include personal names and companies.

Magazine Index
Belmont, Calif.: Information Access Company. Distributed on microfilm.
Computer-produced cumulative indexing (May 1983 to the present) of more than 400 magazines covering a wide variety of subject fields including business, economics, and related topics. Also includes product reviews and book reviews.

Index to U.S. Government Periodicals
Chicago: Infordata International. Issued quarterly; fourth-quarter edition is cumulative for the year.
Indexes by author and subject articles published in over 170 periodicals published by the federal government. A good source for information on national and international business and economic conditions.

Monthly Catalog of U.S. Government Publications
Washington, D.C.: Superintendent of Documents, U.S. Government Printing Office. With semiannual and annual indexes.
Provides "official" access to U.S. government documents. The format has varied in the past several years, but usually has indexes by author, title, and subject. Indexes provide short titles and accession number. With accession number, user locates full descriptions of documents and SuDoc numbers. A good source for access to publications of the Department of Commerce.

Congressional Information Service Index (CIS)
Washington, D.C.: Congressional Information Service. Issued monthly, cumulating quarterly.
A comprehensive subject index and abstract to the working papers of Congress, consisting of committee hearings, reports, and prints as well as publications of joint committees and subcommittees, executive documents, and special publications. Good source for tracing legislation pertaining to business and industry.

SELECTED JOURNALS AND PERIODICALS

Business and Society Review
New York: Warren, Gorhan & Lamont. Published quarterly.
Contains articles covering a wide range of topics on the role of business in a free society. The Company Performance Roundup in each issue briefly reviews notable achievements or failures of specific companies in areas of public

concern. An annual list of African-American corporate directors is included in the fall issue.

Business Week
New York: McGraw-Hill. Published weekly.
An excellent source for information on the business outlook and economic developments as well as information on specific companies and industries. Special features include Corporate Scoreboard (quarterly—third issue in March, May, August, and November), Bank Scoreboard (annual—mid-April issue), International Scoreboard (annual—mid-July issue), and Investment Outlook Scoreboard (annual—last December issue).

Dun's Business Month
New York: Dun & Bradstreet Publications. Formerly *Dun's Review.* Published monthly.
Contains short, readable articles on a wide range of topics of interest to business persons, including management, company news, money and markets, communications, industries, and more. Special features include an annual article on the five "best-managed companies" (December issue) and a list of current job offerings (November issue).

Economist
London: The Economist Newspaper. Published weekly.
Contains information on world business and finance, world politics, and current affairs. Also gives state of the economy for various countries and stock market indexes for major exchanges.

Forbes
New York: Forbes. Published biweekly.
Special features include Special Report on International Business, consisting of ranked lists of the 100 largest foreign investments, U.S. multinationals, and foreign companies (July, first issue); Earnings Forecast for the Forbes 500 Companies (November, last issue); and the Annual Forbes 400, with brief data on the richest Americans (mid-September issue).

Fortune
Chicago: Time-Life, Inc. Published biweekly.
Excellent source for information on U.S. and international companies, economic and financial trends, industries, new products, government regulations, and other news. Special features include First 500 Largest Industrial Corporations (May, first issue); Second Largest 500 Industrial Commercial Banks, Life Insurance Companies, Diversified-Financial, Retailing, Transportation and Utility Companies (July, second issue).

Harvard Business Review
Boston: Harvard University, Graduate School of Business Administration. Published biweekly.
One of the most outstanding professional management journals, with practical articles by recognized authorities on all aspects of general management

policy. Topics of special interest include business policy, ethics for executives, executive compensation, human relations, marketing, planning and strategy, and mergers and acquisitions.

Journal of Business Strategy
Boston: Warren, Gorham & Lamont. Published quarterly.
Contains scholarly, in-depth articles on both theory and application of corporate strategy. The articles focus on such topics as acquisitions, competition, market share, and other areas of interest in the field of strategic management.

Journal of Small Business Management
Morgantown, W.V.: International Council for Small Business. Formerly *JSB. Journal of Small Business.* Published quarterly.
Each issue contains about eight articles on a special theme such as financial management, computerization, or small business and society of interest to members of the International Council for Small Business. Also includes book reviews, a Resources section on the theme topic, and small business news notes.

Mergers and Acquisitions
Philadelphia: Information for Industry. Publication frequency varies.
Contains articles on the state of the art in merger, acquisition, and divestiture methodology. Also contains a roster of U.S. mergers and acquisitions, joint ventures, and cooperation agreements in each issue. It includes reports on corporate sell-offs, a Washington update, information on the world scene, and other business news.

Nation's Business
Washington, D.C.: Chamber of Commerce of the United States. Published monthly.
Publishes the Economic Outlook each January forecasting markets and business. Contains popular articles on business, economics, finance, politics, government activity, and so on. Best features include interviews with business and government officials.

Strategic Management Journal
New York: Wiley. Published bimonthly.
Publishes articles on all aspects of strategic management theory and practice. Topics covered include strategic resource allocation, organization structure, leadership, entrepreneurship and organization purpose and processes, and strategic decision processes.

ECONOMIC AND BUSINESS STATISTICS

Statistical Abstract of the United States
Washington, D.C.: U.S. Department of Commerce, Bureau of the Census. Available from the U.S. Government Printing Office.

The most comprehensive compilation of industrial, social, political, and economic statistics of the United States. This source is divided into subject sections, each of which is preceded by a brief summary giving an explanation of terms used, major source, and origin of data used. Most of the tables are on an annual basis with data for preceding years included for historical comparisons. Numerous specialized supplements are also published (for example *State and Metropolitan Area Data Book*).

Handbook of Basic Economic Statistics
Washington, D.C.: Bureau of Economic Statistics. Issued monthly.
A compilation of current and historical statistics condensed from federal government data on American industry, commerce, labor, and agriculture. More than 1,800 statistical series are included, with some data going as far back as 1913 or to the first year when the statistics were published. Cumulates monthly with the previous year appearing in the January issue.

American Statistics Index (ASI)
Washington, D.C.: Congressional Information Service. Published annually.
A comprehensive, descriptive guide and index to the statistics published by all government agencies, congressional committees, and statistics-producing programs. Each issue is composed of two parts: The Index section provides access by detailed subjects and names, by categories, by titles, and by report numbers; the Abstract section is arranged by issuing agency and gives full descriptions of statistics in each publication, including time period covered, geographical breakdown, and other indicators.

Business Statistics
Washington, D.C.: U.S. Department of Commerce, Bureau of Economic Analysis. Available from the U.S. Government Printing Office. Published biennially.
A supplement to the monthly *Survey of Current Business* providing a historical record of approximately 2,500 statistical series appearing currently in the S-pages of the *Survey*. Tables give annual data beginning with 1947, quarterly beginning with 1966, and monthly beginning with 1973.

Survey of Current Business
Washington, D.C.: U.S. Department of Commerce, Bureau of Economic Analysis. Available from the U.S. Government Printing Office. Published monthly.
A comprehensive statistical summary of national income and product account of the United States, including national income by industry, personal consumption expenditures by major type, government expenditures by type of function, foreign transactions, savings and investment, income and employment by industry, and more. Statistics usually cover the past four years. A supplement, *Business Statistics,* is issued biennially.

Federal Reserve Bulletin
Washington, D.C.: Board of Governors of the Federal Reserve System. Published monthly.
Presents current articles on economics, money and banking, policy, and other

"official" statements issued by the U.S. Board of Governors of the Federal Reserve System. The Financial and Business Statistics section, the second half of each issue, is composed of current U.S. banking and monetary statistics.

Economic Indicators
Washington, D.C.: U.S. Government Printing Office. Available from the Superintendent of Documents. Prepared for the Joint Economic Committee by the Council of Economic Advisers.

Gives the state of the economy and the business outlook. Presents statistical tables and charts for basic U.S. economic indicators such as total output, income, and spending; employment, unemployment, and wages; production and business activity; and currency, credit, security markets, and federal finance.

CASE 1

CARMIKE CINEMAS, INC.　　　　　　　MARILYN L. TAYLOR

Mike Patrick, president of Carmike Cinemas, Inc., put the September 1986 month-end reports in his drawer. He glanced at the pile of notes he had handwritten as he went through the reports. He would ask his secretary, Jo, to distribute them to various company managers. For the most part, the notes asked for the reasons behind specific expenditures in September or gave directions regarding expense reduction.

In half an hour Mike planned to join Carl Patrick, his father, chairman of Carmike. The father and son team had purchased Carmike, then named Martin Theatres, in 1982. At the time of the purchase Martin was the seventh largest U.S. theatre circuit and had been a Fuqua Industries Inc. subsidiary for over 12 years. Fuqua was a large diversified company. The equity in Carmike was held entirely by Carmike, Inc., a private Georgia company owned by the Patrick family and a New York investment company.

Mike knew his father would spend some time on the issue of taking the company public. There were a number of issues to be considered before making the decision. Jay Jordan and others at the investment company wanted to withdraw all or a major part of their investment. His own family would likely be able to reduce their investment in Carmike by offering some of their stock in a secondary issue. However, the Patrick family owned 51% of Carmike's stock and Mike felt strongly that he wanted to be clearly in charge of the company. Mike wondered how the broader investment community would view the various strategic and operational moves undertaken at Carmike over the previous four years. He thought briefly of the acquisition of the video movie chain. An infusion of cash and reduction of debt would position Carmike to take advantage of other potential acquisitions on a timely basis. Mike also realized that resiliency was important as the company faced numerous challenges including difficult industry conditions and continuing capital require-

---

Source: **Prepared by Professor Marilyn L. Taylor, University of Kansas, as a basis for classroom discussion. The research for the case was partially supported by the University of Kansas School of Business Research Fund provided by the Fourth National Bank and Trust Company, Wichita, Kansas.** © **Marilyn L. Taylor, 1989.**

ments. However, going public entailed some costs including potentially more scrutiny by shareholders, public disclosure of company moves, and the costs of required reports and public relations with shareholders, the investment community, and the general public.

Whether to go public was a dilemma. He began to jot some notes under the heading "Pros and Cons of Going Public in Fall, 1986."

HISTORY OF THE COMPANY

Carmike Theatres was originally founded as the Martin Theatres circuit in 1912. Mr. C. L. Patrick, the company's chairman of the board, joined Martin Theatres in 1945 and became the general manager and director in 1948. Fuqua Industries, Inc. purchased the Martin family business holdings including Martin Theatres in 1969. Mr. Patrick served as president of Fuqua from 1970 to 1978 and as vice chairman of the board of directors of Fuqua from 1978 to 1982.

During the 13 years that Martin was a part of Fuqua the subsidiary had been a cash generator for its parent company. Fuqua sold a number of the Martin properties. In 1981 Fuqua completed the sale of three TV stations which had come with the original purchase. Only the theatre circuit remained.

Mike strongly felt that the executives at Martin had largely kept the theatre chain in a holding pattern during its time as a Fuqua subsidiary. The treasurer, for example, had been promoted because he was "sort of in the right place at the right time ... when the previous treasurer, a brilliant man," had a stroke in 1969. Further, Mike explained that when Carl Patrick moved to Atlanta in 1970 as president of the parent company Fuqua, Ron Baldwin as next Martin president was "good in real estate but very poor in accounting."

The purchase price for Martin Theatres was $25M. Financing arrangements for purchasing Martin Theatres were very favorable. The total investment by the Patrick family was less than $250,000. However, the purchase of the theatres was highly leveraged (see financial statements in Exhibit 1). Early efforts were directed toward improving the company's cash flow in order to reduce the debt. At the same time the company had significant capital improvement requirements. To make the venture viable, the Patricks undertook a number of changes in operations which are described in the ensuing sections of this case. Success was by no means assured, as Mike Patrick explained:

> When we bought Martin, Martin was going downhill. It looked bad. And I want you to know that it looked pretty bad for us for a while. I mean it really did. For a while there we were asking ourselves, "Why are we in this mess?" Not only were we leveraged 100%, but we realized that we had to spend somewhere in the neighborhood of $25M more dollars to renew the company.

At the time of Carmike's acquisition of Martin Theatres, the circuit had 265 screens (excluding 26 drive-in theatre screens) located in 128 theatres.

EXHIBIT 1 CARMIKE CINEMAS, INC.: FINANCIAL STATEMENTS 1982–1986

	FISCAL YEARS ENDED				
	March 25, 1982	March 31, 1983	March 29, 1984	March 28, 1985	March 27, 1986
INCOME STATEMENT DATA					
Revenues					
Admissions	$33,622	$40,077	$43,778	$49,040	$42,828
Concessions and other	13,595	15,490	16,886	19,917	18,150
	47,217	55,567	60,664	68,957	60,978
Costs and expenses					
Cost of operations (exclusive of concession merchandise)	36,436	39,981	44,760	50,267	45,902
Cost of concession merchandise	2,695	2,703	3,117	3,566	3,004
General and administrative	2,522	2,878	3,008	2,702	2,760
Depreciation and amortization	2,348	1,964	2,868	3,140	3,385
	44,001	47,526	53,753	59,675	55,051
Operating income	3,216	8,041	6,911	9,282	5,927
Interest expense	380	2,569	2,703	2,337	2,018
Income before income taxes	2,836	5,472	4,208	6,945	3,909
Income taxes	1,323	2,702	1,615	3,054	1,745
Net income	$ 1,513	$ 2,770	$ 2,593	$ 3,891	$ 2,164
Earnings per common share	—	$ .65	$ .61	$ .92	$ .51
Weighted average common shares outstanding	—	4,200	4,200	4,200	4,200
BALANCE SHEET DATA (at end of period)					
Cash and cash equivalents	$(1,317)	$ 433	$ 767	$ 770	$ 786
Total assets	34,742	27,754	35,324	34,953	40,665
Total long-term debt	3,656	18,853	22,125	16,969	18,843
Redeemable preferred stock	—	405	405	405	405
Common shareholders' equity	27,752	2,829	5,382	9,233	11,357

Carmike had acquired or constructed an additional 215 screens and closed or disposed of 44 screens since 1982.

MIKE PATRICK'S BACKGROUND

Mike Patrick had worked in Martin Theatres first as a high school student in Columbus, Georgia, later in Atlanta as a student at Georgia State University, and still later back in Columbus as he finished his studies in economics at

Columbus College. He explained these time periods in his life and how he became acquainted with the company:

> Movie theatres was the only business in which I wanted really to work ... it's a fun business. If you are in construction, no one cares about your business. But if you tell someone that you are in the theater business, then everybody has seen a movie. Everyone has something they want to talk about. So it's an entertaining industry. Plus when I got into it, I was in the night end of it. I wasn't into administrative. So I got captured, as I called it. If you have never worked at night, then you don't understand. I really went to work at 8 a.m. and got off at 10 a.m. and then went back at 2 p.m. and got off at 11 p.m. at night. So your whole group of friends is a total flip flop. You have nighttime friends. Before you know it, you are trapped into this life. All your friends work at night. So your job becomes a little more important to you because that's where you spend all your time. Working in a theater ... is a lot of fun. It really is, especially when you are 19 and you get to handle the cash. A theatre is a cash business.
>
> My father was president of Martin. In 1970 he became president of Fuqua and moved to Atlanta. My father wanted to sell the house in Columbus and my mother did not want to. I was very homesick for Columbus.... So I said, "I will go to Columbus College and I will live in the house." I moved back here in the summer of 1970 and worked in the accounting department because I wanted to understand the reports, why I filled out all these forms, and where they went. I learned then that the treasurer of the accounting department did not understand the paper flow at all.

The Patrick family and a limited number of investors acquired Martin Theatres in April 1982 in a leveraged buy-out for $20M in cash and a 10% note in the principal amount of $5M. Mike Patrick became president of Carmike Theatres, as the new company was called. He explained the advantage of working so long in the company.

> I had done every job in this company except that of Marion Jones, our attorney. But my brother is an attorney, so I have someone in the family to talk to if I have a question. No one can put one over on me.... I've fired them too, and I want to tell you something—I do my own firing ... and firing a man who is incompetent when he doesn't know it is hard. He breaks down because he thinks he's good. When I first became president there was a member of my family who had to go. The other management noticed that.

POST-BUYOUT—STREAMLINING THE ORGANIZATION

In considering the purchase of Martin, Mike Patrick had described the firm to his father as "fat." Mike described what he did after purchase of the firm:

> It appeared that each layer of management got rid of their responsibilities to the next echelon down. For example, I could not figure out what the president did.... I kept looking at senior management trying to figure out what they did. I sort of took an approach like you call zero budgeting. Instead of saying my budget was $40,000 last year and I need 10% more this year, I required that each individual justify everything he did. For example, there is now only

one person in our financial department. The young man in there makes less than the guy that had the job as vice president of finance three years ago, and the current guy does not have a subordinate. The advertising department went from a senior level vice president level to a clerk. You are talking about the difference between $80K and a $19K salary.

When we got hold of the company, we let go the president, the financial vice president, and the senior vice president. At the same time the film procurement people retired, because they were over 65. So I have streamlined the organization tremendously. When we got Martin, Martin had 2,100 employees. Since then we bought a circuit called Video out in Oklahoma. They had 900 employees. Today I have 1,600 employees. Let me double check that number. As of October 31, I had 1,687 and the year before I had 1,607. So I actually have 80 more employees than I had last year. But when I got the company, it had 2,100 and the other company had 900.

Of the employees approximately 65% were paid minimum wage. Another 9% were paid sub-minimum wage. About 8% of the employees were in a managerial capacity and the company was totally non-union. Employee relationships were generally good. Initially, however, there were difficulties. Mike Patrick recalled the initial time period.

Management was not well disciplined when we came into Martin. I had to almost totally clean house: I eliminated all of top management but it took about six months to get second-level management to where it felt secure and at the same time develop a more aggressive attitude. I call it a predator attitude. But that first year we had some great hits, such as "E.T." We did so well that first year breaking all previous records so that the management team, even though it was new, became really confident, maybe too confident. Today they don't believe we can lose. Here's a list of the directors and key employees (see Exhibit 2).

The company also implemented improved technology in order to trim the number of employees. Mike Patrick explained what happened in one city when he wanted to replace the projectionists with totally automated projec-

EXHIBIT 2   CARMIKE CINEMAS, INC.: BACKGROUNDS OF DIRECTORS, OFFICERS AND KEY EMPLOYEES

C. L. Patrick (61), who has served as chairman of the board of directors of the company since April 1982, joined the company in 1945, became its general manager in 1948, and served as president of the company from 1969 to 1970. He served as president of Fuqua from 1970 to 1978, and as vice chairman of the board of directors of Fuqua from 1978 to 1982. Mr. Patrick is a director of Columbus Bank & Trust Company and Burnham Service Corporation.

Michael W. Patrick (36) has served as president of the company since October 1981 and as a director of the company since April 1982. He joined the company in 1970 and served in a number of operational and film booking and buying capacities prior to becoming president.

EXHIBIT 2 (continued)

Carl L. Patrick, Jr. (39) has served as a director of the company since April 1982. He was the director of taxes for the Atlanta, Georgia, office of Arthur Young & Co. from October 1984 to September 1986, and is currently self-employed. Previously, he was a certified public accountant with Arthur Andersen & Co. from 1976 to October 1984.

John W. Jordan, II (38) has been a director of the company since April 1982. He is a co-founder and managing partner of The Jordan Company, which was founded in 1982, and a managing partner of Jordan/Zalaznick Capital Company. From 1973 until 1982, he was vice president at Carl Marks & Company, a New York investment banking company. Mr. Jordan is a director of Bench Craft, Inc. and Leucadia National Corporation, as well as the companies in which The Jordan Company holds investments. Mr. Jordan is a director and executive officer of a privately held company which in November 1985 filed for protection under Chapter 11 of the Federal Bankruptcy Code.

Carl E. Sanders (60) has been a director of the company since April 1982. He is engaged in the private practice of law as chief partner of Troutman, Sanders, Lockerman & Ashmore, an Atlanta, Georgia, law firm. Mr. Sanders is a director and chairman of the board of First Georgia Bank and a director of First Railroad & Banking Company of Georgia, Fuqua Industries, Inc., Advanced Telecommunications, Inc., and Healthdyne, Inc. and a former governor of Georgia.

David W. Zalaznick (32) has served as a director of the company since April 1982. He is a co-founder and general partner of The Jordan Company, and a managing partner of Jordan/Zalaznick Capital Company. From 1978 to 1980, he worked as an investment banker with Merrill Lynch White Weld Capital Markets Group, and from 1980 until the formation of The Jordan Company in 1982, Mr. Zalaznick was a vice president of Carl Marks & Company, a New York investment banking company. Mr. Zalaznick is a director of Bench Craft, Inc. as well as the companies in which The Jordan Company holds investments. He is a director and executive officer of a privately held company which in November 1985 filed for protection under Chapter 11 of the Federal Bankruptcy Code.

John O. Barwick, III (36) joined the company as controller in July 1977 and was elected treasurer in August 1981. In August 1982 he became vice president–finance of the company. Prior to joining the company, Mr. Barwick was an accountant with the accounting firm of Ernst & Whinney from 1973 to 1977.

Anthony J. Rhead (45) joined the company in June 1981 as manager of the film office in Charlotte, North Carolina. Since July 1983, Mr. Rhead has been vice president–film of the company. Prior to joining the company he worked as a film booker for Plitt Theatres from 1973 to 1981.

Lloyd E. Riddish (58) has been employed by the company since 1948. He served as a district manager from 1971 to 1982 and as eastern division manager from 1982 to 1984, when he was elected to his present position as vice president–General Manager.

Marion Nelson Jones (39) joined the company as its general counsel in December 1984 and was elected secretary of the company in March 1985. Prior to joining the company, Mr. Jones was a partner in the law firm of Evert & Jones in Columbus, Georgia, from 1979 to 1984.

tion booths. He consulted with the company attorney regarding action the projectionists could take in retaliation:

> I called our attorney in and I asked him "What is the worst that could happen?" The attorney said, "You might have to reinstate the projectionists and pay them the back pay." I said, "You mean there is no million dollar fine?" He replied "No, you just got to worry about reinstatement and back pay." He went on to say, "Well, why are you going to get rid of the projectionists?" I said, "There is automated projectionist equipment for showing movies that will work very similar to an eight-track player. If we convert the theatres, we won't need projectionists." And he said, "Well, you can do it."
>
> However, the city had a code which said to be a projectionist you must take a test from the city electrical board to be certified. That law was put in about 1913 because back in the old days, they didn't have light bulbs. A projector then used two carbon arcs and it was a safety issue because back then film was made out of something that burned. That was before my time that film burned like that. Often they had fires in the lamp house. Now we have Zenith bulbs. The projectionists hadn't gone and gotten their certification from the electrical board for years. But the rule was on the books. So I figured the only problem we had was the city. As soon as we fired the projectionists, they went to the Council. They complained that the managers were doing the projectionist job without certification from the electrical board. The police raided my theater. I sued the City of Nashville.... In the meantime we sent an engineer up from Columbus and started teaching all our managers how to pass the electrical board test. As they began to pass the board, the rule became a moot question.

Martin had already leased and installed all the needed equipment except an automatic lens turn. The cost of $15,000 per projector was not justified when it took only a few seconds to change the lens. The new equipment eliminated the position of projectionist. The theatre managers took over the job of changing the lens. Mike explained how he was able to get the theatre managers to cooperate.

> I told our managers that once the automated projectionist booth was in operation and the job of projectionist eliminated I would give them a raise consisting of 40% of whatever the projectionists had made. So all of a sudden the manager went from being against the program of converting to automated projectionist booths to where I got a flood of letters from managers saying, "I passed the projectionist test. I'm now certified by the electrical board. Fire my projectionist."

IMPROVING THEATRE PROFITABILITY

At the time they purchased the Martin Theatre circuit, the Patricks were well aware that some of the theatres were losing money and that much of Martin's facilities were quickly becoming outmoded. A 1981 consulting report on Martin underscored that during the 1970s Martin had not aggressively moved to multiplexing. In addition, one of the previous presidents had put a number of theatres into "B-locations" where according to Mike Patrick there were "great leases . . . but the theatres were off the beaten track." Mike explained his approach for handling the situation:

> I looked at all the markets we were in, the big markets where the money was to be made, and I said, "Here's what we will do. First, let's take the losers and make them profitable. At the time the losing theaters were a $1.2M deficit on the bottom line. So I decided to experiment. . . . Phenix City is a perfect example. I took the admission price from $3.75 to $.99. Everybody said I was a fool. The first year it made $70K which I thought was a great increase over the $26K it had been making. The next year what happened was the people in Phenix City are poor, very poor blue collar workers, but the theater is as nice as anything I have over here (in Columbus). So as word of mouth got going that theater kept getting better, and better. Now it almost sells out every Friday, Saturday, and Sunday. And I still charge $.99. That theatre will make over $200K this year.

As Mike put it, the conversion to "dollar theatres" was "a new concept. No one else is doing that." By 1986, Carmike had twenty "99 theatres." The company also offered a discount in admission prices on Tuesdays and discount ticket plans to groups. Two facilities called "Flick 'n' Foam" had restaurants and bar services in the theatre.

In addition, Mike Patrick continued to consider potential acquisitions.

> I'm looking at a circuit of theaters in a major metropolitan area. Now the owner hasn't told me that it is for sale yet. He wants me to make him an offer and I won't do it. I want him to make me the first offer. He has no new facilities. All his theatres are twins except one and that's a triple. He's getting killed. A large chain is coming against him with a twelve-plex. He's located all around the metro area and he's getting killed. He had that town for years and now he's almost knocked out of it. His circuit is going to be worthless. I've been up there. There are no 99 or dollar theaters anywhere. His locations are good for that. You see for a 99 theater, the location must not be a deterrent. It cannot be downtown, because downtown cannot support a night life so that's a deterrent. In the south, you don't want to be in a black area. White people won't go there. In Port Arthur you don't want to be in the Vietnamese area. Basically you don't want to be anywhere there is a minority.

FACILITY UPGRADING

When the Patricks purchased Martin Theatres in 1982, its facilities were quickly becoming outmoded. As Mike put it, "We were basically non-competitive . . . we were just getting hit left and right in our big markets . . . the biggest thing we had was a twin and we had competitors dropping four and six-plexes on us." One reason for Martin's earlier reticence to convert to multi-screen theatres was the tendency to put emphasis on the number of theatres rather than screens. In addition, management of the theatre company, although not so required by the parent company, had managed the circuit for its cash flow. Patrick explained, "Ron (Baldwin) really never understood working for a $2B company. He still managed the firm as though it were privately owned."

Mike Patrick explained the difficulties in the early 1980s:

> Oh, we were just outclassed everywhere you went. Ron Baldwin told me that Columbus Square was doomed. It was going black. I made it an eight-plex. With our nice theater, the Peachtree, I added one screen but I didn't have any more room. But I took the theater no one liked and made it an eight-plex. It is also one of our most profitable theaters we have today.

New theatres, either replacements or additions, were undertaken usually through build, sale, and leaseback arrangements. Carl Patrick explained that in 1985 the theatres were about 75% leased and about 25% company owned.

By 1986 the company had become the fifth largest motion picture exhibitor in the United States and the leading exhibitor in the southern United States in terms of number of theatres and screens operated. The company operated 156 theatres with an aggregate of 436 screens located in 94 cities in 11 southern states with a total seating capacity of 125,758 (see Exhibit 3).

All but 22 theatres were multi-screen. Approximately 95% of the company's screens were located in multi-screen theatres, with over 62% of the company's screens located in theatres having three or more screens. The company had an average of 2.79 screens per theatre. The company's strategy was designed to maximize utilization of theatre facilities and enhance operating efficiencies. In the fiscal year ending March 27, 1986, aggregate attendance at the company's theatres was approximately 15.3 million people.

The company owned the theatre and land for 37 of its 156 theatres. The

EXHIBIT 3 CARMIKE CINEMAS, INC.: THEATRES AND SCREENS, 1986

State	NUMBER OF SCREENS PER THEATRE						Total	Percent of Total Screens
	1	2	3	4	5	6–8		
Alabama	1	16	9	12	0	15	53	12.2%
Florida	1	0	3	0	0	0	4	0.9%
Georgia	3	12	15	4	10	16	60	13.8%
Kentucky	0	2	0	4	5	6	17	3.9%
New Mexico	0	2	0	0	0	0	2	0.4%
North Carolina	0	28	9	4	0	0	41	9.4%
Oklahoma	9	24	3	12	10	18	76	17.4%
South Carolina	0	10	6	0	0	0	16	3.7%
Tennessee	6	24	12	32	0	18	92	21.1%
Texas	2	16	3	28	0	18	67	15.4%
Virginia	0	8	0	0	0	0	4	1.8%
	22	142	60	96	25	91	436	100.00%
Percent of total screens	5.0%	32.6%	13.8%	22.0%	5.7%	20.9%	100.0%	

company owned 30 other theatres which were built on leased land. Another 78 theatres were leased. In addition, Carmike shared an ownership or leasehold interest in 11 of its theatres with various unrelated third parties.

Exhibit 4 describes the scope of the company's theatre operations at the end of five fiscal years.

Carmike's screens were located principally in smaller communities, typically with populations of 40,000 to 100,000 people, where the company was the sole or leading exhibitor. The company was the sole operator of motion picture theatres in 55% of the cities in which it operated, including Montgomery, Alabama; Albany, Georgia; and Longview, Texas. The company's screens constituted a majority of the screens operated in another 22% of such cities, including Nashville and Chattanooga in Tennessee and Columbus, Georgia. The locations of the company's theatres are indicated in Exhibit 5.

Carmike gave close attention to cost control in construction, as Mike Patrick explained:

> Under Fuqua Martin usually owned the theatre. In some instances the land was also owned; in others the company had a ground lease. Since theatres were basically the same from one site to another, the cost of construction of the building was fairly standardized once the site, or pad, was ready.

Mike Patrick built his first theatre in 1982 at a cost of $26/s.f. At the time the usual price in the industry was $31/s.f. He explained that even his insurance company had questioned him when he turned in his replacement cost estimate. In order to reduce his costs Mike Patrick had examined every element of cost. Initially the Patricks worked with the E&W architectural firm as Martin theatres had done for years. Mike Patrick explained that their costs were so favorable that other theatre companies began to use E&W. Eventually E&W costs went up. In 1985 Mike employed a firm of recent University of Alabama graduates to be the architects on a new theater in Georgia.

Costs were also carefully controlled when a shopping center firm built a theatre Carmike would lease. The lease specified that if construction costs would exceed a certain amount, Carmike had the option of building the theatre. Without that specification there was, as Mike Patrick explained, no incen-

EXHIBIT 4 CARMIKE CINEMAS, INC.: OPERATIONS, 1982–1986

DATE	THEATRES	SCREENS
March 25, 1982	128	265
March 31, 1983	126	283
March 29, 1984	158	375
March 28, 1985	160	407
March 27, 1986	156	415

EXHIBIT 5 CARMIKE CINEMAS, INC.: THEATRE LOCATIONS

The Company currently operates 156 theaters with an aggregate of 436 screens in 11 southern states. Those communities in which the Company operates theaters are indicated on the map below.

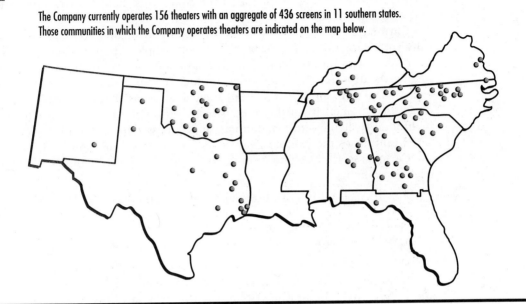

tive for the development firm to contain costs. Carmike's lease payment was based on a return on investment to the development firm. On a recent theatre the estimated costs had come in at $39/s.f. versus the $31/s.f. that the lease specified. Mike Patrick convinced the development company to use one of his experienced contractors in order to reduce the $39/s.f.

ZONE STRATEGY

The orientation under Martin management in the 1970's had been a system wide operations approach. Mike Patrick's approach to theatre location and number of screens was zone by zone and theatre by theatre.

Mike explained that the basic strategic unit in a theatre chain was a geographic area called a zone. A small town would usually be one zone. Larger cities usually had two or more zones. Considering competitive activity in a zone was critical. Mike explained what happened over a period of two years in one major metropolitan area (see Exhibit 6).

> This city has a river which divides it in two. There is only one main bridge and so there are automatically two zones. There is also a third zone which is isolated somewhat. When we first bought Martin there were seven theatres and fourteen screens.
>
> Let me tell you what happened in that Zone A. A strong competitor came in and built a six-plex against me in a shopping center. [See #1 in Exhibit 6.] I leased land, built a six-plex theater [#2], and did a sale lease-back. I built the

EXHIBIT 6 CARMIKE CINEMAS, INC.: MAP OF THE CITY WITH THREE ZONES

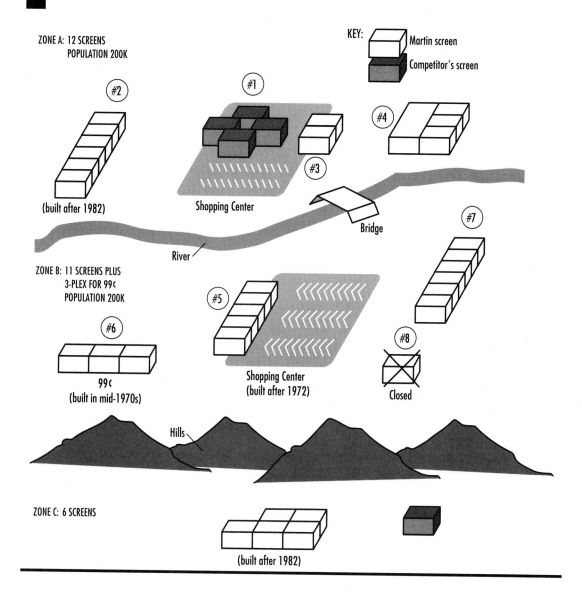

six-plex here right off one of the two shopping centers. I leased the equipment and I leased the building. I actually have no investment. Last year that theater made $79K. Think about the return you have with no investment!

I took the single theater in the shopping center [#3] and put a wall down the middle of it. That cost me $30K. I added an auditorium to a triple [#4]. Both of these theatres are near the competitor's six-plex. Now it's six—four here and two here. So that is six against his six. So now I have twelve screens in Zone A. That's about the number of screens the population in Zone A can support. So no one else can come in. My competitor has no advantage over me in negotiations with Warner Brothers and Paramount. In fact, I have an advantage over him. He's only here in one location and I am in three.

In the other zone I took a twin and added three auditoriums [#5]. Then I took a triple theater and made it a dollar house, $.99 discount.... It was way off the beaten track, way off [#6]. So I had eight screens against the competitor theatres [#7]. There was an opposition single screen, but he closed [#8]. We now have twenty screens in those two zones.

If you are playing Rocky, you can sell three prints to this town. If you choose your theatres carefully as to where you show it, you can make a lot more money. That's something the previous president (of Martin) never understood.

EXPANSION

In May 1983 Carmike acquired the outstanding stock of Video Independent Theatres, Inc. The purchase price included $1.1M cash and $2.7M in a note. The note was at 11% payable in three equal installments. Mike talked about the acquisition:

During the 1970s Martin had not been aggressive. In our industry if you are not on the attack you are being attacked. Then you are subject to what the industry does. We believe in making things happen.

Video was owned by a company which had bought Video for its cable rights. In the mid 1970s the management was killed in an air crash. I went up and talked to the guy in charge of Video. He said he told me the parent company wasn't interested in theatres.

The circuit had a lot of singles and a lot of profitable drive-ins. We borrowed $1M as a down payment and the parent accepted a note for the remainder due in three equal yearly installments.

We immediately looked at all the drive-ins and sold two drive-ins for about $1.5M. So immediately we paid back the down payment. We planned to use the cash flow to meet the installment payments and the depreciation to rebuild the circuit. Today Video is completely paid for.

In some of the towns we went into a tremendous aggressive buying program for film which was very successful. In another we bought out an independent who was building a five-plex. In others we converted twins into four-plexes. We closed singles and in some instances over-built with four, five, or six-plexes. Our revenue per screen as a result is low.

In one town we went in with a new six-plex which cost $620K. We had used basic cement block construction and furnished the facility beautifully. An independent had put in a four-plex, about the same size facility, which has cost $1.1M. A large circuit also had a twin. I attacked with a six-plex during a time when the state economy was down. In addition, there was a lot of bad pictures. The two companies really beat each other up during the period bidding up what pictures were available. The independent went under. We'll pick up that theatre from the bank. The circuit was bought by a larger company which wants to concentrate on larger cities. They've offered us their twin.

CONTROL SYSTEMS

The company also put considerable emphasis on budgeting and cost control. As Mike Patrick explained, "I was brought up on theatre P&L's." The systems he set in place for Carmike theatres were straightforward. "Every theatre had what Mike called "a PL . . . I call them a Profit or Loss Statement." Results came across Patrick's desk monthly and results for the theatres were printed out in descending order of amount of profit generated for that month. No overhead was charged to the theatres. As Mike explained, "if you can charge something to an overhead [account], then no one cares, no one is responsible." Rather, each administrative department had a monthly statement. Mike Patrick explained his approach:

> I used something like zero budgeting on every department. For example, here's the Martin Building. It cost me $18,700 for the month. The report for the Martin Building even has every person's name. . . . What they made last year, what they made this year, what they made current month, every expense they have. . . . For example I know what my dad's office cost me each month and mine also.
>
> Everyone must answer, be responsible, for everything they spend. They can't come to me and say, "Well, we've done it every year this way." Since 1982 we have become more efficient and more efficient each year.

Every department head received a recap each week. Mike noted that in a recent weekly report he had a charge for $2,000 for new theatre passes reading Carmike instead of Martin. Charges for business lunches appeared on the statement of the person who signed the bill. Mike checked the reports and required explanations for anything out of line. Theatre expenses also received close scrutiny, as he explained.

> Then I go a step beyond that. All district managers have a pet peeve. They all want their facilities to look brand new. You can write them letters, you can swear, you can cuss. It makes no difference. They are in that theater and that's the only thing they see. It's their world. They want new carpet every week. They want a new roof every week. They want a new projector and a new ticket machine every week. . . . the government says you have to capitalize those expenditures [but] I hate to capitalize on expenses. The government says if the air conditioning breaks, you capitalize it. Bullshit. I wrote the check for $18K. The money is gone.
>
> So, now I give every district manager a repair report. It shows anything charged to repairs. Yes, I could probably accomplish the same thing with a cash flow statement, but they wouldn't understand it.

MANAGING THE THEATRES

The company did not have a nepotism policy. Indeed, Mike Patrick encouraged the hiring of family. Especially in smaller towns where there might be several family members in visible positions, hiring family was seen as a deterrent to theft. As Mike Patrick explained:

I will let them hire family for two reasons: One, they don't want to quit me. They're married to me as much as they are the family. Second, you get people who just would not steal. They have more to lose than just the job. None of the family will steal from me because it would have a direct bearing on the father, the uncle, the whole family. I am in a lot of little towns and in a small town a son is either going to work on a farm, a grocery store, a filling station, or a theater, cause there is no industry there. The cleanest job in town is the theater manager. Also, in a small town we allow the manager to look like he owns the theatre. Cause I don't go in and act like "Here's the boss" and all that.

Theater managers are paid straight salary. Under Fuqua ownership the manager's salary was linked to theatre performance. But changes in company operations led to the change. Theater managers don't make the theater profit; the movie does. Theatre managers used to select the movies. But now they don't have anything to do with selection. I am the only theater chain in the United States in which the booking and buying for the circuit is done by computer from right here on my desk. This computer is hooked to Atlanta and Dallas, which are my two booking offices.

Mike Patrick had hired both booking managers after retirements of the previous incumbents. He explained how one came to work for Carmike:

Let me tell you how I got Tony Reed. Tony Reed was the biggest SOB I went against. He was the booker in a small city and that circuit was the best in town. He used to give me fits. And I used to spend more time trying to figure out how to get prints away from him than anybody else. So what did I do? I hired him. He made $19K/year working for a competitor and he makes $65K working for me. That's a lot of difference.

The planning system for booking films was set up so that past, current, and future bookings could be called up by theatre, zone, or film. In addition, competitors' bookings were also available. The system allowed interaction between home office and the two booking offices, one in Atlanta and the other in Dallas.

THE OUTLOOK IN 1986

As the 1985 year came to close, Carmike, like much of the industry, faced disappointing year-end results. Part of the problem was attributed to the number of executive turnovers in the movie production companies. Mike explained:

A number of production executives changed jobs within a 90-day period. That meant that production stopped. Production is like developing a shopping center. It takes 18 months from the time you decide to do it to the time it opens. This year is off because there were no pictures out there. I believe that it will get better ... Rocky IV has just come out so we will end the year on an upbeat.

The industry faced a number of challenges that affected Carmike. Lack of films was a negative factor. However, the increase in ancillary markets for films, such as video purchase and rental, was viewed as a positive factor, as Mike explained:

> By 1979–80 the ancillary market became very big. I understand the ancillary market is now about $3B and our side is $4B . . . [but] I talked to a man in Home Box Office when he first started. He told me that they could not figure a way to sell a movie on its first run at all. If it was a bad movie, he couldn't give it away. If it was a good movie, he had all the attendance watching it he needed. He told me, "Mike, I want you to do better every year. The more blockbusters you get, the more demand I have. If you get 'Who Shot Mary' and it dies in your theater, no one will watch it on Home Box Office." The theatre is where you go to preview a movie. That establishes the value. So I realized then that CBS will pay more for a big movie than they will a lousy one so anything that comes through the tube, is no problem with me. I love it because [the revenues] help create more new movies.

An increase in films might be offset by the unabated increase in number of screens. However, the Patricks did not, as did others, foresee the demise of the movie theatre. Mike especially felt that the difficult times offered opportunities to those who were prepared:

> There is more opportunity in bad times than in good times. The reason is that no one wants to sell when business is good and if they do the multiples are too high. So you want to buy when business is bad [and] . . . you got to plan for those times.
>
> I have to know where my capital is. I run this company through this set of reports. This is every financial thing you want to know about Carmike Theaters—construction coming up, everything we are going to spend, source of cash, where it's going to go, everything. One of the critical things we are thinking about is how to expand. I know that if industry business goes bad, within 90 days, three or four more circuits are going to come up for sale. I must be in a position to buy them and I must have the knowledge to do it with. I will not bet the store on any deal.
>
> I am trying to buy a theatre circuit right now [it's priced] at $16M. At $16M I am paying a premium for that circuit, a big premium because it loses money every year, but I am going to fire its management. I could buy it as part of Martin [but] if Martin would buy it then Martin would be liable for the money, so I don't want to do that. So what's my alternative? . . . I will take $2 or $3M out of Carmike or have Carmike borrow $13M and purchase the theatre circuit. Then we expect that the cash flow from the purchased circuit will pay back the $13M.

Mike Patrick was on the continuous outlook for new opportunities. One of those opportunities was outside the theatre industry, as he explained:

> Our new office building is 100% financed with an Industrial Revenue 20-year bond issue. In case the theater business goes bad, I want to own an asset that is not a theater.

CASE 2

LIZ CLAIBORNE, INC. DAVID W. GRIGSBY

"We like to think of ourselves as the IBM of the garment district," stated Jay Margolis, president of Liz Claiborne, Inc.'s women's sportswear division in a 1989 interview.[1] If financial success and industry dominance were the criteria, the comparison was an apt one for the thirteen-year-old company. Liz Claiborne, Inc., led by its glamorous namesake, had topped $1 billion in sales for the second year in a row, a remarkable feat in the apparel industry. Since going public in 1981, the company had become the largest U.S. industrial firm headed by a woman and, in 1985, had been declared the second-most-admired corporation in America by *Fortune* magazine. By 1989, Liz Claiborne controlled an estimated one-third of the $2 billion better women's sportswear market and had added a line of men's sportswear and the company's own cologne label. With her clothes selling in over 3,500 stores across the country, Liz Claiborne had become a household name.

ELISABETH CLAIBORNE ORTENBERG

The company's founder and namesake was the daughter of a European banker and, as such, spent much of her early childhood in Europe. Her family later moved from Brussels to New Orleans and then to Baltimore, giving the young Claiborne a wide exposure to culturally diverse societies and experiences, which had a lasting affect on her sense of style. Before finishing her high school education, Claiborne left the United States and returned to Brussels to pursue her interests in the fine arts. At the age of 20, she won a *Harper's Bazaar* design contest that fueled her ambition to become a leading designer. Against the wishes of her parents, she continued to pursue this interest and went to work as a sketcher and model in a New York design firm. Discovering her self-

---

Source: Prepared by Professor David W. Grigsby, Clemson University, as a basis for classroom discussion and not to illustrate either effective or ineffective handling of administrative situations. © David W. Grigsby, 1990.

identity, Claiborne decided to change her image and cut her long dark hair into the shorter style that became her trademark.

In the mid 1950s, Claiborne became a designer for a large women's sportswear company. Shortly thereafter, she and her boss, Arthur Ortenberg, were married. Claiborne's success in design eventually landed her the position of chief designer at Youth Guild, a junior dress division of Jonathan Logan, Inc. She remained at Logan until Liz Claiborne, Inc. was born in 1976.

Liz Claiborne is not an open, gregarious person. Her associates see her as very private and shy, yet friendly to those around her. As Arthur Lefkowitz, her old boss at Jonathan Logan, stated: She was a "very private girl, low key, not pushy, and a hard worker." She "wasn't a playgirl." [2] Despite her retiring personality, Liz Claiborne has adjusted well to the celebrity that accompanied her firm's meteoric rise. By 1988, her popularity had surpassed that of all other American designers. Few chief executives were as recognizable as Liz Claiborne, whose appearance at the age of 59 reflected her success and personality. The image was a familiar one in the fashion world: close-cropped black hair, strong, sculptured face, and a voice that was firm, low, and very precise. Wearing her trademark oversized glasses, she appeared slim, tanned—a vigorous personality. On one occasion in 1988, she made a personal appearance at Macy's New York store on Herald Square and was greeted by crowd of 600 women who behaved as if she were a rock star.

FROM START-UP TO INDUSTRY LEADERSHIP: 1976–1983

Liz Claiborne, Inc. was founded in 1976 by Claiborne, her husband Arthur Ortenberg, and manufacturing expert Leonard Boxer. Marketing specialist Jerome Chazen was added to the firm a year later. Launched with an investment of $255,000 the company's mission was to provide an alternative to the stuffy business suits career women were wearing to the office. Designers had looked on businesswomen as "mini-men" dressed in female versions of men's suits, complete with bows for ties. Claiborne perceived a more casual trend in women's business wear and advocated leaving the structured suit-and-tie outfit to the high-powered law and business firms. She designed a classic line of related components both for business and for leisure that were designed around a "more feminine look" concept, and she offered them at affordable prices.

With experienced management and some of the best designers in the business, the company's presence in the apparel industry had an immediate impact. Its headquarters building, featuring clean lines and lots of white, was located one block off of Times Square, in the heart of New York's Garment district. By September of the first year, the firm was already running in the black.

Claiborne's initial designs were in sportswear, divided into four lines—Spectator, Casual, Lizwear, and Lizsport—all of which were priced in the "better" price range. Pricing was targeted to be just below other well-known designers such as Ralph Lauren and just above mass-market designers such as

Bernard Chaus. A Petites Division was also created to offer fashions designed for the smaller figure. Each division was run by separate management staffs, but all lines were coordinated at the corporate level to assure a consistent image for the company's various products.

The company grew rapidly over the first five years. In 1981 the firm decided to go public with an offering at $19 a share and raised $6.5 million. At the time of the stock offering, earnings had increased tenfold since 1976 and the company boasted an average compounded annual rate of sales growth of more than 40 percent. In 1982 a new dresses line was added to the sportswear segment. Claiborne was hesitant at first to move into this line, but Ortenberg persuaded her to do so. The line turned out to be one of the company's most successful segments, grossing $10 million in its first year. That same year, the company licensed its name for the production of accessories, including belts, scarves, and gloves. In 1983 the company added the new label Lizkids, a better sportswear line for children. Liz Claiborne's product categories are summarized in Exhibit 1.

FURTHER GROWTH AND CONSOLIDATION, 1984–1988

In 1984, the company concentrated on building its reputation as a fashion merchandiser and solidifying its markets. Closer relationships with retailers were cultivated, and plans for expanding the company still further were laid.

In 1985, sales rose to over $550 million, and the company earned a 10.9-percent return on sales, which turned out to be one of the highest net profit margins in the industry. The apparel industry was experiencing a number of problems at the time. For most companies, production costs were skyrocketing while sales levels fell or remained relatively stable. Contributing to Claiborne's success in spite of flat industry sales were several changes initiated during

EXHIBIT 1 LIZ CLAIBORNE, INC.: PRODUCT CATEGORIES AS A PERCENTAGE OF SALES

	1987	1986	1985
Misses Sportswear	53%	54%	64%
Petite Sportswear	12	13	16
Dresses	14	16	16
Accessories	13	10	—
Menswear	7	5	2
Girls	1	2	2
Total	100%	100%	100%

Source: Liz Claiborne, Inc., 1987 Form 10-K.

the year. The accessories line, which had previously been licensed to outside companies, was bought outright in an effort to gain more control over the company's products. It brought in an additional $50 million in sales revenue. Claiborne realized that accessories have greater appeal during down cycles in their basic clothing lines. Accessories allow women to purchase fewer individual pieces of clothing, yet ultimately have more outfits by using accessories as interchangeable accents.

A new line, Claiborne fashions for men, was added to the company's collection in 1985. The line was composed of sweaters, shirts, and slacks designed to be worn as complete outfits. According to Jerome Chazen, "We discovered that 70% of our women customers also bought clothes for their husbands."[3] Claiborne began shipping men's clothing to retailers at the close of 1985. Plans were also being made at that time to enter into a joint venture with Avon for the distribution of a new fragrance the following year.

1986 brought more success to Liz Claiborne, Inc. The new Claiborne men's line hit the market in the early part of the year and earned $40 million in sales its first year. The accessories line brought in $82 million only one year after being acquired from its licensees. Total revenues for 1986 jumped up to $813 million, $100 million over projections. Liz Claiborne led all firms in the apparel industry on net profit margin (10.6 percent), return on equity (34.8 percent), and return on investment (25.7 percent). The firm was listed on the Fortune 500 for the first time (#437), at only eleven years of age. It led all Fortune 500 firms that year in return on investment.

In 1986, Claiborne debuted its joint venture with Avon as planned. The first product, the fragrance, hit the market in September. The company undertook the first national advertising campaign in its history to promote this product as a light, "workday" scent. The campaign was a straightforward, honest sell, costing approximately $5 million, with no sexual motifs apparent. In some circles the firm was criticized for its lackluster ad campaign with no "glitz."

In the apparel industry, 1987 will not be remembered with fondness. There was a general problem of overstocking in the stores, and too many stores carried similar items, which caused customers simply to stop buying. In addition, most designers misread the consumer market and offered much shorter hemlines, similar to the miniskirts of the 1960s. Liz Claiborne, along with her competitors, fell prey to a rebellion against the shorter skirts. A company spokesman noted that this might have been an indication that the firm was losing touch with its customers, who were "a bit older and more conservative than was previously thought."[4]

Claiborne's stated objectives in 1987 were twofold: to improve the product and to train sales personnel in the "Claiborne way," which was to understand the customer and "see the clothing through Claiborne eyes."[5] While other apparel firms in the industry suffered through an unfortunate year, Liz Claiborne, Inc. posted remarkable sales gains in spite of its misreading of hemline preferences. Total sales for the year were up 29.5 percent over 1986 to $1.05 billion, making Liz Claiborne, Inc. a billion-dollar sales company for the first time.

The Petites Division strengthened its position over the year by making changes in its operations. A new designer was hired, and the division's offices and showroom space were expanded. Reporting patterns were restructured so the Petites Division would report directly to the Sportswear Group. Claiborne, the menswear segment, posted a sales increase of 79 percent in 1987, its second full year of production, bringing in $75 million. Encouraged by the line's early success, Claiborne decided to expand it to include men's furnishings—dress shirts, hosiery, ties, and underwear. The accessories line also did well in 1987, posting a 66-percent increase over 1986 sales, at $136 million. Handbags proved to be the best seller. Dresses posted an 11-percent increase over 1986 and brought in $141 million. Liz Claiborne Cosmetics Division had sales of $26 million for the year and gained significant market share. Its product was one of the top five fragrances sold in the U.S. Claiborne planned to continue this line, but because of unusual acquisitions made by Avon decided to discontinue the joint venture and seek another supplier for the product.

In September 1987, Claiborne introduced a new line of bridge sportswear under the Dana Buchman label. This merchandise was priced to capture a niche just above Liz Claiborne's better-priced lines and just below designer sportswear. Although it recognized this venture as somewhat risky, the firm felt confident that it could capture a reasonable market share in this niche. Projections were for the new line to bring in approximately $5 million in sales for the first four months and then steadily build market share.

A number of problems were corrected in 1987. The Claiborne men's line experienced problems when customers complained that the men's pants fit poorly and were basically too baggy. New pants designs were tried for the following season. Lizkids sales, at $15 million, were disappointing. The company determined that the Lizkids problem was twofold. First, the fashions were merely scaled-down versions of womens' styles and, as such, were too sophisticated for children. Second, retail stores had no system for effectively displaying "better" children's fashions. The most common means of display was to separate by size, not price. Claiborne found her "better" childrens sportswear hanging next to lower-quality and lower-priced styles. To correct this problem, Claiborne began working directly with retailers to set up Lizkids boutiques.

In 1988, the company continued to experience some fallout from the apparel industry's slump. In spite of that, 1988 brought moderate (by Claiborne standards) financial success. Sales rose 13.2 percent over 1987 levels, to a total of over $1.18 billion. The company rose from #312 to #299 on the Fortune 500 listing. Profits, however, declined 3.6 percent, from $114.4 to $110.3 million. (Selected financial data for the company are presented in Exhibit 2.) A number of factors were behind the decline in profitability. Women's sportswear sales, which accounted for 60 percent of Claiborne's total revenue, had increased by only 3 percent, in contrast to the usual 20 percent annual rate. Many analysts thought that the firm's size was making it increasingly unable to respond to the market's needs and that Liz Claiborne would never again grow at its past rate. Liz Claiborne's management, on the other hand, felt confident that, with the support of new ventures, the company could rebound. Plans were

EXHIBIT 2 LIZ CLAIBORNE, INC.: SELECTED CONSOLIDATED FINANCIAL HIGHLIGHTS, 1983–1988

	1988	1987	1986	1985	1984	1983
Net sales	$1,184,229	$1,053,324	$813,497	$556,553	$391,272	$228,722
Gross profit	425,944	397,755	311,250	214,853	147,517	84,064
Net income	110,341	114,414	86,194	60,580	41,938	22,398
Earnings per common share	1.26	1.32	1.00	.71	.50	.27
Working capital	402,069	320,802	213,171	151,950	97,299	57,887
Total assets	629,082	482,369	247,787	225,910	142,826	91,320
Long-term debt	14,107	14,464	–0–	10,000	–0–	–0–
Stockholders' equity	457,826	356,956	247,787	162,729	104,417	64,498
Dividends per common share	.18	.16	.12	.08	.05	–0–
Weighted average common shares	87,484,695	86,933,364	86,270,552	85,395,824	84,577,140	84,013,344

Note: All dollar amounts are in thousands except per-share data.
All common-share data has been adjusted to reflect all stock dividends previously paid.
Source: Liz Claiborne, Inc., *1988 Annual Report.*

already in the works to open its own stores and to offer a new line of clothes for larger women. Wall Street, however, was not that optimistic. Claiborne's stock price fell from $35 to $17 during the year.

The general malaise in the apparel industry was expected to continue into 1989. Most industry analysts believed that sales would rock along at their present levels unless some new fashion trend emerged to create some excitement in the stores. Liz Claiborne's sales were expected to increase by only 4 percent in 1989.

Despite its somewhat disappointing showing for the year, further recognition was bestowed on the company in 1988. When *Fortune* magazine asked 8,000 executives, outside directors, and financial analysts to rate the ten largest firms in their respective industries on eight attributes for its list of "America's Most Admired Corporations," Liz Claiborne, Inc. once again scored at the top of its industry. The company was rated second in quality of management and innovation. Later that year, *Fortune* also named the company one of "America's Fastest-Growing Companies" for 1988.

TOP MANAGEMENT AND ORGANIZATION

The mission of management, as seen through Liz Claiborne's eyes, was to "generate meaningful work by creating products of integrity—to share the rewards of success amply, at all levels."[6]

Brenda Gall, vice-president at Merrill Lynch, attributed Liz Claiborne's success to the fact that it had four key individuals with complementary strengths in different areas of the business. "Usually when you get a start-up, you have a strength in one or two areas—design and sales, or design and finance—you don't have all the bases covered. These people *had* all the bases covered. They've planned their business from day one, and they're still planning."[7]

From its inception, Claiborne has embodied the concept of team management. Liz Claiborne herself was responsible for the designing function; Arthur Ortenberg's strengths were finance, administration, and organization; Jerome Chazen was the sales and marketing expert; and Leonard Boxer was in charge of production and operations. These four individuals shared responsibility for long-range planning and strategic decisions.

By 1986, however, the top management team had become aware of the need to train successors for their jobs. Liz Claiborne began to delegate more and more of her own designing duties to staff members and by 1988 had stepped back to perform only editing functions. Part of the reason for that change was the changing nature of the design trade. What had been a "sketch, take a long lunch, leave at 5:00 and go to parties" type of a day had become a twelve-hour-a-day job because of competitive pressures for larger, more coordinated lines of products. As the demands of managing her rapidly growing company increased, Claiborne found less and less time for actual designing. Ortenberg, continuing his team approach to management, spent much time training a new group of managers to take over the business after his retirement.

Some organizational restructuring took place in 1987. The company's three sportswear divisions—Collections, Lizwear, and Lizsport—were combined into the Sportswear Group, and Jay Margolis was put in charge of this segment. He was given the title executive vice-president, Women's Sportswear Group. Girls sportswear was moved to the Lizwear label. The executive committee, which had been in control of the firm since its founding, was replaced by the policy committee, which reported directly to the board of directors. Its functions were to monitor market share and identify and evaluate business opportunities. Its major objective was to maintain the spirit of Claiborne and Ortenberg after they left the company.

Three new positions were created during 1987. An executive vice-president of operations and corporate planning was added whose primary functions were to oversee production planning, resource acquisition, and manufacturing distribution. Harvey Falk, who succeeded Leonard Boxer, assumed this title. Falk, a certified public accountant, had been with the company since 1982. His previous position was executive vice-president, finance. In addition, a senior vice-president of corporate sales and marketing, responsible for coordinating marketing efforts among the nine divisions, was created. Robert Bernard was appointed to fill this position. Bernard, who had left R. H. Macy's to join Liz Claiborne in 1985, previously served as head of sportswear sales. As noted earlier, Jay Margolis assumed the titles of executive vice-president and president of the Women's Sportswear Group. Margolis had been at Claiborne since 1984, serving in various management capacities in the Sportswear Division. Before coming to Liz Claiborne, Margolis had been a division president at Ron Chereskin, Inc., a sportswear manufacturer. Exhibit 3 lists the corporate officers of Liz Claiborne, Inc.

MARKETING STRATEGY

The Claiborne marketing strategy is straightforward: Know your customer. Claiborne's customer is "about 35 years old and not a perfect size 8."[8] Capitalizing on the trend of increasing numbers of women entering the work force,

EXHIBIT 3   LIZ CLAIBORNE, INC.: CORPORATE OFFICERS (JANUARY 1, 1989)

NAME	AGE	POSITION(S)
Elisabeth Claiborne Ortenberg	59	Chairman of the board, president and chief executive officer
Arthur Ortenberg	62	Vice-chairman of the board and secretary
Jerome A. Chazen*	62	Vice-chairman of the board and, effective June 1989, chairman of the board
Harvey L. Falk*	54	Executive vice-president, Operations and Corporate Planning and, effective June 1989, president and vice-chairman
Jay Margolis*	40	Executive vice-president; president, Women's Sportswear Group and, effective June 1989, vice-chairman and president, Women's Sportswear Group
Robert Abajian	57	Senior vice-president, Women's Sportswear, design
Robert Bernard	38	Senior vice-president, corporate sales and marketing
Ellen Daniel	53	Senior vice-president; Collections Division
Kenneth Ganz	54	Senior vice-president, corporate distribution
Matthew Langweber	37	Senior vice-president; president, Retail Division
Jack Listanowsky	41	Senior vice-president, operations
Alois J. Lohn	54	Senior vice-president, manufacturing
Larry McDonald	54	Senior vice-president, corporate textile engineering
Nina E. McLemore*	43	Senior vice-president; president, Accessories Division
Allen McNeary*	41	Senior vice-president; president, Dress Division
Jo Miller	38	Senior vice-president; First Issue, Retail Division
Samuel M. Miller	51	Senior vice-president, finance
Hank Sinkel	43	Senior vice-president, sportswear, sales
Kathry D. Connors		Vice-president, human resources
Roberta Schuhalter Karp		Vice-president, corporate counsel
Walter L. Krieger		Vice-president, financial operations
Jeffrey H. Shendell		Vice-president, allocations and sales support
Claudia Wong		Vice-president, corporate Far East operations
Elaine H. Goodell		Controller
Robert P. McKean		Treasurer

*Member, policy committee

Sources: Liz Claiborne, Inc., *1988 Annual Report*; 1988 Form 10-K.

Claiborne offers stylish, classic clothes tailored for the working woman. Its marketing strategy is to sell clothes through leading department stores and specialty stores. The selections must be designed with consistent highly individual styling—a "designer line," but at prices a working woman can afford. The working woman, said Liz Claiborne, "isn't going to spend $2,000 on a suit."[9]

Claiborne's vision for her corporation has always been to "create, identify and act upon opportunities for ourselves and our customers." Specifically, the objective is to "provide all needs except formal evening wear, coats, nightwear and bathing suits." Chazen identifies the Claiborne customer as the "executive, professional career woman who is updated in her taste level, as opposed to the traditional customer who wears structured suits." Jack Schultz, general merchandise manager for Sanger Harris, concurs: The fashions are "up-to-date, not avant-garde."[10]

The company prides itself on its close working relationship with its retailers, which is considered to be the best in the industry. Despite the fact that Claiborne refuses to provide them with "markdown money" (funds to cover retailers when they are forced to hold a clearance of slow-selling goods), the relationships hold. Different from other firms in the industry, Claiborne's marketing technique centers around the New York showroom. Refusing to operate a road sales force, Claiborne forces retailers to make initial contact with her in her own showroom. As the stores' top managers usually arrive for the season's showing, the relationship begins at a much higher level than at her competitors. Costs are also reduced by eliminating unnecessary travel.

Mark Shulman, senior vice-president and general merchandising manager for I. Magnin in San Francisco, called it the "best run apparel company on Seventh Avenue today." Other retailers such as Jack Schultz, general merchandise manager for Sanger Harris stores in Texas, stated that Claiborne was the largest and most successful of their accounts. Carol Greer, senior vice-president and general merchandise manager of Rich's in Atlanta, said that "what Claiborne does best is thoroughly understand the customer, her lifestyle, and the price she's willing to pay."[11]

Claiborne provides a great deal of on-site support to its retailers. Fashion specialists travel to all the stores, talking to customers, taking photographs of displays, and giving seminars to the sales people. They take time to discuss the company's goals and fashion point of view. According to Chazen, "The most important thing they get across is that we care about them and we expect them to care in return."[12] In addition, all retailers receive copies of the "Claiboard Receiving Guide," which categorizes names and style numbers by style group and provides buyers with a management tool for keeping up with orders and shipments. Claiborne personnel also help organize the in-store boutiques so that items that go together are displayed properly.

Store displays and groupings are important in the Liz Claiborne marketing system. Within each of the company's seven lines, clothes are grouped by the use of common fabrics and colors. A typical group might consist of a sweater, skirt, pants, and two or more coordinated blouses and T-shirts. Retailers are encouraged to show the items together, as Claiborne representatives believe their clothing sells better that way. Sometimes a single customer will buy an entire coordinated group.

There are six seasons in a Claiborne year: Pre-Spring, Spring One, Spring Two, Fall One, Fall Two, and Holiday. In a recent *New Yorker* article, James Lardner described Liz Claiborne's seasonal planning as follows: "Claiborne bases its production on the number of garments it expects to sell in the two-month period that each season, typically, stays in the stores. Most items are sellouts, and sometimes they sell out very quickly, but there is no provision for increasing output in response to demand; nor is a garment ever repeated in a subsequent season, although its success might inspire something similar."[13] Marketing efforts and sales growth are monitored by a system called SURF (systematic updated retail feedback). Data is gathered on a cross-section of stores representative of size and geographic location. By manipulating the data received weekly, managers can get a good feel of consumer spending habits.

The marketing efforts of the firm reflect both Claiborne and Ortenberg's personalities: intense and somewhat arrogant, driven by a mission of product quality and service. Claiborne herself has always expressed a willingness to be involved with her customer. When preparing clothes for market, she always tries to ask herself, "How much would I pay for that piece?" She frequently travels across the country, stopping in her boutiques, chatting with customers, trying to pick up on the smallest of trends in their buying behavior.

One important part of the winning formula has been the way Liz Claiborne's clothes fit her customers, whose figures often deviate from the ideal image presented by fashion models. Claiborne has said that she has no desire to lead a fashion parade. She prefers "seeing women walking along the streets dressed in my clothes, or coming up to me and saying, 'I love your clothes. Once I start wearing them, that's all I want to buy.' I think that's terrific."[14]

PRODUCTION AND OPERATIONS

Although the company employs over 2,200 workers, it has no manufacturing facilities. Its entire production is contracted out. Claiborne has found that by manufacturing overseas, primarily in the Far East, it can significantly reduce overhead and, by keeping its capital investments low, can post returns on equity of close to 50 percent.

Claiborne's production administration staff, headquartered in the North Bergen, New Jersey, plant, is primarily responsible for maintaining cost and quality among the contractors. Staff members' duties range from production engineering and supplier allocation to quality control. Most of the suppliers to the firm are located in Hong Kong, South Korea, Taiwan, the Philippines, and China. Purchases are made through short-term purchase orders rather than formal long-term contracts. Approximately one-half of the supply of raw materials comes from overseas, specifically Hong Kong, Taiwan, and Japan.

Production lead times in the apparel industry from the time the order is placed to the time the piece arrives for sale can be quite long. Claiborne often makes manufacturing commitments later in the production cycle than some if its competitors in order to assure that the product reflects up-to-date consumer tastes. These constraints understandably can cause problems with some suppliers. It is necessary, therefore, to maintain good relationships with the overseas suppliers that one has found to be reliable. At Claiborne, domestic suppliers' activities are monitored by staff specialists at the North Bergen plant while overseas offices monitor its foreign suppliers. They are located in Hong Kong, Taipei, Tel Aviv, Singapore, Shanghai, Manila, and Florence. Claiborne also works through independent agents located in Korea, Portugal, and Brazil.

Concerns over political and economic conditions abroad were prominent during the 1980s. All incoming merchandise is subject to U.S. Customs duties, and import quotas apply to certain classifications of merchandise, a result of bilateral agreements between the U.S. and exporting countries. Recognizing that escalation of these restrictions could significantly harm the firm, Claiborne tried to allocate as much merchandise as possible to categories not covered by quota regulations. The company's efforts and worries were not unfounded. In 1985 Congress passed legislation calling for tighter restrictions on textile and apparel imports. President Reagan, however, vetoed the referendum. Nevertheless, the danger signals were apparent. Should tighter controls be enforced to protect American jobs, Liz Claiborne, Inc. would suffer repercussions.

DIVERSIFICATION AND STRATEGIC ISSUES

As the company's growth in its primary markets began to level off in the late 1980s, concerns were aired over the level of diversification the company had accomplished and the amount that might be necessary to sustain success in this very volatile industry. Jay Meltzer, industrial analyst at Goldman Sachs & Co., noted that if the firm were to continue to grow, "they'll have to diversify." Yet he also noted that there is an inherent risk in diversification, as management could get farther and farther away from doing what they know best.[15]

Diversification plans were announced in 1988. Liz Claiborne introduced a new sportswear label, sold exclusively through the company's own stores under the First Issue trademark. Stores were located in high-traffic shopping mall locations in major cities. The line was priced just below Liz Claiborne Collections, placing it in direct competition with The Limited, The Gap, and Banana Republic. The first stores were opened in the northeastern U.S. in February 1988, and expansion continued during the year. A total of thirteen stores were opened in 1988, and thirty more were planned to be in operation by the end of 1989. Claiborne estimates the cost of opening one of these stores to be $150,000, with no projected profit until 1990. The possibility of expanding the chain overseas was also being considered.

In 1988, the company assumed full ownership of its fragrance line, thus ending its stormy three-year relationship with Avon. A men's fragrance was being developed and would be introduced in the fall of 1989. The company also expanded its Canadian operations in 1988 and established a jewelry division in 1989.

Another expansion of the Claiborne fashion empire occurred in 1988, when a new line of fashions for larger women was introduced at the end of the year. Called Elizabeth, it offered traditional Liz Claiborne styling at prices comparable to the company's main sportswear lines in a full range of large sizes. It was estimated that between 35 and 40 million women wear size 14 or above, representing a $10 billion market. Claiborne's primary competition in this market is Geoffrey Beane.

A program to expand the company's presence in the marketplace was initiated in 1987. "Project Consumer" was designed to reinforce ties to Claiborne buyers. There were two major thrusts. The first was to increase the number of Claiborne's in-store product specialists, who help train retail sales personnel and display merchandise. The second was to initiate larger in-store boutiques for Liz Claiborne lines in leading department stores. The first boutique was opened in Jordan Marsh's downtown Boston store. This personalized selling space offered the consumer a choice of shopping for dresses, misses sportswear, hosiery, accessories, and fragrances all in one location.

LIZ CLAIBORNE WITHOUT LIZ?

Liz Claiborne and her husband, Arthur Ortenberg, announced in February 1989 that they intended to retire at the end of the year. Although they had scaled back their roles in the firm over the previous few years, their announcement came as something of a surprise to the industry. The couple stated that they wanted to devote more time to environmental projects and personal interests. They planned to remain as board members of the firm. In preparation for their impending retirement, they sold 900,000 shares of stock during 1989, reducing their investment to $82 million.

Leonard Boxer had retired in 1988, and his responsibilities had been assumed by Harvey L. Falk, executive vice-president for operations and corporate planning. Of the four founders, only Jerome Chazen would remain.

Initial response to the retirement announcement was pessimistic, and stock prices dropped by over $1, with 2 million shares changing hands. Although most analysts felt that investors were overreacting, others voiced real concern. In the apparel industry, where products are often very closely identified with the founder's image, firms often face difficult transition periods after their founders retire. Top management at Liz Claiborne is confident, however, that the organization they built will continue to prosper without them, and some in the industry agree. As designer Bill Blass said, "There is a tendency in our business to overstay your welcome. I love the idea of stepping down. I like the idea they know when to do it."[16]

According to a 1988 article in *Fortune*, the quality that makes companies like Liz Claiborne and the other so-called billion dollar kids distinct is the presence of an entrepreneurial atmosphere. The founders frequently have their own strong visions of the future and are very determined to have a piece of action out in the market. Cofounder and vice-chairman Jerome Chazen reflected "We knew we wanted to clothe women in the work force. We saw a niche where no pure player existed. What we didn't know was how many customers were out there."[17]

Given its past dependence on that level of entrepreneurial spirit, the future of Liz Claiborne, Inc. in 1989 was uncertain. Had the company reached the limits of its growth potential, or would the plans made for management succession provide a smooth transition and continued success for Liz Claiborne, Inc. without Liz? Exhibit 4 contains Liz Claiborne's farewell to the stockholders, published in the 1988 Annual Report.

EXHIBIT 4 LIZ CLAIBORNE, INC.: PRESIDENT'S LETTER, 1988 ANNUAL REPORT

As I get ready to close the door behind myself, I find myself compelled to look once more over my shoulder and let my eyes and mind inventory the company I leave. There's Bob Abajian, the new Liz of sportswear, an extraordinary amalgam of talent, integrity, and professional know-how. There's Jay Margolis, the merchant supreme who perfectly synthesizes within himself who we are and what we stand for. There's Harvey Falk, who Jerry, Art, and I feel privileged to have worked with, whose knowledge of operations and whose unsurpassed credibility assures me that our supply base and engineering capabilities will only get better. I am reassured as I bring up mental pictures of our extraordinary team, so many players we love and respect. So many players I owe so much to.

These are the things that are important to me, the things I urge my colleagues to engrave deeply in their memories — that product and engineering are primary; that we are dedicated to coherent, consistent design; that we have the character to bypass fad and trend and live or die by a taste level we can be proud of; that we all learn and relearn the fundamentals of the game —fit, stitching, color matching, fabric evaluation; that top quality makes us proud and shoddy quality is intolerable.

I want all of us to remember that this company was started with pennies and a vision. And respect for our craft. And respect for our suppliers. And a firm regard for the intelligence and good discriminating sense of our ultimate consumer. And let's never forget that what we have demonstrated is that individuals working as a team can bring elegance and vitality to any endeavor.

I have done what I set out to do. I have participated in the building of a company that is certain of successful perpetuation. I thank you for having been, with me, part of a grand adventure.

Signed,
Liz Claiborne
Chairman, President and Chief Executive Officer

Source: Liz Claiborne, Inc., *1988 Annual Report.*

THE APPAREL INDUSTRY

The following statement by Fred Wenzel, chief executive officer of Kellwood Co., a large U.S. apparel manufacturing firm, sums up the state of the industry in early 1989:

> Apparel manufacturing in the U.S. will always be present, but certain ... apparel can best be made in newly industrialized countries. Not only is their direct labor cost substantially lower, but all other costs [as well], resulting in prices that this country cannot meet. Therefore, we must look to design, style, and service as our major weapons against imports.[18]

The U.S. apparel manufacturing industry is a very fragmented, labor-intensive business. The American Association of Apparel Manufacturers estimates that there are over 12,000 firms, only half of which employ twenty or more workers. This top half accounts for over 80 percent of the jobs and most of the business. Competition among U.S. firms and with foreign competitors is, in a word, fierce. Intense price pressure has historically kept prices, operating margins, and wage rates low compared with other manufacturing industries. Most of the smaller companies produce a very narrow range of products, often under contract for a larger firm or a retailer.

The industry is geographically concentrated in the northeastern states. Sixty percent of U.S. apparel is manufactured in New York, California, Pennsylvania, and New Jersey. Practically all of the high-fashion and tailored clothing comes from these states, while factories in the South and Southeast specialize in items amenable to large-volume production runs such as jeans, slacks, and underwear.

Three types of manufacturing operations predominate in the industry: manufacturers, jobbers, and contractors. Manufacturers purchase the material from textile companies and then cut, sew, and sell the finished product to retailers. Jobbers typically buy material and sell the finished product but "job out" the manufacture to outside factory operations, or contractors, who receive the material and make the product according to specifications.

OVERSEAS PRODUCTION

In recent years, production of apparel goods in the United States has declined significantly in real terms as apparel sales companies have sought the cost advantages available through overseas production. U.S. companies have contracted with offshore producers and in a growing number of cases have opened their own production facilities overseas. Apparel imports grew from $5.8 billion in 1980 to $15.8 billion in 1986 while exports of U.S. apparel products actually declined. Exhibit 5 shows import and export totals for textile and apparel goods for the years 1980, 1985, and 1986, the latest year available as of the case date.

Offshore sourcing can be accomplished in two ways. Apparel may be imported under a quota system or under Item 807 of the U.S. Tariff Schedule. Under the quota system, U.S. companies design and market clothing in the

EXHIBIT 5 U.S. EXPORTS AND IMPORTS OF TEXTILES AND APPAREL PRODUCTS, 1980–1986

	1980	1985	1986
EXPORTS			
Textile Mill Products	3,457	2,112	2,347
Apparel	1,001	600	727
Total	4,458	2,712	3,074
IMPORTS			
Textile Mill Products	2,372	4,714	5,517
Apparel	5,767	13,595	15,836
Total	8,139	18,309	21,353
TRADE BALANCE	−3,681	−15,597	−18,279

Source: U.S. Department of Commerce, Bureau of the Census, *Statistical Abstract of the United States, 1988* (Washington, D.C.: Government Printing Office, 1988).

U.S. but contract for their materials and manufacture according to company specifications. Goods are shipped to the U.S. in accordance with quota agreements negotiated with those countries under the Multi-Fiber Agreement, a pact involving fifty-four countries. The quotas are based on a number of variables, including past levels of imports from that country. Liz Claiborne, along with most of its close competitors, manufactures almost all of its clothing in the Far East under this quota system. Although sharp declines in the dollar against other world currencies in the 1980s had a significant effect on world trade, they had little effect on the price of goods purchased abroad by American apparel companies. Most imports come from Asian countries whose currencies are pegged to the dollar.

The quota system of importation, although very economical for outsourcing American production, has some inherent problems. Long lead times are necessary to process orders offshore, so companies must plan their lines far in advance. The advance time often proves to be a hindrance in the rapidly changing world of fashion goods. Another problem is that quotas are sometimes poorly managed by officials in the source countries. If quotas are oversubscribed, even by mistake, U.S. Customs officials may seize the excess. Bernard Chaus, a competitor of Liz Claiborne, had merchandise worth $11.6 million embargoed in 1986 because of inaccurate record keeping in the People's Republic of China. The result was unfilled orders at the retail level and a substantial loss of profits for the company. Manufacturers and labor unions in the U.S. have openly criticized the liberal quota allotments handed out by the U.S. Customs officials in the 1980s, especially those granted to nations in the Far East.

Under Item 807, apparel firms ship cut fabrics to be finished overseas. When the goods are shipped back to the U.S., duty is paid only on the value added. Because the cost of transporting cut fabric is a factor, most of the Item 807 arrangements have been made with factories in Mexico and the Caribbean. Imports of textiles, apparel, and footwear manufactured under Item 807 increased 80 percent between 1980 and 1985. Fashion goods companies such as Claiborne have not used Item 807 sourcing to the extent that other apparel companies, such as Farah Manufacturing, a maker of men's pants, have.

EMPLOYMENT

Increased production abroad has led to loss of jobs in U.S. apparel manufacturing and has kept wage levels below other manufacturing wages. Exhibit 6 details employment and earnings figures for the industry compared to all manufacturing. Although the average wage of apparel workers in 1986, at $5.81, was nearly $4.00 per hour below the average manufacturing wage, comparative wages in the Far East ranged from as little as $0.20 per hour in China to around $2.00 in Hong Kong.

More than half of all production workers in the apparel industry are unionized. The two major unions are the Amalgamated Clothing and Textile Workers Union (ACTWU) and the International Ladies Garment Workers (ILGWU). Both major unions actively support and lobby for increased quota restrictions on imported goods.

The incentive to outsource is not all due to wage differentials. Apparel importers have stated that they cannot get the quality and reliability from domestic sources that is available overseas.

EXHIBIT 6 EMPLOYMENT AND EARNINGS IN U.S. APPAREL INDUSTRY

	APPAREL AND OTHER TEXTILE PRODUCTS		TOTAL MANUFACTURING	
Year	No. Employed (thousands)	Ave. Wage ($)	No. Employed (thousands)	Ave. Wage ($)
1986	1,115	5.81	19,186	9.73
1985	1,162	5.73	19,426	9.52
1984	1,202	5.53	19,590	9.17
1983	1,169	5.37	18,687	8.84
1982	1,158	5.18	18,848	8.50
1981	1,256	4.98	20,281	7.98
1980	1,297	4.57	20,361	7.27
1979	1,313	4.23	21,062	6.69
1978	1,332	3.94	20,505	6.17
1977	1,316	3.62	19,682	5.68

Source: U.S. Bureau of Labor Statistics.

THE MARKET

Estimated at over $166 billion in 1987, the market for apparel goods continued to be one of the largest consumer segments in the U.S. economy in the late 1980s. Although personal consumption expenditures for clothing and related articles had grown each year, the rate of increase had moderated. Furthermore, as a percent of disposable income, apparel expenditures had declined from around 5.6 percent in 1973 to approximately 4.75 percent in 1986. Exhibit 7 shows apparel expenditures for this fourteen-year period. The slowed rate of growth was attributed to a combination of several factors, including the reluctance of consumers to increase their debt loads and the relative lack of big-selling "trendy" goods during the previous few years. Expectations were for the market to remain strong through the late 1980s and early 1990s but for annual increases to be at a more modest level than in the early 1980s.

EXHIBIT 7 CONSUMER APPAREL EXPENDITURES, 1973-1986

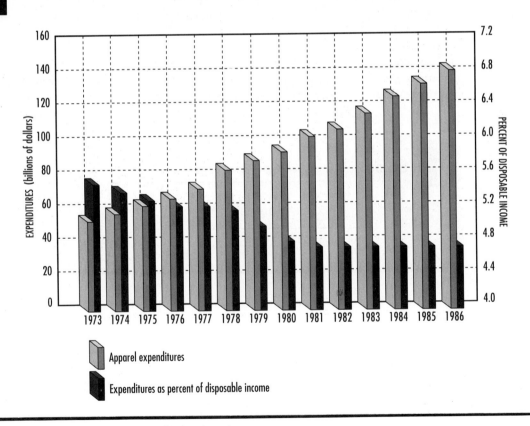

Note: Expenditure amounts represent the seasonally adjusted annual rate.
Source: U.S. Department of Commerce.

Earnings growth was also expected to continue, but also at modest levels. The general outlook was for a quite healthy apparel market in the United States.

THE COMPETITORS

Liz Claiborne's success in designing clothes that appeal to the professional woman attracted a number of significant competitors, including Evan Picone, Donna Karan, Ralph Lauren, and Adrienne Vittadini. Most of them were priced above Claiborne, however. Competition for Liz Claiborne's other lines ranged from designer lines competing with Dana Buchman offerings to specialty lines such as those competing with Claiborne's larger sizes. Surveys of Liz Claiborne customers indicated that they also shopped specialty stores such as Benetton. The competition is therefore hard to specifically identify. In 1989 Liz Claiborne had succeeded in defining and defending a rather unique niche in the market, which could be summarized as "designer clothing at nondesigner prices." The company could legitimately claim to be the "largest women's sportswear manufacturer in the United States" and "the largest better dress company in America."[19]

COMPETITIVE STRATEGIES

As growth stabilized in the industry, manufacturing was further deemphasized in favor of foreign outsourcing. Many companies, such as Kellwood, divested their old manufacturing facilities and looked for acquisitions of other marketing-oriented companies with brand-name products. Competition in the apparel sales industry had come to revolve almost exclusively around design, styling, and service. Another significant marketing innovation of the 1980s was the inclusion of apparel maker and retailer under the same corporate umbrella. Benetton Corp. and The Gap are two companies that have successfully integrated their operations. Liz Claiborne inaugurated its own retail outlets in 1987.

Keener competition among apparel firms also caused more pressure to be placed on manufacturers to tighten their lead times. Designs must be approved and coordinated with the company's other seasonal offerings, a process that can take several months. After samples of goods are shown to buyers in, for instance, a large department store chain and their orders are placed for the company's line, fabrics are ordered for delivery in six to eight weeks. After the fabric is received, the manufacturer typically needs four to six months to finish and ship the goods. In all, the manufacturing part of the cycle can take up to nine months. Adding in design lead times often brings the whole apparel pipeline to around 66 weeks.

One marketing innovation has made lead times even more critical. Traditionally, there have been five seasons for women's wear (summer, early fall, late fall/winter, resort season, and spring). Buying cycles for these seasons have often meant that buyers were placing orders for up to three seasons in the future. Liz Claiborne introduced the six-season fashion year, which increased the number and frequency of seasonal orders to fill at the factory level. Several of Claiborne's competitors followed suit with their own six- and seven-season fashion years.

In the fashion goods segment, a variety of quick response alternatives are being sought to counter long manufacturing lead times. Greater cooperation and communication between retailers and manufacturers has helped some. Large buyers such as Bloomingdale's and Macy's have direct access to the design staffs of such firms as Liz Claiborne and Ralph Lauren. Point-of-sale technology has helped reduce lead times on certain replacement items during the seasonal run.

A number of contractors in the United States have attempted to lure back the apparel business with promises of reduced lead times. Ralph Lauren increased its domestic sourcing in 1987 over previous levels in an attempt to gain a quicker response to the market. Industry analysts predicted that domestic sourcing would also regain favor as sentiment for protectionism grew in Washington. In 1986, The Limited, an integrated manufacturer, announced that it was actively seeking more domestic sources for its contracts. U.S. producers also attempted to be more competitive with foreign contractors through improved technology. Innovations that sought to reduce high-cost labor input were being developed rapidly. Computer-aided garment design was refined through the introduction of improved software packages. Automated marker-making systems and improved water-jet and laser fabric cutting systems were reducing scrap costs as well as labor costs. Programmable sewing units, based on microprocessor technology, were on-line by 1987 in a few plants, although these and most other high-tech innovations were prohibitively expensive for most of the smaller producers.

ENDNOTES

1. Deveny, K., "Can Ms. Fashion Bounce Back?" *Business Week* (January 16, 1989): 64–70.

2. Oberlink, P., "Liz is Big Biz," *Madison Avenue* (October 1986): 29–31.

3. Gannes, S., "America's Fastest-Growing Companies," *Fortune* (May 23, 1988): 28–40.

4. Denveny, "Can Ms. Fashion Bounce Back?" p. 66.

5. Liz Claiborne, Inc., *1987 Annual Report*, p. 6.

6. Ibid.

7. Oberlink, "Liz is Big Biz," p. 29.

8. Deveny, "Can Ms. Fashion Bounce Back?" p. 64.

9. Ibid.

10. Skolnik, R., "Liz the Wiz," *Sales and Marketing Management* (September 9, 1985): 173–176.

11. Ibid., p. 173.

12. Ibid, p. 174.

13. Lardner, J., "Annals of Business: The Sweater Trade—I," *New Yorker* (January 11, 1988): 45.

14. Oberlink, "Liz is Big Biz," p. 30.

15. Skolnik, "Liz the Wiz," p. 176.

16. Trachtenberg, J. A., and T. Agins, "Can Liz Claiborne Continue to Thrive When She is Gone?" *Wall Street Journal* (February 28, 1989): A1.

17. Gannes, "America's Fastest-Growing Companies," p. 30.

18. "Textile, Apparel, and Home Furnishings: Current Analysis," *Standard & Poor's Industry Surveys* (August 27, 1987): T82.

19. Liz Claiborne, Inc., *1987 Annual Report*, p. 4.

ADDITIONAL REFERENCES

"Fortune 500 Largest Industrial Corporations." *Fortune* (April 24, 1989): 346-401.

Lardner, James. "Annals of Business: Global Clothing Industry—Part I." *New Yorker* (January 11, 1988): 39-73.

"Annals of Business: Global Clothing Industry—Part II." *New Yorker* (January 18, 1988): 57-73.

Liz Claiborne, Inc. *1988 Annual Report.*

Liz Claiborne, Inc. *SEC Form 10-K, 1987.*

Schultz, Ellen. "America's Most Admired Corporations." *Fortune* (January 18, 1988).

Sellers, Patricia. "The Rag Trade's Reluctant Revolutionary." *Fortune* (January 5, 1987): 36-38.

Smith, Adam. "How Liz Claiborne Designed an Empire." *Esquire* (January 1986): 78-79.

"Textile, Apparel, and Home Furnishings: Current Analysis." *Standard & Poor's Industry Surveys* (December 11, 1986): T61-T62.

U.S. Department of Commerce. *Statistical Abstract of the United States,* 108th ed. Washington, D.C.: Government Printing Office, 1988.

CASE 3

PIZZA DELIGHTS

JAY HORNE, CHRISTINE PERKINS, KIM GOATES, PETER ASP, KEN SARRIS, JOHN LESLIE, AND JAMES J. CHRISMAN

On the night of April 5, 1986, Earnest Outbanks, manager of the St. George Street Pizza Delights, located in a suburb of Spartanburg, South Carolina, hung up the phone after a two-hour conversation with Leonard Lloyd, owner of three Pizza Delights franchise restaurants in Greer, South Carolina. Outbanks glanced at the clock and noticed that it was almost 11 P.M. There was still a lot of work to be done before closing, and the conversation with Lloyd had put him behind schedule. Although Outbanks tried to concentrate on the job at hand his thoughts kept returning to Lloyd's proposal to purchase the franchise in partnership with him from the Pizza Delights Corporation.

Since assuming control of the company-owned restaurant on St. George Street in 1981, Outbanks had managed to change a sluggish, break-even operation into the second most profitable Pizza Delights in the Greater Spartanburg area (see Exhibit 1 for a map of the area and Exhibit 2 for 1983–1985 income statements). Outbanks' success attracted the attention of Leonard Lloyd, who was interested in acquiring a Pizza Delights franchise in the Spartanburg market. In early 1986, Lloyd contacted Outbanks to discuss the possibility of forming a partnership to purchase the restaurant. Although the two men met on several occasions nothing had yet been resolved. Outbanks had dreamed of owning his own franchise for several years and Lloyd's idea sounded quite attractive. Outbanks was reluctant to give an immediate answer, though. His career with Pizza Delights had been quite successful and he believed that his future with the firm was bright. However, he knew that Lloyd was impatient and that a decision had to be made in the near future.

The remainder of this case describes the history of Pizza Delights, the competitive environment and operations of the St. George Street restaurant, and Leonard Lloyd's business activities and franchise proposal.

Source: **Prepared under the direction of Professor James J. Chrisman, Louisiana State University. The case was prepared for classroom discussion and not to illustrate either effective or ineffective handling of administrative situations. Names and places have been disguised at the request of case subjects. Distributed by the North American Case Research Association. © James J. Chrisman, 1989.**

EXHIBIT 1 AREA MAP

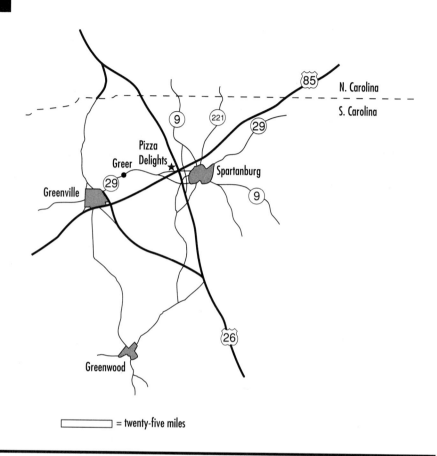

= twenty-five miles

PIZZA DELIGHTS, INC.: COMPANY BACKGROUND AND STRUCTURE

The Pizza Delights chain was established in the greater Omaha, Nebraska, area in the late 1960s. Pizza Delights was one of the first chains to offer customers a limited range of strictly Italian dishes such as pizza and spaghetti. The restaurants enjoyed immediate success because they offered the public a quality pizza with a high level of personal service.

Pizza Delights' early successes caught the attention of a large food manufacturing corporation which, in the late 1970s, purchased the company as well as the rights to their exclusive recipes. With the corporation's financial backing, Pizza Delights restaurants began to appear all over the U.S. Through-

EXHIBIT 2 PIZZA DELIGHTS: THE ST. GEORGE STREET LOCATION INCOME STATEMENTS 1983–1985

INCOME STATEMENTS

	1985	1984	1983
GROSS FOOD SALES	557,278	478,603	422,375
Less allowances	7,869	7,547	7,038
Less sales promotions	34,394	32,982	31,651
NET FOOD SALES	515,015	438,074	383,686
Plus vending machines	1,734	2,103	1,923
Plus game machine	1,582	1,661	1,843
TOTAL REVENUE	518,331	441,838	387,452
COST OF GOODS SOLD	144,406	133,225	117,486
GROSS PROFIT	373,925	308,613	269,966
OPERATING COSTS			
Management Salary	54,373		
Crew labor	56,445	111,391	108,476
Other labor	12,979		
National advertising	7,544		5,637
Coop advertising	12,652	22,880	7,629
Local advertising	9,001		8,538
Operating expenses	12,795		13,330
Utilities cost	19,531		16,343
Maintenance	9,749	40,464	9,019
Uniforms	349		1,113
Other	2,474		2,110
Premiums	5	1,110	210
OPERATING PROFIT	176,028	132,778	97,981
Plus TJTC Credit	4,435	0	0
Less Fixed Costs	47,467*	33,985*	35,647
TOTAL PROFIT	132,996	98,793	62,334

*See Fixed Cost Schedule below.

FIXED COST SCHEDULE FOR 1984–1985 INCOME STATEMENTS

	1985	1984
FIXED COSTS	$47,466	$33,985
T.J.T.C. Expense	161	54
Bank charges	570	615
Personal property tax	221	254
Real estate taxes	3,939	3,939
Licenses & fees	269	289
Equipment depreciation	10,149	7,774
Leasehold amortization	2,618	2,768
Building rental	17,417	15,813
Contigent lease rent	8,442	502
Insurance	2,441	1,909
Abandonment & property	1,236	65
Goodwill amortization	3	0

out this period of rapid expansion, the high degree of quality and service that was Pizza Delights' trademark was maintained.

In the 1980s Pizza Delights introduced several new products including the small pan pizza (1983), the double decker pizza (1984), and the Italian turnover pizza (1985). All of these products met with considerable success in the marketplace.

By 1986 the chain had grown to nearly 1,500 restaurants. Management planned to open 100–200 new restaurants per year over the next decade. Six regional offices, located in major population centers across the United States, had been added since the 1970s in order to accommodate this growth. These regions were subdivided into areas, which were further subdivided into districts (see Exhibit 3). Each region, area, and district had a full-time staff of managers, accountants, inspectors, and other personnel to insure that each individual restaurant fulfilled its duties to the corporation.

HISTORY OF THE ST. GEORGE STREET RESTAURANT

The St. George Street Pizza Delights was built in 1974 primarily to serve customers in the Greater Spartanburg area. It also served commuters and vacationers traveling on Interstate 26 and Interstate 85. In its first few years the restaurant had shown low to moderate profits. The population growth of the Greater Spartanburg area led to increased sales and profits for the restaurant. The growth in population, however, also led to increased competition in the St. George Street restaurant's trade area. By 1981, when Outbanks became manager, the restaurant's net profits before taxes had dipped to $42,680, their lowest level since 1975.

Outbanks inherited a restaurant crew that had been described by the dis-

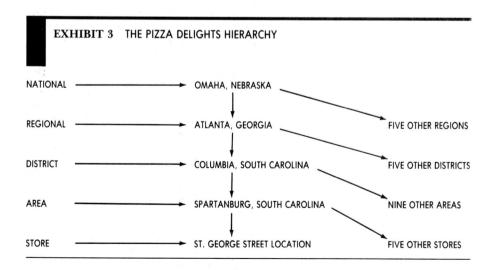

EXHIBIT 3 THE PIZZA DELIGHTS HIERARCHY

trict manager as probably the "most lazy and inhospitable bunch he had ever met." In addition, food costs at the restaurant had been astronomical. Cooks were not preparing the pizzas according to Pizza Delights standards. None of the ingredients were weighed, and Outbanks also suspected that employees were taking pizzas home and giving them away to their friends.

By 1986 most of the obvious problems had been solved and the restaurant's profits had risen steadily under Outbanks' stewardship. His emphasis had been on new policies to improve the efficiency of operations. Although only 20 years old in 1981, Outbanks felt his extensive experience in the pizza business had helped him handle the restaurant's problems. In addition, he had been able to deal effectively with high school and college age employees. Most of the 1986 staff were replacements whom Outbanks had personally selected and trained.

THE GREATER SPARTANBURG ENVIRONMENT

Located in northern South Carolina, Spartanburg was a city of approximately 45,000 people. Situated in an agricultural region that produced cotton, peaches, melons, and feed crops, the city was the seat of Spartanburg County and was part of the tri-county region (Spartanburg, Greenville, and Pickens counties) that made up the Greenville-Spartanburg SMA (Standard Metropolitan Area). A variety of manufacturing businesses in industries such as textiles, metals, rubber, paper, chemicals, clothing, and plumbing supplies were located in the Spartanburg area. The city was also the site for several colleges and universities (see Exhibit 4).

The population of the city of Spartanburg declined by 6.2 percent between 1978 and 1984 (see Exhibit 5). During the same time period the populations of the surrounding county and SMA increased by 8.5 percent and 11.7 percent, respectively. At the same time, the population of the United States grew 8.4 percent.

EXHIBIT 4 COLLEGES & UNIVERSITIES IN SPARTANBURG COUNTY: ENROLLMENTS

INSTITUTION	ENROLLMENT
University of South Carolina — Spartanburg	2,778
Spartanburg Technical College	1,813
Converse College	1,078
Spartanburg Methodist College	1,067
Wofford College	1,034
Rutledge College — Spartanburg	447
TOTAL ENROLLMENT	8,217

Source: South Carolina Statistical Abstract — 1984.

EXHIBIT 5 1978 & 1984 POPULATION STATISTICS FOR SPARTANBURG, SPARTANBURG COUNTY, GREENVILLE-SPARTANBURG SMA, SOUTH CAROLINA, SOUTH ATLANTIC REGION, AND UNITED STATES

Year	Total Population (thousands)	% of U.S.	Total Households (thousands)	% of U.S.	Median Age	% OF POPULATION BY AGE GROUP				
						0–17	18–24	25–34	35–49	≥ 50
SPARTANBURG										
1978	46.9	.02%	16.7	.02%	31.2	26.8%	14.2%	14.6%	16.3%	28.1%
1984	44.9	.02%	17.4	.02%	32.2	24.5%	13.3%	17.0%	16.0%	29.2%
% Change	−6.2%		+4.2%							
SPARTANBURG COUNTY										
1978	196.7	.09%	67.8	.09%	30.6	28.0%	12.6%	16.7%	17.2%	25.5%
1984	213.5	.09%	78.3	.09%	32.1	26.6%	11.1%	17.2%	19.6%	25.5%
% Change	+8.5%		+15.5%							
GREENVILLE-SPARTANBURG SMA										
1978	541.4	.25%	184.5	.24%	29.8	27.9%	13.9%	17.1%	17.1%	24.0%
1984	605.0	.25%	222.1	.26%	31.3	26.2%	12.6%	17.8%	19.5%	23.9%
% Change	+11.7%		+20.4%							
SOUTH CAROLINA										
1978	2,934.8	1.3%	933.8	1.2%	27.7	31.2%	14.5%	15.9%	16.0%	22.5%
1984	3,353.4	1.4%	1,172.0	1.4%	29.8	28.2%	13.3%	17.6%	18.1%	22.7%
% Change	+14.3%		+25.5%							
SOUTH ATLANTIC REGION*										
1978	34,981.7	15.9%	12,186.8	15.9%	30.3	28.2%	13.4%	15.7%	16.3%	26.4%
1984	39,904.5	16.8%	14,612.2	16.8%	32.3	25.4%	12.1%	17.2%	18.5%	26.8%
% Change	+14.1%		+19.9%							
UNITED STATES										
1978	219,768.5	100%	76,904.7	100%	30.1	28.8%	13.2%	15.7%	16.4%	26.0%
1984	238,274.7	100%	86,926.6	100%	31.7	26.3%	12.2%	17.4%	18.3%	25.9%
% Change	+8.4%		+13.0%							

* Includes: Delaware, District of Columbia, Florida, Georgia, Maryland, North Carolina, South Carolina, Virginia, and West Virginia.
Source: "Survey of Buying Power," *Sales & Marketing Management*, 1979 and 1985.

Between 1978 and 1984 per capita incomes increased by about 40 percent in the city of Spartanburg and by more than 50 percent in both Spartanburg county and the Greenville-Spartanburg SMA. By contrast, per capita incomes rose over 60 percent in South Carolina, the South Atlantic region, and the United States during the same period. In 1984, effective per capita buying incomes in the Spartanburg area were approximately $9,000 compared to about $8,500 for the rest of South Carolina (see Exhibit 6).

Sales of eating and drinking places in the city had increased by 5 percent since 1978 (see Exhibit 7). There appeared to be greater opportunities for

EXHIBIT 6 EFFECTIVE BUYING INCOMES IN 1978 & 1984: SPARTANBURG, SPARTANBURG COUNTY, GREENVILLE-SPARTANBURG SMA, SOUTH CAROLINA, SOUTH ATLANTIC REGION, AND UNITED STATES

	TOTAL EBI (IN THOUSANDS)	PER CAPITA EBI	AVERAGE HOUSEHOLD EBI	MEDIAN HOUSEHOLD EBI
SPARTANBURG				
1978	$308,625	$ 6,580	$18,481	$14,721
1984	$410,214	$ 9,136	$23,576	$18,782
% Change	+32.9%	+38.8%	+27.6%	+27.6
SPARTANBURG COUNTY				
1978	$1,127,798	$ 5,734	$16,634	$14,702
1984	$1,943,381	$ 9,102	$24,820	$21,828
% Change	+72.3%	+58.7%	+49.2%	+48.5%
GREENVILLE-SPARTANBURG SMA				
1978	$3,203,011	$ 5,916	$17,360	$15,349
1984	$5,434,481	$8,983	$24,469	$21,540
% Change	+69.7%	+51.8%	+41.0%	+40.3%
SOUTH CAROLINA				
1978	$15,425,876	$ 5,256	$16,519	$14,047
1984	$28,550,182	$ 8,514	$24,360	$20,969
% Change	+85.1%	+62.0%	+47.5%	+49.3%
SOUTH ATLANTIC REGION				
1978	$212,961,331	$ 6,088	$17,475	$14,681
1984	$408,218,168	$10,230	$27,937	$23,576
% Change	+91.7%	+68.0%	+59.9%	+60.6%
UNITED STATES				
1978	$1,439,815,449	$6,552	$18,722	$16,231
1984	$2,576,533,480	$10,813	$29,640	$25,496
% Change	+78.9%	+65.0%	+58.3%	+57.1%

Source: "Survey of Buying Power," *Sales & Marketing Management,* 1979 and 1985.

growth outside the city, as the migration to the suburbs provided increased demand for restaurants in these locations. Between 1978 and 1984 sales for eating and drinking establishments increased by 35 percent in Spartanburg county and by 47 percent in the Greenville-Spartanburg SMA.

COMPETITION IN THE SPARTANBURG AREA

The pizza industry had rapidly expanded in the 1980s. In 1986, the St. George Street restaurant competed with seventeen local and nationally owned pizza restaurants in the Greater Spartanburg area, several other Pizza Delights restaurants, and 170 restaurants of other types. Exhibits 8–10 provide common-

EXHIBIT 7 TOTAL RETAIL AND EATING AND DRINKING PLACES SALES IN 1978 & 1984: SPARTANBURG, SPARTANBURG COUNTY, GREENVILLE-SPARTANBURG SMA, SOUTH CAROLINA, SOUTH ATLANTIC REGION, AND UNITED STATES

	Total Retail Sales	Sales per Capita	EATING & DRINKING PLACES		
			Total Sales	Sales per Capita	% of Total Retail
SPARTANBURG					
1978	$417,207	$ 8,896*	$41,507	$885*	9.9%
1984	$526,485	$11,725*	$43,625	$972*	8.3%
% Change	+26.2%	+31.8%	+5.1%	+9.8%	
SPARTANBURG COUNTY					
1978	$ 635,084	$3,229	$58,911	$299	9.3%
1984	$1,015,451	$4,756	$79,688	$373	7.8%
% Change	+59.9%	+47.3%	+35.3%	+24.7%	
GREENVILLE-SPARTANBURG SMA					
1978	$1,911,506	$3,531	$175,057	$323	9.2%
1984	$3,117,321	$5,153	$257,667	$426	8.3%
% Change	+63.1%	+45.9%	+47.2%	+31.9%	
SOUTH CAROLINA					
1978	$ 9,243,104	$3,149	$ 670,142	$228	7.3%
1984	$15,484,516	$4,618	$1,343,043	$401	8.7%
% Change	+67.5%	+46.6%	+100.4%	+75.9%	
SOUTH ATLANTIC REGION					
1978	$129,343,686	$3,697	$11,434,037	$327	8.8%
1984	$220,144,917	$5,517	$19,950,436	$500	9.1%
% Change	+70.2%	+49.2%	+74.5%	+52.9%	
UNITED STATES					
1978	$ 817,461,457	$3,720	$ 71,602,628	$326	8.8%
1984	$1,296,659,715	$5,442	$124,035,013	$564	9.6%
% Change	+58.6%	+46.3%	+73.2%	+73.0%	

*Retail sales per capita for the city are higher than for the county, SMA, state, region, and nation due to the large number of non-city resident sales.

Source: "Survey of Buying Power," *Sales & Marketing Management*, 1979 and 1985.

size income statements, balance sheets, and financial ratios, respectively, for traditional and fast food restaurants with assets of less than $1 million in 1985. Exhibit 11 shows the locations of competitors in the St. George Street area. Exhibit 12 summarizes the product, service, and pricing strategies of Pizza Delights and its major competitors.

Domino's. Domino's, Inc. was the leading competitor for delivered pizza. The company's strategy was to offer its customers fast delivery (usually less than

EXHIBIT 8 AVERAGE COMMON-SIZE INCOME STATEMENTS FOR TRADITIONAL & FAST FOOD RESTAURANTS IN THE U.S. WITH ASSETS OF LESS THAN $1 MILLION IN 1985

	TRADITIONAL* (N = 481)	FAST FOODS** (N = 301)
Sales	100.0%	100.0%
Cost of Goods Sold	43.8%	39.3%
Gross Profit	56.2%	60.7%
Operating Expenses	52.6%	55.0%
Other Expenses	1.6%	2.7%
Net Profit Before Taxes	2.1%	3.0%

*Includes restaurants selling prepared foods and drinks for consumption on the premises. Caterers and industrial and institutional food service establishments are also included (SIC 5812).

**Includes franchise operations (SIC 5812).

Source: Robert Morris Associates, '86 Annual Statement Studies.

EXHIBIT 9 AVERAGE COMMON-SIZE BALANCE SHEETS FOR TRADITIONAL & FAST FOOD RESTARANTS IN THE U.S. WITH ASSETS OF LESS THAN $1 MILLION IN 1985

	TRADITIONAL* (N = 481)	FAST FOODS** (N = 301)
ASSETS		
Cash & Equivalents	12.1%	14.9%
Trade Receivables (Net)	4.3%	1.9%
Inventory	7.6%	4.8%
All Other Current Assets	2.6%	2.6%
Total Current Assets	26.6%	24.2%
Fixed Assets (Net)	56.3%	53.0%
Intangibles (Net)	4.5%	6.2%
All Other Non-Current Assets	12.6%	16.6%
Total Assets	100.0%	100.0%
LIABILITIES & OWNERS' EQUITY		
Current Liabilities	40.0%	38.6%
Long-Term Debt	32.8%	35.6%
All Other Non-Current Liabilities	2.9%	2.1%
Total Liabilities	75.7%	76.3%
Owners' Equity (Net Worth)	24.3%	23.7%
Total Liabilities + Owners' Equity	100.0%	100.0%

*Includes restaurants selling prepared foods and drinks for consumption on the premises. Caterers and industrial and institutional food service establishments are also included (SIC 5812).

**Includes franchise operations (SIC 5812).

Source: Robert Morris Associates, '86 Annual Statement Studies.

EXHIBIT 10 FINANCIAL RATIOS FOR TRADITIONAL & FAST FOOD RESTAURANTS IN THE U.S. WITH ASSETS OF LESS THAN $1 MILLION IN 1985

Ratios	TRADITIONAL RESTAURANTS*			FAST FOOD RESTAURANTS**		
	Upper Quartile	Median	Lower Quartile	Upper Quartile	Median	Lower Quartile
Current	1.3	0.7	0.3	1.2	0.6	0.3
Quick	0.8	0.4	0.2	0.9	0.4	0.1
Sales/Receivables	INF	451.0	74.9	INF	INF	507.1
Cost of Sales/Inventory	46.1	27.4	16.1	59.6	42.7	28.2
Sales/Working Capital	51.0	−38.5	−12.1	56.2	−31.4	−11.8
Times Interest Earned	4.9	2.0	0.4	5.9	2.5	1.0
Cash Flow/Current Portion of LT Debt	4.5	1.6	0.7	5.4	2.4	1.2
Debt/Equity Ratio	1.0	3.2	−26.2	1.2	3.8	−14.5
Asset Turnover	5.2	3.5	2.2	5.1	3.3	2.4
Return on Equity (%)	62.1%	23.1%	4.6%	81.6%	36.7%	15.9%
Return on Assets (%)	17.1%	5.3%	−3.1%	20.0%	9.6%	1.0%

INF = Infinite.

*Includes restaurants selling prepared foods and drinks for consumption on the premises. Caterers and industrial and institutional food service establishments are also included (SIC 5812). 481 establishments were studied.

**Includes franchise operations (SIC 5812). 301 establishments were studied.

Source: Robert Morris Associates, '86 Annual Statment Studies.

30 minutes) and medium priced pizza. Domino's sold only pizza; the firm did not include other Italian dishes on its menu. Domino's pizza was considered low to medium quality.

Little Caesar's. Little Caesar's was a chain restaurant which catered to the take-out customer; it did not make deliveries or provide facilities for eat-in dining. Its pizza was considered average quality and was priced accordingly. The chain also offered special Greek and Italian salads, sandwiches, and sliced pizza. Little Caesar's frequently placed two-for-one coupons in local newspapers.

Pizza Factory. Located in the nearby Stephenson Plaza, this national chain restaurant provided take out services as well as eat-in dining facilities. Customer service was low, however, as the restaurant did not employ waitresses. Pizza Factory offered low priced, medium quality pizza, a variety of sandwiches, a salad bar, and alcoholic beverages.

EXHIBIT 11 LOCATIONS OF THE ST. GEORGE STREET PIZZA DELIGHTS AND ITS COMPETITORS

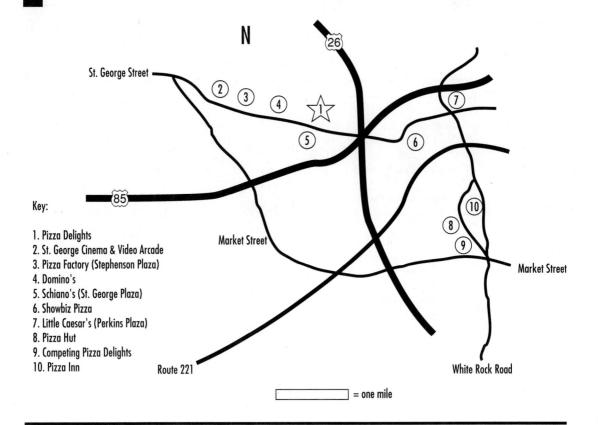

Key:

1. Pizza Delights
2. St. George Cinema & Video Arcade
3. Pizza Factory (Stephenson Plaza)
4. Domino's
5. Schiano's (St. George Plaza)
6. Showbiz Pizza
7. Little Caesar's (Perkins Plaza)
8. Pizza Hut
9. Competing Pizza Delights
10. Pizza Inn

Showbiz Pizza. Showbiz Pizza was a national chain restaurant catering to children. Its dining room decor included dancing bears, games, and other attractions. Showbiz offered a medium quality pizza at a medium to high price.

Pizza Hut. Pizza Hut was Pizza Delights' largest competitor. Pizza Hut was a full-service pizza restaurant, offering high levels of service and a quality product at a medium to high price. In the 1980s the company successfully introduced several new pizza products, each of which it advertised heavily.

Pizza Hut's White Rock Road location was only a few miles to the east of the St. George Pizza Delights. This Pizza Hut was more successful than the other Pizza Delights restaurant located nearby. Because of the growing population in the area, the Pizza Hut Corporation had considered building a new restaurant on St. George Street. These plans had concerned Outbanks because 30–35% of his customers were from the immediate area. After conducting a

EXHIBIT 12 COMPARISONS OF PRODUCT, SERVICE AND PRICING STRATEGIES OF PIZZA COMPETITORS

	PIZZA DELIGHTS	DOMINO'S	LITTLE CAESAR'S	PIZZA FACTORY	SHOWBIZ	PIZZA HUT	PIZZA INN	SCHIANO'S
Services								
Eat-In	yes	no	no	yes	yes	yes	yes	yes
Take-Out	yes	yes	yes	yes	no	yes	yes	yes
Delivery	no	yes	no	no	no	no	yes	no
Buffet	no	no	no	no	no	no	yes	no
Luncheon Menu	yes	no	no	yes	yes	yes	yes	no
Salad Bar	yes	no	no	yes	no	yes	yes	no
Service Level	high	high (delivery only)	low	low	high	high	high	high
Products (Dinner only)								
Quality	med/high	low/med	medium	medium	medium	med/high	low/med	high
# of Pizzas on Menu	6	2	6	6	5	10	12	6
Types of Pizzas	2	1	1	1	1	3	2	2
Sizes	3	2	3	3	3	3	4	3
Slices	no	no	yes	no	no	no	no	no
Meat/Fish Toppings	6	4	6	9	4	7	6	5
Vegetable Toppings	6	7	7	10	6	8	7	6
Italian Dishes	spaghetti	no	no	no	no	spaghetti, cavatini	spaghetti, lasagna	parmigiana, calzone, lasagna
Sandwiches (# × sizes)	4	0	3 × 2	4	5	3 × 2	4	6 × 2
Salads (exc. Bar)	no	no	3 × 3	no	1	no	1	2
Alcoholic Beverages	beer	no	no	beer	beer	beer	beer, wine	beer, wine
Other Beverages	soft drinks, tea, milk, coffee	coke	soft drinks	soft drinks, tea	soft drinks, tea, milk, coffee	soft drinks, tea, milk, coffee	soft drinks, tea, milk, coffee	soft drinks

(continued)

EXHIBIT 12 (continued)

	PIZZA DELIGHTS	DOMINO'S	LITTLE CAESAR'S	PIZZA FACTORY	SHOWBIZ	PIZZA HUT	PIZZA INN	SCHIANO'S
Prices								
Med. Cheese Pizza	$7.45	$6.02	$6.78	$6.70	$8.09	$7.05–7.25	$5.80–7.80	$4.95–6.45
Med. 5–7 Toppings (#)	$10.00 (6)	—	$10.29 (5)	$9.55 (6)	$10.99 (6)	$9.80 (6)	$9.35–9.75 (7)	$9.20–10.70 (6)
Med. 8–11 Toppings (#)	$10.80 (9)	$11.12 (9)	—	$11.25 (11)	—	$10.60 (9)	$10.20–10.70 (9)	$10.20–11.70 (8)
Lg. Cheese Pizza	$9.85	$8.17	$9.28	$8.00	$9.99	$9.45–9.65	$9.00–9.50	$7.20–8.70
Lg. 5–7 Toppings (#)	$12.70 (6)	—	$13.52 (5)	$10.95 (6)	$12.99 (6)	$12.50 (6)	$11.85–12.35 (7)	$12.20–13.70 (6)
Lg. 8–11 Toppings (#)	$13.55 (9)	$15.42 (9)	—	$13.25 (11)	—	$13.35 (9)	$12.80–13.40 (9)	$13.20–14.70 (8)
Toppings — Med./Lg.	$.85/.95	$1.02/1.45	$.77/.96	$.85/.95	$.90/1.00	$.90/1.00	$.85/.95	$.85/1.00
Italian Dishes	$1.99–3.39	—	—	—	—	$2.09–4.49	$1.89–3.89	$3.29–6.95
Sandwiches	$2.89	—	$2.25–2.69	$2.49	$1.39–2.59	$2.79–3.79	$0.79–2.59	$2.15–4.55
Salads	$2.49	—	$1.20–4.69	$2.59	$2.29	$2.79	$1.99	$1.79–3.49
Alcohol (Glass)	$.95	—	—	$.75	$.99	$1.00	$1.00	$.95–1.60
Other Beverages	$.50–$.75	$0.65	$.48–$.87	$.55–$.75	$.50–$.79	$.50–$.80	$.45–$.80	$.65

market survey Pizza Hut decided against building the new restaurant in 1986. The project, however, was still under consideration for the future.

Pizza Inn. Besides Pizza Hut, Pizza Inn was Pizza Delights' most formidable competitor. Pizza Inn offered a variety of services including eat-in dining, take-outs, home delivery (started in early 1986), a salad bar, a luncheon buffet during the weekdays, and a dinner buffet every Tuesday. Its pizza was low to medium quality and was priced accordingly.

Schiano's. Schiano's was part of a chain which offered high quality, high priced "New York" style pizza and extensive service. This restaurant was still under construction but was scheduled to open in late 1986. The site was located directly across the street from Outbanks' restaurant in the new St. George Street Plaza.

Grocery Stores. The grocery stores in the area stocked a diverse line of pizzas and pizza products including microwave pizzas, store-made pizzas, and national brands of frozen pizzas. For the do-it-yourself customers, grocers also offered pre-packaged pizza ingredients such as instant pizza crust, sauces, grated pizza cheese, and sliced pepperoni. These products were generally of lower quality than the pizzas served in restaurants. Prices for store-bought and do-it-yourself pizzas generally ranged from $.79 to $4.00.

DELIVERY

In the 1980s several pizza delivery stores, such as Domino's, were opened in the Greater Spartanburg area. To penetrate this segment of the market, Pizza Delights had opened a delivery store in August 1984 in the northeastern section of Spartanburg. This store produced pizzas for delivery only to households within a ten-mile radius of the store. This delivery area included about 70 percent of Greater Spartanburg but excluded most of the area served by the St. George Street restaurant.

In order to save transportation and delivery costs, the delivery store held orders until a large number of pizzas could be delivered to one area. As a result, delivery times sometimes exceeded one hour, and pizzas were frequently delivered cold. According to market research, approximately 75 percent of the customers surveyed were dissatisfied with the Pizza Delights delivery service.

THE ST. GEORGE STREET RESTAURANT

Although pizza was the primary product, the St. George Street restaurant also offered other items such as sandwiches, spaghetti, and a salad bar. Menu items and prices at the St. George Street restaurant are listed in Exhibit 13.

EXHIBIT 13   THE ST. GEORGE STREET LOCATION: MENU ITEMS & PRICES

	SMALL	MEDIUM	LARGE*
Pizza			
Double Decker (3 varieties)	$8.00	$10.80	$13.55
Pan Pizzas:			
—Cheese	$5.05	$ 7.45	$ 9.85
—Delight (6 toppings)	$7.30	$10.00	$12.70
—Super Delight (9 toppings)	$8.00	$10.80	$13.55
Additional toppings	$ .75	$ .85	$ .95

(Pepperoni, Ham, Pork, Beef, Italian Sausage, Mushroom, Onion, Green Pepper, Black Olive, Jalapeno Pepper, Anchovy, Extra Cheese)

	SMALL	REGULAR
Spaghetti		
w/ Meat sauce	$1.99	$3.19
w/ Meatballs	$2.39	$3.39
Salad bar		
as a meal	$2.49	
with a meal	$1.99	
children under 12	$ .99	
Sandwiches (4 varieties)	$2.89	

Drinks	Soft Drinks:	Pitcher $2.25	Coffee	$.50	Beer: Glass	$ .95
		Large $ .75	Milk	$.55	Pitcher	$3.95
		Medium $ .70	Ice Tea	$.65		
		Small $ .65				

LUNCHEON SPECIALS: MONDAY–FRIDAY

	ONLY	W/SALAD BAR (ONE TRIP)
Italian Turnover**		
Cheese	$2.49	$3.88
Sausage	$2.49	$3.88
Small Pan Pizza		
Pepperoni	$1.79	$3.18
Supreme		$3.58
(6 toppings)	$2.19	

*Small pizzas served 1–2 persons; medium 3–4 persons; large 5–6 persons.
**Guaranteed to be ready in 10 minutes or the lunch is free.

Exhibit 14 provides a per-item breakdown of food and beverage sales and costs for 1984–1985.

According to Outbanks, the restaurant did not have a specific target market; all types of people frequented the restaurant. The store was convenient to area residents, shoppers of the two nearby plazas, commuters, and theatergoers. Almost 50% of the St. George Street restaurant's customers drove between three and five miles to the restaurant. Market research sponsored by the corporation indicated that regular customers composed 58% of the cus-

EXHIBIT 14 THE ST. GEORGE STREET LOCATION: GROSS PROFIT BY PRODUCT LINE

	1985	1984
Pizza		
Eat-in Pizza	$204,886	$168,174
Carry-Out Pizza	215,806	181,774
Net Pizza	$420,692	$349,948
Plus: Pizza Allowances	5,772	4,806
Coupon Sales	31,213	30,241
Total Prom/Adv Sales	36,985	35,047
Gross Pizza Sales	$457,677	$384,995
Cost of Pizza Dough	20,530	17,793
Cost of Toppings	38,066	30,666
Cost of Cheese	47,944	41,698
Cost of Paper-Pizza	6,580	5,663
Freight	99	1,157
Total Pizza Cost	$113,219	$ 96,977
GROSS PROFIT ON PIZZA	$344,458	$288,018
Beer: Sales	$ 13,747	$ 13,236
Costs	4,453	4,004
GROSS PROFIT ON BEER	$ 9,294	$ 9,232
Drinks: Sales	$ 39,599	$ 33,200
Costs	8,162	6,584
GROSS PROFIT ON SOFT DRINKS	$ 31,437	$ 26,616
Other: Salad Sales	26,295	27,012
Pasta Sales	9,069	9,873
Sandwich Sales	5,615	4,805
Other Prom/Adv. Reven.	5,278	5,482
Total Other Sales	$ 46,257	$ 47,172
Cost of Other Sales	18,572	20,649
GROSS PROFIT ON OTHER SALES	$ 27,685	$ 26,523

tomer base and that they ate at the restaurant once a month on average. Quality and service were the two most frequently cited reasons why customers visited the St. George Street location.

SALES PATTERNS

Sales at the St. George Street restaurant were seasonal. The winter months of January, February, and March accounted for only 13% of yearly revenues. The months of April through June accounted for 24% of sales while 31% of sales occurred between October and December. The peak season for sales was in the months of July to September with 32% of sales. September was typically the best month for the restaurant (18% of annual sales) because of the weekly football games at the nearby high school. After the games spectators and students often met for a evening snack at Pizza Delights.

Average weekly sales were approximately $10,500. As shown in Exhibit 15 the slowest day of the week was Monday, which accounted for only about 8.5% of sales. Friday was the busiest day, accounting for 23.4% of weekly revenues.

Lunch sales were always low. The best day for lunchtime sales was Friday, but even on this day lunch sales averaged only 3.3% of weekly revenues. The slowest day for lunch was Tuesday, which accounted for only 1.8% of weekly sales. The Pizza Delights Corporation had introduced the Italian turnover pizza as a strictly lunchtime item to boost lunch sales at its restaurants. Lunch sales had not increased at the St. George Street location, however; sales had simply shifted from the small pan pizzas to the Italian turnovers.

ADVERTISING AND SALES PROMOTION

The St. George Street restaurant spent over $29,000 on national, co-op, and local advertising in 1985 (see Exhibit 2). All national and co-op advertising for

EXHIBIT 15 DAILY SALES BREAKDOWNS

	LUNCH		DINNER	
	$	%	$	%
Monday	198	1.9	692	6.6
Tuesday	186	1.8	716	6.8
Wednesday	191	1.8	874	8.3
Thursday	260	2.5	1,390	13.3
Friday	350	3.3	2,105	20.0
Saturday	308	2.9	1,761	16.8
Sunday	205	1.9	1,277	12.1

Average sales per week: $10,513

the Pizza Delights chain restaurants was coordinated by an advertising firm in Washington, D.C., and was financed by the restaurants on a percentage-of-sales basis. This policy applied to both company-owned and franchised restaurants, neither of which had any input into these decisions. A sample announcement of a new promotional campaign for the Italian turnover is provided in Exhibit 16.

National advertising was arranged by the corporation to familiarize people with the Pizza Delights name and products. It consisted primarily of commercials aired on national television during prime-time and the weekends.

Co-op advertising was done on a district-by-district basis to promote individual restaurants and products. The bulk of the Greater Spartanburg area co-op advertising was done in the peak fall season. The main component of the co-op advertising was a monthly four-color, free-standing insert in the city

EXHIBIT 16   PROMOTIONAL ANNOUNCEMENT TO SPARTANBURG PIZZA DELIGHTS

HOT NEWS FROM YOUR FRIENDS AT BEAUMONT GREEN ADVERTISING
TO: Pizza Delights Managers & Employees/Spartanburg
DATE: February 26, 1986
SUBJECT: Advertising for the Italian Turnover

Background
Many of you will recall the tremendous success that the introduction of the small pan pizza had on our business in 1983. In 1986, the opportunity to stimulate both trial and frequency at lunch lies mainly in the area of menu expansion. Therefore, the Italian Turnover has been developed. This new product will increase your sales and profits at lunch. You have all shown your operational strength with the Double Decker Pizza introduced in 1984. Let's make the Italian Turnover the success story of 1986!

Television
Starting March 14, 1986 and running through May 1, 1986 three new TV commercials focusing on the Italian Turnover will be run.

Radio Promotions
A radio promotion has been developed and implemented. This promotion is provided free of charge in exchange for Italian Turnovers for giveaways. Details of the promotion are provided below:
WASQ-FM will encourage listeners to be the "X" number caller that spotted the WASQ logo on one of the Italian Turnover outdoor billboards. Winners receive two Italian Turnovers and two medium soft drinks. There are to be three giveaways per day, Monday thru Friday, for a total of 60 giveaways.

Outdoor
There will be outdoor boards strategically placed in the area. The message will be "Turn over a new lunch with the Italian Turnover," which is the main print advertising theme for the introduction of the Italian Turnover. These boards will be posted from March 26, 1986 to May 10, 1986.

newspaper. This ad usually was accompanied by coupons which allowed customers a 15–20% discount off regular prices.

Local ads were paid by the individual restaurants and placed in local papers. Franchise owners had greater discretion than managers of company-owned restaurants concerning the types and amounts of local promotions used.

Outbanks had tried a variety of promotional techniques to increase sales. For example, if a child read five books in one month he or she would receive a free small pan pizza. During birthday parties at the restaurant participants were given the opportunity to create their own pizzas in the kitchen. Two other past promotions were "family night" and "football night." Family night was a dinner promotion in which a family could buy a large pizza and a pitcher of soft drinks for $9.95. According to Outbanks this promotion was a huge success at the St. George Street restaurant but was discontinued by the corporation because of low response on a national level. On "football night" small pan pizzas and soft drinks were sold at high school football games for 99 cents. This promotion was also discontinued because the district office felt that it would ruin Pizza Delights' high quality/high service image. Despite the district office's concerns, Outbanks noted that the football night promotion generated additional sales of around $800 per game.

PURCHASING

According to Outbanks, all the supplies used at company-owned restaurants had to be obtained from the parent company. These items included everything from straws and napkins to pizza dough and pepperoni. If an emergency situation occurred, such as a shortage of green peppers, the restaurants were allowed to make purchases from outside suppliers as long as these purchases, in total, did not exceed one percent of yearly sales for the individual restaurant. However, the practice of outside buying was not encouraged by the corporation.

All purchases at company-owned restaurants in excess of $500 had to be approved by the area supervisor, the district manager, and the regional vice-president before the restaurant manager could proceed with the investment. The lag between requests and approvals sometimes created problems for Outbanks. For example, the new small pan pizzas, double decker pizzas, and Italian turnover pizzas required a great deal of refrigerator space for storage. According to Outbanks, however, Pizza Delights had not provided his restaurant with the additional freezer capacity needed to store these items.

Franchised restaurants had more flexibility in purchasing than company-owned restaurants. To insure standardization, items such as printed napkins and pizza ingredients still had to be purchased from the parent corporation but other items, such as pizza cutters, could be purchased from outside sources. Outbanks believed that certain items such as sauce ladies (an $8 item) could be purchased from outside suppliers at prices that were 10–20% less than the prices charged by the corporation.

EXHIBIT 17 THE ST. GEORGE STREET LOCATION: RESTAURANT LAYOUT

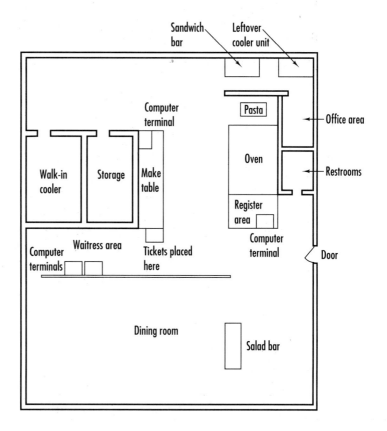

OPERATIONS

Order Processing. The layout of the St. George Street restaurant is shown in Exhibit 17. Orders were processed as follows:

After taking an order the waitress punched it into one of the computer terminals located near her station or the cash register. Tickets were printed out on printers located over the cook's make table and at the waitress station. If the order was for a pan pizza, the cook had to walk twenty feet to the walk-in cooler and get a dough shell. If the order was for a double decker pizza, the dough was rolled out on the table at that time. The pizza, whether it was double decker or pan, was then made on the table and placed in the oven. Next, the ticket was moved to an order stand at the end of the make table where an employee-in-charge would place it on a ticket holder. During busy nights tickets were often misplaced.

Pizzas were cooked on a conveyor oven which was two years old and in good repair. The oven had two conveyors. The upper conveyor was kept in operation at all times; the lower conveyor was used only during peak periods. Both conveyors were ten feet long. Uncooked pizzas were loaded on the first two feet of each conveyor. The oven was six feet long and could accommodate up to six pizzas at a time, per conveyor. The last two feet of the conveyors were used to allow the pizzas to cool off before serving.

After the pizza was cooked, it was given to take-out customers at the cash register where payment was made. Waitresses took the pizza and ticket to the tables of dine-in customers who made payment after they finished dining.

Operating Concerns. Outbanks realized that there were several capacity problems that needed to be resolved if sales and profits at the restaurant were to increase. For example, oven capacity was limited by the speed of the conveyors and this constrained sales on busy nights. Even though the conveyor-type oven cooked pizzas faster (eight minutes for cooking and one minute for cooling) than traditional pizza ovens under normal circumstances, the speed of the conveyors could not be adjusted up or down. With traditional ovens it was possible to "stack" cook the pizzas. Although this procedure sometimes lowered the quality of the final product (e.g. burnt pizzas) and created confusion among the workers, it did allow many more pizzas to be cooked during the course of an evening. Furthermore, while the conveyor oven produced a more uniform quality pizza, the traditional oven was better for cooking items such as spaghetti and hot sandwiches. Outbanks had considered purchasing another conveyor oven at an installed price of $12,500 but had not discussed this idea with the area supervisor. Outbanks estimated that a traditional oven would cost $8,200 installed.

Cooler space was another problem. Outbanks stated that the constant traffic in and out of the cooler made it difficult to keep items cold. For example, customers consistently complained that the beer was too warm. Outbanks speculated that this was one reason why beer sales had not increased as rapidly as the sales of other items. Warm beer was not the only concern, however. According to Outbanks, because pizza ingredients and other foods were not kept cold enough, inventory spoilage, which amounted to about $175–$200 per month, was increasing. The problem was especially noticeable on the peak nights of Friday and Saturday. On these nights employees had to shuffle items around in the walk-in freezer to make room for the dough shells. This situation often caused older stock to be used last.

Outbanks had spoken to the district manager about purchasing a new walk-in cooler for the restaurant but had no idea how long it would take for the Pizza Delights hierarchy to approve the purchase. The new walk-in cooler was estimated to cost approximately $11,000.

Outbanks also noted that dining room seating and parking capacity at the restaurant was limited. The dining room consisted of 22 tables which could seat 88 customers. During busy nights customers were forced to form a line out the door, waiting for an empty table. Furthermore, the parking lot had only thirty spaces, which created havoc on Friday and Saturday nights as take-out and dine-in customers tried to find a place to park. Due to the limited parking, employees were required to park in a dirt field behind the restaurant. Outbanks estimated that it would $8,000 to pave the field and that this area would provide 15 additional parking spaces.

EMPLOYEES

Outbanks' staff included two assistant managers, Pete Gorman and Betty Franks, who were responsible for supervising the restaurant when Outbanks was not working and for helping him with other managerial chores such as purchasing, inventory, and scheduling. Both assistant managers were required to work a minimum of 55 hours per week for which they were paid $5.80 per hour. Assistant managers were paid time-and-one-half for any additional hours worked.

Gorman was a 36-year old ex-high school teacher. He had been an assistant manager at another Pizza Delights for several years prior to joining Outbanks' staff. Gorman was characterized by one employee as a stringent, rule-oriented manager who was actively seeking a promotion. Franks was a recent graduate of Clemson University. According to Outbanks she had brought many innovative ideas to the restaurant, including the idea to weigh out the cheese instead of using cheese cups. Although Outbanks had not yet tried this idea, he knew of a manager in another location who had cut his cheese costs by 10% using this technique.

In addition to Outbanks, Gorman, and Franks, the St. George Street restaurant employed 17 hourly workers, including six waitresses, seven cooks, two dishwashers, and two "employees-in-charge" (EICs). Most of these employees worked on a part-time basis. All employees were evaluated twice each year and received an automatic ten-cent raise regardless of performance.

The waitresses were responsible for seating customers, taking orders, and serving the meal to the customer. Although their base pay was below the minimum wage, after tips waitresses usually earned well above the minimum wage of $3.35 per hour. Cooks were hired to do prep-work, cook the food, and maintain the cleanliness of the facility. Their starting pay was at or slightly above the minimum wage. Besides washing dishes, dishwashers were responsible for keeping the dining room and other work areas clean. They were usually hired at minimum wage and promoted to cook after a few months. The EICs were cooks or waitresses who, through experience and expertise, had shown that they could handle additional responsibilities. Paid in excess of $4.00 per hour, they were responsible for the supervision of the cooking and the daily bookkeeping.

Commenting on his staff Outbanks said, "The St. George Street Pizza Delights is a quality restaurant because everyone from me to the dishwashers work as a team to provide the best product, with the best service, to our customers." The cooks and waitresses, however, were generally young and often had conflicting responsibilities, such as school or another job. Consequently, Outbanks realized that maintaining a high level of commitment among them would be difficult.

LABOR COSTS

In accordance with company policy, all labor costs were computed daily. Pizza Delights had established a labor grid which stipulated how many employees were needed each day during lunch and dinner (see Exhibit 18). Outbanks used these labor grids and the average break times given to employees to calculate his daily labor needs and prepare the work schedule. At the end of each

EXHIBIT 18 PIZZA DELIGHTS PROJECTED LABOR SCHEDULE: LUNCH & DINNER

LUNCH		DINNER	
Projected Sales per hour 11 AM–4 PM	*Projected Labor Needs (# of workers)*	*Projected Sales per hour 4 PM–Closing*	*Projected Labor Needs (# of workers)*
$ 0– 41	2	$ 0– 95	2
42– 61	3	96– 143	3
62– 87	4	144– 190	4
88– 119	5	191– 211	5
120– 156	6	212– 255	6
157– 180	8	256– 295	8
181– 202	9	296– 338	9
203– 245	10	339– 379	10
246– 298	11	380– 423	11
299– 342	12	424– 461	12
343– 387	13	462– 507	13
388– 450	14	508– 547	14
451– 519	15	548– 589	15
520– 614	16	590– 631	16
615– 695	17	632– 673	17

Average total hours of breaktime per week:

Monday	Tuesday	Wednesday	Thursday	Friday	Saturday	Sunday
2.6	2.6	2.9	3.5	4.6	4.2	1.9

Average hourly pay scale per position:

Assistant Managers	$5.80
Employees-in-charge	$4.10
Cook	$3.45
Waitresses	$2.30 plus tips
Dishwasher	$3.35

day, the actual number of employee hours were compared to the suggested labor grid hours, given the daily sales volume. All variances had to be explained to the district manager.

The number of employees needed per sales dollar was higher during lunch hours because of the lower per item price of lunchtime products, and because of the extra demands in providing a ten-minute guarantee for serving the small pan and Italian turnover pizzas.

Since the introduction of the Italian turnover pizza, each Pizza Delights restaurant was required to have a minimum of ten employees present during the guaranteed hours of 11 A.M. to 1:30 P.M., Monday thru Friday, in order to better promote the new product. As a result, an average of 55 employee hours were needed on the weekdays between 8 A.M. and 4 P.M. No minimum was specified for the weekends, however. Before the Italian turnover was introduced, the St. George Street restaurant operated with a total of 28 employee hours between 8 A.M. and 4 P.M. on Monday, Tuesday, Wednesday, Saturday, and Sunday, 33 total employee hours on Thursdays, and 38 total employee hours on Fridays.

LLOYD'S GREER AREA PIZZA DELIGHTS FRANCHISE OPERATIONS

Leonard Lloyd had been involved in the pizza business for five years prior to his interest in the St. George Street Pizza Delights. In 1986 he owned three Pizza Delights franchises, all of which were profitable. The first Pizza Delights franchise Lloyd acquired was built in 1978 in Greer, South Carolina, a small rural town of about 10,000 people. The restaurant was company-owned during its first three years of operation. Recognizing the potential of the restaurant, Lloyd, an area businessman, purchased the franchise from Pizza Delights in 1981 for $375,000, plus $1.2 million for the right to use the company's brand name.

In his first year of operation Lloyd increased the seating capacity at the restaurant from 65 to 150 people. He felt that the demand for pizza in the Greer area could easily accommodate a dining area of that size. Sales revenues increased 7 percent that year.

In 1982, disenchanted by the slow growth in sales, Lloyd decided to offer customers more specials and new dining options. Two-for-one coupons were placed in the local newspapers on a regular basis. Taking advantage of his two ovens and massive dining area, Lloyd also began to offer a lunch buffet during the weekdays to attract students from a nearby community college. Sales revenues increased by 10 percent almost immediately, and many customers began inquiring about the possibility of a Sunday buffet. Lloyd's decision to extend the buffet to Sundays allowed him to capture a larger share of the after-church market, increasing sales during a time of the week that had traditionally been slow.

According to Lloyd, the Greer franchise was very successful and the outlook for the future was bright. Restaurant sales had increased by about 33 percent since 1982. Its only direct pizza competitor, Papa Joe's, offered relatively little service and relied almost entirely on take-out business.

In 1983 and 1984 Lloyd purchased the franchises to two additional Pizza Delights restaurants in two small rural communities, both approximately 5–10 miles outside of Greer. Both of these restaurants followed the same strategy as the Greer restaurant and both were profitable. Lloyd had been able to retain the managers of these restaurants by giving them minority ownership positions in the business.

THE FRANCHISING PLAN

Although neither Outbanks nor Lloyd had worked out all the details of the franchising plan, Lloyd expected that many of the same strategies he had used at the Greer restaurants would be feasible at the St. George Street location. Lloyd wanted to offer a buffet-style dinner or lunch to customers at least once or twice a week. He also wanted to use more coupons and promotions to increase sales during slow periods. Outbanks had considered these options in the past, but company policy had prevented him from implementing them.

Lloyd was also considering setting up a delivery service at the St. George Street location. Spartanburg was the home of six colleges, and Lloyd expected that such a service would be welcomed by students in the area. A delivery operation would require two half-time employees paid at the minimum wage, plus the purchase of two used cars for approximately $5,000 apiece. Gas, maintenance, depreciation, and other related operating expenses associated with the vehicle were estimated at 20 cents per mile.

FRANCHISE FINANCING ARRANGEMENTS

Lloyd had some initial inquiries at the Pizza Delights' district office in Columbia, South Carolina, to determine if purchasing the restaurant would be feasible. The district office quoted Lloyd a price of $725,000 for the physical facilities plus an annual payment amounting to 12% of the restaurant's net profits before taxes. The Pizza Delights brand name was valued at over $1 million. However, Lloyd knew he would not have to pay this fee since he had already purchased the brand rights for the Greer restaurants.

Lloyd was prepared to invest $250,000 in the restaurant. Outbanks' financial commitment would be considerably less as he had only around $25,000 to $30,000 to invest. Lloyd planned to borrow the balance of the funds from one of the financial institutions in the area.

A Spartanburg banker stated that for a commercial loan her bank would require Lloyd and Outbanks to provide at least 25 percent of the total funds needed to purchase the franchise. In addition, both Lloyd and Outbanks would be required to give the bank a first mortgage on the restaurant, as well as pledge all their personal assets as security. The loan itself would probably be a term loan amortized over 15 years with a balloon payment after 3–5 years. In 1986 the prime rate for commercial borrowing was 7.5%. Lloyd realized that he would probably have to pay at least 1.5–2.5% over prime. Lloyd figured that payments for a straight 15 year amortized loan of $500,000 at 10% interest would amount to $5,373 per month or almost $65,000 per year.

The Spartanburg banker also informed Lloyd that franchise loans were not frequently approved by her bank, citing an example of another Pizza Delights franchise in Greenwood, South Carolina (population approximately 20,000), that was recently denied a loan. Exhibits 19 and 20 provide the 1985 income statement and balance sheet for the Greenwood Pizza Delights

EXHIBIT 19 1985 INCOME STATEMENT FOR THE GREENWOOD PIZZA DELIGHTS

SALES		$638,284
Food In	$322,928	
Food Out	239,260	
Food Delivery	14,064	
Food Sub-Total	$576,252	
Beverages In	$ 61,612	
Beverages Delivery	120	
Beverages Sub-Total	$ 61,732	
Premiums	300	
COST OF GOODS SOLD		$184,400
Food Cost	$167,600	
Beverage Cost	$ 16,800	
Premiums	0	
GROSS PROFIT		$453,884
OPERATING EXPENSES		$303,560
Advertising	$ 22,000	
Auto & Delivery Expenses	600	
Payroll	198,325	
Repairs	19,403	
Utilities & Telephone	30,504	
Operating Supplies	10,320	
Other Operating Expenses	22,408	
OPERATING PROFIT		$150,324
ADMINISTRATIVE EXPENSES		$131,080
Royalty Fee	$ 19,000	
Insurance	12,450	
Interest	7,770	
Depreciation	27,250	
Rent	42,000	
Taxes & Licenses	4,000	
Other Administrative Expenses	18,610	
NET PROFIT BEFORE TAXES		$ 19,244

EXHIBIT 20 1985 BALANCE SHEET FOR THE GREENWOOD PIZZA DELIGHTS

ASSETS		$119,820
Cash in Bank	−$14,200	
Cash on Hand	1,000	
Investments	2,700	
Accounts Receivable	1,500	
Inventory	7,500	
Total Current Assets	−$ 1,500	
Automobiles	$17,500	
less Depreciation	− 9,500	
Net Automobiles	$ 8,000	
Equipment	$150,000	
less Depreciation	− 70,000	
Net Equipment	$ 80,000	
Leasehold Improvements	$10,200	
less Depreciation	− 3,000	
Net Leasehold	$ 7,200	
Total Fixed Assets	$95,200	
Deposits	$ 220	
Insurance Reserve Fund	1,700	
Prepaid Insurance	3,000	
Prepaid Rent	4,200	
Franchise Fees	17,000	
Total Other Non-Current Assets	$26,120	
LIABILITIES		$ 63,950
Accounts Payable	$ 650	
Other Current Liabilities	13,300	
Total Current Liabilities	$13,950	
Long-Term Liabilities	$50,000	
EQUITY		$ 55,870
LIABILITIES + EQUITY		$119,820

franchise. Lloyd was not particularly worried by the banker's pessimism, however. He had a successful track record in business and had never experienced problems obtaining financing in the past. He saw no reason why it would be different this time.

FRANCHISE OWNERSHIP AND MANAGEMENT

Based on his conversations with Lloyd, Outbanks anticipated that he would receive a one-quarter to one-third interest in the business, plus his normal salary, for managing the restaurant. Outbanks also expected to have complete control over day-to-day operations. With respect to strategy and policy matters, Outbanks believed that both he and Lloyd would have an equal voice, an arrangement Outbanks felt was similar to the deal Lloyd had made with the other franchise managers.

OUTBANKS' DILEMMA

After weighing the pros and cons of the situation in his mind, Outbanks still was not sure whether he should join Lloyd in the franchising venture or try to advance in the company. Outbanks felt that he was responsible for most of the restaurant's current success and deserved a share of the profits. Yet he admired Lloyd for his success with the Greer Pizza Delights franchises. On the other hand, Outbanks wondered if Lloyd's plans, which had worked so well in Greer, would be successful at the St. George Street restaurant. He also knew the Pizza Delights was growing rapidly and that there might soon be an area supervisor position open for a young, energetic manager with a proven track record.

Personal problems also caused Outbanks to wonder whether he would continue to have the time, money, and motivation to devote to such a venture. A major dispute with his recently estranged wife had greatly taxed Outbanks' mental and physical endurance. This dispute, which Outbanks expected to end in divorce, was also likely to deplete his financial resources once it had been settled.

Despite all of his problems, as Outbanks prepared for closing time he resolved to give Lloyd an answer before the end of the following week.

CASE 4

THE UTAH JAZZ ARENA

GARY McKINNON,
GARY CORNIA,
ROBERT PARSONS,
AND DALE WRIGHT

Larry H. Miller, owner of the Utah Jazz NBA franchise, enthusiastically drove back to his office located at his Toyota auto dealership. He had just come from a successful meeting with the heads of various city, county, and state government agencies. The weather was cold but clear in Salt Lake City, typical of a last Friday in January. "It's a break-through day," he thought to himself. "It looks as though everything is falling into place for an October 31, 1991, opening of the new Jazz Arena." As he parked his car and made his way past the 1989 Toyotas to his office building, a thought passed through his mind. "Everything is on target, but I still need to come up with $40–45 million in the next six months."

As usual, he offered a pleasant greeting to those he passed on his way to his office. As he sat down at his desk he paused to reflect back on his involvement with the NBA franchise. Three major events of the past year had forced him to rethink his original plans for the Utah Jazz.

THE NBA BOARD OF GOVERNORS MEETING

The NBA Board of Governors meets officially three times each year: first at the all-star game, next in mid-April in New York City, and finally in September in a designated city.

The major agenda item for the 1988 spring meeting in New York City had focused on the contract agreement with the Players Association. Two months prior to the 1988 all-star game, the old collective bargaining agreement had

---

Source: **This case material is prepared for class discussion and is not designed to present illustrations of either effective or ineffective decision making. This case was written by Professors Gary Cornia, Gary McKinnon, Robert Parsons, and Dale Wright, all of the Marriott School of Management, Brigham Young University (1990). Kelly Sessions, Stacy Stickler, Jeff Ferguson, and Mick Berry assisted in gathering case materials. Financial support for the case research assistants was provided by the Marriott School of Management Entrepreneurial Founders.**

expired. The NBA players continued to play without a contract while preliminary negotiations took place. The owners came to New York to discuss several options related to player contracts. Owners could renegotiate, give in to player demands, or "go dark," which meant locking out the players and thereby interrupting league play.

It was common knowledge among owners, players, and basketball enthusiasts that the players make their money during the regular season while the owners make their money during the play-offs. Owners were concerned with rumors that the players would continue to play without a contract for a few additional weeks (until they had earned most of their salary) and then strike as the 1988 season ended. This action would place great pressure on the owners for a quick agreement so the play-offs could take place. Without the play-offs, the owners would have to write off the income generated from the play-off games, and most teams would end the season with a deficit.

Prior to the meeting, several NBA owners contacted Miller to explain that if the owners were to gain bargaining power, they needed to go dark, or lock out the players and not wait for the players to initiate a strike near the end of the season. Miller didn't like the idea of going dark, but he knew that was about the only way the owners could bargain from a position of strength.

As the dinner meeting began, David Stern, NBA commissioner, surprised the owners with a bombshell when he outlined a new collective bargaining agreement. Commissioner Stern was ready to present the new agreement to the owners for formal ratification. He described it as "a significant compromise." Larry Fleisher of the NBA Players Association later stated he was more than satisfied with what he called "a breakthrough agreement." (See Exhibit 1 for details of the meeting.)

Miller listened to what he later called "a triple whammy." First, the new agreement limited the draft to three rounds the first year and then to two rounds in subsequent years. Second, new free agent rules were introduced that clearly favored the seasoned player, which meant higher salaries for free agents. A player could become an unrestricted free agent after four years. That meant teams in large TV markets and those with large arenas had a major advantage over the other teams. Third, the new agreement changed the salary cap and the related revenue-sharing formula as players were guaranteed at least 53 percent of the defined gross revenue (revenue from national TV, cable TV, and gate receipts). The salary cap formula was complicated, but it was clear to Miller that under the new cap, salaries for the Utah Jazz would go from $4.9 million to $9.8 million in just four years. The change in the salary cap was clearly advantageous to the teams in large metro-markets, teams with large arenas, and expansion teams.

As the details of the players' agreement were being presented, Miller's initial thought was "I am listening to the death warrant of the Jazz in Utah." He first wondered if the franchise could even survive in the second-smallest market in the NBA (see Exhibit 2). He then wondered how much time he had before he had to make major changes. Would a larger arena solve his problem? Miller knew he couldn't just give up and sell without meeting the chal-

EXHIBIT 1   A BREAKTHROUGH AGREEMENT

N.B.A. AND UNION IN ACCORD
By Robert McG. Thomas Jr.

After more than a year of stalled negotiations and legal clashes, the National Basketball Association and the players' union yesterday announced an unexpected agreement on a new six-year contract. Both sides said that the accord would virtually assure increased prosperity for the teams and the players.

The agreement in principle, which was worked out in a seven-hour bargaining session Monday and is subject to formal ratification by the players, contains the following major provisions:

The draft of college players, which the union had sought to abolish altogether, will be cut from seven rounds to three this year and to two rounds thereafter, leaving undrafted players free to negotiate with any team.

The league's salary cap, which the union had also sought to remove, will be continued, but with a schedule of minimum annual increases that, together with projected increases in team revenues, is expected to bring the average players' salary to almost $1 million by 1993, or almost double the current $520,000 average.

The teams' right of first refusal, which had made so-called free agents virtual chattels of their original teams, will be eliminated at the end of their second N.B.A. contracts for players with at least seven years of service initially and three years eventually.

Those three issues had been the focus of negotiations that began in February 1987 and spilled over into the courts. As a part of the agreement, the league and the Union will discontinue their litigation once a final pact has been ratified.

Describing the agreement as "a significant compromise" by both sides, David Stern, the N.B.A. commissioner, said he was proud that "the players and the owners worked together that growth might continue" for professional basketball.

Larry Fleisher, the founder and general counsel of the N.B.A. Players' Association, echoed the point. "Owners who have been selling their teams for $45 million will now be able to get $80 million," he said.

Although the union appeared to achieve far less than its original demands, particularly on the question of free agency, Fleisher said he was more than satisfied with what he called "a breakthrough agreement."

"For the first time in history," he said, "players will be free to choose the teams they want to play for after a certain period of time."

Under the previous contract, which expired after the 1986–1987 season, players who became technical free agents when their contracts expired were virtually tied to their original teams by a provision that gave those teams the right to retain a player simply by matching a rival club's offer.

Stern said the owners had ratified the agreement by a substantial margin in a meeting in New York.

In addition to ratification by the players, the agreement is also subject to the approval of the Federal District Court in Newark. The union and the league have been engaged in litigation in that court over the union's charges that the so-called labor exemption to the antitrust laws—the legal underpinning of the salary cap, the teams' rights of first refusal and the draft—had ended with the expiration of the previous contract. A ruling against the union has been appealed.

Limiting the draft to three rounds this year and two years thereafter is not expected to have a major impact since few players taken after the second round have been able to make an N.B.A. team in recent years.

On the salary cap and the related revenue-sharing formula, which guarantees that the players receive at least 53 percent of gross league revenues in either salary or benefits, the agreement closes two loopholes. One, which simply codified a court ruling, bars so-called backloading of contracts in which teams had sought to get around the cap by paying a player a small salary in the first years of a multiyear contract with what amounted to large balloon payments in the later years. Under the new agreement, salaries in each year of a multiyear pact may be no more than 30 percent above the previous year's salary.

In addition, in figuring the team salary level, teams will no longer be able to omit the previous salary of a free agent, unless they renounce their right to re-sign the free agent.

Source: New York Times, April 27, 1988.

EXHIBIT 2 THE NBA MARKETS

TEAM	METRO POP.	HOME COURT ATT.	YR. CONST.	87-88 GAMES SOLD OUT
Atlanta Hawks	2,565,000	16,371	1972	4
Boston Celtics	2,841,700	14,890	1928	9
Charlotte Hornets	1,091,000	23,388	1988	1
Chicago Bulls	6,199,000	17,339	1929	3
Cleveland Cavaliers	1,851,000	20,273	1974	2
Dallas Mavericks	3,456,000	17,007	1980	12
Denver Nuggets	1,644,500	17,022	1975	11
Detroit Pistons	4,361,600	21,454	1988	5
Golden St. Warriors	1,500,000	15,025	1966	6
Houston Rockets	3,228,100	16,611	1975	14
Indiana Pacers	1,228,000	16,912	1974	3
Los Angeles Clippers	8,504,500	15,310	1959	6
Los Angeles Lakers	8,504,500	17,505	1967	13
Miami Heat	2,954,000	15,008	1988	3
Milwaukee Bucks	1,389,100	18,633	1988	4
Minnesota Timberwolves	2,335,600	25,559	1989	0
New Jersey Nets	1,870,000	20,039	1981	3
New York Knicks	8,528,800	18,351	1968	4
Orlando Magic	934,700	15,500	1989	0
Philadelphia 76ers	4,866,500	18,168	1967	9
Phoenix Suns	1,989,600	14,487	1965	9
Portland Trailblazers	1,167,800	12,880	1982	7
Sacramento Kings	1,336,500	16,517	1986	7
San Antonio Spurs	1,306,700	15,861	1968	10
Seattle Supersonics	1,795,900	14,250	1986	8
Utah Jazz	**1,044,500**	**12,444**	**1969**	**40**
Washington Bullets	3,646,000	18,756	1984	4

lenge. He had often been the underdog as he built his auto dealerships, and he wasn't about to give up on keeping the Jazz.

LARRY H. MILLER

The 1989–90 *Utah Jazz Media Guide* provided the following information about Larry H. Miller, owner of the Utah Jazz.

> With a firm personal commitment to professional basketball in Salt Lake, Utah Jazz owner Larry H. Miller has built a successful professional sports franchise in this, the smallest of major league cities. (*Note:* The Orlando franchise was added in 1989).
>
> Miller's commitment to keeping professional basketball in Utah was first

evidenced in the spring of 1985, when he purchased a 50 percent interest in the franchise from then-owner Sam Battistone and his StratAmerican Corporation. Then, a little over a year later, he bought out Battistone's remaining share in the team, assuming full ownership, and saving the team from a possible move to Minnesota at the hands of a Minneapolis-based group of investors interested in buying the team.

In the three years since he assumed full ownership of the team, Miller's unique managing and promoting abilities have been instrumental in building the Jazz into one of the league's most respected and admired teams. And with a new state-of-the-art, 18,000+ seat arena in the works, Miller's commitment to the Jazz' future is as strong and solid as ever.

A native of Salt Lake City, Miller is the owner of the LHM Group, a network of auto dealerships in Murray, Utah; Albuquerque, New Mexico; Denver, Colorado; and Phoenix, Arizona as well as several other related businesses.

Miller believes in a "hands-on" approach to business and is actively involved in all aspects of each of his endeavors, from the dealerships to the Jazz. It is not uncommon to see him on the showroom floor or in a service bay at one of his dealerships, or at a Jazz practice session or team meeting. And he is now personally spearheading the effort in all aspects of the new arena project.

Miller's interest in competitive sports is not limited to the basketball court. In fact, for many years prior to his involvement with the Jazz, Miller participated in fast-pitch softball, and was a nationally recognized pitcher. He hung up his glove only recently, as the pressures of his businesses and the team consume an increasing amount of his time, but continues to sponsor several teams.

A devoted family man, Larry and his wife Gail are the parents of five children, four sons and one daughter, and they are very proud grandparents. The Millers reside in Sandy, Utah, a suburb of Salt Lake City.

HISTORY OF THE UTAH JAZZ

EARLY YEARS AND THE MOVE TO SALT LAKE CITY

In 1974, the New Orleans Jazz became the eighteenth member of the National Basketball Association when a nine-member group paid $6.15 million for an expansion team. With "Pistol Pete" Maravich leading the expansion players, the Jazz ended the season with a 23–59 record. Total home attendance that first year was 203,141 (see Exhibit 3).

Attendance jumped the following year to 513,000 as the team's record improved to 38–44 (see Exhibit 4), but the attendance fluctuated for the next three years. In the 1978–79 season the win-loss record was 26–53, and attendance fell to 364,205 fans.

In 1979, after five difficult seasons, co-owners Sam Battistone and Larry Hatfield announced plans to move the Jazz from New Orleans to Salt Lake City. They anticipated better fan support in the new location. Games were played at the Salt Palace, and the first sellout (12,015) in Utah Jazz history took

EXHIBIT 3   JAZZ ATTENDANCE FIGURES

YEAR	TOTAL HOME ATTENDANCE	AVERAGE HOME ATTENDANCE	NO. OF GAMES SOLD OUT
1974–75	203,141	4,955	0
1975–76	513,383	12,519	0
1976–77	444,138	10,833	0
1977–78	527,351	12,862	0
1978–79	364,205	8,883	0
1979–80	320,649	7,821	4
1980–81	307,825	7,508	4
1981–82	313,864	7,665	3
1982–83	355,819	8,697	4
1983–84	407,818	9,947	8
1984–85	373,808	9,117	6
1985–86	477,842	11,655	22
1986–87	491,382	11,985	30
1987–88	503,969	12,292	40

Seating capacity for the New Orleans Jazz (Super Dome): approx. 35,000.
Seating capacity for the Utah Jazz (Salt Palace): 12,212 through 1987, then 12,444.

EXHIBIT 4   JAZZ TEAMS' RECORDS

1974–75:	23–59	1981–82:	25–57
1975–76:	38–44	1982–83:	30–52
1976–77:	35–47	1983–84:	45–37
1977–78:	39–43	1984–85:	41–41
1978–79:	26–53	1985–86:	42–40
1979–80:	24–58	1986–87:	44–38
1980–81:	28–54	1987–88:	47–35

place as the Lakers beat the Jazz. Adrian Dantley, obtained in a trade with the Los Angeles Lakers, led the Jazz in scoring. The Jazz finished their first season in Utah with a 24–58 mark.

The management of the Jazz continued to strengthen the club personnel in 1980–81. Darrell Griffith was drafted (named NBA rookie of the year by *Sporting News*), but the season record did not improve much, and the Jazz record stood at 28–54.

During the 1981–82 season, Sam Battistone bought out Larry Hatfield and became the sole owner of the Jazz. The record of the Utah Jazz did not improve in the 1981–82 season (25–57), but both Ricky Green and Adrian Dantley were leaders in their respective areas (scoring and assists). Battistone hoped there was a light at the end of the tunnel.

Before the 1982–83 season, the Jazz drafted Dominique Wilkins and then traded him to Atlanta for two players and a large cash payment. Battistone was criticized by fans and sports writers for the trade. Attendance figures were just above 300,000 (see Exhibit 3) during the early years in Utah, and the Utah Jazz were rumored to be in financial difficulty. Mark Eaton, a 7'4" center, was drafted in the fourth round. At the end of the season the Jazz requested permission from the NBA Board of Governors to play selected home games at the Thomas and Mack Center in Las Vegas, Nevada, for 1983–84. Battistone was searching for creative ways to save the Utah Jazz.

In the 1983–84 season, the Utah Jazz improved to a 45–37 mark and played their first ever play-off game against Denver. The Jazz beat Denver in five games and went on to lose to Phoenix in the next round. Season attendance rose to 407,818.

Before the 1984–85 season the Jazz surprised many fans and sports writers by drafting John Stockton as their first pick. In another major move, the NBA Board of Governors approved the sale of 50 percent ownership of the Utah Jazz to Larry H. Miller, a relative unknown in NBA circles. With his purchase of 50 percent of the Utah Jazz the organization seemed solvent. The Utah Jazz then ended the experiment of playing selected home games in Las Vegas.

In the 1985–86 season Karl Malone was drafted. In a gesture of appreciation Jazz Jersey #7 was retired in honor of "Pistol Pete" Maravich. With Dantley, Malone, Stockton, and Eaton, the Jazz finished above .500 for only the second time in franchise history and entered into the play-off games for the third straight year.

A CHANGE IN OWNERSHIP AND BUSINESS EXPANSION

In 1986, a major change took place that strengthened the financial health of the Utah Jazz. Larry H. Miller purchased the remaining 50 percent of the Jazz. He was prepared to move forward with plans to make the Utah Jazz a solid NBA franchise so it could remain in Salt Lake City. Miller had learned from his auto dealerships that marketing was a key to success in business. He planned to more effectively market the Jazz and develop associated businesses.

The Jazz Sports Channel was formed with the world's largest cable company (TCI). TCI provided service to about 250,000 subscribers in the Jazz viewing area, but it was estimated that there were an additional 280,000 potential subscribers in Salt Lake Valley itself. In the first year TCI paid $25,000 to broadcast each of 25 games. Advertising revenues from cable television commercials generated another $300,000. Jazz officials estimated that as the number of subscribers increased, multiyear contracts with TCI would eventually approach $1 million per year.

On April 1, 1987, the Utah Jazz purchased four retail stores known as the Pro Image. The product line consisted of official NBA, NFL, NHL, and collegiate athletic merchandise. The retail operation resulted in a loss of $150,000 during the first three months and $130,000 the following year. However, a change in management resulted in a $300,000 profit and a return on investment of over 25 percent.

For several years the National Basketball Association was a co-sponsor of the Youth Basketball Association. When that relationship was severed in 1986, a local YMCA official approached the Jazz management with the idea of forming an independent youth basketball program. A Junior Jazz league was formed with the basic noncompetitive philosophy that all team players would play in each game. By 1988 over 30,000 youths had participated in Jr. Jazz, the largest program of its kind in the nation. Each Jazz player was contracted to make appearances to the numerous Jr. Jazz leagues. Each youth participant received free Jazz game tickets, certificates of participation, Jazz team posters, and other tokens.

Revenue from the Jr. Jazz program came from selling advertising on game shirts and from fees charged to each participant. Most of the detail of administering league play rests with community recreation personnel, resulting in little administrative expense. Net income to the Jazz was approximately $40,000 to $60,000 per year.

AN INTEGRATED PRODUCT OFFERING

Player personnel changes were also made after Miller purchased 100 percent of the Jazz. Adrian Dantley, after some disagreements with the likeable Jazz coach Frank Layden, was traded. The nucleus of a competitive NBA club was in place, and Miller was eager to continue to expand the marketing efforts of the Utah Jazz.

The attendance figures for the 1987–88 season grew to 503,969, and the record was 47–35. Stockton and Malone were each named NBA players of the month (February and March). The Jazz beat Portland in the first round of the play-offs, and the Jazz took the LA Lakers to the seventh game before being eliminated. It was probably the greatest period of Jazz history. As "Hot Rod" Hundley, the voice of the Utah Jazz stated so well, "You've got to love it baby!!"

COMPETITION

Four major universities (Brigham Young University, University of Utah, Utah State University, and Weber State University) are located within 75 miles of Salt Lake City. Each sponsors an NCAA basketball team that plays in large and fairly new arenas.

The Golden Eagles Hockey team, a minor league team, plays at the Salt Palace, but Jazz officials do not view them as a major competitive force. They believe NBA games have little direct competition from other athletic events in the Rocky Mountain region.

Ticket prices for the Utah Jazz are shown in Exhibit 5.

Ticket prices (1989–90) for selected NBA teams are shown in Exhibit 6.

EXHIBIT 5 UTAH JAZZ TICKET PRICES*

Season	Prices
1979–80	$9.00, 7.00, 5.00
1980–81	$9.00, 7.00, 5.00
1981–82	$12.00, 10.00, 9.00, 7.00, 5.00
1982–83	$30.00, 20.00, 12.00, 10.00, 7.50, 5.00
1983–84	$30.00, 20.00, 12.00, 10.00, 7.50, 5.00
1984–85	$22.50, 17.50, 12.50, 10.00, 7.50, 5.00
1985–86	$22.50, 17.50, 12.50, 10.00, 7.50, 5.00
1986–87	$25.00, 20.00, 17.50, 15.00, 10.00, 5.00
1987–88	$25.00, 20.00, 17.50, 15.00, 10.00, 5.00
1988–89	$30.00, 25.00, 20.00, 17.50, 12.50, 7.50
1989–90	$35.00, 30.00, 25.00, 17.50, 12.50, 7.50

*Not including VIP tickets.

EXHIBIT 6 TICKET PRICES OF SELECTED NBA TEAMS, 1989–90

Team	Prices
Atlanta Hawks	$75.00 (VIP), 35.00 (VIP), 25.00 (VIP), 20.00, 15.00, 10.00, 5.00
Boston Celtics	$30.00, 24.00, 23.00, 18.00, 17.00, 13.00, 10.00
Chicago Bulls	$135.00, 60.00, 32.50, 19.50, 14.50, 10.50
Dallas Mavs	$75.60, 29.16, 24.84, 21.00, 17.00, 14.00, 13.00, 10.00, 7.00, 5.00
Denver Nuggets	$100.00, 27.00, 24.00, 22.00, 20.00, 18.00, 15.00, 11.00, 8.00
LA Lakers	$350.00 (VIP), 90.00, 52.50, 32.50, 18.50, 14.50, 11.50, 8.50
New Jersey Nets	$50.00, 30.00, 25.00, 22.00, 18.00, 15.00, 13.00, 10.00, 6.00
Phoenix Suns	$27.00, 22.00, 18.00, 17.00, 13.00, 7.00
San Antonio	$50.00, 40.00, 32.00, 28.00, 21.00, 18.00, 15.00, 11.00, 8.00, 5.00
Seattle	$25.00, 20.00, 18.00, 15.00, 12.00, 9.00, 5.00

THE SALT LAKE METROPOLITAN AREA

DEMOGRAPHICS

As of 1988, population for the Salt Lake metropolitan statistical area (MSA) made up 61.8 percent of the entire population of Utah, which was estimated to be 1,695,000. The population for the Salt Lake MSA is forecasted to grow at a rate of .94 percent annually between the years of 1989 and 1999, reaching 1,150,000 persons by the turn of the century.

The 1988 median household family income for the Salt Lake MSA is $30,500. Although household income is lower than the national average of $35,400, the cost of living index is also lower, at 97.3. The combined personal income for individuals within the Salt Lake MSA is approximately $15 billion. The amount is expected to grow by 7.64 percent per year, reaching $31 billion by 1999.

ECONOMY

In 1989, Utah and Salt Lake experienced impressive economic growth following six years of economic slowdown. The new job expansion was third in the nation, at 4.4 percent, translating new jobs into greater income and the expansion of sales and services.

Utah's construction industry has also started to grow and was at 14.7 percent in the first nine months of 1989. The new-found growth was centered primarily in the commercial community, where construction value was up 32 percent at $277.7 million. Residential construction was $346.5 million, up 7.3 percent over the previous year.

The real estate market rose 1.4 percent in values and 0.4 percent in number compared to the previous year. The selling price of the average home was $80,746.

WORK FORCE

Utah's work force of 305,000 is recognized as hard working and educated. Projections place the work force at over 1,000,000 by the year 2000.

The overall change in the Utah economy's employment picture shows movement away from the state's traditional extraction, manufacturing, and government economic base toward services and trade. Industries projected to have the fastest growth rates are machinery and electronic equipment, air transportation, transportation services, hotels and lodging, business services, and health services.

TRANSPORTATION

Geographically centered in the western United States, Salt Lake City is easily accessible through various modes of travel. The Salt Lake International Airport sustains 550 daily flights, with 56,000 airline seats and connections with 148 U.S. cities. Salt Lake serves as a major hub for Delta Airlines. The airport is located six miles west of the major hotel district. The Salt Palace is at the center of that district.

Salt Lake is also at the intersection of Interstate 80 and Interstate 15 with access to cities in all directions. Amtrak and the Denver and Rio Grand Western Railroad provide passenger train service.

TOURISM

Tourism and conventions add more than $1 billion to the Salt Lake economy, provide 29,000 jobs, and generate a payroll of over $417 million. Over 6 million tourist, convention, and business travelers come to the Salt Lake Valley and its mountain resorts annually. There are 12,166 hotel and motel rooms in Salt Lake County.

THE SKI INDUSTRY

Utah has 15 ski resorts and 7 cross-country touring centers, with 8 of the ski resorts and 5 of the cross-country centers no more than 60 minutes from downtown Salt Lake City. The ski industry accounts for more than $250 million in tourism annually. The average ski tourist spends 3.7 days skiing in Utah and spends $98 per day. Significant media attention on the Utah ski industry and a bid for the 1998 winter Olympic games should contribute to an increased growth in the Utah ski industry.

SELECTING AN ARENA SITE

THE SALT PALACE

Plans for a new civic auditorium in Salt Lake City were first proposed in January 1929, but the idea was shelved with little fanfare until the late 1930s, when arguments for an auditorium again surfaced. With the outbreak of World War II, however, the plans were again put on hold and were not considered for several years after the war in hopes that the cost of building the center would come down. Finally, in 1958, advocates again proposed the idea of building a civic auditorium for Salt Lake City, and in 1961 a committee was appointed to study the feasibility of such a project.

After a year and a half of study, the committee concluded the community needed a two- or three-building complex, and in November 1963, voters approved (by a 59 percent to 41 percent majority) a $17 million bond to fund the project. A downtown site was approved in 1964, ground breaking commenced in March 1967, and the Salt Palace celebrated its grand opening on July 11, 1969.

In its early days, the Salt Palace was considered to be one of the finest civic auditoriums in the nation. The building consisted of a circular 13,075-seat sports/show arena and a 70,000-square-foot convention hall with room for an additional 5,266 seats. The sports area featured a portable basketball floor, an NCAA-sanctioned indoor track floor, and an ice hockey rink. With slight modifications, the arena could be used for other events such as rodeos, circuses, and horse shows. The exhibit hall was used to attract events such as car and boat shows, business conventions, and manufacturers' displays.

Six years after the Salt Palace opening, voters approved a general obligation bond to expand the overall facilities to include an adjacent symphony hall and art center. The bond totalled $8.675 million, and the state matched an appropriation of $7.5 million. The entire complex became known as the Salt Palace Center.

The Salt Palace Center proved itself to be a lucrative investment for Salt Lake County. With the original price tag of $17 million, the Salt Palace by 1979 had brought over $850 million into Salt Lake County, a 50-to-1 return on investment.

By the mid-1970s, the limited size of the original buildings of the Salt

Palace Center was preventing large trade shows and conventions from being booked. Large events were becoming more common at other centers across the nation. A second expansion was needed in order to keep up. In 1980, voters approved $16.5 million of general revenue bonds for construction of two more exhibit halls and to add an additional 200,000 square feet of exhibit space as well as to expand parking facilities. Ground breaking began in 1981, and the new center was completed in 1987. Exhibit 7 lists the 20 largest conventions held in Salt Lake City in 1987–1988.

By 1989 the Salt Palace Center again faced the serious threat of losing out to competition from civic centers in neighboring states. Reports showed that because of inadequate space, the Salt Palace Center had lost 25 major events since 1985, which resulted in a direct loss of an estimated $40 million to the county. The county, therefore, commissioned Coopers and Lybrand, a Minneapolis-based public accounting firm, to do a study of the issue and make recommendations.

Among other things, the Coopers and Lybrand report called for demolishing the original Salt Palace Arena, expanding the existing 200,000 square feet of exhibit space to 300,000 square feet, and increasing the available number of meeting rooms from 35 to 50. Additionally, the existing exhibit and assembly halls would need to be renovated in order to lure more out of state dollars

EXHIBIT 7 TWENTY LARGEST CONVENTIONS HELD IN SALT LAKE CITY, 1987-88

GROUP	ATTEND.	ROOM NIGHTS	$ IMPACT
Teachers of Math	7,000	15,925	$3,619,116
Natl. Tour Assn.	3,100	15,580	3,540,711
Presbyterians	6,000	13,728	3,119,825
Sweet Adelines	6,500	10,125	2,301,008
U.S. Figure Skating	3,000	7,272	1,653,317
School Librarians	3,100	6,100	1,386,286
INGRES Users	1,000	5,420	1,231,749
Adult Educators	3,000	5,349	1,215,614
Sports Medicine	3,500	5,305	1,205,614
Mining Engineers	2,500	4,865	1,105,620
Electrical Dist.	3,000	4,593	1,043,805
Prof. Secretaries	1,800	4,486	1,019,488
Student Information	1,200	4,050	920,403
State Governments	1,000	3,391	770,639
Outdoor Writers	1,000	3,150	715,000
Equipment Dealers	1,300	3,135	712,460
Nu Skin	1,500	3,101	704,733
Information Assoc.	900	2,765	628,374
Child Abuse Conf.	3,000	2,604	591,785
Insurance Commis.	1,500	2,308	524,516

with a large modern facility that could handle more than the present facility could, one convention at a time.

One important key to the Coopers and Lybrand report was that it was made under the assumption that the Jazz would be playing in their own arena, which would also handle the rodeos, tractor pulls, and concerts and would thus free up the Salt Palace Arena for other uses. However, even with the full expansion into the Salt Palace Arena, Salt Lake would still rank thirteenth out of the 16 western convention centers. Undaunted, county planners considered other city amenities and predicted the new Salt Palace would be a "premier" facility and could compete "not only with Denver, Houston, Phoenix, and Albuquerque, but also with the big boys; Los Angeles, Las Vegas, San Francisco, and Anaheim."

ALTERNATIVE ARENA SITES

Soon after acquiring full ownership of the Utah Jazz in 1986, Larry Miller had been casually looking at potential sites for a new arena. He knew that someday (probably by the year 2000) he would need additional seating, but he didn't foresee a radical new players' agreement like the one presented by Commissioner Stern. Miller thought there was less than a 20 percent chance he would need a larger arena by 1995.

During his early exploration he was surprised to find that about eight sites were still available in the Salt Lake Valley that met the criteria for a new arena. A new arena required 54 acres for parking about 6 acres for the rest of the complex. The eight sites also met the need for easy freeway access and utility hook-up. (Exhibit 8 shows site locations.) One major developer wanted to enter into a joint venture with Miller with the Jazz Arena anchoring an industrial park.

During his preliminary site search, Miller contacted NBA owners who had recently built new arenas. These included franchise owners in Milwaukee, Charlotte, Miami, Sacramento, and Detroit. From his discussions with other team owners, he estimated the cost of the new arena to be between $60 million and $70 million. He thought he could handle about $40 million himself, but he questioned where he would get assistance with the remaining $20 million to $30 million.

A DOWNTOWN SITE SELECTION

After Miller returned from the April 1988 New York meetings, he knew he must move rapidly to a larger arena to generate additional revenue for the new salary cap. The other alternative was to sell the Jazz franchise and see the team move to a larger metro-market. The personal challenge of keeping the Jazz in Utah pushed Miller to immediately select one of the preliminary sites he had already identified and to begin construction of a larger arena as soon as possible.

Miller didn't publicize the search, but the word on the street was that he

EXHIBIT 8 SALT LAKE CITY

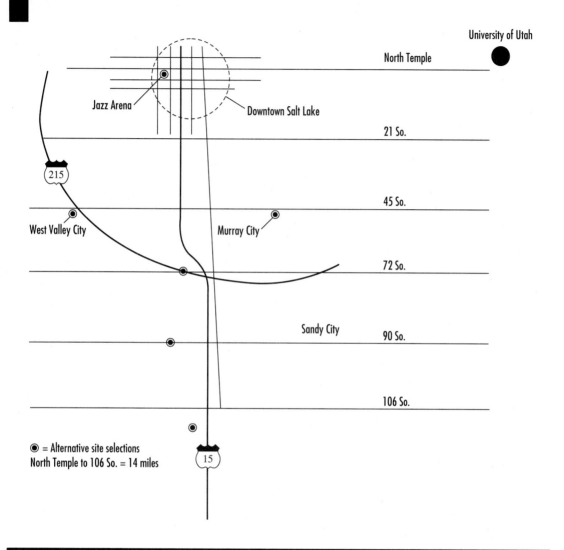

● = Alternative site selections
North Temple to 106 So. = 14 miles

was looking for a site for a new arena. Palmer DePaulis, mayor of Salt Lake City, received numerous telephone calls from downtown merchants suggesting the Jazz needed to remain downtown. In late June 1988 Mayor DePaulis telephoned Miller and asked, "Are you looking at any downtown sites for the new arena?" Miller told the mayor the most attractive sites were outside the downtown area, but after some persuasion Miller said he would keep an open mind about the two downtown locations. The mayor suggested Miller would receive much cooperation and support for the city locations.

Although Miller had little formal education beyond high school, his ownership and expansion of his auto dealership had made him politically astute. He understood that a downtown arena was very important to the community and therefore had almost automatic support from all government units and agencies. But Miller's values were such that he personally felt uncomfortable using power for an unfair advantage. Another dilemma faced by Miller was that he had a major aversion to taxpayers subsidizing private enterprise. He had never used political power or pressure and had always avoided government assistance. That personal philosophy made it more difficult as he thought about the financial help he needed in raising $65 million for the new arena.

During those summer months of 1988 Larry Miller experienced a 180-degree turn: He became convinced that downtown Salt Lake City needed the arena to remain a strong capital city. He later stated to a close associate, "I am convinced that the health of a capital city is crucial to the health of the state, especially in a western state. The central city has a special role in Utah, it must remain strong. Downtown Salt Lake City needs the Jazz Arena."

Miller was involved in meetings with many government officials during the late summer. The main players were Palmer DePaulis, mayor of Salt Lake City, and Bart Barker, a senior county commissioner. Miller became frustrated that the various city, county, and state agencies were more concerned about "jockeying" for power positions than offering a downtown site proposal Miller could accept.

Although Miller had received support for the arena from Utah governor Norman Bangerter, he knew the decisions rested at the county and city level. In late September, Miller informed Mayor DePaulis, Commissioner Barker, and other heads of the various governmental agencies that he was running out of time and needed a decision by October 31. DePaulis balked at the time frame, knowing of the difficulty of assembling all who needed to be in attendance. However, John Rosenthal, Bart Barker's personal assistant, said, "I can do it." In less than a week Rosenthal had 80 high-profile government and civic leaders at a meeting, where they were organized into committees and subcommittees. They had one month to prepare a site package for Miller.

During October everyone cooperated and loose ends began to come together. Two downtown sites were identified, and public hearings were held about the new arena location. By October 31, most of the details had been worked out and Miller had agreed to the downtown location. Miller was impressed with how things worked so well. He later commented, "I wish I had paid better attention in my high school civics class. I really learned how different agencies cooperate with each other when the need is there."

OTHER ALTERNATIVES FOR THE JAZZ

As Miller was waiting for all the parts of the arena puzzle to come together, he tried not to think about other alternatives still open to him. Several friends had suggested that the Salt Lake market was too small to support an NBA franchise. Miller was aware that Toronto and several major cities in the U.S. (St. Louis, Memphis, Anaheim, and Dayton) were interested in an NBA team.

George Shinn and partners paid $32.5 million for the new franchise in North Carolina. On July 10, 1989, the press reported that Bertram M. Lee and Peter C. Bynoe had purchased the Denver Nuggets for $65 million. The health of the NBA was never better, and Miller knew if he sold the club his profit would be substantial.

Miller became aware of a study by *Financial World* magazine that estimated the value of various sports franchises (see Exhibit 9). He thought with a new arena the value of the Jazz would increase beyond their estimates. He also knew that *Financial World* estimated the worth of the Jazz in Salt Lake City. It could be worth more in another location. He had paid approximately

EXHIBIT 9 VALUE OF NBA FRANCHISES (ALL FIGURES IN MILLIONS)

FRANCHISE	PLAYER SALARIES	TOTAL REVENUE	OPER. EXPEN.	PROFIT OR (LOSS)	FRANCHISE VALUE
1. L.A. Lakers	12.6	62.2	32.0	30.2	200.0
2. Boston Celtics	10.5	30.7	21.9	8.8	180.0
3. Detroit Pistons	10.9	47.3	24.0	23.3	150.0
4. Chicago Bulls	9.3	27.4	20.1	7.3	100.0
5. N.Y. Knicks	13.3	25.6	22.2	3.4	100.0
6. Phoenix Suns	8.8	20.7	16.8	3.9	99.0
7. Philadelphia 76ers	9.8	20.4	16.3	4.1	75.0
8. Cleveland Cavaliers	9.0	22.6	16.5	6.1	61.1
9. Orlando Magic	6.2	22.5	13.3	9.2	60.8
10. Portland Trail Blazers	11.2	21.4	20.0	1.4	59.9
11. Charlotte Hornets	7.2	22.8	16.3	6.4	59.6
12. Miami Heat	6.3	21.7	14.2	7.5	58.6
13. Houston Rockets	9.8	22.3	19.0	3.3	58.0
14. Dallas Mavericks	8.9	20.9	18.2	2.7	54.4
15. Atlanta Hawks	10.0	19.1	17.9	1.2	53.5
16. Milwaukee Bucks	8.7	19.1	14.8	4.3	53.5
17. Minnesota Timberwolves	5.7	19.0	14.3	4.7	51.2
18. Golden State Warriors	9.9	19.5	18.4	1.1	50.7
19. Sacramento Kings	8.7	18.9	13.7	5.2	49.1
20. San Antonio Spurs	9.7	17.2	16.9	0.3	46.5
21. Utah Jazz	**8.8**	**16.0**	**15.1**	**0.9**	**44.9**
22. Los Angeles Clippers	8.9	16.5	15.3	1.1	42.9
23. New Jersey Nets	8.4	16.4	14.6	1.8	42.6
24. Denver Nuggets	8.9	15.6	17.4	(1.8)	40.6
25. Washington Bullets	7.9	13.9	16.3	(2.4)	37.5
26. Seattle SuperSonics	8.4	13.8	15.6	(1.8)	37.3
27. Indiana Pacers	8.6	12.8	16.3	(3.5)	33.3

Source: Financial World, "Valuation of Professional Sports Franchises," July 9, 1991, pp. 42–43.

$22 million in two segments, purchasing 50 percent in 1984 and taking complete ownership in 1986. Some suggested that he would be wise to sell and reap the profits from his investment, but Miller knew if he sold the Jazz, Salt Lake City would never be the home of a major league franchise. Exhibit 10 contains the financial history of the Utah Jazz franchise from the 1985–86 season to the 1988–89 season.

THE JANUARY 27, 1989 MEETING

January 27, 1989, was a breakthrough day. In an important meeting of various government agencies, some important details had been finalized. The Redevelopment Agency (RDA) agreed to provide $20 million of the $65 million for land acquisition, water and utility hookups, plaza development, and on-site parking. It was a complicated arrangement because the RDA needed the cooperation of the school board because of the property tax issues involved with the agreement. At the conclusion of the meeting, Miller was pleased that everyone had "bought off" on the proposal. The deal had been struck. Only an additional $45 million stood in the way of the October 31, 1991, opening of the new Jazz Arena. In fulfillment of Miller's dream, the Jazz would remain in Utah! "Forty-Five Million Dollars," he thought; "I wonder which bank to call first."

EXHIBIT 10 UTAH JAZZ FINANCIAL HISTORY (DECEMBER 21, 1989)

	(A) 1985–86	% OF TOTAL REVENUE	(B) 1986–87	% OF TOTAL REVENUE	(C) 1987–88	% OF TOTAL REVENUE	(D) 1988–89	% OF TOTAL REVENUE
DIVISION 1 REVENUE:								
TICKET REVENUE	4,604,588	50.18%	5,334,727	46.30%	5,372,046	39.96%	7,107,506	41.50%
NBA REVENUE	1,857,025	20.24%	2,477,069	21.50%	3,077,879	22.90%	3,262,893	19.05%
EXHIBITION REVENUE	86,235	0.94%	186,041	1.61%	399,255	2.97%	514,235	3.00%
IN ARENA REVENUE	164,565	1.79%	220,127	1.91%	189,341	1.41%	202,392	1.18%
OTHER REVENUE	213,846	2.33%	187,631	1.63%	163,434	1.22%	257,052	1.50%
JAZZ 100 CLUB REVENUE	93,945	1.02%	237,185	2.06%	311,254	2.32%	302,795	1.77%
TOTAL DIVISION 1 REVENUE	7,020,204	76.50%	8,642,780	75.01%	9,513,209	70.77%	11,646,873	68.01%
DIVISION 2 GROSS PROFIT:								
SALT PALACE	31,180	0.34%	43,333	0.38%	74,745	0.56%	182,061	1.06%
FASHION PLACE	0	0.00%	9,932	0.09%	93,191	0.69%	123,623	0.72%
ZCMI	0	0.00%	9,340	0.08%	57,327	0.43%	91,516	0.53%
UNIVERSITY	0	0.00%	9,988	0.09%	87,909	0.65%	123,106	0.72%
SOUTH TOWNE	0	0.00%	4,328	0.04%	42,761	0.32%	51,392	0.30%
COTTONWOOD	0	0.00%	2,146	0.02%	95,523	0.71%	124,090	0.72%
VALLEY FAIR	0	0.00%	0	0.00%	95,541	0.71%	184,945	1.08%
SANDY MALL	0	0.00%	0	0.00%	0	0.00%	8,469	0.05%
TOTAL DIVISION 2 GROSS PROFIT	31,180	0.34%	79,067	0.69%	546,997	4.07%	889,202	5.19%
DIVISION 3 REVENUE:								
TV	839,133	9.14%	706,207	6.13%	826,194	6.15%	1,307,394	7.63%
RADIO	630,906	7.09%	461,806	4.01%	415,939	3.09%	529,027	3.09%
CABLE	0	0.00%	403,022	3.50%	637,482	4.74%	797,774	4.66%
TV PRODUCTION	0	0.00%	198,682	1.72%	268,600	2.00%	274,153	1.60%
PROMOTIONAL	483,724	5.27%	738,881	6.80%	886,940	6.60%	1,150,056	6.72%
OTHER MEDIA	0	0.00%	46,587	0.40%	110,551	0.82%	140,754	0.82%
TOTAL DIVISION 3 REVENUE	1,973,763	21.51%	2,600,185	22.57%	3,145,706	23.40%	4,199,158	24.52%

(continued)

EXHIBIT 10 (continued)

	(A) 1985-86	% OF TOTAL REVENUE	(B) 1986-87	% OF TOTAL REVENUE	(C) 1987-88	% OF TOTAL REVENUE	(D) 1988-89	% OF TOTAL REVENUE
DIVISION 4 REVENUE:								
JR. JAZZ	129,377	1.41%	107,120	0.93%	224,237	1.67%	378,531	2.21%
PRO AM	22,000	0.24%	24,265	0.22%	24,733	0.18%	12,550	0.07%
OTHER SPECIAL EVENTS	474	0.01%	67,861	0.59%	(12,704)	−0.09%	0	0.00%
TOTAL DIVISION 4 REVENUE	151,851	1.65%	200,246	1.74%	236,266	1.76%	391,081	2.28%
TOTAL REVENUE	9,176,998	100.00%	11,522,278	100.00%	13,442,178	100.00%	17,126,314	100.00%
DIVISION 1 EXPENSES:								
PLAYER SALARIES	2,782,656	30.32%	3,871,062	33.60%	5,303,227	39.45%	6,073,672	35.46%
OTHER BASKETBALL EXPENSES	1,340,075	14.60%	1,507,903	13.09%	1,994,179	14.84%	2,139,148	12.49%
EXHIBITION EXPENSES	113,908	1.24%	171,966	1.49%	244,005	1.82%	372,294	2.17%
GAME NIGHT	787,823	8.58%	863,526	7.49%	916,723	6.82%	1,121,203	6.55%
PUBLIC RELATIONS	75,319	0.82%	268,246	2.33%	292,234	2.17%	362,165	2.11%
MARKETING	596,917	6.50%	520,714	4.52%	567,528	4.22%	591,681	3.45%
IN ARENA EXPENSES	50,665	0.55%	68,437	0.59%	73,047	0.54%	17,797	0.10%
JAZZ 100 CLUB	130,944	1.43%	199,012	1.73%	216,883	1.61%	227,798	1.33%
CUSTOMER SERVICE CENTER	198,598	2.16%	192,976	1.67%	229,639	1.71%	262,948	1.54%
GENERAL AND ADMINISTRATIVE	2,283,920	24.89%	1,896,931	16.46%	2,462,364	18.32%	2,584,919	15.09%
TOTAL DIVISION 1 EXPENSES	8,360,825	91.11%	9,560,773	82.98%	12,299,829	91.50%	13,753,625	80.31%
DIVISION 2 EXPENSES:								
SALT PALACE	28,075	0.31%	36,825	0.32%	20,660	0.15%	28,922	0.17%
FASHION PLACE	0	0.00%	19,778	0.17%	78,908	0.59%	102,442	0.60%
ZCMI	0	0.00%	12,829	0.11%	54,889	0.41%	68,109	0.40%
UNIVERSITY	0	0.00%	14,445	0.13%	69,638	0.52%	82,835	0.48%
SOUTH TOWNE	0	0.00%	11,537	0.10%	43,079	0.32%	51,296	0.30%
COTTONWOOD	0	0.00%	9,140	0.08%	83,830	0.62%	101,814	0.59%
VALLEY FAIR	0	0.00%	0	0.00%	75,516	0.56%	128,696	0.75%
SANDY MALL	0	0.00%	0	0.00%	0	0.00%	12,154	0.07%
OVERHEAD	0	0.00%	69,245	0.60%	217,095	1.62%	199,772	1.17%
TOTAL DIVISION 2 EXPENSES	28,075	0.31%	173,799	1.51%	643,615	4.79%	776,040	4.53%

DIVISION 3 EXPENSES:										
TV	423,932	4.62%	387,103	3.36%	436,578	3.25%	560,202	3.27%		
RADIO	152,197	1.66%	99,695	0.87%	179,968	1.34%	282,026	1.65%		
CABLE	0	0.00%	248,297	2.15%	335,361	2.49%	349,422	2.04%		
TV PRODUCTION	0	0.00%	166,369	1.44%	198,900	1.48%	234,640	1.37%		
PROMOTIONAL	340,547	3.71%	327,319	2.84%	320,685	2.39%	515,182	3.01%		
OTHER MEDIA	70,682	0.77%	88,157	0.77%	136,009	1.01%	126,214	0.74%		
SALES OVERHEAD	23,134	0.25%	192,960	1.67%	337,064	2.51%	466,648	2.72%		
BROADCASTING OVERHEAD	285,972	3.12%	522,696	4.54%	270,919	2.02%	233,496	1.36%		
TOTAL DIVISION 3 EXPENSES	1,296,464	14.13%	2,032,596	17.64%	2,215,484	16.48%	2,767,830	16.16%		
DIVISION 4 EXPENSES:										
JR. JAZZ	105,513	1.15%	163,970	1.42%	174,240	1.30%	255,468	1.49%		
PRO AM	14,953	0.16%	25,574	0.22%	34,473	0.26%	13,117	0.08%		
OTHER	0	0.00%	71,784	0.62%	5,633	0.04%	0	0.00%		
TOTAL DIVISION 4 EXPENSES	120,466	1.31%	261,328	2.27%	214,346	1.59%	268,585	1.57%		
TOTAL EXPENSES	9,805,830	106.85%	12,028,496	104.39%	15,373,274	114.37%	17,566,080	102.57%		
NET PROFIT (LOSS)	(628,832)	−6.85%	(506,218)	−4.39%	(1,931,096)	−14.37%	(439,766)	−2.57%		
TOTAL DEPRECIATION	565,563	6.16%	628,546	5.46%	725,338	5.40%	781,166	4.56%		
OPERATING PROFIT (LOSS)	(63,269)	−0.69%	122,328	1.06%	(1,205,758)	−8.97%	341,400	1.99%		
RECONCILLIATION OF NET PROFIT OR LOSS TO AUDITED STATEMENT										
NET PROFIT (LOSS) FROM ABOVE	(628,832)	−6.85%	(506,218)	−4.39%	(1,931,096)	−14.37%	(439,766)	−2.57%		
ADD BACK EXPANSION REVENUE	0	0.00%	0	0.00%	2,826,087	21.02%	2,826,087	16.50%		
ADD BACK PLAY-OFF REVENUE	433,164	4.72%	658,814	5.72%	1,588,410	11.82%	674,377	3.94%		
ADD BACK PLAY-OFF EXPENSES	(252,376)	−2.75%	(362,570)	−3.15%	(784,197)	−5.83%	(309,562)	−1.81%		
ADD BACK CLIPPERS SETTLEMENT	0	0.00%	0	0.00%	128,459	0.96%	128,459	0.75%		
ROUNDING	0	0.00%	0	0.00%	0	0.00%	(11)	0.00%		
AUDITED NET PROFIT (LOSS)	(448,044)	−4.88%	(209,974)	−1.82%	1,827,663	13.60%	2,879,595	16.81%		

CASE 5

THE RISE AND FALL OF YUGO AMERICA, INC.

CAROLYN SILLIMAN
AND JEFFREY S.
HARRISON

> The five years that I invested in the Yugo project were rewarding and maturing for me, although I had a modest financial equity and a large amount of sweat equity invested in the company. In hindsight, there were areas where we failed, but I feel as though it all made a significant impact on the product and pricing aspect of the automobile industry.

William E. Prior, cofounder, former chief executive, and president of Yugo America, Inc. collected his thoughts and reflected on the past five years as he glanced across a crowded airport. It was June 1989, only five months after his company had declared bankruptcy. Looking back, he noted that the privately held company had traveled a rocky road, yet made the most significant impact on the automobile industry in the decade.

It was 1983 when Prior and his two partners, Malcolm Bricklin and Ira Edelson, stumbled upon the idea of a company featuring a low-priced import. Bricklin, who was probably best known for the flashy sports car prototype that bears his name, was heading up the project as its main financial backer. Prior was the former president and general manager of Automobile Importers from Subaru, the nation's second largest Subaru distributor, a company Bricklin had founded after the collapse of his sports car project. Edelson was Briklin's accountant and financial advisor. The three men had been researching the automobile industry, looking for a niche in the already crowded new car market. From their research, the men came to the conclusion that there was no "entry level car"; that is, there was not a new automobile inexpensive enough for the average first-time buyer. Bricklin, Prior, and Edelson concluded that they had discovered "a market in search of a product."

Once the concept was conceived, the three entrepreneurs began their

---

Source: Prepared by Carolyn Silliman and Professor Jeffrey S. Harrison, Clemson University, as a basis for classroom discussion and not to illustrate either effective or ineffective handling of administrative situations. © Jeffrey S. Harrison, 1990.

search for a low-priced, "no frills" mode of basic transportation. They determined that production costs would be too high in the United States, so they began evaluating the possibility of importing. In looking for a country which manufactured such a product, they wanted to meet three requirements:

1. The foreign company was not presently exporting to the United States, but desired to do so.
2. The overall quality of the car would be inferior to American and Japanese cars but could meet United States standards and consumer requirements.
3. The foreign company would be able to sell the cars at a low enough price for the new company to make marginal profits.

Bricklin, Prior, and Edelson spent four months investigating and traveling to countries in pursuit of the "right" country and product that met the three requirements. They researched manufacturing plants in Brazil, Japan, Mexico, Poland, France, Rumania, Czechoslovakia, England, and the Soviet Union before they discovered the Zastava car factory in Yugoslavia. Zavodi Crvena Zastava, Yugoslavia's leading automobile manufacturer, had been producing the Yugo GV model for five years and was quite receptive to Bricklin's proposal. Bricklin, Prior, and Edelson toured the Yugoslavian plant in May 1984 and began discussing the terms of a contract that same month.

Yugoslavian officials were eager to hear of the Yugo America venture. The country's economy was weak, and it owed (in 1985) approximately $19 billion to the Western world. In order to purchase goods from the West, such as oil, steel, and electronics, Yugoslavia had to have "hard" currency (a universal currency of choice). The dinar, Yugoslavia's monetary unit, was not considered hard currency, so the country had to earn dollars by exporting. Yugoslavia's modest exports, including jewelry, tourism, furniture, leather, and sporting guns, did not contribute a significant sum in terms of national debt. Since cars are an expensive item, Yugoslavian officials saw the venture as a profitable method of increasing the supply of hard currency in their monetary economy.

Bricklin and Zastava agreed that 500 Yugos should be shipped to a Baltimore port in early August 1985, so that the cars would be in showrooms and ready to sell later that month. In addition, technicians would be trained at the Zastava's plant prior to the launch in America, in order to guarantee customer satisfaction when the cars were sold and serviced. Bricklin and his partners returned to the United States in late May 1984 and began setting up operations.

COMPETITIVE STRATEGY

Competitive maneuvering among car manufacturers revolves around such factors as innovative options and styles, pricing, and brand name/reputation. Of these factors, Yugo's strategy focused on pricing. Innovative options and styles were not considered important, since the car was an older model and had no fancy options included in the base price. The company could not rely on reputation, since the company did not have an established name.

Yugo America took advantage of a pricing scheme which set it apart from other automobile manufacturers. At $3,995, it was the lowest priced car in America. Because price is important to most car buyers, Yugo felt that its low price strategy gave the company an advantage over other small cars. Major price competitors included the Toyota Tercel, Volkswagen Fox, Chevrolet Sprint, and, later, the Hyundai Excel; however, the Yugo GV was priced below all of these competitors. Instead of targeting families or status-conscious individuals, Yugo America made its car appealing to the first-time buyer looking for an economical subcompact.

OPERATIONS BEGIN

Four strategic decisions were made at the onset of operations:

1. The cars would be sold through "dual dealerships"; that is, Yugo would be a partner to an established retailer, such as Ford or Subaru. In this manner, Yugo America's executives hoped the public would associate its name with another successful manufacturer's name and reputation.
2. Prior, Bricklin, and Edelson decided that the company would import regionally rather than nationally. More specifically, Yugo America, with a home base in Upper Saddle River, New Jersey, would establish itself among Northeastern dealers. Approximately 23% of all import cars are sold in this region, and the Northeastern coast is the closest to Yugoslavia.
3. There would be a small number of dealers selling a large number of Yugos. The idea behind this decision was that the dealers would be making a substantial profit from the large number of cars, which would motivate them and encourage them to sell more.
4. The price of the car would be low, but the company would stress the fact that the car was of acceptable quality.

The first task to accomplish before announcing the introduction of the Yugo GV in America was to set up a management hierarchy. As mentioned previously, Malcolm Bricklin was Yugo America's chief financial backer. As chairman, he owned 75% of the company. William Prior, who would act as president and head of operations, owned 1%. Ira Edelson owned 2% of the company and held the title of financial administrator. The remaining 22% was held by investors who were not involved in the management of the company.

In February 1985, the company began recruiting automobile dealers. (The company's founders had been reviewing dealers for over four months, but the actual signing did not take place until February.) Tony Cappadona was hired as dealer development manager and given the responsibility of locating established dealers who were interested in selling the Yugo. In addition, extensive surveys helped Mr. Cappadona determine the best area placement of Yugo franchises. By the end of July, the first 50 dealers were contracted in Pennsylvania, Massachusetts, New York, New Jersey, Connecticut, Rhode Island, Delaware, Maryland, and Washington, D.C.

Some dealers were hesitant to sign because of the financial commitment involved. Pressure from Manufacturers Hanover Trust Company required that Yugo America produce 50 letters of credit by December 1985. By the terms of agreement, dealers had to produce a $400,000 stand-by letter of credit to cover at least two months of vehicle shipments. The dealer also had to pay $37,000 for a start-up kit and arrange financing for a floor plan. A floor plan is an agreement between a financial institution and an auto dealership to finance the vehicles that are on the lot. The financial institution retains title to the automobiles until they are sold, which allows the financial institution to offer extremely attractive rates to the dealership, usually one to two percentage points above the prime lending rate. A typical floor plan would only require $600,000 of credit. However, the commitment of funds was excessive for such a risky operation. In response to these concerns, Yugo executives assured dealers that the Yugo GV would sell itself.

Bricklin contacted Leonard Sirowitz, a New York advertiser, to write and launch a $10 million campaign prior to the debut of the Yugo GV. Sirowitz, who helped to create the Volkswagen Beetle advertisements during the 1960s, expected the Yugo ads to reach a potential one million buyers via newspapers, magazines, and television. He hoped to convince Americans that, despite their views of Communist Yugoslavia, the $3,995 car was of sound quality.[1] Yugo's first slogan intended to catch the consumer's eye by asking, "The Road Back to Sanity: Why Pay Higher Prices?"

In addition to trained technicians, Yugo's support system of quality parts and service was comprehensive. The company received 180 tons of spare parts to distribute among dealers during the summer of 1985. The company implemented the industry's first Universal Product Code inventory system, which enhanced the accuracy and efficiency of inventory processing. In addition, service schools were developed so that technicians would have no problems or questions when repairing the cars. For the "do-it-yourself" consumers, Yugo America published its own repair manuals and included a toll-free telephone number for assistance.

THE YUGO ARRIVES IN AMERICA

The first shipment of 500 cars from the Zastava plant arrived in mid-August 1985 (a picture of the Yugo is found in Exhibit 1 and its features are listed in Exhibit 2). Ten cars were sent to each of the fifty dealers in the Northeast. Each dealer was instructed to reserve two cars as demonstration vehicles and to uphold this condition at all times. By the end of August, the cars were polished and ready for their national debut.

Yugo's official entry into the automobile industry was announced on August 26, 1985. It was a long-awaited moment, and consumers were equally as

EXHIBIT 1　THE YUGO GV

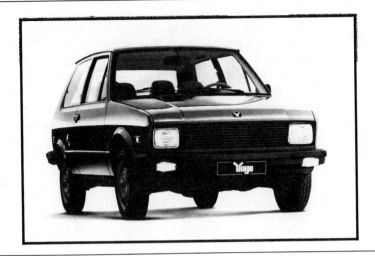

excited about the car as the Yugo employees. The Yugo frenzy spread so quickly that thirty-three dealerships were added and 3,000 orders were taken for cars by September 9. Customers paid deposits in order to reserve their cars, and by the end of 1985, a six-month waiting list was tallied. Indeed, Yugo's founders had discovered "a market in search of a product."[2]

During its first year of operations, which ended July 31, 1986, Yugo America, Inc. grossed $122 million from the sale of 27,000 automobiles and parts and accessories. The Yugo was hailed as the "fastest selling import car in the history of the U.S."[3] The company employed 220 dealers throughout the Southeast and East Coast, and it was estimated that the consumer credit divisions of Chrysler, Ford, and General Motors financed one-third of the Yugo retail sales.[4] At the end of July, Prior announced the expansion of the New Jersey home office to include a corporate planning department. He also informed reporters of Yugo's new slogan, "Everybody Needs a Yugo Sometime."[5]

PROBLEMS BEGIN

In February 1986, *Consumer Reports* published the first of two articles criticizing the Yugo GV. Reporters mocked Malcolm Bricklin for his other car ventures (the Subaru 360 and the Fiat Spider) which had recently failed. The writers pointed out that, after adding destination charges, dealer preparation fees, and a stereo, the price of the car exceeded $4,600. The magazine's personal test evaluation was also published. It stated that the transmission was "sloppy," the steering was "heavy," the ride was "jerky," and the heating system was "weak and obtrusive."[6]

EXHIBIT 2 YUGO GV STANDARD FEATURES

VEHICLE TYPE
Front-engine, front-wheel drive, four passenger, three-door hatchback.

DIMENSIONS AND CAPACITIES
Wheelbase: 84.6 inches
Overall Length: 139.0 inches
Overall Height: 54.7 inches
Overall Width: 60.7 inches
Headroom: Front: 37.0 inches
         Rear: 36.0 inches
Legroom: Front: 39.0 inches
         Rear: 39.0 inches
Ground Clearance: 4.8 inches
Luggage Capacity: 18.5+9.0 cubic feet
Fuel Capacity: 8.4 gallons
Curb Weight: 1,832 pounds

ENGINE
Type: Single overhead cam, 1.1 liter 4-cylinder with aluminum cyl. head. Dual barrel carburetor
Bore & Stroke: 80 × 55.5 mm.
Displacement: 1116 cc.
Compression Ratio: 9.2:1
Horsepower: 54hp at 5,000 rpm.
Torque: 52 lbs. at 4,000 rpm.

DRIVE TRAIN
Transmission: 4-speed Manual
Final Drive Ratio: 3.7
Gear Ratios: 1st-3.5, 2nd-2.2, 3rd-1.4, 4th-1.0, Reverse-3.7

SUSPENSION
Front: Independent, MacPherson struts, anti-sway bar.
Rear: Independent, transverse leaf spring with lower control arms

BRAKES
Front: 8.0" disc, power-assisted
Rear: 7.2" drum, power-assisted
Rear brake proportioning valve

WHEELS AND TIRES
Wheels: Steel
Tires: Tigar 145SR-13, steel-belted radials with all-weather tread design.

ELECTRICAL
Bosch electronic ignition
Alternator: 55 amp
Battery: 12 volt, 45 amp

(continued)

EXHIBIT 2 (continued)

ECONOMY
City: 28 mpg
Highway: 31 mpg

STANDARD EQUIPMENT
1.1 liter 4-cylinder overhead cam engine
Front-wheel drive
4-wheel independent suspension
Power assisted brakes, disc front, drum rear
Front anti-sway bar
Rack and pinion steering
Color-coordinated fabric upholstery
Full carpeting, including carpeted luggage compartment
Reclining front seats
Folding rear seats—27.5 cu. ft. luggage space
3 grab handles
2 dome lights
Visor vanity mirror
Analog instrument gauges
Low fuel warning light
Steel-belted radial tires (145 × 13)
Lexan bumpers
Plastic inner front fender shields
Bosch electronic ignition
Rear brake proportioning valve
Full-size spare tire
Front spoiler
Hood scoop
Hub caps
PVC undercoating
Opening rear quarter windows
Rear window electric defroster
Quartz halogen headlights
Body side molding
Special owner's tool kit
Cigarette lighter
Locking gas cap
Dual storage pockets
Concealed radio antenna
Spare fuse and bulb kit
Night/day rear-view mirror
Electric cooling fan
Console

Source: Yugo America, Inc. promotional materials.

The writers continued by criticizing almost every aspect of the car, from seat coverings to the "not-so-spacious" trunk. The safety of the car was questioned, but could not be verified by government crash tests. It was noted, however, that the impact of a collision at 3 mph and 5 mph severely twisted and crushed the bumpers. It was estimated that repairing the damage to the front and rear bumpers was $620 and $461, respectively.[7] Twenty-one other defects were discovered, ranging from oil leaks to squealing brakes. A survey by J. D. Power and Associates (included in the article) concerning customer satisfaction revealed that over 80% of Yugo buyers had reported problems. In short, the writers did not recommend the Yugo GV at *any* price.

The Yugo was facing increasing competition as well. In late 1985 Hyundai Motor America, a subsidiary of the giant South Korean industrial company, announced the American introduction of the Hyundai Excel for $4,995. The Excel was a hatchback model that included standard features which were comparable to the Yugo GV. Therefore, the Excel posed a direct threat to the Yugo GV in the lower priced automobile market.

By mid-October 1986, Yugo America responded to the *Consumer Reports* article and increasing consumer complaints by making 176 improvements to the car without raising its price.[8] Prior stated that Yugo spent between $2.5 and $3 million to improve its image through advertisements and national incentives. Independent dealers offered additional rebates, as well, in an effort to boost sagging sales.

Looking ahead, Yugo America had hoped to introduce some new models, all within the lower price range. For 1987, the Yugo GV would be given a "face lift" to take on an aerodynamic look, and a convertible GV would be available later in the year. In order to meet the needs of couples and small families, Yugo anticipated the 1988 debut of a five-door hatchback, which would compete with the Honda Accord. A four-door sedan would be added to the line between 1989 and 1990, and a two-seater sports car named "TCX" would be the highlight of 1990.[9]

During 1986, there were rumors that Yugo America was considering a move to "go public" by issuing common stock, since the company was beginning to experience financial tension. The proposal was later cancelled for two reasons. First, Bricklin did not want to surrender any of his equity (75%). Second, the company was starting to feel the effects of negative publicity, and financial consultants felt that the stock would not bring a fair price. For the time being, Yugo would remain a private company.

MORE TROUBLE

In April 1987, *Consumer Reports* released its annual survey of domestic and foreign cars, and once again, Yugo's image was tainted. The writers criticized the Yugo GV from bumper to bumper, stating that "the manual transmission was very imprecise . . . the worst we've tried in years." As for comfort, "small, insufficiently contoured front seats" contributed to an "awkward driving position." In addition, the ride of the car was described as "noisy" and "harsh."[10]

Besides the negative description of the car's driving performance, the article publicized the results of an independent crash test. This test, which was not mandated by law, disclosed the results of a crash at 35 miles per hour among domestic and foreign automobiles. (The National Highway Traffic Safety Administration requires that all cars pass the national standard impact at 30 miles per hour.) The Yugo GV was among the 40% which did not pass the test. In fact, it received the lowest possible ranking with respect to driver and passenger protection. The report indicated that the steering column "moved up and back into the path of the driver's head," and the seats "moved forward during the crash, increasing the load on occupants."[11]

Consumer Reports also reported that damage to the front and rear bumpers when hit at an impact of 3 and 5 mph was $1,081, the highest in its class. This was particularly embarrassing to Yugo America, since many of its foreign competitors (including Toyota, Mazda, and Saab) escaped the collisions without a scratch.[12]

Before the second *Consumer Reports* articles, Yugo sold every car coming into its ports every month. Sales in 1987 were the highest to date. From there, Yugo's problems started to catch up with the company. The negative image of the Yugo was apparent, and dealers were forced to offer $500–750 rebates as an incentive to buy. In addition, several new programs and extended warranties were offered to entice customers. Monthly sales levels started to decline, and waiting lists became virtually obsolete.

Through all of these problems, William Prior remained an exemplary figure for all of the Yugo-Global employees. As Tony Cappadona stated, "Bill added a lot of charisma and dedication to the company. He let the employees know that everyone was working to achieve a mission. They (the employees) didn't mind working 10 or 12 hours a day, because they saw Bill putting in twice as much."

CHANGES IN OWNERSHIP

The 1987 year was marked by the acquisition of Yugo America, Inc. by Global Motors, Inc., a company founded by Malcolm Bricklin. Bricklin established Global Motors as an umbrella corporation for importing cars worldwide. Gaining 91% of Yugo America, Global became its parent, distributor, and holding company, and it helped with the coordination and distribution of Yugos as they arrived at the Baltimore port.

By 1988, Yugo America and Global Motors began contemplating the sale of a substantial portion of the company in an effort to avoid bankruptcy. In April, Mabon Nugent and Company, a New York investment firm, purchased Global Motors for $40 million.[13] Bricklin sold 70% of his equity for $20 million, and a debenture was purchased from Global for an additional $20 million. A management group headed by Prior and Edelson agreed to contribute

$2.1 million to obtain 5.5% of the company. The management group would be awarded stock options periodically over the following three years, to bring the group's total ownership to 22%. Prior was named chief executive officer during the acquisition.[14]

THE FINAL YEAR

By April 1988, the company's operating problems had also increased. Not only had the *Consumer Reports* articles thrashed the Yugo GV again, but dealers were beginning to undermine the company as well. William Prior stated that dealers would often persuade buyers to purchase one of their other brands instead of a Yugo. To make things worse, Consumers could only receive 36-month financing with the purchase of a Yugo. Conversely, Ford Motor Credit and other financiers offered 60-month plans on their own cars, which resulted in lower payments. The thought of lower monthly payments was incentive enough for a prospective Yugo buyer to change his decision to purchase. If the former tactic did not persuade the buyer, the salesperson would criticize the Yugo directly and accentuate the features of the other line. Higher commissions on more costly brands increased the motivation of salespeople to move away from the Yugo.

Even after deciding to buy a Yugo, many consumers ran into additional difficulties when they tried to obtain financing. Because the typical Yugo customer was a young, low-income, first-time buyer, lending institutions were hesitant to make high-risk loans to persons in this segment of the market. It was estimated that as many as 70% of all Yugo customers were declined for credit, since the majority had no previous credit history and a debt-income ratio of over 50%. This common scenario was discouraging for both the customers and dealers. Enticing advertisements lured customers in, and yet many could not obtain financing. The dealers became frustrated because of the amount of time and effort contributed to "put the deal together." Prior described the situation as "an inefficiency in the market."

In an effort to hurdle these financing roadblocks, Yugo America announced in June 1988 that it would design its own program for financing. The first-time buyer plan was administered through Imperial Savings Association, a $10-billion institution based in San Diego. Yugo and Imperial intended to protect themselves by charging a higher annual percentage rate—as much as four percentage points higher than those of other finance companies. In doing so, Yugo America could establish a "higher-than-average" reserve for loan defaults. Though the annual percentage rate was higher, buyers could finance the loan over 60 months so that monthly payments remained low.[15]

Approximately 50 dealers were enrolled in the program. Imperial was hesitant to allow all of the dealers to take advantage of Yugo Credit, since there were still some "bugs" in the system. Also, each state required separate licensing, and Yugo did not have the time to wait for acceptance in each state.

The financing program was terminated after 90 days. One of the provisions of the plan required Yugo America to be "in good standing" financially. Bills were accumulating at Yugo and company debt was becoming unmanageable. Imperial Savings had to pull out.

In November 1988, William Prior and 71 other employees were released from the company, leaving a skeleton crew of 71 remaining. Mabon Nugent's intentions were to cut costs in an effort to relieve cash-flow pressures and generate additional funds for product development. Marcel Kole, senior vice president and chief financial officer of Global Motors, temporarily replaced

EXHIBIT 3 GLOBAL MOTORS, INC. BALANCE SHEET, DECEMBER 31, 1988 (UNAUDITED)

ASSETS	
Cash	0
Due to/from subsidiaries	27,145
Due from manufacturer	15
Inventories	0
Prepaid and other current assets	48
	27,208
Property, plant and equipment (at cost)	8
Less: Accumulated depreciation	(1)
	7
Investment in subsidiaries	223
Deferred charges	
Total Assets	27,438
LIABILITIES AND EQUITY	
Acceptances payable	0
Accounts payable and accrued expenses	1,429
Notes payable	11,825
Due to/from subsidiaries	0
Estimated warranty (current)	0
	13,254
Estimated warranty (long-term)	0
Long-term debt	11,000
Minority interest	0
Shareholders' deficiency	3,184
Total Liabilities and Equity	27,438
	0

Note: Amounts are given in thousands of dollars.

Source: Bankruptcy Docket Number 89 00680, filed January 30, 1989, United States Bankruptcy Court, District of New Jersey.

Prior as president and chief executive of Yugo America. Turnover within the company was high, and national advertising was brought to a halt.[16] Norauto LP of Ohio agreed to finance two shipments of Yugos backed by letters of credit. Norauto, a firm which aids bankrupt, terminated, or distressed companies, took possession of the cars until Yugo America could repay the $14.3 million letter of credit.[17]

Mabon Nugent and Company had written off $10.5 million as a loss in Global Motors by January 30, 1989. It was estimated that Global would need $10 million to get back on its feet, but Mabon Nugent did not feel that contributing more money to a dying company was a worthy investment. The firm's partners considered selling the company to Zastava or private investors, but neither of the ideas were pursued.[18] Global officially filed for Chapter 11 bankruptcy on January 30, 1989.[19] Global's unaudited balance sheet reported in the petition for bankruptcy is contained in Exhibit 3.

A HAZY FUTURE FOR YUGO AMERICA

After declaring bankruptcy in January 1989, parent company Global Motors, Inc. discharged 250 (of 300) Yugo America employees. Zastava, honoring the warranty of the cars, began seeking financial backing so that the company could remain afloat. By February 1989, three lawsuits had been filed against Global Motors and Mabon Nugent and Company. William Prior sued the companies for breach of contract and Turner Broadcasting System in Atlanta filed suit demanding $182,000 for unpaid bills. A third lawsuit, by Imperial Savings, alleged that Mabon Nugent was "involved in the day-to-day operations of the company (Global)" before it (Mabon Nugent) actually took control of Yugo-Global in 1988. Mabon Nugent denied the charge.[20]

John A. Spiech became Yugo's new president and chief executive, succeeding Marcel Kole. Spiech, a veteran of the automobile industry, had full confidence in the company and its product, stating, "Whatever happened wasn't the car's fault. It is still good, low-cost, reliable transportation."[21] He intended to take the company to the top, even though he was starting from the very bottom.

ENDNOTES

Much of the information in this case is based on personal interviews with William Prior and Tony Cappadona, conducted in June 1989.

1. J. Fierman, "Can A Beetle Brain Stir a Yearning For Yugos?" *Fortune* (May 13, 1985): 73.
2. "The Price is Right," *Time* (September 9, 1985): 58.
3. J. L. Kovach, "We Don't Overpromise," *Industry Week* (October 13, 1986): 73.
4. Ibid.
5. J. A. Russell, "Yugo Grosses $122 Million in First Year," *Automotive News* (September 1, 1986): 42.
6. "How Much Car for $3990?" *Consumer Reports* (February 1986): 84–86.
7. Ibid.
8. Kovach, "We Don't Overpromise."

9. J. A. Russell, "Zastava to Construct Plant For U.S. Yugos," *Automotive News* (May 20, 1985): 2.

10. "The 1987 Cars," *Consumer Reports* (April 1987): 200–215.

11. Ibid., p. 200.

12. Ibid., p. 208.

13. J. A. Russell, "Bricklin's Import Firm Sold in $40 Million Deal," *Automotive News* (April 18, 1988): 1, 56.

14. Ibid.

15. J. Henry, "Low Finance: Yugo Offers Loans to Spur Buyers," *Automotive News* (August 1, 1988): 1, 51.

16. C. Thomas, "Prior Ousted: Shaky Global Trims Ranks," *Automotive News* (November 14, 1988): 1, 58.

17. J. Henry, "Yugo, Liquidator in Accord," *Automotive News* (March 27, 1989): 1.

18. J. Henry, "Global Struggles to Remain Afloat," *Automotive News* (January 30, 1989): 1, 257.

19. Henry, "Yugo, Liquidator in Accord."

20. J. Henry, "More Yugo Grief—Maker Plans Termination," *Automotive News* (February 20, 1989): 1, 51.

21. D. Cuff, "A Car Industry Veteran Will Try to Revive Yugo," *New York Times* (March 17, 1989): D4.

CASE 6

FROM AIRLINE TO EMPIRE: UNITED AIRLINES UNDER RICHARD FERRIS

GARY E. WILLARD

Richard Ferris, chairman and chief executive officer of Allegis Corporation, arrived in New York on June 9, 1987, to attend another meeting in a series of meetings with the board of directors. This one had been hastily called by Charles Luce, the board's senior member. Ferris was prepared to discuss flaws that had appeared in Allegis's defenses against a hostile takeover. Several groups had emerged as threats to Allegis: the pilots of United Air Lines (Allegis's airline subsidiary), Coniston Partners (an investment firm that owned 13% of Allegis's stock), and a group of large institutional investors who were dissatisfied with the firm's stock price performance. Ferris planned to meet the next day with some of these investors to try to regain their support. He would never get the chance.

Less than two months previously, Luce had written to the *Wall Street Journal*, pledging the board's support for Ferris's total travel company strategy. As this meeting started, Ferris realized that things had changed. Some of the directors openly criticized his strategy and takeover defenses. When Luce joined them, Ferris knew that his strategy was doomed.

The directors had a final offer for Ferris. If he would divest the nonairline divisions and concentrate on United's affairs, he could remain as chairman and CEO. That was unacceptable. Rather than abandon the fly-drive-sleep concept that he believed would revolutionize the travel industry, Richard Ferris resigned.

THE AIRLINE INDUSTRY: DEREGULATION

The decade prior to 1987 had been one of significant change within the airline industry. Before 1978, the industry was tightly regulated by the Civil Aeronautics Board (CAB). CAB approval was required for any changes in routes or

Source: **This case was prepared by the author and research assistants David Krueger and Tim Schoenecker as a basis for class discussion rather than to illustrate either effective or ineffective handling of a management situation.** © 1987, Purdue University.

even significant adjustments in fares. The review process was a long and costly one for the applicants. However, the passage of the Airline Deregulation Act of 1978 was the first step in the process of deregulating the industry. This legislation was the federal government's first attempt in decades to deregulate an entire industry.[1] The target date for ending all regulation of carriers' route structures was 1981.

During the mid-1970s government regulation of industry had come under increasing criticism. Most airline executives, however, strongly opposed deregulation, even though the CAB sharply limited their flexibility.[2] Their rationale was simple: Restricted competition on certain routes served to protect inefficient carriers. Deregulation would end monopolies, force increased price competition, and lead to poorer financial performance.[3] One airline executive who favored deregulation was Richard Ferris. He told the *Wall Street Journal,* "Deregulation will be the greatest thing to happen to airlines since the jet engine."[4]

Response to deregulation by most of the major carriers was similar. Short, low-profit routes to smaller cities were abandoned as the major airlines focused on longer routes between larger markets. United was a leader in this move toward consolidation, adding more flights from its "hubs" (key airports in geographic regions) in Chicago and Denver while eliminating service to many smaller cities.[5] (Exhibit 1 shows new routes added by United Airlines in 1978 and 1979.) However, the major airlines found an unexpected result of this tactic was that it "opened the door" to new airlines building their customer base from these smaller markets. It also put at risk the airlines' traditional "hub and spoke" strategy, since many of the discontinued routes had served to feed travelers into major hubs. By reducing their overall networks, the majors inadvertently gave passengers more freedom in choosing an airline.

Deregulation did have its intended effect on fares. Increased competition among the major carriers and the emergence of low-cost carriers like People Express and Britt led to heavy discounting and price wars. This period saw the development of "super-saver" fares (discounts of up to 50%) as well as other pricing innovations. The airline industry changed from one that had competed primarily on service to one that competed on price.

The financial performance of the airlines in the years after deregulation made Ferris's rosy prediction seem foolish. In 1981, the industry registered a record $362 million in operating losses (see Exhibit 2). This was surpassed the following year, when nearly $700 million in operating losses were recorded. Approximately 18,000 workers were laid off during these two years. It would be unfair to place the blame for all of this red ink on deregulation, however. Concurrent with the fare wars was a general slowdown in the nation's economy and a strike by the Professional Air Traffic Controllers Organization (PATCO). This and the subsequent firing of the PATCO strikers by President Reagan sharply reduced the capacity of the air traffic system. The airlines were forced to cancel many flights.

THE AIRLINE INDUSTRY: DEREGULATION

EXHIBIT 1 ROUTES ADDED BY UNITED AIRLINES (1979)

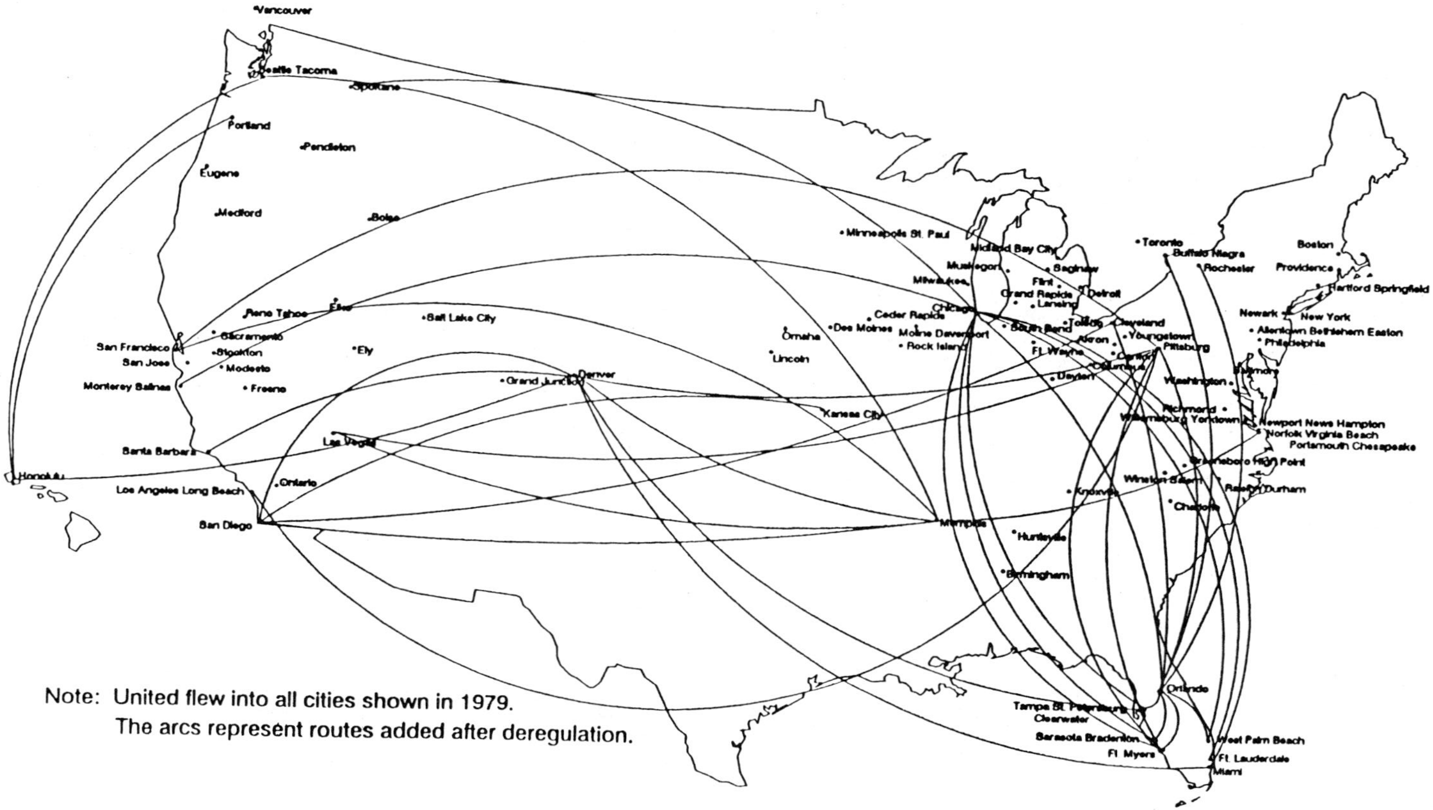

Note: United flew into all cities shown in 1979.
The arcs represent routes added after deregulation.

EXHIBIT 2 AIRLINE INDUSTRY PERFORMANCE

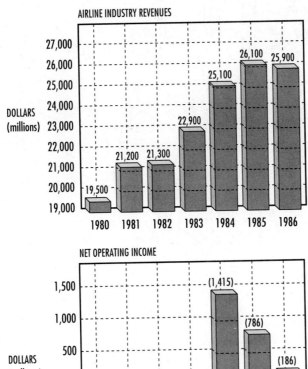

THE AIRLINE INDUSTRY: LATER DEVELOPMENTS

The airline industry's performance improved significantly after the hard times of those transition years. In 1984, the industry posted a record $1.4 billion in operating profits, although profits declined in 1985 and 1986. Revenue passenger miles grew throughout the mid-1980s with a 33% overall gain from 1980 to 1986. Passenger load factors (the percentage of seats filled), a key to profitability, climbed to 61% in 1986 from a low of 57% in 1981.[6] Finally, a decline of nearly 20% in fuel prices between 1981 and 1985 eased the upward pressure on a major component of operating costs.[7]

When deregulation was first instituted, some observers predicted consolidation to a maximum of seven primary carriers.[8] Consolidation became the trend as several carriers merged or were acquired by others. For example, Texas Air transformed itself from a regional carrier into a megacarrier by acquiring Continental, Eastern, and People Express.

Throughout the 1980s, the development and use of computerized travel registration systems became increasingly important. Each of the five largest carriers had its own system (Northwest and TWA shared one), with American's Sabre and United's Apollo being the largest. These systems were not only marketing and distribution tools, they also generated revenue since airlines pay for tickets reserved on a competitor's system. This revenue could be significant. American's Sabre system produced revenues of over $400 million in 1986,[9] nearly 7% of parent AMR's total revenue.

The result of the changes in the market during the decade was the consolidation that the experts had predicted. Over 70% of the market was now concentrated among the top five carriers (see Exhibits 3 and 4). Brief sketches of the United's top competitors follow:

TEXAS AIR

Through aggressive acquisition tactics focused solely on the air transportation industry, Texas Air became the largest airline (in terms of revenue passenger miles) in the United States. It was divided into two divisions—Continental (which included Frontier and People Express) and Eastern. The Continental division was non-union and noted for its low costs. Texas Air experienced problems integrating Eastern into its corporate structure, primarily because it was unionized.

AMERICAN

American Airlines was known as an innovator in the industry. It pioneered the price war tactic of "super saver" fares as well as the two-tiered wage scale (discussed later) as a way to control labor costs. American had the highest operating income of the top five, 7.9% of revenues. American relied on internal growth for expansion, acquiring only one regional carrier, Air Cal, during this period. American was the largest subsidiary of its parent cor-

EXHIBIT 3 AIRLINE INDUSTRY COMPETITION, 1986 SELECTED DATA ON THE TOP 5 DOMESTIC CARRIERS (ALL NUMBERS IN MILLIONS)

AIRLINE	MARKET SHARE*	REVENUE PASS MILES	PASSENGER REVENUES	OPERATING INCOME	LABOR COSTS AS % OF REV.	NUMBER OF EMPLOYEES	MAJOR HUBS
Texas Air	20.0%	66,300	$4,030	$237	0.32	68,000**	Denver, Houston, Miami, Newark
United	17.9%	59,300	$5,960	$407	0.43	87,000**	Chicago, Denver, San Francisco, D.C.
American	14.7%	48,800	$4,960	$392	0.41	54,300	Dallas, Chicago, Nashville
Delta	9.6%	31,800	$4,200	$237	0.47	38,901	Atlanta, Dallas, Salt Lake City
Northwest	8.7%	28,800	$2,920	$167	0.35	33,427	Detroit, Memphis, Minneapolis

*Based on revenue passenger miles.
**Average number of employees for the year. All others are the number of employees at year end.

poration, AMR, accounting for approximately 88% of AMR's revenues in 1986.

DELTA

Delta was traditionally strong in the Southeast; it controlled a majority of the traffic at Atlanta's huge Hartsfield Airport. Its acquisition of Western Airlines gave Delta a new and strong presence in the West. This airline had a reputation for high-quality service as well as high profits; however, in 1986 it had the lowest return of sales of the major carriers. Some thought that this was the result of its labor costs, which were the industry's highest even though it was non-union. Delta was virtually undiversified in 1986; only 2% of its revenues were generated from nonairline business.

NORTHWEST

From its hubs in Minneapolis, Detroit, and Memphis, the Northwest/Republic team moved from being a strong regional carrier to a major player in the industry with a 9% market share. Much of its strength lay in its Pacific routes and well-integrated feeder network. Northwest also had moderate labor costs in comparison with its rivals. Northwest was the major subsidiary of NWA. Northwest's passenger revenues accounted for 81% and its freight revenues 14% of parent NWA's revenues in 1986.

UNITED AIRLINES: BEFORE DIVERSIFICATION

The idea of airlines owning hotel chains did not begin with UAL. In 1946, Pan American initiated the trend with its Intercontinental Hotel subsidiary. TWA followed by acquiring Hilton International in 1967, American Airlines had its Flagship Hotels, and Braniff owned a group of hotels in Latin America. This diversification was more than just a sideline. It was an important source of earnings intended to offset the cyclical nature of the airline industry.

United Airlines was the last major airline to follow suit with its 1970 acquisition of Western International, a hotel chain that outranked all but Sheraton and Hilton (U.S.) in the number of rooms available. For $82 million in stock, United acquired 71 major hotels in 13 countries, approximately one-half in cities served by United. United also acquired two Western International executives, Edward Carlson and Richard Ferris, who would play significant roles in the operation of the airline.

However, 1970 was not a good year for United. The airline suffered a $46 million loss, its worst ever. A recession, new competition on its Hawaii and California routes, and the cost of financing a large fleet of jumbo jets combined to squeeze United.

Shortly before the end of 1970, United's outside directors felt that CEO George Keck was not moving aggressively enough to solve the airline's problems. A bitter boardroom struggle ended when Keck, aloof and introverted, resigned and was replaced by Carlson. Carlson's lack of airline experience led United's employees to joke that he was going to ground all the 747's and make them into hotels.

Carlson promptly canceled all orders for jets, eliminated 300 of United's 1,800 daily flights, reorganized and decentralized the company's management, and cut the number of employees by 9%. These actions helped turn United

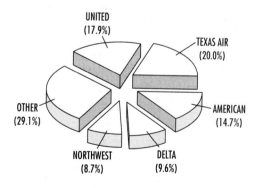

EXHIBIT 4 AIRLINE INDUSTRY MARKET SHARE, 1986*

UNITED (17.9%)
TEXAS AIR (20.0%)
AMERICAN (14.7%)
DELTA (9.6%)
NORTHWEST (8.7%)
OTHER (29.1%)

* Based on revenue passenger miles.

around, and the company suffered only a small loss in 1971 and was profitable again in 1972.

UAL's next diversification move was in 1975. Carlson acquired GAB Business Services, a small ($100 million) but profitable insurance business.

UNITED AIRLINES: RICHARD FERRIS TAKES OVER

Richard Ferris traveled an unusual route to the helm of United Airlines and Allegis. After graduating from Cornell University's hotel management program in 1962, he went to work for Western International (later Westin) Hotels. Ferris quickly moved up the corporate ladder, managing hotels domestically and overseas. When Carlson was named CEO of Western's new parent, Ferris followed him to the airline and became the head of United's food service division. "Here was an industry being managed by the federal government through regulation," Ferris said. "I thought that it would be stifling."[10]

Ferris's next job at United was vice-president of marketing. Then, in 1974, Carlson named Ferris president while he remained chairman and CEO. Industry observers were surprised at the selection of Ferris, since he had never held an operating position in the airline before taking over.[11] This, plus his background in hotels, made Ferris somewhat of an outsider in the close-knit airline industry. After two years as president, he became CEO of United and in 1979 replaced Carlson as chairman of UAL, Inc., the holding company.

To overcome his lack of experience in the airline industry, Ferris placed heavy emphasis on employee relations during his early days as president. He traveled extensively to cities served by United, meeting with employees and discussing their problems. He was often a cockpit companion of the pilots during flights. He even obtained a pilot's license to increase his rapport with the pilots. But he would need more than just flying skills to guide United through the turbulent skies that lay ahead.

UNITED UNDER FERRIS

United remained profitable for most of the decade, registering record operating earnings of $296 million in 1978. But, as Carlson stepped aside in 1979, Ferris faced a stormy introduction. Starting with an operating loss of $235 million that year, the airline lost half a billion dollars in Ferris's first three and a half years as Chairman of UAL, Inc. (see Exhibit 5). The losses were the result of several factors:

1. Deregulation (discussed earlier).
2. A long strike by the International Association of Machinists, who rejected two pacts endorsed by their leaders before finally settling the strike.
3. The crash of a DC-10 flown by American Airlines. All such aircraft

were subsequently grounded. United, with 38 of these planes, was deprived of more than one-third of its long-haul capacity.
4. The PATCO strike, which severely limited the capacity at Chicago's O'Hare Field. Since one-third of United's revenues flowed through this airport, the effect on United was severe.

Ferris responded by cutting costs. The number of employees dropped from 54,500 in 1979 to 42,500 by the summer of 1982. The company negotiated a new contract in 1982 with its 4,500 pilots, improving work rules in exchange for a no-layoff guarantee. For example, the new rules cut the cockpit costs of a Boeing 737 by 37%, from $430 to $270 per hour. Ferris also delayed shipment of twenty 767's on order. The situation began to turn around during the second half of 1982. After a disastrous first half, the consolidated operating loss for the full year was a modest $9 million.

By May 1985, United's turnaround was complete and the picture so rosy that *Business Week* featured Ferris as the chief executive officer who returned shareholders the most for the pay received. In the same article, *Business Week* noted that UAL was the subject of leveraged buyout speculation. Fueling this speculation was the price of UAL's stock. It closed on May 1 nearly 15% below its book value of $47 per share.

In an attempt to enhance UAL's market value, Ferris sought additional productivity gains and wage concessions from the pilots' union. He felt that such concessions were necessary if the company was to compete with the new low-cost, no-frills airlines such as People Express. A two-tier pay proposal for pilots became the focal point of the negotiations.

United proposed hiring new pilots at a scale 40% below that of its 6,000 existing pilots. The lower scale would exist for the first 20 years of service, by which time the pilots should have attained the rank of captain. New hires would also receive fewer fringe benefits, different work rules, and smaller pensions. Worried about the effects that this proposal might have on other airlines, the ALPA (the pilots' union) called a strike in May 1987. The walkout was strongly supported by the union membership. Of approximately 6,000 pilots, only 250 plus a handful of trainees crossed the picket lines. United's flight schedule was reduced by more than 85%.

In an attempt to keep the airline going, United recruited pilots away from other airlines by offering comparatively high wages and flexible working hours. United also announced that all of the trainee pilots who supported the strike would not be reinstated. These actions quickly became the focus of the strike as an agreement was reached on the two-tier wage plan. The ALPA was adamant that the trainees be reinstated and that the recently recruited pilots be made subject to the new wage agreement. These demands were important to the ALPA since losing on these points would damage its ability to successfully organize strikes in the future. Ferris was unyielding on these issues as well. He stated, "We would never forsake those who kept this airline going during the work stoppage. That is the word of this corporation and it is worth something."[12]

EXHIBIT 5 UAL, INC. FINANCIAL DATA, 1979–1987

CONSOLIDATED BALANCE SHEETS
(IN THOUSANDS OF DOLLARS)

YEAR ENDED DECEMBER 31

	1979	1980	1981	1982	1983	1984	1985	1986	1987
ASSETS:									
Cash & cash equivalents	$355,121	$318,923	$194,621	$308,801	$292,146	$442,230	$750,511	$218,144	$2,208,016
Receivables	565,272	605,219	593,222	599,408	766,800	721,479	933,716	1,100,609	816,547
Prepaid expenses	232,606	285,832	180,787	165,928	194,835	262,502	307,652	390,171	402,455
Refundable taxes	11,051	2,556	0	0	0	0	78,163	61,118	0
Rental automobiles	0	0	0	0	0	0	1,019,418	1,378,468	0
Total Current Assets	1,164,050	1,212,530	968,630	1,074,137	1,253,781	1,426,211	3,089,460	3,148,510	3,427,018
Net assets of discontinued operations (A)									426,747
Owned equipment	4,017,495	4,085,781	4,453,980	5,120,131	5,718,546	5,891,084	6,829,915	7,672,264	7,214,028
Leased equipment	820,986	886,931	959,542	921,627	917,616	823,418	725,146	666,977	643,134
Accumulated depreciation	(2,258,137)	(2,300,283)	(2,581,767)	(2,785,527)	(2,983,258)	(3,171,040)	(3,439,077)	(3,650,639)	(3,851,278)
Net Equipment	2,580,344	2,672,429	2,831,755	3,256,231	3,652,964	3,543,462	4,115,984	4,688,602	4,005,884
Other assets	118,055	156,499	175,392	248,526	226,898	189,369	668,775	879,405	366,620
	$3,862,449	$4,041,458	$3,975,777	$4,578,894	$5,133,643	$5,159,042	$7,874,219	$8,716,517	$8,226,269

	1979	1980	1981	1982	1983	1984	1985	1986	1987
CURRENT LIABILITIES:									
Short term borrowings	$	$152,192	$178,704	$75,985	$187,940	$297,518	$602,912	$987,819	$1,010,311
Current portion of LTD	102,114	105,247	116,406	84,672	130,585	81,525	409,164	146,938	47,198
Advance ticket sales	360,812	396,680	358,731	352,181	453,232	432,979	432,782	561,322	581,333
Accounts payable	699,690	752,832	813,989	945,267	1,152,024	1,059,241	1,451,411	1,857,303	496,216
Accrued/deferred taxes	13,840	23,409	22,005	8,482	10,455	80,390	76,951	207,285	1,274,803
Total Current Liabilities	1,176,456	1,430,360	1,489,835	1,466,587	1,934,236	1,951,653	2,973,220	3,760,667	3,409,861
LONG TERM DEBT	1,234,291	1,176,086	1,181,346	1,794,899	1,311,267	986,803	2,642,234	2,066,008	1,427,295
DEFERRED TAXES & OTHER LIABILITIES	294,219	264,737	204,131	196,452	290,795	326,373	465,552	593,734	464,005
SHAREHOLDER'S EQUITY:									
Preferred stock	9,532	8,850	8,441	8,038	200,737	251,296	234,345	3,498	3,021
Common stock	147,578	147,598	147,925	148,049	172,423	173,974	176,566	251,118	292,354
Paid in capital	419,290	419,507	420,677	421,100	555,427	560,456	578,258	1,260,595	1,678,306
Retained earnings	583,201	596,438	525,540	545,887	670,876	908,821	804,378	781,231	1,073,760
Treasury stock	(2,118)	(2,118)	(2,118)	(2,118)	(2,118)	(334)	(334)	(334)	(122,333)
Total Equity	1,157,483	1,170,275	1,100,465	1,120,956	1,597,345	1,894,213	1,793,213	2,296,108	2,925,108
	$3,862,449	$4,041,458	$3,975,777	$4,578,894	$5,133,643	$5,159,042	$7,874,219	$8,716,517	$8,226,269

(A) Consists primarily of the Westin Hotels sold January 31, 1988, for $1,350.

Source: Company Annual Reports

EXHIBIT 5 UAL, INC. FINANCIAL DATA, 1979–1987 (continued)

CONSOLIDATED BALANCE SHEETS
(IN THOUSANDS OF DOLLARS)

YEAR ENDED DECEMBER 31

	1979	1980	1981	1982	1983	1984	1985	1986	1987
Operating Revenues	$3,831,523	$5,041,335	$5,141,174	$5,319,709	$6,021,840	$6,967,599	$6,383,405 (C)	$9,196,233	$11,013,028 (D)
Operating Expenses:									
Aircraft fuel	804,380	1,342,529	1,346,205	1,289,577	1,266,700	1,368,099	1,143,568	1,099,441	
Depreciation	283,061	305,102	315,509	368,124	411,324	445,623	540,648	781,938	
SG&A	609,769	740,347	851,371	956,332	1,082,922	1,224,598	1,247,342	1,853,350	
Other	2,295,094	2,635,448	2,706,100	2,715,064	3,044,577	3,285,953	3,555,270	5,054,305	
Total Expenses	3,992,304	5,023,426	5,219,185	5,329,097	5,805,523	6,324,273	6,486,828	8,789,034	10,501,727
Operating Income (Loss)	(160,781)	17,909	(78,011)	(9,388)	216,317	643,326	(103,423)	407,199	511,301
Interest Expense	79,725	105,746	116,218	168,766	171,401	142,620	213,793	318,968	(365,722)
Other Income/(Expense)	54,792	92,045	46,699	187,916	202,729	2,382	222,133	2,069	
Income before Taxes	(185,714)	4,208	(147,530)	9,762	247,645	503,088	(95,083)	90,300	145,579
Income Taxes	(112,900)	(16,800)	(77,000)	(21,000)	105,600	220,700	(46,400)	78,700	80,956
Gain on sale of discontinued operations, net of income taxes						282,388			270,494
Net Income (Loss)	(72,814)	21,008	(70,530)	30,762	142,045		(48,683)	11,600	335,117

SELECTED SEGMENT INFORMATION
(IN THOUSANDS OF DOLLARS)

YEAR ENDED DECEMBER 31

	1979	1980	1981	1982	1983	1984	1985	1986	1987
Airline:									
Revenues	$3,295,278	$4,458,832	$4,541,668	$4,695,294	$5,372,774	$6,218,720	$5,291,609	$7,105,141	$8,292,790
Operating Profit	(235,390)	(65,558)	(148,819)	(66,748)	160,097	564,130	(242,656)	73,281	231,248
Hotels:									
Revenues	383,740	425,921	454,378	462,086	485,284	556,504	503,833	491,566	N/A
Operating Profit	63,790	72,591	74,634	58,631	52,239	69,398	63,414	54,980	N/A
Hertz (A):									
Revenues							496,506	1,599,526	N/A
Operating Profit							75,836	278,938	N/A
Business Services (B):									
Revenues	152,505	145,128	156,582	162,329	163,782	192,375	91,457		
Operating Profit	10,819	10,876	(3,826)	(1,271)	3,981	9,798	(17)		

(A) Four months in 1985.
(B) Six months in 1985.
(C) Allegis changed the manner in which they reported in 1987. The information shown is the only comparable information publicly available.
(D) Aircraft fuel expense was $1,243,579 in 1987.
Note: Hertz was sold December 30, 1987 for $1,300; Hilton International on October 14, 1987 for $1,070; Westin Hotels in January, 1988 for $1,300.

Source: Company Annual Reports

After 29 days the union agreed to end the strike. A modified two-tier wage system was instituted, and the issues regarding the trainees and recently recruited pilots were to be taken to an arbitrator. Although the airline was successful in obtaining the right to implement the new wage system, the strike cut deeply into operating revenues. It caused an estimated $92 million loss in the second quarter of 1985 and decreased revenues for the rest of the year as the company ran a series of promotions such as half-fare coupons, doubling frequent flyer mileage credits, and reducing advance purchase requirements to regain lost market share.

UNITED AIRLINES DIVERSIFICATION

HERTZ

The same day United was outlining these promotions to the press, UAL announced that it was acquiring Hertz from RCA for $587.5 million. Originally, RCA had asked $700 million but Ferris's team had negotiated a 16% reduction. Ferris claimed that Hertz was a natural addition to UAL's portfolio. He pointed out that 80% of all car rentals relate to an airline trip. Hertz was the undisputed leader in its industry with a 33% market share (although that was a decrease from its 42% share of 1975). The company, with 4,500 locations, rented a car every two minutes somewhere in the 122 countries in which it operated.

The business press raised questions regarding UAL's choice of industries in which to diversify. These concerns included:

1. The common cyclical swings of the two industries as the result of cars being rented in connection with air travel. In response to this criticism, UAL director Andrew Brimmer, a Washington-based economic consultant, said, "Certainly the Hertz business will add some cyclical component to earnings, but this will be offset by added cash flow. We think the return on investment will justify the purchase."[13]
2. The car rental industry's overcapacity. The industry was in its second price war in three years. A senior vice-president for marketing at Hertz stated, "We are signing contracts at rates lower than we have since 1978."[14]
3. The policy of corporate discounting. Corporate discounting was the opposite of the airlines' philosophy, which discouraged discounts to business travelers.
4. Hertz had $1.1 billion of existing long-term debt that would have to be assumed by UAL.
5. Hertz was a partner with other airlines in frequent flier programs and could not afford to lose their business.
6. In 1984, Hertz earned only $50 million in pretax earnings on revenues of $1.3 billion.

PACIFIC ROUTES

In April 1985, Ferris and UAL surprised the airline industry with the announcement that United was acquiring Pan American Airways' Pacific Division (excluding its Mainland-Hawaii routes) for $750 million plus the assumption of $136 million in lease obligations. United had long desired such Pacific routes, and adding them would boost its share to 16.5% of the Pacific traffic (Northwest Airlines led with 19%). It would have taken United years to establish a comparable presence since international airline routes require landing rights for each city served negotiated under near-treaty conditions. National airlines would almost certainly have opposed such landing rights, adding years to the process, if not killing it. In this transaction, United purchased preexisting landing rights in 60 cities in 10 countries, in a region with enormous growth potential.

Pan Am had been having financial difficulties for several years, last reporting a profit in 1980. In view of Pan Am's financial condition and need for cash, some analysts felt that Ferris paid too much for what United received. Some felt that the price (22 times the pretax earnings of the division) was too high. Even Ferris conceded that the majority of the planes purchased might not be suitable for trans-Pacific flights because of their limited seating capacity.

United expected to benefit from these routes since many travelers bound for Asia prefer the same airline for flights from the interior of the country to a departure destination on the West Coast. Expansion into the Pacific seemed natural for United with its strength in the western part of the U.S. One competitor agreed when he said, "With their very large domestic route system, the people at United will have an automatic control on the domestic scene. They could wind up with huge profits and a huge ability to control fares."[15]

In lengthy public hearings regarding the sale, United and Pan Am argued that the public would benefit because a relatively weak carrier was being replaced by a strong one. They saw it as a golden opportunity to break the Japanese stranglehold over trans-Pacific air routes. Ultimately the Department of Transportation approved the sale, and it became the largest route exchange in the history of U.S. aviation.

In addition to the Pacific routes, United received 18 planes, $50 million worth of spare parts, and all Pan Am interests in Pacific ground facilities and equipment (except those in Hawaii). The planes had an average age of about 7 years (compared to an average age of 12 years for United's existing fleet). United also agreed to hire 2,600 Pan Am employees.

In addition to this expansion, Ferris continued to search for other expansion opportunities. For example, UAL tried to acquire Frontier Airlines in 1986. The deal fell through when Frontier's pilots would not agree to concessions that Ferris felt were essential.

HILTON INTERNATIONAL

In 1986, United acquired Hilton International, the hotel chain that Transworld (formerly TWA) first acquired in 1968. Transworld was selling its subsidiary in an effort to prevent a hostile takeover.

Hilton International (a separate entity from the domestic Hilton chain) operated 90 luxury hotels in 41 countries with 1985 revenues of $700 million. Transworld had originally signed an agreement to sell the unit to the Dutch

Airline KLM for $975 million. When KLM backed out, UAL purchased the hotels for $980 million.

DIVERSIFICATION SYNERGIES

Ferris expressed enthusiasm for the acquisitions. (See Exhibit 6 for changes in revenues and assets as a result of diversification.) He stated that the operating synergies of the three divisions outweighed the cyclical risks. He recalled that after a family trip to Vail, he pulled his Hertz car into the return lot at Denver's Stapleton International Airport. There he paid for his car, deposited his luggage (including five sets of skis), and picked up his boarding passes for a United flight—all at an uncrowded Hertz counter. He argued that such travel experiences would be more pleasurable for the customer and create brand loyalty for UAL. Ferris expected to have such installations in other major cities by the end of 1986.

To the surprise of no one, UAL selected Hertz as its car rental firm in Hawaii for 1987, replacing Alamo. United flew 60,000 passengers to Hawaii in 1986 on package tours and expected to double that number in 1987. All of

EXHIBIT 6 UAL, INC.: RELATIVE SEGMENT INFORMATION BEFORE AND AFTER DIVERSIFICATION

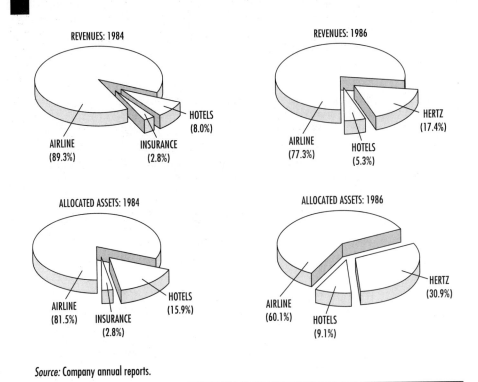

Source: Company annual reports.

these passengers would not rent cars, but Hertz still expected a significant increase in rentals. This action generated a competitive reaction, however. Budget Rent-a-Car and Hyatt hotels canceled their participation in United's mileage-plus program.

Among the reported synergistic results was the combined efforts of Hertz and United to reposition 600 cars from Denver to Phoenix in the fall of 1986. Hertz offered a midsize or larger car for one week, 1,500 free miles and two one-way airline coach tickets from Phoenix to Denver—all for $59. The airline tickets alone were regularly $89 each. Despite restricting the travel to a six-week period ending October 15, the offer sold out in three days. Without this combination, Hertz would have relied on its previous method of transferring the vehicles via truck or rail.

Critical to the attainment of these operating synergies would be the Apollo reservation system, now renamed Covia. Upgrading the system to include all travel-related needs would allow for better customer service. Ferris expected to invest up to $1 billion in the reservation system over the next five years. This upgrade would help ensure that an adequate number of airplane seats, rental cars, and hotel rooms would be available in the right place at the right time. Additionally, a database would be compiled to keep a record of frequent travelers' preferences concerning travel-related needs. This information would help Allegis implement the total travel strategy. Ferris felt that Allegis might eventually bypass travel agents and go directly to corporations with discounted full-service travel packages that no competitor could match.[16]

UNITED AIRLINES: PROBLEMS BEGIN

UAL needed cash to pay for these acquisitions. Ferris also wanted to make the company less attractive to raiders, since some analysts insisted the stock, which closed at $57\frac{5}{8}$ on August 1, 1985, was still undervalued. He began by pulling more than $500 million out of the company's overfunded pension plans. He sold GAB Business Services for a $28 million pretax gain and announced that UAL would sell some Westin hotels. Merrill Lynch was retained to form partnership trusts containing two or more hotels. The trusts would then be sold to investors, netting UAL between $300 million and $500 million per trust. Westin was to be the general partner, would continue to manage the hotels, and would share in any appreciation of property values under this arrangement. Two hotels were packaged and sold in 1986 with UAL realizing net proceeds of $225.7 million.

Overall, 1986 proved to be a difficult year for Ferris and United. The Pacific route acquisition proved to be far more costly than anyone had estimated. Veteran Pan-Am employees absorbed by United came in at the top of United's pay scales. A trans-Pacific captain, for example, received up to $170,000 per year. Maintenance, repair, and refitting of the aircraft acquired also proved to be more expensive than estimated. For the year, the Pacific Division's losses topped $100 million.

After losing $13 million in the fourth quarter in 1986, United laid off 1,016 white collar employees and placed a freeze on management salaries. UAL asserted that these actions would generate $100 million in savings. They also hoped the unionized employees would grant additional concessions.

The announcement of these cost-cutting measures came only hours after Texas Air disclosed new discounted fares. These fares were up to 80% off full coach prices and 20% to 40% less than the previously low-priced super saver fares. Industry executives, including those at United, were concerned that such discounts would spread to the business traveler, producing a free-for-all during the slack winter flying season. United, following its policy of matching price reductions, immediately matched the new fares where they competed directly with Texas Air's Eastern and Continental units.

THE BEGINNING OF THE END

Wall Street was unimpressed by Ferris's strategy. During a period when most airlines shared in a significant overall rise in stock prices, UAL's value rose less than 9% from $49\frac{3}{8}$ to $53\frac{3}{4}$, between the start of the diversification program (May 30, 1985) and the end of February 1987. In contrast, the value of AMR, the parent of American Airlines, increased nearly 24% during the same period. Further, a Salomon Brothers analyst was quoted as saying that UAL paid $1 billion above the fair market value for the businesses it had acquired.

On February 18, 1987, Ferris announced that UAL, Inc. would be renamed Allegis Corp. The new name, reported to cost UAL over $7.2 million to select and adopt, was intended to identify the company as more than just an airline. Ferris expected this new awareness to help drive the company's stock price up. Perhaps the plan was working. On April 1, Allegis offered 5.5 million shares to the public at $56.50. The offering sold almost immediately.

On April 6, United's pilots made headlines by offering to purchase United Airlines from Allegis for $4.5 billion. This was nearly 50% more than the market value of the entire company. Outlining the proposal in a letter to management, the pilots cited concerns over the direction of the airline and the potential takeover threats to Allegis. The head of the union joked, "It's our belief that they've been buying hotels so they can have more room for dissatisfied passengers."[17]

Allegis countered by claiming that the pilots' offer was an out-of-the-blue publicity stunt. The market took the pilots more seriously. The company's stock increased nearly 17% to $70 per share in the next week. There was no doubt that Ferris was concerned. He and seven others negotiated employment agreements. These "golden parachutes" assured the officers that they would receive their current compensation until April 1992 or retirement, whichever was earlier. For Ferris that meant nearly $600,000 per year. Thirty-seven others were made eligible for severance pay of one to three times their base salary.

In announcing the agreements, the company said that they would enable management "to devote the necessary attention to the business of the corporation by giving them an objective, distraction free environment."[18] Ferris also hired Morgan Stanley & Co. to help ward off any takeover attempts.

Charles Luce, the senior member of Allegis's board, was appalled by a front-page story in the April 17 *Wall Street Journal* that said Ferris's job was on the line. In a letter published in *WSJ* on April 20, Luce stated that the directors fully supported Ferris, his management team, and his long-range strategy.

Three weeks after the pilots' offer, Allegis's board rejected the bid as grossly inadequate. Its advisors, Morgan Stanley & Co. and First Boston Corporation, concurred. The company asserted that the union proposal was subject to a number of conditions and uncertainties and was not in the best interests of shareholders.

The day after the rejection was announced, a minor shareholder filed suit against Allegis. The suit asked that the company be required to bargain with the pilots and requested that the employment contracts be enjoined. That same day, the pilots said they were reviewing their options, one of which was to buy the entire company and then sell the airline to themselves.

On May 1, less than a week after rejecting the pilots' bid, Allegis held its annual meeting. Ferris said that the pilots' offer would wreck the company's long-term growth prospects. In an effort to appease the pilots, he announced that the company was considering ways to offer its employees an ownership stake. After the meeting, Ferris answered questions from the stockholders for nearly four hours. Several stockholders wanted to know if the company would be worth more if it were broken apart. There were also complaints about the employment contracts.

Less than two weeks later, Allegis made headlines again. The company signed a $1.5 billion order for 11 Boeing 747-400 jumbo jets, the largest order ever for such aircraft. Delivery was scheduled to begin in 1995; the planes would be used on the Pacific routes. While the size of the order was newsworthy, the contract details generated surprise among airline analysts. As part of the agreement, Boeing would be issued $700 million in notes, convertible to 16% of Allegis stock. The stock, when issued, would contain special provisions requiring Boeing's approval of any takeover attempt. Boeing also agreed not to pursue a takeover bid of Allegis, the company that had once been Boeing's parent.

A Boeing spokesman indicated that the agreement was simply the result of fierce competition to sell aircraft. He said, "We had to put together a deal that would win the business."[19] A United executive had a somewhat different view. The *Wall Street Journal* quoted him as saying, "It's quite a coup for Ferris. He's improved the equity of the company and placed it in a better defensive posture with regard to takeovers."[20]

On May 27, the friendly skies hit new turbulence. Coniston Partners, an investment firm that had become known on Wall Street as an audacious and successful raider, announced it had acquired 13% of Allegis's stock and planned to seek control of Allegis's board. *Business Week,* in a December 1986 article, had portrayed Coniston as controlling only about $300 million, "hardly enough to do more than give a company a good scare." Success to Coniston, however, lay in convincing other shareholders that what they wanted to do made sense.

Coniston filed a plan with the SEC, outlining their belief that Allegis's three businesses would be stronger and significantly more valuable as independent companies. They also filed a lawsuit attacking the Boeing agreement, contending that the arrangement was for the purpose of entrenching management and that it gave Boeing control of Allegis.

Allegis considered others with more resources as bigger threats. A spokesman said, "If Coniston bought 13 percent, we're assuming that's probably the maximum they could pull together at this time."[21] The company appeared to "believe that the Coniston Partners simply want to be bought out at a premium to market price, a practice known as greenmail. Coniston denied it, saying they would not accept greenmail if it were offered."[22]

Ferris recognized, though, that his long-term strategy was in trouble. He asked Boeing to vote against Coniston, but Boeing was not yet ready to convert its notes to voting stock. Boeing may have faced a conflict of interest. How would other airlines, customers of Boeing, respond if Boeing took an equity position in one of their major competitors?

The same day, May 27, the company announced plans to pay a special dividend of $60 cash per share. However, Allegis did not have the $3 billion required for such a dividend. The company would have to borrow it, raising its long-term debt to more than $5 billion. If it completed such a deal, the company would be one of the most debt-ridden companies in the airline industry. There was also the question of whether the plan would violate the provisions of the Boeing agreement. In any case, it would require shareholder approval.

The stock price continued to climb, reaching $87 per share on May 28, a 22% jump in just one week. Ferris thought that Coniston would take their profits and run. Coniston, however, said Allegis was worth still more and that Coniston would continue to seek control of the company.

During this period, United was in the midst of negotiations with the International Association of Machinists. The machinists, who had spurned attempts by the pilots to involve them in the purchase of the company, were alarmed by the company's payout plan. They raised the possibility of a strike if Allegis went ahead with the recapitalization. At the height of the publicity and speculation surrounding Allegis, the company retained a proxy solicitor to informally poll the company's shareholders. Reportedly, institutional investors owned just under 75% of Allegis's outstanding stock, and a majority expressed support for the Coniston plan. They reported the company was likely to lose a shareholder vote.

On June 4, the pilots sweetened their bid to buy the company, offering $70 per share plus stock in the airline. Their new strategy was similar to Coniston's plan—break up the company to generate cash for the proposed payout. They considered their offer to be competing with that of the company's $60 dividend and sought to have it submitted to the shareholders. Anticipating questions regarding the financing of such a payout, they obtained an opinion from the Salomon Brothers investment firm indicating that the proposed offer could be financed. The pilots also announced that they had a cash offer of $1 billion for the Hilton International hotels.

Allegis was having trouble raising the $3 billion needed for its recapitalization plan. Bankers were demanding an impossible guarantee that the company could win wage reductions from its increasingly antagonistic unions. Without such reductions, the banks contended that the company's cash flow would not justify the debt.

Ferris scheduled a trip to New York for June 10 and to Boston the following day to lobby institutional shareholders for support. The trips were canceled when Luce called a special board meeting for June 9.

After meeting with the board for seven hours, Ferris resigned. He later confided to an associate, "I thought Luce was in my corner but instead, he stabbed me in the back."[23] Reflecting on the turbulent events of the past two months, Richard Ferris wondered what he should have done differently.

ENDNOTES

1. *Fortune,* November 20, 1978.
2. *Forbes,* August 15, 1977.
3. *Fortune,* November 20, 1978.
4. *Wall Street Journal,* March 2, 1979.
5. *Business Week,* August 18, 1980.
6. *Standard & Poor's Industry Surveys,* October 1987.
7. UAL Annual Report, 1986.
8. *Air Transport World,* July 1977.
9. *Fortune,* May 11, 1987.
10. *Wall Street Journal,* March 2, 1979.
11. Ibid.
12. *Business Week,* June 10, 1985.
13. *Fortune,* September 30, 1985.
14. *Business Week,* May 6, 1985.
15. Ibid.
16. *Fortune,* September 30, 1985.
17. *Wall Street Journal,* April 8, 1987.
18. *Wall Street Journal,* April 21, 1987.
19. *Wall Street Journal,* May 13, 1987.
20. Ibid.
21. *Wall Street Journal,* May 27, 1987.
22. Ibid.
23. *Wall Street Journal,* June 11, 1987.

CASE 7

NCNB, INC.
FRANK C. BARNES

In 1960, American Commercial Bank, which was later to become NCNB, was a medium-sized state bank with assets of $480 million in a southern state, hardly known to the major money-center banks of New York or Chicago. American Commercial had its hands full competing with its two state rivals, rock-solid Wachovia Bank & Trust and third-place First Union National Bank. Although most states restricted banks to one county, North Carolina had allowed statewide banking since 1804. This fact had important implications in size and operating style for the banks.

In 1960, Hugh McColl was a C-student college kid from Bennettsville, South Carolina, who was just free from his hitch in the military. He was ready with his new bride to move into the big city, Charlotte, North Carolina, to see if he could hold onto a job with American Commercial.

By 1990, American Commercial was NCNB and the seventh-largest bank in the nation, with $64 billion in assets. Wachovia was in third place in the state with $24 billion, behind First Union, with $39 billion. NCNB had a worldwide reputation for initiative, ambition, and aggressiveness stemming from such achievements as beating every other bank in the nation into the lucrative Florida market by two years and outwitting the largest U.S. bank, Citicorp of New York, in acquiring failing First RepublicBank of Texas in what some called "the deal of the century." The rapid growth of all three North Carolina banks increased the chances that they would be among the survivors from the revolution of banking in the deregulated environment.

By 1990, Hugh McColl was at the top of NCNB and the most famous of a new breed of bankers. His 1989 compensation was $1.5 million, and his stock was worth $8 million. His reputation for aggressiveness and frankness of

---

Source: **This case was prepared by Frank C. Barnes, professor of operations management at the University of North Carolina at Charlotte. It was presented to the North American Case Research Association. All rights are reserved to the author. © 1990, Frank C. Barnes.**

speech made him a prime target for newspaper controversy and was reported to make him feared by the managers in acquisition targets. The military jargon he used to describe strategic moves was emphasized by the press and upset the traditional "country club" banker. Numerous writers played up the idea of merger targets taking the attitude of "anyone but NCNB." They reported that in 1985 First Atlanta took a $30 per share offer from Wachovia instead of $33 from NCNB in rejection of McColl. But people at NCNB disagreed and were solidly behind McColl.

NCNB reportedly had a corporate culture that emphasized competitiveness and aggressiveness. It was among the most active in recruiting talent on college campuses, was an innovator in policies such as employee child care, and valued entrepreneurial behavior. Acquisitions were firmly integrated into the NCNB culture.

By 1990 the first great wave of regional bank mergers across state lines was subsiding. The survivors, like NCNB, were working to strengthen their financial position and integrate all the new banks and people into their organizations. It wasn't exactly clear who had won, though states like Florida and South Carolina, whose banks had been acquired by others, might have lost. In a few years, a larger wave of mergers was expected as the U.S. went to full interstate banking and the "super regional" NCNBs and First Unions would have to go head to head with the money-center Citicorps. Interstate mergers might eliminate 80% of existing banks; many wondered who would survive. Exhibit 1 contains information about the ten largest southern banks and their national competitors.

A January 1989 article in *Business—North Carolina* suggested NCNB had the answer: "You make things happen. You don't sit and wait. You lead by example. You go out, you compete, and you do your damnedest to win. This is more than Hugh McColl's approach to banking; it is his approach to life. This is why NCNB is one of the most aggressive, feared competitors in banking today. This is why NCNB succeeds when others don't even try."

Some analysts predicted the entire 1990s would be bearish for banking. However, stock prices were off in September 1990, with NCNB down 43%, First Union down 23%, and Wachovia down 14%. The savings and loan crisis, the slowing economy with its continuing budget deficit, and the increased competition from banks and nonbank financial companies all created a challenging situation. McColl was concerned about the path NCNB must take to succeed.

BACKGROUND

The predecessor to NCNB, Commercial National Bank, was formed in 1874 in Charlotte. American Trust Company opened in Charlotte in 1901. In 1957, American Trust, which had become the largest unit bank in the Carolinas and primarily a wholesale (commercial) bank, merged with Commercial National,

EXHIBIT 1 VIEWS OF BANKING LEADERS

THE SOUTH'S TOP 10—'NEW' BANKS AND OLD, 1985

RANK	BANK	ASSETS*	MERGERS	ASSETS*	TOTAL
1.	NCNB Corp. Charlotte, N.C.	16,900	Bankers Trust (S.C.) Pan American (Fla.) Southern National Bankshares (Ga.)	2,081 1,658 93	20,732
2.	Sun Trust Banks Inc. Atlanta, Ga.	16,293	(SunBanks Inc. (Fla.) and Trust Co. of Ga.)		16,293
3.	First Wachovia Corp. Winston-Salem, N.C.		Wachovia Corp. (N.C.) First Atlanta Corp. (Ga.)	8,932 7,106	16,038
4.	First Union Corp. Charlotte, N.C.	8,250	Northwestern Financial Corp. (N.C.) Atlantic Bancorp (Fla.)	2,983 3,777	15,010
5.	Barnett Banks of Florida Inc. Jacksonville, Fla.	13,190			13,190
6.	Citizens & Southern Georgia Corp. Atlanta, Ga.	8,480	Landmark Banking Corp. (Fla.)	3,844	12,324
7.	Southeast Banking Corp. Miami, Fla.	10,204			10,204
8.	Sovran Financial Corp. Norfolk, Va.	8,700	DC National Bancorp (D.C.) Virginia Southern Bank (Va.)	400 50	9,100
9.	United Virginia Bankshares Richmond, Va.	6,600	NS&T Bank of Washington, D.C.	900	7,500
10.	Florida National Banks Jacksonville, Fla.	5,367			5,367

*Figures in millions as of 6/30/85.
**Merger completed

Source: *Winston-Salem Journal*, August 26, 1985. From *Jenks Southeastern Business Letter* and other sources.

MARKET CAPITALIZATION

RANK	BANK	MKTCAP*
1.	Sun Trust	1.74
2.	First Wachovia	1.71
3.	First Union	1.60
4.	NCNB	1.40
5.	Barnett Banks	1.20
6.	Citizens and Southern	1.10
7.	Sovran	.74
8.	Southeast	.52
9.	United Virginia	.51
10.	Florida National	.46

*in billions

(*continued*)

EXHIBIT 1 VIEWS OF BANKING LEADERS (continued)

MARKET CAPITALIZATION LEADERS, 1985

BANK	ASSETS* IN BILLIONS	MARKET CAPITAL** IN BILLIONS	STOCK PRICE/ BOOK VALUE
Citicorp	$159.9	$5.7	89%
J.P. Morgan	$64.3	$4.4	115%
First Interstate	$46.8	$2.3	95%
BankAmerica	$120.6	$2.2	55%
Chase Manhattan	$86.4	$2.2	59%
Banker's Trust	$48.4	$2.1	100%
Chemical	$57.3	$2.0	80%
Security Pacific	$47.9	$1.9	93%
First Wachovia	$16.0	$1.8	170%
Sun Trust	$16.3	$1.7	165%
First Union	$18.8	$1.6	164%
Manufacturers	$75.9	$1.5	55%
NCNB	$19.1	$1.5	144%
FNC Financial	$16.7	$1.5	132%
Mellon	$30.5	$1.3	82%
Banc One	$9.6	$1.3	174%
Barnett	$12.8	$1.3	168%
Sovran	$11.9	$1.2	129%
First Bank System	$24.4	$1.2	100%
Wells Fargo	$29.2	$1.2	93%
First Chicago	$39.9	$1.1	69%
C&S Georgia	$13.8	$1.1	120%

Note: Figures assume all announced mergers were completed.
*As of June 30, 1985.
**As of October 16, 1985

Source: Atlanta Journal & Constitution, October 23, 1985. From Keefe, Bruyette and Woods Inc.

which had become primarily a retail bank. American Commercial added First National of Raleigh in 1959.

In 1933, Security National Bank had been formed in Greensboro, later adding offices in six cities from Burlington to Wilmington. Security merged with a Durham bank in 1959. Then on July 1, 1960, American Commercial merged with Security to form North Carolina National Bank, NCNB. This merger created the second-largest bank in the state, with assets of $480 million and 1,300 employees in 40 offices in 20 North Carolina cities.

During the 1960s, NCNB, headquartered in Charlotte, acquired or opened 51 more offices and doubled deposits as it completed a statewide expansion strategy. The holding company, NCNB Corp., was formed in 1969. In the 1970s it added 82 more offices, increased assets to $6 billion, and achieved a 20% market share. First Union National Bank (FUNB) and Wachovia Bank had similar market shares.

It was generally agreed that this merger activity by NCNB (and FUNB) was in response to the competitive dominance of Wachovia. In the 1930s, under the presidency of Robert Hanes of the hosiery family, Wachovia had become the largest bank in the state, with a reputation for quality. Wachovia's managers were slow to jump on fads and instead sought growth through conservative management, soundness, and profitability. They were considered the "corporate bankers" in the state. Tom Storrs, chairman of NCNB through the 1970s, said this history explained the competitiveness of the North Carolina banks.

GOVERNMENT REGULATION AND DEREGULATION: 1982

Banking had always been closely regulated by government. For many years the government set the interest rates that all banks could pay or charge customers. At the same time the government also controlled the price and quantity of money. In this way banks and savings and loans were shielded from most competition and were pretty much guaranteed a profit. The activities that banks could undertake were narrowly defined, but the banks were protected from nonbank competitors.

Historically, bank regulations were concerned with the impact of bank failures on the economy. In recent years, in addition to the safety issue, regulation has been concerned with the size and distribution of banks (structure issues) and consumer protection issues. Congress periodically enacted new legislation. The process was a political one of treating differences in viewpoints between rich and poor states, large and small banks, North versus South, East versus Midwest and West, and so on. Since 1970, banking had undergone dramatic change. Information technology was speeding and simplifying financial activities and eroding the separation between commercial banks and investment banks. The entire system was becoming international. The financial system was subject to greater volatility and the risk it involved.

Interest rates had been the subject of much regulation. The 1933 Banking Act prohibited banks paying interest on demand deposits and placed ceilings on rates on other accounts. This part of the law, Regulation Q, did not apply to S&Ls, which gave them a small edge in this area until 1984. In the 1970s, inflation caused the market rate for money to increase beyond bank ceiling rates. Other nonbank financial institutions, such as brokerage houses, that were not subject to federal regulations raised rates and took deposits from banks. Congressional acts of 1980 and 1982 responded to this situation by phasing out interest rate ceilings, lessening the regulatory difference between banks and nonbanks, and reducing regulatory burdens.

The activities permitted to banks had also changed. In 1960, only banks provided checking accounts and provided installment and business loans. Banks and S&Ls provided savings accounts. Banks and retailers had credit cards. Insurance companies provided insurance, and stockbrokers bought and sold stocks. In September 1990, J. P. Morgan became the first bank since the

Depression to receive government permission to underwrite corporate stock. In 1990 all of these activities could be provided by some nonbank institutions. Banks, or bank holding companies, were providing all of these services except insurance, which was expected in the near future.

The bank holding companies increased significantly after the Bank Holding Company Act of 1956. This act, designed to restrict holding companies, actually encouraged their growth. One-bank holding companies, as opposed to multibank ones, were excluded from the act, which gave them the right to engage in most nonbanking activities. This loophole was closed by a 1975 act.

Holding companies had three potential advantages: avoiding restrictive state laws on interstate banking, diversifying into nonbank activities, and lowering tax burdens. An acquisition by a holding company could leave the acquired bank with a "president" instead of a "branch manager." It was possible for a holding company to delete some of the usual bank activities from a bank and create a bank that was not subject to the Bank Holding Company acts. This "nonbank bank" could engage in a much wider range of activities, such as providing insurance, providing data processing services, underwriting, consulting, gold and silver futures trading, and securities brokerage. After the rapid growth in bank holding companies, a 1987 act put a moritorium on the creation of new holding companies and slowed their growth.

In 1982 Congress enacted major deregulation that left banks substantially free to pay what they wanted on interest-bearing accounts and charge what they wished for their services. A profit was no longer guaranteed; instead, it had to be achieved, as in any business, by good management. In this environment, fees charged for services were expected to be a major source of income. There would be a movement toward charging for traditionally free services, such as check writing, in addition to the creation of new services, such as credit and financial services. In succeeding years, laws would also less sharply distinguish between the banks and nonbank financial institutions. Banks would move into discount brokerage while stockbrokers would move into checking accounts. All of these changes were expected to have a major impact on the financial landscape of the U.S.

HUGH McCOLL AND NCNB

Hugh McColl was closely associated with the development and style of NCNB. His tenure covered the last 30 years of strategic development. McColl came from a competitive family. He told the story of proudly coming home from school one day to tell his grandmother about coming in second in something. She responded, "You'll do better next time." He was expected to win. His father, Hugh McColl, Sr., told *Business—North Carolina,* "I think he got his fighting spirit from his mother; I give her credit for a lot of Hugh's ability and success." Hugh McColl spoke of her as a talented and "very, very competitive" woman born in the wrong era. All of the men in the family had been small town bankers: his grandfather, his father, and his two brothers.

In high school in Bennettsville, S.C., he was active in everything from the Latin Club and Radio Club to almost every sport (though only five feet, seven inches) and was voted Best All-Round. In the graduation yearbook, he is nicknamed "Happy" and recognized with "He who's talented in leadership/Holds the world's dreams in his grip."

In 1953 he went off to UNC–Chapel Hill, like most of the family had, without much thought. He was cut from the basketball and baseball teams and lost his bid for freshman class president. He worked hard at intramural sports since he was "more interested in athletics than anything else." He wasn't very interested in his business major or in the required ROTC, using "minimum maintenance" to make mostly Cs. "It just didn't matter"; he figured after graduation he would go home and run the family business.

He went into the military because it was practically required, but chose the Marines for his two years. He thoroughly enjoyed the "maturing" experience and had his eyes opened by living with people from all over the country. It was an important lesson for the young southerner from a well-off family. "It was a great graduate school, a great management training program, to be an officer and to be responsible for other people." Leadership, he learned, required that he be out with his people all the time.

When he returned home in 1959 from the Marines to join the family business, his father surprised him by telling him to look elsewhere. McColl says, "He did me the greatest favor in the world, sending me off." His father sent him to the bank with which he did his business, American Commercial Bank in Charlotte. He was interviewed by president Addison Reese, but not hired. Hugh, Sr. called another contact in the bank, and Hugh had the job. He didn't report until September because he and a friend were headed to Europe for the summer. As the trip started, he met a girl from South Carolina he would end up marrying that fall. In Belgium, he bought her a whole cart of flowers.

His first job at American Commercial was scouring South Carolina for corporate accounts. He left Charlotte in his VW by 6:00 a.m. and returned at night to the office to look for new leads. Long hours away from home was the pattern for many years. "It cost me a lot of my family time; my wife had to be both father and mother." But success wasn't guaranteed. In 1983 he remembered for the *Charlotte Observer*, "What drove me was feeling inadequate. I remember telling Jane not to get too comfortable in Charlotte, that I might not make it here."

When Addison Reese became chairman of CNB in 1957, it was still a small wholesale and commercial bank. His aim was to make the bank large enough to compete with Wachovia. Reese hired Tom Storrs in 1960 as an executive vice-president to lead the expansion across North Carolina with acquisitions and mergers. Storrs's 25-year career had been split between the Federal Reserve Board in Richmond and wartime navy duty as an executive officer on a destroyer. He was a professional economist with a master's and a doctorate in economics from Harvard. In 1960, Storrs was working with a merger partner in Greensboro and having trouble with bickering between Greensboro and Charlotte. He called McColl with a task and got immediate cooperation: "He stood out, he responded." Storrs became his mentor as McColl took on more responsibilities.

In 1968, NCNB was the third bank in the country to form a one-bank holding company. It was the first to use commercial paper to finance the activities of its nonbank subsidiaries and the first to go to the long-term debenture market to raise money for the holding company, setting a pattern that others followed. In 1969 Storrs became president.

In 1973 Storrs succeeded Reese as chairman and named McColl and two other rising stars, Luther Hodges, Jr. and Bill Dougherty, to run the bank. Each expected to succeed Storrs. Hodges, son of a former governor, was seen as an "outside" P.R. man, while Dougherty, a CPA, was more of a back-office expert. During the 1974–75 recession, a company with a $28 million loan got into trouble and McColl helped them reorganize without bankruptcy. McColl said, "Losing that $28 million would have taken us out. We only made $16 million the year before." This was one example of McColl's performance, which Storrs said the executive committee viewed as the "best track record of the three."

Nineteen seventy-nine was a pivotal year. NCNB's 1979 annual report proposed "An Orderly Approach to Interstate Banking" in recognition of the fact that continued rapid growth could be achieved only by crossing state lines, though interstate branching was still not permitted. NCNB began to build equity for out-of-state expansion and looked for opportunities. In December 1980, as chairman Storrs completed a stock sale in anticipation of eventual opportunities to go into interstate banking, he stated, "Two things are going to be very important to financial institutions in the 1980s as regulations change and opportunities for expansion arise: the quality of their people and the adequacy of their capital. NCNB has done a good job of attracting and developing competent people. And we are committed to continuing that effort. With the stock sale ... we have strengthened the capital base that will also be required for future asset expansion."

McColl was president of NCNB bank, the retail operation, and active in carrying out Storrs's statewide acquisitions. In 1981, McColl was named vice-chairman, which indicated he would be the one to succeed Storrs. In 1981, Hodges left the chairmanship of the bank to run, unsuccessfully, for governor. Dougherty left his presidency of the holding company in 1982. On September 1, 1983, McColl became chairman and CEO of the corporation.

Bill Weiant, who followed NCNB for First Boston, noted that McColl had spent his entire career with the bank in the headquarters city and predicted he would be a "hands-on" chief executive: "He is the kind of guy who gets involved in every detail." McColl believed in being in touch with all parts of the organization. He noted that too many executives forgot that information is filtered as it comes up through the organization. He said, "I try to remove some of the filters. I'm an in-the-field manager. There's never a day I'm not out in someone's area. I go and look; it keeps people honest. If I've seen it myself no one's going to say it isn't so."

People in the bank describe him as demanding and impatient to get on with decisions. He wanted consensus and was impatient with people who didn't contribute. "He's quick to have an opinion, and he's very perturbed if others involved don't participate," one executive told *Business—North Carolina*. Another added, "He always says what he has to say. He's open, honest, and forthright. You always know where he stands. It's gotten him into trouble outside the bank, but that's how it is." For example, in discussing expansion with reporters, he said he didn't need to be in "every pig path" in Georgia. When this was reported a big flap developed.

People inside and outside the bank credited him with creating the entrepreneurial "can-do" culture. His style had no critics inside the bank. He was described as being very accessible and valuing his associations with employees at all levels. He jogged and entered "fun runs" with others from the bank, played racquetball with young employees at lunch, and visited sick employees in the hospital. He was energetic and inquisitive. Employees commented that it was hard to mention a book he hadn't read. If a trip to a foreign country was ahead, he would be studying the maps and reading several books about it. His bank had been a leader in providing for its employees. For example, in 1990 *Good Housekeeping* magazine praised NCNB as among the best companies for working mothers. Its policies addressing family needs included parental leave, daycare at or near work, flex-time, and counseling support.

McColl had his style. He told *Business—North Carolina* about being at the beach in the summer of 1988 and going by a newly opened office. He didn't see a sign on the building, and the manager said it was being made. It irritated McColl so much that he went to a hardware store and got some letters, board, and paint. Then he returned, where he made and installed a sign. "It's a graphic lesson. You don't wait until things happen. It's part of what leading by example is all about. It would never occur to me to have an office without a sign. I want my managers to feel they can do what it takes to get the job done and not be impeded by bureaucracy and I'll back them up. You are responsible. Be responsible."

EXPANSION INTO FLORIDA: 1981–84

Interstate banking would not be allowed until 1985, but NCNB was able to expand into Florida in 1981. In 1972, Florida had enacted statutes to prevent acquisition of their banks by out-of-state banks. Just prior to this, NCNB had bought small Orlando Trust Company. In July 1981, NCNB took the position it was a Florida bank because of the Orlando company and offered to buy First National Bank of Lake City. Banks in Florida and across the country opposed NCNB getting this early start at interstate branching. But by December the Federal Reserve Board had ruled in NCNB's favor, and NCNB became the first bank to expand into the lucrative Florida market.

NCNB moved quickly in 1982 to buy three banks with 67 branches and over $2 billion in assets. In 1984 it added Ellis Banking Corporation with 75 offices and $1.8 billion in assets and in 1985 a $2 billion Miami bank with 51 offices. By 1987 NCNB National Bank of Florida was the fourth largest in the state with $9.9 billion and over 200 offices.

In June 1982 McColl had stated, "Our purpose is to build a banking company of a size that can compete more effectively with the money-center banks in providing a range of services to customers here in the southeast, across the nation and in the world markets." Chairman Storrs warned of the dangers of overemphasizing short-run earnings and ignoring long-term needs: "You would leave your successor with the problem of doing the building that you should have been doing.... What we are doing is what Addison Reese did twenty years ago—always building on the foundation for the next decade." McColl forecasted, "By 1984, we will have this ship running hot and heavy. Between now and then we will not divert ourselves with casual mergers. We will pay back our debt, and get in good shape to start over when they drop the barriers on interstate banking." Dick Stillinger, a New York banking specialist, told the *Charlotte Observer*, "I think they will have a tough row to hoe for the next couple of years. I am skeptical if NCNB can make it pay off fast enough to offset the dilution of earnings."

But some people saw a problem with McColl. A former NCNB executive reported to *Business—North Carolina* "a deal in which a Florida banker was ready to sell, only to pull out after listening to McColl over dinner dictate what changes NCNB would make after the acquisition." In acquisitions, the NCNB name would go on the bank, many services would be centralized, and the policies would be those set by Charlotte. After NCNB's Florida expansion, it was reported that 41 of 45 top executives left Gulfstream bank after the 1982 acquisition and that over 150 of Exchange Bancorporation's 300 managers left after its 1983 takeover. Gulfstream's ex-CEO was quoted as saying that "NCNB's corporate culture was "a snotty-nosed kid aching for a fight." Exchange's ex-CEO complained of NCNB's military style. "Many of our people didn't stay because they didn't like the NCNB culture. There was one way to do things—the NCNB way."

In 1983, as he became CEO, McColl told the *Charlotte Observer* that he was working at toning down his image, softening his statements, trying to adopt a posture more appropriate for a CEO. "I have been working on that," McColl said. "But part of our images get to be caricatures. I think people think I'm aggressive. I don't think of myself that way." Yet he was energetic and competitive and admitted to being "downright hostile in competition." He said, "I would probably hurt fewer people's feelings. I might modify my behavior by being less aggressive. But if I tried to be somebody else, I wouldn't do very well at that."

As 1984 began, NCNB showed plans to target services for "middle market" firms, $5 million to $250 million, under the direction of 37-year-old Ken Lewis. It already did business with 70% of North Carolina companies with $50 million and had the largest market share of business with southeastern firms that size. Lewis said, "The banks that survive are the ones that pick those market segments they can best compete in."

In the summer of 1984, NCNB stated that it planned to concentrate on increasing shareholder wealth and planned no major acquisitions through 1985. Year-end earnings were projected at $3.85 per share, representing about a 4% dilution due to acquisitions. Loan officers had been opened in Washington and Memphis. NCNB told *American Banker:* "We would think we have to have a presence in Atlanta, but don't think it's necessary to have a big branch system in Georgia."

GOVERNMENT REGULATION AND INTERSTATE BANKING

Interstate banking had long been banned by the federal government. However, many experts saw the need for nationwide banks like those common outside the U.S., and some bankers wanted the growth opportunity. By 1980, it was clear that interstate banking was coming. In early 1981, the Southern Growth Policies Board, an important regional study group, recommended that southeastern states let other southeastern banks cross their borders. It was expected that Congress would approve full interstate banking by the end of the decade. This regional expansion was expected to strengthen the regional banks before full competition came. In 1982, Massachusetts and Connecticut approved regional interstate banking. When the Supreme Court upheld the legality of regional compacts in 1985, Justice Rehnquist wrote, "One predictable effect of the regionally restrictive statutes will apparently be to allow the growth of regional multistate bank holding companies which can compete with the established banking giants of New York, California, Illinois and Texas." In a 1984 meeting Hugh McColl stated: "Our industry is simply not ready for all-out national interstate banking."

Other advantages were put forth for mergers. In 1982, Tom Storrs who was the chairman of NCNB, cited the "obvious" advantages of creating bigger banks. But the *Charlotte Observer* reported that a senior economist for the Federal Reserve Board had yet to discover any advantages. He pointed out that studies had indicated supposed economies of scale were achieved at the $100 to $200 million size and not beyond. Surprisingly, the data showed smaller banks tended to be more profitable; there was an inverse correlation between size and profitability. Some felt the mergers would concentrate political power and stifle competition. A community banker asked, "Why would bigger be better? Banking is a people business." But others spoke of the access to larger amounts of capital for big projects, participation in the total economy, and the ability to have a role in the direction of change in the banking industry.

REGIONAL BANKING BEGINS

In February 1984, Georgia was about to become the first southeastern state to approve a regional reciprocal interstate banking law. Under these laws, southeastern banks could expand into another southeastern state if a reciprocal expansion were allowed. The entry of other states' banks, primarily major money-center banks like the nation's largest, $150 billion Citicorp of New York, was carefully excluded. Some large northern banks were expected to oppose the move in federal courts if provision were not made for eventual full interstate banking. Two of Atlanta's major banks, Citizens and Southern (C & S) and First Atlanta, expressed support for the legislation and took steps to prepare for it. The *Wall Street Journal* reported that NCNB was opposing the legislation, fearing that since North Carolina wasn't expected to consider a reciprocal law until 1985, NCNB would not have a chance at the best merger opportunities in Georgia. NCNB was considering using its Florida operation, where there would soon be a reciprocal agreement, to get around this problem. This idea met resistance from Georgians. One executive told the *WSJ*, "The way for NCNB to come into Georgia is through its home state of North Carolina. If NCNB managed to get into Georgia through Florida, you can be sure they'll fight claw and nail to defeat regional banking in North Carolina."

In June 1985, the U.S. Supreme Court ruled that state legislatures could set up reciprocal regional agreements allowing banks from states in their region to merge across their borders but excluding out-of-region banks. In July, six southeastern states enacted such laws, and there was immediate action by the region's largest banks: NCNB, SunTrust, Wachovia, First Union, and Citizens and Southern. The race for mergers began immediately. By July, C&S of Atlanta had acquired a Florida bank and Wachovia had announced a merger with First Atlanta. The CFO of C&S of South Carolina told the *WSJ*, after agreeing to be acquired by C&S of Atlanta: "Being part of a large institution gives us the marketing and capital resources to continue being a broad based bank." NCNB and FUNB appeared not to have succeeded in moving into Atlanta. NCNB commented, "It would be advantageous to have a bank in Atlanta but we don't think a major presence is required. We do an awful lot of business there without a loan production office." But rumors were active that NCNB had made a bid for First Atlanta and lost out to Wachovia. While all the banks remained quiet, a New York analyst said, "NCNB was caught off guard a little (by Wachovia). They are disappointed that they are not going to have as big a presence in Atlanta."

Many reporters alluded to McColl's aggressive, military-jargoned style as a real turnoff. On October 3 the *Wall Street Journal* commented on NCNB as the most aggressive bank in the Southeast:

> But Hugh McColl, Jr., the combative ex-Marine who heads NCNB, often rubs more genteel bankers the wrong way. "He's a little bit more aggressive than the rest of us," says Mr. Poelker [John Poelker, president of Citizens and Southern Georgia Corp.]. The executive has tended to shake up management and insist on the NCNB name on acquired banks. As a result, some banks have taken an anyone-else-but-NCNB stance. First Atlanta rejected a $33.50 a share bid from NCNB in favor of a $30 bid from Wachovia Corp. "Some of NCNB's attitudes came back to haunt it," says a First Atlanta executive.

In response, NCNB's communication chief, Rusty Page, stated that the policies on using one name and on centralizing were those of the scholarly, soft-spoken Tom Storrs, not McColl. He believed the approach was sound and that the opportunity to become a part of the South's largest and strongest bank would continue to attract merger partners.

In mid-July *American Banker* reported: "Wachovia and First Atlanta bent over backwards to try to demonstrate that the transaction is a merger of equals in which there is no clear buyer or seller." It had been assumed that First Atlanta would dominate in any merger it pursued. However, the stock prices behaved to indicate Wachovia was the buyer, according to *American Banker*. Earlier, FUNB's Crutchfield and McColl had indicated they had no interest in any merger of equals. McColl commented, "I have to say it's like getting married and promising not to sleep with each other."

First Atlanta, with assets of $7 billion, and Wachovia, with assets of $8.7 billion, would be merged into a holding company called First Wachovia. There would be legal addresses in both states, and corporate functions would be located wherever they could be performed best. John Medlin, 51, of Wachovia would be president and CEO, and Tom Williams, 56, of First Atlanta would be chairman. Wachovia, with 60% of the shares, would name 60% of the directors, and First Atlanta would name 40%. Board meetings would alternate between the two states.

The *Atlanta Journal* reported on June 23, 1985, that First Atlanta had been eyeing Wachovia for some time. Williams had been educating the directors for months about criteria for merger partners; management compatibility being one of three. "The studies we went through showed us the best combination was unquestionably Wachovia." Earlier in the year, the two banks had discussed a combination, but decided to wait for the Court's decision on interstate mergers. On the day of the decision, Medlin called Williams; two days later they met in Greensboro. The *Charlotte Observer* noted that analysts such as John Maseir in New York gave the leadership high marks: "I think Tom Williams is one of the most intelligent, statesmanlike individuals I've come across. Medlin is one of the great heroes of the South. It's a combination of two very intelligent men."

In October 1985, the *Wall Street Journal* noted the South was the most active region in mergers because of fear and opportunity:

> The Southeast long has had the smallest banks in the poorest area of the nation. The region's largest bank, NCNB, was only the nation's 25th largest. However, the region now had some of the most attractive retail banking markets in the nation, Atlanta, Nashville, all of Florida. The big, money-center banks, already very active in lending activity in the region, wanted into the retail part of the market. The Executive Director of the Southern Growth Policies Board told the WSJ: "We don't want our capital resources dominated by money-center banks. The South has a long history of being exploited by corporate interests outside the region."

McColl believed the entry of money-center banks and nationwide banking was inevitable; some said as soon as the early 1990s. He felt his state's big three banks had ensured their long-term survival by these mergers. Twenty billion dollars in assets was often mentioned as the minimum size to assure continued competitiveness against the large banks and avoid being takeover targets.

The race to acquire the most attractive merger candidates had stretched NCNB's resources. McColl said, "There's a limit to what anyone can do in a reasonable time frame." Some dilution of earnings was expected and there were questions of adequate depth of management to run the operations.

In July 1985, NCNB announced plans to acquire Bankers Trust of South Carolina, the state's third largest with assets of $1.9 billion and 110 branches. NCNB paid 12 to 13 times earnings, which was expected to result in a 2% dilution in their earnings. Bankers Trust was a leader in the industry in profitability, unlike the Florida banks. It was the first in the state to install automatic teller machines and the third in the nation to provide personal cash management accounts. The South Carolina papers stressed the friendly nature of the merger. Bankers Trust chairman "Hootie" Johnson told *The State* (Columbia, S.C.) that he and McColl had been the closest of friends for many years. McColl praised Bankers Trust's leadership in marketing, especially the aggressive marketing of its credit cards. He added, "They are way ahead of a lot of people, including us" in financial services. The bank would operate as an independent subsidiary, NCNB Bankers Trust of South Carolina. He told the *Columbia Record*, "We will be separate banks with the basic same philosophy. All of us will actually be doing business the same way." Johnson, in addition to being chairman of the South Carolina bank, would become chairman of the executive committee of NCNB Corporation, a position held by Tom Storrs. His CFO would move to Charlotte to become an executive vice-president of NCNB Corporation. Two of their directors would become directors of NCNB Corporation.

In November 1985, Bankers Trust's shareholders overwhelmingly (96%) approved the merger. The merger would take place after January 1, 1986, when South Carolina's reciprocal banking laws went into effect. NCNB was awaiting approval by regulators of its plan to acquire Southern National Bankshares of Atlanta and Pan American Bank of Miami.

On September 8, 1985, the *Miami Herald,* in the article "North Carolina Banks Take the Lead," noted that while Florida had none of the region's top four banks, North Carolina had three. "Who's going to be around in five, ten years?" asked Hugh McColl. "It's quite clear the North Carolina banks, because they're stronger and better managed, with more capital." The *Herald* noted that NCNB tried to be a bank for everyone, while Wachovia was regarded as one of the nation's finest corporate banks. FUNB positioned itself between the two, with its strength in mortgage operations. FUNB's Ed Crutchfield explained the source of the three banks' strengths: "We're at each other's throats on a lot of street corners and that intense competition breeds strength." The rich Florida market bred a group of banks with less drive.

Observers tended to see a race between the three North Carolina banks to see who could be biggest (see Exhibit 1). By 1985, NCNB and FUNB had jumped ahead of Wachovia, the traditional leader. In December, FUNB claimed to be the second biggest behind NCNB. A Wachovia executive referred to "bragging rights," but all disclaimed growth for growth's sake. The pace of expansion in 1985 brought some concern as FUNB faced a 15% dilution in earnings, Wachovia 6%, and NCNB 4%. McColl told analysts, "Instead of concentrating on making money, many banks seem to be concentrating on acquisitions activity. This is certainly not the case at NCNB." He noted the high prices FUNB had paid late for acquisitions, 2.8 times book compared to NCNB's 1.8. The *Charlotte Observer* reported Crutchfield's quick response: "If he [McColl] isn't making acquisitions in 1985, I must be reading the wrong papers."

In October 1985, McColl gave up the job of president of NCNB Corporation to 45-year-old Francis "Buddy" Kemp, a Davidson College graduate with a Harvard MBA. McColl planned no major acquisition in the coming 18 months, but spoke of an interest in the northern Virginia market. Ken Lewis moved to Tampa as executive vice-president of the Florida banking group. As 1985 ended, NCNB reported earnings up 23% to $4.60 per share, in line with expectations. Assets reached $19.8 billion and would be $22 billion with the January 2 Bankers Trust acquisition. McColl was "very pleased ... with another year of improved profitability and well-planned growth."

THE TEXAS COUP

During planning meetings in December 1987, NCNB, then the eighteenth largest U.S. bank with $29 billion in assets, found itself short of opportunities for further acquisitions. Targets above $10 billion were considered too large and those below $1 billion were felt to be too small to have any impact. The chief strategic planner, Frank Gentry, considered the pool to be only 20 southeastern banks, some not in good markets. The idea of considering wider options, such as savings and loans or insolvent banks, was discussed.

First RepublicBank, a Texas bank that was the thirteenth largest in the nation with 171 offices, was on the FDIC's list of troubled banks because of the depressed Texas economy and other problems. In March 1988, the FDIC put $1 billion into First Republic as it sought a solution. A number of large banks became interested, including Citicorp, the nation's largest, and Wells Fargo. Gentry and John Mack, NCNB treasurer, had McColl's support in examining some role for NCNB, though McColl considered the odds slim. As the smallest bank bidding, they knew their plan must be innovative and secret to win. The other potential buyers planned to divide First Republic into a "good" bank and a "bad" bank and buy only the "good" one. This would leave the FDIC the expensive task of liquidating the "bad" one. NCNB offered to acquire the whole bank, 20% at once and the rest over five years. A key feature would be NCNB getting tax credits for First Republic's operating losses. This was considered impossible in the legal opinion of the trade journals and New York lawyers. A private Charlotte tax lawyer thought it was possible.

In April 1988, Gentry, accompanied by McColl, went on an early negotiating trip to the FDIC in Washington. Gentry noted, "The staff guy was shocked when Hugh walked in." A question that would require a decision arose and the staff man said only the FDIC chairman, Siedman, could decide the point. McColl replied, "Well, is he here?" Soon they met face to face to discuss their positions. An FDIC official told *Business—North Carolina* in January 1989: "McColl's presence made a difference. I don't think John Reed [Citicorp's chairman] or Wells Fargo's guy ever came by and said, 'We're interested,' at least at that stage of negotiation."

Examination of feasibility went forward in absolute secrecy. Earlier, Ross Perot, the Texas billionaire, had been approached by First Republic and briefly considered buying the bank. Lacking banking expertise, he thought of the man he would want for the task, Hugh McColl. He had met and befriended McColl earlier in the year at a dinner in Charlotte. Perot soon dropped the idea but later played an important role by guaranteeing NCNB's $210 million offer.

In June, the IRS ruled in favor of NCNB on the tax credit issue and then only the FDIC's decision remained. One of the three directors of the FDIC who would decide which offer to take was C. C. Hope, retired head of FUNB. He could help or hurt. Ultimately he would vouch for the depth of the NCNB's management.

As the time for a decision approached, NCNB prepared to move fast. They wanted to have an NCNB person at all 171 Texas offices on the first day to reassure everyone that they did not plan to make any major changes. After three false starts, on Thursday, July 28, McColl briefed 200 employees in Charlotte for two hours and sent them off to Texas to wait. On Friday, McColl waited nervously at his command center in the Dallas Sheraton. By noon he began to worry that NCNB had lost. At 12:00 the call came: "Your bank has been selected." By 1:30 all but seven NCNB people were at the branches, and all were in place by 3:30. Within a few days, Buddy Kemp, the NCNB executive chosen to head the Texas operation, had sent a yellow rose to each First Republic employee.

William Dougherty, who had left NCNB in 1982 when McColl won out in the competition to head NCNB, told *Business—North Carolina* in June 1989, "He has put his job on the line; if he pulls it off, he could be the banker of the century, not just the decade." A year later on May 15, 1989, *U.S. News and World Report* summed it up:

> NCNB's biggest banking coup came last year in acquiring insolvent First RepublicBank of Dallas with the aid of the Federal Deposit Insurance Corporation. Frank Gentry, NCNB's director of corporate planning, calls it the "banking deal of the century." For $210 million, NCNB bought 20 percent of the biggest bank in Texas and received options to buy the rest for another $840 million. For a relative pittance, NCNB has acquired effective control of the bank, all the assets unclouded by bad loans, nearly $2 billion in tax credits and generous incentives to help the FDIC recoup some of the $10 billion in loans that went sour. NCNB's giant foothold in Texas has given it tremendous advantages at just the right time. The state's economy is beginning to recover from its energy-based depression; branch banking, long prohibited in the

state, is now allowed, and NCNB Texas has been able to lend aggressively, becoming the biggest lender in the state at a time when other Texas banks have been financially hobbled. If NCNB buys the rest of First Republic, it will become the 10th-largest bank holding company in the country. Its Texas earnings will account for 60 percent of its profits by 1992, estimates Bear Stearns banking analyst Mark Alpert. The deal has already fattened NCNB's bottom line in 1989 and has driven its stock price up by 50 percent to nearly $40 a share.

INTO A NEW DECADE

In April 1989, NCNB made a try for C&S of Atlanta. McColl reportedly told C&S chairman Bennett Brown, "You have three hours to answer, or I will launch my missiles." A few hours later couriers delivered letters from NCNB across the Southeast to C&S's 15 directors. McColl insisted the offer was friendly but C&S resisted and refused to negotiate. NCNB's planner, Gentry, said, "We felt it was time to move ahead; if something is worth doing, sooner is better than later." A merger "would be bad for our shareholders, bad for our bank, bad for our community, and bad for the banking industry," C&S's chairman declared. C&S was expected to resist with Georgia's antitakeover provisions, including staggered director's terms, arguing that NCNB shouldn't be able to use its Texas tax breaks to finance the offer and the NCNB's stock was overpriced. However, NCNB's offer represented a 36% premium over C&S's current stock value, and the institutions that held 47% of C&S's stock might force C&S to accept the offer. NCNB's stock fell about 10% during the first two weeks of the battle. A C&S employee pointed out that the cultures of the organizations were entirely opposite. Within a few days NCNB gave up trying to overcome C&S's opposition. In McColl's view, "We offered them an exciting and unique opportunity. We are going to make a lot of money here in the Southeast. We're going to make a lot of money in Texas, and we're going to keep it for ourselves."

Business Week saw the pursuit of C&S as evidence of pressure for NCNB to keep up its earnings momentum with whatever acquisitions remained in the Southeast. *United States Banker* reported that NCNB had captured the imagination of investors worldwide with its aggressive interstate expansion, resulting in its stock's price having one of the highest multiples of any banks, 12 against 9.6 for the seven largest southeastern banks. NCNB noted that its employees and directors held 20% of its shares. During 1989 it increased its capitalization by $1.65 billion by adding some subordinated debt and selling 15 million new shares of common stock for $700 million. Approximately $1 billion was used to complete the purchase of the remaining 80% of the Texas banks, giving NCNB $3 billion in tax-loss carryovers.

In the 1989 Annual Report, McColl said, "The 1980s will be remembered as the decade the company built the foundation for a national financial service company" and pointed out with pride that during the decade shareholders had received a yearly compound growth rate of 21.1% in stock price and 13.5% in dividends. But the 1990s promised rigorous challenges in banking. NCNB's Rusty Page predicted the 14,000 U.S. banks would be reduced to 1,500. Kenneth Guenther of the Independent Bankers Association described 1990 to the *Charlotte Observer* as a lull before the storm, "a transitional year looking to cataclysmic banking legislation in 1991." Deregulation had removed the guarantees of profit that banking had enjoyed, and bank managers took increasing risks to hold onto profits, sometimes unwisely. Over 1,000 banks had failed in the last 10 years, costing the government over $20 billion. In that time the top 10 U.S. banks wrote off $40 billion in bad loans while earning less than $30 billion. The cost of the savings and loan debacle was raising questions about the government's role in insuring deposits. Regulators were reviewing banks' portfolios to see that reserves were truly in line with the amount of risk. Most banks were already moving to increase reserves to handle "nonperforming" assets (bad loans). Some analysts saw banking at the start of a multiyear decline. Exhibit 2 lists the assets and earnings of the top 25 U.S. banks.

As 1990 unfolded, NCNB continued to round out acquisitions. The prior October it had acquired a $3.5 billion savings and loan in Houston and Austin from the government's Resolution Trust Corporation. In June it won a bidding battle for nine insolvent banks in the San Antonia area, making NCNB/Texas the largest bank in Texas. There was talk that NCNB was preparing to make a private placement of $150 million in preferred stock in anticipation of buying Florida's largest S&L. It completed a realignment of senior management in which there would be an executive in charge of each line of business, such as real estate or trust, instead of a geographical region. Thus Ken Lewis, president of NCNB Texas in Dallas, was responsible for real estate lending wherever it occurred. McColl saw the opportunities for the 1990s to be in fee-income business and nontraditional lines such as investment banking and trust activity. Against the challenges, McColl saw opportunities. He told stockholders, "Now is not the time to rest. The thing we must guard against is complacency—believing we have arrived. Actually, we still have a long way to go." The Appendix contains information from NCNB's 1989 annual report.

EXHIBIT 2 TOP 25 BANK HOLDING COMPANIES BASED ON TOTAL ASSETS AS OF MARCH 31, 1990 (ASSETS IN BILLIONS AND NET INCOME IN MILLIONS)

ASSET RANK 3/31/90	ASSET RANK 12/31/89		TOTAL ASSETS 3/31/90	TOTAL ASSETS 12/31/89	PERCENT CHANGE	NET INCOME 1Q90	NET INCOME 1Q89	PERCENT CHANGE
1	1	Citicorp, New York	$233.1	$230.6	+1.1	$231.0	$529.0	−56.3
2	2	Chase Manhattan Corp., New York	106.5	107.4	−0.8	44.0	132.0	−66.7
3	3	BankAmerica Corp., San Francisco	101.1	98.8	+2.3	218.0	208.0	+4.8
4	4	J. P. Morgan & Co., New York	90.8	89.0	+2.0	399.0	179.6	+122.2
5	5	Security Pacific Corp., Los Angeles	86.5	83.9	+3.1	188.4	179.3	+5.1
6	6	Chemical Banking Corp., New York	74.2	71.5	+3.8	151.7	117.9	+28.7
7	7	NCNB Corp., Charlotte, N.C.	63.7	66.2	−3.8	140.1	75.8	+84.8
8	8	Manufacturers Hanover Corp., New York	59.7	60.5	−1.3	96.0	103.0	−5.8
9	10	Bankers Trust New York Corp.	59.3	55.7	+6.5	198.0	164.3	+20.5
10	9	First Interstate Bancorp., Los Angeles	57.4	59.1	−2.9	97.1	94.3	+3.0
11	12	Wells Fargo & Co., San Francisco	50.2	48.7	+3.1	159.8	141.5	+12.9
12	13	First Chicago Corp.	50.0	47.9	+4.4	68.6	124.7	−45.0
13	11	Bank of New York Co., Inc.	47.8	48.9	−2.2	102.3	101.1	+1.2
14	14	PNC Financial Corp., Pittsburgh	46.6	45.7	+2.0	74.5	123.6	−39.7
15	17	First Union Corp., Charlotte, N.C.	39.1	32.1	21.8	77.6	72.2	+7.5
16	15	Bank of Boston Corp.	37.3	39.2	−4.8	43.6	89.1	−51.1
17	16	Fleet/Norstar Financial Group Inc., Providence, R.I.	36.5	33.4	+9.3	(98.1)	92.4	−206.2

INTO A NEW DECADE

18	19	SunTrust Banks Inc., Atlanta	30.9	31.0	−0.3	87.9	84.0	+4.6
19	18	Mellon Bank Corp., Pittsburgh	30.8	31.5	−2.2	65.0	53.0	+22.6
20	20	First Fidelity Bancorp., Newark, N.J.	30.2	30.7	−1.6	21.1	61.9	−55.9
21	23	Barnett Banks Inc., Jacksonville, Fla.	29.3	29.0	+1.0	15.5	62.4	−75.2
22	22	Continental Bank Corp., Chicago	29.0	29.5	−1.7	56.7	75.6	−25.0
23	26	Banc One Corp., Columbus, Ohio	27.2	26.6	+2.3	101.8	87.2	+16.7
24	28	Republic New York Corp.	26.2	25.5	+2.7	44.5	41.8	+5.5
25	27	NBD Bancorp., Inc., Detroit	25.7	25.8	−0.4	66.6	63.5	+4.9
		Totals for the Top 25	$1,469.1	$1,448.2	+1.4	$2,650.7	$3,057.2	−13.3
		Dropping out of the Top 25						
26	25	Marine Midland Banks Inc., Buffalo, N.Y.	25.7	27.1	−5.2	6.0	31.7	−81.1
29	24	Shawmut National Bank, Hartford, Conn.	24.9	27.9	−10.8	32.1[1]	64.7	−50.4
30	21	Bank of New England Corp., Boston	24.9	29.8	−16.4	(46.6)	42.3	−210.2
		Pro forma ranking-merger in progress						
12	13	Avantor Financial Corp.[2]	49.5	44.7	10.7	128.2	119.7	7.1

Net income is income after taxes and minority interest but before preferred dividends and extraordinary items. Income from discontinued operations is excluded. First-quarter net income for 1989 is as reported in 1989. **Total assets** for Dec. 31, 1989, are as originally reported and have not been restated for mergers, changes in accounting practices, etc.

[1]Excludes an $8.5 million extraordinary credit arising from the utilization of a net operating loss carry-forward.
[2]On 9/26/89 Citizens and Southern Corp., Atlanta, and Sovran Financial Corp., Norfolk, Va., announced a definitive agreement to merge. The deal expected to be completed at the end of the third quarter, will create Avantor Financial Corp.
( ) indicates a net loss.

Source: Earnings releases from the companies. Compiled by American Banker, Copyright 1990.

APPENDIX

Excerpts from NCNB Corporation 1989 Annual Report

Principal Officers

NCNB Corporation

Hugh L. McColl Jr.
Chairman of the Board and Chief Executive Officer

Francis B. Kemp
President, NCNB Corporation Chairman, NCNB Texas

James W. Thompson
Vice Chairman
NCNB Corporation
Chairman, Southeastern Banking

Timothy P. Hartman
Vice Chairman, NCNB Corporation
Vice Chairman and Chief Financial Officer, NCNB Texas

James M. Berry
Corporate Executive Vice President
NCNB Corporation
Vice Chairman, NCNB Texas

Fredric J. Figge II
Chairman, Credit Policy

James H. Hance Jr.
Executive Vice President and Chief Financial Officer
NCNB Corporation

Kenneth D. Lewis
President, NCNB Texas

William P. Middlemas
President, Southeastern Banking

Charles J. Cooley
Executive Vice President
Corporate Personnel

James W. Kiser
Executive Vice President
Corporate Counsel and Secretary

Joseph B. Martin III
Executive Vice President
Corporate Affairs

NCNB Southeast

James W. Thompson
Chairman, Southeastern Banking

William P. Middlemas
President, Southeastern Banking

John G.P. Boatwright
President, NCNB Carolinas

Edward J. Brown III
President, Corporate Bank

Robert L. Kirby
President, NCNB Florida

G. Patrick Phillips
President, NCNB Services, Inc.

Joel A. Smith III
President, NCNB South Carolina

F. William Vandiver
President, Investment Bank

William L. Maxwell
Executive Vice President
Funds Management

James B. Sommers
Executive Vice President
Trust, Private Banking, Securities

Craig M. Wardlaw
Executive Vice President
Corporate Investments

NCNB Texas

Francis B. Kemp
Chairman

Timothy P. Hartman
Vice Chairman and Chief Financial Officer

Kenneth D. Lewis
President

James M. Berry
Vice Chairman, Houston

Ralph M. Carestio
Corporate Executive Vice President
Specialized Banking

John D. Dienes
Corporate Executive Vice President
Corporate Banking

James R. Erwin
President, Special Asset Bank

Raleigh Hortenstine III
Corporate Executive Vice President
Funds Management

William G. Kelley
Corporate Executive Vice President
Credit Policy

Robert B. Lane
Corporate Executive Vice President
General Banking

Joseph R. Musolino
Vice Chairman, Dallas

O. Darwin Smith
Corporate Executive Vice President
Support

Samuel J. Atkins
Executive Vice President
Energy

David W. Fisher
Executive Vice President
Trust

Harry J. Grim
Executive Vice President
General Counsel

Calvin C. Hunkele
Executive Vice President
Control

Harris A. Rainey Jr.
Executive Vice President
Administration

Boards of Directors

NCNB Corporation

William M. Barnhardt
President, Southern Webbing Mills Inc. (textiles)

Thomas M. Belk
President, Belk Stores Services Inc. (retailing)

Wilbur L. Carter Jr.
Retired President, Southern Life Insurance Company (insurance)

Charles W. Coker
President, Sonoco Products Company (manufacturer of paper and plastic products)

H.L. Culbreath
Chairman, TECO Energy Inc. (electric utility holding company)

Alan T. Dickson
President, Ruddick Corporation (diversified holding company)

W. Frank Dowd Jr.
Chairman of the Executive Committee, Charlotte Pipe & Foundry Company (manufacturer of cast iron and plastic pipe and fittings)

A.L. Ellis
Senior Chairman, NCNB National Bank of Florida

Timothy P. Hartman
Vice Chairman
NCNB Corporation
Vice Chairman and Chief Financial Officer, NCNB Texas

Edward A. Horrigan Jr.
Former Vice Chairman of the Board, RJR Nabisco Inc. (consumer products)

W.W. Johnson
Chairman of the Executive Committee, NCNB Corporation

Francis B. Kemp
President, NCNB Corporation
Chairman, NCNB Texas

William A. Klopman
Retired Chairman and Chief Executive Officer, Burlington Industries Inc. (textiles)

Hugh L. McColl Jr.
Chairman of the Board and Chief Executive Officer
NCNB Corporation

Robert E. McNair
Chairman of the Board
McNair Law Firm P.A.

John C. Slane
President, Slane Hosiery Mills Inc. (textiles)

Albert E. Sloan
Chairman and Chief Executive Officer, Lance Inc. (snack food products)

W. Roger Soles
Chairman and President, Jefferson-Pilot Corporation (insurance)

Meredith R. Spangler
Trustee and Volunteer

Robert H. Spilman
Chairman and Chief Executive Officer, Bassett Furniture Industries Inc. (furniture manufacturer)

Thomas I. Storrs
Retired Chairman
NCNB Corporation

James W. Thompson
Vice Chairman
NCNB Corporation
Chairman, Southeastern Banking

Wilson C. Wearn
Retired Chairman of the Board
Multimedia Inc. (diversified communications company)

Michael Weintraub
(private investor)

NCNB National Bank of Florida

Jack M. Berry Sr.
Chairman, The Berry Companies

Tully F. Dunlap
Corporate Trustee
Representative, Alfred I. du Pont Testamentary Trust

R.M. Elliott
Chairman and Chief Executive Officer, Leviz Furniture Corporation (nationwide chain of retail furniture stores)

A.L. Ellis
Senior Chairman

Edward L. Flom
Chairman and Chief Executive Officer, Florida Steel Corporation (steel manufacturers and reinforcing steel fabricators)

Timothy L. Guzzle
President and Chief Executive Officer, TECO Energy Inc. (electric utility holding company)

James H. Hance Jr.
Managing Director

Frank W. Harvey
(private investor)

John J. Hudzberg
Former Chairman and Chief Executive Officer, Florida Power & Light Company (electric utility)

George W. Jenkins
Founder and Chairman of the Board, Publix Super Markets Inc. (chain of supermarkets)

Robert L. Kirby
President

Hugh L. McColl Jr.
Chairman

William P. Middlemas
Managing Director

Richard L. Schmidt
Certified Public Accountant

John W. Temple
President and Chief Executive Officer, VMS/TEMPLE Development Company (real estate development and land acquisition)

James W. Thompson
Managing Director

Dr. Israel Tribble Jr.
President, Florida Endowment Fund for Higher Education

NCNB National Bank of North Carolina

Dr. Robert L. Albright
President, Johnson C. Smith University

E. James Becker Jr.
President and Chief Executive Officer, Geneva Corporation (financial holding company)

John G.P. Boatwright
President

Dr. G. John Coli
Chairman and Chief Executive Officer, Armira Inc. (producer of fashion leather products)

James H. Hance Jr.
Managing Director

John W. Harris
President, The Bissell Companies Inc. (real estate development)

J.R. Hendrick III
President, Hendrick Management Corporation (automobile mega dealer management company)

Charles W. Howard Jr.
Retired Tobacco Executive

Robert L. Jones
President, Davidson and Jones Corporation (general contractors and developers)

Hugh L. McColl Jr.
Chairman

Harold M. Messmer Jr.
Chairman and Chief Executive Officer, Robert Half International Inc. (financial personnel services)

William P. Middlemas
Managing Director

Jerome J. Richardson
President and Chief Executive Officer, TW Services, Inc. and Spartan Food Systems (food service)

A. Pope Shuford
President, Shuford Mills Inc. (textiles and pressure sensitive tapes)

Robin W. Sternbergh
Vice President and Area General Manager, IBM Corporation (information-handling systems, equipment and services)

James W. Thompson
Managing Director

John T. Warmath Jr.
Executive Vice President-Investments, Jefferson-Pilot Life Insurance Company (life insurance)

INTO A NEW DECADE

NCNB National Bank of South Carolina

Bill L. Amick
Chief Executive Officer, Amick Farms, Inc. (poultry processing)

John G.P. Boatwright
Managing Director

W. Melvin Brown Jr.
President, American Development Corporation (defense manufacturing)

Madge Chase DeFosset
(personal investments)

James H. Hance Jr.
Managing Director

Richardson M. Hanckel
Planters Three (farming)

Dwight A. Holder
Chairman of the Board and President, Carolina Financial Corporation (diversified investors)

D. Welhman Johnson
Vice Chairman, The Abney Foundation

George Dean Johnson Jr.
President, Johnson Development Associates, Inc. (property development)

W.W. Johnson
Chairman, NCNB South Carolina Chairman of the Executive Committee, NCNB Corporation

R.M. Laffitte
Chairman of the Board, The Exchange Bank, Estill, South Carolina

Edgar H. Lawton Jr.
President, Hartsville Oil Mill (manufacturers of cottonseed and peanut products)

Hugh L. McColl Jr.
Chief Executive Officer

Robert E. McNair
Chairman of the Board McNair Law Firm P.A.

William P. Middlemas
Managing Director

Dr. M. Maceo Nance Jr.
President Emeritus, South Carolina State College

Donald S. Russell Jr.
Attorney

James C. Self Jr.
Chairman of the Board Greenwood Mills Inc. (textiles)

Henry R. Sims II
Attorney

Joel A. Smith III
President

James W. Thompson
Managing Director

NCNB Texas Corporation

Robert H. Dedman
Chairman and Chief Executive Officer, ClubCorp International (owns and manages private clubs)

Timothy P. Hartman
President, NCNB Texas Corporation

Ray L. Hunt
Chairman and Chief Executive Officer, Hunt Consolidated, Inc. (oil and gas, real estate, agriculture and ranching)

Francis B. Kemp
Chairman of the Board NCNB Texas Corporation

Kerney Laday Sr.
Vice President and Regional General Manager, USMG Xerox Corporation (multi-national business products and services)

Irvin L. Levy
President, NCH Corporation (international manufacturer of chemical specialties)

Kenneth D. Lewis
President
NCNB Texas National Bank

Hugh L. McColl Jr.
Chairman
NCNB Corporation

Allen T. McInnes
Executive Vice President Tenneco, Inc. (diversified industrial corporation)

John J. (Jack) Murphy
Chairman, President and Chief Executive Officer, Dresser Industries, Inc. (energy-related products and services)

William T. Solomon
Chairman, President and Chief Executive Officer Austin Industries, Inc. (general contractor)

V.H. (Pete) Van Horn
President and Chief Executive Officer, National Convenience Stores, Inc. (retail convenience stores)

John F. Woodhouse
Chairman and Chief Executive Officer, SYSCO Corporation (wholesale food service marketing and distribution)

NCNB Texas National Bank

James M. Berry
Vice Chairman, Houston
NCNB Texas National Bank

Timothy P. Hartman
Vice Chairman and Chief Financial Officer, NCNB Texas National Bank

W.W. Johnson
Chairman of the Executive Committee, NCNB Corporation

Francis B. Kemp
Chairman of the Board
NCNB Texas National Bank

Kenneth D. Lewis
President, NCNB Texas National Bank

Hugh L. McColl Jr.
Chairman
NCNB Corporation

Joseph R. Musolino
Vice Chairman, Dallas
NCNB Texas National Bank

NCNB National Bank Georgia

Edward J. Brown III
Chairman

Graham W. Denton Jr.
Executive Vice President NCNB National Bank of Florida

William B. Heberton
(private investor)

Blaine Kelley Jr.
Chairman of the Board and Chief Executive Officer, The Landmarks Group (real estate development and management)

Jerry R. Sarrum
President and Chief Operating Officer, Georgia Gulf Corporation (commodity and specialty chemical manufacturer)

R. Edwin Spears
President

NCNB National Bank of Maryland

William F. Blue
Attorney, Ober, Kaler, Grimes & Shriver

H. Lee Boatwright III
President

Catherine B. Doehler
Retired Director of Fund Development, American Red Cross

C. Franklin Eck Jr.
President, American Lubrication Equipment Corporation (auto parts distributor)

Charles C. Fenwick
President, Towson Valley Motors

Dr. Lawrence F. Halpert
Chairman, Periodontal Associates

Craig Lewis
President, Investment Counselors of Maryland (investment management)

Larry W. Mallard
Managing Director

William P. Middlemas
Chairman

William H. Morrison III
Managing Director

Harrison M. Robertson Jr.
Retired Attorney, Niles, Barton & Wilmer

F. Bradford Smith
President, Environmental Elements Corporation (waste treatment purifying equipment manufacturers)

J. Richard Thomas
Senior Partner, Thomas Associates (insurance)

Otis Warren Jr.
President, Otis Warren Real Estate Services

NCNB Virginia

H. Lee Boatwright III
President, NCNB National Bank of Maryland

William M. Johnston
District Manager, Virginia Power Company

Larry W. Mallard
Chairman

William V.H. White
Magazine Editor

Robert L. Williams
President

NCNB Corporation and Subsidiaries

Six-Year Consolidated Statistical Summary

	1989	1988	1987	1986	1985	1984
Taxable-Equivalent Yields Earned						
Loans and leases, net of unearned income:						
Commercial	11.85%	10.02%	9.40%	9.65%	11.20%	13.17%
Real estate–construction	11.88	10.22	9.21	9.43	11.59	13.73
Real estate–commercial mortgage[1]	10.80					
Real estate–residential mortgage	10.70	10.25	10.63	11.56	11.89	12.61
Consumer	11.68	11.19	11.29	12.57	13.81	15.44
Bank card	16.59	17.67	17.61	19.02	15.97	15.60
Lease financing	7.92	8.53	8.33	9.90	14.56	14.91
Foreign loans	11.53	12.27	7.74	9.64	9.94	13.01
Total loans and leases, net	11.77	10.71	10.12	10.75	11.93	13.71
Taxable investment securities	8.97	7.86	7.57	8.75	10.63	11.03
Tax-exempt investment securities	10.72	11.10	12.84	13.54	12.96	11.98
Total investment securities	9.10	8.44	8.52	9.79	11.07	11.21
Federal funds sold and securities purchased under agreements to resell	9.14	7.51	6.65	6.63	8.14	10.55
Time deposits placed	9.83	8.22	7.12	7.39	9.02	10.75
Trading account securities	9.26	8.16	7.16	7.83	9.36	12.07
Total earning assets	10.90	9.97	9.49	10.13	11.39	12.82
Rates Paid						
Savings and interest-bearing demand deposits	6.08	5.09	4.92	5.45	6.32	7.38
Time deposits	8.71	7.43	6.83	7.56	9.00	10.23
Total domestic savings and time deposits	7.76	6.42	5.92	6.55	7.72	8.88
Foreign time deposits	9.78	7.98	7.28	7.73	9.10	10.55
Total savings and time deposits	7.88	6.53	6.04	6.64	7.87	9.11
Federal funds purchased and securities sold under agreements to repurchase	9.03	7.25	6.40	6.42	7.84	10.15
Commercial paper	9.21	7.49	6.55	6.71	8.43	10.60
Other notes payable	9.17	6.95	6.56	6.56	7.89	11.12
Total borrowed funds	9.05	7.24	6.42	6.44	7.88	10.29
Capital leases	11.63	12.34	11.71	11.85	11.32	11.04
Long-term debt	10.31	9.73	9.80	10.99	11.68	11.86
Total interest-bearing liabilities	8.22	6.81	6.25	6.70	7.98	9.47
Profit Margins						
Domestic spread	2.83	3.20	3.45	3.64	3.62	3.63
Foreign spread	.01	2.08	.02	.70	1.37	1.15
Consolidated spread	2.68	3.16	3.24	3.43	3.41	3.35
Domestic net interest yield	3.79	3.88	4.15	4.42	4.71	4.95
Foreign net interest yield	.50	2.49	.21	.83	1.47	1.35
Consolidated net interest yield	3.61	3.83	3.91	4.17	4.43	4.57
Year-End Data						
(Dollars in millions)						
Loans and leases, net of unearned income	$34,409	$18,908	$17,087	$15,765	$12,134	$10,362
Investment securities	16,170	4,727	6,826	5,653	3,336	2,386
Time deposits placed	2,966	963	855	1,630	979	988
Total earning assets	54,159	26,101	25,491	24,065	17,255	14,559
Total assets, excluding Special Asset Division	61,491	29,848	28,915	27,472	19,754	17,354
Demand deposits	8,439	3,913	3,862	4,510	3,354	3,137
Domestic savings and time deposits	37,988	15,900	14,383	12,542	9,396	8,200
Foreign time deposits	2,149	857	1,305	1,467	1,200	1,361
Total savings and time deposits	40,137	16,757	15,688	14,009	10,596	9,561
Total deposits	48,576	20,670	19,550	18,519	13,950	12,698
Borrowed funds	11,735	5,899	6,542	6,596	3,767	2,583
Obligations under capital leases	35	36	35	36	33	31
Long-term debt	1,430	457	533	537	401	319
Total shareholders' equity	2,962	1,942	1,510	1,309	1,039	902

[1]Commercial mortgage loans were included with commercial loans for 1988 and previous years.

	1989	1988	1987	1986	1985	1984
Earnings Ratios						
Return on average:						
Total assets[1]	1.01%	.88%	.62%	.84%	.92%	.84%
Earning assets[1]	1.14	.99	.71	.95	1.06	1.00
Common shareholders' equity	20.45	15.55	11.70	16.31	17.23	16.30
Earnings Analysis (Taxable-Equivalent)						
Noninterest income as a percentage of net interest income	48.37	37.31	36.29	35.29	38.24	28.62
Noninterest expense as a percentage of net interest income	95.11	83.21	82.78	80.30	78.40	78.71
Overhead ratio: noninterest expense less noninterest income divided by net interest income	46.74	45.90	46.49	45.01	40.16	50.09
Net income as a percentage of net interest income	25.13	25.78	18.22	22.82	23.98	21.88
Asset Quality						
For the year:						
Net charge-offs as a percentage of average loans and leases	.45	.83	1.08	.66	.45	.36
Net charge-offs as a percentage of the provision for loan and lease losses	61.52	121.38	90.83	89.49	43.34	55.92
At year-end:						
Allowance as a percentage of total loans and leases	1.35	1.22	1.50	1.50	1.53	1.22
Allowance as a percentage of nonperforming loans	117.67	131.19	96.88	146.23	141.06	93.37
Nonperforming assets as a percentage of loans and leases, net of unearned income	1.30	1.14	1.67	1.10	1.21	1.44
Nonperforming assets as a percentage of total assets[2]	.73	.72	.99	.63	.74	.86
Nonperforming assets (in millions)	$ 446	$ 215	$ 286	$ 173	$ 146	$ 149
Capital Ratios						
Primary	5.69%	7.82%	6.56%	6.47%	7.17%	6.44%
Total	7.74	8.98	7.69	7.77	8.55	8.11
Common shareholders' equity as a percentage of total assets at year-end[2]	4.41	5.67	5.22	4.76	5.26	5.20
Dividend payout ratio (per common share)	23.81	32.41	42.36	30.83	29.78	29.85
Shareholders' equity per common share:						
Average	$22.58	$18.67	$17.38	$15.50	$13.35	$11.99
At year-end	26.79	19.60	17.87	16.42	14.23	12.74
Other Statistics						
Number of full-time employees (not restated for acquisitions)	27,002	12,979	12,334	12,107	9,981	9,329
Rate of increase in average:						
Total loans and leases, net of unearned income	83.29%	8.54%	16.43%	30.39%	20.65%	32.79%
Earning assets	92.82	9.03	12.10	35.13	16.06	22.87
Total assets[2]	92.43	7.93	12.55	32.77	12.57	22.94
Total deposits	123.27	7.19	14.51	25.75	12.46	22.60
Total shareholders' equity	41.27	16.07	17.00	27.67	16.70	26.76
Average foreign assets as a percentage of average total assets[2]	5.70	4.37	6.92	6.78	9.13	12.25
Average foreign liabilities as a percentage of average total liabilities	6.05	6.09	7.50	6.70	9.92	12.83
Common Stock Information						
Market price of common stock:						
High for the year	$ 55	$ $29\frac{1}{8}$	$ $29\frac{1}{8}$	$ $27\frac{3}{4}$	$ $23\frac{5}{8}$	$ $18\frac{1}{4}$
Low for the year	27	$17\frac{1}{2}$	$15\frac{1}{2}$	20	17	$11\frac{1}{2}$
Close at the end of the year	$46\frac{1}{4}$	$27\frac{1}{4}$	$17\frac{1}{4}$	$21\frac{1}{2}$	$22\frac{5}{8}$	18
Daily average trading volume	303,599	189,043	210,644	209,938	132,402	80,834
Number of shareholders of record	29,064	29,344	29,789	28,732	21,004	19,896

[1]Includes FDIC's interest in earnings of NCNB Texas for 1989; excludes Special Asset Division assets.
[2]Excludes Special Asset Division assets.

Taxable-Equivalent 12-Month Data
(Income and Expense Amounts in Thousands, Balance Sheet Amounts in Millions)

	1989			1988			1987			1986			1985			1984			Five-Year Compound Growth Rate 1984/89	
	Average Balance Sheet Amounts	Income or Expense	Yields/Rates	Average Balance Sheet Amounts	Income or Expense	Yields/Rates	Average Balance Sheet Amounts	Income or Expense	Yields/Rates	Average Balance Sheet Amounts	Income or Expense	Yields/Rates	Average Balance Sheet Amounts	Income or Expense	Yields/Rates	Average Balance Sheet Amounts	Income or Expense	Yields/Rates	Average Balances	Income or Expense
Earning assets:																				
Loans and leases, net of unearned income:																				
Commercial	$16,703	$1,979,025	11.85%	$10,107	$1,012,939	10.02%	$ 9,464	$ 889,397	9.40%	$ 7,836	$ 757,898	9.65%	$ 5,945	$ 666,009	11.20%	$ 4,713	$ 620,567	13.17%	33.3%	30.1%
Real estate—construction	2,144	254,609	11.88	1,537	157,073	10.22	1,425	131,221	9.21	1,307	123,200	9.43	868	100,621	11.59	509	69,888	13.73	33.3	29.5
Real estate—commercial mortgage[1]	3,099	334,804	10.80																	
Real estate—residential mortgage	2,506	268,206	10.70	1,172	120,114	10.25	953	101,380	10.63	954	110,249	11.56	840	99,877	11.89	791	99,707	12.61	25.9	21.9
Consumer	5,654	660,557	11.68	3,469	388,091	11.19	3,037	342,902	11.29	2,448	307,802	12.57	1,985	274,162	13.81	1,785	251,691	15.44	25.9	19.1
Bank card	1,311	217,442	16.59	968	171,070	17.67	762	134,215	17.61	717	136,388	19.02	365	58,305	15.97	267	41,657	15.60	37.5	39.2
Lease financing	404	31,944	7.92	288	24,567	8.53	279	23,254	8.33	254	25,155	9.90	225	32,736	14.56	211	31,461	14.91	13.9	.3
Foreign loans	787	90,729	11.53	249	30,609	12.27	470	36,388	7.74	541	52,152	9.64	568	36,472	9.94	672	87,454	13.01	3.2	.7
Total loans and leases, net	32,608	3,837,316	11.77	17,790	1,904,463	10.71	16,390	1,658,757	10.12	14,077	1,512,844	10.75	10,796	1,288,202	11.93	8,948	1,226,425	13.71	29.5	25.6
Investment securities:																				
Taxable	11,232	1,007,828	8.97	4,702	369,676	7.86	3,936	298,316	7.57	3,450	301,857	8.75	2,299	244,413	10.63	2,152	237,604	11.03	39.2	33.5
Tax-exempt	895	95,937	10.72	1,014	112,524	11.10	857	110,030	12.84	960	129,973	13.54	540	69,978	12.96	472	56,494	11.98	13.7	11.2
Total investment securities	12,127	1,103,765	9.10	5,716	482,200	8.44	4,793	408,346	8.52	4,410	431,830	9.79	2,839	314,391	11.07	2,624	294,098	11.21	35.8	30.3
Federal funds sold and securities purchased under agreements to resell	1,957	178,839	9.14	1,093	82,105	7.51	839	55,852	6.65	1,020	67,636	6.63	820	66,784	8.14	813	85,725	10.55	19.2	15.8
Time deposits placed	2,037	200,285	9.83	735	60,374	8.22	1,094	77,862	7.12	963	71,235	7.39	821	74,008	9.02	829	89,050	10.75	19.7	17.6
Trading account securities	517	47,873	9.26	206	16,844	8.16	310	22,228	7.16	426	33,326	7.83	188	17,588	9.36	110	13,327	12.07	36.3	29.1
Total earning assets	49,246	5,368,078	10.90	25,540	2,545,986	9.97	23,426	2,223,045	9.49	20,896	2,116,871	10.13	15,464	1,760,973	11.39	13,324	1,708,625	12.82	29.9	25.7
Cash and cash equivalents	3,597			1,723			1,706			1,547			1,232			1,152			25.6	
Other assets, less allowance for loan and lease losses and excluding Special Asset Division	2,673			1,587			1,598			1,307			1,192			1,415			13.6	
Total assets, net of Special Asset Division	$55,516			$28,850			$26,730			$23,750			$17,888			$15,891			28.4	
Interest-bearing liabilities:																				
Consumer savings and other time deposits	$ 3,165	190,260	6.01	$ 2,499	149,007	5.96	$ 2,269	140,342	6.19	$ 1,744	115,456	6.62	$ 1,305	92,787	7.11	$ 1,261	87,349	6.93	20.2	16.8
Negotiable order of withdrawal and money market deposit accounts	10,087	635,414	6.30	4,715	241,106	5.11	4,833	236,625	4.90	4,392	241,379	5.50	3,303	216,100	6.54	2,542	204,847	8.06	31.7	25.4
Consumer certificates	10,260	882,211	8.60	3,849	278,723	7.24	3,173	209,685	6.61	3,104	240,549	7.75	2,468	226,180	9.16	2,136	214,791	10.06	36.9	32.7
Negotiable CDs, public funds and other time deposits	10,259	911,749	8.89	3,768	283,834	7.53	2,943	196,162	6.66	2,182	150,428	6.89	1,631	136,927	8.39	1,431	147,560	10.31	48.3	43.9
Foreign time deposits	2,157	211,004	9.78	1,092	87,088	7.98	1,271	92,585	7.28	975	75,350	7.73	1,080	98,299	9.10	1,192	125,805	10.55	12.6	10.9
Borrowed funds	11,870	1,074,699	9.05	6,533	472,844	7.24	5,847	375,549	6.42	5,703	367,060	6.44	3,324	261,986	7.88	2,700	277,941	10.29	34.5	31.1
Capital leases and long-term debt	1,035	107,265	10.36	548	54,165	9.89	568	56,301	9.91	504	55,719	11.06	368	42,872	11.65	348	41,030	11.79	24.4	21.2
Special Asset Division net funding allocation	(5,164)	(423,553)	(8.20)																	
Total interest-bearing liabilities	43,669	3,589,049	8.22	23,004	1,566,767	6.81	20,904	1,307,249	6.25	18,604	1,245,942	6.70	13,479	1,075,151	7.98	11,610	1,099,323	9.47	30.3	26.7
Noninterest-bearing sources:																				
Noninterest-bearing deposits	7,246			3,415			3,551			3,357			2,742			2,578			23.0	
Other liabilities	1,851			776			849			570			712			885			15.9	
FDIC interest	412																			
Shareholders' equity	2,338			1,655			1,426			1,219			955			818			23.4	
Total liabilities and shareholders' equity	$55,516			$28,850			$26,730			$23,750			$17,888			$15,891			28.4	
Net interest spread			2.68			3.16			3.24			3.43			3.41			3.35			
Impact of noninterest-bearing sources			.93			.67			.67			.74			1.02			1.22			
Net interest income/yield on earning assets		$1,779,029	3.61		$ 979,219	3.83		$ 915,796	3.91		$ 870,929	4.17		$ 685,822	4.43		$ 609,302	4.57		23.9

[1]Information on real estate—commercial mortgage loans is included with commercial loans for 1988 and previous years.

CASE 7. NCNB, INC.

NCNB Corporation and Subsidiaries
Consolidated Statement of Cash Flows
(Dollars in Thousands)

	Year Ended December 31		
	1989	1988	1987
Operating Activities			
Net income	$ 447,069	$ 252,471	$ 166,852
Reconciliation of net income to net cash provided by operating activities:			
FDIC interest in earnings of NCNB Texas	116,164		
Provision for loan and lease losses	239,123	121,538	194,632
Depreciation	91,416	43,657	39,419
Amortization of intangibles	39,358	37,575	37,260
Deferred income tax expense (benefit)	14,568	(3,582)	(9,277)
Net (increase) decrease in trading securities	(163,048)	(10,348)	258,573
Net increase in interest receivable	(237,690)	(23,351)	(12,288)
Net increase (decrease) in interest payable	(111,255)	45,590	42,157
Other operating activities	(164,924)	(54,253)	(15,456)
Net cash provided by operating activities	270,781	409,297	701,872
Investing Activities			
Proceeds from maturities of investment securities	1,836,644	394,977	549,726
Proceeds from sales of investment securities	14,921,349	8,936,643	7,744,388
Purchases of investment securities	(24,523,399)	(6,986,789)	(9,197,560)
Net (increase) decrease in federal funds sold and securities purchased under agreements to resell	1,503,498	(769,719)	34,298
Net (increase) decrease in other short-term investments	(1,269,017)	(209,805)	799,111
Net increase in bank card receivables	(449,637)	(203,894)	(68,261)
Net collections (originations) of longer-term loans	107	(1,904,191)	(1,502,360)
Proceeds from sale of factored receivables		82,308	
Net sales (purchases) of premises and equipment	(247,940)	79,624	(132,630)
Purchase of NCNB Texas	(790,000)	(210,000)	
Purchase of banking and financial organizations	(173,088)	(591)	101,566
Other investing activities	3,443	(859)	6,926
Net cash used by investing activities	(9,188,040)	(792,296)	(1,664,796)
Financing Activities			
Net increase in deposits	7,431,461	1,074,811	635,637
Net increase (decrease) in federal funds purchased and securities sold under agreements to repurchase	2,386,409	(941,558)	(134,007)
Net increase in other borrowed funds	52,045	298,812	76,889
Proceeds from issuance of long-term debt	1,003,318		
Repayment of long-term debt	(122,486)	(72,593)	(23,591)
Proceeds from issuance of common stock	690,051	22,423	116,041
Proceeds from issuance of preferred stock		250,000	
Cash dividends paid	(122,308)	(85,238)	(70,569)
Assistance refunded to FDIC	(262,607)		
Other financing activities	1,912	(3,962)	7,173
Net cash provided by financing activities	11,057,795	542,695	607,593
Effect of exchange rate changes on cash and cash equivalents	(592)	(548)	1,780
Net increase (decrease) in cash and cash equivalents	2,139,944	159,148	(353,551)
Cash and cash equivalents at beginning of year	1,971,324	1,812,176	2,165,727
Cash and cash equivalents at end of year	$ 4,111,268	$ 1,971,324	$ 1,812,176

See accompanying notes to consolidated financial statements.

NCNB Corporation and Subsidiaries
Consolidated Statement of Income
(Dollars in Thousands Except Per-Share Information)

	Year Ended December 31		
	1989	1988	1987
Income from Earning Assets			
Interest and fees on loans	$3,776,266	$1,851,394	$1,592,580
Lease financing income	31,379	23,750	21,275
Interest and dividends on taxable investment securities	987,623	352,266	293,605
Interest on investment securities exempt from federal income taxes	71,088	78,493	66,817
Time deposits placed	200,285	60,374	77,862
Federal funds sold	123,031	50,784	35,274
Securities purchased under agreements to resell	55,808	31,321	20,578
Trading account securities	46,449	16,069	20,580
Total income from earning assets	5,291,929	2,464,451	2,128,571
Interest Expense			
Deposits	2,830,638	1,039,758	875,399
Borrowed funds	1,074,699	472,844	375,549
Capital leases and long-term debt	107,265	54,165	56,301
Special Asset Division net funding allocation	(423,553)		
Total interest expense	3,589,049	1,566,767	1,307,249
Net interest income	1,702,880	897,684	821,322
Provision for Loan and Lease Losses			
Bank provision	239,123	121,538	194,632
Loans transferred to Special Asset Division	216,699		
Assistance from FDIC	(216,699)		
Total provision for loan and lease losses	239,123	121,538	194,632
Net credit income	1,463,757	776,146	626,690
Noninterest income	860,517	369,055	332,372
Noninterest expense	1,692,042	814,806	758,085
Income before taxes and FDIC interest in earnings of NCNB Texas	632,232	330,395	200,977
Special Asset Division			
Net adjustment for asset valuation allowance	(332,390)		
Other net costs	(616,445)		
Assistance from FDIC	948,835		
Net costs associated with Special Asset Division	—	—	—
Earnings			
Income before taxes and FDIC interest in earnings of NCNB Texas	632,232	330,395	200,977
Income tax expense	68,999	77,924	34,125
Income before FDIC interest in earnings of NCNB Texas	563,233	252,471	166,852
FDIC interest in earnings of NCNB Texas	(116,164)		
Net income	$ 447,069	$ 252,471	$ 166,852
Earnings Per Common Share			
Primary	$ 4.62	$ 2.90	$ 2.03
Fully diluted	$ 4.44	$ 2.87	$ 2.01
Dividends per common share	$ 1.10	.94	.86
Average Common Shares Outstanding			
Primary	92,491,551	85,210,165	82,073,254
Fully diluted	100,791,654	88,269,581	83,096,742

See accompanying notes to consolidated financial statements.

CASE 8

SONOCO PRODUCTS, INC.

MYRA REGISTER, LISA SCOTT, SHERYL WEST, AND DAVID W. GRIGSBY

In early 1988, Charles W. Coker, president and CEO of Sonoco Products Company, had reason for celebration. The previous year had seen his company set records in sales growth and profits, with sales reaching over $1 billion for the first time and profits reaching an all-time high of over $60 million. The future also looked good for Sonoco. The company was becoming a worldwide leader in the consumer packaging industry and held a commanding share of the fast-growing plastic grocery bag market. Sonoco's April 1987 acquisition of the Consumer Packaging Division of Boise Cascade had been the largest in its history. Coker also had reason to be a bit more apprehensive about the future than ever before. To finance the Boise Cascade purchase, Sonoco had increased its long-term debt by 4.5 times. Although Sonoco's basic markets looked strong, industry analysts had begun to wonder if this traditionally conservative company, still led by descendants of its founder, could assimilate its recent growth and continue to expand.

HISTORY OF THE COMPANY

After the Civil War, Major James Lide Coker came home to Hartsville, South Carolina, from a Union prison with a shattered hip and a determination to help rebuild the war-torn South. Over time, he opened a country store, a bank, a cotton mill, and a college, but he was convinced that the South's future hinged on scientific farming and the development of industry. In the 1890s, Coker's eldest son, James, became interested in the processes of pulping and paper making, using the region's abundant pine forests. The major soon became involved in the development of this idea and raised $20,000 to begin a

---

Source: Prepared under the direction of Professor David W. Grigsby, Clemson University, as a basis for classroom discussion and not to illustrate either effective or ineffective handling of administrative situations. The authors acknowledge the assistance and cooperation of officials of Sonoco Products Company, but take full responsibility for the accuracy of information contained in the case. © David W. Grigsby, 1990.

pulp and paper venture. They hoped to market the pulp commercially, but this idea soon had to be abandoned. Instead, they decided to focus their efforts on making paper. Their first machine turned out between five and eight tons of paper per twenty-four-hour day. This first mill became known as the Carolina Fibre Company. Shortly thereafter, an agreement was reached to form a company to use the paper manufactured by the Carolina Fibre Company to produce paper cones for the textile industry. These cones, made of a thick cardboard-like paper, were used to wind yarns in the manufacturing process of various fabrics. Paper cones would gradually replace the heavier and more costly wooden cones used in the textile industry. The new company was designated the Southern Novelty Company, a name that was later abbreviated to Sonoco.[1]

Through the early 1900s, the textile industry grew rapidly and Sonoco grew with it. After Major Coker's death in 1918, his son Charles was named President. Under his leadership, Sonoco grew from a one-product company to be a leading supplier of textile-related manufacturing supplies. When Charles Coker died in 1931, he left a solid foundation for the future growth of Sonoco. Charles's two sons, James Lide Coker and Charles Westfield Coker, had grown up in Sonoco, working for the company in the summers during high school and college. After their father's death, James Coker, the eldest of the two, was named president. Under James Coker's leadership, Sonoco began yet another period of growth. The introduction of manmade fibers spurred rapid growth in the textile industry, increasing the demand for Sonoco's products. Sonoco began expanding, opening eight plants in new locations outside of Hartsville. After James Coker's death in 1961, his younger brother, Charles, took over the presidency and served until 1970, when he stepped aside to become honorary chairman of the board. His son, Charles W. Coker, then became the fourth generation of the Coker family to head Sonoco.[2] In 1988, Charles W. was beginning his nineteenth year as president and CEO. The directors and executive officers of Sonoco are listed in Exhibit 1.

In the 1960s, Sonoco's composite paper core process, which had been used to produce wound paper tubes for rolls of cloth and carpet and other industrial applications, was adapted to produce composite paper cans for concentrated fruit juices, motor oils, refrigerated dough, and dozens of other applications. This entry into the packaging industry began a diversification program that, by the 1980s, had taken Sonoco into virtually every area of consumer packaging, including plastic bottles and grocery bags.

Sonoco's growth and diversification in the 1970s and 1980s was accomplished through a combination of internal innovation and strategic acquisition. By acquiring key companies in critical new technological areas to supplement its own internal research and development in new packaging processes, Sonoco managed to position itself among the top two or three competitors in several segments of the consumer packaging industry while maintaining its leadership in specialized industrial products. Until the Boise Cascade merger, however, Sonoco's acquisitions, although numerous, had been relatively small ones.

In 1988, Sonoco was ranked 240th in the Fortune 500[3] and employed more

EXHIBIT 1 THE OFFICERS OF SONOCO PRODUCTS COMPANY, 1988

CORPORATE OFFICERS
Charles W. Coker, 55, President
Thomas C. Coxe, III, 58, Executive Vice President
Russell C. King, Jr., 54, Senior Vice President
F. Bennett Williams, 58, Senior Vice President
J. Gary Caudle, 51, Vice President-Corporate Development
Peter C. Coggeshall, Jr., 45, Group Vice President
C. William Claypool, 53, Vice President-Paper Division
H. Gordon Dancy, 49, Vice President-High Density Film Products Division
Harris E. DeLoach, Jr., 44, Vice President-Administration and General Counsel
Robert C. Elmers, 41, Vice President-Human Resources
F. Trent Hill, Jr., 36, Vice President-Finance
Ronald E. Holley, 46, Vice President-Industrial Products Division
Harry J. Moran, 56, Vice President-Consumer Products Division
Earl P. Norman, Jr., 52, Vice President-Technology and Planning
John R. Tinnell, 49, Vice President-Drum Operations
James L. Coker, 48, Secretary
Charles J. Hupfer, 42, Treasurer

Source: Sonoco Products Company, *1988 Annual Report*

than 14,000 workers in 200 operations in the U.S. and abroad. Some 150 branch plants were strategically located throughout the U.S. in order to take advantage of transportation efficiencies and to provide services to its wide range of customers. Internationally, Sonoco operated in 20 foreign countries.[4]

Despite its size and dominance in several of its markets, Sonoco is far from being a household word. Adding to its relative obscurity is the company's frequent confusion with Sun Oil Company, which is often referred to as "Sunoco." Nevertheless, millions of consumers unknowingly come in contact with Sonoco products every day as they pull aluminum foil from a Sonoco tube, open a Sonoco composite can of orange juice, refill their car's crankcase from a Sonoco plastic oil bottle, or carry their groceries home in a Sonoco Polysack bag.

Sonoco is the largest producer of spiral tubes in the world. The company is also a major manufacturer of paperboard, producing over 800,000 tons annually in some 300 grades of paper. Sonoco is also one of the largest users of recycled wastepaper in the country, an accomplishment that has earned the company praise from several environmental groups.

ORGANIZATION

Sonoco is organized into seven distinct operating groups and divisions: Industrial Products Division, Consumer Packaging Group, Drum Operations, Paper Group, International Division, High Density Film Products Division, and Special Products Operations. According to Peter Coggeshall, senior executive vice-president, Sonoco can be considered "almost completely integrated, producing its own paper, adhesives, lacquers, and varnishes; and designing and building its converting machinery." Russell King, senior vice-president, says, "The company is no longer considered just a paper company that also makes some packaging products. This perception is gradually changing and Sonoco is becoming known as a packaging company that happens to make a lot of its own paper." Sonoco, in essence, can be described as a "packaging job shop."

INDUSTRIAL PRODUCTS DIVISION

The Industrial Products Division is Sonoco's traditional business. This division produces paper and plastic tubes and cones, which are used by a variety of industries for winding products such as paper, film, foil, textiles, and tape. Sonoco tubes are also used as shipping and storage containers and for certain operations in the construction industry such as forms for casting large concrete columns. Sonoco is the only national manufacturer of products of this type, with a network of more than forty plants in twenty-eight states. Primary competition for the division is from numerous regional producers. Besides its national network of plants, Sonoco's vertical integration and strong technology base are two other major competitive advantages. Sonoco has excellent relationships with almost every major textile, paper, film, and tape manufacturer in the United States.[5]

The Industrial Products Division produces its products according to customer specifications and therefore carries no inventory of finished goods. Depending on the grade of paper, special coatings, and the build-up of the tube or core, the customers' orders can be manufactured to resist heat, certain chemicals, and moisture.

A guiding principle of the Industrial Products Division is to help its customers reduce their manufacturing costs. Much of Sonoco's success can be attributed to its ability to create a paper or plastic product that does the same job as an existing one, but at a lower cost. For instance, cones used in the textile industry for winding yarn were originally heavy, expensive, wooden ones. With Sonoco's paper cones, the customer got a lightweight, less expensive cone. Likewise, when plastics became a more economical solution for certain industrial applications, Sonoco shifted some of its products to plastic. This same principle has been applied in other Sonoco divisions. The Fibre Drum Division, for example, promotes its products as replacements for steel drums in some markets, and has begun shifting many of its customers to plastic drums. The IPD sales force is trained to look for possibilities of improvement in a customer's operation and focuses on innovative ways of improving a customer's product or production system.

The IPD is organized geographically in order to keep a local focus on competition. Since plants in different regions of the country often concentrate on a single product or group of products, there is also an underlying departmentalization by process. IPD departments at the home plant in Hartsville—spiral department, parallel department, convolute department, and cone department—supply technical expertise to plants in other localities. All salespeople, however, are responsible for generating orders of all the division's products. Sales territories are divided geographically throughout the U.S. Account representatives in the field are supported by an inside sales force. The Industrial Products Division's largest customers include DuPont, Hoechst-Celanese, 3M, International Paper, and Burlington Industries.

With its forty-four plants, Sonoco's Industrial Products Division is able to meet its customers' needs on a timely basis, often on a just-in-time basis. Some customers, such as DuPont or 3M, can call in an order for a truckload of tubes and have it the next day. Quality is also an important consideration. For example, the spiral paper cores used to wind plastic film are required to fit very precise specifications, to thousandths of an inch. Sonoco has improved the reliability of this technology to the point that 3M has "officially certified" Sonoco as a supplier. This means that 3M will not inspect any of the cores shipped to its Greenville, South Carolina, plant from Sonoco's spiral tube plant located in nearby Fountain Inn.[6] Although the Industrial Products Division could be considered to be operating in a mature market, by applying innovative solutions to customers' problems its business has continued to increase. Sonoco estimated that in 1988 it had "over 80% of the cone market, and over 50% of the tube and core market."[7]

CONSUMER PACKAGING GROUP

The Consumer Packaging Group consists of the Consumer Products Division, Petroleum Products Division, and the business development and technology area. Among the division's customers in 1988 were practically every major food and oil company, including Proctor & Gamble, General Foods, Coca Cola, Pillsbury, Pennzoil, and Kraft. Primary products produced by the Consumer Products Division are composite and plastic cans and fiber and plastic caulking cartridges. The Petroleum Products Division's main products are one-quart plastic oil bottles. Both of these operations are clear industry leaders in their markets. According to the Sonoco's 1987 annual report, "A major strategy of this group is to develop long-term relationships with customers which allow for innovative package development. Such innovation is a key to successful competition in the packaged goods marketplace".[8]

Many of the Consumer Packaging Group's innovations come out of its research facility located at Sonoco headquarters in Hartsville, South Carolina. The Packaging Development Center was established in 1987 as a separate facility to respond to customers' needs for more innovative packaging. A major thrust of the facility has been to increase Sonoco's technological strength in plastics so that it will match the company's expertise in paperboard technology. Plastic products accounted for 15 percent of Sonoco's total sales in 1987. Company officials expect this percentage to rise significantly in the 1990s.

An example of a packaging innovation developed by Sonoco is its new TablePak™ product line developed in 1987 for the frozen foods industry. TablePak containers are made from a new combination of paper and plastics. The containers are made to be taken directly from the freezer and placed in either conventional or microwave ovens.

Overall, the Consumer Packaging Group has been the fastest growing division of the company, with most of the growth coming in the 1980s. By 1988, its total revenues equalled that of the Industrial Products Division, and it was estimated that consumer packaging and industrial products each represented 40 percent of Sonoco's total operations. Paper production and other products comprised the remaining 20 percent.

General sales manager Ray McGowan explains that a disruption in the packaging industry resulted when companies such as American Can and Continental Can began shifting their focus toward financial services and making acquisitions outside of packaging. "Sonoco saw a void in the overall marketplace for somebody who was *just* a packaging company. The growth took place, with the composite can business as the base, through acquisitions to a large degree." Composite cans are basically paper tubes that have been sealed airtight with some type of metal or plastic ends.

Many of Sonoco's most recent acquisitions have been in this area of the business. Some of these include the can division of Container Corporation of America, General Can Corporation, certain Owens-Illinois plants, and Continental Fibre Drum. The largest acquisition, on April 1, 1987, was that of the Consumer Packaging Division of Boise Cascade Corporation. Boise Cascade apparently wanted to leave the packaging industry and return to being strictly a paper company. Although the purchase cost Sonoco over $170 million in cash plus the assumption of $6.6 million in long-term debt, the company considered it an excellent opportunity to increase its share of the consumer packaging industry. The acquired operations manufacture composite cans and/or plastic bottles used in packaging motor oil, frozen juice concentrate, snack foods, refrigerated dough, and other products.

Sonoco was able to make the transition to consumer packaging by taking the winding technology used for making tubes and cones and applying it to the manufacture of composite cans. In 1963, Coker recognized a movement from metal cans to the lighter weight, less expensive composite cans and decided to enter what he saw as an emerging business. Sonoco's first composite can plant was built in Charleston, South Carolina, for the purpose of making motor oil cans. From there, Sonoco moved into other consumer packaging areas that were beginning to use composite cans. For over twenty years, composite cans afforded Sonoco a stable product with little technological change.

By the 1980s, however, packaging technology had become far more volatile, with packages changing every three to four years. As McGowan acknowledged, "The growth will come with the new packages—not what is currently being made." It has been estimated that over 22,000 new products are introduced every year—2000 in the grocery area alone. Approximately one-third of them will require new packages. Dick Puffer, director of public relations and corporate advertising, voiced a similar view: "If we are going to be a vital force in the packaging industry, we have to be ready to give the customer a package in whatever material a customer wants that package—in a very short span of time."

McGowan explained that Sonoco's objective for this division "is not to be known as a composite can manufacturer, but as a package supplier for consumer products." It is willing to grow and change as long as there continues to be a demand for different types of packages.

HIGH DENSITY FILM PRODUCTS DIVISION

One of Sonoco's most promising new ventures is its High Density Film Products Division, which changed its name in 1988 from the Polysack Division. This division is responsible for the manufacture and distribution of plastic bags for the grocery and retail sales industries. Its most successful product has been grocery bags sold under the trade name QuickMate. As of 1988, more than 60 percent of all U.S. grocery chains were using plastic bags, and industry reports noted that plastic held a 50% percent share of the market. Sonoco held a leading share of the national market in 1988 and was by far the dominant supplier in the Southeast. Of the top twenty-five grocery operators in America, Sonoco's Polysack bags were in twenty-one of the chains. The company opened its fourth and fifth Polysack plants in 1987 and its sixth plant in 1988.

Sonoco plastic bags are promoted in the grocery industry as a way to reduce costs and increase productivity for the grocery chains. The bag has proven to be valuable in several ways. Grocers benefit from lower per-unit cost per bag, as compared to paper bags. In addition, the shipping, handling, and storage costs for bags is reduced because Polysack bags require only one-eight the space of paper bags. The actual number of bags used in a store can also be reduced because the stronger plastic bag eliminates the need for double-bagging heavy items.

Despite these obvious advantages, the acceptance of plastic grocery bags has been slow. In fact, the battle with traditional paper grocery bags resulted in Polysack Division losses in its first four years.[9] Sonoco did not expect the transition to plastic to take as long as it did. In a 1987 interview, Charles W. Coker said, "We knew we had an excellent product that was cost advantageous. What we did not anticipate is we had to sell each individual store on the concept and had to sell it store by store."[10]

Sonoco's studies indicated that use of its plastic bags, if properly implemented, could result in a significant reduction in the number of bag set-up motions required of a store employee. This translates into quicker packing of groceries and therefore shorter checkout lines for the store. The Polysack Division's marketing effort was extended to include a total redesign service for a customer's check-out lines. Switching to the QuikMate system has improved front-end productivity as much as 25 percent for some stores.[11] Sonoco also provides training for stores making the change from traditional paper bags. Sonoco teams teach the store's employees how to set up and pack the new bags properly. In an additional effort to further the acceptance of the new bags, Sonoco experts have also assisted a manufacturer of store equipment in designing checkout counters especially made for the new bags.[12]

Sonoco's dominance in the plastic grocery bag segment has been attributed to its early decision to use high-density, high-molecular plastic, which has proven to be the preferred material. According to Rick Brown, marketing manager for the division, of all grocery chains using plastic bags, 84 percent were using high-density plastic bags in 1988.

In 1987, the Polysack Division more than doubled its 1985 profits as a result of volume increases and high capacity utilization. According to industry sources, Sonoco held 35% percent of the plastic grocery bag market in 1988 and was the industry leader. Mobil Corp. occupied second place, but the gap between the companies was widening dramatically. As for the future of the Polysack Division, management projected that it would account for 10 percent of Sonoco's total profits by 1990.[13]

Building on its success in the grocery industry, the Polysack Division introduced a line of plastic bags for department and discount stores in 1987. Marketed under the label Rollmate, these bags come in several sizes in the familiar "t-shirt" shape and are wound on Sonoco paper cores and dispensed through a counter system developed by the division. According to Sonoco Polysack executives, retail sales represent a potential market that could be as large as the market for grocery bags.[14]

DRUM OPERATIONS

In 1985, Sonoco acquired Continental Fibre Drum as an entry into the semi-bulk packaging market. In 1987, the operation changed its name to Sonoco Fibre Drum. By 1988, Sonoco Fibre Drum operated thirteen plants around the country. The company expanded its role in semi-bulk packaging with the addition of plastic drum operations in 1986, and by 1988 it operated three plants under the name Sonoco Plastic Drum.[15]

Primary markets for Sonoco drums are the chemical, pharmaceutical, and food industries. Besides general economic and market share growth, the division seeks growth from conversions of steel drum users to fiber and plastic. Sonoco is seen as the technology leader in the fibre drum industry, which is a competitive advantage in markets having special requirements.

Sonoco competes with one other national fibre drum manufacturer and several smaller, regional firms. Besides its recognized technological leadership, its complete lines of fibre and plastic drums and its reputation for quality are some of its competitive advantages.[16]

An example of product innovation in the fibre drum division is the ResponsePak, a nest of five heavy-duty drums that range in size from seven to fifty-five gallons. The drums were developed to withstand the ravages of almost anything that can be shoveled into them. They provide safe, temporary containment of spilled hazardous waste materials until final disposal is possible. ResponsePak drums are being marketed to local fire departments, which, under new federal guidelines, are required to have emergency toxic waste disposal capability.[17]

PAPER GROUP

The Paper Group consists of Sonoco's U.S. paper mills, which produce paperboard from recycled wastepaper; the company's corrugating medium production operation; Paper Stock Dealers, a wastepaper packing subsidiary; and Sonoco's relatively small forest products operations.

One of the world's largest producers of uncoated cylinderboard, Sonoco generates approximately 565,000 tons annually when its eleven U.S. paperboard mills operate to capacity. Cylinderboard is sold mostly to internal operations for conversion into paperboard packaging products. The division benefits from long, cost-effective production runs, made possible by this "captive" market. Cylinderboard capacity has grown in step with the company's consumer products growth. In 1988 Sonoco added 6 percent additional tonnage to its capacity through new manufacturing strategies and capital improvement at its existing mills.

The corrugating medium operation is a joint venture with Georgia-Pacific, which takes all the output, approximately 15,000 tons of corrugated paperboard, from the machines for use in its cardboard carton facility. Wastepaper, mainly from old corrugated containers, is one of Sonoco's primary raw materials. The company collects about 85 percent of its supply through its wastepaper subsidiary. Sonoco annually consumes more than one million tons of wastepaper in its operations, making it one of the largest users of recycled materials in the world.[18]

SPECIAL PRODUCTS OPERATIONS

Sonoco's smaller activities are grouped together under the Special Products Operations umbrella. The Baker Division is a major producer of nailed wood, plywood, and metal reels for the wire and cable industry. The Fibre Partitions Division produces solid fiber and corrugated partitions for shipping cartons. Sonoco produces aluminum and steel beams for the textile industry and a variety of castings for a multitude of other industries through its Briggs-Shaffner Division. The Adhesives Division and Machinery Manufacturing Operations are part of the company's vertical integration, although both have some outside sales as well.

INTERNATIONAL DIVISION

Mike Bullington, director of international staff at Sonoco, describes the company, with its operations located in twenty countries, as a "multidomestic" company. It is multidomestic in the sense that its international operations are replicas of the company's U.S. operations rather than support activities.

Sonoco's first international extension came about in the 1920s and was an effort to follow Sonoco's traditional customers to other parts of the world. In time, the company's international operations were extended to include overseas counterparts to practically every market that the company serves in the U.S.

Sonoco's international operations are organized according to four world regions: Europe, Canada, Latin America, and the Pacific. Most of the company's foreign operations are carried out through wholly owned subsidiaries. European operations are the oldest and largest segment. There are six converting plants and three major paper-making facilities in England producing both industrial and packaging products. There are also three converting plants in the Netherlands, one in Norway, and one in Spain, and a paper mill in Germany.

Until 1987, European profits were not as high as Sonoco desired. The year ended, however, with sales of $31.4 million, a 53.2-percent gain over 1986. Operating profits for 1987 were over $2 million. The European group moved its headquarters to Brussels in 1988 in order to have better access to Sonoco's continental customers and to place more emphasis on continental European opportunities (the headquarters of the European Community (EC) are located in that city). Although the company held a leading share of the converted paper market in England, its presence on the continent was minimal prior to 1988. Sonoco's plans at that time were to expand its European activities through acquisitions.

The International Division's second largest operation is in Canada. Canadian operations stretch from Newfoundland to Vancouver Island. Its major customers are paper mills. Sonoco makes packaging materials for the Canadian paper mills and supplies Canadian textile firms with paper tubes and cones. Sonoco also holds a 49-percent share in Domtar Sonoco Containers, Inc., a company that makes composite cans and other products.

Latin America is the third largest of Sonoco's international operations. The company has five plants in Mexico: two paper mills, two converting plants, and a fibre drum plant. Operations in Columbia include a small paper mill, several converting plants, and a major composite can operation. The composite oil can business is attractive in Colombia. Because unscrupulous dealers often resell used oil to unsuspecting customers, Colombians are leery of plastic bottles or any other package that can be refilled. Sonoco solved this problem by offering composite oil cans with easy-open tops similar to potato chip cans. Sonoco also has small operations in Venezuela and Puerto Rico.

Sonoco's newest international group is the Pacific region. Although it is the smallest international operation, it is one with great potential for growth. It is estimated that half of the world's population is in this area. Sonoco has three plants in New Zealand, six plants in Australia, and one plant in Singapore. Until recently, Sonoco had a 45-percent share in a major packaging company in Australia. It was sold in order to buy 100 percent of the company's industrial packaging division. Sonoco has plans to increase its presence in the Pacific Rim and is conducting market surveys in Korea, Thailand, and Indonesia.

Each of the International Division's four regions—Europe, Canada, Latin America, and the Pacific—has its own president, who reports to Jim McGee, Sonoco's group vice-president for international operations, who is located at corporate headquarters in Hartsville. A support group under the direction of Mike Bullington is also located in Hartsville. It is comprised of four major groups: an operations support group, consisting of engineers whose job is to make sure that technology is exchanged between the U.S. and the foreign operations and vice versa; a marketing group, which is responsible for market surveys and various worldwide trade shows; a project manager, who is in charge of organizing and implementing an entire special project such as a new plant installation; and a financial group, which handles all of the budgeting, forecasting, capital analysis, and consolidations of earnings for the international operations.

To combat language and cultural barriers, Sonoco prefers to manage its international operations with local personnel wherever possible. Two of the four group presidents are natives of host countries, as are all second-line managerial personnel.

Sonoco's basic philosophy of business extends to the international arena. Mike Bullington explains that Sonoco is basically trying to do two things internationally. The first is "to leverage Sonoco's capabilities worldwide." All of the many products, the new markets, and the methods of satisfying customers that are developed in the U.S. are spread throughout the world. By spreading the development costs over a much larger base, a cost reduction occurs. Also, as many of the countries in which Sonoco operates are not as economically developed or technologically integrated as the U.S., Sonoco can often use obsolete equipment or machinery in many of the foreign operations where much lower labor costs offset any productivity gains that are realized with much of the company's modern equipment used in the U.S.

The second goal that Sonoco is trying to accomplish by operating internationally is to stay abreast of new developments in other countries. For instance, the world's leaders in high-performance and high-speed paper-making machinery happen to be in the Scandinavian countries. Sonoco can learn about the technologies of the machinery in each country while satisfying the customers' needs. Sonoco capitalizes on what it learns overseas by transferring the new technology to its domestic operations.

COMPETITION

Sonoco's competition lies in several directions. The company is simultaneously involved in the paper, packaging, plastics, partitions, and corrugated products industries, as well as several others. Its focus since 1986, however, has been in the packaging industry. The packaging industry can be divided into four segments, categorized by materials:

1. **Metal Containers (cans).** Sonoco is not involved in this segment. The largest metal container producer in the U.S. market is Triangle Industries.
2. **Glass Containers.** Sonoco does not compete in this segment, either. The glass industry has recently undergone much restructuring and consolidation. Ball Corporation is the leader in glass containers.
3. **Paperboard Products.** This segment includes corrugated boxes, folding cartons, tubes, cores, and cans. It is Sonoco's traditional business and remains the company's strongest area. Sonoco is the industry leader in terms of tubes, cores, and cans, but it does not compete in the carton and box areas, except through one joint venture with Georgia-Pacific. The largest competitor for paperboard products is Jefferson-Smurfit Corporation.
4. **Plastics.** Sonoco considers plastics the wave of the future in packaging and strives to be well positioned for new technology and opportunities for alternative packaging forms. There are many competitors in the plastic packaging business, which has no clear leader. In the Polysack business, Sonoco competes primarily with Mobil Corporation and Surrey Industries.

According to Warren Hayslip, director of planning, all of these areas—metal, glass, and paper—are converging rapidly on plastics. Traditional packaging materials in each of the first three segments are being replaced by plastic products. For this reason, Sonoco's competition for new business can be considered dispersed across the entire packaging industry.

As Sonoco is among the dominant competitors in most of its present markets, much of the company's competition has sought to imitate Sonoco. As Hayslip put it, "The competitors in many markets tend to be smaller, less well capitalized, and often not as advanced in their manufacturing and quality." Overall, Sonoco places more emphasis on its customers than its competition. Dick Puffer stated, "We worry about competition in that Sonoco doesn't want to be surprised. This often means monitoring all segments of the packaging industry. In many of its markets, but especially in converted paper products, Sonoco could end up competing with a company in the metal or glass industry simply because both companies are converging on plastics."

Acknowledging the fact that the $60 billion packaging industry has many players in it, Sonoco strives to compete by differentiating its products. According to Puffer, Sonoco sells value, not just a package. Sonoco attempts to set itself apart from its competition by constantly seeking new and better ways of producing both its industrial and its consumer packages.

Sonoco is the only international producer of paper and industrial packaging products. Consequently, international competition basically comes from local producers within the various countries. This local competition is one of the main reasons that the international operations are set up autonomously.

Sonoco's goal to be in the number one or two position in each of its markets holds true for the international arena as well. Sonoco holds leading market positions in England, Australia, Canada, and Mexico and has good positions in several other countries.

MARKETING

Although Sonoco's products are used in a wide array of packaging and industrial applications, the company name is not well known. Sonoco executives do not consider this lack of identity a problem, however. Increasing the general public's awareness of Sonoco would not generate more sales. It would only inform people about, for example, who manufactures the can in which their Pillsbury biscuits are packaged. Marketing efforts are therefore geared exclusively toward industrial buyers. The primary marketing vehicles used in that effort are industry journals, trade show presentations, brochures, and direct mail campaigns. Following a recent reorganization, each division has its own marketing staff with total responsibility for the division's marketing program.

As a result of its focused diversification within the packaging industry, Sonoco enjoys a remarkable degree of independence and stability in relation to its customer base. No segment of its business is dependent, to any material degree, on a single or few customers, and none of the company's products are seasonal.[19]

A concept shared by the marketing staffs of all divisions is the idea of selling not just a product, but an entire service package. For the most part, the products will sell themselves; especially industrial products, as they are necessary to the manufacturing process and are manufactured to the customer's specifications. The primary task of the marketing force is to persuade and reassure customers that Sonoco is the best company from which to purchase the products. This is done by promoting the company's unique service assets, two of which are just-in-time delivery and statistical process control. The customer is assured that Sonoco will deliver the highest quality products on a dependable delivery schedule. Just-in-time delivery can eliminate expensive inventory carrying costs as well.

With over 200 branch plants worldwide, Sonoco is considered to have an abnormally high number of plants per dollar volume of sales. Having such a great many plants increases overhead, but Sonoco's management believes the advantages of lower transportation costs far outweigh these increases. An important benefit is that the branch plants are located near some of their large customers, enabling Sonoco to quickly meet customers' needs. Few competitors can match Sonoco's just-in-time delivery system. Although expensive in terms of increased scheduling and labor costs, this system has significantly improved Sonoco's reputation for reliable delivery and service.

With its highly trained staff of packaging scientists, Sonoco offers customers a commitment to insuring their products' success. Engineers work with customers to adapt their packing equipment to new packages. The Consumer

Packaging Division runs field checks in the marketplace to discover consumer response to new packages. The Polysack Division offers training programs to increase the efficiency of those using the new grocery bags. Sonoco sells a complete package of services because, as Ray McGowan, general sales manager in consumer products, states, "If we don't, our competitors will." As of 1988, the company had 238 employees engaged in new product development and technical support for existing products. Sonoco's new packaging research facility in Hartsville, which became operational in 1988, added significantly to the customer support effort.

FINANCIAL MANAGEMENT

Through the 1970s and 1980s, Sonoco's growth rate varied between 10 and 15 percent, with prospects for future growth considered excellent. Sonoco passed the $1 billion sales mark in 1987 for the first time. One of management's primary goals is to achieve $3 billion in sales by the mid-1990s. The company's growth history is detailed in Exhibit 2. In 1988, Sonoco's net income was $96,277,000, compared with $61,482,000 in 1987, $54,676,000 in 1986, and $49,409,000 in 1985. This represents an average increase of over 19 percent. Current assets in 1988 totaled nearly $378 million, and Sonoco had over $533 million in property, plant, and equipment. Current liabilities totaled $189.8 million, while long-term debt totalled $275.5 million after quadrupling to $263.5 million the year before. Sonoco's consolidated statements of income for the year ended December 31, 1988, are presented in Exhibit 3, and its consolidated balance sheets for the same period are presented in Exhibit 4 (page 457). Consolidated changes in shareholders' equity are shown in Exhibit 5 (page 458) and cash flows in Exhibit 6 (page 459).

The huge increase in long-term debt was due to the 1987 acquisition of the Consumer Packaging Division of Boise Cascade. The purchase price was $175 million, almost all of which was financed through long-term debt. While the acquisition strengthened Sonoco's position as a major packaging company and increased the size of the company by one-third, a side effect was that substantial cost reductions had to be made. These reductions involved closing eight plants, consolidating activities, and eliminating over 400 jobs. Adjustments also included a $10 million pretax write-off in the fourth quarter of 1987, which translated to almost 13 cents per share.[20]

In the past, debt related to acquisitions had been absorbed by the company's rapid growth in sales. For example, Sonoco's 1985 acquisition of Continental Fibre Drum, for $72 million, was also debt financed. Sonoco generated enough cash, however, to pay off over half the loan within the first year. Absorption of the much larger Boise Cascade acquisition will be more difficult.

The Tax Reform Act of 1986 had no significant effect on Sonoco. Lower tax rates were offset by changes in international tax provisions and by the loss of the Investment Tax Credit. In the future, however, Sonoco expects its overall effective tax rate to drop approximately 40 percent.

EXHIBIT 2 SONOCO'S GROWTH

YEAR	NET SALES	NET INCOME
1900	$17,000	$2,000
1910	132,000	29,000
1920	908,000	304,000
1930	1,598,000	200,000
1940	5,018,000	540,000
1950	18,895,000	1,635,000
1960	38,200,000	2,460,000
1970	125,027,000	6,600,000
1971	135,808,000	8,140,000
1972	154,820,000	8,729,000
1973	188,559,000	11,188,000
1974	225,669,000	13,588,000
1975	199,550,000	14,524,000
1976	242,425,000	18,881,000
1977	270,634,000	20,910,000
1978	344,204,000	23,263,000
1979	421,480,000	27,238,000
1980	490,397,000	32,511,000
1981	533,349,000	38,716,000
1982	538,617,000	29,070,000
1983	668,628,000	37,274,000
1984	740,869,000	42,535,000
1985	869,598,000	49,409,000
1986	963,796,000	54,676,000
1987	1,312,052,000	61,482,000
1988	1,599,751,000	96,277,000

Sources: *The Story of Sonoco* (company publication) and Sonoco Products Company, 1988 Annual Report.

HUMAN RESOURCE MANAGEMENT

A unique aspect of Sonoco is that its personnel department does not measure turnover. According to Jack Westmoreland, director of corporate personnel, "If we ever start having turnover, we'll know it." He went on to explain that when he previously measured personnel turnover, the numbers were almost insignificant. Gradually he reduced the number of times per year it was measured until now it is not reported at all. "Our people stay with us," says Westmoreland.

Traditionally, Sonoco's policy has been to promote from within. The majority of its personnel are hired to fill entry-level positions. Rarely is an experienced manager hired from outside the company and, if so, only for higher-level

EXHIBIT 3 SONOCO PRODUCTS COMPANY CONSOLIDATED BALANCE SHEETS

	1988	1987
ASSETS		
Current Assets		
Cash and cash equivalents	$ 20,375	$ 14,447
Receivables	164,252	140,046
Inventories	163,706	134,427
Prepaid expenses	29,514	32,585
	377,847	321,505
Property, Plant and Equipment	533,427	482,357
Cost in Excess of Fair Value of Assets Purchased	45,809	42,714
Investments in Affiliates	6,642	15,143
Other Assets	13,734	15,906
	$977,459	$877,625
LIABILITIES AND SHAREHOLDERS' EQUITY		
Current Liabilities		
Payable to suppliers and others	$154,013	$160,074
Notes payable and current portion of long-term debt	22,465	10,850
Taxes on income	13,284	6,609
	189,762	177,533
Long-Term Debt	275,535	263,489
Deferred Income Taxes	57,676	56,691
Shareholders' Equity		
Common shares, no par value		
Authorized 75,000,000 shares		
Issued 45,920,440 shares	7,175	7,175
Capital in excess of stated value	45,982	45,847
Translation of foreign currencies	(3,516)	(9,137)
Retained earnings	417,115	348,884
Treasury shares at cost (1988–2,059,607, 1987–2,154,779)	(12,270)	(12,857)
	454,486	379,912
	$997,459	$877,625

Note: Amounts are in thousands.

Source: Sonoco Products Company, *1988 Annual Report.*

EXHIBIT 4   SONOCO PRODUCTS COMPANY CONSOLIDATED INCOME STATEMENTS

	1988	1987	1986
Sales	$1,599,751	$1,312,052	$963,796
Cost and expenses			
Cost of products sold	1,263,978	1,044,556	761,121
Selling, general and administrative expenses	148,417	129,176	96,957
Interest expense	25,175	18,593	8,552
Acquisition consolidation charges		10,000	
Income from operations before income taxes	162,181	109,727	97,166
Taxes on income	67,029	48,714	44,435
Income from operations before equity in earnings of affiliates	95,152	61,013	52,731
Equity in earnings of affiliates	1,125	469	1,945
Net income	$ 96,277	$ 61,482	$ 54,676
Average shares outstanding	43,816,224	43,865,245	43,806,380
Net income per share	$2.20	$1.40	$1.25
Dividends per share	$.64	$.50	$.41

Note: Dollars in thousands except per share.

Source: Sonoco Products Company, *1988 Annual Report.*

positions. In recent years, however, rapid growth has forced Sonoco to depend more on outside hiring, especially in new technical areas such as plastics. When interviewing for a salaried position, a prospective employee meets and talks to eight to ten people during the first visit, estimates Westmoreland. Upon being hired, every new salaried employee meets individually with the president, vice-presidents, and chief officers of the company.

Sonoco communicates with its employees through posted notices and through *Sonoco News,* published monthly by the public relations department. The company also encourages feedback from its employees. By using the "Sonofone" system, employees can complain or ask questions. A secretary takes the calls and, if the caller chooses to be identified, will receive a personal response that day from an executive who is qualified to answer. If the employee does not wish to be identified, a response to the question or complaint will be posted in each department. Sonoco's open door policy, which is printed in the company's policy manual, states that employees can approach any manager—even the president—with a problem or inquiry.

Sonoco's employee benefits package includes fully paid health and dental plans. A thrift and savings plan is also offered, in which the company will match a percentage of each dollar saved in Sonoco's credit union. The credit

EXHIBIT 5 SONOCO PRODUCTS COMPANY CONSOLIDATED STATEMENTS OF CHANGES IN SHAREHOLDERS' EQUITY

	COMMON SHARES	CAPITAL IN EXCESS OF STATED VALUE	TRANSLATION OF FOREIGN CURRENCIES	RETAINED EARNINGS	TREASURY SHARES
January 1, 1986............	$7,175	$45,802	$(19,428)	$272,631	$(10,437)
Net income...................				54,676	
Dividends, $.41 per share...				(17,963)	
Translation gain (net of $631 in taxes)..............			427		
Issuance of treasury shares under stock option plan.		(127)			134
December 31, 1986.........	7,175	45,675	(19,001)	309,344	(10,303)
Net income...................				61,482	
Dividends, $.50 per share...				(21,942)	
Translation gain (net of $879 in taxes)..............			9,864		
Issuance of treasury shares under stock option plan.		172			475
Treasury shares acquired...					(3,029)
December 31, 1987.........	7,175	45,847	(9,137)	348,884	(12,857)
Net income...................				96,277	
Dividends, $.64 per share...				(28,046)	
Translation gain (net of $171 in taxes)..............			5,621		
Issuance of treasury shares under stock option plan.		135			587
December 31, 1988.........	$7,175	$45,982	$ (3,516)	$417,115	$(12,270)

Note: Dollars in thousands.

Source: Sonoco Products Company, *1988 Annual Report.*

union also extends loans to employees at low rates of interest. An employee stock ownership plan is offered to key employees. At the end of 1987, some 4,808 employees participated in the plan.[21]

Sonoco's relations with organized labor have always been placid. The company's main plant at Hartsville is nonunion. Sonoco's approach to preventive labor relations is straightforward: "If we treat employees right—give them fair pay, good benefits—they won't need a union," says Westmoreland. Although its main plant has remained nonunion, employees at many of the subsidiaries acquired in expansion are represented by collective bargaining contracts. In 1988, approximately half of Sonoco's eligible employees were unionized. The

EXHIBIT 6 CONSOLIDATED STATEMENTS OF CASH FLOWS

	1988	1987	1986
Cash Flows From Operating Activities			
Net income	$ 96,277	$ 61,482	$ 54,676
Adjustments to reconcile net income to net cash provided by operating activities:			
Depreciation, depletion and amortization	69,055	57,086	35,654
Gain on sale of stock of affiliated companies	(3,980)	(1,224)	
Loss on assets retired	340	1,540	1,259
Dividends from affiliates	807	1,437	312
Equity in earnings of affiliates	(1,125)	(469)	(1,945)
Exchange (gain) loss	(62)	713	(1,961)
Increase in deferred taxes	413	1,945	7,284
Provision for losses on accounts receivable	962	1,908	774
Changes in assets and liabilities net of effects from acquisitions and foreign currency adjustments:			
(Increase) in accounts receivable	(17,270)	(29,401)	(8,127)
(Increase) decrease in inventory	(24,530)	(14,901)	2,196
(Increase) in prepaid expenses	(62)	(13,582)	(15,735)
Increase in payables and taxes	5,685	28,041	16,846
(Increase) in other assets and liabilities	(2,777)	(4,440)	(304)
Net cash provided by operating activities	123,733	90,135	90,929
Cash Flows From Investing Activities			
Purchase of property, plant and equipment	(93,599)	(104,757)	(45,072)
Cost of acquisitions, exclusive of cash	(35,266)	(170,517)	(22,217)
Sale (purchase) of stock of affiliated companies	16,275	3,995	(969)
Proceeds from the sale of assets	4,583	2,166	2,201
Net cash used by investing activities	(108,007)	(269,113)	(66,057)
Cash Flows From Financing Activities			
Proceeds from issuance of debt	51,171	214,971	25,010
Principal repayment of debt	(32,642)	(22,781)	(27,585)
Cash dividends	(30,243)	(20,841)	(16,868)
Treasury shares acquired		(3,029)	
Other	710	713	(1,961)
Net cash (used) provided by financing activities	(11,004)	169,033	(21,404)
Effects of exchange rate changes on cash	1,206	4,083	(2,230)
Increase (decrease) in Cash and Cash Equivalents	5,928	(5,862)	1,238
Cash and Cash Equivalents at beginning of year	14,447	20,309	19,071
Cash and Cash Equivalents at end of year	$ 20,375	$ 14,447	$ 20,309
Supplemental cash flow disclosure			
Interest paid	$ 24,185	$ 17,373	$ 5,836
Income taxes paid	$ 63,086	$ 48,110	$ 28,337

Note: Dollars in thousands.

Source: Sonoco Products Company, *1988 Annual Report.*

company has a good reputation of getting along well with these unions, stressing cooperation instead of confrontation.

CORPORATE CULTURE AT SONOCO

In an address to the operations committee on July 20, 1987, P. C. Coggeshall, Sr., former senior executive vice-president, presented a list of words he felt described the culture at Sonoco. Included in this list were, of course, such ideas as honesty, integrity, and fairness. Coggeshall also mentioned other characteristics that, although not unique to Sonoco, have been instrumental in the company's success. One of these terms is "family control." Through the years the Coker sons have not only been willing to be involved in the family business, but have also been fully capable of managing this ever-growing company. Although each man had his own particular insights, this handing down of leadership has kept individual talents focused on the company's primary goals and has lent stability to the overall operation.

Another characteristic is the "organizational pride" that Sonoco instills in its employees. Ever since its beginnings during the Reconstruction period, the company has been forced to deal with adverse and changing conditions. According to Coggeshall, "This history and pride allows teamwork to flourish. . . . Performance stimulating pride, stimulating performance."[22] Employees at Sonoco "work hard but enjoy what they're doing," explains Westmoreland. "This is true at every level."

The concept of teamwork is a guiding principle at Sonoco. Evidence of this idea appears in *Sonoco News*, where headlines read, "Teamwork Makes a Good Idea Work," and "To Build the Championship Team."[23] Company president C. W. Coker has expressed to the shareholders the importance of having employees who are committed to achieving the goals of both their specific division and the company as a whole. "We believe that our mission and our goals are understood by our employees. This is important, because our chances of success are enhanced as our employees all pull in the same direction." As Coker explains, one of the goals at Sonoco "is to foster an atmosphere of teamwork . . . and maintain the loyalty and dedication that is tradition among all Sonoco employees."[24] It is the recognition of this fact that has led the company to be people oriented. Westmoreland claims that although many businesses say they have a people orientation, at Sonoco this is not simply a philosophy but a "genuine, sincere approach" to operating the business. Management practices are based on treating every individual with respect and consideration.

From its inception, Sonoco has had strong ties with its people. It started as a family-run business, and early employees, growing up in the small town of Hartsville, knew the Coker family personally. The company has tried to hold on to this relationship with its people in spite of its growth and success. While tradition remains important, the company is also aware of the benefits of embracing new attitudes. Coggeshall points out that after the acquisition of another company, the plan is not to make new employees into traditional Sonoco workers. Instead, an attempt is made to merge the new cultures, drawing on the strengths of each possibly very different way of corporate life.

Employees are encouraged to develop their talents and ideas through Sonoco's program of incentive compensation. Employees are given monetary awards for suggestions adopted by the company. In December 1986, the second-largest award ever earned ($19,118) was received by a worker in the cone department. The employee commented that his supervisors had been very cooperative in working on the idea. "I was proud to be able to help the company as well as myself. I am fortunate to work for a company that has such a fine suggestion system."[25]

Another form of incentive compensation is the company's program for educational reimbursement. Under Sonoco's educational policy, the company will reimburse an employee for 75 percent of the expenses involved in job-related training. Safety is also an important part of employee development. Prizes are awarded for having a perfect safety record. Loyalty and faithful service are recognized in a unique way. After working for the company for twenty-five years, employees can become members of the "Old Timers Club," which allows them to participate in special company-sponsored events. The team spirit concept is supplemented through the company's sponsorship of bowling teams and both men's and women's softball teams.

The team concept at Sonoco goes beyond the workers and the company and extends to its customers. "Giving them what they have a right to expect and a little more" defines Sonoco's "customer orientation." "We will focus on our customers," claims Coker. "We exist to help them achieve their goals, and only if they grow profitably will we have the opportunity to do likewise. It is absolutely essential that we provide products and services which are responsive to present and longer term needs of our customers."[26] Sonoco personnel often work with customers to develop new products and applications. Says Coker, "Change is a way of life with us and, if anything, the rate of change will only accelerate in the future."[27]

STRATEGY

By focusing its growth in activities with which it is familiar, Sonoco has maintained a first- or second-place market share in all of its markets. Starting with paper cores in 1899 and moving gradually into other areas (such as packaging), the company has grown consistently at a rate of 15 percent in recent years. Maintaining this growth, however, has not been without problems. Until 1985, the company's marketing, engineering, and personnel functions were staffed at the corporate level. Each division would "pay" the company for the use of these services. With growth and the addition of new divisions such as Polysack and Consumer Packaging, the demand for these services became greater and more diverse. The task of coordinating the services in order to meet the needs for various departments became increasingly cumbersome. In

1985, it was decided that many of the divisions had grown large enough to be responsible for staffing these functions on their own. The process of "divisionalization" was begun.

At first it was a struggle for those working in corporate offices to start new departments in these areas. People were forced to become very specialized in areas they barely had been exposed to previously. Toby Reynolds, manager of marketing services for IPD, explained that he had never developed an ad or created a brochure before the divisionalization took place. Although in 1988 his department was still in what he called a "learning mode," he predicted that by the following year the transition would be complete.

In spite of the difficulty of adjustment, Sonoco management feels that the new system will be of great benefit to the company. According to Ray McGowan, each division will be able to "manage business more clearly and be more focused on what our needs are rather than fit into a mode that has to meet everyone's needs." Having these skills more readily available has made it easier to accomplish many tasks that formerly required a few feet of red tape.

The staffing aspects of implementing a rapid growth strategy can be very problematic. Sonoco believes that the key to effective hiring is to find the right type of management talent first, and then allow the managers to staff their own departments. In a rapid growth situation, this process can be prohibitively time consuming. Fortunately for Sonoco, much of its growth has come through acquisitions that happened to have very talented managers. McGowan, who came to the company in its acquisition of Container Corporation of America, estimates that three-fourths of the people in the Consumer Packaging sales department came to Sonoco via acquisitions.

With most acquisitions there is a period of adjustment in which to discover how the strengths of the two companies can best be combined to achieve the company's overall strategy. Customers' expectation of "business as usual" from the day of the purchase can cause frustrations for all involved. The management at Sonoco feels that its strategy of balanced growth—combining acquisitions such as Boise Cascade with internal growth, such as its Polysack Division—is the most effective one for lessening these effects while capitalizing on acquisition opportunities.

Sonoco's growth pattern has changed through the years. Initially, the company was known as a paper company that also made a few packaging products. In 1986, senior management decided to refocus the strategy of Sonoco to a "packaging company that happens to be vertically integrated." Much of Sonoco's business in the 1970s was still concentrated in the textile industry; if this had not changed, it is questionable where the company would be today. By focusing on the packaging industry, especially consumer packaging, Sonoco's competitive position has improved greatly. In addition, as one industry analyst has noted, as many of the consumer packaging products are linked to lower-cost or staple items such as food and cleaning agents, economically troubled times should not affect Sonoco as dramatically as they will some companies.[28]

The term "focused diversification" has been used to describe Sonoco's strategy. All of its products are either directly in the packaging industry or are packaging related. While plastic packaging products are, for example, different from the company's typical products, the commonality of their end use is the same. Sonoco's decision to focus on packaging meant divesting some of its subsidiaries. A metal building subsidiary, although very profitable, was divested in 1985. A common carrier trucking subsidiary was also sold.

In addition to Sonoco's diversification strategy, the company seeks to be a low-cost producer. This strategy is apparent through the many branch plants located throughout the U.S. and overseas. The plants are often located near major customers, allowing for just-in-time delivery. Sonoco also has what are called "focused factories" that produce only one product, thus providing increased efficiency and decreased complexity in the manufacturing process.

Even though "responsiveness" is one of the driving forces in Sonoco's plants, it can cause problems. With very short lead times, methods for predicting the future demands of customers are not much help. Therefore, when a sudden influx of orders occurs, scheduling work can be difficult. Certain customers have priority, and when one of them calls in an order to be delivered the next day, not only are other orders pushed behind, but overhead costs are increased due to overtime. Just-in-time delivery is a distinct advantage for Sonoco and its customers and its customers is an important means of differentiating Sonoco's products, but in 1988 its implementation had not yet included long enough lead times for production processes to be scheduled efficiently.

There are three main determining factors in the company's strategic decision making process. The first is the concept of leadership. According to Dick Puffer, "Sonoco wants to be the top producer in the market if it can be." A second-place position in the market is also acceptable, and third place will be reluctantly accepted if the business is a profitable one. If Sonoco's position is any lower, it will sell the business. Sonoco bases this objective on an analysis of the PIMS database, which indicates that in order to accumulate reasonable returns, a company must be among its market's top three competitors. Puffer says that the second factor in the company's decision to venture into a business is whether or not it can "become the low-cost producer or one of the low-cost producers." As mentioned earlier, Sonoco operates at very high efficiency levels. The company prides itself on producing a quality product at a low cost. The third determining factor in the decision-making process is value. Top executives ask themselves "what kind of value can Sonoco offer to the customer to make it worth the customer's while to buy from a new person entering the market." Basically, the question of what new business to enter goes back to the customer.

The formal strategic planning process at Sonoco also has been decentralized along division lines. Each of twelve operating groups is responsible for planning its own future and making its own business-level strategic decisions. A corporate planning group looks at the overall company and considers issues that cannot be addressed by the operating groups. The corporate planning department decides both what businesses to enter and which to avoid or divest. Warren Hayslip, director of planning, says that strategic thinking must take place throughout the organization, for every decision. "It is not simply, 'we want to be bigger or we would like to make these products'; there is an in-depth justification of capital and in-depth analysis."

As the company operates in a global economy, its strategy also has an international dimension. The International Division of Sonoco expects continued growth. Hayslip states that "Sonoco's worldwide strategy is multidomestic in the sense that we have separate operations that are linked together by technology, by know-how, by financial resources, etc., but the operations are autonomous to a large extent in that they have their own marketing team, their own manufacturing team, their own plants, and they function as a separate operating unit." The International Division's strategy basically is to leverage what Sonoco has in the U.S. According to Mike Bullington, International Operations are expected to grow geographically at a "10–12 percent compounded growth rate for the next 5 years." In many of the countries, Sonoco will attack a specific niche in a market. For example, surveys have shown that in Taiwan Sonoco could not be a broad-line producer of products. Consequently, Sonoco will try to segment this market by focusing on products that cannot be made by local producers. The niche will be high-quality, specialty products such as sophisticated film cores.

CONCLUSION

From its beginnings as a small producer of paper tubes and cones for the southeastern textile industry at the dawn of the twentieth century, Sonoco has become a supplier of industrial products, consumer packages, and plastic containers for corporations throughout the U.S. and overseas. With Sonoco's goal of becoming the leading U.S. packaging company, one would expect its management to be one that gambles, jumping at every opportunity for expansion. Sonoco's management has, however, traditionally chosen to let the company grow slowly, concentrating on the products and technologies most familiar to the company.

Sonoco's focus has undergone a series of related shifts over the years. The first was the step from industrial products to consumer packaging, primarily the manufacture of composite cans. The company used its technological expertise in converted paper products to enter this new market. Once it was established in the new industry, Sonoco began acquiring expertise to enter new segments of the packaging arena, such as plastic oil containers.

Sonoco's acquisition of Boise Cascade's consumer packaging activities in 1987 represents a departure from the company's slow-growth policy. The merger will potentially place Sonoco at the top of several of its most important business segments, but at a high cost. The company has taken on more debt than it has ever had. Although Sonoco officials feel that the company has sufficient resources for much more growth, the restrictions that increased debt places on top management are significant. Higher fixed obligations for debt service will necessitate more attention to cash flow and may restrict the amount of capital the company can invest in new packaging technology. Further strategic expansion may be limited as a result of the company's higher leverage position.

It took Sonoco eighty-seven years to reach the billion-dollar sales mark. Coker expects the company's sales to reach $3 billion by the mid-1990s and states that the company will continue to grow because a growing company provides the best security for employees, customers, and suppliers. This is not the goal of a complacent, inward-looking company. In 1988 the question remained as to whether or not this family-run corporation can continue to absorb its newly initiated rapid growth while maintaining its reputation for quality and service.

ENDNOTES

Much of the information for this case was derived from interviews conducted in March 1988 with the following Sonoco personnel:

- Rick Brown, marketing manager, Polysack Division
- Mike Bullington, director of international staff
- P. C. Coggeshall, senior executive vice-president
- Warren Hayslip, director of planning
- Charlie Hupfer, director of tax and audit
- Ray McGowan, general sales manager, Consumer Products Division
- Dick Puffer, director of public relations and corporate advertising
- Toby Reynolds, manager of marketing services, Industrial Products Division
- J. E. Westmoreland, director of corporate personnel

1. *The Story of Sonoco Paper Products Since 1899* (Hartsville, S.C.: Sonoco Products Company, 1977): 3.
2. Ibid., pp. 4–5.
3. "The Fortune 500," *Fortune* (April 24, 1989): 362.
4. Sonoco Products Company, *Form 10-K, 1987*.
5. Sonoco Products Company, *1987 Annual Report*, p. 5.
6. "Sonoco Named Certified Supplier for 3M," *Sonoco News* (January 1988): 7.
7. *Investment Research* (Hartsville, S.C.: Sonoco Products Company, 1988.)
8. Sonoco Products Company, *1987 Annual Report*, p. 5.
9. "NYC Grocer Cuts Operating Costs 10% with Sonoco Plastic Sacks," *Sonoco Solutions* (Hartsville, S.C.: Sonoco Products Company, 1988): 1.
10. Fladung, Thom. "Sonoco on Front Line in Battle to Woo Customers," *The State* (Columbia, S.C.) (December 21, 1987): B1.
11. *You Get More Out of Packaging with Sonoco*. Sonoco publication no. SP1212, 1987.
12. "Oklahoma Grocer Increases Front-end Productivity, Frees Up Labor with New Express Lane Check-out and Plastic Sacks," *Sonoco Solutions* (Hartsville, S.C.: Sonoco Products Company, 1988): 1.
13. "Sonoco Products Company," *NCNB Investment Research* (November 16, 1987): 3.
14. Sonoco Products Company, *1987 Annual Report*, p. 7.
15. Ibid., p. 6.
16. Ibid.
17. Sonoco Products Company, *1985 Annual Report*, inside cover.
18. Sonoco Products Company, *1987 Annual Report*, pp. 6–7.
19. Sonoco Products Company, *Form 10-K, 1987*.
20. Sonoco Products Company, *1987 Annual Report*, p. 13.
21. Sonoco Products Company, *Form 10-K 1987*.
22. Matthews, R. W., "To Build the Championship Team," *Sonoco News* (February, 1988): 3.
23. *Sonoco News* (February 1988).
24. "Coker Credits Company Success to Loyal, Dedicated, Employees," *Sonoco News* (May 1987): 5.
25. "Teamwork Makes a Good Idea Work," *Sonoco News* (February, 1988): 7.
26. *Sonoco News* (January, 1987).
27. "Coker Credits Company Success to Loyal, Dedicated, Employees."
28. Fladung, "Sonoco on Front Line."

CASE 9

EASTMAN KODAK COMPANY: THE STERLING DRUG ACQUISITION

DAVID W. GRIGSBY AND
CHARLES G. CARTER

By any measure one cares to choose, Eastman Kodak Company is one of the premier success stories of American business. Begun in 1877 as a part-time venture by the photographic pioneer and inventor, George W. Eastman, the company quickly became the foremost producer of photographic equipment and supplies in the world, a position it has held ever since. By 1989, Eastman Kodak had diversified into a wide range of high-technology products and services. Its sales in 1988 were over $17 billion, and it was listed as #18 on the Fortune 500.

Eastman Kodak's story has not been without its ups and downs, however, and the 1980s proved to be especially troubling times for the photographic giant. Competitive challenges in Kodak's basic product markets and new technological challenges to its dominance of the industry caused top executives to rethink the company's basic mission and objectives. The result was a number of important changes at Eastman Kodak, some of which have significantly altered the way the company does business. These changes include the complete reorganization of the company's operating divisions, the repositioning of many of Kodak's product lines, and the multibillion-dollar acquisition of Sterling Drug Co., a major producer of pharmaceuticals and household products.

Early in 1989, as the company entered its 100th year of incorporation, Colby Chandler, Kodak's CEO and chairman of the board, had reason to be pleased with the way these changes were going. He also knew, however, that the once-complacent giant company would face even greater challenges in its next 100 years.

Source: Prepared by Professor David W. Grigsby and Research Assistant Charles G. Carter, Clemson University, as a basis for classroom discussion and not to illustrate either effective or ineffective handling of administrative situations. © David W. Grigsby, 1990.

HISTORY OF THE COMPANY

Eastman Kodak's founder, George Washington Eastman, was born in Waterville, New York, on July 12, 1854.[1] His family moved to Rochester in 1860, where his father had established the city's first commercial college. George's father died two years later, leaving his mother to take in boarders to supplement the family's modest income. The deprivation of his childhood impressed upon Eastman the importance of thrift, which, in time, came to be one of his most notable characteristics. After seven years in the public schools, Eastman took a job in a Rochester insurance office. At the age of 20 he secured a position as junior bookkeeper at the Rochester Savings Bank, where he advanced rapidly. By age 21, Eastman had managed to save over $3,000, which was over twice his annual salary.

At the age of 23, Eastman became fascinated with photography and spent ninety-four of his carefully saved dollars on photographic equipment. He began developing his own prints and soon was experimenting with new methods of reducing the weight and size of photographic equipment in use at the time. By 1879 Eastman had obtained patents on a coating machine, which he used to begin a part-time business preparing photographic plates. In 1880, Eastman left his job with the bank to devote all of his time to the business.

In 1884, Eastman began experimenting with various substitutes for the bulky glass "dry plates" in widespread use at the time. That year he developed a paper-backed flexible film that could be cut into strips and wound on rollers. He renamed his company the Eastern Dry Plate and Film Company and raised new capital of $200,000 to market his inventions. The company introduced its first camera the following year, 1885. Film rolls for 100 pictures were mounted inside a small box camera called the Kodak, which sold for $25. The camera had to be returned to the company for developing. National advertising was launched featuring the slogan "You push the button, we do the rest." The age of amateur photography had begun, although photography was still a relatively expensive hobby.

Further research at the Eastman Company resulted in rapid advances in film and photographic equipment. At the request of Thomas A. Edison, a transparent film was developed in 1887 to be used in his then-experimental motion picture camera. The Eastman Company was incorporated in 1890 with a capital stock issue of $1 million and reorganized two years later as Eastman Kodak Company with capital of $5 million. Expansion continued despite the financial panics of the 1890s, and a second reorganization occurred in 1898, with capital stock of $8 million.

In 1891 a daylight-loading film, which eliminated the necessity of sending cameras back to the company for developing, was introduced. Cheap pocket Kodaks priced as low as $5 put photography within every person's reach by 1895, and photography then became a mass-market hobby. The company continued to expand through the first three decades of the twentieth century, with capital doubling every few years.

By 1900, Eastman Kodak employed 3,000 workers. The original factory on State Street in Rochester was expanded, and a new facility known as Kodak Park was developed north of the city. A branch plant was opened in Harrow, England, to manufacture equipment and film for the rapidly growing European market.

At times, Eastman had difficulty exercising control over his greatly expanded business. He made decisions independently on the board of directors and summarily fired anyone who disagreed with his views. Eastman sought loyalty among his employees, however, through liberal employee benefit programs and some of the most progressive wage bonus plans in existence. Although he refused to allow collective bargaining, Eastman sought to reduce turnover with up-to-date medical facilities, social programs, improved lunchroom facilities, and shorter working hours. Loyalty was high among Eastman Kodak employees, who numbered 15,000 by 1920.

Instrumental in the early growth of Eastman Kodak were a number of successful battles fought for dominance of the photographic equipment market. From the earliest days of the company, George Eastman had been fiercely protective of his position in the industry. In 1892, he discharged Henry Reichenbach, one of his closest assistants, along with two others, when it was disclosed that the three were planning to form a rival company. A number of other rival companies were simply bought out, usually at premium prices. In 1898, Eastman bought out all the photographic paper producers in the United States and contracted with a European cartel to buy all of its product shipped to the U.S. Photographic equipment dealers were required to sign exclusive contracts with Kodak. An arrangement with Edison also assured Eastman of exclusive access to the burgeoning motion picture film market. The result of these dealings was a 75- to 80-percent share of the home photography market and virtually all of the photographic paper and motion picture film markets. Eastman Kodak's profit margin in 1912, averaged across all product lines, was over 71 percent.

Antitrust sentiment began to grow, and in 1915 the firm was found to be in violation of several antitrust regulations by a federal court. Upon appeal, Eastman agreed to sell off several subsidiaries and modify his business practices. In return, the Justice Department agreed to drop the case.

Eastman, who was a lifelong bachelor, became one of the country's leading philanthropists, dispensing most of his vast fortune during his lifetime. His gifts added substantially to the endowments of M.I.T., the University of Rochester, and a number of other institutions.

At the time of Eastman's death, the company he founded had grown to enormous size. In addition to the Rochester and Harrow facilities, there were manufacturing plants in Kingsport, Tennessee, and in France, Germany, Australia, and Hungary. The main plant at Kodak Park covered 240 acres and held 120 buildings. Over 9,500 workers were employed in the Rochester area alone. Eastman committed suicide on March 12, 1932, at the age of 77. He left a note that read, "My work is done, why wait?"

Kodak continued to grow and prosper after Eastman's death, and became, in every sense of the word, the giant of the photographic industry. The company enjoyed a virtual monopoly from the time the silver halide photographic imaging process became a manufacturing reality. So invincible was the company that employees within the company referred to Kodak as "The Great Yellow Father."

A significant milestone in photography, as well as in the growth of the company, was the advent of reliable color processing, which put color photography within the budgets of advertisers, magazine publishers, and amateur photographers. In the 1940s, Eastman Kodak scientists invented and patented the Kodacolor process, which quickly became the standard color film processing system. Following the advent of Kodacolor, the vast majority of all color processing in the U.S. was done in Kodak's labs. In the mid-1950s, Eastman Kodak was ordered to divest much of its photoprocessing capacity under an antitrust consent decree handed down in the federal courts. Kodak then began licensing the process to independent photoprocessing firms throughout the country and selling them photographic paper and supplies to use in the process.

Kodak continued to grow throughout the 1950s and 1960s despite a number of other unfavorable antitrust rulings. Its Instamatic and Pocket Instamatic cameras made higher-quality amateur photography easier for millions of consumers, and the company's professional products maintained their reputation for high quality and dependability. A series of incidents beginning in the late 1960's, however, rocked the company to its very foundation.

COMPETITION WITH JAPAN

Around 1967, the two Japanese photographic companies Konishiroko and Fuji began targeting the United States photographic market. Their first target was the very profitable photographic paper market, in which Kodak held a virtual monopoly. Kodak, with its hold on the market, had concentrated on high product quality, developing the best papers for true color representation in finished photographs. The Japanese entered the market with lower-quality papers and began competing for the photofinishers' paper business on the basis of lower price. In most cases, the amateur photographers served by the photofinisher could not discern a difference in the end product (their Christmas pictures of Aunt Jane and the family still looked like Aunt Jane and the family). Meanwhile, the profit margins of the photofinishers increased as they bought larger and larger amounts of the cheaper Japanese papers.

Konishiroka and Fuji concentrated their quality control efforts on improving the batch-to-batch consistency of their product. This innovation reduced set-up costs for the photofinisher. Kodak continued to stress the overall quality of its papers, ignoring the batch-to-batch consistency dimension. Kodak's share of the photographic paper market continued to decline. In the early 1970s, Konishiroka acquired Photomat Corporation, a chain of photofinishers, to further solidify its share of the U.S. photographic paper industry.

On another front, Fuji Photo Film Corporation, which was a familiar company in the Far East but not well known in the U.S., concluded from market studies in the early 1970s that Kodak had diverted its attention from the retail photo film business. According to Fuji, Kodak spent little time and effort merchandising film at retail locations. Sensing this as a weakness, Fuji launched a drive to gain placement of its film in the same stores that carried Kodak. To gain retail acceptance, Fuji merchandised its products in multiroll packages using colorful point-of-sale displays. The strategy worked. Fuji Photo Film USA, Inc. quickly grabbed nearly 10 percent of the retail film business. Kodak countered the measures, but never fully recaptured the market share loss.

At the same time, Kodak, lulled to sleep by its dominance in the industry, allowed manufacturing costs to increase. Suppliers were recruited out of provincialism and convenience to plants rather than low cost/quality bidding. Since gross margins were near 70 percent for film and photographic paper, cost considerations were not of the utmost importance and the high mark-up covered many unfortunate choices.

Kodak also was vulnerable in its foreign markets. International sales, which accounted for a substantial portion of Kodak's revenue, dropped as Agfa, a West German Film manufacturer, aggressively pushed for shelf space in Europe and South America.

Other product lines within Kodak suffered as well. In the early 1970s the company elected not to develop a 35mm camera line, only to see Japanese 35mm cameras replace the Pocket Instamatic as the amateur camera of choice. In an attempt to reestablish its dominance in the camera market, Kodak introduced its disk-format camera in 1982. Kodak also allowed Polaroid to develop the instant photo concept without challenge until 1983. When Kodak did release its own version of the instant-picture camera, Polaroid sued Kodak for patent infringement.

Kodak has always seen quality as an essential product ingredient. This rigid adherence to high quality has sometimes cost the company dearly, however. For example, Kodak, targeting the high end of the photocopier market, continued to make copier parts from metal rather than the less expensive molded plastic while Xerox, Sharp, Canon, and others found that profits were much higher at the lower end of the market, where lower manufacturing costs were important to stay competitive. Kodak's refusal to shift its focus and sacrifice quality cost it competitive position by pricing its product out of the largest and most profitable segment of the photocopier market.

Kodak's woes were exacerbated by two unforeseen economic events. In the 1960s and 1970s, silver, one of the main ingredients in photographic film, sold in the twenty- to thirty-dollar range per ounce. By 1980, silver had risen to just over fifty dollars per ounce, due in large part to a scheme by the Hunt brothers of Texas to control the silver market. This high price persisted for nearly a year. Eventually, shortages of silver eased and prices began to return to historic levels. Just as silver prices adjusted downward and gross margins were returning to former levels, however, the dollar rose relative to foreign currency making foreign goods cheaper in the U.S. and U.S. goods more expensive overseas. Fuji, recognizing this unique opportunity, sharply reduced prices of its basic consumer film. Kodak was forced to compete in price with Fuji, but at a staggering cost. The *New York Times* estimated that the combined effects of the silver shortage plus the dollar value fluctuation cost Kodak in the neighborhood of $3.5 billion over a five-year period.

Kodak's problems were not limited to product considerations. The company's management style reflected the culture of a slow-moving, lumbering giant. As the mainstay of the product line had remained stable for over a quarter of a century, there had been little incentive to innovate, take risk, or move quickly. At best, Kodak's cradle-to-grave, paternalistic, insular attitudes generated loyalty and stability in the work force. At worst, this management style stifled entrepreneurial spirit, a desire to compete, and the ability to respond to market changes quickly.

As Kodak had grown in the post–World War II economy, the company had added layers to the management organization. What resulted was the classic deep and tall organization structure. Much of the power within the organization resided in top management and staff positions, however. Corporate planning and research managers controlled the flow of information within the organization and authorized spending for new products. The financial staff determined product prices, and research staffs often had the final say as to whether and when new products were to be released. These managers often forced product decisions through the chain of command all the way up to the corporate management committee. Exhibit 1 illustrates the company's organizational structure up to 1981.

Even with the thoroughness of Kodak's approach to manufacturing and quality control and an army of corporate managers, some important business functions were not being done. Robert Murray, a corporate financial executive in 1976, noticed that no one had the responsibility to track corporate market share and competitive activity.

KODAK IN THE 1970s AND 1980s

Two major threats faced the company in the late 1970s. The first was a threat to its technological dominance in the photographic industry, and the second was the introduction of electronic imaging as a replacement for traditional chemical imaging processes. In terms of the first threat, Kodak had long been the leader in silver halide processes, but the Japanese had made significant strides in the last few years. Fuji had successfully developed the first commercially viable 1000-speed film, and there had been other breakthroughs that suggested that Kodak's technological leadership might be questioned.

A more significant threat was the replacement of silver halide photography with electronics. In the early 1970s, Kodak's management become convinced that electronic imaging would someday replace traditional chemical imaging. Although electronic photography still had a long way to go, in terms of resolution and color rendering, before it matched the quality available in

EXHIBIT 1 EASTMAN KODAK, 1981

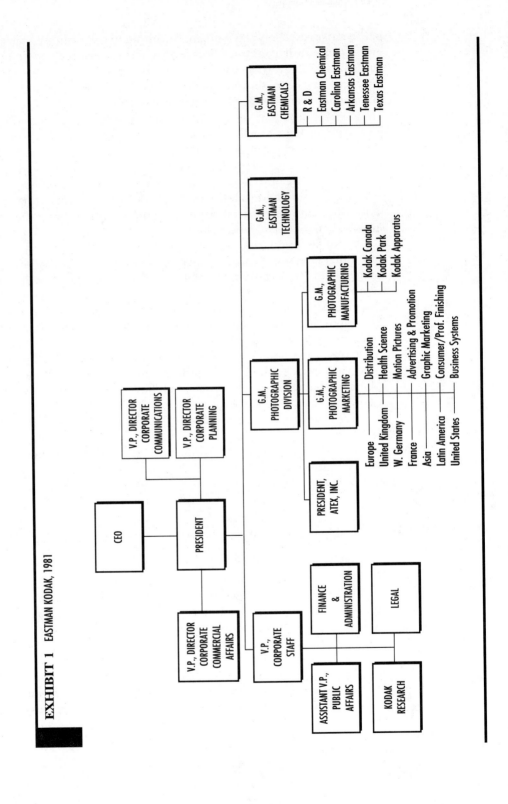

chemical imaging, advances were being made rapidly. Electronic imaging, when fully developed, would have advantages over chemical processes. Electronic images would be available for use instantaneously (no chemical processing), and they could be transmitted electronically in digital format over telephone lines and computer networks. The advantages, moreover, were significant to heavy users of Kodak products, such as the print journalism industry. It was clear to Kodak's management that if the company wanted to remain in the imaging business, it would have to acquire an expertise in electronics.

Accompanying this anticipated redefinition of the company's principal business were a multitude of other reasons for expanding the technological base of the company. One of the most compelling was the opportunity to draw on Kodak's considerable expertise in organic chemicals, an area that could be applied in a number of businesses.

In 1972, Kodak management adopted a plan for expanding the company's range of activities into other areas. Three industries were targeted for expansion: (1) electronic imaging and computer mass storage devices, (2) pharmaceuticals and biotechnology, and (3) photofinishing. To provide a vehicle for the purchase of enterprises within these three targeted industries, Eastman Kodak organized Eastman Technology, Inc.

The Technology Group's first purchase was Spin Physics of San Diego, California, in 1972. Spin Physics developed and manufactured high-technology magnetic recording disks for computer technology. In 1981, Eastman Kodak purchased Atex, Inc., a developer of computer-based text and graphics equipment. Along with Eikonix, purchased in 1985, these two companies served the newspaper printing business and expanded into desktop publishing and word processing equipment and software. Recognizing the tremendous growth of personal computers and the mass storage needed to store data within computers, Kodak purchased Verbatim Corporation, makers of the well-known Data-Life floppy disks for $175 million in 1985.

Several acquisitions were made in the pharmaceutical and biotechnology industries. BioImage Corporation, a maker of analytical equipment for medical and biotechnology applications, was acquired in 1986. Genecor, an industrial biotechnology research and development company, and International Biotechnologies, a manufacturer of biological agents and molecular instrumentation for universities, hospitals, and research firms, were both acquired in 1987. To supplement internal development of pharmaceutical products, Eastman Kodak also entered into joint ventures with Halcon International, ICN Pharmaceuticals, and Immunex Corporation to develop pharmaceuticals for the heart and immune systems and radiographic diagnostic dyes.

The photofinishing industry, closest to Eastman Kodak's original core photographic film business, received perhaps the most noticeable attention. Fox Photo Labs was acquired in 1986 for $91 million. Fox was a large photofinisher with wholesale and mini–photo labs in twenty-three states. That same year, Kodak purchased American Photographic Group for $43 million. This company was a privately held photofinishing firm operating in seventeen states. Joint ventures with Fuqua Industries and Magese KK of Japan, announced in 1987, further expanded photofinishing capabilities and technology in both the U.S. and Japan. The grouping of Fox's Ektra photofinishing labs, Fuqua's Colorcraft, American Photographic Group, and Kodak's own processing labs provided the company with a dominant position in this fast-growing segment of the industry.

ORGANIZATIONAL AND MANAGEMENT CHANGES

Colby H. Chandler became chief executive officer and chairman of the board at Eastman Kodak in 1983. Chandler's career at Kodak had begun in 1950, when he joined the company after serving as a Marine in World War II and completing a degree in engineering physics at the University of Maine. Starting in the Quality Control Division, Chandler was steadily promoted through the ranks. In the early 1970s, he served as project manager for Kodak's foray into office copiers. So successful was this venture that in 1977, Chandler was made president of the company.

Chandler has been described by his colleagues as a "corporate visionary." He recommended that Kodak reshape its organization structure to emphasize the uniqueness of each product group. Another key to Chandler's vision was to replace old-guard executives with more vigorous and aggressive line managers. Enter J. Phillip Samper.

Like Chandler, Samper was a career Kodak employee. He rose through the marketing and international ranks. Samper spent fourteen years overseas, mostly in Latin America. On his return to Rochester, Samper recognized the effects bureaucracy and lack of response had had on the organization. In 1980, Samper went on a campaign to shake up the organization and remove the complacent attitude. The silver market cooperated with Samper, and line managers began to get the message. Samper is quoted as saying that "it is easier to get people to sign onto a culture change in bad times."

Faced with a falling stock price, a devaluation of both Moody's and Standard & Poor's debt rating, heated competition in the film industry, and spiraling costs, Chandler and Samper orchestrated a revolutionary reorganization of the company in 1984. The first action was to split the company into twenty-four separate operating units. (See Exhibit 2.) At the head of each unit was a manager charged with the responsibility to make decisions. This process often involved promoting managers over the heads of previous supervisors. For instance, W. J. Prezzano moved from a middle manager position in international marketing to head Kodak's Photographic Products Group. Charles Trowbridge, also a middle manager in marketing, moved to the general manager's position in the Commercial and Information Systems Division. Bill Fowle, previously far down the manufacturing hierarchy, was named to head manufacturing. These moves signalled a change in promotion policy from the old seniority system to one stressing performance and vision.

Another departure from the Kodak of old was the building of entrepreneurial spirit within the divisions, starting with the general manager's posi-

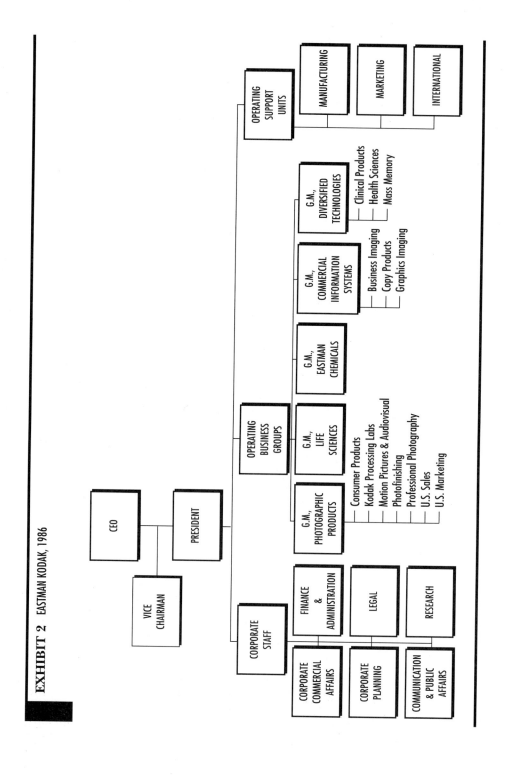

EXHIBIT 2 EASTMAN KODAK, 1986

tion. Chandler wanted the new general managers to think small. Each GM would be responsible for both costs and quality. He wanted them to be "fast on their feet." Risk taking would now be acceptable. A team approach to product development would be used instead of chain-of-command decision making. To assist the development of new products, Kodak set up a New Ventures Division to provide seed money and technical assistance. Part of this division was a technology assessment department to help new product champions incorporate the latest technology into designs.

The results of the new plan manifested themselves quickly. New products hit the market much faster than before. For instance, in 1986 and 1987, 250 new products were introduced. Kodak's newest color copier took only two and a half years from conception to delivery of the first model. The lithium battery took only three to four years to develop and was promised to last ten years. The previous management structure would have taken more than ten years to develop the product. Finally, the Fling 35, Kodak's new disposable camera, was completely designed by CAD (computer aided design) at substantial time savings.

Perhaps most traumatic were the personnel changes instituted by Chandler and Samper. Gone were the employee bowling alley, guarantees of lifetime employment, and nearly 25,000 jobs from 1984. The large corporate staffs that had dominated the organization before Chandler and Samper took over were reassigned to the operating units. Samper admits the changes were not easy. He says, "There's been an enormous amount of pain and trauma. And the culture's not completely changed yet."

Other elements in the reorganization included a significant reduction in slow-moving or highly specialized products; the buying back of 22 million shares of stock; divestiture of a textile dye company; and the assumption of $1.1 billion dollars of additional debt.

After completing the reorganization phase, Chandler shifted emphasis to a repositioning phase. A significant move toward repositioning the company was the acquisition of Sterling Drug Company in 1988.

LIFE SCIENCE DIVISION AND THE STERLING DRUG ACQUISITION

Kodak's expansion into pharmaceuticals and biotechnology seemed to many to take the company far afield from its traditional business of photography. There are, however, very close technological ties between the two industries. The foundation of the silver halide photographic process is chemical transformation. Over the years, Kodak has made substantial improvements to the technique, nearly to the point of perfection.

Photographic chemicals are, by nature, highly unstable; the slightest light, heat, or moisture variation will affect the film emulsion. To control the filmmaking process Kodak produces and mixes most of its own raw chemicals. Additionally, Kodak researchers have aggressively sought new methods to record images on a chemical film emulsion. These same researchers look for not only innovative photographic imagery products, but also new chemical compounds and processes to improve current technology. In sum, Kodak's expertise in chemicals and chemical processes extends substantially beyond the photographic film product category. Success in the chemical film process led Kodak to pursue the manufacture of other chemicals basic to American industry. In 1988, for instance, sales of Kodel, a synthetic textile fiber, and other plastics and chemicals accounted for over 18 percent of all Kodak sales.

An outgrowth of this expertise in chemicals was Kodak's desire to pursue products in the pharmaceutical industry. Most proprietary drugs are synthetic chemical products. In 1984, Kodak started its Life Science Division with the express charter to broaden the company's product mix beyond basic manufacturing chemicals and photographic chemicals. Leo J. Thomas, a leading Kodak researcher, was selected to head the unit. To supplement research from Kodak's other divisions, Thomas hired top managers from Ciba-Geigy and Merck.

Thomas pursued a strategy of modest growth by joint venture and equity investments in small, undercapitalized, start-up biotechnology firms. As Kodak had ample resources for this type of investment, the strategy was sound. Thomas's major criteria for joint venture was a firm that was small and had products nearly ready for chemical trials. More specifically, Kodak targeted companies developing products in the immune system, cardiovascular system, and central nervous system.

Kodak's Life Science Division, however, remained mostly a research unit with very little in the way of commercial products to show for its efforts. In 1985, Kodak's board made a strategic decision to diversify into pharmaceuticals. CFO Paul Smith led a discreet search for suitable pharmaceutical companies to acquire. Sterling was high on the list. Kodak, however, felt that Sterling Drug was unavailable and did not pursue the company at that time.

On January 4, 1988, Kodak's acquisition search priority changed drastically. On that day, Hoffman-LaRoche, a large Swiss drug company, made a hostile bid for Sterling Drug at $72.00 per share. Hoffman-LaRoche would eventually sweeten the bid to $81.00 per share as Sterling fought the takeover attempt. Kodak reacted to Hoffman-LaRoche's move by focusing total attention on the company. Knowing that Sterling was now on the "available" list, Chandler called John M. Pietruski, its CEO, to discuss a potential merger. Pietruski reacted favorably to Kodak's courting because Sterling was looking for a "white knight" to fend off the unwanted attack from Hoffman-LaRoche.

Sterling Drug seems to be a good fit for Kodak. It manufactures ethical drugs (25 percent of sales); household products, cosmetics, and toiletries (48 percent of sales); and proprietary drugs (27 percent of sales). Within the ethical drug group, Sterling sells Bayer, Panadol, Phillips Milk of Magnesia, Haley's M-O, and Midol. Lysol, Mop & Glo, and d-Con are well-known household products. In the proprietary drug market, Sterling Drug offers the well-known analgesics Talwin and Demerol as well as other products such as pHiso-Hex and NegGram. When questioned later why he pursued Sterling Drug so aggressively, Chandler said, "The merger will accelerate our entry into the $100 billion per year pharmaceutical industry."

During the 1984–1987 period, the proprietary drug group had a higher growth rate, at 33.6 percent, than any other division in Sterling Drug. The ethical drug business, however, had the highest gross margin of all divisions, ranging from 20.5 percent in 1984 to 23.3 percent in 1985. In addition, Sterling is aggressively seeking new proprietary drugs. Milrinone, an ACE inhibitor that could challenge Squibb's leading drug Capoten, may be successful in the treatment of congestive heart failure. Omnipaque iohexal is a new low-ionic imaging agent for radiodiagnostic procedures. Sterling Drug will provide Kodak's credibility and expertise in applying for a federal Food and Drug Agency (FDA) license for new products.

On January 22, 1988, after the stock market had closed, Kodak offered $89.50 per share for Sterling Drug. This amount represents $8.50 per share, or a 10.5 percent increase, over Hoffman-LaRoche's second offer of $81.00 per share. Furthermore, Chandler pledged to keep Sterling Drug intact, ending speculation that the household products division would be sold. Sterling Drug closed at $78.75, down $0.125 on Friday, January 22, 1988.

At the bid price, Kodak had to raise $5.1 billion to purchase all of the outstanding shares of Sterling Drug stock. To raise this amount in cash, Kodak approached Banker's Trust Co. to work out a three-year revolving credit arrangement. Banker's Trust, in turn, syndicated the loan to a many as thirty different banks. The problem with the $5.1 billion loan was not the credit worthiness of Kodak or the "business judgment" of this acquisition, but the first year's interest payment, calculated to be nearly $330 million. To obtain the best possible interest rate, Kodak negotiated with Banker's Trust several alternatives for the interest rate. According to the agreement, Kodak can choose one of these options:

1. As base rate, Banker's Trust prime rate or the Federal Funds rate, whichever is higher, plus 0.25 percent
2. The reserve adjusted London Interbank offered rate plus 10 points
3. Competitive bid by another bank, with Banker's Trust Co. acting as broker/agent

Financial analysts reacted with mixed feelings to the Kodak–Sterling Drug merger. On the one hand, many though it was a wise acquisition on Kodak's part because Sterling's businesses fit with Kodak's and filled in some strategic gaps. On the other hand, many felt that Kodak overpaid. Analysts are concerned about stock dilution as Kodak amortizes $4.07 billion in good will. At a thirty-year rate, this amortization results in a dilution of $0.31 per share. The acquisition also changes Kodak's capital structure so that Kodak's debt-to-capital ratio would be around 57 percent. Accordingly, both Moody's and Standard & Poor's lowered their investment rating of Kodak.

EASTMAN KODAK IN 1988

Kodak made significant progress during 1988 in fulfilling its goal to expand into related markets. The purchase of Sterling Drug on February 23, 1988, dramatically added to net sales, which were up 28 percent to $17.034 billion, and profits, which rose 39 percent to $2.938 billion. A summary of Kodak's financial statements for the years 1981 through 1988 are shown in Exhibit 3. Sterling Drug Company's sales and gross margins, by division, are shown in Exhibit 4.

In addition to the Sterling Drug purchase, Kodak also acquired IBM's copier service business for an undisclosed amount in 1988. This acquisition was consistent with Kodak's goals for its existing copier business and, in essence, eliminated a competitor at the high end of the copier equipment market, a segment Kodak pursues vigorously.

Kodak's worldwide employment increased in 1988 to 145,300, up 17 percent from the previous year. Most of the increase in employment was attributed to the Sterling Drug acquisition.

Kodak also continued its expansion in photofinishing laboratories. It gained twenty-five photofinishing labs in France by acquiring Les Laboratoires Associés. Also, Kodak solidified business in a joint venture with Fuqua Industries and others by forming an independent company known as Qualex, Inc.

On a per-share basis, Eastman Kodak's profit performance increased from $3.52 per share to $4.31 per share, a 22.4 percent increase. Total consumer spending for photographic equipment, supplies, and services was estimated at approximately $10 billion in 1987. According to *Standard & Poor's Industry Surveys*, recent growth in the industry was attributable to two factors: "new and improved products and services, and a population mix that has increasingly shifted toward a relatively affluent and free-spending 25- to 40-year-old age group."[2]

THE PHOTOGRAPHY INDUSTRY

Total consumer spending for photographic equipment, supplies, and services was estimated at approximately $10 billion in 1987. According to *Standard & Poor's Industry Surveys*, recent growth in the industry was attributable to two factors: "new and improved products and services, and a population mix that has increasingly shifted toward a relatively affluent and free-spending 25- to 40-year-old age group."[2]

An estimated 13.3 billion pictures are taken each year by amateur photographers, 97 percent of which are color photographs. A large proportion of them (65 percent) are taken using 35mm equipment. The largest share of consumer spending, some 39 percent, goes for photofinishing—chemically processing exposed film and printing slides and prints. Expenditures for photography are detailed by segment in Exhibit 5. Although retail innovations such as "minilabs," which offer speedy on-site film processing, account for a growing percentage of the market, traditional retail outlets still predominate in the industry. Exhibit 6 shows the relative shares of various retail outlets in a recent year.

One of the most significant trends in the industry in recent years has been the shift toward 35mm cameras and equipment. The 35mm market is

EXHIBIT 3   EASTMAN KODAK COMPANY AND SUBSIDIARIES: FINANCIAL SUMMARY, 1981–1988

	1988	1987
Sales	$ 17,034	$ 13,305
Earnings from operations	2,938	2,111
Earnings before income taxes	2,236	1,984
Net earnings	1,397	1,178
EARNINGS AND DIVIDENDS		
Net earnings—percent of sales	8.2%	8.9%
—percent return on avg. shareowner's equity	21.8%	19.0%
—per common share	4.31	3.52
Cash dividends declared—on common shares	616	572
—per common share	1.90	1.71
Common shares outstanding at close of year	324.2	324.1
Shareowners at close of year	174,110	168,517
Earnings retained	781	606
BALANCE SHEET DATA		
Current assets	$ 8,684	$ 6,791
Properties at cost	15,667	13,789
Accumulated depreciation	7,654	7,126
Total assets	22,964	14,698
Current liabilities	5,850	4,140
Long-term obligations	7,779	2,382
Total liabilities and deferred credits	16,184	8,685
Total net assets (shareowners' equity)	6,780	6,013
SUPPLEMENTAL INFORMATION		
Sales—Imaging	$ 10,575	$ 9,711
—Chemicals	3,033	2,600
—Health	3,691	1,230
Research and development expenditures	1,147	992
Additions to properties	1,914	1,652
Depreciation	1,057	962
Taxes (excludes payroll, sales, and excise taxes)	973	911
Wages, salaries and employee benefits	5,469	4,645
Employees at close of year—in the United States	87,900	81,800
—worldwide	145,300	124,400
SUBSIDIARY COMPANIES OUTSIDE THE U.S.		
Sales	$ 7,748	$ 5,572
Earnings from operations	997	797
Eastman Kodak Company equity in net earnings (loss)	661	439

Note: Dollar amounts and shares given in millions, except per-share figures.
Source: 1988 Annual Report.

EXHIBIT 3 (continued)

1986	1985	1984	1983	1982	1981
$11,550	$10,631	$10,600	$10,170	$10,815	$10,337
724	561	1,547	1,027	1,860	2,060
598	530	1,624	1,020	1,872	2,183
374	332	923	565	1,162	1,239
3.2%	3.1%	8.7%	5.6%	10.7%	12.0%
5.8%	4.8%	12.6%	7.5%	16.2%	19.4%
1.10	.97	2.54	1.52	3.17	3.41
551	553	578	587	581	566
1.63	1.62	1.60	1.58	1.58	1.55
338.7	338.5	350.0	372.5	372.5	365.6
172,713	184,231	189,972	200,005	203,788	220,513
(177)	(221)	345	(22)	581	673
$ 5,857	$ 5,677	5,131	$ 5,420	$ 5,289	$ 5,063
12,919	12,047	10,775	10,049	9,344	7,963
6,643	6,070	5,386	4,801	4,286	3,806
12,994	12,142	10,778	10,928	10,622	9,446
3,811	3,325	2,306	2,172	2,146	2,119
981	988	409	416	350	93
6,606	5,580	3,641	3,408	3,081	2,676
6,388	6,562	7,137	7,520	7,541	6,770
$ 8,352	$ 8,531	$ 8,380	$ 8,097	$ 8,935	$ 8,258
2,378	2,348	2,464	2,285	2,151	2,349
1,056	...	...	...	...	...
1,059	976	838	746	710	615
1,438	1,495	970	889	1,500	1,190
956	831	758	652	575	452
329	297	793	543	801	1,026
4,912	4,482	4,148	4,340	4,446	4,099
83,600	89,200	85,600	86,000	93,300	91,900
121,450	128,950	123,900	125,500	136,500	136,400
$ 4,387	$ 3,429	$3,367	$ 3,410	$4,279	$ 4,017
400	169	113	60	302	450
167	(9)	25	(65)	72	188

EXHIBIT 4 STERLING DRUG: SALES AND GROSS MARGINS, 1984–1987

	1984		1985		1986		1987	
	Sales (mill).	Gross Marg.	Sales (mill).	Gross Marg.	Sales (mill).	Gross Marg.	Sales (mill).	Gross Marg.
Proprietary Drug	269.4	(10.4%)	280.0	(15.0%)	326.5	(16.8%)	360	(17.0%)
Household	509.6	(17.9%)	566.4	(18.0%)	588.7	(16.5%)	640	(16.5%)
Foreign	681.9	(11.9%)	656.6	(10.8%)	774.1	(10.6%)	900	(10.5%)
Ethical Drug	267.7	(20.5%)	268.8	(23.3%)	301.1	(21.9%)	340	(22.0%)

Source: *Value Line* (1988).

EXHIBIT 5 U.S. CONSUMER EXPENDITURES IN PHOTOGRAPHY

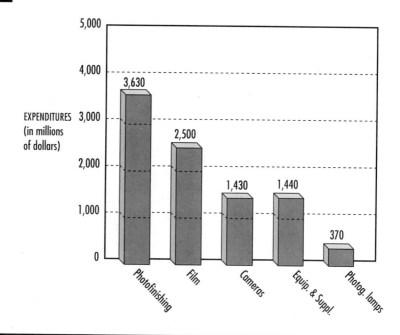

Source: 1985 Wolfman Report.

composed of both the lens/shutter rangefinder ("point-and-shoot") cameras and the more sophisticated single-lens reflex (SLR) cameras favored by professionals and advanced hobbyists. Although SLR sales were sluggish in the late 1980s, technological improvements in "point-and-shoot" cameras such as automatic film loading, built-in flash units, and autowinding caused sales for those cameras to mushroom. By 1987, sales of the once-popular disk camera had declined precipitously, as had those of cartridge film cameras. Polaroid's introduction of its "Spectra" line, with its improved picture quality, breathed new life into the instant camera market. Exhibit 7 shows relative market shares in 1985 and 1987 by camera type.

A number of technological advances in photography and related products were made in the late 1980s. Videocassette recorders (camcorders) grew rapidly during the 1980s and by 1987 had virtually replaced 8mm home movies in the marketplace. Camcorder sales had little impact on the conventional "still" camera business, however. According to *Standard & Poor's Industry Surveys*, "This is likely due to the familiarity, portability, and permanent images provided by still cameras, as well as improvements in products and services for still camera users."[3] Recent development in electronic still-picture imaging may prove to be a threat to traditional chemically processed photography, however. In 1986 several companies introduced electronic still cameras that record and store images on a two-inch diameter magnetic video disk. Images

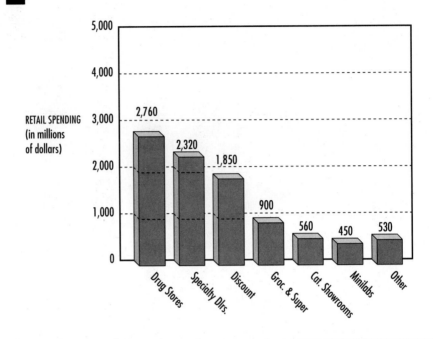

EXHIBIT 6 U.S. RETAIL SPENDING IN PHOTOGRAPHY

Source: 1985 Wolfman Report.

may be viewed on a television set, enchanced electronically, and then reproduced using special printers, or they may be transmitted over telephone lines. At around $40,000, the systems were targeted for professional and publishing markets. As new developments in still-imaging technology in the 1990s bring about reduced costs, the new electronic still cameras could become competitive with traditional photographic processes.

The introduction of simpler-to-use 35mm cameras and improved film accounted for significant increases in the photofinishing segment in the 1980s. Between 1981 and 1985, retail photofinishing grew at a compound annual rate of 11 percent, reaching $3.63 billion in 1985. Estimates placed total retail photofinishing sales at over $4 billion in 1986 and at nearly $4.5 billion in 1987. The new minilabs, most of which are located in shopping malls, were the fastest-growing part of this segment and by 1987 accounted for nearly $1 billion in sales. Leading chains of minilabs include MotoPhoto, CPI Corp., and Fox Photo, each with around 200 to 300 locations. The total number of minilabs in operation stood at about 12,000 in 1986.

The majority of all photographs are still developed by large wholesale labs, which receive exposed film from drug and discount stores and by direct mail. A large amount of consolidation took place among the wholesale labs in the late 1980s, with Eastman Kodak leading the way. In December 1986, Kodak acquired Fox Photo for $91 million, divesting Fox's minilab business but keep-

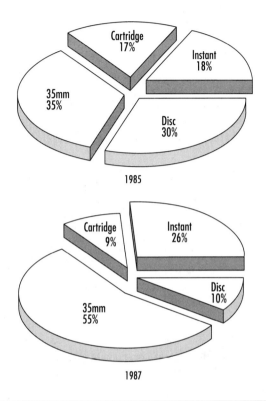

EXHIBIT 7 U.S. CAMERA SALES, 1985 AND 1987

Source: *Photographic Trade News*, 1986 and 1988.

ing its large wholesale photofinishing operations. American Photographic Group, another large wholesale photofinisher, was purchased by Eastman Kodak for $43 million in October 1987. Kodak also announced in December 1987 that it planned to launch a joint venture with Fuqua Industries' Colorcraft wholesale photofinishers. The combination would have given the two companies over $600 million in photofinishing business. This announcement caused Phototron Corp., a California photofinisher, to raise antitrust objections, claiming that the joint venture, combined with Kodak's 80-percent share of the retail film business, gave it too powerful a hold on amateur photography. A federal district court in Ft. Worth, Texas, ordered a preliminary injunction against the joint venture.

ENDNOTES

1. Most of the information in this section is taken from Ingham, J. N., *Biographical Dictionary of American Business Leaders* (Westport, Conn.: Greenwood Press, 1983).

2. "Photography," *Standard & Poor's Industry Survey* (March 10, 1988): L48.

3. Ibid., p. L46.

CASE 10

LINCOLN ELECTRIC COMPANY, 1989   ARTHUR D. SHARPLIN

People are our most valuable asset. They must feel secure, important, challenged, in control of their destiny, confident in their leadership, be responsive to common goals, believe they are being treated fairly, have easy access to authority and open lines of communication in all possible directions. Perhaps the most important task Lincoln employees face today is that of establishing an example for others in the Lincoln organization in other parts of the world. We need to maximize the benefits of cooperation and teamwork, fusing high technology with human talent, so that we here in the USA and all of our subsidiary and joint venture operations will be in a position to realize our full potential (George Willis, CEO, Lincoln Electric).

The Lincoln Electric Company is the world's largest manufacturer of arc-welding products and a leading producer of industrial electric motors. The firm employs 2,400 workers in two U.S. factories near Cleveland and an equal number in eleven factories located in other countries. This does not include the field sales force of more than 200. The company's U.S. market share (for arc-welding products) is estimated at more than 40 percent.

The Lincoln incentive management plan has been well known for many years. Many college management texts make reference to the Lincoln plan as a model for achieving higher worker productivity. Certainly, the firm has been successful according to the usual measures.

James F. Lincoln died in 1965 and there was some concern, even among employees, that the management system would fall into disarray, that profits would decline, and that year-end bonuses might be discontinued. Quite the contrary, twenty-four years after Lincoln's death, the company appears as strong as ever. Each year, except the recession years 1982 and 1983, has seen high profits and bonuses. Employee morale and productivity remain very

---

Source: Prepared by Professor Arthur D. Sharplin, McNeese State University, as a basis for classroom discussion and not to illustrate either effective or ineffective handling of administrative situations. © Arthur D. Sharplin, 1990.

good. Employee turnover is almost nonexistent except for retirements. Lincoln's market share is stable. The historically high stock dividends continue.

A HISTORICAL SKETCH

In 1895, after being "frozen out" of the depression-ravaged Elliott-Lincoln Company, a maker of Lincoln-designed electric motors, John C. Lincoln took out his second patent and began to manufacture his improved motor. He opened his new business, unincorporated, with $200 he had earned redesigning a motor for young Herbert Henry Dow, who later founded the Dow Chemical Company.

Started during an economic depression and cursed by a major fire after only one year in business, the company grew, but hardly prospered, through its first quarter century. In 1906, John C. Lincoln incorporated the business and moved from his one-room, fourth-floor factory to a new three-story building he erected in east Cleveland. He expanded his work force to thirty and sales grew to over $50,000 a year. John preferred being an engineer and inventor rather than a manager, though, and it was to be left to another Lincoln to manage the company through its years of success.

In 1907, after a bout with typhoid fever forced him from Ohio State University in his senior year, James F. Lincoln, John's younger brother, joined the fledgling company. In 1914 he became active head of the firm, with the titles of general manager and vice-president. John remained president of the company for some years but became more involved in other business ventures and in his work as an inventor.

One of James Lincoln's early actions was to ask the employees to elect representatives to a committee which would advise him on company operations. This "Advisory Board" has met with the chief executive officer every two weeks since that time. This was only the first of a series of innovative personnel policies which have, over the years, distinguished Lincoln Electric from its contemporaries.

The first year the Advisory Board was in existence, working hours were reduced from fifty-five per week, then standard, to fifty hours a week. In 1915, the company gave each employee a paid-up life insurance policy. A welding school, which continues today, was begun in 1917. In 1918, an employee bonus plan was attempted. It was not continued, but the idea was to resurface later.

The Lincoln Electric Employees' Association was formed in 1919 to provide health benefits and social activities. This organization continues today and has assumed several additional functions over the years. In 1923, a piecework pay system was in effect, employees got two weeks paid vacation each year, and wages were adjusted for changes in the Consumer Price Index. Approximately 30 percent of the common stock was set aside for key employees in 1914. A stock purchase plan for all employees was begun in 1925.

The board of directors voted to start a suggestion system in 1929. The program is still in effect, but cash awards, a part of the early program, were discontinued several years ago. Now, suggestions are rewarded by additional "points," which affect year-end bonuses.

The legendary Lincoln bonus plan was proposed by the Advisory Board and accepted on a trial basis in 1934. The first annual bonus amounted to about 25 percent of wages. There has been a bonus every year since then. The bonus plan has been a cornerstone of the Lincoln management system and recent bonuses have approximated annual wages.

By 1944, Lincoln employees enjoyed a pension plan, a policy of promotion from within, and continuous employment. Base pay rates were determined by formal job evaluation and a merit rating system was in effect.

In the prologue of James F. Lincoln's last book, Charles G. Herbruck writes regarding the foregoing personnel innovations:

> They were not to buy good behavior. They were not efforts to increase profits. They were not antidotes to labor difficulties. They did not constitute a "do-gooder" program. They were expression of mutual respect for each person's importance to the job to be done. All of them reflect the leadership of James Lincoln, under whom they were nurtured and propagated.

During World War II, Lincoln prospered as never before. By the start of the war, the company was the world's largest manufacturer of arc-welding products. Sales of about $4 million in 1934 grew to $24 million by 1941. Productivity per employee more than doubled during the same period. The navy's Price Review Board challenged the high profits. And the Internal Revenue Service questioned the tax deductibility of employee bonuses, arguing they are not "ordinary and necessary" costs of doing business. But the forceful and articulate James Lincoln was able to overcome the objections.

Certainly since 1935 and probably for several years before that, Lincoln productivity has been well above the average for similar companies. The company claims levels of productivity more than twice those for other manufacturers from 1945 onward. Information available from outside sources tends to support these claims.

COMPANY PHILOSOPHY

James F. Lincoln was the son of a Congregational minister, and Christian principles were at the center of his business philosophy. The confidence that he had in the efficacy of Christ's teachings is illustrated by the following remark taken from one of his books:

> The Christian ethic should control our acts. If it did control our acts, the savings in cost of distribution would be tremendous. Advertising would be a contact of the expert consultant with the customer, in order to give the customer the best product available when all of the customer's needs are considered. Competition then would be in improving the quality of products and increasing efficiency in producing and distributing them; not in deception,

as is now too customary. Pricing would reflect efficiency of production; it would not be a selling dodge that the customer may well be sorry he accepted. It would be proper for all concerned and rewarding for the ability used in producing the product.

There is no indication that Lincoln attempted to evangelize his employees or customers—or the general public for that matter. Neither the chairman of the board and chief executive, George Willis, nor the president, Donald F. Hastings, mention the Christian gospel in their recent speeches and interviews. The company motto, "The actual is limited, the possible is immense," is prominently displayed, but there is no display of religious slogans, and there is no company chapel.

ATTITUDE TOWARD THE CUSTOMER

James Lincoln saw the customer's needs as the *raison d'être* for every company. "When any company has achieved success so that it is attractive as an investment," he wrote, "all money usually needed for expansion is supplied by the customer in retained earnings. It is obvious that the customer's interests, not the stockholder's, should come first." In 1947 he said, "Care should be taken . . . not to rivet attention on profit. Between 'How much do I get?' and 'How do I make this better, cheaper, more useful?' the difference is fundamental and decisive." Willis, too, ranks the customer as management's most important constituency. This is reflected in Lincoln's policy to "at all times price on the basis of cost and at all times keep pressure on our cost." Lincoln's goal, often stated, is "to build a better and better product at a lower and lower price." "It is obvious," James Lincoln said, "that the customer's interests should be the first goal of industry."

ATTITUDE TOWARD STOCKHOLDERS

Stockholders are given last priority at Lincoln. This is a continuation of James Lincoln's philosophy: "The last group to be considered is the stockholders who own stock because they think it will be more profitable than investing money in any other way." Concerning division of the largess produced by incentive management, he wrote, "The absentee stockholder also will get his share, even if undeserved, out of the greatly increased profit that the efficiency produces."

ATTITUDE TOWARD UNIONISM

There has never been a serious effort to organize Lincoln employees. While James Lincoln criticized the labor movement for "selfishly attempting to better its position at the expense of the people it must serve," he still has kind words for union members. He excused abuses of union power as "the natural reactions of human beings to the abuses to which management has subjected them." Lincoln's idea of the correct relationship between workers and managers is shown by this comment: "Labor and management are properly not warring camps; they are parts of one organization in which they must and should cooperate fully and happily."

BELIEFS AND ASSUMPTIONS ABOUT EMPLOYEES

If fulfilling customer needs is the desired goal of business, then employee performance and productivity are the means by which this goal can best be achieved. It is the Lincoln attitude toward employees, reflected in the following comments by James Lincoln, which is credited by many with creating the success the company has experienced:

> The greatest fear of the worker, which is the same as the greatest fear of the industrialist in operating a company, is the lack of income.... The industrial manager is very conscious of his company's need of uninterrupted income. He is completely oblivious, evidently, of the fact that the worker has the same need.

> He is just as eager as any manager is to be part of a team that is properly organized and working for the advancement of our economy.... He has no desire to make profits for those who do not hold up their end in production, as is true of absentee stockholders and inactive people in the company.

> If money is to be used as an incentive, the program must provide that what is paid to the worker is what he has earned. The earnings of each must be in accordance with accomplishment.

> Status is of great importance in all human relationships. The greatest incentive that money has, usually, is that it is a symbol of success.... The resulting status is the real incentive.... Money alone can be an incentive to the miser only.

> There must be complete honesty and understanding between the hourly worker and management if high efficiency is to be obtained.

LINCOLN'S BUSINESS

Arc-welding has been the standard joining method in shipbuilding for decades. It is the predominant way of connecting steel in the construction industry. Most industrial plants have their own welding shops for maintenance and construction. Manufacturers of tractors and all kinds of heavy equipment use arc-welding extensively in the manufacturing process. Many hobbyists have their own welding machines and use them for making metal items such as patio furniture and barbecue pits. The popularity of welded sculpture as an art form is growing.

While advances in welding technology have been frequent, arc-welding products, in the main, have hardly changed. Lincoln's Innershield process is a notable exception. This process, described later, lowers welding cost and improves quality and speed in many applications. The most widely used Lincoln electrode, the Fleetweld 5P, has been virtually the same since the 1930s. The most popular engine-driven welder in the world, the Lincoln SA-200, has been a gray-colored assembly including a four-cylinder continental "Red Seal" engine and a 200 ampere direct-current generator with two current-control knobs for at least four decades. A 1989 model SA-200 even weighs almost the same as the 1950 model, and it certainly is little changed in appearance.

The company's share of the U.S. arc-welding products market appears to have been about 40 percent for many years. The welding products market has grown somewhat faster than the level of industry in general. The market is highly price-competitive, with variations in prices of standard items normally amounting to only a percent or two. Lincoln's products are sold directly by its engineering-oriented sales force and indirectly though its distributor organization. Advertising expenditures amount to less than three-fourths of a percent of sales. Research and development expenditures typically range from $10 million to $12 million, considerably more than competitors.

The other major welding process, flame-welding, has not been competitive with arc-welding since the 1930s. However, plasma-arc-welding, a relatively new process which uses a conducting stream of super heated gas (plasma) to confine the welding current to a small area, has made some inroads, especially in metal tubing manufacturing, in recent years. Major advances in technology which will produce an alternative superior to arc-welding within the next decade or so appear unlikely. Also, it seems likely that changes in the machines and techniques used in arc-welding will be evolutionary rather than revolutionary.

PRODUCTS

The company is primarily engaged in the manufacture and sale of arc-welding products—electric welding machines and metal electrodes. Lincoln also produces electric motors ranging from $\frac{1}{2}$ horsepower to 200 horsepower. Motors constitute about 8 to 10 percent of total sales. Several million dollars has recently been invested in automated equipment that will double Lincoln's manufacturing capacity for $\frac{1}{2}$ to 20 horsepower electric motors.

The electric welding machines, some consisting of a transformer or motor and generator arrangement powered by commercial electricity and others consisting of an internal combustion engine and generator, are designed to produce 30 to 1,500 amperes of electrical power. This electrical current is used to melt a consumable metal electrode with the molten metal being transferred in super hot spray to the metal joint being welded. Very high temperatures and hot sparks are produced, and operators usually must wear special eye and face protection and leather gloves, often along with leather aprons and sleeves.

Lincoln and its competitors now market a wide range of general purpose and specialty electrodes for welding mild steel, aluminum, cast iron, and stainless and special steels. Most of these electrodes are designed to meet the standards of the American Welding Society, a trade association. They are thus essentially the same as to size and composition from one manufacturer to another. Every electrode manufacturer has a limited number of unique products, but these typically constitute only a small percentage of total sales.

Welding electrodes are of two basic types: (1) Coated "stick" electrodes, usually fourteen inches long and smaller than a pencil in diameter, which are held in a special insulated holder by the operator, who must manipulate the electrode in order to maintain a proper arc-width and pattern of deposition of the metal being transferred. Stick electrodes are packaged in six- to fifty-pound boxes. (2) Coiled wire, ranging in diameter from .035" to 0.219", which is designed to be fed continuously to the welding arc through a "gun" held by the operator or positioned by automatic positioning equipment. The wire is packaged in coils, reels, and drums weighing from fourteen to 1,000 pounds and may be solid or flux-cored.

MANUFACTURING PROCESSES

The main plant is in Euclid, Ohio, a suburb on Cleveland's east side. The layout of this plant is shown in Exhibit 1. There are no warehouses. Materials flow from the half-mile-long dock on the north side of the plant through the production lines to a very limited storage and loading area on the south side. Materials used on each work station are stored as close as possible to the work station. The administrative offices, near the center of the factory, are entirely functional. A corridor below the main level provides access to the factory floor

EXHIBIT 1 MAIN FACTORY LAYOUT

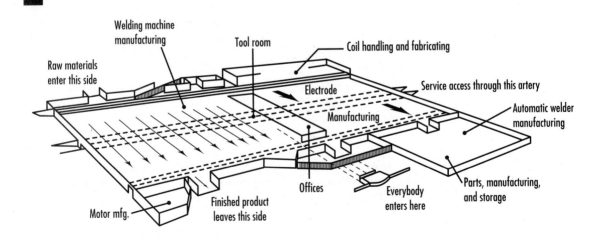

from the main entrance near the center of the plan. *Fortune* magazine recently declared the Euclid facility one of America's ten best-managed factories, and compared it with a General Electric plant also on the list:

> Stepping into GE's spanking new dishwasher plant, an awed supplier said, is like stepping "into the Hyatt Regency." By comparison, stepping into Lincoln Electric's 33-year-old, cavernous, dimly lit factory is like stumbling into a dingy big-city YMCA. It's only when one starts looking at how these factories do things that similarities become apparent. They have found ways to merge design with manufacturing, build in quality, make wise choices about automation, get close to customers, and handle their work forces.

A new Lincoln plant, in Mentor, Ohio, houses some of the electrode production operations, which were moved from the main plant.

Electrode manufacturing is highly capital intensive. Metal rods purchased from steel producers are drawn down to smaller diameters, cut to length and coated with pressed-powder "flux" for stick electrodes or plated with copper (for conductivity) and put into coils or spools for wire. Lincoln's Innershield wire is hollow and filled with a material similar to that used to coat stick electrodes. As mentioned earlier, this represented a major innovation in welding technology when it was introduced. The company is highly secretive about its electrode production processes, and outsiders are not given access to the details of those processes.

Lincoln welding machines and electric motors are made on a series of assembly lines. Gasoline and diesel engines are purchased partially assembled but practically all other components are made from basic industrial products, e.g., steel bars and sheets and bar copper conductor wire.

Individual components, such as gasoline tanks for engine-driven welders and steel shafts for motors and generators, are made by numerous small "factories within a factory." The shaft for a certain generator, for example, is made from raw steel bar by one operator who uses five large machines, all running continuously. A saw cuts the bar to length, a digital lathe machines different sections to varying diameters, a special milling machine cuts a slot for the keyway, and so forth, until a finished shaft is produced. The operator moves the shafts from machine to machine and makes necessary adjustments.

Another operator punches, shapes, and paints sheetmetal cowling parts. One assembles steel laminations onto a rotor shaft, then winds, insulates, and tests the rotors. Finished components are moved by crane operators to the nearby assembly lines.

WORKER PERFORMANCE AND ATTITUDES

Exceptional worker performance at Lincoln is a matter of record. The typical Lincoln employee earns about twice as much as other factory workers in the Cleveland area. Yet the company's labor cost per sales dollar in 1989, twenty-six cents, is well below industry averages. Worker turnover is practically nonexistent except for retirements and departures by new employees.

Sales per Lincoln factory employee currently exceed $150,000. An observer at the factory quickly sees why this figure is so high. Each worker is proceeding busily and thoughtfully about the task at hand. There is no idle chatter. Most workers take no coffee breaks. Many operate several machines and make a substantial component unaided. The supervisors are busy with planning and record keeping duties and hardly glance at the people they "supervise." The manufacturing procedures appear efficient—no unnecessary steps, no wasted motions, no wasted materials. Finished components move smoothly to subsequent work stations.

Appendix A includes summaries of interviews with employees.

ORGANIZATION STRUCTURE

Lincoln has never allowed development of a formal organization chart. The objective of this policy is to insure maximum flexibility. An open door policy is practiced throughout the company, and personnel are encouraged to take problems to the persons most capable of resolving them. Once, Harvard Business School researchers prepared an organization chart reflecting the implied relationships at Lincoln. The chart became available within the company, and present management feels that had a disruptive effect. Therefore, no organizational chart appears in this report.

Perhaps because of the quality and enthusiasm of the Lincoln workforce, routine supervision is almost nonexistent. A typical production foreman, for example, supervises as many as 100 workers, a span-of-control which does not allow more than infrequent worker-supervisor interaction.

Position titles and traditional flows of authority do imply something of an organizational structure, however. For example, the vice-president, sales, and the vice-president, Electrode Division, report to the president, as do various staff assistants such as the personnel director and the director of purchasing. Using such implied relationships, it has been determined that production workers have two or, at most, three levels of supervision between themselves and the president.

PERSONNEL POLICIES

As mentioned earlier, it is Lincoln's remarkable personnel practices which are credited by many with the company's success.

RECRUITMENT AND SELECTION

Every job opening is advertised internally on company bulletin boards and any employee can apply for any job so advertised. External hiring is permitted only for entry level positions. Selection for these jobs is done on the basis of personal interviews—there is no aptitude or psychological testing. Not even a high school diploma is required—except for engineering and sales positions, which are filled by graduate engineers. A committee consisting of vice-presidents and supervisors interviews candidates initially cleared by the personnel department. Final selection is made by the supervisor who has a job opening. Out of over 3,500 applicants interviewed by the personnel department during a recent period fewer than 300 were hired.

JOB SECURITY

In 1958 Lincoln formalized its guaranteed continuous employment policy, which had already been in effect for many years. There have been no layoffs since World War II. Since 1958, every worker with over two years' longevity has been guaranteed at least thirty hours per week, forty-nine weeks per year.

The policy has never been so severely tested as during the 1981–1983 recession. As a manufacturer of capital goods, Lincoln's business is highly cyclical. In previous recessions the company was able to avoid major sales declines. However, sales plummeted 32 percent in 1982 and another 16 percent the next year. Few companies could withstand such a revenue collapse and remain profitable. Yet, Lincoln not only earned profits, but no employee was laid off and year-end incentive bonuses continued. To weather the storm, management cut most of the nonsalaried workers back to 30 hours a week for varying periods of time. Many employees were reassigned and the total workforce was slightly reduced through normal attrition and restricted hiring. Many employees grumbled at their unexpected misfortune, probably to the surprise and dismay of some Lincoln managers. However, sales and profits—and employee bonuses—soon rebounded and all was well again.

PERFORMANCE EVALUATIONS

Each supervisor formally evaluates subordinates twice a year using the cards shown in Exhibit 2. The employee performance criteria, "quality," "dependability," "ideas and cooperation," and "output," are considered to be independent of each other. Marks on the cards are converted to numerical scores which are forced to average 100 for each evaluating supervisor. Individual merit rating scores normally range from 80 to 110. Any score over 110 requires a special letter to top management. These scores (over 110) are not considered in computing the required 100 point average for each evaluating supervisor. Suggestions for improvements often result in recommendations for exceptionally high performance scores. Supervisors discuss individual performance marks with the employees concerned. Each warranty claim is traced to the individual employee whose work caused the defect. The employee's performance score may be reduced, or the worker may be required to repay the cost of servicing the warranty claim by working without pay.

COMPENSATION

Basic wage levels for jobs at Lincoln are determined by a wage survey of similar jobs in the Cleveland area. These rates are adjusted quarterly in accordance

EXHIBIT 2 MERIT RATING CARDS

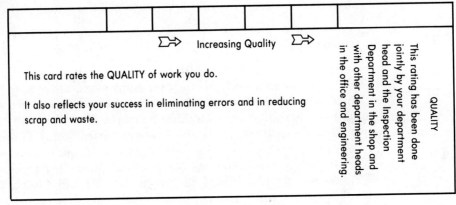

⇨ Increasing Quality ⇨

This card rates the QUALITY of work you do.

It also reflects your success in eliminating errors and in reducing scrap and waste.

This rating has been done jointly by your department head and the Inspection Department in the shop and with other department heads in the office and engineering.

QUALITY

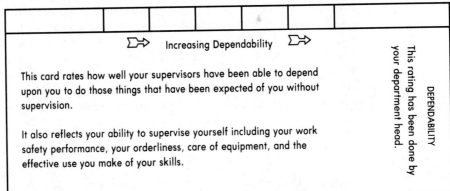

⇨ Increasing Dependability ⇨

This card rates how well your supervisors have been able to depend upon you to do those things that have been expected of you without supervision.

It also reflects your ability to supervise yourself including your work safety performance, your orderliness, care of equipment, and the effective use you make of your skills.

This rating has been done by your department head.

DEPENDABILITY

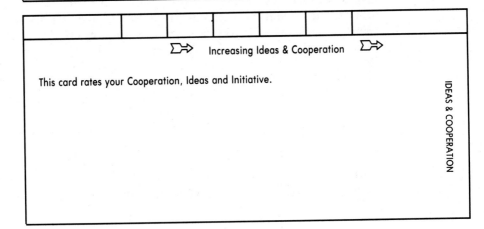

⇨ Increasing Ideas & Cooperation ⇨

This card rates your Cooperation, Ideas and Initiative.

IDEAS & COOPERATION

EXHIBIT 2 (continued)

→ Increasing Output → Days Absent

This card rates HOW MUCH PRODUCTIVE WORK you can actually turn out. It also reflects your willingness not to hold back and recognizes your attendance record.

New ideas and new methods are important to your company in our continuing effect to reduce costs, increase output, improve quality, work safety and improve our relationship with our customers. This card credits you for your ideas and initiative used to help in this direction.

It also rates your cooperation—how you work with others as a team. Such factors as your attitude towards supervision, co-workers and the company, your efforts to share knowledge with others, and your cooperation in installing new methods smoothly, are considered here.

This rating has been done jointly by your department head and the Production Control Department in the shop and with other department heads in the office and engineering.

OUTPUT

---

with changes in the Cleveland area wage index. Insofar as possible, base wage rates are translated into piece rates. Practically all production workers and many others—for example, some forklift operators—are paid by piece rate. Once established, piece rates are never changed unless a substantive change in the way a job is done results from a source other than the worker doing the job.

In December of each year, a portion of annual profits is distributed to employees as bonuses. Incentive bonuses since 1934 have averaged about 90 percent of annual wages and somewhat more than after-tax profits. The average bonus for 1988 has $21,258. Even for the recession years 1982 and 1983, bonuses had averaged $13,998 and $8,557, respectively. Individual bonuses are proportional to merit-rating scores. For example, assume the amount set aside for bonuses is 80 percent of total wages paid to eligible employees. A person whose performance score is 95 will receive a bonus of 76 percent (0.80 × 0.95) of annual wages.

VACATIONS

The company is shut down for two weeks in August and two weeks during the Christmas season. Vacations are taken during these periods. For employees with over twenty-five years of service, a fifth week of vacation may be taken at a time acceptable to superiors.

WORK ASSIGNMENT

Management has authority to transfer workers and to switch between overtime and short time as required. Supervisors have undisputed authority to assign specific parts to individual workmen, who may have their own preferences due to variations in piece rates. During the 1982–1983 recession, fifty factory workers volunteered to join sales teams and fanned out across the country to sell a new welder designed for automobile body shops and small machine shops. The result—$10 million in sales and a hot new product.

EMPLOYEE PARTICIPATION IN DECISION MAKING

Thinking of participative management usually evokes a vision of a relaxed, nonauthoritarian atmosphere. This is not the case at Lincoln. Formal authority is quite strong. "We're very authoritarian around here," says Willis. James F. Lincoln placed a good deal of stress on protecting management's authority. "Management in all successful departments of industry must have complete power," he said. "Management is the coach who must be obeyed. The men, however, are the players who alone can win the game." Despite this attitude, there are several ways in which employees participate in management at Lincoln.

Richard Sabo, assistant to the chief executive officer, relates job enlargement/enrichment to participation. He said, "The most important participative technique that we use is giving more responsibility to employees. We give a high school graduate more responsibility than other companies give their foremen." Management puts limits on the degree of participation which is allowed, however. In Sabo's words:

> When you use "participation," put quotes around it. Because we believe that each person should participate only in those decisions he is most knowledgeable about. I don't think production employees should control the decisions of the chairman. They don't know as much as he does about the decisions he is involved in.

The Advisory Board, elected by the workers, meets with the chairman and the president every two weeks to discuss ways of improving operations. As noted earlier, this board has been in existence since 1914 and has contributed to many innovations. The incentive bonuses, for example, were first recommended by this committee. Every employee has access to Advisory Board members, and answers to all Advisory Board suggestions are promised by the following meeting. Both Willis and Hastings are quick to point out, though, that the Advisory Board only recommends actions. "They do not have direct authority," Willis says. "And when they bring up something that management thinks is not to the benefit of the company, it will be rejected."

Under the early suggestion program, employees were awarded one-half of the first year's savings attributable to their suggestions. Now, however, the value of suggestions is reflected in performance evaluation scores, which determine individual incentive bonus amounts.

TRAINING AND EDUCATION

Production workers are given a short period of on-the-job training and then placed on a piecework pay system. Lincoln does not pay for off-site education, unless very specific company needs are identified. The idea behind this latter policy, according to Sabo, is that everyone cannot take advantage of such a program, and it is unfair to expend company funds for an advantage to which there is unequal access. Recruits for sales jobs, already college graduates, are given on-the-job training in the plant followed by a period of work and training at one of the regional sales offices.

FRINGE BENEFITS AND EXECUTIVE PERQUISITES

A medical plan and a company-paid retirement program have been in effect for many years. A plant cafeteria, operated on a break-even basis, serves meals at about 60 percent of usual costs. The Employee Association, to which the company does not contribute, provides disability insurance and social and athletic activities. The employee stock ownership program has resulted in employee ownership of about 50 percent of the common stock. Under this program, each employee with more than two years of service may purchase stock in the corporation. The price of these shares is established at book value. Stock purchased through this plan may be held by employees only. Dividends and voting rights are the same as for stock which is owned outside the plan. Approximately 75 percent of the employees own Lincoln stock.

As to executive perquisites, there are none—crowded, austere offices, no executive washrooms or lunchrooms, and no reserved parking spaces. Even the top executives pay for their own meals and eat in the employee cafeteria. On one recent day, Willis arrived at work late due to a breakfast speaking engagement and had to park far away from the factory entrance.

FINANCIAL POLICIES

James F. Lincoln felt strongly that financing for company growth should come from within the company—through initial cash investment by the founders, through retention of earnings, and through stock purchases by those who work in the business. He saw the following advantages of this approach:

1. Ownership of stock by employees strengthens team spirit. "If they are mutually anxious to make is succeed, the future of the company is bright."
2. Ownership of stock provides individual incentive because employees feel that they will benefit from company profitability.
3. "Ownership is educational." Owners-employees "will know how profits are made and lost; how success is won and lost.... There are few socialists in the list of stockholders of the nation's industries."

4. "Capital available from within controls expansion." Unwarranted expansion would not occur, Lincoln believed, under his financing plan.
5. "The greatest advantage would be the development of the individual worker. Under the incentive of ownership, he would become a greater man."
6. "Stock ownership is one of the steps that can be taken that will make the worker feel that there is less of a gulf between him and the boss. ...Stock ownership will help the worker to recognize his responsibility in the game and the importance of victory."

Until 1980, Lincoln Electric borrowed no money. Even now, the company's liabilities consist mainly of accounts payable and short-term accruals.

The unusual pricing policy at Lincoln is succinctly stated by Willis: "At all times price on the basis of cost and at all times keep pressure on our cost." This policy resulted in the price for the most popular welding electrode then in use going from 16 cents a pound in 1929 to 4.7 cents in 1938. More recently, the SA-200 Welder, Lincoln's largest selling portable machine, decreased in price from 1958 through 1965. According to Dr. C. Jackson Grayson of the American Productivity Center in Houston, Texas, Lincoln's prices increased only one-fifth as fast as the Consumer Price Index from 1934 to about 1970. This resulted in a welding products market in which Lincoln became the undisputed price leader for the products it manufactures. Not even the major Japanese manufacturers, such as Nippon Steel for welding electrodes and Osaka Transformer for welding machines, were able to penetrate this market.

Substantial cash balances are accumulated each year preparatory to paying the year-end bonuses. The bonuses totaled $54 million for 1988. The money is invested in short-term U.S. government securities and certificates of deposit until needed. Financial statements are shown in Exhibit 3. Exhibit 4 shows how company revenue was distributed in the late 1980s.

HOW WELL DOES LINCOLN SERVE ITS STAKEHOLDERS?

Lincoln Electric differs from most other companies in the importance it assigns to each of the groups it serves. Willis identifies these groups, in the order of priority ascribed to them, as (1) customers, (2) employees, and (3) stockholders.

Certainly the firm's customers have fared well over the years. Lincoln prices for welding machines and welding electrodes are acknowledged to be the lowest in the marketplace. Quality has consistently been high. The cost of field failures for Lincoln products was recently determined to be a remarkable 0.04 percent of revenues. The Fleetweld electrodes and SA-200 welders have been the standard in the pipeline and refinery construction industry, where price is hardly a criterion, for decades. A Lincoln distributor in Monroe, Louisiana, says that he has sold several hundred of the popular AC-225 welders, which are warranted for one year, but has never handled a warranty claim.

Perhaps best-served of all management constituencies have been the employees. Not the least of their benefits, of course, are the year-end bonuses, which effectively double an already average compensation level. The foregoing description of the personnel program and the comments in Appendix A further illustrate the desirability of a Lincoln job.

While stockholders were relegated to an inferior status by James F. Lincoln, they have done very well indeed. Recent dividends have exceeded $11 a share and earnings per share have approached $30. In January 1980, the price of restricted stock, committed to employees, was $117 a share. By 1989, the

EXHIBIT 3 LINCOLN ELECTRIC: CONDENSED COMPARATIVE FINANCIAL STATEMENTS

	BALANCE SHEETS								
	1979	*1980*	*1981*	*1982*	*1983*	*1984*	*1985*	*1986*	*1987*
ASSETS									
Cash	2	1	4	1	2	4	2	1	7
Bonds & CDs	38	47	63	72	78	57	55	45	41
N/R & A/R	42	42	42	26	31	34	38	36	43
Inventories	38	36	46	38	31	37	34	26	40
Prepayments	1	3	4	5	5	5	7	8	7
Total CA	121	129	157	143	146	138	135	116	137
Other assets**	24	24	26	30	30	29	29	33	40
Land	1	1	1	1	1	1	1	1	1
Net buildings	22	23	25	23	22	21	20	18	17
Net M&E	21	25	27	27	27	28	27	29	33
Total FA	44	49	53	51	50	50	48	48	50
Total assets	189	202	236	224	227	217	213	197	227
CLAIMS									
A/P	17	16	15	12	16	15	13	11	20
Accrued wages	1	2	5	4	3	4	5	5	4
Accrued taxes	10	6	15	5	7	4	6	5	9
Accrued div.	6	6	7	7	7	6	7	6	7
Total CL	33	29	42	28	33	30	31	27	40
LT debt		4	5	6	8	10	11	8	8
Total debt	33	33	47	34	41	40	42	35	48
Common stock	4	3	1	2	0	0	0	0	2
Ret. earnings	152	167	189	188	186	176	171	161	177
Total SH equity	156	170	190	190	186	176	171	161	179
Total claims	189	202	236	224	227	217	213	197	227

(continued)

EXHIBIT 3 (continued)

INCOME STATEMENTS

	1979	1980	1981	1982	1983	1984	1985	1986	1987
New sales	374	387	450	311	263	322	333	318	368
Other income	11	14	18	18	13	12	11	8	9
Income	385	401	469	329	277	334	344	326	377
CGS	244	261	293	213	180	223	221	216	239
Selling, G&A**	41	46	51	45	45	47	48	49	51
Incentive bonus	44	43	56	37	22	33	38	33	39
IBT	56	51	69	35	30	31	36	27	48
Income taxes	26	23	31	16	13	14	16	12	21
Net income	30	28	37	19	17	17	20	15	27

Note: Amounts are given in millions of dollars. Column totals may not check and amounts less than $500,000 (0.5) are shown as zero, due to rounding.
*Includes investment in foreign subsidiaries, $29 million in 1987.
**Includes pension expense and payroll taxes on incentive bonus.

stated value, at which the company will repurchase the stock if tendered, was $201. A check with the New York office of Merrill Lynch, Pierce, Fenner and Smith at that time revealed an estimated price on Lincoln stock of $270 a share, with none being offered for sale. Technically, this price applies only to

EXHIBIT 4 LINCOLN ELECTRIC: REVENUE DISTRIBUTION

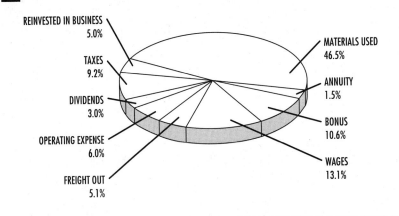

the unrestricted stock owned by the Lincoln family, a few other major holders, and employees who have purchased it on the open market. Risk associated with Lincoln stock, a major determinant of stock value, is minimal because of the small amount of debt in the capital structure, because of an extremely stable earnings record, and because of Lincoln's practice of purchasing the restricted stock whenever employees offer it for sale.

A CONCLUDING COMMENT

It is easy to believe that the reason for Lincoln's success is the excellent attitude of the employees and their willingness to work harder, faster, and more intelligently than other industrial workers. However, Sabo suggests that appropriate credit be given to Lincoln executives, whom he credits with carrying out the following policies:

1. Management has limited research, development, and manufacturing to a standard product line designed to meet the major needs of the welding industry.
2. New products must be reviewed by manufacturing and all producing costs verified before being approved by management.
3. Purchasing is challenged to not only procure materials at the lowest cost, but also to work closely with engineering and manufacturing to assure that the latest innovations are implemented.
4. Manufacturing supervision and all personnel are held accountable for reduction of scrap, energy conservation, and maintenance of product quality.
5. Production control, material handling, and methods engineering are closely supervised by top management.
6. Management has made cost reduction a way of life at Lincoln, and definite programs are established in many areas, including traffic and shipping, where tremendous savings can result.
7. Management has established a sales department that is technically trained to reduce customer welding costs. This sales approach and other real customer services have eliminated nonessential frills and resulted in long-term benefits to all concerned.
8. Management has encouraged education, technical publishing, and long range programs that have resulted in industry growth, thereby assuring market potential for the Lincoln Electric Company.

Sabo writes, "It is in a very real sense a personal and group experience in faith—a belief that together we can achieve results which alone would not be possible. It is not a perfect system and it is not easy. It requires tremendous dedication and hard work. However, it does work and the results are worth the effort."

APPENDIX A

Employee Interviews

Typical questions and answers from employee interviews are presented below. In order to maintain each employee's personal privacy, fictitious names are given to the interviewees.

INTERVIEW 1

Betty Stewart, a 52-year-old high school graduate who had been with Lincoln thirteen years and who was working as a cost accounting clerk at the time of the interview.

- Q: What jobs have you held here besides the one you have now?
- A: I worked in payroll for a while, and then this job came open and I took it.
- Q: How much money did you make last year, including your bonus?
- A: I would say roughly around $25,000, but I was off for back surgery for a while.
- Q: You weren't paid while you were off for back surgery?
- A: No.
- Q: Did the Employees Association help out?
- A: Yes. The company doesn't furnish that, though. We pay $8 a month into the Employee Association. I think my check from them was $130.00 a week.
- Q: How was your performance rating last year?
- A: It was around 100 points, but I lost some points for attendance for my back problem.
- Q: How did you get your job at Lincoln?

A: I was bored silly where I was working, and I had heard that Lincoln kept their people busy. So I applied and got the job the next day.

Q: Do you think you make more money than similar workers in Cleveland?

A: I know I do.

Q: What have you done with your money?

A: We have purchased a better home. Also, my son is going to the University of Chicago, which costs $13,000 a year. I buy the Lincoln stock which is offered each year, and I have a little bit of gold.

Q: Have you ever visited with any of the senior executives, like Mr. Willis or Mr. Hastings?

A: I have known Mr. Willis for a long time.

Q: Does he call you by name?

A: Yes. In fact he was very instrumental in my going to the doctor that I am going to with my back. He knows the director of the clinic.

Q: Do you know Mr. Hastings?

A: I know him to speak to him, and he always speaks, always. But I have known Mr. Willis for a good many years. When I did Plant Two accounting I did not understand how the plant operated. Of course you are not allowed in Plant Two, because that's the Electrode Division. I told my boss about the problem one day and the next thing I knew Mr. Willis came by and said, "Come on, Betty, we're going to Plant Two." He spent an hour and a half showing me the plant.

Q: Do you think Lincoln employees produce more than those in other companies?

A: I think with the incentive program the way that it is, if you want to work and achieve, then you will do it. If you don't want to work and achieve, you will not do it no matter where you are. Just because you are merit rated and have a bonus, if you really don't want to work hard, then you're not going to. You will accept your ninety points or ninety-two or eighty-five because, even with that you make more money than people on the outside.

Q: Do you think Lincoln employees will ever join a union?

A: I don't know why they would.

Q: So you say that money is a very major advantage?

A: Money is a major advantage, but it's not just the money. It's the fact that having the incentive, you do wish to work a little harder. I'm sure that there are a lot of men here who, if they worked some other place, would not work as hard as they do here. Not that they are overworked—I don't mean that—but I'm sure they wouldn't push.

Q: Is there anything that you would like to add?

A: I do like working here. I am better off being pushed mentally. In another company if you pushed too hard you would feel a little bit of pressure, and someone might say, "Hey, slow down; don't try so hard." But here you are encouraged, not discouraged.

INTERVIEW 2

Ed Sanderson, a 23-year-old high school graduate who had been with Lincoln four years and who was a machine operator in the Electrode Division at the time of the interview.

Q: How did you happen to get this job?
A: My wife was pregnant, and I was making three bucks an hour and one day I came here and applied. That was it. I kept calling to let them know I was still interested.
Q: Roughly what were your earnings last year including your bonus?
A: $45,000
Q: What have you done with your money since you have been here?
A: Well, we've lived pretty well and we bought a condominium.
Q: Have you paid for the condominium?
A: No, but I could.
Q: Have you bought your Lincoln stock this year?
A: No, I haven't bought any Lincoln stock yet.
Q: Do you get the feeling that the executives here are pretty well thought of?
A: I think they are. To get where they are today, they had to really work.
Q: Wouldn't that be true anywhere?
A: I think more so here because seniority really doesn't mean anything. If you work with a guy who has twenty years here, and you have two months and you're doing a better job, you will get advanced before he will.
Q: Are you paid on a piece rate basis?
A: My gang does. There are nine of us who make the bare electrode, and the whole group gets paid based on how much electrode we make.
Q: Do you think you work harder than workers in other factories in the Cleveland area?
A: Yes, I would say I probably work harder.
Q: Do you think it hurts anybody?
A: No, a little hard work never hurts anybody.
Q: If you could choose, do you think you would be as happy earning a little less money and being able to slow down a little?
A: No, it doesn't bother me. If it bothered me, I wouldn't do it.
Q: Why do you think Lincoln employees produce more than workers in other plants?
A: That's the way the company is set up. The more you put out, the more you're going to make.
Q: Do you think it's the piece rate and bonus together?
A: I don't think people would work here if they didn't know that they would be rewarded at the end of the year.

Q: Do you think Lincoln employees will ever join a union?
A: No.
Q: What are the major advantages of working for Lincoln?
A: Money.
Q: Are there any other advantages?
A: Yes, we don't have a union shop. I don't think I could work in a union shop.
Q: Do you think you are a career man with Lincoln at this time?
A: Yes.

INTERVIEW 3

Roger Lewis, a 23-year-old Purdue graduate in mechanical engineering who had been in the Lincoln sales program for fifteen months and who was working in the Cleveland sales office at the time of the interview.

Q: How did you get your job at Lincoln?
Q: I saw that Lincoln was interviewing on campus at Purdue, and I went by. I later came to Cleveland for a plant tour and was offered a job.
Q: Do you know any of the senior executives? Would they know you by name?
A: Yes, I know all of them—Mr. Hastings, Mr. Willis, Mr. Sabo.
Q: Do you think Lincoln salesmen work harder than those in other companies?
A: Yes. I don't think there are many salesmen for other companies who are putting in fifty- to sixty-hour weeks. Everybody here works harder. You can go out in the plant, or you can go upstairs, and there's nobody sitting around.
Q: Do you see any real disadvantage of working at Lincoln?
A: I don't know if it's a disadvantage but Lincoln is a spartan company, a very thrifty company. I like that. The sales offices are functional, not fancy.
Q: Why do you think Lincoln employees have such high productivity?
A: Piecework has a lot to do with it. Lincoln is smaller than many plants, too; you can stand in one place and see the materials come in one side and the product go out the other. You feel a part of the company. The chance to get ahead is important, too. They have a strict policy of promoting from within, so you know you have a chance. I think in a lot of other places you may not get as fair a shake as you do here. The sales offices are on a smaller scale, too. I like that. I tell someone that we have two people in the Baltimore office, and they say, "You've got to be kidding." It's smaller and more personal. Pay is the most important thing. I have heard that this is the highest paying factory in the world.

INTERVIEW 4

Jimmy Roberts, a 47-year-old high school graduate who had been with Lincoln seventeen years and who was working as a multiple-drill press operator at the time of the interview.

Q: What jobs have you had at Lincoln?
A: I started out cleaning the men's locker room in 1967. After about a year I got a job in the flux department, where we make the coating for welding rods. I worked there for seven or eight years and then got my present job.
Q: Do you make one particular part?
A: No, there are a variety of parts I make—at least twenty-five.
Q: Each one has a different piece rate attached to it?
A: Yes.
Q: Are some piece rates better than others?
A: Yes.
Q: How do you determine which ones you are going to do?
A: You don't. Your supervisor assigns them.
Q: How much money did you make last year?
A: $53,000.
Q: Have you ever received any kind of award or citation?
A: No.
Q: Was your rating ever over 110?
A: Yes. For the past five years, probably, I made over 110 points.
Q: Is there any attempt to let the others know . . . ?
A: The kind of points I get? No.
Q: Do you know what they are making?
A: No. There are some who might not be too happy with their points and they might make it known. The majority, though, do not make it a point of telling other employees.
Q: Would you be just as happy earning a little less money and working a little slower?
A: I don't think I would—not at this point. I have done piecework all these years, and the fast pace doesn't really bother me.
Q: Why do you think Lincoln productivity is so high?
A: The incentive thing—the bonus distribution. I think that would be the main reason. The pay check you get every two weeks is important too.
Q: Do you think Lincoln employees would ever join a union?
A: I don't think so. I have never heard anyone mention it.
Q: What is the most important advantage of working here?
A: Amount of money you make. I don't think I could make this type of money anywhere else, especially with only a high school education.
Q: As a black person, do you feel that Lincoln discriminates in any way against blacks?

A: No. I don't think any more so than any other job. Naturally, there is a certain amount of discrimination, regardless of where you are.

INTERVIEW 5

Joe Trahan, 58-year-old high school graduate who had been with Lincoln thirty-nine years and who was employed as a working supervisor in the tool room at the time of the interview.

Q: Roughly what was your pay last year?
A: Over $56,000; salary, bonus, stock dividends.
Q: How much was your bonus?
A: About $26,000.
Q: Have you ever gotten a special award of any kind?
A: Not really.
Q: What have you done with your money?
A: My house is paid for—and my two cars. I also have some bonds and the Lincoln stock.
Q: What do you think of the executives at Lincoln?
A: They're really top notch.
Q: What is the major disadvantage of working at Lincoln Electric?
A: I don't know of any disadvantage at all.
Q: Do you think you produce more than most people in similar jobs with other companies?
A: I do believe that.
Q: Why is that? Why do you believe that?
A: We are on the incentive system. Everything we do, we try to improve to make a better product with a minimum of outlay. We try to improve the bonus.
Q: Would you be just as happy making a little less money and not working quite so hard?
A: I don't think so.
Q: Do you think Lincoln employees would ever join a union?
A: I don't think they would ever consider it.
Q: What is the most important advantage of working at Lincoln?
A: Compensation.
Q: Tell me something about Mr. James Lincoln, who died in 1965.
A: You are talking about Jimmy Sr. He always strolled through the shop in his shirt sleeves. Big fellow. Always looked distinguished. Gray hair. Friendly sort of guy. I was a member of the advisory board one year. He was there each time.
Q: Did he strike you as really caring?
A: I think he always cared for people.
Q: Did you get any sensation of a religious nature from him?
A: No, not really.

Q: And religion is not part of the program now?
A: No.
Q: Do you think Mr. Lincoln was a very intelligent man, or was he just a nice guy?
A: I would say he was pretty well educated. A great talker—always right off the top of his head. He knew what he was talking about all the time.
Q: When were bonuses for beneficial suggestions done away with?
A: About eighteen years ago.
Q: Did that hurt very much?
A: I don't think so, because suggestions are still rewarded through the merit rating system.
Q: Is there anything you would like to add?
A: It's a good place to work. The union kind of ties other places down. At other places, electricians only do electrical work, carpenters only do carpenter work. At Lincoln Electric we all pitch in and do whatever needs to be done.
Q: So a major advantage is not having a union?
A: That's right.

CASE 11

CARNIVAL CRUISE LINES

BARBARA-JEAN ROSS,
CHEKITAN S. DEV, AND
KATHLEEN M. DENNISON

INTRODUCTION

In early 1990, Bob Dickinson, senior vice-president of sales and marketing, looked out of his Miami office window. He reflected on recent changes and considered future options for Carnival Cruise Lines (CCL).

Since the premiere of the Fun Ship Fleet® in 1984, CCL had been a significant player in the cruise industry. It had a 24% market share, based on available berths, and annual growth rates of 20% or more. The company's financial history is shown in Exhibit 1 and in Appendix A and Appendix B.

Prior to 1985, Carnival had concentrated its operations in the contemporary, entry-level segment. In 1989, the company embarked on an aggressive expansion plan, acquiring two cruise lines and ordering three new superliners. However, this expansion plan did not guarantee success. Holland America Line, one of CCL's acquisitions, came on line during the winter, its off season. Consequently, its short-term profit contributions were small. Wartsila, the Finnish shipyard contracted to build the superliners, declared bankruptcy in October 1989. Wartsila's bankruptcy delayed construction of the new superliners and increased production costs.

Carnival's acquisitions placed it in all segments of the cruise industry and gave CCL the opportunity to compete in the premium and luxury segments. Carnival also operated land-based tours and a casino. This case will focus on the Carnival Cruise Lines business unit (CCL), which operates eight ships from the ports of Miami, Ft. Lauderdale, Los Angeles, and San Juan, Puerto Rico. These ships are the *Mardi Gras, Carnivale, Festivale, Tropicale, Holiday, Jubilee, Celebration,* and *Fantasy.*

Source: This case was prepared by the authors at Cornell University's School of Hotel Administration as a basis for class discussion rather than to illustrate either effective or ineffective handling of a managerial situation. © 1990, Chekitan S. Dev.

EXHIBIT 1 FIVE-YEAR SUMMARY OF SALES AND INCOME, CARNIVAL CRUISE LINES (1985–1989)*

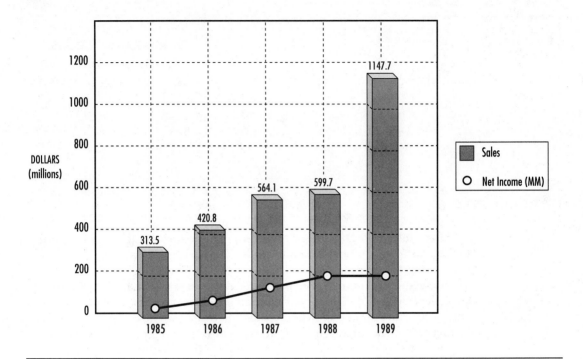

*All business units.
Source: CCL 10-K; Robinson-Humphrey Company, Inc., *Equities Research*.

As CCL enters the 1990s, it faces a critical period, not only for CCL, but for the entire cruise industry. Rapid expansion of capacity and softening of the U.S. economy are making competition fierce in this once-booming industry. Dickinson and Carnival's executive management face the major task of selecting both a short-term plan to guide the company through the immediate challenges and a long-term strategy to carry the firm into the twenty-first century.

HISTORY

Ted Arison founded Carnival Cruise Lines (CCL) in 1974 after approximately ten years in the shipping industry. The company has been operated by the Arison family since its inception. Ted Arison has been chairman of the board since 1974. Arison's son, Micky, held several positions with the company before being named chief executive officer in 1979.

Carnival was launched at the height of the energy crisis with one aging transatlantic liner christened the *Mardi Gras*. The ship proved to be a gas guzzler so its ports of call and cruising speed were reduced. Arison decided to add on-board activities to compensate for the cutbacks. The activities included a disco, a casino, a movie theatre, and nightclubs. The marketing team dubbed the *Mardi Gras* the Fun Ship®, and a new era of cruising began.[1]

From 1974 to 1985, CCL expanded its fleet by adding a new ship every two to four years. CCL also entered the gaming industry in 1983 when it built the Crystal Palace Resort and Casino and Nassau, the Bahamas. In 1985, the company crafted a strategy of further expansion, which was to be financed by the public offering of common stock in July 1987. The stock offering raised approximately $400 million. In the quest for expansion, Carnival attempted to acquire Royal Caribbean Cruise Lines (RCCL) and Holland America Cruise Operations, which operates both Holland America Line (HAL) and Windstar Sail Cruises (WSC). CCL was unsuccessful in its bid to acquire RCCL because of RCCL's large size and financial strength. However, Carnival successfully acquired Holland America Cruise Operations. Consequently, the company now operates three separate cruise lines: (1) Carnival Cruise Lines, which competes in the Caribbean market; (2) Holland America, which competes in the Alaskan and Caribbean market; and (3) Windstar Sail Cruises, which operates in the Caribbean, Mediterranean, and South Pacific markets.

The acquisition of HAL and WSC increased the company's total number of berths to 13,909. A summary of the CCL ships, including the year each entered service and its passenger capacity, is shown in Exhibit 2. To further augment supply, Carnival placed construction orders for three new superliners—*Fantasy, Ecstasy,* and *Sensation*—to begin operations in 1989, 1990, and 1991, respectively. *Fantasy* (passenger capacity 2,044) came on line in 1990. The estimated cost for each ship was $200 million, including start-up costs.

CARNIVAL CRUISE LINES, INC.: BUSINESS BREAKDOWN

In 1990, Carnival Cruise Lines, Inc. was the largest operator of cruise ships sailing to North American destinations. This North American market made up 60–75% of the worldwide cruise market. In the Caribbean market, CCL

---

car‑ni‑val (kâr′nə vəl) n. 2a. any merrymaking, feasting, or masquerading. 3a. a traveling enterprise consisting of such amusements as sideshows, games of chance.... 3b. an organized program of entertainment or exhibition. (*Webster's Third New International Dictionary*, 1986)

---

fantasy (fan tə see) n.1. imagination or fancy, esp: the free play of creative imagination as it affects perception and productivity. 3a. a fanciful design or invention. 4. a whimsical or capricious mood. 5. daydream. (*Webster's Third New International Dictionary, 1986*)

EXHIBIT 2 SUMMARY OF CCL SHIPS

NAME	YEAR ENTERED SERVICE	PASSENGER CAPACITY
CARNIVAL CRUISE LINES		
Celebration	1987	1,486
Jubilee	1986	1,486
Holiday	1985	1,452
Tropicale	1982	1,022
Festivale	1978	1,146
Carnivale	1976	950
Mardi Gras	1974	906
Total CCL		8,448
HOLLAND AMERICA LINE		
Westerdam	1988	1,494
Noordam	1984	1,214
Nieuw Amsterdam	1983	1,214
Rotterdam	1959	1,095
Total HAL		5,017
WINDSTAR SAIL CRUISES		
Wind Spirit	1988	148
Wind Song	1987	148
Wind Star	1986	148
Total WSC		444
GRAND TOTAL CLL		13,909

Source: CCL 1989 10-K.

represented a contemporary, entry-level offering. In Alaska and the Caribbean, Holland America Line represented a premium offering. In the worldwide market, Windstar Sail Cruises offered luxury cruises on small, sail-powered vessels.

In addition to cruises, CCL also operated in the following industries: tours, transportation, hotels, and gaming. The tour and transportation unit was Westours, which offered tours in Alaska, Washington, and the Canadian Yukon. These land tours were sold as stand-alone tours and as part of land/cruise packages. Carnival's Crystal Palace Resort represented the hotel and gaming business unit. (The percentage of company revenue attributable to each of CCL's business segments is shown in Appendix C.)

Carnival Cruise Lines and its subsidiaries are incorporated in Panama and Liberia and thus exempted from most U.S. taxes. The company is traded on the American Stock Exchange under the ticker symbol CCL.

THE CRUISE INDUSTRY

The cruise industry was once considered a dying industry due to the efficiency and convenience of air travel. However, today cruising has become the fastest growing and most dynamic segment of the travel industry because only 5% of the U.S. leisure/vacation market has been on a cruise. Growth has been so dramatic that the Cruise Lines International Association (CLIA) termed the years between 1970 and 1982 the "Cruise Revolution" era. *Fortune* magazine reported, "The number of Americans who file up the gangplank annually has gone up 600% since 1980, to more than three million, well above the growth rate of any other hospitality business."[2] The *Journal of Travel Research* noted, "Passengers on cruise ships tripled between 1970 and 1982 from 500,000 to 1,500,000 and the number continues to grow."[3] The popularity of the "Love Boat" television show also contributed to this rapid growth in the cruise industry. The significant increase in cruise passengers is illustrated in Exhibit 3, which shows the number of cruise passengers traveling in the North American market.

EXHIBIT 3 NUMBER OF CRUISE PASSENGERS, NORTH AMERICAN MARKET

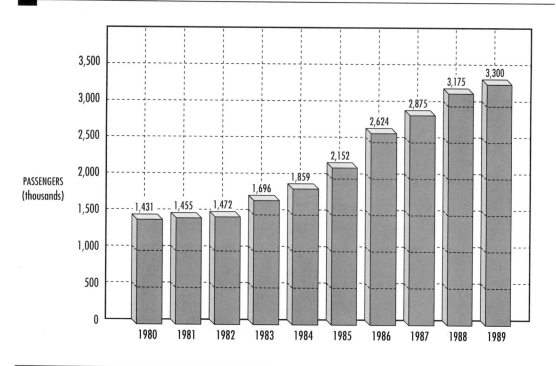

Source: Robinson-Humphrey Company, Inc., *Equities Research.*

A major factor in this dramatic growth has been word-of-mouth recommendations from satisfied cruise passengers. When asked to compare cruises with other types of vacations, passengers provide cruises with the highest satisfaction ratings in the travel industry.[4]

Along with the dramatic growth in passengers, there has been an accompanying growth in berth space. All of the major cruise lines have added ships or berths to existing ships to exploit the upswing in customer demand. The number of berths in the North American market is illustrated in Exhibit 4.

In the 1990s, the industry projects a 14% increase in berth space. Until 1989, passenger growth kept pace with berth increases. However, berth increases are expected to outpace passenger growth due to the entry of new lines into the industry and the aggressive expansion plans of present competitors. The projected growth in number of available berths is depicted in Exhibit 5.

In this rapidly growing industry, cruises to North American destinations represent the fastest growing segment. Within North America, Caribbean destinations remain the most popular. Major players in the Caribbean cruise market include Carnival, Royal Caribbean, Norwegian Caribbean, Premier, Epirotiki, Holland American, Princess, and Cunard.

EXHIBIT 4 TOTAL NUMBER OF BERTHS, NORTH AMERICAN MARKET

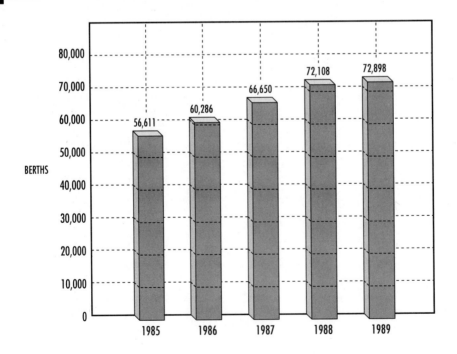

Source: Robinson-Humphrey Company, Inc., *Equities Research.*

EXHIBIT 5 PROJECTED TOTAL NUMBER OF BERTHS IN 1990, NORTH AMERICAN MARKET

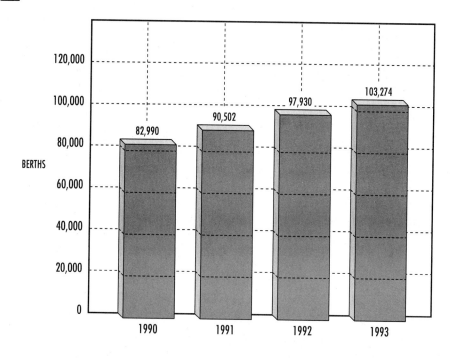

Source: Robinson-Humphrey Company, Inc., *Equities Research*.

It is a widely held belief that cruise passengers are "newly wed or nearly dead." In fact, the profile of cruise passengers is varied, as shown by a 1990 CLIA market study of passengers who had taken a cruise in the previous five years.[5] CLIA found that the age of cruisers was almost uniformly distributed between the ages of 25 and 60-plus. The major portion of passengers (39%) earned between $20,000 and $40,000, and 28% earned more than $60,000. However, significant demographic differences did exist in the categories of sex, marital status, and household composition. Fifty-six percent of cruisers are female, 65% are married, and 69% do not have children at home.

THE PRODUCT

Cruises are designed to be all-inclusive packages. The typical cruise product offers room, board, and entertainment. Most cruises offer exotic ports of call, on-board events, or special programs. Alcohol, gambling, and gift shop purchases are not included in the base price.

CURRENT INDUSTRY SEGMENTATION

The cruise industry can be segmented by number of cruise days and dollar amount per day for each cruise type. Exhibit 6 displays the positioning of the main competitors, based on the duration and price of their cruises.

Flexibility in packaging gives the industry additional segments. When existing segments incorporate different ports of call, the industry is able to attract diversified markets by responding to each market's needs with different packages. The ability to change packages to reflect changing customer profiles allows the industry to swiftly capitalize on demographic and social trends.

SUBSTITUTE PRODUCTS

Many substitute products are available to the potential cruise passenger. Some of the industry-related substitutes include airlines (for transportation), hotels, destination resorts, all-inclusive resorts, time-shares, and casinos. Be-

EXHIBIT 6 CURRENT CRUISE INDUSTRY SEGMENTATION

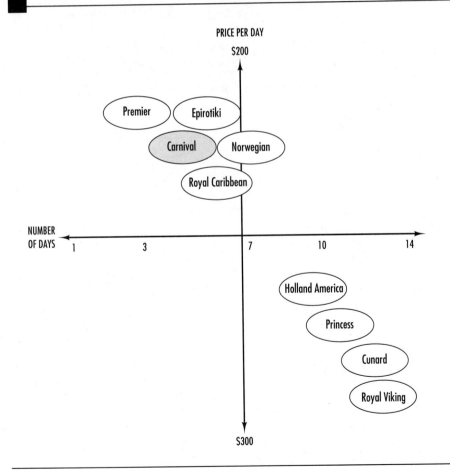

cause cruises are usually discretionary purchases, especially in times of economic recession, passengers can also decide to stay at home in lieu of taking a cruise.

Many people have the misconception that cruising is an expensive proposition. One element of the perception problem exists because of leftover images from the cruise industry when it was an expensive, elitist vacation option. Another factor is that the price of a cruise is almost all inclusive. For example, "the up-front cost of a seven-day Caribbean cruise can easily run $1,600 per person [including airfare]."[6] The price tag may seem exorbitant unless the potential customer takes the time to calculate the cost of a non-inclusive, land-based vacation.

POTENTIAL NEW ENTRANTS

Due to the performance of the industry over the past ten years, many new entrants have begun or plan to begin operations. For example, Crystal and Seabourn are new entrants in the luxury market. Each new entry into the cruise industry has some impact on Carnival because the entry represents additional berth space and competition for passengers.

COMPETITION

CCL competes directly with up to seven cruise lines offering cruises from Florida and California. Each cruise line focuses on different aspects of the cruise product, such as food, ports of call, or on-board experiences. Because of its emphasis on on-board activities, CCL characterizes itself as The Fun Ship® Fleet and use the slogan "Ain't we got fun." The profiles and slogans of primary and secondary competitors are described below.

Norwegian Caribbean Lines (NCL). NCL is one of three cruise lines operated by Kloster Cruise Line. NCL is in the contemporary market and operates six ships (6,490 berths) in the Caribbean and West Coast markets. Itineraries range from three to seven days and feature sporting activities and nighttime entertainment. The line specializes in Broadway-style shows and theme cruises, focusing on ideas such as jazz, chocolate, Big Bands, and the 1950s. NCL also owns a private island in the Bahamas that is visited only by NCL ships. Snorkeling, sailing, and windsurfing are key attractions of the private island. A pride of the line is the *Norway,* formerly the *France,* reputed to be one of the grandest cruise liners afloat. NCL's newest ship, built in 1988, is the *Seaward.* It its slogan, NCL boasts, "We are going to spoil you."

Royal Caribbean Cruise Line (RCCL). RCCL is one of two cruise lines operated by Royal Admiral Cruises (8,950 berths). Royal Admiral Cruises was the largest cruise company in the world, based on number of berths, until CCL acquired HAL. RCCL operates six ships in the contemporary market. Its itineraries range from three to twelve days and include destinations in the Caribbean, Bermuda, and Europe. The line's focal point is the *Sovereign of the Seas,* the world's largest cruise ship with passenger capacity of 2,282. RCCL planned to expand its fleet in 1991, adding another ship similar in size to the *Sovereign of the Seas*. RCCL claims to offer "The it's all here vacation."

Secondary Competitors. Premier Cruise Lines operates in the contemporary market, offering short cruises in Florida and the Caribbean. Most cruises include a land tour to Walt Disney World. Epirotiki Cruises, also in the contemporary market, allows passengers to "Cruise to a different beat." It offers three-, four-, and seven-day Caribbean cruises departing from Trinidad. Princess, Cunard, and Royal Viking Line feature Caribbean as well as worldwide itineraries. These lines operate in the luxury market.

FACTORS THAT AFFECT THE CRUISE INDUSTRY

There are many potential external threats to the cruise industry. First, the industry is sensitive to general economic conditions. Since cruise and tour travel is discretionary, it can be curtailed in times of recession.

Second, the cruise industry is subject to fuel costs. For most cruise lines, fuel expenses represent 3–5% of revenue. Since cruises are sold in advance, if expenses rise after the cruise is sold, the company has no way to recover the additional fuel expense.

Weather can affect the demand for cruising. Since the Caribbean is the predominant destination in North America, hurricanes can play a major role. Though the cruise experience may not actually be affected, the perception in the consumer's mind is important. For example, Hurricane Hugo had a negative impact on bookings in 1989 and 1990. The negative press associated with the hurricane and the resulting destruction reduced cruise bookings.

Finally, cruises do not originate in passengers' home cities. Thus cruise companies are extremely dependent on air transportation to deliver their passengers. For example, Carnival found that "the Eastern Airline strike reduced fiscal 1989 earnings by about $0.05 per share for CCL since [it was] forced to purchase airline tickets in the open market."[7] The airfare portion of Carnival's cruise packages accounted for 30% of its revenues.[8] Thus, interruption of service (strikes) or rate increases by airlines negatively impact both bookings and profits.

EXTERNAL OPPORTUNITIES

The industry faces four potential opportunities for growth. The largest opportunity is the changing demographics in North America as the baby boomers grow into middle age. This group begins to have more disposable or discretionary income that may be spent on a cruise. The next opportunity is the estimate that only 5% of the leisure travel market (70 million Americans) has been on a cruise—which leaves a vast untapped market available to the cruise industry. Third, due to the flexibility of cruise packaging, many diverse segments can be targeted. Fourth, since ships are mobile by nature, the ports of call can be altered each season. Many cruise lines, such as Princess and Holland America, feature cruises to the Caribbean during winter and to Alaska during summer.

SUPPLIERS

The potential for adding new ships has been severely limited by the bankruptcy of Wartsila shipyard in Finland. Other shipyards exist, predominantly in Germany, Hong Kong, and the United States, but the cost of new ship construction has risen dramatically and the number of new berths that can be constructed has been reduced.

BUYERS

The cruise industry is dependent on its relationship with three buyers. Travel agents and wholesalers sell roughly 90% of all bookings for premium and contemporary cruises. Airlines are also influential because they transport people to ports of embarkation. Additionally, due to heavy discounting by some liners, knowledgeable consumers have learned to shop for price, thereby creating more power for the individual cruise product purchaser.

MARKETING

THE PRODUCT

With its invention of the Fun Ship® Fleet, Carnival pioneered shorter (three, four, and seven days) and less expensive cruises. The Fun Ship® was designed to have broad market appeal by emphasizing on-board entertainment, activities, and gambling. Ports of call were less important to the overall cruise experience. CCL cruises were designed as an all-inclusive package, making the cost of a cruise very favorable when compared to foreign travel or domestic land-based, non-inclusive vacations.

Carnival characterized its product in the following way:

> As befits their status as destination rather than mere transportation, Carnival's ships are floating resorts.... The company reinforces the notion of the ship as a resort by swamping the passengers with service. The ratio of guests to crew is 2 to 1.... Eating, drinking, and a daunting number of activities go on nonstop. There are eight bars, room service is available 24 hours a day versus 16 for some lines, dining rooms serve three full meals daily and two midnight buffets. Sandwiches, salad, and snacks are available from 6:30 am. Every afternoon pie-eating events, pillow fights, and contests to select the woman with the shapeliest legs and the man with the hairiest chest take place at poolside. Passengers can play bingo or shuffle board, shoot skeet, or visit a fully equipped gym and sauna, a beauty parlor, or gambling casino.[9]

PROMOTION

"'Our job is kind of like telling a hermit about sex.' quips Dickinson. 'He won't know what you're talking about at first, but once he tries it, he's going to like it.'"[10] Because of this large potential market base for cruise vacations, Carnival broke with tradition and moved away from the industry standard of newspaper advertising toward mixed-media advertising. Carnival also capitalized on the popularity of the "Love Boat."

In 1988, Carnival spent approximately $30 million on advertising, more than any other cruise line. Carnival's 1989 expenditure of $15 million on television advertising was more than all the other players in the cruise industry combined. (Appendix D compares advertising expenditures for CCL and its competitors. Note that these data are from 1985, the latest year available for CCL's competitors. In the late 1980s, Holland America, Princess, and Royal Caribbean started television campaigns.)

Currently, only 2% of the money spent in the U.S. leisure market ($100 billion per year) is spent on cruises, as reported by CLIA. CLIA forecasts a segment of 30 million first-time cruisers. Consequently, Carnival has targeted its efforts toward those Americans and Canadians who would be first-time cruise patrons.

Carnival targeted a mass market by using aggressive marketing to emphasize the shipboard experience. As one cruise industry leader stated, what Carnival sells is "fun," and it sells fun relentlessly. Carnival's television advertising and promotion attempted to convey the message that a Carnival holiday at sea is within reach of nearly every American.[11]

"'The average age [of a cruiser] used to be deceased' is a favorite line of Dickinson. . . . 'We're marketing to a younger clientele than the cruise industry.' About 30% of Carnival's passengers are under 35; 30% are over 55, and the balance is in the middle."[12] Carnival made several changes in its operations to attract the younger market. It went against industry norms by giving its ships nontraditional names such as *Mardi Gras, Festivale,* and *Jubilee*. New names were even more exotic, including *Ecstasy, Fantasy* (the latest addition), and *Sensation*, still to be built. CCL also instituted singles cruises, parties, and packages.

DISTRIBUTION

CCL became the industry's most forceful marketer to travel agents. A survey on the *Jubilee* revealed that virtually all of the passengers said Carnival Cruise Lines was recommended by their travel agent.[13] Travel agents sell 99% of CCL's cruises; thus, selling these agents on the Carnival product was paramount for the lines' success.

Carnival was very supportive of travel agencies as a distribution channel. None of CCL's advertising had a direct-response pitch; its advertisements referred readers to their travel agents. Commissions and other payments to travel agents accounted for Carnival's second-largest cost of sale (approximately 20–24% of revenue).

Dickinson developed an extremely successful long-term promotion geared toward travel agents. "Mystery vacationers" visited travel agencies. If a travel agent recommended a cruise first, he/she received $10. If the agent's initial suggestion was a Carnival Cruise, the "mystery vacationer" gave the agent $1,000. Carnival has awarded more than $500,000 to agents since the "mystery vacation" program began in 1981.

However, there were problems with this distribution system. At a travel industry meeting in Cancun, Dickinson made these comments about travel agents and their sales skills:

> Most travel counselors really don't know how to sell. The average agency isn't converting anywhere close to its potential sales ... only about 10 percent of leisure travel enquiries are converted to sales. There are agencies out there that are converting 50 percent, 60 percent of their enquiries. (Agency managers) need to make sure (travel counselors) get selling technique seminars and learn how to qualify prospects; without spending an additional dollar in advertising or promotion, agencies could triple their volume of vacation business by taking the conversion rate from 10 percent to 30 percent.[14]

Research quoted by Dickinson revealed that travel agents convert only 3–15% of their sales opportunities into actual sales. Any other industry has a standard conversion rate of 30%. In contrast, Dickinson pointed out the success of Liberty Travel as a positive example of what can be accomplished: Agents made $30,000 and up strictly on commission.[15]

Passengers making direct purchases represented a second channel of distribution. However, for CCL, this channel was almost nonexistent.

PRICING AND UTILIZATION

Discounting of prices has increased dramatically in recent years. Carnival already offered cruises priced at least 20% below competitors, but had to drop prices to as low as $599 for a seven-day cruise (normally, the price would start at $995). However, cruise lines are willing to discount fares because the average passenger spends an extra $50 per day on board the ship. Carnival gained 14% of its revenue from passengers' on-board expenditures.

The average industrywide utilization factor is 78%. In 1989, Carnival completed its twelfth year of 100%-plus capacity. Utilization figures, also referred to as occupancy figures, are based on two people per cabin. Thus, a ship is at 100% capacity if all berths (rooms) are sold with double occupancy. Numbers over 100% are obtained because some cabins have three or four beds. Carnival had the lowest break-even point in the industry at 60% utilization.

CONCLUSION

As Dickinson considers the future of CCL, what course should he chart? Should his long-term pricing strategy hinge on the current wave of discounting, or should he steer Carnival in a new direction? How will demographic changes affect CCL's market position in the future? Is CCL poised to defend its dominance of the contemporary cruise market? These are the questions Dickinson pondered as he turned away from the Miami skyline and returned to his desk.

ENDNOTES

1. F. Rice, "How Carnival Stacks the Decks," *Fortune* (January 16, 1989): 109.
2. Ibid.
3. R. Santangelo, "What's Happening in the Cruise Industry," *Journal of Travel Research* (Fall 1984): 3.
4. Cruise Lines International Association, *The Cruise Industry—An Overview* (July 1990):8.
5. Ibid., p. 14.
6. R. Christie, "Cruise Operators Hope Marketing Push Will Put the Wind Back in Their Sales," *Wall Street Journal* (April 3, 1990):B1.
7. J. D. Parker, *Carnival Cruise Lines, Inc., Equities Research, Basic Report* (Atlanta: The Robinson-Humphrey Co., 1990).
8. Rice, "How Carnival Stacks the Decks."
9. Ibid.
10. P. Schnorbus, "Liner Notes," *Marketing & Media Decisions* (January 1987): 64.
11. Santangelo, "What's Happening."
12. Schnorbus, "Liner Notes."
13. P. Schnorbus, "Ain't We Got Fun!" *Marketing & Media Decisions* (March 1988): 101–106.
14. Judi Bredemeier, "Adapting to Change," *ASTA Agency Management* (July 1990): 59.
15. Ibid.

APPENDIX A CARNIVAL CRUISE LINES INCOME STATEMENT* ($ THOUSANDS)

FISCAL YR ENDED	11/30/89	11/30/88	11/30/87	11/30/86	11/30/85
Net Sales	1,147,675	599,731	564,080	420,837	313,503
Cost of Goods	659,947	326,872	305,072	232,525	188,291
Gross Profit	487,728	272,859	259,008	188,312	125,212
Sell Gen & Admin. Exp	180,285	87,309	82,355	70,541	58,289
Inc Bef Dep & Amort	307,443	185,550	176,653	117,771	66,923
Depreciation & Amort	66,705	27,468	24,506	16,552	9,982
Non-operating Income	18,939	40,150	14,037	3,938	2,694
Interest Expense	59,657	1,838	13,378	7,466	4,028
Income before tax	200,020	196,394	152,806	97,691	55,607
Income Taxes	6,415	0	0	0	0
Net Income	193,605	196,394	152,806	97,691	55,607

*All business units.
Source: CCL 10-K.

APPENDIX B CARNIVAL CRUISE LINES BALANCE SHEET* ($ THOUSANDS)

	FISCAL YEAR ENDED NOVEMBER 30		
	1989	*1988*	*1987*
ASSETS			
Cash	101,148	90,406	153,379
Marketable Securities	11,600	266,262	195,821
Receivables	35,786	8,877	8,269
Inventories	26,833	10,905	10,611
Other Current Assets	35,950	18,585	7,276
Total Current Assets	211,317	395,035	375,356
Net Prop. Plant & Equip	1,703,201	568,654	474,188
Deposits Other Assets	305,641	85,783	91,486
Total Assets	2,220,159	1,049,472	941,030
LIABILITIES			
Accounts Payable	72,233	37,590	30,830
Current Long Term Debt	183,236	13,717	13,775
Accrued Expense	106,534	27,375	24,706
Other Current Liability	142,044	142,128	146,010
Total Current Liability	504,047	220,810	215,321
Long-Term Debt	822,956	76,392	90,177
Total Liabilities	1,327,003	297,202	305,498
SHAREHOLDERS' EQUITY			
Common Stock Net	1,362	1,362	1,362
Capital Surplus	420,242	419,360	419,360
Retained Earnings	493,470	353,724	236,792
Treasury Stock	−14,396	−15,001	−14,056
Shares to be Vested	−7,522	−7,175	−7,926
Shareholder's Equity	893,156	752,270	635,532
Total Liabilities and Net Worth	2,220,159	1,049,472	941,030

*All business units.

Source: *CCL 1989 Annual Report* and 10-K.

APPENDIX C CARNIVAL CRUISE LINES FINANCIAL HIGHLIGHTS, 1985-1989*

FISCAL YR	1989	1988	1987	1986	1985
Revenue (MM)					
Cruise	901.7	574.2	525.9	383.9	281.2
Tour	155.0	0.0	0.0	0.0	0.0
Resort & Casino	91.0	25.5	38.2	36.9	32.3
Total	1,147.7	599.7	564.1	420.8	313.5
Operating income (MM)					
Cruise	234.6	163.0	152.9	103.7	60.2
Tour	16.9	0.0	0.0	0.0	0.0
Resort & Casino	−10.7	−4.9	−0.7	−2.5	−3.3
Total	240.7	158.1	152.1	101.2	56.9
Operating Margin	21%	26%	27%	24%	18%
Other Income (Expense%)**	−40.7	38.3	0.7	−3.5	−1.3
Pre-tax Margin	17%	33%	27%	23%	18%
Net Income (MM)	193.6	196.4	152.8	97.7	55.6
Net Margin	17%	33%	27%	23%	18%
EPS	$1.44	$1.46	$1.30	$0.89	$0.51
Operating Statistics (Cruise)					
Passengers	73,485	579,034	552,774	483,339	310,242
Capacity Utilization	107%	112%	112%	110%	113%
Revenue per passenger per day	$186.06	$172.10	$166.48	$161.75	N.A.

*All business units, except as noted.

**1989 figures reflect the disposition of cash and interest expense associated with the acquisition of Holland America, effective January 1, 1989.

Source: CCL 10-K; Robinson-Humphrey Company, Inc., *Equities Research*.

APPENDIX D MEDIA EXPENDITURES, 1985 ($ THOUSANDS)

CRUISE COMPANY	MAGAZINES	NEWSPAPER	TELEVISION	MEDIA TOTAL
Carnival	**25.1**	**6,429.1**	**8,659.0**	**15,113.2**
Cunard	0.0	8,791.4	0.0	8,791.4
Holland America	611.2	3,766.4	0.0	4,377.6
Princess	0.0	6,197.7	0.0	6,197.7
Royal Caribbean	2,964.9	6,591.0	0.0	9,555.9
Royal Viking	2,254.1	4,899.1	0.0	7,153.2
Totals	5,855.3	36,674.7	8,659.0	51,189.0

Source: Paula Schnorbus, "Liner Notes," *Marketing and Media Decisions* (January 1987).

CASE 12

TOYS "R" US, 1989

CARON H. ST. JOHN

In 1948, Charles Lazarus began selling baby furniture in the back of his father's Washington, D.C., bicycle repair shop, located below the apartment where the Lazarus family lived. Within a few months, and in response to customer requests, he added a few toys to his line of baby furniture. Before long he realized parents who bought toys returned for more toys—but parents who bought furniture rarely came back. "When I realized that toys broke," he said, "I knew it was a good business."[1] Soon his entire business was focused on toys.

After the success of his first store, he opened his second store in Washington as a self-serve, cash-and-carry business. In 1958, he opened his third store—a 25,000-square-foot "baby supermarket" with discount prices and a large selection of products. Within a few years, a fourth supermarket-style store was opened. By 1966, the four stores in the Washington, D.C., area were achieving $12 million in annual sales.

In order to have the capital necessary for continued growth, Lazarus sold his four stores in 1966 to Interstate Stores, a retail discount chain, for $7 million. Lazarus stayed with Interstate and maintained operating control over the toy division. Between 1966 and 1974, the Toys "R" Us division of Interstate Stores grew from 4 to 47 stores through internal growth and a merger with Children's Bargain Town.

In 1974, the parent company, Interstate Stores, filed for bankruptcy. When Interstate completed reorganization and emerged from bankruptcy in 1978, the new company name was Toys "R" Us (TRU) and Charles Lazarus was chief executive officer. Since then, all but four of the Interstate Stores have been divested and all creditors have been paid.

Between January 1979 and January 1984, Toys "R" Us grew from 63 stores with sales of just under $350 million to 169 stores with sales of over $1.3 billion, for a compound annual growth rate of 30%. During the same years, profits increased from $17 million to $92 million for a compound annual

---

Source: Prepared by Professor Caron H. St. John, Clemson University, as a basis for classroom discussion and not to illustrate either effective or ineffective handling of administrative situations. © Caron H. St. John, 1990.

growth rate of 40%. TRU stock, which traded for $2 per share in 1978, split 3 for 2 for 4 years in a row and consistently traded above $40 per share. A $2 TRU stock investment made in 1978 was worth $200 in the spring of 1984.

After 1984, Toys "R" Us continued to grow and gain share of market in the toy retailing market. By 1988 sales had more than doubled to $3.14 billion with earnings of $204 million. At that time, Toys "R" Us operated 313 U.S. toy stores, 37 international toy stores, 74 Kids "R" Us clothing stores, and 4 department stores. As of 1988, Toys "R" Us was the largest toy retailer in the world with an estimated U.S. market share of greater than 21%.

Charles Lazarus has consistently been the motivating force behind the growth of Toys "R" Us. His vision is for Toys "R" Us to become the McDonald's of toy retailing: "We don't have golden arches, but we're getting there."[2] He credits his success in toy retailing to his love of the business. "What we do is the essence of America—making a business grow," he says. "If you're going to be a success in life you have to want it. I wanted it. I was poor. I wanted to be rich.... My ego now is in the growth of this company."[3]

TOY INDUSTRY

The U.S. toy industry saw the best of times and the worst of times during the decade of the eighties. Between 1980 and 1984, sales growth in the toy industry, fueled by electronic games and Cabbage Patch Kids, was very strong. Including electronic games, sales growth in those years exceeded 18% per year. Excluding the electronic games category, industry sales growth averaged 11%. While electronic games accounted for 18.4% of total U.S. toy sales in 1980, by 1982 they represented 30.9%—almost one-third—of total toy sales. During those same years, highly publicized toys such as Cabbage Patch Kid dolls, ET the Extra-Terrestrial toys, and the Trivial Pursuit board game accounted for 50% of non-electronic game sales. Traditional toys such as Slinky and Etch-A-Sketch accounted for the remaining 50%.

In 1984 and 1985, interest in electronic games fell sharply. This trend, combined with a dearth of blockbuster new toys of the caliber of Cabbage Patch Kids and Trivial Pursuit, resulted in relatively flat sales for the industry from 1985 to 1987. Total retail toy sales in 1988 were just over $13 billion.

TOY MANUFACTURING

During the slow growth years, many toy manufacturers suffered financially. Several companies posted losses in 1986 and 1987, and two large companies, Coleco and Worlds of Wonder, were forced into Chapter 11 bankruptcy.

By 1988, the industry had turned much of its energies toward cost control. Hasbro and Mattel closed facilities to reduce overhead costs and Tonka shifted much of its production to contract vendors in the Far East. Product development efforts focused on traditional favorites with considerably less emphasis on promotional games and toys, and licensed dolls and action figures (see

Exhibit 1). The movement toward traditional toys and cost containment was fueled by the bankruptcies of Coleco and Worlds of Wonder, the creator of the talking Teddy Ruxpin bear. The consensus in the industry was that both companies had become overly dependent on their promotional toys and had neglected cost controls.

TOY RETAILING

Until recently discount stores were the primary outlet for toy sales in the U.S. As shown in Exhibit 2, toy stores, particularly toy supermarkets such as Toys "R" Us and Lionel, have made major inroads into the retail toy market. Although all categories of retailers compete with each other, they use different approaches to appeal to customers. The national toy chains offer a large selection of products at low prices with a minimal level of in-store service. The discount stores frequently offer similar low prices and minimal service, but their selection is not as extensive as that of the toy chains. The small, independent toy stores provide personalized service and specialty items but ask higher prices. The larger department stores compete on the basis of convenience—the customer can purchase toys while shopping for other items. Toy depart-

EXHIBIT 1   TOY SHIPMENTS IN LEADING PRODUCT CATEGORIES (MILLIONS OF DOLLARS)

	1986	1987	% CHANGE
Plush (electronic; traditional)	$1,062	$1,174	10.5
Activity toys (educational, building sets, model kits, art)	850	1,092	28.5
Vehicles (remote control, battery, nonpower)	764	923	20.8
Dolls (baby, fashion)	1,663	920	(44.7)
Games & puzzles	760	861	13.3
Infant/preschool	816	840	2.9
Figures (action, robots)	1,105	702	(36.5)
Ride-on toys, except bicycles	288	570	97.9
Guns (weapons, accessories)	71	78	9.9
Other (playground, furniture, sports, audiovisual)	944	1,041	10.3
Total toy industry	$8,323	$8,201	(1.5%)

Source: Exstein, Michael B., "Toys "R" Us," *Shearson Lehman Hutton Investment Analysis* (August 19, 1988). (Original source: Toy Manufacturers of America, February 1988.)

EXHIBIT 2 U.S. TOY SALES BY TYPE OF STORE, PERCENT SHARE OF MARKET

	1982	1987
Toy, hobby, and game stores, including toy supermarkets	19	39
Discount	38	34
Other, including department stores	43	27

Source: Exstein, Michael B., "Toys "R" Us," *Shearson Lehman Hutton Investment Analysis* (August 19, 1988).

ments in the large department stores are small with minimum inventory and a limited product selection. Some large retailers such as J. C. Penney have dropped toy departments altogether.

There are approximately 85,000 retail toy outlets in the United States. With 313 U.S. outlets in 1988, Toys "R" Us is the largest national toy chain with 21.6% of total U.S. retail toy sales (see Exhibit 3). Child World, a division of Cole National, follows TRU with 6.0% of the market. Kay-Bee, a specialty toy retailer usually located in shopping malls, accounts for 4.9% of toy sales. Lionel Corporation, a large toy supermarket chain similar to Toys "R" Us, has 2.7% of the market. Between 1984 and 1986, Lionel was reorganizing under Chapter 11 of the Bankruptcy Act. When the company emerged from bankruptcy, it announced that it would attempt to grow and increase its share of the toy market by building 15 to 20 new stores per year.

Child World and Lionel have attempted to imitate Toys "R" Us by building similar warehouse-style stores. With few exceptions, TRU is the strongest competitor in those markets where the companies are in direct competition. Although all three competitors operate stores of similar size, TRU achieves an average of $8.4 million in sales a year per store compared to $4.4 million for Lionel and $4.9 million for Child World. In 1987, Child World attempted a price war that undercut the prices of TRU across several product categories.

EXHIBIT 3 MARKET SHARES OF MAJOR U.S. TOY RETAILERS IN 1987 (PERCENT)

Toys "R" Us (U.S. sales only)	21.6
Child World	6.0
Kay-Bee	4.9
Lionel	2.7
Circus World	1.1

Source: Exstein, Michael B., "Toys "R" Us," *Shearson Lehman Hutton Investment Analysis* (August 19, 1988).

The attack worked to increase sales at Child World stores at the expense of Toys "R" Us but profits were reduced so much at Child World that they are unlikely to try it again.

Toy retailing is a very seasonal business. Well over 50% of toy sales are reported in the fourth quarter—with much of those sales generated in the 6 weeks before Christmas. To balance the unevenness of toy sales, most toy stores sell other seasonal items such as swimming pool supplies and lawn furniture. The best selling toys, as of October 1988, are shown in Exhibit 4.

INDUSTRY TRENDS

Some demographic and industry trends that are expected to continue to influence demand for toys in the next several years are:

1. *Numbers of children.* The number of households headed by people aged 35 to 44 grew by 38% between 1980 and 1988. Since the late seventies, many of these members of the baby boom generation, who delayed having children while in their twenties, started having babies. Consequently, the 2-to-5-year-old age group has grown steadily for several years and may now be slowing down. Although the number of married couples of child-bearing age is expected to increase through 1990, by

EXHIBIT 4   TOP SELLING TOYS IN OCTOBER 1988

1. Nintendo Entertainment System (Nintendo)
2. Barbie (Mattel)
3. Micro Machines (Galoob)
4. Pictionary (Games Gang)
5. Real Ghostbusters (Tonka's Kenner)
6. G.I. Joe (Hasbro)
7. Win, Lose or Draw (Hasbro's Milton Bradley)
8. Hot Wheels (Mattel)
9. Starting Lineup (Tonka's Kenner)
10. Dolly Surprise (Hasbro's Playskool)
11. Teenage Mutant Ninja Turtles (Playmate)
12. Fun With Food (Fisher-Price)
13. Lil Miss Makeup (Mattel)
14. Kitchen (Fisher-Price)
15. Transformer (Hasbro)
16. Dyno-Rider (Tyco)
17. Super Mario Brothers, II (Nintendo)
18. Atari 2600 (Atari)
19. Sega Master System (Sega)
20. Koosh Ball (OddzOn)

Source: Pereira, Joseph, "Toy Makers Brace For a Blah Christmas," *Wall Street Journal* (November 22, 1988): B1.

2000 the number will have dropped precipitously as the baby bust generation replaces the baby boom.
2. *More money to spend on toys.* Many parents are having children after their households are formed and careers are established, so family incomes are higher. In many families, both parents are employed full-time. The higher family incomes mean there is more money for discretionary items such as toys.
3. *Broader market appeal of toy stores.* The toy market has joined with the video games and home electronics markets to form a broader category of "toys." The objective is to appeal to the teen and young adult market segment and draw this new group of buyers into the toy stores. While the industry was hurt badly by the decline in the video game market in 1984 and 1985, industry forecasters are predicting a resurgence of interest in the video game segment. The revival of the video game market is being led by a Japanese company, Nintendo, with 70% of the market. Analysts argue that companies are more technologically sophisticated and market-wise than they were in the early eighties and should be able to manage product demand.
4. *Licensing.* Licensing, or basing a product on a motion picture, television program, or comic strip character, accelerated in importance in the early eighties and is expected to continue to play a significant role in toy sales. According to manufacturers, toys based on popular characters appeal to an already established market. In recent years, however, toy retailers have criticized manufacturers for relying too heavily on licensed toys. They argue that there are too many licenses in the market and too large a variation in quality among them. Many retailers have cut back their stock of licensed products by as much as 10 to 30%, characterizing many licensed toys as "junk with stickers on it."

TOYS "R" US

The aim of Toys "R" Us is to be the customer's only place of purchase for toys and related products. Management says it is proud that TRU attracts the least-affluent purchasers because of the everyday discount prices and also attracts the most-affluent purchasers because of the extensive product selection. In order to provide total service to all customer segments, the company maintains tight operating procedures and a strong customer orientation.

RETAILING OPERATIONS

According to Charles Lazarus, "Nothing is done in the stores."[4] What he means is that all buying and pricing decisions are made at corporate headquarters in Rochelle Park, New Jersey. The corporate buying and pricing decisions are made using an elaborate computerized inventory control system where sales by item and sales by store are monitored daily. Those actual sales numbers are compared to forecasts, and when substantial differences exist, the slow items are marked down to get them out of the stores and the fast-selling items are reordered in larger quantities.

By closely following the buying habits of the consumer, TRU is able to pick up on trends before the crucial Christmas buying season and maintain more flexibility than competitors. In 1980, when sales of hand-held video games fell off sharply before Christmas, Toys "R" Us had been forewarned by its extensive monitoring system and had moved much of its stock of video games, at reduced prices, before the Christmas season. TRU was fully stocked with the big Christmas items that year—the Rubik's Cube and Strawberry Shortcake—unlike virtually all its competitors.

Toys "R" Us has gained a formidable reputation with toy manufacturers because of management's ability to predict the success or failure of new toys. Before the 1988 Christmas season, Toys "R" Us executives informed Hasbro that its $20 million new product, Nemo, aimed at the Nintendo market was dull and too expensive. Hasbro canceled the Nemo line and took a $10 million write-off. In August of 1988, TRU used its market-by-market sales data to show Ohio Arts Co. that its newly developed commercial for its new plastic building set was ineffective. Ohio Arts pulled the new commercial and substituted an older one that had been tried in Canada. Sales increased by 30%.

The TRU stores are regionally clustered with a warehouse within one day's driving distance of every store (see Exhibit 5). The company also owns a fleet of trucks to support its warehousing operations. The regional warehouses allow TRU to keep the stores well stocked and make it possible for TRU to order large quantities of merchandise early in the year, when manufacturers are eager to ship. Since most manufacturers will defer payments for 12 months on shipments made in the months immediately following Christmas, TRU is able to defer payment on about two-thirds of its inventory each year. TRU's competitors typically buy closer to Christmas, when buying terms are tighter.

All TRU stores have the same layout with the same items arranged on exactly the same shelves—according to blueprints sent from the corporate office. A TRU store is typically 43,000 square feet and is characterized by wide aisles and warehouse-style shelving stocked to the ceiling with over 18,000 different items. A substantial percent of the floor space is devoted to computers and computer-related products, and to non-toy items such as diapers, furniture, and clothing. However, toys, games, books, puzzles, and sports equipment are the major focus of the stores.

Each store is jointly managed by a merchandise manager and an operations manager. The merchandise manager has full responsibility for the merchandising effort in the store: content, stock level, and display. The operations manager is responsible for the building, personnel, cash control, customer service, and everything else that is not directly related to merchandise. Area supervisors oversee the total operations of three or four stores in a given area, and area general managers are responsible for the performance and profitability of all the TRU stores in a given market.

Toys "R" Us has little turnover among its middle and upper managers. In

EXHIBIT 5 TOYS "R" US STORES IN EACH OF THE COMPANY'S 22 U.S. REGIONS

WAREHOUSE/DISTRIBUTION REGION	NUMBER OF STORES
Washington, D.C., Virginia, Maryland	19
Southern California #1	13
Southern California #2	13
Northern California #1	9
Northern California #2	10
Illinois–Indiana	23
Wisconsin–Illinois	9
New York–New Jersey	30
Southern Texas–Louisiana	19
Michigan	19
New England	15
Northern Texas–Oklahoma	14
Pacific Northwest	11
Philadelphia	17
Northern Florida	9
Southern Florida	10
Georgia–Alabama–Tennessee	18
Western Ohio–Kentucky	18
Upstate New York	7
Carolinas	11
Cleveland–Pittsburgh	14
Phoenix	5

Source: Toys "R" Us, 1988 Form 10K.

the past 10 years, more than 40 employees have become millionaires through the company's employee stock option plan. According to TRU president, Norman Ricken, the company wants people who want to work. He says, "Toys "R" Us is not a 9-to-5 but an 8-to-faint job."[5]

MARKETING

As indicated earlier, each Toys "R" Us store carries over 18,000 items. Although toys represent, by far, the majority of the items stocked, other products include baby furniture, diapers, and children's clothing. The feeling at TRU is that the parent will go to the store to buy a necessity or nonseasonal item and will leave with at least one toy purchase. The average TRU customer spends over $40 per visit.

The product line at TRU includes home computers and software as well as traditional toys. This serves to broaden the company's customer base to include teenagers and adults, and to create add-on business at each retail unit. According to company statistics, products for these "older children" account for more than 15% of sales. TRU strongly feels this is not a change in its basic business—computers and software are toys for adults.

This strategy of carrying a wide selection of merchandise has benefited TRU in another way. The company has been successful in encouraging year-round buying at its stores. In 1980, 7.5% of profits were made in the nine months of January through September compared with 25% in fiscal year 1988.

TRU has a strong policy of year-round discount prices. Because TRU buys most of its merchandise during the off-season, when manufacturers are offering discounts, the company is able to pass the discounts on to the customer. TRU has a policy of not having store sales. Individual items will be marked down if they are not selling, but TRU does not have sales that are category-wide or store-wide.

Virtually all Toys "R" Us stores are located on an important traffic artery leading to a major shopping mall. A location of this type serves two purposes: it allows TRU to attract mall patrons without paying high mall rents, and it gives TRU the space to do business the way it wants to—as a large "supermarket" for toys, complete with grocery type shopping carts.

Other customer conveniences include the stock availability and return policies. Product availability is virtually guaranteed. Because of extensive inventory monitoring and attention to consumer buying habits, TRU rarely has a "stock out." Also, TRU boasts of a liberal return policy. The company claims it will accept all returns with no questions asked—even if a toy with no defect is broken by a child after several months of play.

Toys "R" Us does no national advertising. Before entering a new region, TRU promotes the opening of the new stores through heavy television and newspaper advertising. Once the stores are open, TRU may continue very limited television and newspaper advertising.

DOMESTIC AND FOREIGN EXPANSION

Toys "R" Us pursues a corporate objective of 18% expansion of retail space per year. In order to meet this objective, it has opened more than 35 new toy stores in the U.S. each year for several years (see Exhibit 6) and now has stores in 33 of the 50 states.

All of the expansions are made as a total entry into a new region. First, TRU builds a warehouse, then it clusters several stores within one day's driving distance of the warehouse so that prompt merchandise delivery is ensured. Typically, the warehouse and all the stores are up and running within the same fiscal year and in time for the Christmas season. Once TRU enters a local market with more than one store, it immediately becomes the low price leader in the area—forcing competitors to bring down their prices.

Charles Lazarus keeps a file of locations that have already been selected as potential sites for future U.S. stores. The regions are selected on the basis of demographic patterns and toy buying statistics. The individual store locations are decided after an analysis is completed of the area shopping malls, traffic patterns, and local retail toy competition. During fiscal 1988, TRU

EXHIBIT 6 NUMBER OF STORES AT YEAR-END

	1988	1987	1986	1985	1984	1983	1982	1981	1980
Toys "R" Us United States	313	271	233	198	169	144	120	101	85
Toys "R" Us International	37	24	13	5					
Kids "R" Us	74	43	23	10	2				

Source: Toys "R" Us, *1988 Annual Report.*

opened 42 new stores in the U.S. including five stores in a new market centered around Phoenix, Arizona. Long term plans call for regional expansion into Kansas City, Denver, Memphis, St. Louis, Minneapolis–St. Paul, and Salt Lake City. Charles Lazarus believes there is sufficient market demand for Toys "R" Us to build and operate a total of 700 stores in the United States.

In addition to domestic expansion, TRU is embarking on a plan of growth into the large non-U.S. toy market. The first Canadian and European stores were opened in late 1984. At the end of fiscal 1988, TRU operated 37 stores in Canada, Europe, and the Far East—13 more than in 1987. In 1989 TRU plans to build 15 more stores in Canada, West Germany, and the United Kingdom. (Company financial information is given in Exhibits 7 and 8.)

KIDS "R" US, TOO

TRU's only venture outside of toy retailing has been into children's clothing—a more than $6 billion industry in the United States alone. The corporate objective in creating Kids "R" Us was to "provide one stop shopping with an overwhelming selection of first quality, designer and brand name children's clothing in the season's latest styles at everyday prices.... We have taken the knowledge and systems we have refined for our toy stores over the past 30 years and applied some of these principles to our Kids "R" Us stores."[6]

In 1983, TRU opened its first two Kids "R" Us stores in the New York area. As of 1988 the company operated 74 Kids "R" Us stores in various markets in the U.S. with plans for 35 more stores in fiscal 1989. Each store offers a full assortment of first-quality, discount-priced clothing and accessories for children up to age twelve. The surroundings are spacious and well decorated with neon signs, color-coded departments, fitting rooms with platforms for small children, changing areas for infants, play areas for children, and color-coded store maps.

Some observers felt TRU would meet more resilient competition in children's clothing than it did in toys. Department and discount stores make more money on children's clothing than they do on toys and are not willing to give

EXHIBIT 7 TOYS "R" US, INC. AND SUBSIDIARIES: STATEMENTS OF CONSOLIDATED EARNINGS

	FISCAL YEAR ENDED		
	January 31 1988	February 1 1987	February 2 1986
(In thousands except per-share information)			
Net sales	$3,136,568	$2,444,903	$1,976,134
Costs and expenses:			
Cost of sales	2,157,017	1,668,209	1,322,942
Selling, advertising, general and administrative	584,120	458,528	408,438
Depreciation and amortization	43,716	33,288	26,074
Interest expense	13,849	7,890	6,999
Interest income	(8,056)	(7,229)	(8,093)
	2,790,646	2,160,686	1,756,360
Earnings before taxes on income	345,922	284,217	219,774
Taxes on income	142,000	132,000	100,000
Net earnings	$ 203,922	$ 152,217	$ 119,774
Net earnings per share	$1.56	$1.17	$.93

up that market easily. "Department stores fight when it comes to soft goods. That's their bread and butter, it's the guts of their business."[7] Some department store managers feel the purchase of children's clothing sets a family's buying patterns for years—so the implication of losing the children's department as a way to draw in families goes beyond the immediate loss of profits in that area.

After five years the Kids "R" Us move is finally beginning to show a profit. Kids "R" Us sells 85% of its clothing at a profit with 15% marked down to clear inventory. The industry average for markdowns is 22%. Kids "R" Us sales in fiscal 1987 were roughly $200 million with earnings of about $7 million.

COMPETITOR REACTION

TRU has an excellent reputation with consumers—a reputation that precedes the company into new market areas. Toys "R" Us also is feared and respected by its competitors. Examples of comments from competitors include:

- Toy store owner: "We were going, 'oh, nooo,' because they were coming in right across the street from us."[8]
- President of a buying guild about a children's store owner: "All I can tell you is his face turned white. You come up against a giant like this,

EXHIBIT 8 TOYS "R" US, INC. AND SUBSIDIARIES: CONSOLIDATED BALANCE SHEETS

	FISCAL YEAR ENDED	
	January 31 1988	February 1 1987
ASSETS		
Current Assets:		
Cash and short-term investments	$ 45,996	$ 84,379
Accounts and other receivables, less allowance for doubtful accounts of $1,386 and $1,133	62,144	37,502
Merchandise inventories	772,833	528,939
Prepaid expenses	5,050	3,566
Total Current Assets	886,023	654,386
Property and Equipment		
Real estate, net of accumulated depreciation of $31,238 and $22,400	762,082	600,747
Other, net of accumulated depreciation and amortization of $116,980 and $86,207	351,037	240,218
Leased Property Under Capital Leases, net of accumulated depreciation of $16,840 and $15,797	11,397	12,440
Other Assets	16,520	15,175
	$2,027,059	$1,522,966
LIABILITIES AND STOCKHOLDERS' EQUITY		
Current Liabilities:		
Short-term notes payable to banks	$ 17,657	$ —
Accounts payable	403,105	305,705
Accrued expenses, taxes and other liabilities	167,280	118,260
Federal income taxes	71,003	73,059
Current portion:		
Long-term debt	876	973
Obligations under capital leases	1,071	968
Total Current Liabilities	660,992	498,965
Deferred Income Taxes	53,356	40,321
Long-Term Debt	159,788	63,966
Obligations Under Capital Leases	17,602	18,673
Commitments		
Stockholders' Equity		

Common stock par value $.10 per share:
  Authorized 200,000,000 shares
  Issued 130,530,467 and 127,110,608
	13,053	12,711

Additional paid-in capital	252,493	239,721
Retained earnings	854,421	650,499
Foreign currency translation adjustments	23,586	8,449
Treasury shares, at cost	(5,929)	(5,571)
Receivable from exercise of stock options	(2,303)	(4,768)
	1,135,321	901,041
	$2,027,059	$1,522,966

Note: Figures are given in thousands.

with every major line discounted, and where do you go? If you're the average kiddy shop next door, do you take gas or cut your throat?"[9]
- Manufacturer about a buyer: "one department store buyer, arriving at the [TRU] store, said it caused her instant depression."[10]
- Atlanta toy retailers about TRU's entry into the Atlanta market:

  I admire Toys "R" Us. They will own the town.
  I hope they take the business from Zayre, Richway, Lionel and not us. We may have to start looking outside Atlanta for locations.
  The new Toys "R" Us will saturate the market.[11]

- Michael Vastola, chairman of the board of Lionel Corporation: "They have paid a lot of attention to real estate and location, and it has paid off. You have got to say that they have a very disciplined, well-managed operation."[12]

ENDNOTES

1. Sherman, Stratford P., "Where the Dollars "R"," *Fortune* (June 1, 1981): 45–47.

2. Fesperman, Dan, "Toys "R" Us is a Giant in Kids' Business," *Miami Herald* (November 22, 1982).

3. Chakravarty, Subrata N., "Toys "R" Fun," *Forbes* (March 28, 1983): 58–60.

4. Sherman, "Where the Dollars "R"."

5. Pereira, Joseph, "Toys "R" Us, Big Kid on the Block, Won't Stop Growing," *Wall Street Journal* (August 11, 1988): B1.

6. "Kids "R" Us—The Children's Clothing Store Both Parents and Kids Will Choose," Press Release from Toys "R" Us, July 1983.

7. Ricci, Claudia, "Children's Wear Retailers Brace for Competition from Toys "R" Us," *Wall Street Journal* (August 25, 1983).

8. Fesperman, "Toys "R" Us is a Giant."

9. Ricci, "Children's Wear Retailers."

10. Ibid.

11. "A New Hat in Atlanta's Toy Ring," *Toys, Hobbies & Crafts* (May 1983): 5–8.

12. Kerr, Peter, "The New Game at Toys "R" Us," *New York Times* (July 4, 1983).

CASE 13

DELTA AIR LINES, INC.

MICHELE BOREN,
REGINA BRUCE,
BARRON GREEN,
VICTOR KHOO,
SEXTON ADAMS,
AND ADELAIDE GRIFFIN

INTRODUCTION

It was 6:40 P.M. on August 2, 1985, and the first officer of cabin crew Flight 191 spotted lightning from a thunderstorm. The flight proceeded on into the thunderstorm and was caught by a sudden downburst of air which was blowing in the opposite direction. The cockpit voice recorder quoted the captain as saying "Push it up, push it way up," followed by "togo," which means to take up the plane at a higher altitude and go around the other direction.[1]

However, eight seconds later the aircraft struck a hill, emerged from the thunderstorm, and touched down on State Highway 114 and struck a vehicle. Then the plane burst into a ball of flames and collided with a water tower on the airport grounds. This was a flashback of Delta Air Lines Flight 191 as reported by the National Transportation Safety Board.[2] Ron Allen was glad that this unpleasant memory of Delta's worst aircrash in its history, which left 137 dead and 29 survivors, was almost over. But was it really over?

INDUSTRY OVERVIEW

> We have not seen the total results of deregulation, by a long shot. The experiment in deregulation is not completed yet.[3]

Airports these days can be exciting places, especially if you happen to encounter an airline desk right after it has announced a flight cancellation. Riots, police, and arrests are not uncommon. The situation is becoming so bad that some of the major airlines are training their employees in crowd control.[4]

Source: Prepared under the direction of Professor Sexton Adams, University of North Texas, and Professor Adelaide Griffin, Texas Woman's University, as a basis for classroom discussion and not to illustrate either effective or ineffective handling of administrative situations. © Sexton Adams and Adelaide Griffin, 1990.

The airline industry had undergone tremendous changes since deregulation in 1978. Increased demand had caused serious problems for the industry in terms of service. In 1987, 126 million adults, 72% of the population, had flown at least once in their lives as compared to only 10% in 1967.[5] Fifty-three million adults made at least one airplane trip in 1986, as compared to 38 million in 1977.[6] As a result of this increase, congestion problems have been occurring.

There were several reasons for the congestion. Deregulation has made flying cheaper for the average citizen. According to the Air Transport Association, the average fare fell by 9.6% in 1986, the largest one year drop ever.[7] Combine the drop in general fares with the discount wars and a very attractive ticket was produced. Adding to this problem was the fact that airlines were changing their routes to a hub and spoke system. Hubbing means that several flights will converge on the same location at the same time, resulting in severe congestion.[8] When a delay occurs in the hub, the spoke location also will have a delay, causing a domino effect throughout the system.

GOVERNMENT REGULATION

The process of airline deregulation began in 1978 under President Jimmy Carter. Prior to deregulation, competition among airlines was limited by the Civil Aeronautics Board (CAB ceased to exist by 1985) in two of the three major areas of airline marketing—route authority and pricing—leaving only the amount of capacity (number of flights) up to the judgment of individual carriers. Also, there was tight control over the entrance of new airlines. The results were predictable: A fairly small number of major airlines—flying medium to large size jets—who served a broad network of large cities and small towns. In many cases, an airline's dealings with the CAB were more important than its dealings with customers. However, since the deregulation acts, customer service was viewed as a crucial element in an airline success story.

ECONOMIC FACTORS

The economy has clearly had a major impact on the airline industry. Many of the major airlines performed poorly during the recessionary period of 1980–1982. In 1985, the economy began to improve and oil prices reached record lows. These factors coupled with increased passengers led to record profits for some of the major carriers. But the profits of 1985 would be lowered in the following year due to the reduced prices brought on by the fare wars. Fares were being lowered while operating expenses were going up (see Exhibit 1).

During the first half of 1987, the economy continued to grow at a moderate pace. The Dow Jones Industrial Average had more than tripled since 1982. The energy and agricultural sectors had begun to regain strength. While the trade imbalance had improved slightly and the value of the dollar had begun

EXHIBIT 1 COMPOSITE INDUSTRY STATISTICS: AIR TRANSPORT INDUSTRY

	1987 (Est.)	1986	1985	1984
Revenues ($ mil)	45,800	42,405	45,826	42,059
Load factor	57.0%	57.7%	56.0%	58.2%
Operating margin	11.0%	10.8%	10.3%	11.6%
Depreciation	3320.0	3006.0	2881.8	2584.2
Net profit ($ mil)	525	143.9	584.7	913.3
Income tax rate	35.0%	—	40.6%	42.5%
Net profit margin	1.1%	0.3%	1.3%	2.2%
Long-term debt ($ mil)	19,000	17,593	15,452	12,173
Net worth ($ mil)	14,500	13,020	11,930	9,587.4
% Earned ttl. cap.	14.5%	2.5%	4.7%	7.0%
% Earned net worth	3.5%	32.0%	4.9%	9.5%

Source: Marilyn M. McKellin, "Air Transport Industry," *Value Line* (July 3, 1987): 251.

to rise, economists were still concerned that the trade balance might worsen and that the value of the dollar would fall, pushing the U.S. into a recession. On October 19, 1987, the Dow Jones Industrial Average fell 508 points, 22.6% of market value.[9] The stock prices of several airline carriers were adversely affected. Were the predictions of recession coming true? What would the effects of a recession be on the airline industry?

FARE WARS

Prior to deregulation, the pricing of airline fares was controlled by the CAB with zero price competition among the airlines. Since deregulation, pricing strategies have become a very important factor in the airline strategy game. Deregulation has allowed many new entrants into the industry. Many of these new entrants had lower cost structures which allowed them to offer substantially discounted fares. The major carriers had to respond to these low fares in order to maintain their market shares. This resulted in the first fare war during the winter of 1982. Various approaches such as the frequent flier program and advance discount tickets were initiated.

Since most of the airline management teams were trained during the period of regulation, they did not have the experience to deal with these complex pricing strategies. Consequently, the prices of fares varied greatly within the industry and even within a given flight. Fare wars severely damaged many of the major carriers, who suffered decreased passenger revenues without a corresponding increase in the number of passengers.

With the advent of highly sophisticated computer systems, major carriers are currently tackling the pricing game much more effectively.[10]

INDUSTRY STRUCTURE

The airline industry was made up of three different leagues. They included major, national, and regional airlines. (See Exhibit 2.) This grouping was not set in stone and fluctuated considerably. The biggest example of this would be Braniff, dropping from a major airline to a national airline. The merger game was very prevalent in this time of deregulation. Since 1985, there have been more than eight major mergers which have decreased the number of major carriers from 20 to 8.[11] These acquisitions have not been cheap. The majors have spent or gone into debt for nearly $6 billion to buy each other.[12]

The number of independent major airlines was shrinking. Eight megacarriers existed and represented 91.7% of the nation's scheduled jet air travel.[13] This growth was coming at the expense of the national and regional lines. Many were either bought by larger airlines or made marketing agreements with them. In 1986, 75 airlines in this group were involved in code-sharing or other agreements with a larger airline.[14] The number of these lines has dropped by 59, from a high of 238 in 1981 to a low of 179 in 1985.[15]

The major airlines constituted most of the domestic flights between the large metropolitan areas as well as most of the international flights. They were by far the most expensive lines and recorded the most passenger miles and revenues. The national lines consisted mostly of domestic flights, concentrating upon the major metropolitan areas as well as the smaller hubs such as Cincinnati and Charlotte. The national price structure is lower than the majors, in general, with some airlines going strictly no-frills. The regional lines are the low-cost carriers of the industry. They usually operate only a few routes and act as feeders to the larger lines.

EXHIBIT 2   AIRLINE INDUSTRY LEAGUES

MAJOR AIRLINES	NATIONAL AIRLINES	REGIONAL AIRLINES
Texas Air	Southwest	Aspen Airways
United	American West	Metro Airways
American	Hawaiian	Florida Express
Delta	Alaska	SkyWest
Northwest	Midway	ASA
TWA	Braniff	Comair
Pan Am	Aloha	Business Express
USAir		

Source: James P. Woolsey, "Airlines Enjoy Modest Traffic, Financial Gains, Benefits of Lower Fuel Costs," *Air Transport World* (June 1987): 64.

FLIGHT SCHEDULES

> We will resist in every appropriate way any implication that Delta misleads the public.[16]

Competing with each other in flight schedules was nothing new to the airlines. Since deregulation, airlines were expanding their routes and increasing the frequency of flight schedules. This was achieved through acquiring additional aircraft for the company. As a result, several major airports' traffic was increasingly congested with more planes on their runways and terminals than they could accommodate. This problem triggered a new call for a possible reregulation on flight schedules at several major airports.

According to Department of Transportation (DOT) officials, there was an increasing trend in flight delay problems since December 1986. Delays at 22 airports were increased by 24.4 percent to 367,000 delays by 1986, and for the first three months of 1987, more than a third of customers' complaints against airlines were contributed by delays and cancellations.[17] The delay problems prompted the DOT to take some steps against flight scheduling at several major airports. The department chose Hartsfield Atlanta International Airport as the first of 13 airports to be investigated.

Upon investigation at Atlanta, Transportation Secretary Elizabeth Dole accused Delta of setting unrealistic flight schedules. The department said its investigation showed that more than 55 Delta flights to and from Atlanta arrived at least 15 minutes late 70 percent of the time during a 30-day sampling period. In addition, two Delta flights were late 100 percent of the time.[18]

Delta was "appalled" by Ms. Dole's accusation that it may be engaging in deceptive practices. The carrier maintained that its Atlanta schedules had not increased significantly since 1984. Delta said the transportation department was engaged in "a misguided effort to shift responsibility for airline delays away from the government's failure to staff and maintain an adequate air traffic control system."[19]

DELTA AIR LINES, INC.

MANAGEMENT

> The attitude of our people is unusual. Delta people pitch in where they are needed.[20]

Ron Allen was elected by the board of directors to become Delta's chairman of the board and chief executive officer on August 1, 1987. He was the successor of David Garrett, who reached mandatory retirement age after serving Delta for 41 years. Garrett exhibited strong leadership and nourished Delta through some bad times into a healthy, growing airline. His management style brought Delta through a time of uncertainty and changing environment caused by the Airline Deregulation Act of 1978. Delta encountered its first major net loss of $86.7 million in 1983, after 36 years of profitable operations.

Nevertheless, Delta was quick in responding to this crisis situation and bounced back in 1984 with a net income of $175.6 million, a $262.3 turnaround from 1983. According to Garrett, there were several factors contributing to this turnaround in profitability, which included an improvement in marketing strategy, increased computer application in travel agent programs by using DATAS II automated reservations system, significant fleet change, and dependence on commuter carriers in feeding passengers at Delta's major hubs. Garrett retired on July 31, 1987, but he plans to remain active as a member of the board and serve as chairman of the executive committee.

Allen, who was appointed as Delta's first-hand man, was a veteran in the airline business. He has been with Delta for 24 years, beginning his career in the Personnel Division and moving to the position of senior vice president for administration and personnel. By November 1983, he was promoted to president and chief operating officer, and after four years, he has become the new chief executive officer of Delta.[21]

Allen's successor was Hollis Harris, who was elected by the board as Delta's president and chief operating officer. Harris was a Delta veteran of 33 years. He worked his way up the corporate ladder from transportation agent in the Technical Operations, Operations, and Passenger Service divisions, to senior vice president of operations.

Delta's organization was set up with seven functional divisions—Finance, Marketing, Personnel, Technical Operations, Operations, Information Services and Properties, and General Counsel and Secretary. Each of these division is supervised by senior vice presidents and a chief financial officer who directly reports to the president and chief operating officer. Several subdivisions exist in each functional area, which are supervised by either vice presidents or assistant vice presidents.[22] An illustration of Delta's organization chart is shown in Exhibit 3.

Delta had always been very centralized. Ron Allen and his senior management group had always made the critical decisions. Even though the organization was very centralized, the senior management group was accessible to the rest of the company. Delta's management maintained an "open door" policy for its employees to discuss their problems and concerns.

In addition, Delta's management had generally maintained a policy of delegating the maximum degree of responsibility to its crew members. In September 1987, the FAA noted in its report that "this management style has worked well, and the airline has enjoyed an excellent reputation in the industry."[23]

OPERATIONS

The competitive requirement today is to have a strong, high-frequency operation in major centers. You have to control a good deal of traffic in order to survive in a very volatile, competitive environment.[24]

Delta Air Lines, Inc. was the fourth largest air carrier providing scheduled air transportation for passengers, freight, and mail over a network of routes

EXHIBIT 3 ORGANIZATION CHART OF DELTA AIR LINES, INC.

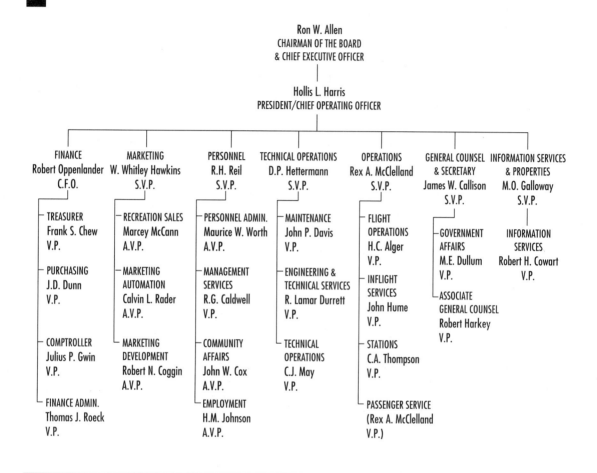

throughout the United States and overseas. Delta serves 132 domestic cities in 42 states, the District of Columbia, and Puerto Rico, and also operates flights to 20 international cities in 9 foreign countries.[25]

Expansion and Routes. Delta, in compliance with its strategic plan to become a major international airline, acquired Western Airlines in 1987. This acquisition increased Delta's presence in areas where it previously lacked strength. Forty-four new cities were added, including cities in Alaska, Hawaii, western Canada, and Mexico. New hubs were added at Salt Lake City and Los Angeles.

In addition to the new routes added by the merger with Western, Delta added new service from Atlanta through Portland, Oregon, to Tokyo, Japan, and Seoul, South Korea. New service was also added from Cincinnati to London.

The Cincinnati hub has undergone tremendous expansion and upgrade. Now Delta will compete head-on with other major carriers in the midwest. Delta more than doubled its daily flights to Cincinnati.[26]

Delta invented and currently operates under the hub and spoke system which has become the keystone of route development in the airline industry.[27] The hub and spoke system allows for fewer planes than if each regional base had to be connected with all the others by a direct flight.[28]

Major hubs for Delta are Dallas/Forth Worth, Atlanta, Salt Lake City, and Los Angeles. More than half of all Delta flights either begin or end at one of these cities.[29]

Delta uses four regional carriers to increase the efficiency of its hub operations: Atlantic Southeast Airlines, Comair, Business Express, and SkyWest. These carriers serve 93 cities and operate more than 1,400 flights per day.[30]

Cargo operations and mail carrier service continue to increase in 1987. Delta signed a new agreement with the United States Postal Service for the carriage of mail which is expected to increase the number of mail ton miles throughout 1988. Delta also continued its push into the special passenger markets such as conventions and groups, military and government, tour and cruise passengers, and family and senior citizen travelers.[31]

In an effort to support continued growth, Delta has expanded several facilities during 1987. Federal Inspection Service facilities were added in Atlanta and Dallas/Forth Worth and plans were made to add one to Cincinnati. Gate expansion occurred in Cincinnati, Dallas/Fort Worth, Portland, and Los Angeles. New terminal facilities were opened in Mobile and Fort Lauderdale.[32]

Aircraft. In order to facilitate this expansion, Delta took delivery of 35 new aircraft in addition to 92 aircraft gained in the acquisition of Western.[33] The company now has use of 368 planes which consist of 132 B-727s, 36 DC-9s, 9 DC-10s, 12 DC-8s, 35 L-1011s, 22 B-767s, 86 B-737s, 28 B757s, and 8 MD-82/88s.[34] This represents over 59,000 passenger seats available to Delta.[35]

Delta has 63 aircraft on order and options on another 101 aircraft from 1988 through 1992.[36]

During 1987, Delta decreased its average cost per seat mile by 14%. This decrease along with a decline from the reduction in fuel prices and greater productivity from personnel helped Delta to decrease its unit cost and increase its operating revenues.[37]

Customer Service. According to United States government records, Delta for the thirteenth consecutive year had the best customer service record. Delta was voted as the best airline by the readers of *Travel Holiday* magazine.[38] Delta was also one of the best airlines in not overbooking flights. Overbooking results in bumping some passengers from the flight, usually late arrivals. Delta did this to 1.3 passengers our of every 1,000 on an involuntary basis and 6.4

passengers our of 1,000 on a combined voluntary and involuntary basis. These numbers were second and first in the airline industry.[39]

Flight delays have continued to plague Delta. Delta has one of the worst records in overall percentage of reported flights arriving on time. In September of 1987, Delta only had 72.3% of reported flights that arrived on time. It ranked eleventh out of 13 airlines. Delta also had 4.7% of its regularly scheduled flights arriving late 70% of the time or more. This was the third worst percentage. Finally, Delta had 6 flights which arrived late 96% to 100% of the time. This was the most of any airline.[40]

COMPETITOR PROFILES

AMERICAN AIRLINES

American Airlines was the second largest domestic carrier. It had major hubs in Dallas/Fort Worth, Chicago, Nashville, Raleigh-Durham, and San Juan. American had international service to Canada, Mexico, the Caribbean, and Europe. American had been very profitable over the past four years, posting total profits of $1.09 billion.[41] In 1986, American purchased AirCal for $225 million. This was the major event of 1986 for the company and represented a new and stronger push into the west coast area.[42]

American filed suit this year against Texas Air Corporation claiming they illegally induced travel agencies to break contracts with American's Sabre reservation system. The suit seeks millions in actual claims that Texas Air used illegal methods to coerce travel agencies into using the Sabre system.[43]

Third quarter results for AMR, the parent company of American Airlines, showed a 27.8% drop in earnings. Revenues were up to $1,975.4 million while operating income was down $7.1 million.[44] Traffic increased almost 15%. Load factor, or percentage of seats filled, was unchanged at 66.0%.[45] American placed a large aircraft order in 1987, agreeing to take 15 767-300FRs from Boeing and 25 A300-600Rs from Airbus. Both deals were leases with easy-return provisions.[46] American was reportedly going to use the Airbus planes in the Caribbean and use the replaced jets for domestic expansion. The Boeing jets were to be placed in service in North America for European routes. The jets currently in that position had been used also for domestic purposes.

New routes have been established for 1987 to Zurich, Geneva, Paris, Frankfurt, and Tokyo.

UNITED AIRLINES

United Airlines was the largest single domestic airline in the United States. United had hubs in Chicago, Denver, San Francisco, and Washington, D.C., where flights serve North America as well as Europe, Mexico, and the Far East.

United Airlines' parent had changed its name from UAL, Inc. to Allegis Corporation and since that time it had also decided to divest the Hertz operations, the Westin and Hilton International hotel chains, and perhaps all or part of their computerized reservations system (CRS). The Hilton International hotel chain was sold to Ladbroke Group PLC of Britain for $1.07 billion.[47] Hertz was recently sold to a group including Ford Motor Co. and Hertz management for $1.2 billion.[48] The proceeds of the sale went to the shareholders. These moves were designed to protect the company from takeover by hostile entities.[49] The original plan was designed to give the company a full line of services which could meet all the needs of the passenger.

PAN AM CORPORATION

Pan Am was the seventh largest airline in the United States. The airline recently sold off its Pacific routes to United Airlines. It has concentrated its efforts upon the Atlantic and European routes. In 1987, Pan Am has shown relatively good growth with demand increasing from the Europeans due to the weaker dollar.[50] Improved feed systems to the JFK and Miami hubs has also helped increase growth. (Pan Am has made agreements with regional airlines which act as feeders to their main hubs of JFK and Miami.)[51]

Pan Am was determined to improve its future by decreasing labor costs.[52] Pan Am had tried to secure labor savings of $180 million over the time period 1985–1987.[53] Management feels that this is key to the long-term survival of the airline.[54]

A group of airline experts and a coalition of Pan Am's unions had negotiations on taking the company over. The airline experts, led by Kerk Kerkorian, were requiring greater concessions from the unions than current management. The situation was placed on hold until a more viable solution could be worked out.[55]

TEXAS AIR CORPORATION

Texas Air Corporation was ranked as the largest multi-airline corporation in the United States. The corporation was made up of Continental, Eastern, Frontier, People Express, New York Air, and Texas International. Texas Air's major hubs were in Houston, Denver, Atlanta, Miami, Kansas City, and Newark. The corporation serves primarily the domestic corridor. The massive growth that this company had undergone in the past year had caused several problems to occur. First, Texas Air is the owner of the most complained about airline—Continental.[56] Labor disagreements plague Eastern. Service and schedule disruptions, along with misplaced luggage had driven many passengers to other airlines.[57]

In 1987, Continental posted a passenger load drop to 56.2% from 60.4% in 1986.[58] Traffic increased 83.3%, which reflects Continental's merged operations with People Express and New York Air.[59] Eastern also reported a decline in traffic while reducing available seat miles. Eastern's load factor improved to 58.2% from 54.5% a year earlier.[60]

Continental reported that its September 1987 on-time performance was

80%, and that it completed 98.9% of flights, and transported 99.3% of its passenger bags to the right airport at the right time.[61]

NORTHWEST

By acquisition of Republic Airlines, Northwest Airlines had become the fifth largest airline company in the United States.[62] The carrier services all the major metropolitan areas in the United States and also serves the Far East and Canada.

Northwest is preparing to upgrade its fleet by ordering 100 Airbus A320s. The company will order up to 20 Airbus A340 widebodies in 1987, with delivery expected to occur in 1992.[63]

Northwest earned $76.9 million in 1986, up from 1985. Yields had increased with the integration of Republic and are thought to have had a good chance of increasing in 1987. Northwest appears to be in a good position with its marketing agreement with TWA, concerning its PARS computer reservation system. This will enable Northwest to have the travel agent leverage needed to compete with the other computer reservation system giants.[64]

USAIR

USAir was the ninth largest domestic carrier. USAir recently purchased PSA, which was a west coast carrier and owns 51% of Piedmont. These acquisitions give USAir a very competitive strategy.[65] USAir will enjoy a very strong west coast presence and with the addition of Piedmont, USAir's east coast network will be greatly enhanced.[66] When the acquisitions are completed, USAir will become the seventh largest domestic carrier.

In 1987, USAir was developing a new hub in Philadelphia and starting service to Atlanta, Jacksonville, Manchester, and Portland.

USAir increased its passenger boarding as well as load factors and revenues. USAir had to perform adequately in order to service its increased debt.[67]

TWA

Transworld Airlines was the sixth largest domestic airline. TWA services the continental United States, Europe, Mideast, India, and the Caribbean.

TWA owned Ozark Airways, which gave it a major hold in St. Louis. Since international service was very cyclical, Ozark gave TWA some stability in the domestic market.

TWA's flight attendants went on strike in March 1986, over wage cuts imposed by controlling owner Carl Icahn. Management eventually won by hiring new replacements, which cut costs by 10%.[68]

In spite of the labor union strike and the decreased international passenger mileage caused by anti-American terrorism, TWA still posted a net profit of $85 million in the fourth quarter of 1987, which reduced the overall deficit by $76 million.[69] This was good considering the losses in 1985 and 1986. With

FINANCE/ACCOUNTING

> Financial strength is very important in a marketing war. It permits you to create an unprofitable price to fight off interlopers in a market.[71]

Delta's balance sheets and income statements are shown in Exhibits 4 and 5. For the fiscal year ending June 30, 1987, Delta had total operating revenues of $5,318,712,000. Net income was $263,729,000 compared with $47,286,000 in fiscal 1986. In addition, earnings per share of common stock was $5.90.[72]

Debt has long been used by Delta to finance its fleet expansion programs. As of June 30, 1983, Delta's long-term debt was in excess of $800 million. This debt generated approximately $62 million in interest expense for fiscal 1987.[73]

On December 18, 1986, Delta purchased all 61,331,334 outstanding shares of Western stock for $787 million by paying $384 million in cash and issuing 83 million shares of Delta stock for the balance. In addition, Delta assumed Western's long-term debt of $228 million, capital lease obligations totaling $199 million, and other non-current liabilities of $29 million.[74]

Delta's operating financial strength was demonstrated in the significant decrease in its unit cost during fiscal 1987. As shown in Exhibits 6 and 7, average cost per available seat mile was 7.12 cents, down 14% from the 8.30 cents average in fiscal 1986. The decline in seat mile cost is extremely important as airlines struggle to compete by providing the lowest fares to travelers.[75]

Delta continued to use lease financing to acquire new aircraft due to the fact that the company had a significant amount of investment tax credit and net operating loss carryovers. During fiscal 1987, all new aircraft acquired were sold and leased back from the purchaser using operating leases.[76]

MARKETING/SALES

> We have determined that much of Delta's future success will depend on the imagination and skill we bring to the use of fast-paced developments in the information management technologies.[77]

Delta had recently taken several actions to enhance its competitive situation for the future. The company's marketing plan called for expansion of the Dallas/Fort Worth and Cincinnati hubs. On July 30, 1986, Delta announced that it would double its operations at the Cincinnati airport by the end of the 1986 calendar year.[78]

In September 1987, Delta launched a new marketing campaign to counteract some of the negative press resulting from the crash of Flight 191 and the near mishaps earlier in 1987. The theme line "Delta: we love to fly and it shows" will replace Delta's two-year-old theme, "Delta gets you there." The company is expected to spend about $70 million on the new campaign.

Acquiring Western Airlines provided Delta with a significant improvement in its route system. Western added 44 cities to the 108 already served by Delta. Western's domestic operations were centered in the western half of the United States in areas were Delta did not have substantial operations.[79]

EXHIBIT 4 CONSOLIDATED BALANCE SHEETS, 1987 AND 1986

	JUNE 30	
	1987	1986
ASSETS		
Current Assets:		
Cash and temporary cash investments	$ 379,928	$ 61,315
Accounts receivable, net of allowance for uncollectible accounts	626,139	425,912
Refundable income taxes	—	10,485
Maintenance and operating supplies, at average cost	42,337	35,503
Prepaid expenses and other current assets	131,170	49,660
Total current assets	1,179,574	582,875
Property and Equipment:		
Flight equipment owned	4,485,898	4,174,632
Less: Accumulated depreciation	1,951,494	1,939,205
	2,534,404	2,235,427
Flight equipment under capital leases	221,811	—
Less: Accumulated amortization	16,307	—
	205,504	—
Ground property and equipment	1,078,185	965,980
Less: Accumulated depreciation	451,643	390,324
	626,542	575,656
Advance payments for new equipment	307,461	323,399
	3,673,911	3,134,482
Other Assets:		
Investments in associated companies	55,427	37,976
Cost in excess of net assets acquired, net of accumulated amortization of $5,529	371,756	—
Funds held by bond trustees	8,308	7,677
Other	53,407	22,452
	488,898	68,105
	$5,342,383	$3,785,462

(*continued*)

EXHIBIT 4 (continued)

	JUNE 30	
	1987	1986

LIABILITIES AND STOCKHOLDERS' EQUITY

Current Liabilities:

Current maturities of long-term debt	$ 8,406	$ 10,921
Current obligations under capital leases	12,921	—
Short-term notes payable	11,000	9,000
Commercial paper outstanding	14,836	41,055
Accounts payable and miscellaneous accrued liabilities	455,686	270,445
Air traffic liability	506,669	286,579
Accrued vacation pay	110,835	88,595
Transportation tax payable	60,705	39,342
Total current liabilities	1,181,058	745,937

Non-Current Liabilities:

Long-term debt	837,201	868,615
Capital leases	181.216	—
Other	80,320	38,949
	1,098,737	907,564

Deferred Credits:

Deferred income taxes	590,876	427,339
Unamortized investment tax credits	98,525	150,594
Manufacturers credits	137,611	146,844
Deferred gain on sale and leaseback transactions	297,050	104,742
Other	614	496
	1,124,676	830,015

Commitments and Contingencies

Stockholders' Equity:

Common stock, par value $3.00 per share—Authorized 100,000,000 shares; outstanding 48,639,469 shares at June 30, 1987, and 40,116,383 shares at June 30, 1986	145,918	120,349
Additional paid-in capital	484,398	93,333
Reinvested earnings	1,307,596	1,088,264
	1,937,912	1,301,946
	$5,342,383	$3,785,462

Note: Amounts given in thousands.

Source: Delta Air Lines, Inc., *1987 Annual Report.*

EXHIBIT 5 DELTA AIR LINES, INC.: CONSOLIDATED STATEMENTS OF INCOME, 1987, 1986, AND 1985

	YEAR ENDED JUNE 30		
	1987	1986	1985
Operating Revenues:			
Passenger	$4,921,852	$4,132,284	$4,376,986
Cargo	280,271	240,115	235,199
Other, net	116,049	87,663	71,930
Total operating revenues	5,318,172	4,460,062	4,684,115
Operating Expenses:			
Salaries and related costs	2,228,814	1,963,575	1,856,243
Aircraft fuel	672,004	796,883	892,182
Aircraft maintenance materials and repairs	127,856	91,590	66,022
Aircraft rent	150,653	68,518	57,090
Other rent	145,473	109,778	92,839
Landing fees	89,519	65,879	60,908
Passenger service	219,834	180,409	170,163
Passenger commissions	432,066	359,299	350,690
Other cash costs	569,453	425,723	422,840
Depreciation and amortization	277,975	363,920	349,128
Total operating expenses	4,913,647	4,425,574	4,318,105
Operating Income	404,525	34,488	366,010
Other Income (Expense):			
Interest expense	(94,000)	(79,113)	(84,081)
Less: Interest capitalized	32,092	23,758	22,028
	(61,908)	(55,355)	(62,053)
Gain on disposition of aircraft	96,270	16,526	94,343
Miscellaneous income, net	8,312	7,775	6,863
	42,674	(31,054)	39,153
Income Before Income Taxes	447,199	3,434	405,163
Income Taxes (Provided) Credited	(219,715)	2,228	(186,624)
Amortization of Investment Tax Credits	36,245	41,624	40,914
Net Income	$ 263,729	47,286	$ 259,453
Net Income Per Common Share	$5.90	$1.18	$6.50

Note: Amounts given in thousands, except per-share data.
Source: Delta Air Lines, Inc., *1987 Annual Report.*

EXHIBIT 6 DELTA AIR LINES, INC.: OPERATING STATISTICS

	1987	1986	PERCENT CHANGE
Revenue plane miles (000)	407,773	311,347	+31%
Available seat miles (000)	69,013,669	53,336,135	+29
Available ton miles (000)	8,999,668	6,934,047	+30
Fuel gallons consumed (000)	1,435,801	1,126,876	+27
Avg. fuel price gallon	46.80	70.72	−34
Passenger load factor	55.66%	56.48%	−1
Breakeven load factor	51.09%	56.01%	−9
Cost per avail. seat mile	7.12	8.30	−14

Source: Delta Air Lines, Inc., *1987 Annual Report.*

Delta Air Lines signed a ten-year agreement to become the official airline of Walt Disney World. Many marketing opportunities will be provided as a result of the association with Walt Disney World such as: service personnel, on-site ticketing, etc.[80]

DELTA PROBLEMS

While we would like to put the series of safety incidents behind us, we will not and cannot allow ourselves to forget them, but rather we must learn from the experience.[81]

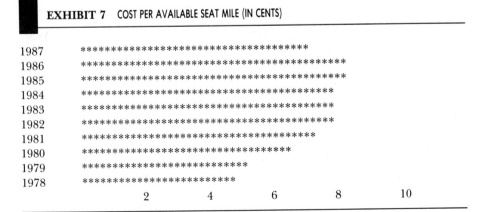

EXHIBIT 7 COST PER AVAILABLE SEAT MILE (IN CENTS)

Source: Delta Air Lines, Inc., *1987 Annual Report.*

According to the Federal Aviation Administration (FAA) investigation of Delta's training program on flight safety, numerous problems were uncovered with pilot-crew coordination, lapses in discipline, and poor cockpit communication. This investigation was triggered by a series of safety incidents at Delta in June and July of 1987. The report indicated the shortcomings as primarily due to a lack of clear-cut, definitive guidance from those responsible for developing and standardizing cockpit procedures. The inspection team also blamed the airline's management philosophy for the crew problems.[82]

Delta's management philosophy was to delegate a maximum degree of responsibility to its crew members. According to the FAA, this philosophy worked well in the past but there is a limit to this approach due to an increasingly complex and stressful environment. The report suggested that this philosophy caused crew members to work independently rather than functioning as team members.[83]

The series of safety incidents at Delta were recorded as follows:

- July 8, 1987. A Delta jumbo jet flying from London to Cincinnati strayed 60 miles off course and came within 100 feet of a Continental Airlines jet off the coast of Newfoundland.
- July 7, 1987. A Delta pilot heading for Lexington, Kentucky, mistakenly landed 20 miles away at Frankfort, Kentucky.
- June 30, 1987. The crew of a Delta jet accidentally turned off the engines while climbing over the Pacific Ocean after leaving Los Angeles. The pilot managed to restore power 600 feet above the ocean.
- June 18, 1987. A Delta jet had to abort its takeoff run as another jet passed 100 feet overhead while taking off in the opposite direction on the same runway.[84]

Delta was the brunt of much negative publicity due to the intense media coverage of the preceding events. Delta management identified breakdown in cockpit communication as the primary cause of the safety incidents. The firm has taken corrective action and individual disciplinary action in response to the incidents. While the negative coverage of these events was short-lived, Delta has been and continues to receive negative coverage in connection with the August 2, 1985, crash of Flight 191. The National Transportation Safety Board has reported the probable causes of the accident, which left 137 dead, as the flight crew's decision to initiate and continue the approach into a cumulonimbus cloud that they observed to contain lightning; the lack of specific guidelines, procedures, and training for avoiding and escaping low-altitude wind shear; and the lack of definitive, real-time wind shear hazard data.[85] Recent reports regarding the pre-trail events (a trial to determine liability in the accident is set for February 1, 1988) state that an expert witness for the plaintiffs, family of accident victims, will testify that the pilot, Captain Edward M. Connors, had been taking a prescription tranquilizer called Stelazine and that it affected his flying.[86] Delta spokesman Jim Lundy defended Connors by stating, "There is no indication that Connors was on medication at the time of the accident."[87] The National Transportation Safety Board said that if enough new evidence was revealed they might reopen the crash investigation.[88] Coverage of the Flight 191 accident will likely continue until all the lawsuits have been settled. Will such coverage cloud Delta's image?

ENDNOTES

1. James Ott, "Recorder Reveals Lightning Preceded Delta L-1011 Crash," *Aviation Week and Space Technology* (October 7, 1985): 26.

2. Ibid.

3. "Delta's Soft Landing," *Management Today* (July 1985): 71.

4. Jonathan Dahl, "Battling Crowds at the Airports," *Wall Street Journal* (October 19, 1987): 29.

5. Holman Jenkins, Jr., "Setting Course for Smoother Skies," *Insight* (October 26, 1987): 8.

6. Ibid.

7. "Merger Myopia," *Wall Street Journal* (October 19, 1987): 27.

8. Jenkins, "Setting Course for Smoother Skies," p. 9.

9. Amy Stromberg, "How Panic Swept Wall Street," *Dallas Times Herald* (October 20, 1987): A7.

10. Kenneth Labich, "Winners and the Air Wars," *Fortune* (May 11, 1987): 74.

11. James P. Woolsey, "Airlines Enjoy Modest Traffic, Financial Gains, Benefits of Lower Fuel Cost," *Air Transport World* (June 1987): 64.

12. Ibid., p. 58.

13. Donald L. Pevsner, "Merger Mania is Putting Lower Air Fares in a Tailspin," *Dallas Morning News* (October 11, 1987): 10G.

14. Woolsey, "Airlines Enjoy Modest Traffic," p. 59.

15. Ibid.

16. Laurie McGinley, "U.S. Weighs Penalizing Delta, Eastern Over Scheduling at Airport in Atlanta," *Wall Street Journal* (April 10, 1987): 3.

17. James Ott, "Airlines View Flight Adjustments as Trend Toward Reregulation," *Aviation Week and Space Technology* (February 9, 1987): 34.

18. McGinley, "U.S. Weighs Penalizing Delta, Eastern," p. 3.

19. Ibid.

20. "Delta's Soft Landing," p. 70.

21. Delta Air Lines, Inc., *1987 Annual Report*, p. 10.

22. Ibid, p. 15.

23. David Tarrant, "FAA Faults Delta But Reports No Finable Offense," *Dallas Morning News* (September 19, 1987): 1.

24. Bruce A. Smith, "Delta Agrees to Acquire Western for $860 Million," *Aviation Week and Space Technology* (September 15, 1986): 31.

25. Delta Air Lines, Inc., *1987 Form 10-K*, p. 1.

26. Delta Air Lines, Inc. *1987 Annual Report*, p. 12.

27. Ibid., p. 4.

28. Jenkins, "Setting course for Smoother Skies," p. 9.

29. Delta Air Lines, Inc., *1987 Annual Report*, p. 12.

30. Ibid.

31. Ibid., p. 13.

32. Ibid., pp. 13–14.

33. Ibid., pp. 9–10.

34. Marilyn M. McKellin, "Air Transport Industry," *Value Line* (July 3, 1987): 259.

35. Delta Air Lines, Inc., *1987 Annual Report*, p. 10.

36. Ibid.

37. Ibid., p. 5.

38. Ibid.

39. Francis C. Brown III and Jonathan Dahl, "New Data on Airline Performance May End Up Misleading Travelers," *Wall Street Journal* (November 23, 1987): 25.

40. Laurie McGinley and Jonathan Dahl, "Delay Date: Airlines' Figures Hold Surprises—and Spark Controversy," *Wall Street Journal* (November 11, 1987): 22.

41. "U.S. Majors," p. 100.

42. Ibid., p. 110.

43. Dennis Fulton, "American Files Suit Against Texas Air," *Dallas Morning News* (October 16, 1987): 1D.

44. Dennis Fulton, "AMR Earnings Sag 27.8% in Quarter," *Dallas Morning News* (October 15, 1987): 6D.

45. "AMR's American Air Traffic," *Wall Street Journal* (October 12, 1987): 6.

46. "U.S. Majors," p. 100.

47. "Allegis Completes Hilton Sale," *Wall Street Journal* (October 15, 1987): 5.

48. James P. Miller, "Ford to Acquire U.S. Leasing for $68 a Share," *Wall Street Journal* (October 12, 1987): 2.

49. McKellin, "Air Transport Industry," p. 257.

50. Ibid., p. 265.

51. Ibid.

52. Ibid.

53. Ibid.

54. Ibid.

55. "Pan Am Proposal Requires Greater Worker Concessions," *Dallas Morning News* (October 15, 1987): 3D.

56. Laurie McGinley, "Consumer Gripes About Air Service Fell in September," *Wall Street Journal* (October 12, 1987): 29.

57. McKellin, "Air Transport Industry," p. 268.

58. Paulette Thomas, "Texas Air's Continental Unit Posts Drop in September Passenger Load to 56.2%," *Wall Street Journal* (October 7, 1987): 6.

59. Ibid.

60. Ibid.

61. Dennis Fulton, "Continental Reports September Performance," *Dallas Morning News* (October 16, 1987): 4D.

62. "U.S. Majors," p. 108.

63. Ibid.

64. Ibid.

65. McKellin, "Air Transport Industry," p. 271.

66. "U.S. Majors," p. 115.

67. Ibid.

68. Ibid.

69. Ibid.

70. McKellin, "Air Transport Industry," p. 270.

71. Delta's Soft Landing," p. 71.

72. Delta Air Lines, Inc. *1987 Annual Report,* p. 6.

73. Ibid., pp. 17–18.

74. Ibid., 8.

75. Ibid., p. 5.

76. Ibid., p. 4.

77. "Delta's Soft Landing," p. 69.

78. Delta Air Lines, Inc. *1986 Annual Report,* p. 2.

79. Delta Air Lines, Inc., *1987 Annual Report,* p. 12

80. Ibid., p. 13.

81. "FAA Faults Delta," p. 1A

82. Ibid., p. 1A.

83. Ibid., p. 28A.

84. Clemens P. Work, "The Gremlins in the Sky," *U.S. News and World Report* (July 20, 1987): 12–13.

85. "NTSB Documents Observations of Weather Prior to Delta Crash," *Aviation Week and Space Technology* (November 10, 1986): 89.

86. Ann Reeks, "Tranquilizer Affected Captain of Flight 191, Witness Contends," *Dallas Morning News* (December 9, 1987): 29A.

87. David Tarrant, "Delta 191 Pilot Used Tranquilizer," *Dallas Morning News* (November 15, 1987): 37A.

88. Ibid.

CASE 14

SUN MICROSYSTEMS

WILLIAM C. HOUSE AND
WALTER E. GREENE

INTRODUCTION

In 1982, four 27-year-old entrepreneurs combined forces to found Sun Microsystems. The objective was to produce and market computer workstations to scientists and engineers. Two of the four were Stanford MBA graduates—Michigan-born Scott McNealy and Vinod Khosla, a native of India. They were joined by Andreas Bechtolsheim, a Stanford engineering graduate who had constructed a computer workstation with spare parts in order to perform numerical analysis, and UNIX software expert William Joy from the Berkley campus. Sun's founders believed there was demand for a desktop computer workstation costing between $10,000 and $20,000 in a market niche ignored by IBM, Data General, DEC, and Hewlett-Packard.

Sun Microsystems, the market leader in the fast-growing workstation industry, expects sales revenue growth of 30% annually during the next five years, compared to 5–10% for the personal computer industry. Workstations can be used in stand-alone fashion or as part of networked configurations. The product lines range from low-priced diskless units to higher-powered graphics-oriented stations at the top of the line.

In contrast to personal computers, workstations are characterized by 32-bit instead of 16-bit microprocessors, a strong tendency to use the UNIX operating system instead of MS/DOS, more sophisticated software and graphics capabilities, larger storage capacities, faster processing speeds, and the ability to function effectively in a networking environment. The principal users of workstations have been engineers and scientists. However, price reductions

---

Source: The research and written case information was prepared by the authors for presentation at the North American Case Research Association Symposium, Atlanta, 1991. © 1991, William C. House.

and technological improvements have broadened the appeal of workstations so that they are finding use in financial trading, desktop publishing, animation, mapping, and medical imaging applications.

Sun, the fastest growing company in the computer hardware industry, has revenues that are increasing at a five-year compounded rate of 85% and income that increased at a 67% rate from 1985 to 1990 (Markoff, 1991). For fiscal year 1991, Sun's revenues were $3.2 billion and net income was $190 million (Zachary, 1991). The company's rapid growth rate, however, has severely drained its cash resources.

SUN'S MANAGEMENT

SCOTT MCNEALY, CHAIRMAN AND CEO

Scott McNealy, the current chairman of Sun, is a native of Detroit and grew up on the fringes of the U.S. automobile industry. Originally rejected by both Harvard and Stanford business schools, he graduated from Harvard with a major in economics. Between his Harvard and Stanford academic careers, he accepted a job as a foreman at a truck plant. After two months of hectic workplace activity, he was hospitalized with hepatitis. He entered Stanford University in 1978 on his third try.

In 1981, at the age of 26, McNealy became manufacturing director at Onyx Systems, a small minicomputer maker. The company was faced with serious quality problems. In two months, the operation showed drastic improvement as McNealy probed work rules and production bottlenecks, encouraging workers to identify problems and overcome obstacles on the way toward improving workplace efficiency.

In 1982, former Stanford classmates Andy Bechtolsheim and Vinod Khosla asked him to join them as director of operations in a new company to be called Sun Microsystems. Two years later, McNealy was chosen by the board of directors to be CEO over Paul Ely, now executive vice-president of Unisys. During the first month after McNealy became CEO, one of the three cofounders resigned, the company lost $500,000 on $2 million in sales, and two-thirds of its computers didn't work.

McNealy is a workaholic, working from daylight to dark, seven days a week, rarely finding time for recreational, activities. The frantic pace at Sun engendered by McNealy is sometimes referred to as "Sunburn." There is a tendency for Sun executives to take on too many projects at once, thereby creating tremendous internal pressure and organizational chaos.

McNealy's philosophy can be capsuled in the following company sayings:

1. On decision making—Consensus if possible, but participation for sure.
2. On management cooperation—Agree and commit, disagree and commit, or just get the hell out of the way.

3. On market response—The right answer is the best answer. The wrong answer is second best. No answer is the worst.
4. On individual initiative—To ask permission is to seek denial.

He has stated that the company is trying to achieve four goals: significant increases in revenue and in book value, improved product acceptance, and higher profit margins.

ANDREAS BECHTOLSHEIM, CHIEF COMPUTER DESIGNER

Andreas Bechtolsheim, chief computer designer, was one of Sun's cofounders. At age 35 he has the title of vice-president of technology. A native of West Germany, Bechtolsheim designed his first computer in 1980 while still a graduate student at Stanford University. It was a workstation designed for scientists and engineers. However, he was unable to sell the idea to any computer company then in existence. Shortly after, he joined Joy, Khosla, and McNealy in founding Sun Microsystems. The company's first product was based on his machine.

Initially, Bechtolsheim persuaded Sun to use off-the-shelf products to develop its workstations instead of following the usual industry practice of utilizing proprietary components. This meant that company products would be easy for competitors to copy, but it also allowed quick entry into the marketplace. As nonproprietary open systems came to be more widely accepted, competitors such as Apollo, DEC, and IBM encountered problems in keeping pace with product lines that lacked the flexibility and performance of Sun's products. When Steve Jobs formed Next, Inc. and announced the development of a desktop workstation, Bechtolsheim urged Sun officials to build a truly desktop computer. There was considerable resistance to the project, and he almost left the company at that point.

Almost at once, he began working on the new computer on his own. He spent $200,000 of his own funds on the project without official company backing. He also formed a small company called Unisun to provide the vehicle for marketing his new computer and persuaded Khosla, a member of Sun's board of directors, to become president of Unisun. Khosla offered Sun the right to invest in or purchase the smaller company outright. Sun seriously considered both possibilities, but McNealy was fearful that the new venture might be considered a competitor of Sun.

In view of the possible negatives of a smaller company selling an identical clone of Sun, the larger company finally agreed to build the new computer and call it Sparcstation I. Initially, restrictions were placed on the project and only engineers who said that they would resign otherwise were allowed to join the project. Because the company has had a culture based on building bigger boxes, the Sparcstation was widely criticized within the company as being too small. However, Bechtolsheim stubbornly refused to change the specifications, and he eventually prevailed.

CAROL BARTZ, FIELD OPERATIONS DIRECTOR

Carol Bartz, national sales director and the number-two executive at Sun Microsystems, has about half of the company's 12,000 employees reporting to her. Although many outsiders feel that she will soon be named chief operating officer, she abruptly dismisses the idea, observing that she doesn't believe the company needs as COO. At 42, the hard-driving and aggressive female seems to be reaching new heights in her career.

Bartz attended the University of Wisconsin, receiving a Bachelor of Computer Science degree in 1971. After that, she spent seven years with Digital Equipment Corporation. Since joining Sun in 1983, she has become intimately involved in marketing operations, including supervising field support activities and a subdivision that sells to federal governmental agencies. Bartz has indicated that her relationship with McNealy permits her to tell him what he is doing wrong as well as what he's doing right. According to Bob Herwick, an investment analyst, Bartz is a very effective problem solver. She has turned around a sluggish service organization and is ensuring that the company is fully exploiting the market potential in the government sector.

TEAM AND CONSENSUS MANAGEMENT AT SUN

McNealy, current Sun chairman, attended Cranbrook, a North Detroit prep school. While there, he excelled in a variety of activities including music, tennis, golf, and ice hockey. According to Alan De Clerk, a high school classmate, McNealy developed a strong self-image and competitive spirit as a result of participating in sports activities and competing with two brothers and a sister. Through the years he has approached all activities as if they were team sports.

McNealy's father, William McNealy, was the vice-chairman of American Motors. Scott followed his dad on the golf course, listened to automobile industry discussions, and found himself pouring over internal company memos along with his father, who was heavily involved in AMC's battle to stay alive. William McNealy ruled his household with an iron hand. McNealy's brother William, who is an architect in St. Louis, says that Scott's strong commitment to consensus management may be a reaction to the type of environment in which they were raised.

McNealy's efforts to build consensus among executives before a decision is made have become famous throughout the company. As he has stated, "Give me a draw and I'll make the decision but I won't issue an edict if a large majority is in favor of an alternative proposal." A frequently quoted example occurred in 1988 when he stubbornly resisted changing prices at a time when rapidly increasing memory costs were reducing profit margins. With a consensus arrayed against him, he finally agreed to some product price increases, which were enacted without reducing sales. In fact, he has a hard time saying no to any project pushed by one or more company groups. He demands complete loyalty within his concept of teamwork and becomes very angry if he believes that individuals or teams have let him down.

PRODUCT LINE FOCUS

The Sparcstation I was introduced in April 1989 at a stripped-down price of $9,000. A lower-priced version was introduced in May 1990 costing $5,000. The machine processes data at 12 mips and runs about twice as fast as personal computers. Sun expects the lower price to facilitate sales to large companies who base computer purchases on quantity discounts. However, the low-end Sparcstation does not have disk drives, color monitors, or add-in slots. Therefore, it must be networked and cannot be used as a stand-alone unit.

An improved version of Sparc I was introduced in summer 1990 with an improved graphic interface, a color monitor, and a price of $10,000. Sun has asserted that a personal computer with the same characteristics as the SPARCSTATION IPX would cost $15,000 to $20,000 and would have only about one-third the processing power of this workstation model. The Sparcstation is now Sun's top seller among all its product lines, and Sparcstation products produce 80% to 90% of total company revenues.

Exhibit 1 shows prices and specmarks (a measure of processing power and speed) for two Sun models as well as for the latest Hewlett-Packard and IBM workstation models. From this table, the relative performance of the Sun computers in terms of computing power per dollar can be compared with their major competitors.

COMPANY STRATEGY

Early on, Sun executives believed that they had only a short time to focus on growing demand for computer workstations from scientists and engineers before large companies such as IBM, DEC, and Hewlett-Packard would aggressively move into that market niche. Therefore, company strategy was designed to emphasize gaining market share, concentrating on all-out sales growth, no matter what the cost. At one point, the organization was adding more than 300 employees and a new sales office each month. Company engineers developed a steady stream of innovative but sometimes impractical prototypes.

EXHIBIT 1 A COMPARISON OF PERFORMANCE MEASURES FOR MAJOR WORKSTATION MAKERS

	PRICE	SPECMARKS	PRICE PER SPECMARK
Hewlett-Packard 9000	$11,990	55.5	216.00
Sun Sparcstation ELC	$ 4,995	20.1	248.50
IBM RS/6000	$13,992	32.8	426.50
Sun Sparcstation IPX	$13,495	24.2	557.60

Source: J. A. Savage, "Price Takes Backseat with Users," *Computerworld*, September 2, 1991, p. 4.

Products were sold largely by word of mouth with virtually no formal sales promotion programs.

As part of the market share focus, in the mid-1980s the company began creating autonomous divisions to develop and market its products. This policy allowed rapid movement into such market areas as sales to government agencies, universities, and financial institutions. A special team was created in 1986 to successfully counter the threat posed by Apollo. Sun can win market share battles in such cases, noted F. H. Moss, formerly vice-president for software development at Apollo, because it has no strong preconceptions about what can or cannot be done. The autonomous groups created unnecessary duplication and contributed to development costs that were almost twice the industry average. When attempts were made to consolidate functions, fierce turf battles resulted, and top executives were forced to step in and referee the conflicts.

The market share/sales growth emphasis created many unexpected problems. Needed investments in customer service and data processing activities had to be postponed. The existence of independent, autonomous divisions caused numerous difficulties for both sales and manufacturing activities. At one point, the company had more than 10,000 computer and option combinations to keep track of. Three different product lines based on three different microprocessors—Sparc, Motorola 68000, and Intel 386—required excessive investment and extensive coordination to ensure that they all worked on the same network. Overlaps and duplications in marketing and finance made forecasting all but impossible. As it grew, the company could no longer scramble madly to meet shipping deadlines at the last minute.

By summer 1989, the company was experiencing production bottlenecks as discounted sales of older products mushroomed. Demand for newer products also increased faster than expected. Large backlogs of sales orders prevented the company from knowing how many or what kinds of products it needed to produce.

In the last quarter of 1989, Sun experienced a $20 million loss due to misjudgment of consumer demand for its new Sparcstation and parts shortages. A new management information system produced inaccurate parts forecasts that contributed to order snafus and lower earnings. Even so, Sun posted a $5 million profit in the first quarter of 1990. It produced revenues of $2.5 billion in fiscal 1990 and was expected to achieve revenues of $3.3 billion in 1991.

Sun is now changing its approach to place more emphasis on profitability and less on growth and to expand customer service and hire fewer employees. Sun president McNealy has recently tied executive pay to before-tax return on investment. In the 1989 annual report he stated that he desired performance to be judged on the basis of significant increases in revenues, acceptance of new products, improvements in profit margins, and increases in book value.

McNealy was one of the early pioneers pushing open systems that would allow computers of many different manufacturers to be linked together in networks. In fact, Sun has actually encouraged competition with itself through its focus on open systems development and invited the industry to build Sparc-based clones in order to expand the position of the workstation industry. As the percentage of total Sparc-based computers sold by Sun has begun to decline, Sun appears to be changing its position on clones. Recently, it told its own dealers that they would incur Sun's displeasure if they sold Sun clones along with Sun workstations. Many of these dealers are angry at what they perceive to be Sun's arrogance.

Sun has consistently maintained a narrow product line focus. It has gradually phased out all microprocessors except Sparc and has concentrated on low-end workstations with the greatest market share growth possibilities. It has avoided entering markets for higher-priced lines and markets for the personal computer segment with their emphasis on low price and compactness. However, recently Sun announced plans to move into high-end workstation markets where processing speed and power requirements necessitate linking a series of microprocessors and using sophisticated software. Sun may encounter problems in this market similar to those it experienced in product upgrades of its lower-level models, since it does not have a good record in managing product introductions.

As workstations become more powerful and less expensive, workstation manufacturers face a serious challenge in maintaining profit margins. Current models now combine high functionality with high volume, in contrast to an earlier focus on producing highly functional units in small quantities. Extensive use of application-specific integrated circuits with fewer components reduces system size, increases reliability, and lowers product costs. Sun and other companies increasingly follow the practice of involving manufacturing representatives in the design process as early as possible in order to minimize manufacturing problems. Increased attention is also being paid to maintaining product quality and improved product testing before systems are shipped.

In past years, Sun's strategies have included a focus on lower prices, well-developed marketing programs, and third-party software development. From 1,500 to 2,000 applications are available for the Sun Sparcstation, compared to approximately 1,000 for Hewlett-Packard and DEC. The company is licensing its Sparc chip to third-party clone companies with the aim of expanding the installed RISC computer base. The overall company goal is to deliver a complete processing solution, including graphics, input/output, software, and networking.

DISTRIBUTION CHANNELS AND CUSTOMER SERVICE

Workstation makers traditionally have sold their units using manufacturers' sales forces and specialized hardware resellers, who repackage specialized software with other companies' workstations. Sun has about 300 VARS (value added resellers), compared to more than 500 for Hewlett-Packard, with Digital and IBM falling somewhere between. Some authorities think the majority of VARs are not capable of selling workstations. Sun is now considering the possibility of selling some of its models through retailers such as Microage in a manner similar to personal computer sales now made by IBM, COMPAQ, and

Apple. Such a move would reduce selling and inventory costs but is meeting initial resistance from dealers unaccustomed to handling complex workstation models.

Sun still sells a large number of workstations through its 1,000-person sales force. In July 1990, Sun selected 200 dealers from three retail chains and gave them training in selling workstations. The company expected to sell $30 million of workstations through retail dealers in FY 1990, but a full-fledged dealer network may require several years to develop. Because of the higher average selling price, greater product differentiation, and the uniqueness of workstations compared to personal computers, many PC vendors are expressing interest in handling workstations in spite of the small volumes generated.

One area of concern has been Sun's field service organization, which has not been very effective in supporting customer software. Bartz has stated that the company wants to improve on customer service without making large monetary expenditures or building a dinosaur service group. In line with this, Sun has announced plans to start using company-trained, third-party service personnel who can be dispatched to customer locations on demand.

CUSTOMER CATEGORIES

The workstation market for engineers and scientists is rapidly becoming saturated. About one-third of Sun's customers now come from the commercial side, up from only 10% several years ago. The company is now concentrating more of its efforts on airlines, banks, and insurance and finance companies, trying to persuade users to utilize Sun workstations to solve new problems. Sun vice-president Eric Schmidt says that Sun tends to get early adopters of new technology. Often, by starting with a pilot program that proves successful, workstations can be expanded to other areas in a customer's operations. Eastman Kodak began using Sun workstations in engineering design and soon expanded their use in marketing databases and mailroom operations.

Sun machines are being used by Wall Street firms Merrill Lynch, Shearson Lehman Hutton, and Bear Sterns on the trading floor. Northwest Airlines uses 500 workstations in Minneapolis to monitor ticket usage and check the correctness of air fare charges and the impact of flight delays or cancellations on revenues and profits. To increase customer satisfaction, Sun has had to change product designs to make its machines easier to install and to improve understandability of product manuals. As Sun has discovered, commercial customers need more help than engineers.

Dataquest says that by 1994, 29.1% of workstation sales will be made to commercial users as opposed to scientific/engineering users in a market expected to reach $22 billion. Workstation makers are moving into the personal computer area by offering UNIX versions that will run on both workstations and personal computers. Workstations provide much greater computing power at a lower cost than would be required to enhance a personal computer to the equivalent capability. Workstations seem to be making their biggest inroads into CPU-intensive applications formerly done on mainframes (e.g., stock transactions and airline reservations).

Sun's first major TV advertising effort in April 1991 took the form of a 30-second commercial seen on CNN, ESPN, and the three major TV networks. The commercial was not directed specifically at a consumer audience, but instead was an attempt to get broad exposure for a new message aimed at the business market. Sun expected the advertisement to reach 59% of U.S. households and 42% of the target market of senior-level corporate and computer executives. The campaign also included an eight-page insert in the *Wall Street Journal*.

Sun's advertising budget of approximately $4.6 million in 1990 was spent on computer and general interest business publications. Sun's advertising budget is only about .25% of sales revenues, compared to 1% to 1.5% spent by its major competitors. Some observers have questioned the cost effectiveness of a high-priced TV advertisement by a company that sells high-priced computers to a limited group of customers.

SOFTWARE DEVELOPMENTS

Availability of software still remains a major problem in expanding sales of workstations. Only about 5% to 10% of UNIX-based software is designed for business and commercial applications. Sun is trying to sign up software developers to produce UNIX-based versions of many common personal computer products. It now has UNIX-based versions of popular PC software, including Lotus 1-2-3 and DBase IV. It hopes the increased availability of software plus the narrowing cost gap between low-end workstations and high-end personal computers will help it penetrate the personal computer market. However, it must sell users on the benefit/cost performance of workstations compared to personal computers and needs to expand its existing base of software developers.

The type of software to be run often is the determining factor in deciding between a personal computer or workstation. For productivity and business applications, PCs can be more cost efficient. For technical and graphics applications, workstations are more appropriate. Differences in costs are no longer a differentiating factor.

An entrenched personal computer MS-DOS operating system base and lack of commercial workstation software has hampered a switch from high-end personal computers to workstations. MS-DOS-based computers appear adequate for a majority of user needs, especially with the advent of the Windows operating environment. PC users are more likely to change if complex applications such as multimedia, integrated database, or windowing become desirable rather than on the basis of price alone. Workstations may become less attractive if 80846-based personal computers with considerably more computing power than today's systems become more widely available.

Product/price performance is no longer as important a differentiating factor as it used to be. Software availability and usability are increasing in importance. In recognition of this development, Sun has formed two software subsidiaries—one for application software and one to concentrate on improvements in the UNIX operating system. The Open Look Graphical Interface has been added to make Sun products more user friendly. The key to maintaining market position seems to be improving systems software and selling software developers and users on the benefits of workstations over other hardware options.

Sun has announced that it will release a new version of its operating system designed to run on Intel-based personal computers. Some analysts say that Sun will face stiff competition from Microsoft's DOS/Windows combination and that Sun's new system is a defensive move, made in realization that Sun no longer can generate enough revenue from its own machines to meet its growth goals. McNealy denies that the Sun announcement is defensive, saying that high-powered PC owners will move to Sun's operating systems to take advantage of advanced capabilities (e.g., running multiple programs simultaneously, which have been vaguely promised by Microsoft Windows' new NT versions. McNealy has sharply criticized Windows NT, referring to it as illusionary.

Sun's Solaris operating system became available in mid-1991 and works on both Intel's X86 series and Sun's Sparc processors. The new operating system makes linking Sun workstations with other computers in a network easier and will increase the number of Sun users. Sun hopes that this will encourage independent software houses to write new programs for Sun systems. So far, approximately 3,500 application programs are available for Sun, compared with more than 20,000 for IBM-compatible personal computers.

COMPETITION IN THE MARKETPLACE

Although still the market leader, Sun is facing increasing competition from much larger computer companies. Sun shipped 146,000 workstations in 1990 (39% of the market) out of a total of 376,000 and was expected to ship 200,000 in 1991. Having fully absorbed Apollo into its organization, Hewlett-Packard is selling about two-thirds as many workstations as Sun, with about 20% of the market, and DEC, which has completely reworked its product lines, has about 17% of the workstation market. Hewlett-Packard has introduced a new workstation model comparable in price to the Sparcstation, which runs about twice as fast as Sun's current model. Exhibit 2 shows the 1989 and 1990 market shares for the major firms in the workstation market.

IBM has made a significant comeback in the workstation market with the RS/6000 after its first workstation model proved to be a slow seller. In 1990, IBM shipped more than 25,000 workstations, producing revenue of $1 billion and attaining a market share of 6.6%, or more than double its 1989 market share. In 1991, some analysts estimate IBM will sell between $2 and $3 billion worth of workstations. IBM has a stated goal of overtaking Sun by 1993, achieving a 30% market share, although some experts predict it is more likely to achieve a 15% market share by that date.

EXHIBIT 2 COMPUTER WORKSTATION MARKET SHARES

COMPANY	1989	1990
Sun Microsystems	30.4%	38.8%
Hewlett-Packard	26.1%	20.1%
Digital Equipment	26.6%	17.0%
Intergraph	7.0%	3.8%
IBM	1.2%	4.5%
Silicon Graphics	5.1%	2.6%
Sony	—	3.3%
Next	—	2.6%
Other	3.6%	7.0%

With the workstation market expected to exceed $20 billion by the mid-1990s, competition will be fierce. IBM's late entry, entrenched positions of competitors in the market, lack of a low-priced entry-level model, and the use of nonstandard operating and graphics environments are likely to hamper IBM's efforts to achieve a market share much above 15%. IBM's service and sales reputation, its large reseller base, and strong position in commercial markets should give the company leverage to enter the fast-growing markets for network servers and small or branch office multiuser systems. However, if IBM focuses its efforts on penetrating these markets with its RS/6000, it runs a serious risk of undercutting sales of its own AS/400.

Cost no longer seems to be the primary factor in decisions to acquire workstations. Workers must become more accustomed to graphic as opposed to character-based systems before adoption by current PC users becomes more widespread. Some companies feel that workstations have yet to demonstrate significant productivity advantages over personal computers. The biggest shortcomings of workstations are lack of application software and integration difficulties.

FINANCIAL ANALYSIS

Exhibit 3 shows Sun's revenues, expenses, and income for the five-year period 1986–1990. Revenues increased at a more rapid rate than net income during the period. Return on sales declined significantly to 4.5% from the peak of almost 7% in 1987, with revenue per shipment also declining in 1990 compared to 1989 and 1988. Book value per share and unit shipments increased significantly during the five years.

Exhibit 4 indicates that Sun's sales, income, and asset growth were higher than the industry average in 1990 and 1989, with market value/equity also above the industry average. However, net income/sales was below the industry average in 1989 and only slightly above the industry average in 1990. As

FINANCIAL ANALYSIS

EXHIBIT 3 SUN MICROSYSTEMS: REVENUES, EXPENSES, AND INCOME, 1986–1990 (BILLIONS OF $)

	1990	1989	1988	1987	1986
Net revenues	2,466	1,765	1,052	538	210
Cost of sales	1,399	1,010	550	273	102
Gross profit	1,067	755	502	265	108
R&D outlays	302	234	140	70	31
Selling, adm. & general expenses	588	433	250	127	57
Total	890	667	390	197	88
Operating income	177	88	111	68	20
Interest income	(23)	(10)	(302)	834	369
Income taxes	43	17	44	33	9
Net income	111	61	66	36	11
Net income/sales	4.5%	3.4%	6.3%	6.8%	5.3%
Net income/share	1.21	0.76	0.89	0.55	0.21
Book value/share	9.82	7.77	4.75	3.57	2.04
Unit shipments (000's)	118.3	80.7	48.4	24.6	9.9
Revenue/unit shipped (000's)	20.8	21.9	21.7	21.8	21.2

Source: Adapted from 1990 Annual Report.

EXHIBIT 4 COMPUTER INDUSTRY DATA FOR 1989 AND 1990

COMPANY	SALES GROWTH		INCOME GROWTH		ASSET GROWTH		NET INC/ SALES		MKT VALUE/ EQUITY	
	1990	1989	1990	1989	1990	1989	1990	1989	1990	1989
Apple	1.07	1.21	1.14	1.05	1.12	1.24	8.7	8.2	4.81	3.21
COMPAQ	1.25	1.39	1.36	1.31	1.30	1.31	12.6	11.6	3.26	3.31
DEC	1.01	1.05	0.00	0.72	1.03	1.10	−.7	6.8	1.21	1.13
Hewlett-Packard	1.10	1.20	0.95	0.97	1.09	1.31	5.7	6.6	1.83	1.98
Intergraph	1.21	1.07	0.79	0.80	1.06	0.97	6.0	9.2	1.79	1.73
IBM	1.10	1.05	1.60	0.68	1.30	1.06	8.7	6.0	1.75	1.62
NCR	1.06	0.99	0.90	0.94	1.01	0.95	5.9	6.9	3.54	3.40
Silicon Graphics	1.41	1.73	1.97	1.94	1.37	0.94	8.3	5.9	3.57	4.30
Sun Microsystems	1.34	1.41	318.00	0.40	1.49	1.50	5.5	1.8	2.72	1.41
Wang	0.87	0.90	0.00	0.00	0.72	0.87	−6.7	−13.9	1.27	0.87
Avg.	1.14	1.20	32.70	0.88	1.15	1.12	5.4	4.9	2.58	2.37

Source: Business Week 1000 Companies, 1990, 1991.

Exhibit 5 indicates, Sun appears to be very close to the industry average in terms of two common productivity measures, sales/assets and sales/employee. In reviewing the common leverage measures, Sun is well above the industry average for R&D expenses/revenues and R&D expenses/employee.

EXHIBIT 5   COMPUTER INDUSTRY DATA FOR 1988 AND 1989

COMPANY	SALES/ ASSETS		SALES/ EMPLOYEE		ADV EXPS/ SALES		R&D EXPS/ SALES		R&D EXPS/ EMPLOYEE	
	1990	1989	1989	1988	1989	1988	1989	1988	1989	1988
Apple	1.82	1.91	364	377	7.34	8.30	8.0	6.7	28937	25233
COMPAQ	1.32	1.38	303	289	1.75	2.87	4.6	3.6	13945	10849
DEC	1.13	1.15	101	94	1.38	1.01	12.0	11.4	12123	10753
Hewlett-Packard	1.22	1.21	125	113	2.69	2.35	10.7	10.4	13358	11713
Intergraph	1.20	1.07	105	110	1.00	1.00	10.6	11.1	11157	12216
IBM	0.79	0.81	164	154	1.17	0.44	8.3	7.4	13572	11415
NCR	1.38	1.32	106	100	1.06	0.53	7.5	7.0	7964	6940
Silicon Graphics	1.22	1.19	180	105	1.00	1.00	11.9	15.8	21150	21908
Sun Microsystems	1.27	1.41	172	148	1.00	0.74	13.3	13.3	22934	19733
Wang	1.35	1.12	109	97	1.00	1.02	9.8	8.7	10543	8510
Avg.	1.27	1.26	173	159	2.64	1.93	9.7	9.5	15568	14027

Source: *Business Week 1000 Companies*, 1990, 1991; Innovation in America (special *Business Week* issues), 1990, 1988.

REFERENCES

Susan E. Fisher, "Vendors Court Reseller Partners as Workstations Go Mainstream," *PC Week*, July 30, 1990.

Jonathan B. Levine, "High Noon for Sun," *Business Week*, July 24, 1989, pp. 71, 74.

John Markoff, "The Smart Alecs at Sun are Regrouping," *New York Times*, April 28, 1991.

Andrew Ould, "IBM Challenges Sun in Workstation Market," *PC Week*, February 28, 1991.

Andrew Ould, "Carol Bartz: Star is Still Rising for Hard Driving Executive," *PC Week*, September 3, 1990.

Andrew Ould, "What's Behind Lower Workstation Prices," *UNIX World*, July 1990.

Julie Pitta, "The Trojan Horse Approach," *Forbes*, April 15, 1991.

Kathy Rebello, "Sun Microsystems on the Rise Again," *USA Today*, April 20, 1990.

"Sun Microsystems Turn on the Afterburners," *Business Week*, July 18, 1988.

G. Paschal Zachary, "Sparc-station's Success is Doubly Sweet for Sun Microsystem's Bechtolsheim," *Wall Street Journal*, May 29, 1990.

Susan E. Fisher, "Vendors Court Resellers as Workstations Go Mainstream" *PC Week*, July 30, 1990.

Robert D. Hof, "Why Sun Can't Afford to Shine Alone," *Business Week*, September 9, 1991.

G. Paschal Zachary, "Sun Challenges Microsoft's Hold Over Software," *Wall Street Journal*, September 4, 1991.

Bob Francis, "Big Blue's Red Hot Workstation," *Datamation*, October 15, 1990.

Lawrence Curran, "HP Speeds Up Workstation Race," *Electronics*, April 1991.

"Getting Down to Business," *Information Week*, January 14, 1991.

CASE 15

WORDPERFECT FACES THE NINETIES CHARLES BOYD

In early 1990, WordPerfect Corporation was the market leader in word-processing software. Yet signals in the rapidly changing personal computer (PC) software market indicated that no firm could rest on past successes. Computer-savvy customers wanted products with more features for their faster and more powerful machines. At the same time, the advent of laptop computers required that scaled-down versions of popular programs fit on a single floppy disk. It was not enough to have a single successful product, such as a word-processing package. Many users had become sophisticated enough to integrate spreadsheet and database files into their documents, which indicated a need for a family of programs that could be integrated easily.

The combination of these forces caused WordPerfect and its competitors to upgrade their products constantly and provide excellent support service for their customers. Management at WordPerfect had to keep particularly close watch on its closest competitor, Microsoft Word (often called Word). In recent performance tests, Word compared very favorably to WordPerfect.

A BRIEF HISTORY OF WORD PROCESSING[1]

In 1961, IBM introduced the Selectric typewriter. For the first time, typists could control the typeface they used by changing a print ball. It was another ten years before the next notable advance in document preparation would occur: Wang Labs' introduction of the Wang 1200. This small-screen typing workstation could retrieve documents stored on cassette tape. Five years later, the Wang WPS (Word Processing System) was introduced. This machine permitted storage of up to 4,000 pages on disk.

Source: **This case was prepared by the author as a basis for classroom discussion rather than to illustrate either effective or ineffective handling of an administrative situation. © Charles Boyd, 1991.**

The 1975 introduction of the Altair marked the beginning of the era of PCs. Disks became the storage system of choice for PCs when Digital Research Corporation introduced the CP/M (Computer Program Management) System in 1976. Dedicated word-processing systems dominated the corporate office market until the introduction of the IBM PC in 1981. By that time, users had become comfortable with the available word-processing packages they had used on CP/M equipment. These included the IBM Displaywriter System, Wang Labs' WangWriter, and the popular WordStar. Users were reluctant to switch from these programs to new ones written for the IBM PC such as Easy-Writer and Volkswriter. In fact, many users installed a "Baby Blue" card in their early IBM PCs that permitted the machines to run CP/M programs.

Meanwhile, vendors were busy rewriting their programs so they would run on the PC. By 1982, several word-processing programs were available for the PC: Micropro's WordStar 2.3, Wang's Wordmate (now named Multimate), and WordPerfect Corporation's program. Micropro was the first to capture the heart of the corporate PC word-processing market with the release of WordStar 3.3 in 1983. About the same time, PFS:Write became the first personal word-processing program to make full use of the PC's capabilities with its "what you see is what you get" (WYSIWYG) screen displaying margins, line spacing, and other attributes. Microsoft Corporation also entered the arena in 1983 by introducing Microsoft Word. Word further expanded the WYSIWYG concept by enabling the user to see attributes on the screen. Bold and underlined words appeared on screen as they would on the printed page.

Advances in the speed and power of word-processing software and PC hardware continued to occur during the 1980s. IBM's introduction of the Personal System/2 (PS/2) line of computers in 1987 marked a crossroad for word-processing and other software. Existing software will run on PS/2 machines, but more powerful software could be written to run only on PS/2 machines. Software companies must now decide which way to orient new versions of their products. They can write separate versions for PCs and PS/2 equipment or write versions that will run only on PS/2 machines.

HISTORY AND MANAGEMENT OF WORDPERFECT CORPORATION

In 1975, Alan Ashton, then a Brigham Young University professor, met a young music student named Bruce Bastion. Bastion was trying to write software to choreograph the university's marching band. The two men created the first version of WordPerfect in a garage operation in a Salt Lake City suburb in 1979. Initial sales reached $36,000 and have grown rapidly every year since 1980, reaching $178 million in more than 20 countries in 1988.[2] WordPerfect's 1989 sales reached $281 million. WordPerfect passed Ashton-Tate during the second quarter of 1989 to attain third place in the microcomputer software market on quarterly sales of $67 million. The firm's share of the word-processing software market increased from 35 percent in early 1988 to 60 percent by the fall of 1989.[3]

WordPerfect is a closely held corporation, and management will not release its financial statements. The firm does make available some performance data. Exhibit 1 reports WordPerfect's meteoric growth in sales, number of employees, and user base (the number of its programs in use).

Computer-industry writer Will Fastie remembers that Bruce Bastion was the person who answered the company telephone to field users' questions back in 1979. He was always friendly, had time to talk, and asked for suggestions that might improve the product. Mr. Fastie has found that the firm's friendly atmosphere has prevailed through the years. WordPerfect employees staff trade-show booths. Other software companies use attractive young women known as spokesmodels for this purpose. Mr. Fastie has found the employees friendly and excited about their work and their product, both at trade shows and during his many company visits over the years. He believes this attitude trickles down from the two company founders at the top.[4]

WordPerfect's corporate culture is largely a result of the Mormon virtues of hard work and loyalty. Alan Ashton and Bruce Bastion are Mormons, as are most WordPerfect employees. In fact, WordPerfect is only one of several successful firms and recent scientific achievements that have their roots in Utah's Salt Lake Valley: two other word-processing companies, Software Systems and Electronic Word Corporation; Linguatech and Alpnet, two leaders in language-translation software that is selling well in Europe; the Jarvik-7, the first reliable artificial heart; and the controversial 1989 discovery of a cold fusion process that has the possibility of producing vast amounts of cheap energy. Many of the founders of these innovations come from either Brigham Young University or the University of Utah. The Mormon Church owns Brigham Young University, and the University of Utah is in a state where the governor, the two senators, and 85 percent of the state legislators are Mormons.[5]

Managers at WordPerfect encourage initiative and creativity from employees and reward achievers with incentives and promotions. This work ethic has paid off time and again as the firm has surpassed competitors in this highly competitive—sometimes ruthless—industry. Bruce Bastion has commented,

EXHIBIT 1 WORDPERFECT'S GROWTH IN SALES, EMPLOYEES, AND USER BASE

	1979	1980	1981	1982	1983	1984	1985	1986	1987	1988	1989
Annual sales (million)	$.036	$.45	$.85	$1	$3.5	$9	$23	$52	$100	$178	$281
Employees	3	6	11	18	47	84	199	306	554	1,130	1,612
User Base (000 omitted after 1982)	5	85	260	605	11	47	175	485	1,159	2,621	3,856

Source: "Company Outline," WordPerfect Corporation, undated.

"We treat our programmers with respect and win their loyalty. Their heads are not clouded by the drugs and alcohol so common in this business."[6] David Tebbut, consulting editor of Europe's *PC Dealer,* has said of WordPerfect employees, "They are the most dedicated, bubbly bunch of people I have ever met in my life."[7]

WordPerfect Corporation also has been successful in Europe. Aggressive marketing has captured 30 percent of the British and West German markets, 60 percent of the market in Holland, and 70 percent of the Scandinavian market. WordPerfect translates its word-processing packages into the language of a local market. Many competitors don't take the time and effort to do this.[8] "International expansion is essential to the life of this company, and we see Europe as a prime market," Alan Ashton said. "We want to become the standard for word processing in Europe and we are confident we can do it."[9] In mid-1989, management projected that the firm would own 80 percent of the European market within five years.[10] Exhibit 2 illustrates WordPerfect's international expansion.

EXHIBIT 2   WORDPERFECT'S INTERNATIONAL EXPANSION

INTERNATIONAL VERSIONS RELEASED

1982: Finnish
1983: French, German, Norwegian
1984: Spanish
1985: Danish, Dutch
1986: UK English
1987: Icelandic, Swedish, Canadian French
1988: Italian, Portuguese

INTERNATIONAL TERRITORIES OPENED

1980: Canada
1981: Finland, France, Switzerland, Sweden
1982: West Germany, United Kingdom
1983: Denmark, Norway, The Netherlands
1984: Australia, Brazil, New Zealand, Belgium/Luxembourg
1985: Mexico, Spain
1986: Hong Kong
1987: Italy, Japan, Austria
1988: Malaysia, Singapore
1989: Argentina, Bolivia, Botswana, Brazil, Chile, Colombia, Ecuador, India, Lesotho, Mexico, Mozambique, Namibia, New Caledonia, Paraguay, Peru, South Africa, Swaziland, Switzerland, Uruguay, Venezuela, Zambia, and Zimbabwe.

WPCORP INTERNATIONAL OFFICES

WordPerfect Denmark
WordPerfect Iberica
WordPerfect Europe
WordPerfect Switzerland
WordPerfect Japan
WordPerfect Pacific
WordPerfect Sweden
WordPerfect Norway
WordPerfect U.K.
WordPerfect France
WordPerfect Nederland
WordPerfect Software GmbH (Germany)

Source: "Company Outline," WordPerfect Corporation, undated.

WordPerfect's incursion into Europe has not been without problems. The firm created some ill will at first by offering only short-term contracts to small distributors. This approach saved capital investment costs and allowed WordPerfect to switch distributors quickly if sales were disappointing. It failed to generate much loyalty and enthusiasm from the distributors, however. Now WordPerfect distributes differently in Europe. Managers have concluded that they will need to spend some money to win the European market. Peter Ferguson, managing director of WordPerfect U.K., says, "Previous distributors failed miserably because they had little incentive to perform. Our approach is very different; we invest in advertising, offer free training to dealers, and we go to twelve computer shows each year."[11]

Pete Peterson, a WordPerfect vice-president and the firm's chief financial planner, says, "We treat our people with decency and we reward them for good work. We've only lost one programmer in the last eight years."[12] Peterson started working for the company in 1980, earning $5 an hour to organize the company's accounts. He has resisted offering a public stock issue by exercising the Mormon value of thriftiness. He has said, "Innovative companies should never be answerable to investors, because investors only think of short-term profit while innovation requires time and patience. So we have to be careful: We always budget from the previous quarter's receipts and, above all, we never borrow money."[13] This financial philosophy stands in stark contrast to the huge amounts of venture capital that often fund the start-up of many high-tech firms. Such capital dilutes the entrepreneur's ownership. It also places entrepreneurs under pressure to produce returns on investment in the 40–50-percent range early in the firm's life. WordPerfect's philosophy also contrasts with the heavy doses of debt many more-established firms incur to fuel impressive growth rates. WordPerfect has grown the old-fashioned way: by selling a good product and backing it with excellent service after the sale.

THE WORD-PROCESSING SOFTWARE INDUSTRY IN 1990

By 1989, the word-processing software market for PCs was well developed and competition was keen. The market was divided into three segments: lower-priced, limited-function programs; high-end programs rich with features; and a middle market consisting of programs fitting between the other two segments in price and features. WordPerfect was the market leader at the high end of the market. This segment mostly appeals to corporate users and professional writers.

The dividing lines between these three market segments are not distinctly drawn. For example, the latest version of WordPerfect lists for $495, but an excellent shareware product with a good reputation, PC-Write, sells for $99. Shareware products are made available by their authors at a nominal fee for a trial period, usually 30 days. If users like the product, they pay the asking price and become registered owners. Shareware is one of the few products a customer can try before buying. A customer can buy a trial copy of PC-Write from a mail-order house. PC-Write offers many of the features found in high-end products, including a manual, tutorial, spelling checker, extensive printer support, and macros (keystroke-saving functions). PC-Write released a new version in 1989 that offered users 500 new features. A condensed version, PC-Write Lite, sells for $69. PC-Write has been respected in the market for years. It is site licensed at the *Los Angeles Times,* where all the paper's reporters use it.[14] With 500,000 registered copies in use, PC-Write has 13 percent as much user base as does WordPerfect.[15] This example illustrates just how competitive the PC software industry can get.

Heavy competition was taking place at the high end of the market as the 1980s drew to a close. Organizations and individuals using the latest computers with fast microprocessors and large disk storage capacity could take the best advantage of the many of features the latest programs offered. New features are periodically accumulated and incorporated into a new version of a product. For example, WordPerfect 5.0 was released in May 1988, followed by version 5.1 in late 1989. Chief competitor Microsoft Word had released version 5.0 earlier in 1989.[16] Each vendor tries to add more impressive features in each new version than its competitors have in their current versions.

WordPerfect 5.1 lists for $495 and Microsoft Word 5.0 lists for $450. Registered owners of the previous versions can upgrade to WordPerfect 5.1 for $85 and to Word 5.0 for $75. These reduced upgrade prices are typical for most software products. They foster customer loyalty by allowing current users to benefit from new features without paying the full price for an upgraded version, which few probably would do anyway. Still, customers have incentives to stay with their current programs. Becoming proficient in using a word-processing program takes many hours. For this reason, it is extremely difficult to entice users to abandon their present programs unless they can see many advantages in doing so. This problem is multiplied for an organization that has purchased a package and trained hundreds of employees to use it effectively. Both increased cost and temporarily lowered productivity would result from changing to a new program. Managers would have to see tremendous benefits before changing programs. This reluctance to change helps software companies hold their customers. Still, they must add new features as the state of word-processing software and the computer hardware that runs it improves.

Hard disks for desktop PCs have enabled users to store and use larger programs with more features. The advent of laptop and notebook computers in the late 1980s created a new need. Some of these smaller computers have hard disks, but prices for these machines start about $2,500. Many users choose a less-expensive computer with one or two floppy disk drives and no hard disk. These machines could be purchased for as little as $1,000 in early 1990. Students, traveling executives, and professionals find these smaller, portable computers desirable. Software vendors had to respond to this trend by "trimming down" their programs to fit on a floppy diskette. WordPerfect responded with WordPerfect Executive. This program retained the most commonly used features from version 4.3. Advanced word-processing features were omitted, and the spelling checker dictionary was reduced. The program also included a limited version of WordPerfect's spreadsheet package, PlanPerfect, and some features from WordPerfect Library 1.1, the company's desktop tools program. The entire package fits on one standard $3\frac{1}{2}$-inch floppy diskette and lists for $249.[17] Failure to offer programs like WordPerfect Executive would leave the growing laptop and notebook computer market to the lower and middle segments of the software market.

EVERYONE WANTS A PIECE OF THE ACTION

Another advantage enjoyed by users of best-selling software programs is the availability of third-party, add-in programs. Some of these programs simplify program functions. A disk of macros would do this. Others are utilities, such as menu systems that make it easier to select program functions or that offer functions not available within the program itself. For example, a program called Sideways is packaged with the popular Super-Calc spreadsheet program. As the name implies, this program permits large spreadsheets to be printed sideways on a standard 80-column printer. This permits all of the columns to be displayed on one page. Lotus packages the program Allways with the latest version of its popular 1-2-3 spreadsheet program. Allways enables the user to create more eye-appealing spreadsheet printouts.

The popularity of WordPerfect has attracted a host of such third-party software. These include menu programs that can be popped to the screen when the user needs to execute some program functions. Up to 70 WordPerfect macros can be purchased on a single floppy diskette. Shareware diskettes containing WordPerfect utilities and macros are also available.

Software programs typically come packaged with explanatory user manuals and have on-line help that users can access on screen from within the programs. Despite this, many explanatory manuals are published by other companies. These third-party manuals go into extensive detail explaining the programs' functions in very accessible language. Many of them are available in local bookstores and are typically priced in the $20–$30 range. Several such books are available for WordPerfect. WordPerfect 5.1 was first released in mid-November 1989, and books for it were available by April 1990.

Keyboard templates are another popular third-party item. These cardboard or plastic templates fit over a computer keyboard's function keys. The primary functions the program will execute when certain keys are pressed are printed on these templates.

These third-party books, add-in software, and keyboard templates bolster the confidence of potential customers as they consider the purchase of a program. They confirm the popularity of the programs for which they are written; no one would bother to write products to support a program that did not have huge market share. The software add-ins also help WordPerfect and other vendors of popular software in two ways: They increase sales of the current version of their programs, and they help vendors see what new features users want in the next version. It doesn't hurt to get this free information when competing in such a volatile market. Exhibit 3 provides a partial list of third-party, add-in software and books for WordPerfect.

A FRIEND FOR LIFE

WordPerfect and other quality software vendors compete fiercely in providing customers with toll-free telephone support. Users can call these numbers when they encounter problems using the software. Microsoft, the largest software firm, uses 2,200 employees to answer such calls. This costs the firm $8–$10 million per year. Fifteen percent of Ashton-Tate's employees provide user support.

EXHIBIT 3 SELECTED THIRD-PARTY SOFTWARE AND BOOKS FOR WORDPERFECT

COMMERCIAL SOFTWARE

NAME	TYPE	PUBLISHER	PRICE
Perfect Complement	multipurpose utility	Perfect Complement Corporation	$149.95
Perfect Addition	pop-up menus	Applause Software	$54.95
Winning WordPerfect 5.0	20-lesson tutorial	T. S. MicroTech, Incorporated	$29.95
Grammatik IV*	grammar checker	Reference Software	$97.00
RightWriter*	grammar checker	RightSoft	$95.00

*Grammatik IV and RightWriter work with several other word-processing programs in addition to WorkPerfect.

SHAREWARE

WordPerfect Macros	Available for versions 4.2 and 5.0
WordPerfect 5.0 Tools	Multipurpose utilities
WordPerfect 5.0 Clip-Art	Graphic images that can be inserted into documents
WordPerfect 5.0 Business Letters	More than 70 fill-in-the-blanks form letters
HelpPerfect for WordPerfect	Memory-resident pull-down menus, file search utility, calculator, 300-number phone book and dialer, more. Available for 4.1, 4.2, and 5.0.
WP Learning System	WordPerfect tutorial
WordPerfect 5.0 Menu/Mice	Menu system and mouse drivers

BOOKS AND MANUALS

Alvieri, Vincent, revised by Ralph Blodgett. *The Best Book of WordPerfect 5.1,* 2nd ed. Hayden Books, 1989.

Kelly, Susan Baake. *Mastering WordPerfect 5.* Sybex, 1988.

Mincberg, Mella. *WordPerfect Secrets, Solutions, Shortcuts: Series 5 Edition.* Osborne McGraw-Hill, 1988.

———. *WordPerfect Made Easy: Series 5 Edition.* Osborne McGraw-Hill, 1989.

Neibauer, Alan R. *WordPerfect 5.1 Tips and Tricks,* 4th ed. Sybex, 1990.

Parker, Roger C. *Desktop Publishing with WordPerfect.* Ventana Press, 1988.

Between the May 1988 release of version 5.0 and November of the year, WordPerfect's support staff increased from 200 to 420, which was 37 percent of total employees.[18] By the end of the first quarter of 1989, 450 employees were answering 10,000 calls per day.[19] Utah's entire telephone system was once shut down due to the number of incoming calls to WordPerfect Corporation.[20] The cost of providing this support equals 5 percent of the firm's gross revenues. M. Daniel Lunt, vice-president of marketing at WordPerfect, said, "I view the expense of support as a marketing expense, similar to advertising."[21] WordPerfect maintains many toll-free numbers around the nation for user support. The average call lasts seven minutes, longer if it is printer related. WordPerfect often hires students at nearby Brigham Young University to answer the calls. Beginning salaries start as low as $13,000 and rise to the mid- to high $20,000s after two or three years' service.[22]

Major hardware and software vendors conducted an informal survey of technical support telephone service. They found that staff at Lotus, Ashton-Tate, Microsoft, AST, and WordPerfect answered the phone on the first ring. Some vendors took up to five rings. AST ranked first in overall service. AST and WordPerfect tied for first in technical competence, with Lotus and COMPAQ tying for last. Microsoft and Ashton-Tate took the least amount of time to solve a problem, while WordPerfect and IBM took the longest.[23]

The Europeans must pay higher wages than those paid in Utah, and Europeans do not share the same work ethic as the employees at WordPerfect's headquarters. In addition, WordPerfect's European sales have grown so fast that it has been difficult for the support to keep up. For these reasons, the firm hasn't been as successful with its European telephone support service as it has been in the U.S.[24] The manager of one European computer store that sells $2 million of equipment to corporate customers each year said, "Even major corporate customers say they cannot get an answer on the help lines, so they come back to us. People are cut off, messages are not returned, and it can sometimes take two or three months to solve a problem."[25] Quality support ultimately will be important to WordPerfect's efforts to win the continent.[26]

As PC hardware and software become increasingly sophisticated, service is expected to become increasingly important to customers. Jim Manzi, president of Lotus Development Corporation, stated, "Service, rather than raw technology, will drive the next cycle of growth in the PC industry."[27] Lotus has a toll-free line for the releases 2.2 and 3.0 of its 1-2-3 program. Service is free for the first six months, after which customers can renew it for $49 per year. In early 1990, the firm was testing a 900 line that will provide quicker response for a small cost to the customer.[28] WordPerfect's telephone support is free for as long as the customer owns the firm's product(s). WordPerfect is the customer's friend for life.

THE COPY PROTECTION ISSUE

During the early and mid-1980s, many software vendors placed copy-protection code in their programs to prevent customers from making more than one or two copies. A customer is always advised to make a working copy of newly purchased software and to store the original diskettes in a safe place. Often customers would place a working copy on their hard disk and later experience a hard disk crash (mechanical disk failure) or accidental erasure of the program. The copy protection code prevented them from replacing the lost copy—which created some unhappy customers. Programs that could strip the copy protection code from commercial software were written to address this problem. Software vendors soon gave in to customers' demands for software without copy protection. The vendors knew that this would result in lost revenue because customers would make illegal copies to distribute to friends and fellow employees. They also knew it would make software piracy (mass copying for black-market sales) easier. The consensus was that these risks would be less of a problem than the customer ill will they had already experienced. As a result, just about all commercial software was being distributed without copy protection by the late 1980s.

It is impossible to know how much revenue software vendors have lost from unauthorized copies. The Association of Data Processing Service Organization estimates that software piracy cost the industry between $800 million and $1 billion in 1985. Research estimates of the percentage of illegal software in use by 1989 range from 50 percent to 80 percent of all programs in use.[29] Copying commercial software for resale or to give to others is a violation of the copyright laws. But like most copyright violations, it is extremely hard to detect and prosecute.

The issue of copy protection surfaced again early in 1990. A group of companies in Europe proposed a strict law to prevent software companies from reverse engineering other companies' software. Reverse engineering, a common industry practice, involves examining the coded instructions in a software program. Companies do it to figure out how to write their own programs so they will interact smoothly with a competitor's program. IBM, Digital Equipment, and Apple Computer were leading the effort to ban this practice in Europe. Together they lead the Software Action Group for Europe (SAGE). They are opposed by another group, the European Committee for Interoperable Systems, which wants the relevant laws to remain as the are. Amdahl, Fujitsu, NCR, and Unisys are key members of this group. The European Commission's ruling on this issue is likely to have profound worldwide results for both software companies and consumers. If the law SAGE wants is passed in Europe, experts expect that a similar law will be passed in the United States. Attorney Michael Jacobs said, "Everything everyone thought was legal is now being called into question."[30] If companies are prevented for examining competitors' software, they can't develop similar interfaces (screens that provide users a common look and feel necessary for interacting with those other programs). As Norbert Kuster, manager of the Association of German Corporate Consultants has said, "Whoever controls the interface controls the market."[31]

The proposed European law also seeks tighter control of software piracy and illegal copying of programs, as practically difficult as that would be. Computer magazine writer John Dvorak believes the software copying issue is surfacing again because of the proliferation of laptop PCs. A customer who buys a software program can legally copy that program for use on only one computer. This means that a person who uses a program on a desktop machine at the office and on a laptop computer used on trips legally must buy two copies of the program, one for each machine. Dvorak considers the laptop an extension of the person's desktop machine and thinks that laptops should be given consideration in software licensing agreements. His position is that copy protection is counterproductive to software companies' marketing efforts and that companies that adopt it will suffer lost sales.[32]

SOFTWARE INDUSTRY OUTLOOK

Analysts expected software sales by U.S.-based vendors to increase worldwide at an average rate of 21.25 percent from 1988 to 1991 (see Exhibit 4). Growth rates were expected to be somewhat stronger outside the U.S.

New versions of high-end software continue to include additional features to attract new customers and retain old ones. Even as features multiply, users want their programs to be easy to use and to include well-documented instructions through manuals and on-line help. They also want training, service, and support from the vendor. Exhibit 5 reports these and other software selection criteria from a survey of 1,900 data processing and other corporate managers responsible for buying and evaluating software. Supplying these customer desires and holding the line on prices will pose a big challenge for software vendors in coming years.

WORDPERFECT'S PRODUCT LINE

Several young software companies that have great success with their first product never develop a successful follow-up product, and sluggish sales soon follow. Continued success in the software industry demands that a vendor continually develop new programs and periodically upgrade existing programs. This

EXHIBIT 4 FORECASTED SOFTWARE SALES, 1990–1991

Year	U.S.			INTERNATIONAL		TOTAL WORLDWIDE	
	Sales (mil.$)	% chg. (from prev.yr.)	% of total	Sales (mil.$)	% chg. (from prev. yr.)	Sales (mil.$)	% chg. (from prev. yr.)
1990	23,095	+18	58	16,590	+23	39,685	+20
1991	27,095	+17	57	20,255	+22	47,350	+19

Source: Standard & Poor's Industry Surveys, June 15, 1989, p. C93.

EXHIBIT 5 SOFTWARE SELECTION CRITERIA, BY SYSTEM SIZE (PERCENT OF RESPONSES CLAIMING "VERY IMPORTANT")

SELECTION CRITERIA	MAINFRAME SOFTWARE	MINICOMPUTER SOFTWARE	MICROCOMPUTER SOFTWARE
Ease of use	67	75	73
Features and performance	69	65	66
Documentation	63	63	66
Vendor support	67	51	39
Compatibility with other software	48	49	46
Error handling	39	33	35
Portability to other hardware	25	30	32
Vendor size, reputation	25	18	17
Price	26	22	20
Site licensing	—	—	16
Removal of copy protection	—	—	31
Limited liability for unauthorized copying	—	—	7
Ability to transfer between mainframes, minis, & micros	—	—	22

Source: *Standard & Poor's Industry Surveys*, June 15, 1989, p. C9.

need is often best met by developing a family of programs that work together and complement one another. Each of these programs typically has a common command structure and familiar screen so users of one program can easily use the others. This compatibility enhances the company's sales and develops customer loyalty.

WordPerfect has developed such a family of products. Its flagship word-processing program is supplemented by its PlanPerfect spreadsheet program, DataPerfect database program, WordPerfect Library desktop utility program, and DrawPerfect graphics program. These programs allow users to integrate spreadsheet data, file data, and graphic images into their word-processing documents. WordPerfect and other quality word-processing programs also will accept these kinds of data from other vendors' popular programs. For example, many word-processing programs will directly import Lotus 1-2-3 spreadsheet files because that program is considered to be the industry standard in spreadsheet software. WordPerfect 5.0 will directly import graphic images from 11 other vendors' graphics programs. In addition, it will capture images directly from the screen from 22 additional graphics programs.[33] Still, having their own spreadsheet and other complementary programs enables WordPerfect and other vendors to offer their users an option many prefer: a familiar interface and command structure in all the types of programs needed to write a professional-looking document. The complementary programs also increase sales and enable vendors to create a presence in additional segments of the software market. This spreads competitive risks.

When it was introduced in 1988, WordPerfect 5.0 had several features that competing packages did not have. The program included the following key features:

1. Screen and keyboard customization.
2. A powerful macro editor and macro language.
3. Outlining capability.
4. The ability to view a full page on screen.
5. The ability to incorporate graphics into a document.
6. Modest desktop publishing capabilities.[34]

WordPerfect 5.0 received the following awards in 1988:

1. *PC World*'s Class Award for word processing
2. *InfoWorld* Product of the Year Award
3. *InfoWorld* MS-DOS Word Processor of the Year Award
4. *PC Computing*'s Most Important Products of 1988 Award
5. *PC Magazine*'s Best of 1988 Award for word processing
6. *Computer Dealer*'s "Best-to-Sell Product"[35]

PlanPerfect 5.0 is a full-featured spreadsheet program that is easy to learn and has a user interface similar to the word processor's. The program also has Lotus 1-2-3–type commands and will read Lotus files (as will most seriously competitive spreadsheets). PlanPerfect also supports all 450 printers that the word processor supports.[36] One evaluator noted that although the program was satisfactory, it had few distinctive features that would attract users who did not use WordPerfect's word-processing program.[37]

DataPerfect is a program for defining and managing many kinds of data: names and addresses, invoices, or whatever can be stored and sorted as the user wishes. Users can print reports in various formats.

WordPerfect Library contains six integrated utility programs: calculator, calendar, file manager, notebook, program editor, and macro editor. Users can easily switch between Library and WordPerfect's other programs. Users can share data among the programs. Library received the following awards in 1987 and 1988:

1. Finalist in *PC Magazine*'s 1987 Awards for Technical Excellence
2. *PC World*'s World Class Award for utilities package (1988)
3. *Commodore Magazine*'s Best Productivity Software Program Award (WordPerfect Library for the Amiga) (1988)[38]

WordPerfect Executive, described earlier, is a condensed program designed for laptop and notebook computers. It features selected word-processing, spreadsheet, and desktop utility functions from WordPerfect's other programs. The entire package fits on the standard $3\frac{1}{2}$-inch floppy diskette.

DrawPerfect was designed to give WordPerfect a presence in the growing field of graphics programs and to improve the desktop publishing capabilities of the firm's word-processing package. The package enables users to incorporate charts and graphic images into presentations or word-processing documents. DrawPerfect contains 500 clip-art images that the user can edit.[39]

WordPerfect Office 2.0 was a groupware package, which means that it was meant to be used simultaneously by many employees in an office setting. Its functions included a scheduler, database program, calculator, file manager, and macro editor.[40] Version 2.1 of WordPerfect Office was scheduled for release in January 1990. This new version would work across several local area networks and use the popular Novell Message Handling Service. This would give users access to electronic mail systems, including MCI and Telenet.[41]

THE BATTLE OF THE WORD PROCESSORS

WordPerfect was clearly the market leader in word-processing software in 1989, but its leadership was being challenged by three competitive forces:

1. Recent upgraded versions of competing word processors.
2. Uncertainty about which operating system for PCs would predominate in the future. The resolution of this issue will affect the number of versions of a software product that must be written and the look and feel of each version to users.
3. The mergers and consolidations among software firms. A realignment of power in the industry is likely to result.

These competitive forces are discussed in the following sections.

RECENT UPGRADES

Software vendors introduced a rash of new versions of popular word-processing packages during the late 1980s. Each of these upgrades packs an array of new features designed to lure first-time purchasers and to attract users of competing products. Persuading a user of another word-processing program to switch is a difficult task due to the time and effort involved in learning a feature-packed, top-quality package.

WordStar was a very popular program during the early 1980s, but the package lost significant market share during the middle and latter part of the decade due to some marketing miscues. Micropro introduced snappy new versions during 1988 and 1989. The latest version is 6.0, which lists for $495. It features more desktop publishing features than previous versions, and it is the first package to support scalable (sizeable) fonts for the new Hewlett-Packard LaserJet III printer.[42]

Ashton-Tate released version 4.0 of its Multimate Word Processing package in spring 1990. The program contains 150 new features, including an electronic mail service and Reference Software's Grammatik IV grammar checker. Suggested retail price is $565. Owners of the previous version can upgrade for $75.[43]

Although there are many excellent word-processing programs on the market, clearly Microsoft Word poses the greatest challenge to WordPerfect. These two programs constantly compete against each other. Perhaps WordPerfect has maintained the market lead because in the past Word seemed always to be a version behind in features and performance. For example, when WordPerfect 5.0 was introduced in May 1988, it had a clear advantage in features over the then-current Word 4.0. But the introduction of Word 5.0 in 1989 made the two packages equal. Word 5.0 featured many improvements in graphics importing and page previewing. The package also offered automatic document saving, automatic pagination, and integrated spell checking. Both programs offer modest desktop publishing capability, although WordPerfect has a slight graphics-handling advantage. Word offers superior group document handling, important to office use. Overall, Word 5.0 effectively closed the features gap between the two packages. As one writer put it, "Word 5.0 matches WordPerfect feature for feature."[44]

Word 5.0 has a list price of $450, while WordPerfect 5.0 lists for $495. Both packages use 384 kilobytes (KB) of memory—a modest amount of computer memory by 1989 standards, especially for the vast array of features that these programs offer. This factor is competitively significant, however, because owners of PCs dating back to the mid-1980s can use these programs. As features multiply, many programs require more computer memory and faster microprocessors. Often only the newer, more expensive PS/2 and compatible computers can run these programs. PS/2s have faster operating speeds, more internal memory, and fixed disk drives with large storage capacities. Version 3.0 of Lotus Development Corporation's popular 1-2-3 spreadsheet program, released in 1989, required PS/2 equipment. When initial sales were disappointing, Lotus released version 2.2. This version contained most of the features of 3.0, printed better, ran on both old and new computers, and cost $100 less than 3.0. Version 2.2 has been Lotus's big 1-2-3 seller since its introduction. Version 3.0 has accounted for only 25 percent of 1-2-3 sales.[45] Like version 2.2 of Lotus 1-2-3, WordPerfect and Word have positioned their products to be available to owners of both newer and older PCs.

The release of Word 5.0 in 1989 put the ball back in WordPerfect's court. The next competitive move was predictable. Later in 1989, WordPerfect released version 5.1. This new version featured pull-down menus that supported the use of a mouse (a convenient device for selecting options from an on-screen menu). Word already had mouse support. WordPerfect 5.1 also contained automated table creation. In addition to many other new features, users could write longer, more descriptive file names.[46] The package lists for $495, the same as 5.0. Upgrades cost $85. Despite its many new features, 5.1 still occupies only 384 KB of memory, the same as 5.0, and will run on just about all PCs in use.

THE OPERATING SYSTEM WARS

Computers must have operating system software. The operating system functions much as a traffic cop. It directs the flow of application software such as word processors and spreadsheets in and out of the computer's memory and enables their commands to be executed. It also performs routine chores such as file and directory management.

Most personal computer software is written for the largest-selling class of PC on the market: the IBM PC and the many compatibles. Many of the top-selling packages also make available versions for other types of computers and for the variety of operating system software that controls IBM and compatible computers. For example, both WordPerfect and Microsoft Word are available for use on the popular Apple Macintosh computer. Both will run on the majority of existing IBM and compatible machines that use the older MS-DOS (Microsoft Disk Operating System). They will also run on newer PS/2s controlled by Microsoft's OS/2 operating system.

The Macintosh computer upped the ante in the PC market with its easy-to-use operating system. The Macintosh features icons (pictures) to present menu choices that a user can select with a mouse. The user does not need to learn text commands to operate the computer. This system is in stark contrast to the almost blank screen with a single command prompt that stares at those who use computers controlled by an older version of MS-DOS. To bridge this difference, Microsoft Corporation developed the new OS/2 operating system when IBM introduced its line of PS/2 computers. Along with OS/2 they introduced a graphical interface called Presentation Manager.

Sales of the OS/2 software were disappointing. The system had not caught on well with users. Industry analysts estimated that Microsoft had shipped 200,000 copies of OS/2 by the end of the first quarter of 1990. Paul Maritz, Microsoft's vice-president of advanced operating systems, stated, "Our early expectations [for the success of OS/2] were incorrect; we did not do ourselves or the industry a service by setting those expectations. We should have realized that moving from DOS is a multilayered decision that takes five to seven years to do."[47]

To address this problem, Microsoft developed another graphical interface named Windows. Windows will operate with later versions of MS-DOS. These versions are widely used and are still being purchased. To date, users have preferred Windows to OS/2 with Presentation Manager. Microsoft estimates there are about 600 OS/2-based software packages on the market. Only a few of them support Presentation Manager. But there are about 20,000 packages available for MS-DOS, around 700 of which run under Windows.[48] Exhibit 6 shows the projected worldwide shipments of DOS and OS/2 through 1997. With MS-DOS and OS/2, Microsoft provided the operating systems running on 87 percent of the world's PCs at the end of the first quarter of 1990.[49]

As if MS-DOS and OS/2 did not provide enough confusion in the market, there is a third contender: the UNIX operating system developed by AT&T. Like OS/2 and Windows, UNIX sports a graphical interface. And like OS/2, UNIX will enable a user to run several programs at once on a PC. This is called multitasking. UNIX will run under MS-DOS. UNIX's major weakness is that many versions are available, leading to confusion and postponed purchases. Some analysts cite this as a reason they expect OS/2 to surpass UNIX in sales.[50]

EXHIBIT 6 PROJECTED WORLDWIDE UNIT SHIPMENTS OF MS-DOS AND OS/2, 1991–1997

	MS-DOS	OS/2
1991	13.9	2.2
1993	16.1	6.1
1995	16.1	11.1
1997	16.3	16.6

Source: Patricia Keefe and Charles Von Simson, "Overblown Promises Give Way to Reality," *Computerworld*, April 30, 1990, p. 1.

This proliferation of operating systems complicates software decisions for both users and software vendors. WordPerfect has developed different versions of its software for a variety of computers. Recent versions of the company's software are available for the Macintosh, Apple IIGS, Amiga, Atari ST, Data General, VAX (Digital Equipment Corporation's minicomputer), and the large IBM 370 mainframe.[51] WordPerfect also made great strides in releasing new products for various operating systems during 1989. These included PlanPerfect 3.0 for VAX/VMS, WordPerfect 5.0 for OS/2, WordPerfect Office for UNIX systems, PlanPerfect for Data General, and DataPerfect 2.1 for MS-DOS. Versions of WordPerfect for IBM and compatible PCs accounted for 70 percent of the firm's 1989 sales.[52]

WordPerfect and other software could run under Microsoft Windows, but software had to be written in a certain way to make full use of this popular graphical interface. In spring 1990, only three word-processing programs could use all the advantages of Windows: Microsoft's Word for Windows 1.0; Samna Corporation's Ami Professional; and NBI, Inc.'s Legend. All three of these programs were released in 1989. They were all priced at $495, the same as WordPerfect 5.1. While they required more computer memory and PS/2 hardware, they added one important feature not possessed by WordPerfect 5.1, Word 5.0, or other character-based packages: true WYSIWYG. The on-screen display revealed exactly how a document would appear when printed. The ability to see both text and graphic images before printing positioned these programs much closer to the higher-priced desktop publishing packages. These programs also provided many layout tools for desktop publishing work. Their main disadvantage was that they ran much more slowly than their character-based counterparts. They would run faster under the new version 3.0 of Windows, which was scheduled to be released by Microsoft in May 1990.[53] Both Word for Windows 1.0 and Ami Professional received *PC Magazine*'s Best Buy Award. Ami Professional also received one of *PC Computing*'s 16 Most Valuable Product awards of 1989. The latter award was for Ami's leadership in Windows word processing and for the overall elegance and design of Ami Professional.[54]

MERGERS AND CONSOLIDATIONS

On November 13, 1989, Lotus Development Corporation announced that it was working with WordPerfect Corporation to develop a similar command structure for Lotus's new version 1-2-3/G spreadsheet program and the forthcoming WordPerfect 5.1. Both programs will run under OS/2 Presentation Manager. Lotus had surprised the executives at WordPerfect a year before this announcement by offering the firm the code to 1-2-3/G. Vice-president Pete Peterson said, "It took us six months to believe they were really sincere."[55] Lotus and WordPerfect are clearly aiming at another word processor–spreadsheet combination: Microsoft Word and Microsoft's Excel spreadsheet package. Excel also runs under Windows and integrates with Word for Windows.

On April 9, 1990, the *Wall Street Journal* reported that Lotus Development Corporation was attempting to acquire Novell, Inc. of Provo, Utah, for $1.5 billion in stock. Novell produced a best-selling networking software program. Networks link the computers in an organization so they can share programs and databases. Networking was a rapidly growing business. "The merger [of Lotus and Novell] rearranges the power structure of the software industry," stated Aaron Goldberg, a market researcher for International Data Corporation.[56] Analysts expected the two companies' sales to exceed $1.2 billion in 1990. This would surpass the $1.1 billion of sales that industry leader Microsoft was predicted to earn.[57] When Lotus announced the merger, it had 65 percent of the $350 million spreadsheet market, even though it still had no product for the Macintosh or for Windows. Novell controlled two-thirds of the PC networks in America's offices at the time. Analysts predicted Novell's sales would reach $500 million during the current fiscal year. Twenty percent of the nation's PCs are networked, and the number is increasing 30 percent each year. Novell's new product, NetWare 386, could link together hundreds of computers. Lotus was expected to help Novell capture some larger corporate accounts by providing better name recognition. The main competition in that market segment was coming from Digital Equipment Corporation's PC Network and IBM's network system. IBM controlled 13 percent of the market.[58]

The Lotus-Novell merger appeared to have great market potential; however, some who are familiar with the two companies expressed concern about the different cultures of New England–based Lotus and Utah-based Novell. A distributor said, "The boys in Cambridge go out drinking every night. That doesn't happen in Provo."[59] Consultant John McCarthy said, "The shortest book of all time is about successful technology mergers."[60]

On April 11, 1990, the *Wall Street Journal* reported that Lotus, Novell, and WordPerfect Corporation would combine their customer service operations. Jim Manzi, Lotus's chief executive officer, said, "Wouldn't it be wonderful if a customer gets to call one place and gets an answer to their [sic] question?"[61] WordPerfect's management team was not interested in merging with the other two companies. Still, Ray Noorda, Novell chief executive, said the three companies "are now in a position where they can help guide the [personal computer] industry."[62]

A few days later, Novell shareholders filed a lawsuit claiming the price management accepted from Lotus for the company was inadequate. Lotus and Novell issued a statement saying that they believed the suit to be without merit.[63] Shareholders of both companies were scheduled to vote on the proposed merger in July 1990.[64]

In May 1990, Lotus announced that it would develop a future version of 1-2-3 that would run under Windows 3.0. Analyst David Readerman of Shearson Lehman Hutton said, "It's a concession by Lotus that the groundswell for Windows is pretty strong."[65]

ENTER THE 1990S

WordPerfect Corporation sat at the top of the word-processing industry after barely a decade of existence. The firm's 1989 sales increased 60 percent over 1988 sales. Marketing Department director Ross Wolfley said, "Considering that WordPerfect 5.1 wasn't released until the middle of November, I think our 1989 sales of $281 million are exceptional. We also expect healthy increases in 1990."[66] About $48 million, or 17 percent, of those 1989 sales came from abroad as WordPerfect opened offices in Denmark, The Netherlands, and the United Kingdom. The firm's products were sold in 22 new countries during 1989.[67]

This continued growth led the company to add 482 new employees, bringing the total to 1,612. The Customer Support Department was over 500 strong by year end. These employees responded to 2.6 million calls during 1989.[68]

It has been said that it is more difficult for World Series and Super Bowl champions to repeat their feats the following year than it is to achieve them the first time. This may be true for WordPerfect in its second decade. Alan Ashton and Bruce Bastion must respond successfully to many uncertainties the firm faces in the 1990s. Their judgment regarding which (if any) of the three major PC operating systems will rise to prominence will help determine how the firm's application programs are written. This is very important because front-end research and development costs are high in the software industry. It is very inexpensive to produce copies of a program after it is developed, so the margins are high as sales volume builds. But volume will not build if the right programs are not written. So each upgrade and each new program must be just right for customers' needs.

Decisions must be made about the future of each program in the family of WordPerfect products. The new ability of WordPerfect's word-processing package to interact with Lotus 1-2-3/G must be considered in this decision.

ENDNOTES

1. This section is adapted from Carol Ellison, "The Trek From Typewriters," *PC Magazine*, February 29, 1988, pp. 96–97.

2. Richard Evans, "Mormon Spearhead," *International Management*, July–August 1989, pp. 30–32.

3. Sandra D. Atchison, "A Perfectly Good Word for WordPerfect: Gutsy," *Business Week*, October 2, 1989, pp. 99–100.

4. Will Fastie, "WordPerfect's Corporate Culture Is a Model," *PC Week*, September 26, 1988, p. 53.

5. "The Mormon Touch," *International Management*, July–August 1989, p. 31.

6. Evans, "Mormon Spearhead," p. 31.

7. Ibid.

8. Ibid.

9. Ibid., p. 30.

10. Ibid., p. 30.

11. Ibid., p. 32.

12. Ibid., p. 32.

13. Ibid.

14. John C. Dvorak, "Tools of the Trade: What PC Writers Use," *PC/Computing*, May 1990, p. 15.

15. Deborah Asbrand, "Six Who Share," *PC Computing*, February 1990, pp. 102–107.

16. Robert L. Scheier, "Rumors Aside, Vendors Spend a Mint on Support," *PC Week*, November 14, 1988, p. 48.

17. Catherine D. Miller, "WordPerfect on the Fly," *PC Magazine*, December 26, 1989, pp. 170–171.

18. Scheier, "Rumors Aside."

19. WordPerfect Corporation newsletter, April 4, 1989.

20. Amy Bermar, "Rapid Success of WordPerfect 5.0 Causes Support Headaches," *PC Week*, September 19, 1988, p. 120.

21. Scheier, "Rumors Aside."

22. Ibid.

23. Robert L. Scheier, "Tech Support or Russian Roulette?" *PC Week*, November 14, 1988, pp. 45–46.

24. Evans, "Mormon Spearhead."

25. Ibid., p. 32.

26. Ibid.

27. "Computer Industry Finds Profits in Customer Service," *PC Resource*, April 1990, p. 17.

28. Ibid.

29. G. Stephen Taylor and J. P. Shim, "Attitudes of Business Faculty and Business Practitioners Toward the Unauthorized Copying of Microcomputer Software," Proceedings of the Southern Management Association, November 1989, New Orleans, pp. 193–195.

30. John W. Verity, "Defense Against Pirates or Death to the Clones?" *Business Week*, May 7, 1990, p. 138.

31. Ibid.

32. John C. Dvorak, column in *PC Magazine*, May 15, 1990, p. 73.

33. *WordPerfect for IBM Personal Computers*, WordPerfect Corporation, 1989, pp. 489–491.

34. Christopher O'Malley, software review, *Personal Computing*, August 1988, pp. 165–166.

35. "Company Outline," WordPerfect Corporation, undated.

36. Janet Lou Darby and Rita Johnson, software review, *Personal Computing*, November 1989, pp. 149–150.

37. "PlanPerfect: A Few Advantages," *Computerworld*, December 11, 1989, pp. 45–46.

38. "Company Outline," WordPerfect Corporation, undated.

39. Lisa Picarille, "DrawPerfect Wins Early Praise for Text-Handling Capabilities," *PC Week*, October 2, 1989, pp. 41–42.

40. M. Keith Thompson, software review, *PC Magazine*, September 26, 1989, pp. 266–267.

41. Lisa Picarille, "WordPerfect Office Gains Remote Links," *PC Week*, November 13, 1989, p. 4.

42. "A Surprise First," *PC/Computing*, May 1990, p. 44.

43. "Upgrades," *PCResource*, May 1990, p. 16.

44. George Campbell, "Word Closes the Gap," *PC World*, September 1989, pp. 98–103.

45. William F. Bulkeley, "Lotus Spreadsheet To Accommodate Microsoft Program," *Wall Street Journal*, May 8, 1990, p. 84.

46. Frank Hayes, "Mouse-Ified and Feature-Laden," *Byte*, December 1989, p. 89.

47. Patricia Keefe and Charles Von Simson, "Overblown Promises Give Way to Reality," *Computerworld*, April 30, 1990, p. 119.

48. Patricia Keefe and Charles Von Simson. "OS/2 Fever Is Burning Slowly But Strongly," *Computerworld*, April 30, 1990, p. 119.

49. Keith H. Hammonds, Richard Brandt, and Sandra Atchison, "Overnight, Lotus Blossoms Into No. 1," *Business Week*, April 23, 1990, pp. 28–29.

50. Charles Von Simson and Patricia Keefe, "And Then There's UNIX," *Computerworld,* April 30, 1990, p. 118.

51. "Company Outline," WordPerfect Corporation, undated.

52. WordPerfect Corporation newsletter, January 15, 1990.

53. George Campbell, "Picture-Perfect World Processing," *PC World,* May 1990, pp. 104–111.

54. Preston Gralla, "Most Valuable Products of the Year," *PC Computing,* January 1990, pp. 69–85.

55. "Why Lotus and WordPerfect Are Suddenly So Cozy," *Business Week,* December 4, 1989, p. 114G.

56. William F. Bulkeley, "Lotus to Acquire Novell for $1.5 Billion; Possible Challenge to Microsoft Is Seen," *Wall Street Journal,* April 9, 1990, p. A3.

57. Ibid. pp. A1, A5.

58. Hammonds, Brandt, and Atchison, "Overnight, Lotus Blossoms Into No. 1."

59. Ibid., p. 29.

60. Ibid.

61. "WordPerfect, Novell, Lotus to Combine Customer Services," *Wall Street Journal,* April 11, 1990, p. B4.

62. Ibid.

63. "Novell Holders Sue To Prevent Takeover By Lotus Development," *Wall Street Journal,* April 17, 1990, p. B7.

64. "WordPerfect, Novell, Lotus to Combine Customer Services."

65. Bulkeley, "Lotus Spreadsheet To Accommodate Microsoft Program."

66. WordPerfect Corporation newsletter, January 15, 1990.

67. Ibid.

68. Ibid.

CASE 16

LANDS' END, INC.
CARON H. ST. JOHN

In 1963, Gary Comer ended his successful 10-year career as a copywriter for Young & Rubicam to found a mail order company specializing in sailing equipment and fittings. Comer and his sailing partner, Dick Stearns, opened a small catalog outlet store in Chicago's old tannery district and called it Lands' End Yacht Stores. The misplaced apostrophe in "Lands' End" was a typographical error in their first printed publicity that they could not afford to correct—so the name stayed with them. Their first catalog was titled "The Racing Sailor's Equipment Guide." Comer explains: "There were a lot of changes taking place [in the sailing industry]—new companies, new ideas, no one really understood them. We set out to not only supply the fittings but show how to use them, so there was a lot of editorial in those books [early Lands' End catalogs]."[1]

After five years of limited success, Comer bought out Stearns and three other partners who had joined the company. He gradually began adding products to the catalog that would appeal to the weekend sailor, such as luggage and clothing. In 1976 Comer pulled out of the intensely competitive sailing equipment segment and focused exclusively on luggage and clothing. He then moved the executive offices to a new location in Chicago and relocated the warehouse and customer service departments to Dodgeville, Wisconsin. In 1981, Lands' End began a national advertising program to describe the company's business philosophy and build a reputation for quality, value, and service. That advertising campaign introduced the phrase "direct merchant" as a way of describing the company's approach to business.

Between January 1984 and January 1986, Lands' End's sales increased by 84% and income increased by 73%. In October of 1986, after 23 years of successfully selling sailing equipment, clothing, and related items as a Sub-

---

Source: **Prepared by Professor Caron H. St. John, Clemson University, with the assistance of Stephen H. Meeker as a basis for classroom discussion and not to illustrate either effective or ineffective handling of administrative situations. © Caron H. St. John, 1990.**

chapter S firm, Lands' End sold 14% of its shares to the public. For the fiscal year that ended January 31, 1987—its first year to pay corporate income tax—Lands' End reported a net income of $18.6 million on sales of $265 million. After 11 months the stock split 2 for 1.

When Lands' End went public in 1986, some analysts criticized Comer for making the move too late. Gene Mueller, a broker with Blunt Ellis & Loewi said, "It would have been better for them to go public five or six years ago, when they were recording seven and eight-fold increases in sales. The problem with such growth is that it reaches a plateau. It's going to be much harder to double sales from $230 million to $500 million than growing from $30 million to $100 million."[2] However, by fiscal year ended January 1989, sales were $456 million, income was 32.3 million, and earnings per share were $1.61—up from $0.56 in 1986. In early 1989, Gary Comer made the cover of *Fortune* magazine as part of a story titled "Getting Customers To Love You."[3]

By late 1989 problems were beginning to surface. In November, Lands' End announced that profits for the first nine months of its fiscal year had fallen 23% from the nine-month period the year before. Sales projection for the 1989 Christmas season were expected to be up by a meager 4% over the 1988 season. One month later, in December 1989, Lands' End announced that profits for the fiscal year ending 1990 would be down by 13% from 1989. When the announcement was made, the company's stock fell $4.62 to $23.75 in one day. A company spokesman commented, "There's no question we've had some slowdown in response to our catalogs. We're not convinced at this point that we know whether its because of macroeconomic factors or something that's related to Lands' End or the way we're marketing the products or the products themselves."[4]

THE MAIL ORDER INDUSTRY

Although many people view catalog shopping as a 20th century phenomenon, shopping by mail can be traced back to the mid-18th century. In 1744, Benjamin Franklin published a catalog of close to 600 books and promised, "Those persons who live remote, by sending their orders and money to said B. Franklin may depend on the same justice as if present."[5] Throughout the 1800s, mail order companies offered the practical product needs of the time such as seeds, sewing machines, and dry goods. In 1872, Aaron Montgomery Ward published his first multi-product catalog. With 163 items, most priced at $1.00, the catalog became a wish book—and the modern era of mail order shopping was under way.

The mail order industry of the late 1980s and 1990s includes a wide array of products and services. Clothing, sports equipment, craft supplies, housewares, gardening products, magazine subscriptions, book and record clubs, auto clubs, insurance, prescription drugs, and film processing are among the many products and services available by mail order.

MAIL ORDER INDUSTRY TRENDS

During the early and mid-eighties, catalog retailing experienced 10–12% annual growth with the number of Americans who shopped by phone or mail increasing from 57.4 million in 1983 to 88.5 million in 1988. During those years, technological developments contributed substantially to the growth trend. Catalog companies made use of computerized databases that allowed them to profile names on mailing lists and select those that met certain demographic characteristics. This ability to segment buyers and focus product and marketing efforts spurred the development of specialty catalogs that were marketed to customer niches.

The convenience of mail order was enhanced by improved computer and communication systems. Toll-free 24-hour 800 numbers and readily available bank cards made catalog shopping easy. Integrated order placement and inventory systems allowed catalog companies to take orders, monitor inventory levels in real time, check a customer's credit, and fill orders quickly.

According to industry observers, the improved service and convenience offered by catalog companies could not have come at a better time. With more women entering the work force, household incomes increased as time available for shopping decreased. As Elsa Gustafson of Lands' End noted, Lands' End management believes families with two working parents and small children are more interested in using their discretionary time to do things together rather than shop. The mail order purchase of gifts, clothing, toys, and books takes pressure off of harried working parents.

The mail order industry attributes much of its growth in the 1980s to the prevalence of these two wage-earner families. For many catalog retailers, the target market is households headed by 25–44-year-old adults with three or more family members and household incomes of more than $30,000 per year. Since 1980, the number of households headed by 35–44 year old adults has increased by 38%—the largest gains of any other age group. (Exhibits 1 and 2 give demographic information on families.)

Studies have indicated that people who use mail order services are generally satisfied with the experience. A Direct Marketing Association–sponsored survey of 2,300 catalog customers revealed that people prefer catalog shopping because they feel they are getting more complete product information.[6] Once a customer has had a positive experience with mail order he or she is more likely to order again—and to try different kinds of products from different companies. However, if a customer's first experience with mail order is unsatisfactory, he or she may be reluctant to try again and may generalize that experience to include all mail order companies.

In 1988, approximately 58% of mail order purchases were made by women (Exhibit 3). As shown in Exhibit 4, clothing, non-food gifts, and gardening supplies are the items customers are most likely to purchase through mail order.

As the decade of the 1980s closed, there were several disturbing trends on the horizon. In 1988, 88.5 million Americans shopped by mail or phone—only

EXHIBIT 1 AGE AND INCOME STATISTICS FOR HOUSEHOLDS BY TYPE IN 1988 AND MEDIAN INCOME IN 1987

	HOUSEHOLDERS AGED 25–34			HOUSEHOLDERS AGED 35–44			HOUSEHOLDERS AGED 45–54		
	Households No. (000)	Median Income	Percent of Type	Households No. (000)	Median Income	Percent of Type	Households No. (000)	Median Income	Percent of Type
Total	20,000	$26,923	100.0	19,323	$34,929	100.0	13,630	$37,250	100.0
% change 1980–1988	11.0	–5.0		36.0	1.0		8.0	3.0	
Families	15,008	28,813	72.9	15,852	36,836	82.0	11,138	37,250	81.7
Married couples with children*	8,665	31,111	42.1	10,121	40,372	52.4	3,980	44,785	29.2
Nonfamily	5,575	22,694	27.1	3,471	24,586	18.0	2,492	20,001	18.3

*(with children under 18 living at home)

Source: Waldrop, Judith, "Inside America's Households," American Demographics 11, No. 3 (March 1989): 20–27.

EXHIBIT 2 PAST AND FUTURE DEMOGRAPHIC TRENDS

DEMOGRAPHIC TRENDS—1980 TO 1988

1. In 1988, there were 91 million households in America, a 13-percent increase over 1980.
2. The number of households headed by people aged 35–44 increased by 38 percent between 1980 and 1988, making it the fastest growing population segment.
3. The number of households headed by people under age 25 fell by 20 percent between 1980–1988.
4. Married couples declined as a share of all households from 61% in 1980 to 57% in 1988.
5. Although the number of married couples with children was predicted to grow during the 1980s, that segment fell from 31% of households in 1980 to 27% in 1988.
6. The median income of younger householders still lags behind what it was in 1979, but the over age 65 segment is gaining in median income faster than any other age group.

FUTURE DEMOGRAPHIC TRENDS

There are three fundamental trends:

1. The number of households headed by 45–54 year olds will increase as the baby boomers enter their mid-forties.
2. The composition of households will continue to change with fewer described as "married couples with children."
3. Household incomes are separating into two categories: those that keep up with inflation and those that do not.

Source: Waldrop, Judith, "Inside America's Households," *American Demographics* 11, No. 3 (March 1989); 20–27.

EXHIBIT 3 NUMBER OF AMERICAN ADULTS WHO SHOPPED BY PHONE OR MAIL

YEAR	MILLION	% MALE	% FEMALE
1988	88.5	42.0	58.0
1987	88.0	46.9	54.1
1986	87.7	41.9	58.1
1985	76.2	41.3	58.7
1984	64.4	40.7	59.3
1983	57.4	40.6	59.4

Source: "Study of Media and Markets, 1983–1988," Simmons Market Research, New York.

EXHIBIT 4 PRODUCT PURCHASES BY CATALOG CUSTOMERS

	% OF CATALOG CUSTOMERS WHO PURCHASED THESE ITEMS
Clothing	93
Non-Food Gifts	80
Gardening	71
Home Furnishings	70
Housewares	66
Food	62
Hardware	61
Sporting Goods	49

Source: "DMA Survey Uncovers Consumers' Attitudes on Catalog Shopping," Press Release, Direct Marketing Association, Inc., New York.

.5 million more than in 1987 and .8 million more than in 1986. This slowdown in the number of new catalog customers suggests a slowdown in mail order shopping and is in sharp contrast to the 10–12% increases that were evident in the early and mid-1980s.

At the same time that market demand seems to be leveling, costs of operating a mail order business are on the rise. In 1991, the U.S. Post Office is expected to increase rates on third-class mail by roughly 17%—which will add millions of dollars to the cost structures of mail order firms and make it much more risky for a company to mail catalogs to customers who do not order. Rising costs will make mailing list management practices more important to the cost control efforts of firms and will further encourage development of specialty catalogs targeted to particular types of customers.

As of now, few states require sales tax on mail order purchases but in 1989 momentum began to gather nationwide to require mail order companies to collect sales taxes. Catalog companies are concerned that the addition of sales tax will price their products out of the market. Purchasing a product by mail order has always required that either the buyer or the catalog company pay for postage and handling. Many customers have rationalized that the postage and handling has not substantially affected the price of the items purchased because in the stores they would have to pay sales tax. If customers are required to pay both, then they may feel they can get equivalent items for a better price at the mall.

COMPETITION

In the past 10 years, thousands of people have started mail order businesses. Estimates of the total number of companies that sell via mail order range from 10,000 to over 13,000.[7] So many new catalog businesses have started up that there is widespread concern in the industry that consumers are becoming overwhelmed by the sheer number of catalogs in their mailboxes. The number of new catalogs is increasing by more than 16% per year. The Direct Marketing Association estimates that catalog retailers mailed more than 12.4 billion catalogs in 1988—which translates into 50 catalogs for every man, woman, and child in America.

The amount of capital required to start up a mail order business is usually much less than that required to open a retail store. Products may be purchased from vendors rather than produced by the company, and the services and supplies required to prepare, print, and mail catalogs are available from list brokers, photographers, and printing houses. In addition to its product inventories and computer system, one of the most valuable assets a mail order company will own is its mailing list. Since mailing lists are frequently valued in the accounting records at $0.00, returns on investments tend to be very high for mail order firms.

With so many companies vying for a position, competition in the mail order industry is intense. Many are small, private companies that specialize in one unique product such as smoked salmon or office calendars. At the other end of the spectrum are large retailers and wholesalers with multi-product mail order divisions such as Bloomingdales and J. C. Penney.

In recent years, large general merchandise catalogs have been replaced by specialized catalogs for very specific customer groups. The trend toward specialty catalog marketing has influenced the planning of the large general merchandise catalog companies. Montgomery Ward discontinued its general merchandise catalog altogether. Spiegel and Bloomingdales, among others, have developed their own specialty catalog groups. As part of a major revamping of its catalog business, Sears is planning to issue six apparel catalogs and one catalog of durable home products called "Home" in 1989.

Most mail order companies deal with two sets of competitors—other comparable mail order companies and retail stores. Mail order companies try to compete with retail stores by offering hard-to-get items, a wider selection than a store can offer, the convenience of shopping from home, and, in some cases, discount prices. To encourage potential customers to try mail order, some companies have begun advertising their products and their shop-at-home convenience in the newspapers and magazines that are purchased by the customers they hope to target. Retailers have begun to take notice. The *Direct Marketing* trade publication quotes Donald Zale, chairman of the Zale's jewelry chain, as saying, "Catalogs are public enemy number one. They are a threat to the existence of retail stores. They are in existence to take customers out of your stores. We must band together to begin to formulate the kinds of strategies to insure our survival!"[8]

Once a customer has been won over to mail order, the company must convince the customer to buy from it rather than one of the many other mail order companies. The techniques that mail order companies use to get the attention of customers are often very creative. Virtually all companies have easy-return policies and toll-free numbers for customers to use when placing orders—but some companies accept telephone orders 24 hours a day, seven days a week, some pay all of the postage required to deliver merchandise, and others provide toll-free numbers for customers to use to check on the status of an order. In the apparel and gift areas, catalogs are mailed out very frequently—almost like the sales fliers that come from local department stores. Most catalogs have full product descriptions and many use loss leaders and free gifts to encourage customers to buy.

Many companies are developing catalogs with more of a "magazine" look. High quality photography and glossy, heavy weight paper are combined with anecdotes and stories to draw potential customers to the catalog as they would be drawn to a magazine. To offset the cost of printing these expensive catalogs, some companies carry advertisements for non-competitive products. Some companies offset costs by charging customers a fee for their catalogs.

COMPETITION IN THE CASUAL APPAREL SEGMENT

The Robinson-Humphrey Company investment firm estimates that consumers spent $2.7 billion on men's and women's apparel from specialty mail order catalogs in 1986—almost twice the amount spent in 1980.[9] In casual apparel, there are four dominant companies: L. L. Bean, Eddie Bauer, J. Crew, and Lands' End.

L. L. Bean is a privately held mail order marketer of outdoor sporting apparel and footwear. Founded in 1912 as a hunting shoe manufacturer, L. L. Bean now manufactures tote bags and a full line of sailing and hunting footwear. As the largest shareholder in this industry segment, the company generates 85% of its sales from mail order with the remaining 15% from its one retail store in Freeport, Maine.[10] In 1989, the company reported a small 3% increase in sales over the previous year.

Excluding its specialty areas, L. L. Bean mails 10 catalogs to its prospective

EXHIBIT 5 CATALOGS AND MAILINGS IN 1987

	NUMBER OF DIFFERENT CATALOGS PRODUCED ANNUALLY	MILLIONS OF COPIES MAILED
Lands' End	13	64
L. L. Bean	22*	85
Spiegel	42	150
J. Crew	12	15

*Includes a variety of specialty camping and equipment catalogs, some of which have very small circulation.
Source: Addis, Ronit, "Big Picture Strategy," *Forbes* (January 9, 1989); 70–89.

customers each year for a total of 60 million catalogs. The product line carried in the catalog includes very traditional denim and khaki pants and skirts, oxford cloth shirts, jackets and overcoats, and boots—with a heavy emphasis on plaids, stripes, all-cotton fabrics, and little fashion influence. Items are priced competitively with the products of other casual apparel mail order firms plus L. L. Bean pays all postage and handling.

Although competition in the casual apparel segment has increased substantially in recent years, L. L. Bean has made very few changes in the way it designs and develops its catalogs. Clothes models look like average people between 30 and 50 years of age. Most clothing items are shown without models. Very few scenic "location shots" are used in the catalogs. While L. L. Bean issues a small, special catalog of casual women's apparel, the primary catalog carries many more items for men. The results of a focus group of non-customers suggested that the L. L. Bean catalog is directed toward serious outdoor sportspeople, particularly older men, while the Lands' End catalog has more fashionable clothing and is targeted toward men and women who enjoy the outdoors.[11]

In addition to its reputation for excellent quality and service, L. L. Bean has developed an image with its catalog that helps it sell merchandise. Many of the items in the catalog do not make money for the company but are there to support the image. A customer browsing through an L. L. Bean catalog sees casual clothing positioned among the axes, sleeping bags, duck decoys, and bird feeders—and the clothing takes on a more rugged, outdoor aura. As one of their senior officers noted, "We would not sell the casual clothing if we didn't have duck decoys in the book."[12] When asked by a team of marketing analysts what she thought about when someone said "L. L. Bean," one customer said, "I see a small log cabin. There's a light in the window. The snow is falling. It is beautiful and calm."[13]

Another strong competitor in casual apparel is Eddie Bauer. Eddie Bauer was started as a family business many years ago and was subsequently sold to General Mills. In 1988, as part of a restructuring at General Mills, Eddie Bauer was sold to Spiegel, the largest U.S. catalog retailer with 1989 revenues of $1.7 billion. Eddie Bauer offers merchandise that is comparable in quality and price to that offered by L. L. Bean but with a higher percentage of items for women and more fashion-conscious styling. The Eddie Bauer catalog has a sleek, magazine appearance. The layouts are beautifully photographed with attractive models dressed in Eddie Bauer fashions surrounded by mountains or sail boats—depending on the season. The clothing receives almost secondary treatment to the upscale, sporting Northern Pacific lifestyle that is portrayed.

Eddie Bauer has successfully operated Eddie Bauer retail stores for several years. The stores offer much of the same merchandise that is in the catalogs including over-stocks. While Eddie Bauer is smaller (less than $200 million in sales) than L. L. Bean, it has been growing rapidly over the last several years through its catalog and retail store sales and is expected to benefit a great deal from its alliance with Spiegel. According to one source,[14] Eddie Bauer has increased its share of market at the expense of Lands' End in recent years. Spiegel experienced a 21% increase in sales, a 29% increase in profits, and a 7.5% gross margin in fiscal year 1989. Exhibit 6 compares prices for selected clothing items at Lands' End, L. L. Bean, and Eddie Bauer.

A third major competitor in the casual apparel mail order segment is J. Crew, a division of the privately held J. Crew, Inc. J. Crew mailed its first catalog in 1983 and since then sales have risen from $3 million to more than $100 million, making it the fourth largest company in the casual apparel mail order segment. J. Crew offers a product mix focused on t-shirts, rugby shirts, sweaters, skirts, pants, and shorts in all-natural fabrics. The company characterizes the image it portrays in its catalogs as "a sports oriented life-style" and uses beautiful location shots and youthful, active models. J. Crew targets college students as well as young adults and families with its catalogs.

As the smallest of the four major casual apparel companies, J. Crew is trying to sustain growth in a maturing market. In 1989, the company cut back some staff positions, was late with payments to some suppliers, and failed in an attempt to sell off a division of the company that was not in mail order. J. Crew recently made an expansion move that concerned some industry observers. Facing the slower expected growth in catalog retailing, J. Crew opened its first retail store in New York City in 1989 and announced plans to open 40 more stores over the next five years. The company says it plans to take advantage of its retail stores to add women's career apparel to its product line. The company's move into store retailing was met with much skepticism because of the troubles other catalog companies have had making a similar move. Last year, Royal Silk, a very successful catalog retailer, was forced to declare Chapter 11 bankruptcy when its attempts to move into store retailing failed.

EXHIBIT 6 SAMPLE MERCHANDISE AND PRICE RANGES—SPRING 1989

	LANDS' END	L. L. BEAN	EDDIE BAUER
Solid, Long Sleeve 100% Cotton Oxford Shirt	$19.50–33.50	$24.50	NA
Madras, Plaid, Gingham Long Sleeve Shirts	21.00–29.00	21.00–37.00	25.00–30.00
100% Cotton Denim Full Skirt	34.50	35.00	36.00
Men's Swim Trunks	14.00–28.00	22.50–28.00	20.00–24.00
Sport Shorts	10.50–28.00	14.00–33.00	15.00
Knit Shirts	12.00–20.00	16.50–23.00	17.00–22.00
Cotton Pullover Sweaters (Crew, Shaker, Fatigue)	29.50–44.50	29.00–39.00	28.00–65.00

Note: Price ranges reflect different weights and styles within product categories.

Source: Prepared by the casewriters from 1989 Spring/Summer catalogs for each of the three companies.

LANDS' END

Lands' End concentrates on traditional, unbranded, high quality clothing such as oxford cloth dress shirts, khaki trousers, heavy-weight sweats, and knit sports shirts and sweaters that are sometimes lower priced than comparable regular-priced items in department and specialty stores. At the request of customers, the company has recently introduced a line of children's clothing and is venturing into some domestic items such as sheets and comforters. Analysts and managers have credited Lands' End's past success to its quality merchandise, commitment to value pricing, and its high level of service to customers. The Lands' End Principles of Doing Business are shown in Exhibit 7.

EXHIBIT 7 THE LANDS' END PRINCIPLES OF DOING BUSINESS

Principle 1: We do everything we can to make our products better. We improve material, and add back features and construction details that others have taken out over the years. We never reduce the quality of a product to make it cheaper.

Principle 2: We price our products fairly and honestly. We do not, have not, and will not participate in the common retailing practice of inflating mark-ups to set up a future phony sale.

Principle 3: We accept any return, for any reason, at any time. Our products are guaranteed. No fine print. No arguments. We mean exactly what we say: GUARANTEED. PERIOD.

Principle 4: We ship faster than anyone we know of. We ship items in stock the day after we receive the order. At the height of the last Christmas season the longest time an order was in the house was 36 hours, excepting monograms which took another 12 hours.

Principle 5: We believe that what is best for our customer is best for all of us. Everyone here understands that concept. Our sales and service people are trained to know our products, and to be friendly and helpful. They are urged to take all the time necessary to take care of you. We even pay for your call, for whatever reason you call.

Principle 6: We are able to sell at lower prices because we have eliminated middlemen; because we don't buy branded merchandise with high protected mark-ups; and because we have placed our contracts with manufacturers who have proved that they are cost conscious and efficient.

Principle 7: We are able to sell at lower prices because we operate efficiently. Our people are hard working, intelligent, and share in the success of the company.

Principle 8: We are able to sell at lower prices because we support no fancy emporiums with their high overhead. Our main location is in the middle of a 40-acre cornfield in rural Wisconsin. We still operate our first location in Chicago's Near North tannery district.

Source: Lands' End, Inc., 1987 Annual Report.

MARKETING

Instead of following the common practice of renting mailing lists from other companies, Lands' End has developed its own proprietary mailing list through a national "space advertising" program. Lands' End advertises in the *Wall Street Journal* and *USA Today* as well as 30 magazines which appeal to the more affluent, "upscale" subscriber. The ads are not used to sell the company's products—instead they are supposed to create an image for the name "Lands' End." The advertisements portray Lands' End as a good neighbor, someone you can count on. At the bottom of the advertisements is a toll-free number to call to get a free "subscription" to the Lands' End catalog. Competitors L. L. Bean and Spiegel also use advertising but the ad focus is on promoting sales and catalogs rather than the company image. Lands' End has used these advertisements to help increase the size of its mailing list in the last three years. In 1989, the company tried national television advertising for a short time.

When a customer receives his or her first catalog from Lands' End, a pamphlet is enclosed that describes the history of the company. The photograph on the front page of the pamphlet is of a country road with old rural mail boxes. It says, "It was really good to hear from you, and have the opportunity to send our catalog and tell you how things are out our way." The pamphlet is filled with photographs of the small town of Dodgeville, Wisconsin, and of employees with their families. The purpose of the pamphlet is to convey a sense of traditional small town values of integrity and service.

The company updates and refines its proprietary mailing list of approximately 10 million names before each catalog mailing. Lands' End monitors the recency, frequency, and dollar amount of purchases by customers as a way of gauging customer interest. The company actively manages its list in this way in an attempt to avoid wasting money mailing catalogs to customers who are unlikely to make a purchase. Of the ten million people who receive catalogs each month, 45% have made purchases within the past 36 months. In 1988 the company mailed 76 million of its 115 page catalogs. The best customers received approximately 13 catalogs during the year—at least one per month.

Lands' End uses its space advertising and list management practices to reach a select target market. Research studies have shown that approximately 40% of Lands' End's customers are in the 35-49 age group with 29% in the 25-34 age group. Median annual income for Lands' End households is almost twice that of the U.S. population, 70% of customers are professionals or managers, and 88% attended college.[15]

Lands' End catalogs have a distinct magazine appearance. One 1989 catalog looked like an old issue of the *Saturday Evening Post*—with a Norman Rockwell cover, volume and issue numbers printed at the top, and a boldface listing of the "features" inside. The catalogs make use of other magazine techniques such as background stories and monthly publication to stimulate the interest of readers. The first eight pages of one catalog was devoted to the "story of cotton" while another profiled a trip through the Sahara desert. The catalogs describe products in detail and offer the company's views about the benefits of the merchandise.

Management at Lands' End feels strongly that the company's major competitors are department and specialty stores—not other mail order companies. There are some inherent disadvantages associated with shopping by mail that the company tries to overcome. To make catalog shopping more like the service customers get in a store, Lands' End included a tear-out guide for matching shirts and ties in a recent catalog. Since customers cannot drape a tie across a shirt like they can in a store, the company developed a template of shirts of different colors with a cut-out opening for the tie. All of the ties described in the catalog were of the correct size to view under the template. This system allowed the customer to compare shirts and ties for color and style.

Lands' End tries to be responsive to the requests of customers. Company volunteers respond personally to the approximately 50,000 letters the company receives from customers each year. When customers wrote in and complained that knit shirts did not have breast pockets, the company added a pocket to its standard knit shirt. Customers protested when a 100% cotton twill skirt was dropped from the catalog so the company brought the skirt back. After receiving several requests, Lands' End added turtlenecks in a sweatshirt fabric to its product line. The company is so proud of its responsiveness to customers that it featured letters from customers in its 1989 annual report.

OPERATIONS

Lands' End owns a 100,000 square foot office building, a 277,000 square foot warehouse, and 78 acres of undeveloped land in Dodgeville, Wisconsin, as well as a 10,000 square foot soft-side luggage manufacturing operation in West Union, Iowa. The company also leases office space and operates seven outlet stores in the Chicago area.

Lands' End provides a toll-free number that may be used 24 hours a day, seven days a week to place orders or request a catalog. Orders are entered online into a computerized inventory control system which updates the company's mailing list and provides a database for tracking product demand and response to mailings.

Lands' End boasts of a 24-hour turnaround time on orders. To achieve this, operators use the real-time inventory data to immediately tell the caller if a product is in stock. If it is not, the screen will tell the operator when the next shipment is expected and show a variety of alternatives including, in some cases, the name of another retailer. If the merchandise is in stock, the order is placed and the inventory files are updated in real time. The system simultaneously checks the credit of the customer through data links with American Express and, for MasterCard and VISA purchases, National Data Corporation.

The processing of orders takes place at night. At midnight, high speed laser printers print two sets of bar-coded tickets for each order—one for picking and one for packing. Warehouse workers use the picking tickets to determine which items must be pulled from storage bins. The warehouse worker affixes the bar-coded picking ticket to the package and places it in a tray on a conveyor belt. A laser scanner reads the bar-codes so that items are automatically sorted by customer order.

With the exception of soft luggage, Lands' End purchases all of its products from approximately 250 independent manufacturers. Nearly 80% of its merchandise is purchased from vendors in the United States with the remainder purchased from Europe and Asia through two trading companies, Mitsubishi Textiles and British Isles Buying Agency. Lands' End management feels that using U.S. vendors when possible gives the company an advantage over its competitors that purchase goods from the Far East. Having production facilities so close by allows them to exercise some control over design, quality, and delivery speed.

Lands' End maintains an extensive quality control group including three airplanes and pilots. Buyers and quality assurance personnel develop the company's own product specifications. Before agreeing to use a vendor, the staff puts garments through rugged quality testing. Inspectors make frequent inspection visits to vendors' plants and if vendors do not uphold the Lands' End commitment to quality, they are dropped. "We don't go two streets over because its a nickel cheaper," Comer says, "If a manufacturer meets our standards, we'll stick with him. Otherwise we move on."[16]

MERCHANDISE MIX

Gary Comer has resisted allowing Lands' End to become fashion driven. In 1983, the company introduced a line of dress clothing for men and women called the Charter Collection. The garments were made from expensive Italian silks with trendier styling than typically found in a Lands' End catalog. Although Charter was spun off into its own catalog and was making money, Comer was uncomfortable with the potential for a diluted company image. He said, "It was developing into this fashion business, and I knew I didn't want that. When they started shooting photographs of models in London, I said, 'That's it, enough.'"[17]

At the specific request of customers, Lands' End has added selected new products to its line such as swimsuits and extra-large and petite sizes. Recently, at the request of customers, Lands' End added a line of children's clothing that met with considerable success—$15 million in sales in 1988. Similar to Eddie Bauer and L. L. Bean, the company has added a line of high quality domestic items such as sheets and comforters that it feels will appeal to its existing customer base.

1989—A YEAR OF CHANGE

Effective January 1, 1989, Richard C. Anderson replaced Gary Comer as president and chief operating officer of Lands' End. Anderson, a director of the company since 1978 and vice-chairman since 1984, was promoted as part of a planned management succession designed to allow Comer to spend more of his time on the broad issues affecting the company's long-range direction. Comer continued as chairman and chief executive officer. As part of the reorganization, Comer became chairman of the company's executive committee which is responsible for strategic and financial planning. Anderson was put in charge of the company's policy committee which is responsible for operations planning.

At the beginning of 1989, management at Lands' End was advocating a conservative approach to growth. The company estimated that its potential market would be about 13.5 million households by 1990 and it planned to use two approaches to further penetrate that market.[18] One approach was to increase the size of its mailing list by using its space advertising techniques to reach more of its target market. A second approach was to add new products that would be of interest to the traditional Lands' End customer—so that they would rely on Lands' End for a larger portion of their household purchases. Movement into retail outlets was not a growth alternative. Comer has indicated for some time that he is not interested in opening retail stores such as the ones operated by Eddie Bauer and others. He sees retail store management as a completely different business.

In 1989 (the fiscal year that ended January 31, 1990) Lands' End added some higher-priced merchandise to its product mix including $200-plus cashmere sweaters. With children's clothing, domestics, and higher-end apparel added to the product line, the catalog grew from an average of 115 pages in 1988 to about 149 pages in 1989. The company mailed 91 million catalogs—15 million more than in 1988.

EXHIBIT 8 LANDS' END STATEMENT OF OPERATIONS

	FOR THE YEAR ENDED JANUARY 31			
	1990	1989	1988	1987
Net Sales	$545,201	$455,806	$336,291	$265,058
Cost of Sales	313,573	261,671	190,348	152,959
Gross Profit	231,628	194,135	145,943	112,099
Selling, G&A	184,910	143,486	107,699	83,454
Income from Operations	46,718	50,649	38,244	28,645
Net interest and other	552	1,493	84	(159)
Income before Income Tax	47,270	52,142	38,328	28,486
Tax Provision	18,199	19,860	16,208	9,836
Adj. for change in accounting			685	
Net Income	$ 29,071	$ 32,282	$ 22,805	$ 18,650
Net income per share	$ 1.45	$ 1.61	$ 1.14	$ 0.73

Note: Dollars in thousands, except per-share amounts.

EXHIBIT 9 LANDS' END INC. BALANCE SHEETS

	JANUARY 31		
	1990	1989	1988
ASSETS			
Current assets:			
Cash and cash equivalents	$ 8,254	$ 32,139	$ 28,175
Receivables	348	755	274
Inventory	85,709	66,820	46,444
Prepaid expenses	5,403	3,967	3,363
Total current expenses	99,714	103,681	78,256
Property, plant & equip. at cost:			
Land and buildings	38,335	31,267	15,114
Fixtures and equipment	41,123	25,192	21,974
Leasehold improvements	1,512	1,234	908
Construction in progress	4,637	3,280	674
Total property, plant and equipment	85,607	60,973	38,670
Less depreciation/amortization	18,389	13,502	9,947
Property, plant and equipment, net	67,218	47,471	28,723
Total assets	$166,932	$151,152	$106,979
LIABILITIES AND SHAREHOLDERS' INVESTMENT			
Current liabilities:			
Current maturities of long term debt	$ 1,775	$ 1,860	$ 1,918
Accounts payable	24,415	25,904	21,223
Advance payment orders	203	350	453
Accrued liabilities	10,568	9,734	7,226
Accrued profit sharing	1,652	3,285	2,646
Income taxes payable	5,302	10,397	5,394
Total current liabilities	43,915	51,530	38,860
Long term debt, less current mat.	5,031	6,806	8,667
Deferred income taxes	3,382	868	2,778
Shareholders' investment:			
Common stock, 19, 881, 394 (1990) and 20,040,294 (1989, 1988) outstnd.	201	200	200
Donated capital	8,400	7,000	—
Paid-in capital	23,340	22,308	22,308
Deferred compensation	(959)	—	—
Retained earnings	87,516	62,440	34,166
Treasury stock, 194,900 shares	(3,894)	—	—
Total shareholders' investment	114,604	91,948	56,674
Total liabilities and shareholders' investment	$166,932	$151,152	$196,979

Note: Dollars are given in thousands.

Expecting an excellent sales year in 1989, the company entered 1989 with a record $66.8 million invested in inventory. When sales volume did not meet expectations, the company mailed four million special mailers to keep sales up and inventories in balance. The sales push increased selling expenses which were not then offset by higher sales volume. In the summer of 1989, employees praised the company as a wonderful place to work but were well aware of increasing pressures to keep down costs. In late fall 1989, customers received catalogs from Lands' End with many of the newer items marked "Sorry, Not Available" across the picture layouts. While there had been an occasional two-page section in the catalog showing "clear the decks" specials (overstocks) in 1988, in late 1989 the overstock sale section of the catalog grew much larger and was included in every catalog.

In early 1990, Lands' End's stock traded around $19 per share compared to its high of $35 per share in April 1989. When the company compiled its performance for fiscal year ended January 31, 1990, sales for the year were $545 million—20% greater than the previous year's sales. Net income for the year was $29.1 million—10% less than what the company earned the year before. For the first time in four years, Lands' End had failed to exceed its goal of 10% pretax return on sales. (Lands' End financial statements are shown in Exhibits 8 and 9.)

Several factors were identified by management and industry analysts as contributing to the problems at Lands' End: an overall slowdown in consumer spending in 1989 and price discounts at department stores of up to 25% which made store purchase more attractive than catalog purchase. Some analysts criticized Lands' End's product mix as "tired" and pointed to the threat of the Spiegel-backed Eddie Bauer. Faced with increasing competition from stores and other catalogers as well as increasing sales and catalog costs, Lands' End entered fiscal 1991 with some very difficult decisions to make.

ENDNOTES

1. Addis, Ronit, "Big Picture Strategy," *Forbes* (January 9, 1989): 72.

2. Freeman, Laurie, "Lands' End a Beacon for Mail-Order Market," *Advertising Age* (December 8, 1986): 74.

3. Sellers, Patricia, "Getting Customers To Love You," *Fortune* (March 13, 1989): 38-49.

4. "Lands' End Says Profit for Fiscal 1990 is Likely to Fall About 13% From 1989," *Wall Street Journal* (December 12, 1989): A5.

5. Ross, Nat, "A History of Direct Marketing," in *Fact Book: An Overview of Direct Marketing and Direct Response Advertising* (New York: Direct Marketing Association, 1986).

6. "DMA Survey Uncovers Consumers' Attitudes on Catalog Shopping," Press Release, Direct Marketing Association, Inc., New York (September 1988).

7. Sroge, Maxwell, "Mail Order Industry Overview," in *Inside the Leading Mail Order Houses*, 3rd ed. (Lincolnwood, Ill.: NTC Business Books, 1987): viii.

8. Raphel, Murray, "Which Came First, the Chicken or the Egg?" *Direct Marketing* (June 1986): 99.

9. Wewer, Dan R., "Lands' End, Inc.," Investment Report, Robinson-Humphrey Company, Inc. (March 1988).

10. Sroge, "Mail Order Industry Overview," p. 51.

11. Takeuchi, Hirotaka, and Merliss, Penny Pittman, "L. L. Bean.: Corporate Strategy," *Harvard Business School Case: 9-581-159* (Boston, Mass: Harvard Business School, Publishing Division, 1981); rev. 5/88.

12. Raphel, "Which Came First," p. 98.

13. Ibid.

14. Bremner, Brian, and Hammonds, Keith H., "Lands' End Looks a Bit Frayed at the Edges," *Business Week* (March 19, 1990): 42.

15. "Lands' End, Inc.: Our Market," Press Release, Lands' End Research, Lands' End, Inc., Chicago, Ill.

16. Caminiti, Susan, "A Mail Order Romance: Lands' End Courts Unseen Customers," *Fortune* (March 13, 1989): 45.

17. Ibid.

18. Interview with Elsa Gustafson, Lands' End Public Relations, spring 1990.

CASE 17

HARLEY-DAVIDSON, INC.

SCOTT DRAPER,
A. SCOTT DUNDON,
ALLEN NORTH,
RON SMITH,
SEXTON ADAMS, AND
ADELAIDE GRIFFIN

COMPANY HISTORY

The year was 1903. Henry Ford introduced the first Model A, the Wright brothers flew over Kitty Hawk, and, in a shack near Milwaukee, Wisconsin, a machine called the Silent Grey Fellow was born. Three brothers, William, Walter, and Arthur Davidson, had invented a machine that would exemplify "the American desire for power, speed and personal freedom"—the Harley-Davidson motorcycle.

The Davidson's first crude machines found a ready market among both individuals and law enforcement agencies, and by 1907, production had reached 150 motorcycles per year. Two years later, a new engine, the V-twin, enabled motorcycles to attain top speeds of 60 mph. Motorcycles were fast becoming the primary source of transportation in the United States.

The Harley-Davidson Motorcycle Company took pride in America. When the U.S. joined Europe in World War I, Harley-Davidson motorcycles helped the U.S. Army chase the Kaiser across Germany. After World War I, however, it was the automobile, not the motorcycle, that gained popularity as America's principal means of transportation. Harley's annual production plunged from 28,000 to 10,000 units immediately after the war. After a decade of struggle, Harley-Davidson again reached prewar production levels, only to be ravaged by the Great Depression. In 1933 only 3,700 motorcycles were produced by Harley-Davidson.

Source: **This case was prepared by students Scott Draper, A. Scott Dundon, Allen North, and Ron Smith under the supervision of Professor Sexton Adams, University of North Texas, and Professor Adelaide Griffin, Texas Woman's University, as a basis for classroom discussion and not to illustrate either effective or ineffective handling of administrative situations.** © 1990, Sexton Adams and Adelaide Griffin.

The economic boost provided by World War II and the military's high demand for motorcycles enabled Harley-Davidson to again match its 1920 production level. But after World War II, the motorcycle industry crashed. As America's heroes returned, their focus was on housing and family necessities, not motorcycles. At one time Harley-Davidson was one of 150 U.S. motorcycle manufacturers, but by 1953, the weak motorcycle market had eliminated Harley's final U.S. competitor, Indian Motorcycle Company. Harley-Davidson stood alone as the sole manufacturer of motorcycles in the United States.

THE AMF REIGN

Harley-Davidson made its first public stock offering in 1965, and shortly thereafter, the struggle for control of Harley-Davidson began. In 1969, Bangor Punta, an Asian company with roots in the railroad industry, began acquiring large amounts of Harley-Davidson stock. At the same time, AMF, an international leader in the recreational goods market, announced its interest in Harley-Davidson, citing a strong fit between Harley-Davidson's product lines and AMF's leisure lines. Bangor Punta and AMF entered a bidding war over Harley-Davidson. Harley's stockholders chose AMF's bid of $22 per share over Bangor Punta's bid of $23 per share because of Bangor Punta's reputation for acquiring a company, squeezing it dry, and then scrapping it for salvage. AMF's plans for expansion initially were perceived as more favorable for Harley-Davidson's long-term existence.

AMF's plans did not, however, correspond with Harley-Davidson's ability to expand. Much of Harley-Davidson's equipment was antiquated and could not keep up with the increase in production. One company official noted that "quality was going down just as fast as production was going up." These events occurred at a time when Japanese motorcycle manufacturers began flooding the U.S. market with high-quality, low-cost motorcycles that offered many innovative features.

Many of Harley's employees felt that if AMF had worked with the experienced Harley personnel instead of dictating orders for production quotas, many of the problems could have been properly addressed. One Harley senior executive stated that "the bottom line was that quality went to hell because AMF expanded Harley production at the same time that Harleys were getting out of date, and the Japanese were coming to town with new designs and reliable products at a low price." Unlike their Japanese competitors whose motorcycles failed to pass inspection an average 5% of the time, Harley's motorcycles failed to pass the end-of-assembly-line inspection at an alarming 50–60% rate.

After a $4.8 million annual operating loss and 11 years under AMF control, Harley Davidson was put up for sale in 1981. A management team led by Vaughn Beals, vice-president of motorcycles sales, used $81.5 million in financing from Citicorp to complete a leveraged buyout. All ties with AMF were severed and Harley-Davidson, Inc. was created.

THE TARIFF BARRIER

Harley-Davidson had managed to obliterate its U.S. competition during the 1950s and 1960s, but the company took a beating from the Japanese in the 1970s. Japanese competition and the recession presiding over the nation's economy had taken nearly all of Harley-Davidson's business. The company's meager 3% share of total motorcycle sales led experts to speculate whether or not Harley-Davidson would be able to celebrate its eightieth birthday. Tariff protection appeared to be Harley-Davidson's only hope. Fortunately, massive lobbying efforts finally paid off in 1983, when Congress passed a huge tariff increase on Japanese motorcycles. Instead of a 4% tariff, Japanese motorcycles would now be subject to a 45% tariff. The protection was to last for five years.

Slowly, Harley-Davidson began to recover market share as the tariff had its impact on competitors. Management was able to relinquish its ownership with a public stock offering in 1986. Brimming with confidence, Harley-Davidson asked Congress to remove the tariff barrier in December 1986, more than a year earlier than originally planned. It was time to strap on the helmet and race with the Japanese head to head.

ACQUISITION AND DIVERSIFICATION

Holiday Rambler was purchased in 1986 by Harley-Davidson, a move that nearly doubled the size of the firm. As a wholly owned subsidiary, the manufacturer of recreational and commercial vehicles provided Harley-Davidson with another business unit that could diversify the risks associated with the seasonal motorcycle market. That move gave Harley-Davidson two distinct business segments, Holiday Rambler Corporation and Harley-Davidson Motorcycle Division. In addition, during the late 1980s, Harley-Davidson attempted to capitalize on its manufacturing expertise by competing for both government and contract manufacturing opportunities in an attempt to further increase the proportion of revenues derived from nonmotorcycle sources.

HOLIDAY RAMBLER CORPORATION

Harley-Davidson implemented many new management techniques at Holiday Rambler. The Yadiloh program was created in 1989. Yadiloh was "Holiday" spelled backwards and an acronym for "Yes Attitude, Deliver, Involvement, Leadership, Opportunity, Harmony." The goal of Yadiloh was to address cost and productivity problems facing Holiday Rambler. The employees of Holiday Rambler seemed to favor the program. "This program will help us solve a lot of problems in the long run. So I think it's a really big step, a positive step," said Raud Estep, a quality control inspector for Holiday Rambler. Another employee, Vickie Hutsell, agreed: "I think that most of the people who've gone through the Yadiloh training session are 'pumped up' about it."

But Holiday Rambler's new owners did more than get employees excited.

They built a new, centralized facility, scheduled to be completed in late 1990 to handle all of the company's manufacturing needs. They also installed more computer aided design (CAD) equipment to support the research and development staff, which led to a $1.9 million increase in operating expenses.

Observers, however, felt that the success of Holiday Rambler was mixed at best. Several strong competitors had entered the RV market in 1988. Holiday Rambler responded by discontinuing its Trail Seeker line of recreational vehicles after the unit experienced a $30 million sales decline in 1988. Holiday Rambler continued to trim poor performing areas. In October 1989, Parkway Distribution, a recreational vehicle parts and accessories distributor, was sold. A $2.8 million decline in revenues from the business units of Creative Dimensions, Nappanee Wood Products, and B & B Molders was recorded in 1989. Holiday Rambler enacted competitive pricing measures and a lower-margin sales mix in 1989. The result was a decrease in gross margin percentage, from 19% to 18.2%.

Some industry experts recognized a possible recovery for the sluggish RV market in 1990. However, the message of H. Wayne Dahl, Holiday Rambler president, was unclear. "Whether our business is RVs, commercial vehicles or a related enterprise, we intend to keep it strong and growing by keeping in close touch with its customers."

In 1986, Harley executives claimed that the acquisition of Holiday Rambler would help diversify the risks associated with the seasonal motorcycle market. However, some industry experts questioned whether such an acquisition was a wise move for Harley. They pointed out that although the acquisition smoothed seasonal fluctuations in demand, cyclical fluctuations caused by the economy were unaffected. One expert asserted, "Because both items [motorcycles and recreational vehicles] are luxury goods, they are dependent on such key economic factors as interest rates, disposable income, and gasoline prices."

In addition to the economy, the demographics of the RV market presented a challenge to Harley. The main consumer of recreational vehicles in the 1970s was the blue-collar worker who worked a steady 40 hours per week. However, economic trends led to a switch from manufacturing to a more service-oriented economy. The trends left most consumers with little time on their hands for recreational activities. Statistics revealed in 1989 that the typical owner of an RV was between 35 and 54 years old with an average income of $39,800. Census projections also indicated that the American population was growing older at the end of the 1980s. The high incomes and older ages gave RV manufacturers the opportunity to include extra features that allowed them to raise total vehicle prices by $20,000 and more.

The RV industry had support from nonconsumer groups that existed specifically to accommodate the RV owner. The Escapees, for instance, offered insurance and cash handling services to members driving RVs. The Good Sam's Club provided road service to RVs in need of repair. RV owners were even treated to their own television program to watch while on the road—"Wish You Were Here." The show, broadcast via satellite by the Nashville channel, highlighted RV lifestyles through interviews with owners across the country.

MANAGEMENT

Vaughn Beals's outward appearance was far removed from the burly image that many might have expected of a Harley chief executive. The middle-aged Ivy Leaguer graduated from MIT's Aeronautical Engineering School and was known in manufacturing circles as a productivity guru. But, on the inside, Vaughn Beals was a "Hog" (a Harley fanatic) in the truest sense of the word. He began working with Harley-Davidson as vice-president of motorcycle sales with AMF. Disgruntled with AMF's declining attention to quality, Beals led a team of 12 others that successfully completed a leveraged buyout from AMF.

But Beals had a difficult mission ahead. Even after receiving tariff protection, Harley-Davidson had to find a way to restore confidence in its products. So Beals decided to hit the high road—literally. He drove Harley-Davidson motorcycles to rallies, where he met Harley owners. In doing so, Beals was able to learn about product defects and needed improvements directly from the consumer. Industry experts believed that these efforts were vital to the resurgence of the company.

Willie G. Davidson, grandson of the company's founder, rode along with Vaughn Beals on Harley's road to recovery. "Willie G." provided a sharp contrast to Beals. If Vaughn Beals looked more at home in a courtroom, Davidson might have looked more at home behind the bars of a jail cell. His appearance was that of a middle-aged remnant of the 1960s. A Viking helmet covered his long, stringy hair, and his beard hid the hard features of a wind-parched face. He wore a leather jacket that, like his face, showed the cracks of wear and tear that the miles of passage over U.S. highways had caused. Nonetheless, Willie G. was named the new vice-president of design for Harley in 1981. Industry observers believed that he was instrumental in instigating much-needed improvements in the Harley Hog.

Beals stepped down as CEO in 1989, passing the reins to Richard Teerlink, who was then serving as chief operating officer for Harley-Davidson Motorcycle Division. Beals, however, retained his position as chairman of the board. After the transition, Harley-Davidson retained a long list of experienced executives. The organizational chart in Exhibit 1 highlights the depth of the Harley-Davidson management team.

In a somewhat ironic turn of events, Beals and other executives of Harley-Davidson had traveled to Japan in 1981 to visit the factories of their competition in an attempt to uncover any secrets. What they found was surprising. The Japanese did not run a low-cost production facility with sophisticated machinery; instead, they simply used effective management techniques to maximize productivity. Armed with a new management perspective from the Japanese, Harley-Davidson began implementing quality circles, statistical operations controls, and Just-In-Time (JIT) inventory.

EXHIBIT 1 HARLEY-DAVIDSON ORGANIZATIONAL CHART

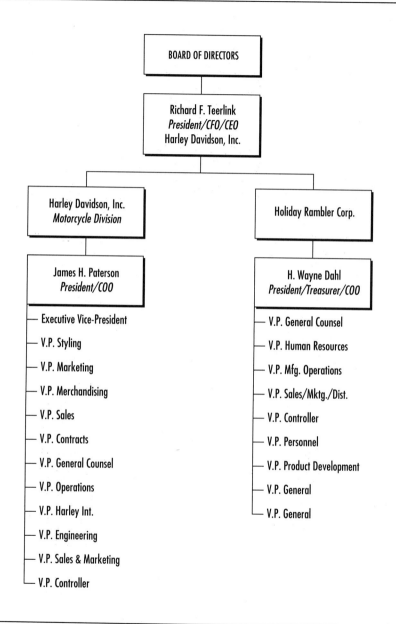

Source: Harley-Davidson, Inc.

The first dramatic change implemented by Harley management was to divide each plant into four to seven profit centers. The managers of each profit center were assigned total responsibility within their particular area. The increase in responsibility gave plant managers more authority and allowed Harley-Davidson to greatly reduce the staff functions previously needed to assist production. Harley-Davidson was able to reduce its employee work force by 40% after implementing these changes. In 1982 the company adopted a Just-In-Time (JIT) system for control of "in-plant" manufacturing and a Materials-As-Needed (MAN) system that dealt with control of all inventories both inside and outside the plants.

Next, Harley-Davidson attempted to increase employee involvement through the formation of quality circles (QCs). Thomas Gelb, Harley's executive vice-president of operations, noted that even though QCs were only a small part of employee involvement programs, they played a significant role in helping break down the communication barriers between line workers and supervisors. Line workers who were previously given quotas from high-level management became involved, through the use of QCs, in setting more realistic quotas based on actual production capacity and needs. Employee involvement gave workers a real sense of ownership in meeting these goals, according to Gelb. Employees were viewed as links in a chain, and through employee involvement programs they could drive quality throughout the organization. Employees were involved, by direct participation, in discussions and decisions on changes that affected them in the performance of their own work. Also, management trained employees on ways to recognize and eliminate waste in the production process. According to 1986 figures, Harley's tab for warranty repairs, scrap, and reworking of parts had decreased by 60% since 1981.

Employee involvement was further increased through a program called Statistical Operator Control (SOC). SOC gave employees the responsibility for checking the quality of their own work within a predetermined range. Employee quality checks took place on the production floor, and on many occasions, the workers themselves were given the responsibility for making the proper correcting adjustments. SOC helped identify errors in the production process on a timely basis and gave line workers more responsibility.

Although employees became more involved at Harley, labor relations remained strained. Management implemented an open-door policy to improve labor relations and increased stock options to include a broader base of employees. Management took a more sensitive stance toward the opinions of all employees. Union relations also improved when management voluntarily agreed to put the union label on all motorcycles produced and to share financial information with union leaders. Harley attempted to deal with all employees, even those affected by layoffs, in a humane way. Several employee assistance programs were put into place. Among these were outplacement assistance to cushion the blow of layoffs, early retirement (age 55) or voluntary layoffs, and drug abuse programs administered by the Milwaukee Council on Drug Abuse.

In order for these changes to work, Harley developed several overall goals.

As stated in the annual report, Harley's 1989 management goals included improvement of quality, employee satisfaction, customer satisfaction, and shareholder return. The company's long-term focus would address four major areas of concern for the 1990s: quality, productivity, participation, and flexibility.

- *Quality.* Management efforts in the late 1980s attempted to overcome the company's reputation for poor quality. Because most of Harley's upper management believed that quality improvement was an ongoing process, they made a commitment to a long-term goal.
- *Participation and productivity.* These two areas were overlapping objectives, according to Harley executives. Because of this connection, the company emphasized employee involvement programs throughout the firm.
- *Flexibility.* The diminishing domestic marketplace and the slowing U.S. economy created the need for flexibility. Harley-Davidson management hoped to explore other options for the firm.

Management hoped to lead rather than follow the competition. In 1990, Harley cultivated the phrase "Do the right thing and do that thing right."

PRODUCTION AND OPERATIONS

After the leveraged buyout, manufacturing was still a major problem. According to one Harley executive, less than 70% of motorcycles were complete when they reached the end of the assembly line. Motorcycle production schedules were often based on the parts that were available instead of the planned master schedule. According to industry experts, "Japanese manufacturing techniques were yielding operating costs 30% lower than Harley's." How did the Japanese do it? Though Beals and other managers had visited Japanese plants in 1981, it was not until they got a chance to tour Honda's assembly plant in Marysville, Ohio, after the buyout that they began to understand Japanese competion. Beals said, "We were being wiped out by the Japanese because they were better *managers.* It wasn't robotics, or culture, or morning calisthenics and company songs—it was professional managers who understood their business and paid attention to detail." Harley managers attributed most of the difference to three specific Japanese practices: quality circles, the use of statistical operations controls to ensure consistently high quality, and Just-In-Time manufacturing. The company quickly began to initiate the Japanese techniques.

THE JUST-IN-TIME (JIT) INVENTORY METHOD

A pilot Just-In-Time (JIT) manufacturing program was quickly introduced in the Milwaukee engine plant. Tom Gelb, senior vice-president of operations, called a series of meetings with employees and told them bluntly, "We have to play the game the way the Japanese play or we're dead."

Gelb's program was met with extreme skepticism. The York, Pennsylvania, plant, for instance, was already equipped with a computer-based control system that utilized overhead conveyors and high-rise parts storage. In a meeting with the work force of the York facility, Gelb announced that the JIT system would replace these effects with push carts. The production floor erupted with laughter. Surely, this was a joke. Plant managers mumbled that Harley-Davidson was returning to 1930.

Observers noted that the overriding principle of the Just-In-Time method was that "parts and raw materials should arrive at the factory just as they are needed in the manufacturing process. This lets the manufacturer eliminate inventories and the costs of carrying them." Anne Thundercloud, the York plant quality circle facilitator, stated that "it is the Harley employees who make JIT work, by having an investment in seeing it work." The same men and women who laughed out loud over the implementation of JIT began to believe in JIT's "exacting discipline." Their belief was justified: Nearly 60,000 square feet of warehouse space were freed, and costs of production plummeted. In 1986, Harley was able to lower its break-even point to 35,000 units, down from 53,000 in 1981.

Supplier cooperation was also critical to JIT success, but Harley-Davidson had a poor track record with its vendors. As one industry observer noted, "Harley was notorious for juggling production schedules and was one of the worst customers when it came to last-minute panic calls for parts." Furthermore, suppliers were wary of their role in the Just-In-Time picture. Edward J. Hay of Rath & Strong, a Lexington, Massachusetts, management consulting firm, stated, "The big problem is that companies treat Just-In-Time as a way of getting the suppliers to hold the inventories." One expert noted that Harley had to "abandon the security blanket that inventory often represented for them and learn to trust their suppliers."

Critics believed that Harley erred initially by taking a legalistic approach in trying to sign up suppliers for a JIT system. The company insisted on contracts that were 35 pages long, devoted largely to spelling out suppliers' obligations to Harley. This strategy was ambitious and too pretentious. Early results did not meet management's expectations, and the animosity was growing between Harley and its suppliers. One Harley supplier contended, "They're constantly renegotiating contracts, and tinkering with the layout of the plant."

Finally, the company took positive steps to improve vendor relations. Contracts were reduced to two pages. According to one Harley executive, "We need to get out of the office and meet face-to-face." Experts noted, "Teams of its buyers and engineers fanned out to visit suppliers: they began simplifying and improving designs and helping suppliers reduce setup time between jobs by modifying equipment to permit quick changes of dies. To improve the quality of the parts, Harley gave suppliers courses in statistics to teach workers how to chart small changes in the performance of their equipment. The practice provides early tip-offs when machines are drifting out of tolerance."

In 1986 Harley-Davidson began pressing some of its suppliers to start passing up the line more of the cost savings that Just-In-Time afforded. "It's time," said Patrick T. Keane, project engineer at Harley's York, Pennsylvania, plant, "to enter an era of negotiated price decreases. And right now we are holding meetings to accomplish that."

After five years of using Just-In-Time, reviews poured in. Between 1981 and 1988 the following results were achieved:

1. Inventory had been reduced by 67%.
2. Productivity climbed by 50%.
3. Scrap and rework were down two-thirds.
4. Defects per unit were down 70%.

Some industry experts believed that "the results for Harley and its suppliers have been good, although the company still has not achieved all its goals." "We are very inefficient," said Keane, "but the comparison of where we were five years ago is phenomenal."

MATERIALS-AS-NEEDED (MAN)

Harley's MAN system was tailored after that of Toyota's and was driven by "Kanban" technology—a control system that used circulating cards and standard containers for parts. The system provided real-time production needs information without the use of costly and complex resources that were typically needed for planning and support. Tom Schwarz, general manager of Harley-Davidson Transportation Company, developed a strategically controlled inbound system for dealing with suppliers. As one executive noted, "Harley's ultimate goal is to control all inbound and outbound shipments themselves. They prefer to keep a minimum (number) of carriers involved. That reduces the chance of delays." Harley-Davidson used its own leased fleet of 26 tractors and 46 trailers for the bulk of its road miles and used contract carriers only to supplement direct point service to its 700 dealers.

Harley-Davidson then began to evaluate its present suppliers based on manufacturing excellence and ability to provide small and frequent deliveries instead of evaluating suppliers strictly on price. Harley's trucks made daily, timed pickups from five to six suppliers on a predetermined route. Over the course of a week, the truck brought in all inbound shipments from 26–30 important vendors within a 200-mile radius of the plant. This type of system also allowed for frequent, small deliveries while helping to reduce freight costs. From 1981 to 1986, MAN cut York's inbound freight costs (mostly from vendor billing) by $50,000.

Other important elements in keeping freight costs down were the elimination of nonproductive travel and Harley's new purchase order system. The company reported in 1986 that only 4% of the 2 million miles that their fleet traveled in the past year were empty. Harley changed its purchase order system in 1986 so that the only prices it would acknowledge were F.O.B. vendors' shipping docks. This prevented suppliers from including freight in their prices and in turn discouraged them from using their own carriers for shipments to the motorcycle maker's plants.

QUALITY

In the 1970s, the running joke among industry experts was "If you're buying a Harley, you'd better buy two—one for spare parts." After the buyout from AMF, Harley-Davidson strove to restore consumer confidence by raising the quality of its motorcycles. Harley-Davidson's quality improvements did not go unnoticed. John Davis, a Harley dealer mechanic, stated, "I've been wrenching on Harley-Davidson motorcycles for 26 years. I think the main key to their success is quality. And since '84 they have been very good." Teerlink boasted in his 1990 letter to shareholders that Harley-Davidson would be competing for the Malcolm Baldrige National Quality Award in 1991. "We will follow the example established by the 1990 winner (Cadillac)."

Harley's commitment to quality may have led management to opt not to carry any product liability insurance since 1987. One Harley executive commented, "We do not believe that carrying product liability insurance is financially prudent." Instead, Harley created a form of self-insurance through reserves to cover potential liabilities.

OTHER PRODUCTION

In 1988, Teerlink proudly stated, "Capitalizing on its reputation as a world class manufacturer, Harley-Davidson is developing a strong contract manufacturing business. In April of 1988, the company became the first Army Munitions and Chemical Command (AMCCOM) contractor to be certified under the U.S. Army's Contractor Performance Certification Program. The company achieved the certification for its application of advanced manufacturing techniques in the production of 500-pound casings for the U.S. Army. Additionally, the company is the sole supplier of high-altitude rocket motors for target drones built by Beech Aircraft."

Harley-Davidson formed an agreement with Acustar, Inc., a subsidiary of Chrysler Corporation, in early 1988 to produce machined components for its Marine and Industrial Division. Harley also manufactured small engines for Briggs & Stratton. The company planned to further broaden its contract manufacturing business by aggressively marketing its proven and innovative manufacturing efficiencies to the industrial community. For 1990, management placed a goal of nonmotorcycle production to reach 25–30%. Teerlink felt strongly that "this goal is actually quite conservative and can be easily accomplished."

INTERNATIONAL OPERATIONS

The international markets of England, Italy, and other European countries were hardly uncharted territory for Harley-Davidson. Since 1915, Harley-Davidson had been selling its products in these overseas markets. Harley-Davidson's international efforts increased significantly during the mid-1980s. In 1984, the company produced 5,000 motorcycles for export; projections for 1990 called for production in the 20,000 unit range.

Several international markets exploded for Harley-Davidson in the late 1980s. In 1989, Harley motorcycle sales grew in France by 92%, England by 91%, and Australia by 32%. Europeans also bought other Harley products, such as T-shirts and leather jackets. Clyde Fessler, director of trademark licensing for Harley-Davidson, said, "In Europe we're considered Americana."

MARKETING

> When it comes to pleasuring the major senses, no motorcycle on earth can compare to a Harley. That's why I've tattooed my Harley's name on the inside of my mouth.
>
> —Lou Reed

Probably not every Harley-Davidson owner has Lou Reed's loyalty. Nonetheless, loyalty to Harley-Davidson has almost always been virtually unparalleled. According to the company's research, 92% of its customers remain with Harley. Even with strong brand loyalty, however, Harley's marketing division did not reduce its advertising. Harley-Davidson limited its advertising focus to print media, opting not to explore a radio or television campaign. The company used print ads in a variety of magazines, including trade magazines and the company's own trade publication, *The Enthusiast*. The advertising department, headed by Carmichael Lynch, had the benefit of a very well known company name. Unfortunately, the company name also carried serious image problems.

One major problem that plagued Harley's marketing efforts was that bootleggers were ruining the Harley-Davidson name by placing it on unlicensed, unauthorized goods of poor quality. Furthermore, society was turning away from the attitudes of the 1960s. With antidrug messages becoming a prevalent theme in American society, Harley-Davidson found itself linked to an image of the pot-smoking, beer-drinking, women-chasing, tattoo-covered, leather-clad biker. One industry expert observed, "When your company's logo is the number one request in tatoo parlors, it's time to get a licensing program that will return your reputation to the ranks of baseball, hot dogs, and apple pie." This image problem was not ignored by management. Kathleen Demitros, who became director of marketing in 1983, stated, "One of our problems was that we had such a hard-core image out there that it was basically turning off a lot of people." Demitros was speaking from experience. The Milwaukee native had been with the company since 1971. Like many of the company executives, she owned a Harley. By her own admission, Demitros chose not to ride her "Hog" to work. She saved it for the weekends.

Harley-Davidson took a proactive approach to solving the image problem. Managers created a licensing division responsible for eliminating the bootlegged products. This new division was led by John Heiman, formerly a mechanical accessories products manager. Goods with the Harley-Davidson logo would have to be sold by licensed dealers to be legal. Using warrants and federal marshals, Heiman went to conventions of motorcycle enthusiasts and began to put an end to the bootleggers.

Harley-Davidson then began to concentrate its efforts on a wide variety of products, ranging from leather jackets to cologne and jewelry, to supplement motorcycle sales. The concept was not new to Harley-Davidson. As far back as the 1920s, Harley had designed and sold leather jackets. The hope was that consumers would buy the other products, get comfortable with the Harley name, and then consider purchasing Harley motorcycles. One company executive said, "It helped pull us through the lean years." In 1988, he continued, "we sold 35,000 bikes and over 3 million fashion tops." For Harley-Davidson, these sales were crucial in offsetting the seasonal market of the motorcycle industry. Industry observers applauded Harley on this marketing ploy. "Historically, the winter months are tough on sales for the motorcycle industry. Harley-Davidson has been successful at selling fashion items." A Harley marketing executive went one step further. "If we can't sell someone a bike in the winter, we'll sell them a leather jacket instead."

Essentially, the licensing division had become an extension of marketing. Heiman said, "If you've got a 6-year-old boy wearing Harley pajamas, sleeping on Harley sheets and bathing with Harley towels, the old man's not going to be bringing home a Suzuki." In addition, retailers found that the licensed goods were popular. Major retail chains began selling Harley-Davidson products. The logic behind the selection of Harley goods was simple: "Harley is the only motorcycle made in the United States today, and I thought with pride in America high, the time was right for the licensed goods," explained one major retailer. However, the hard-core biker image of Harley-Davidson was still a strong influence. For example, when Fifth Avenue Cards, Inc. decided to sell Harley items, they did so in a satirical manner. According to Ethel Sloan, the card store chain's vice-president of merchandising, "We were definitely shooting for tongue-in-cheek, selling this macho, all-black coloration merchandise to bankers in three-piece suits—it was a real hoot!" It may have been this cynical and virtually unexpected market that Vaughn Beals hoped to exploit. Beals predicted the emergence of a new breed of Harley customer. "We're on the road to prosperity in this country, and we'll get there on a Harley."

The customers he spoke of began to buy Harleys in record numbers. The new Harley consumers were bankers, doctors, lawyers, and entertainers who developed an affection for "Hogs." They became known as Rubbies—Rich Urban Bikers. The Rubbies were not frightened by the high price tags associated with the Harley-Davidson product line. The Sportster 883, which was Harley's trademark motorcycle, and the Nova, which was specifically designed to capture the college student market, sold in a price range of $14,000–$15,000 in 1987.

Harley continued to expand its product line in 1988 with the addition of the Springer Softail, the Ultra Classic Electra Glide, and the Ultra Classic Tour Glide. James Paterson, president and chief operating officer of the Motorcycle Division, commented, "The Springer goes to the heart of Harley-Davidson, the custom-cruiser type of motorcycle. The Ultra Classics . . . are aimed at the touring market, . . . a market we couldn't reach previously." Product line expansion continued in 1989 with a move that several industry observers thought to be a questionable marketing decision. Harley-Davidson introduced the Fat Boy, their largest motorcycle with 80 cubic inches of V-twin engine.

The Rubbies brought Harley back into the forefront. By 1989, Harley-Davidson was again the leader in the U.S. super heavyweight motorcycle market, with a nearly 60% market share (see Exhibit 2). One consequence of the Rubbie market was the Rubbies' impact on the demographics of the Harley-Davidson consumer. According to an August 1990 *Wall Street Journal* article, "One in three of today's Harley-Davidson buyers are professionals or managers. About 60% have attended college, up from only 45% in 1984. Their median age is 35, and their median household income has risen sharply to $45,000 from $36,000 five years earlier."

Even with the growth of the Rubbie market, Harley-Davidson was careful not to lose touch with its grass-roots customers. In 1990, roughly 110,000 members belonged to the Harley Owners Group (H.O.G.) The fact that upper management continued to ride alongside their loyal throng was an important marketing tool. Paterson asserted, "Going to rallies and mixing with our customers has more value than you might initially expect. You begin to understand how important the motorcycle is and how important the Harley-Davidson way of life is to them. . . . At a motorcycle rally, everyone's part of the same family—sharing their love for motorcycling and life in general." Paterson's beliefs were shared by Harley owner Pat Soracino. "It's a family affair. My bike rides better with [wife] Vicki riding next to me. And our daughter has grown up with Harleys. It's more than a motorcycle to us. It's our lives."

H.O.G. and Harley-Davidson combined their efforts often in 1989. One

EXHIBIT 2 U.S. MARKET SHARE OF SUPER HEAVYWEIGHT MOTORCYCLES, 1989 (PERCENT)

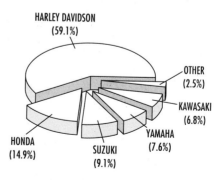

Source: R. L. Polk & Co.

such venture was a series of national forest improvement projects. In addition, the First Annual National Poker Run motorcycle rally received the support of almost 160 Harley dealers nationwide. This rally and others raised about $1.7 million for the Muscular Dystrophy Association, a charity for which Harley-Davidson collected over $6.5 million during the 1980s.

Although high performance was not a strong selling point for Harley-Davidson motorcycles, the company did enhance its reputation on the racing circuit in 1988 and 1989. In both years, Harley's factory-sponsored rider, Scotty Parker, captured the Grand National and Manufacturer's Championship in the American Motorcyclist Association's Class C racing season.

COMPETITION

MOTORCYCLE COMPETITION

Harley faced stiff competition from Japan's big four motorcycle manufacturers—Honda, Yamaha, Suzuki, and Kawasaki (see Exhibit 3). Industry analysts claimed that the Japanese manufacturers held a commanding lead in the world market with 80% of total motorcycle production.

In 1990, Honda was the world's largest motorcycle manufacturer. The president of the company, Shoichiro Irimaziri, attributed Honda's success to his company's philosophy of producing products of the highest efficiency at a reasonable price. In every aspect of the design of both its cars and its motorcycles, the company's engineers endeavored to achieve a reasonable level of efficiency and obtain the last increment of performance. The president also placed a high value on the early involvement of production and engineering. In his vision, the marketing and production departments are part of engineering; production departments are part of a bigger unit aimed at achieving quality and efficiency.

Yamaha grossed $3 billion in sales in 1989, making it the second-largest producer of motorcycles in the world. For decades, Yamaha remained extremely diversified as the leading producer of outboard motors, sailboats, snowmobiles, and golf carts. At Yamaha Motor, many of the products were developed almost exclusively for overseas markets. Why so much diversification? First, Yamaha executives believed that the motorcycle business in the late 1980s was a shrinking one. Second, as voiced by the president of the company, "Diversification is a hobby of my father's. He gets bored with old businesses."

Suzuki made its name selling motorcycles, but in 1987 almost doubled its sales with the introduction of a jeep, the Suzuki Samurai. When it was first introduced, critics thought it would be a modern-day Edsel. "When these odd-ball vehicles first came out; nobody gave them a nickel's chance of success," said Maryann N. Keller, a vice-president and automotive analyst with Furman Selz Mager Dietz & Birney. But the critics were wrong. Suzuki sold a record 48,000 units in 1986. The Samurai was the best model launch in history of any

EXHIBIT 3 HARLEY DAVIDSON'S SHARE OF THE U.S. SUPER HEAVYWEIGHT MOTORCYCLE MARKET

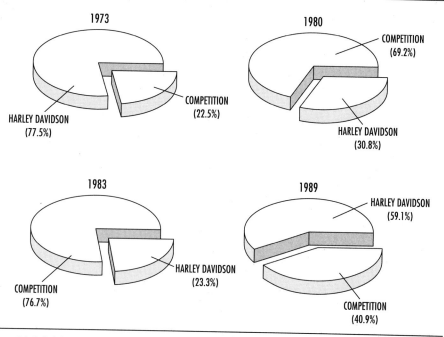

1973: HARLEY DAVIDSON (77.5%), COMPETITION (22.5%)
1980: COMPETITION (69.2%), HARLEY DAVIDSON (30.8%)
1983: COMPETITION (76.7%), HARLEY DAVIDSON (23.3%)
1989: HARLEY DAVIDSON (59.1%), COMPETITION (40.9%)

Source: R. L. Polk & Co.

Japanese auto manufacturer. Despite its success, however, the Samurai was hit with negative publicity in 1988. Specifically, the Consumers Union, a consumer protection organization, gave the Samurai a "not acceptable" rating and pleaded for the recall of 150,000 Samurais and full refunds to all owners. The union claimed that the vehicle was unsafe because it rolled over easily when turning corners. Although the negative publicity caused a temporary decline in sales, Suzuki rebounded in the second half of 1988 through utilization of dealer and customer incentives.

In 1988, Kawasaki's motorcycle sales increased 5% while the overall motorcycle market shrank 20%. Kawasaki's management attributed much of this success to a new service in which dealers could make sales with no-money-down financing. A computer network, Household Finance Corporation, allowed dealers to get nearly instantaneous responses on credit applications. Kawasaki also focused efforts to accommodate its dealers. The K-share program was developed in 1986 to act as a sales support system for dealers. K-share allowed dealers to make payments electronically; as a result, interest expense was reduced and keying errors made by Kawasaki were virtually eliminated because the manual input of checks was no longer necessary.

RECREATIONAL VEHICLE COMPETITION

With its acquisition of Holiday Rambler, Harley nearly doubled its revenues. However, experts indicated that it also bought into a very troubled industry with declining demand. They further claimed that greater competition in the industry would lead to increasing marketing costs and decreasing profit margins. Harley faced three top competitors in the RV industry: Fleetwood, Winnebago, and Airstream.

Fleetwood Enterprises, Inc. was the nation's leading manufacturer of recreational vehicles in 1989. Its operations included 21 factories in 17 states and Canada. For 1989, its sales totaled approximately $719 million.

Winnebago was number one in sales with $420 million in 1988. The company experienced financing problems in early 1990 when Norwest Bank cancelled a $50 million revolving credit line. This situation caused Winnebago to fall to number two in industry sales in 1990.

Airstream ranked third among the RV manufacturers with sales of approximately $389 million for 1989. Thor Industries bought the failing RV manufacturer from Beatrice Foods in 1980. Thor made assembly-line improvements and upgraded components to cut warranty costs and help the RV's image. In 1990, thousands of Airstream owners were members of the Wally Bran Caravan Club International. The club, started by Airstream, held regional rallies and caravans throughout the year. This cult-like following provided a loyal customer base, accounting for 60% of all of Airstreams sold.

THE IMPACT OF THE ECONOMY

Historically, the success of Harley-Davidson has hinged significantly on the performance of the U.S. economy. The company suffered along with everyone else during the Great Depression, and the boom periods of both world wars represented times of prosperity for Harley-Davidson. Changing demands of consumers during the postwar years in the 1940s and 1950s had an adverse effect on the motorcycle industry, and, just when Harley was on the road to recovery in the early 1980s, the economy fell into a recession.

Harley-Davidson proved repeatedly that it was a survivor, having restored peak production levels after each economic downturn. The company reached its highest levels of output in 1989, but, once again, the threat of recession was looming on the horizon. *Standard & Poor's Industry Surveys* warned that "leading indicators have been roughly flat and pointing to little growth, ... recent financial market activity alternates between fears of recession and inflation. Presently, inflation is a bigger worry for the markets, though recession is the larger worry for the moment."

As the summer of 1990 was reaching its peak, a major international crisis unfolded. On August 2, Iraq invaded Kuwait, unleashing a series of events that seriously affected the U.S. economy. In their August 16, 1990, *Trends & Projections,* Standard & Poor's discussed some of the effects of the anxiety in the Middle East: "The economy looks a lot more vulnerable than it did only a month ago. That was true before the Iraqi invasion; it is even truer with oil prices climbing.... A very slow, sluggish economy is predicted for the second half of 1990."

Valueline offered some further insight into the risks of the Middle East situation to Harley-Davidson. "The chief cause for concern would be curtailment of fuel supply in case of a shooting war. In any event, higher oil prices mean more inflation, which increases the risk of recession and with that, a slump in spending for big-ticket recreational goods." Harley-Davidson's products traditionally carried a reputation of producing less fuel efficient bikes than their their Japanese counterparts. "This is no touring bike ... that will take you nonstop from Tucson to Atlantic City."

Other analysts predicted continued pessimism in the recovery of the recreational vehicle market. "Consumers are getting nervous about the economy; recent consumer sentiment reports show deteriorating trends.... In the consumer durables category, weak auto sales are not likely to be reversed soon ... the prospect of higher oil prices means more pressure on consumer spending. Because it is difficult to reduce energy consumption in the short run, many consumers react to higher oil prices by reducing their spending on other items."

LEGAL AND SAFETY ISSUES

SPEED AND HELMETS

In 1988, 21 states had laws that required motorcycles to be operated with their headlights turned on during the daytime as well as nighttime hours. In addition, 20 states required motorcycle riders to wear helmets. Motorcyclists argued that such laws were a violation of their constitutional rights and that helmets actually prevented them from hearing sirens and other important road noises. But such legislation was not without justification. The number of deaths on motorcycles reached 4,500 in 1987—a rate approximately 16 times higher than that for automobiles. Cycle enthusiasts had a tendency to push the blame on unobservant car drivers. However, statistics from the Insurance Institute for Highway Safety (IIHS) showed that 45% of these accidents involved only one vehicle. Of particular concern to the IIHS were the high-speed superbikes that became available to the general public. These bikes accounted for almost twice the number of fatalities as other cycles. Moreover, the IIHS blamed the motorcycle industry for marketing these bikes' high speed and power, claiming that this emphasis encouraged the reckless use of an already dangerous product. The president of IIHS stated, "The fact is motorcycles as a group have much higher death and injury rates than cars, so the last thing we need is this new breed of cycle with even higher injury rates."

But what did all this mean to Harley? With the high revs of the traditional Hog and the production of lighter-weight race-style cycles like the Nova, industry experts claimed that Harley was sure to be hit with the same adverse publicity and criticisms as its Japanese counterparts.

THE RUBBIE (RICH URBAN BIKER) INFLUENCE

> I love riding the motorcycle. What a shame it nearly throws you into the jaws of death.
>
> —Billy Idol

> Every motorcycle rider thinks about the possibility of an accident. But I figured I was sharp enough in my reactions not to have one.... But the fact is, on Sunday, December 4, 1988, there I was, sprawled at the feet of a policeman with paramedics on the way.
>
> —Gary Busey

Both Idol, the international rock star, and Busey, the Academy Award–nominated actor, suffered near-fatal accidents while riding Harley-Davidson motorcycles. Neither Idol nor Busey was wearing a helmet at the time of his accident. An apparent disdain for the safety aspect of motorcycle riding was condoned by these role models. Busey, in fact, continued to be an opponent of helmet laws even after his ordeal. His stance remained with the throng of enthusiasts for whom "the decision to wear a helmet is a matter of personal freedom."

The Rubbies that helped revive Harley-Davidson were a double-edged sword. Well-known personalities such as comedian Jay Leno; actors Sylvester Stallone, Mickey Rourke, Lorenzo Lamas, Kurt Russell, Daniel Day-Lewis, and John Schneider; and Michael Hutchence of the rock group INXS were members of the Rubbie "fraternity." Their high-profile status drew attention to the helmet laws. Many of these celebrities were often seen in photos mounted on their Harleys without wearing helmets. Peter DeLuise, star of television's *21 Jumpstreet*, explained, "Biking is like sliding through the air. When you put a helmet on, it takes away part of the feeling." Ironically, DeLuise's show, which catered to an adolescent audience, often depicted teenagers cruising streets and highways without helmets.

Statistics showed that "142,000 Americans are injured in motorcycle accidents each year." In the early 1970s, Congress used its power over the states to enact legislation that required all motorcycle riders to wear helmets. Federal highway funds were cut in those states that did not pass the laws. Forty-seven states complied with the demand, but in the bicentennial year, aggressive lobbying efforts by biking groups succeeded in influencing Congress to revoke the sanctions. By 1980, 25 of the states had removed or weakened their helmet laws. Federal figures reported an increase in motorcycle fatalities of over 40% during this three-year period (1977–1980). A 1986 study by General Motors revealed that one-quarter of the 4,505 motorcyclists killed that year would have lived if they had worn helmets.

With models that can reach top speeds of 150 mph, Harley-Davidsons continued to satisfy "the American desire for power, speed and personal freedom." The company was never in the business of manufacturing helmets, nor did it take a stance on the helmet issue. Although the contention of prochoice enthusiasts was that the decision was personal, statistics showed that society was absorbing the cost. According to *Time*, a 1985 survey in Seattle found that 105 motorcycle accident victims hospitalized incurred $2.7 million in medical bills, of which 63% was paid from public funds.

FINANCIAL HIGHLIGHTS

Harley-Davidson's financial position improved greatly from 1986 to 1989 (see Exhibit 4). Even after the public stock offering in 1986, insiders continued to maintain some ownership of the company. *Valueline* reported in September 1990 that insiders owned 11.6% of Harley-Davidson's stock. Other major shareholders included FMR Corporation (7.2%) and Harris Association (6.7%). In June 1990, Malcolm Glazer reduced his ownership in Harley-Davidson from 7.29% to less than 1%, earning a $10 million profit in the process.

EXHIBIT 4 HARLEY DAVIDSON, INC.: NET INCOME COMPARISON, 1982–1989

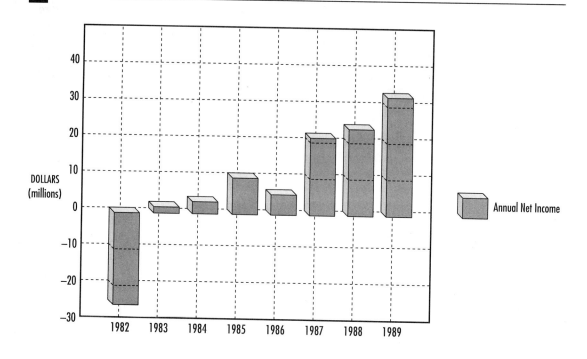

Source: Harley-Davidson, Inc.

Management's concern for employee satisfaction impacted the company's financial statements when in April 1989 Harley paid a $1.3 million signing bonus to the Wisconsin labor unions. Harley lowered its debt-equity ratio considerably in 1989 with the repurchase of $37.1 million of debt during the year, which created a decrease in the debt-equity ratio from 55% to 40%. In 1990, Harley-Davidson's stock was pounded from a high of $34 to a low of $13 before recovering to $18 as 1990 drew to a close. (The company's financial position is shown in the Appendix.)

REFERENCES

Advertising Age (1988). "Crisis Communications." September 5, p. 29.

Airstream Corporation Annual Report (1989). p. 17.

Busey, Gary (1990). "A Near-Fatal Motor Crash Changes an Actor's Life, But Not His Refusal to Wear a Helmet." *People.* May 15, p. 65.

Carey, David (1986). "Road Runner." *Financial World.* November, pp. 16–17.

Fannin, Rebecca (1988). "Against All Odds." *Marketing and Media.* March, pp. 45–47.

Fleetwood Corporation Annual Report (1989). p. 18.

Forbes (1983). "Thunder Road." July 18, p. 32.

Forbes (1987). "Harley Back in High Gear." April 20, p. 8.

Greising, David (1990). "Unhappy Campers at Winnebago." *Business Week.* May 8, p. 28.

Harley-Davidson, Incorporated Annual Report (1988).

Harley-Davidson, Incorporated Annual Report (1989).

Harley-Davidson News (1988).

Hutchins, Dexter (1986). "Having a Hard Time With Just-In-Time." *Fortune.* June 9, p. 66.

Irimaziri, Soichiro. "The Winning Difference." *Vital Speeches.* pp. 650–651.

Kitchen, Steve (1983). "More Than Motorcycles." *Forbes.* October 3, p. 193.

Ludlum, David (1989). "Good Times Roll." *Computer World.* August 7, p. 51.

Marvel, Mark (1989). "The Gentrified Hog." *Esquire.* July, pp. 25–26.

Parola, Robert (1989). "High on the Hog." *Daily News Record.* January 23, p. 74.

Popular Mechanics (1989). "The Harley Priority." June 9, p. 24.

Purchasing (1986). "At Harley-Davidson JIT Is a Fine Tuned Cycle." April 24.

Reid, Peter C. (1988). "Well Made in America: Lessons From Harley-Davidson on Being the Best." Harley Davidson, Inc.

Roberts, John Madock (1985). "Harley's Hogs." *Forbes.* December 7, p. 14.

Rolling Stone (1990). "Billy Idol." July, p. 174.

Rose, Robert L. (1990). "Vrooming Back." *Wall Street Journal (Southwestern Edition).* August 31, p. 1.

Saathoff, John A. (1989). "Workshop Report: Maintain Excellence Through Change." *Target.* Spring, p. 2.

Schwartz, Joe (1986). "No Fixed Address." *American Demographics.* August, pp. 50–51.

Serafin, Raymond (1988). "RV Market Puzzled." *Advertising Age.* July, p. 52.

Spadoni, Marie (1985). "Harley Davidson Revs Up to Improve Image." *Advertising Age.* August 5, p. 30.

Standard and Poor's Industry Surveys (1990). August 16, p. 4.

Standard and Poor's, Trends and Projections (1990). August 16, p. 3.

Stores (1986). "Greeting Card Chain Scores Big With Macho 'Biker' Promotion." February, p. 21.

Tanzer, Andrew (1987). "Create or Die." *Forbes.* April 6, pp. 55–59.

Time (1988). "High Gear." December 19, p. 65.

Willis, Rod (1986). "Harley-Davidson Comes Roaring Back." *Management Review.* March, pp. 20–27.

APPENDIX

HARLEY DAVIDSON, INC. CONSOLIDATED BALANCE SHEETS, 1988 AND 1989

	DECEMBER 31	
	1989	1988
	(In thousands, except share amounts)	
ASSETS		
Current assets:		
Cash and cash equivalents	$ 39,076	$ 52,360
Accounts receivable, net of allowances for doubled accounts	45,565	42,857
Inventories	87,550	89,947
Deferred income taxes	9,662	8,844
Prepaid expenses	5,811	4,795
Assets of discontinued operation	—	12,488
Total current assets	187,674	211,291
Property, plant, and equipment, net	115,700	107,838
Goodwill	66,190	68,782
Deferred financing costs	2,356	4,495
Other assets	7,009	4,307
Noncurrent assets of discontinued operation	—	4,401
	$378,929	$401,114

(continued)

HARLEY DAVIDSON, INC. CONSOLIDATED BALANCE SHEETS, 1988 AND 1989 (continued)

	DECEMBER 31	
	1989	1988
	(In thousands, except share amounts)	
LIABILITIES AND STOCKHOLDERS' EQUITY		
Current liabilities:		
Notes payable	$ 22,789	$ 21,041
Current maturities of long-term debt	4,143	12,188
Accounts payable	40,095	36,939
Accrued expenses and other liabilities	69,334	63,047
Liabilities of discontinued operation	—	3,172
Total current liabilities	136,361	136,387
Long-term debt	74,795	135,176
Accrued employee benefits	5,273	3,309
Deferred income taxes	6,253	4,594
Commitments and contingencies (Notes 4, 7, and 9)		
Stockholders' equity:		
Series A Junior Participating preferred stock, 1,000,000 shares authorized, none issued	—	—
Common stock, 9,155,000 shares issued	92	92
Additional paid-in capital	79,681	76,902
Retained earnings	77,352	44,410
Cumulative foreign currency translation adjustment	508	374
	157,633	121,778
Less:		
Treasury stock (447,091 and 520,000 shares in 1989 and 1988, respectively), at cost	(112)	(130)
Unearned compensation	(1,274)	—
Total stockholder's equity	156,247	121,648
	$378,929	$401,114

Source: Harley-Davidson, Inc.

The accompanying notes are an integral part of the consolidated financial statements.

CONSOLIDATED STATEMENTS OF INCOME

	YEARS ENDED DECEMBER 31		
	1989	1988	1987
	(In thousands, except share amounts)		
Net sales	$790,967	$709,360	$645,966
Operating costs and expenses:			
Cost of goods sold	596,940	533,448	487,205
Selling, administrative, and engineering	127,608	111,582	104,672
	724,546	645,030	591,877
Income from operations	66,421	64,330	54,089
Interest income	3,634	4,149	2,658
Interest expense	(17,956)	(22,612)	(23,750)
Other-net	910	165	(2,143)
Income from continuing operations before provision for income taxes and extraordinary items	53,009	46,032	30,854
Provision for income taxes	20,399	18,863	13,181
Income from continuing operations before extraordinary items	32,610	27,169	17,673
Discontinued operations, net of tax:			
Income (loss) from discontinued operation	154	(13)	—
Gain on disposal of discontinued operation	3,436	—	—
Income before extraordinary items	36,200	27,156	17,673
Extraordinary items:			
Loss on refinancing/debt repurchase, net of taxes	(1,434)	(1,468)	—
Additional cost of 1983 AMF settlement, net of taxes	(1,824)	(1,776)	—
Benefit from utilization of loss carryforward	—	—	3,542
Net income	$ 32,942	$ 23,912	$ 21,215
Per common share:			
Income from continuing operations	3.78	3.41	2.72
Discontinued operation	.41	—	—
Extraordinary items	(.38)	(.41)	.55
Net income	3.81	3.00	3.27

Source: Harley-Davidson, Inc.

The accompanying notes are an integral part of the consolidated financial statements.

CONSOLIDATED STATEMENTS OF CASH FLOWS

	YEAR ENDED DECEMBER 31		
	1989	1988	1987
		(In thousands)	
Cash flows from operating activities:			
Net income	$32,942	$23,912	$21,215
Adjustments to reconcile net income to net cash provided by operating activities			
Depreciation and amortization	20,007	17,958	15,643
Deferred income taxes	821	(1,375)	(2,875)
Long-term employee benefits	2,741	1,037	(439)
Gain on sale of discontinued operation	(5,513)	—	—
Loss on disposal of long-term assets	28	1,451	1,505
Net changes in current assets and curent liabilities	10,051	(30,346)	12,205
Total adjustments	28,135	(11,275)	26,039
Net cash provided by operating activities	61,077	12,637	47,254
Cash flows from investing activities:			
Capital expenditures	(24,438)	(23,786)	(17,027)
Less amounts capitalized under financing leases	819	2,877	—
Net capital expenditures	(23,619)	(20,909)	(17,027)
Proceeds on sale of discontinued operation and other assets	19,475	—	—
Other–net	(2,720)	(1,204)	901
Net cash used in investing activities	(6,864)	(22,113)	(16,126)
Cash flows from financing activities:			
Net increase in notes payable	1,748	1,083	5,891
Reductions in debt	(69,245)	(42,652)	(78,478)
Proceeds from issuance of common stock	—	35,179	18,690
Procceds from additional borrowings	—	—	70,000
Repurchase of warrants	—	—	(3,594)
Deferred financing costs	—	—	(3,265)
Net cash provided by (used in) financing activities	(67,497)	(6,390)	9,244
Net increase (decrease) in cash and cash equivalents	(13,284)	(15,866)	40,372
Cash and cash equivalents:			
At beginning of year	52,360	68,226	27,854
At end of year	$39,076	$52,360	$68,226

Source: Harley-Davidson, Inc.

The accompanying notes are an integral part of the consolidated financial statements.

CONSOLIDATED STATEMENTS OF CHANGES IN STOCKHOLDERS' EQUITY

YEARS ENDED DECEMBER 31, 1989, 1988, AND 1987
(IN THOUSANDS, EXCEPT SHARE AMOUNTS)

	Common stock		Additional paid in capital	Retained earnings (deficit)	Cumulative foreign currency translation adjustment	Treasury stock	Unearned compensation
	Outstanding shares	Balance					
Balance, January 1, 1987	6,200,000	$62	$26,657	$ (717)	$287	$(130)	$ —
Net income	—	—	—	21,215	—	—	—
Net proceeds from common stock offering	1,230,000	12	18,678	—	—	—	—
Repurchase of 230,000 warrants in connection with public debt and common stock offering	—	—	(3,594)	—	—	—	—
Cumulative foreign currency translation adjustment	—	—	—	—	443	—	—
Balance, December 31, 1987	7,430,000	74	41,741	20,498	730	(130)	—
Net income	—	—	—	23,912	—	—	—
Net proceeds from common stock offering	1,725,000	18	35,161	—	—	—	—
Cumulative foreign currency translation adjustment	—	—	—	—	(356)	—	—
Balance, December 31, 1988	9,155,000	92	76,902	44,410	374	(130)	—
Net income	—	—	—	32,942	—	—	—
Issuance of 72,909 treasury shares of restriced stock	—	—	2,779	—	—	18	(1274)
Cumulative foreign currency translation adjustment	—	—	—	—	134	—	—
Balance, December 31, 1989	9,155,000	$92	$79,681	$77,352	$508	$(112)	$(1,274)

Source: Harley-Davidson, Inc.

The accompanying notes are an integral part of the consolidated financial statements.

CASE 18

UNICRE, S.A. AND THE CREDIT CARD INDUSTRY IN PORTUGAL

DAVID W. GRIGSBY AND
VITOR F. C. GONÇALVES

Seated in a conference room on the ninth floor of UNICRE headquarters overlooking Edward VII Park in downtown Lisbon, Sebastião Lancastre reviewed the recent performance of his company. As founding CEO of Portugal's largest credit card company, Lancastre felt he had reasons to be pleased with its performance. UNICRE's revenues had reached their highest-ever levels in 1990, and an improving Portuguese economy showed signs of continuing to boost the company's profits ever higher as the company entered its eighteenth year of operations. A number of critical strategic issues faced the company, however. Lancastre wondered how to deal with rapid changes in the Portuguese banking system and how to react to increased competitive threats on several fronts.

UNICRE (formally known as UNICRE–Cartão International de Crédito, S.A.) was a principal member of eight international credit card organizations, including Visa, MasterCard, American Express, Diner's Club, Carte Blanche, JCB, DKV, and AirPlus. It was a jointly owned subsidiary of Portugal's eighteen largest commercial banks, which together controlled over 95% of the country's total deposits. UNICRE was formed in 1971 to issue credit cards and to process credit card charges in Portugal. Six banks originally formed the company through a consortium arrangement, with each member bank holding one-sixth of the capital stock. By 1991, UNICRE had over 220,000 Visa cards in circulation under the name "UNIBANCO" and maintained an exclusive

---

Source: By David W. Grigsby of Clemson University and Vitor F. C. Gonçalves of the Technical University of Lisbon. Originally presented at a meeting of the North American Case Research Association in 1991. This case was written with the cooperation of management, solely for the purpose of stimulating student discussion. All data are based on field research in the organization. All incidents and events are real. All rights reserved jointly to the authors and the North American Case Research Association (NACRA). © 1992, North American Case Research Association and David W. Grigsby.

arrangement that processed all credit card purchases for a network of over 18,500 merchants.

HISTORY OF THE COMPANY

The concept of UNICRE came about in 1969, when two banks that would later be founding members, Banco Totta & Açores (BTA) and Banco Portugues do Atlantico (BPA), began to investigate the possibility of issuing bank credit cards under one of the two existing major systems, BankAmericard (later Visa) or Interbank/MasterCharge, both of which were based in the United States. At the time, only T&E (travel and entertainment) cards were operating in Portugal. Diner's Club, operating through Banco do Alentejo, had 2,000 cards in circulation, and American Express was set up to process charges on its cards through Banco Borges & Irmão.

By 1971, the bank credit card business had grown rapidly throughout the world, and cards were in widespread use in most of Western Europe. Interest in starting a bank card network in Portugal spread from the original two banks to others. A meeting of the major banks was held to discuss the oncoming credit card revolution and how the Portuguese banking system might respond to it. After the meeting, several banks agreed to set up a bank card network to serve the whole country. The concept was to charter the operation as a separate corporation, jointly owned by the banks. This arrangement would provide a means of avoiding the intense competition that had typified credit card systems in some other European countries.

A single event the previous year had underscored the necessity of moving quickly. Banco Pinto & Sotto Mayor (BPSM) had struck a deal on its own with BankAmericard (Visa) and had launched the first Portuguese bank card in February 1970. Since BankAmericard's policy was to grant a license to only one organization per country, the bank group decided to seek an arrangement through Interbank/MasterCharge, BankAmericard's primary rival.

The name UNICRE was chosen for the venture. It is an acronym for "unido crédito" (united credit). The next step was to set aside start-up capital and hire an executive to found the new company. Unable to agree on any internal candidates from the banks themselves, UNICRE directors decided to seek a chief executive from outside.

"I never thought I would be involved in the banking business. I was trained as a mining engineer," said Lancastre. Following his university training, Lancastre had worked in a family-owned gold mining company in the northern region of Portugal, a rural area known as Tras-as-Montes (literally, "behind the mountains"). After twelve years working there as an engineer, he had moved to Lisbon to assume duties in the mining company's home office. In 1971, Lancastre, who had become dissatisfied with his job, saw a newspaper advertisement that simply stated that a new company was being formed and sought an executive to head up its operations. "If I had known that the company was in banking, I might never have answered the ad, but the idea of being involved in a totally new venture intrigued me. So, I applied."

The primary qualification UNICRE sought in its CEO was the ability to make decisions in an uncertain environment. According to Lancastre, "This was something for which I was well qualified by virtue of my experience in the mining industry. There we made many decisions daily, often ones of a life and death nature." The directors of UNICRE agreed, and Lancastre was hired to head up the new company. When the venture began in 1971, Lancastre, with no experience in the credit card field and no employees, had much to do. Hiring staff, buying equipment, finding office space, and hundreds of other details consumed a three-year start-up period before actual credit card operations could begin. Lancastre traveled extensively, visiting other credit card companies and studying successful operations in the United States and in other European countries.

UNICRE's credit card was named UNIBANCO, an acronym for "unido banco" (united bank), in reference to the cooperative nature of the venture. The founders originally had intended to use the name UNIBANCO as the company's name, but government officials had objected to the word "banco" in the title since the organization was not to be a charted bank.

After putting together a working organization in Lisbon, Lancastre established a merchant network and began issuing credit cards. Operations actually began on April 17, 1974. Eight days later, the Portuguese "revolution" changed everything.

BACKGROUND

On April 25, 1974, a democratic left-wing government, supported by the military, overthrew the Portuguese premier-for-life in a swift, nearly bloodless coup, ending forty-eight years of authoritarian rule and establishing widespread civil and political liberties in Portugal. Within a year, Portugal's African colonies had declared their independence and plunged into civil wars. Seeking asylum from the new African regimes and prosperity under Portugal's newly granted civil liberties, nearly 1 million overseas Portuguese, most of whom had been born in the colonies and lived their entire lives there, streamed into Portugal, increasing its population by nearly 15%.

The influx of these "retornados" brought additional problems to the economy, which was already in disarray. The new socialist government had instituted wholesale economic reforms, including the country's first-ever broad-based social assistance programs, and announced plans to nationalize Portugal's major industries and all Portuguese financial institutions. Despite the radically changed business environment and heavy controls placed on almost every aspect of the banking industry, UNICRE officials decided to continue operating. According to Lancastre, "For five years, we just survived."

Portuguese banks and other financial institutions were nationalized in

March 1975. All systems in the industry were centralized, and complete authority for all decisions was vested in the Ministry of Finance. In order to mitigate outflows of badly needed foreign exchange, the Finance Ministry prohibited the use of Portuguese credit cards outside the country. In December, the ministry went a step further and announced intentions to begin a process that would eventually dissolve all independent credit card operations then in existence and give one organization the sole responsibility for issuing bank credit cards and maintaining the country's merchant network. The period of uncertainty that followed was finally relieved in 1979 when a law was enacted that officially gave UNICRE the sole responsibility for bank credit cards in Portugal. The resulting single operation was, ironically, what the consortium of banks had in mind when it established UNICRE.

The government was slow in enforcing the new law. Diner's Club continued issuing cards until 1977 and finally ceased all operations in 1979. In the meantime, Visa International had relaxed its restrictions against dual operations. This gave UNICRE the opportunity to switch its own card, the UNIBANCO card, to Visa in 1981. BPSM continued to operate its Visa business until 1984, when it was finally forced to abandon it and join UNICRE as a member/stockholder. From that point until 1988, when restrictions were relaxed, UNICRE operated as the sole entity representing international credit card organizations in the country.

Beginning in the mid-1980s, the country entered a period of rapid economic growth and credit expansion. Portugal's entry into the European Community in 1986, which was accompanied by a substantial aid package for infrastructure development, added greatly to its improved economic position. (For more information concerning Portugal and the Portuguese economy, refer to the statistics in Appendix A at the conclusion of the case.)

THE UNICRE CONCEPT

The decision to form one company to launch the credit card era in Portugal was a fortunate one, not only for UNICRE, which enjoyed a unique position, but also in terms of overall market efficiency. In larger markets, competing card companies often operated parallel merchant networks, which vied for the right to process credit card purchases in return for a percentage of the merchant's credit sales. This percentage, known as the "discount," varied from 2% to 5%, depending on the volume of the merchant's credit sales and the intensity of competition between the companies. In a country the size of Portugal, where the total volume of credit sales was small, operational economies of scale were much more difficult to achieve. Under these conditions, competition among credit card networks would probably have resulted in the erosion of profit margins below the break-even level, making survival for the networks impossible.

THE COMPETITIVE ENVIRONMENT

BANK REGULATION AND CREDIT REFORM

In 1988, the Portuguese government relaxed its controls on the banking and credit industry. The major banks that had been nationalized after the 1974 revolution, all of which were member stockholders in UNICRE, were slated to be reprivatized beginning in 1991. The gradual process of reprivatization, which involved selling the stock of public banks on the open market, began with some of the stronger banks. Eventually all eighteen members of UNICRE would be in private hands, with the exception of Caixa Geral de Depositos (CGD), the national savings bank. This meant that for a number of years, UNICRE could expect to have a mixture of private and public banks as its stockholders.

In 1991, the Portuguese banking system was still highly regulated. In order to protect the nationalized banks from competition for deposits from the private banks, maximum interest rates on deposits were set by the government. Lending rates had, however, been deregulated. This situation kept intermediation margins in the banking industry quite high. Consequently, the country's few private banks and several of its national banks had a series of very profitable years beginning in 1988. By 1991, the high profit margins had led to vigorous competition among the banks for deposits, which were still at the relatively low regulated rates around 15%.

As the European Community countries, including Portugal, approached the deadline for economic consolidation in 1992, reforms were being installed rapidly. Deregulation of interest rates on deposits was scheduled to be a part of the overall plan, but government officials delayed that action, fearing that the public banks, which in mid-1991 still controlled a majority of the total bank deposits in Portugal, would be hard pressed to compete in a completely deregulated banking market and that the consequent loss of earnings would depress the value of their stocks upon privatization.

As a part of its 1988 reforms, the government also relaxed its regulation of credit cards. For the first time, Portuguese citizens were permitted to hold more than one bank credit card. In addition, beginning in 1988, banks were permitted to issue their own cards. Some of the banks quickly made arrangements to do so, either in association with UNICRE or as independent members of an international system. UNICRE, however, still held the largest share of the cards in the country by far with its original UNIBANCO card, a standard Visa card, and continued to control the merchant network through which all other card charges were processed.

UNIBANCO

In 1991, UNICRE's regular UNIBANCO card was being issued to qualified applicants for a annual fee of 3,500 escudos (approximately $23), which entitled them to receive two cards. Interest rate charges in 1991 were 3.5% per month on unpaid balances (about 42% annually). The interest rates consisted of three components: a mandatory rate, a flexible rate, and a government tax on credit balances. The mandatory rate, which was 12% in 1991, was a minimum rate imposed by the government. The flexible rate was an additional amount, with no limits, that could be imposed by creditors. UNICRE used a formula of the prime rate plus 1.5% to set the flexible portion. With prime rates at approximately 18.5% in 1991, the flexible rate was 20%. Taxes of 10% were imposed on credit balances in 1991. Total interest charges in 1991 were therefore equal to an annual rate of 42% (the 12% mandatory rate plus the 20% flexible rate, plus the 10% tax.) UNICRE realized revenues of 32% APR on account balances (the total rate minus the 10% tax, which was passed on to the government).

The high prime rate of interest was attributable to the country's overall inflation rate, which in 1991 stood at about 13.5% annually. Credit card operations were able to charge rates well above prime for a number of reasons. First of all, the structure of the industry was not conducive to interest rate competition. Since UNICRE controlled most of the credit cards issued, the ordinary market forces that would inspire price competition were not active. Also, since UNICRE was a subsidiary of the banks, there was little incentive for banks to engage in direct competition with it. The situation was therefore one in which UNICRE acted as price leader, and implicit price setting prevailed. The banks simply followed UNICRE's rates.

In Portugal, most customers paid off credit card balances monthly and did not incur interest charges. This was not entirely due to the high interest rates. In fact, studies conducted by Visa International had shown cardholders to be extremely price inelastic when it came to using credit cards as a source of consumer debt. A large part of the phenomenon was due to a national characteristic; Portuguese consumers avoided accumulating debt. Despite high inflation rates and relatively low average income, the Portuguese savings rate was the highest in Europe—approximately 20% of disposable income.

Another factor that contributed to the lack of carryover balances was UNICRE's very conservative policies for approving credit card applications. Unicre had a practice of granting accounts to only the best risks. Qualification restrictions based on income level and occupation kept many Portuguese citizens from obtaining a card. Also, individual credit limits were set quite low for most customers, a practice that discouraged them from using the card for large purchases and carrying over balances.

Only 220,000 UNIBANCO cards were outstanding in 1991. It was estimated that there were fewer than 300,000 total credit cards held in the country, despite studies indicating that present income levels could justify expanding the number to over 500,000 without changing substantially the conservative credit policies then in effect. A 1990 survey revealed that 84.5% of individuals in Portugal between the ages of 15 and 70 had bank accounts, but only 10.3% had credit cards.

In addition to its standard card, UNICRE also offered a Premier Visa ("gold") card to the top 15% of income earners. Launched in 1991, the UNI-

BANCO gold card offered a comprehensive package of benefits and services to cardholders including health, travel, and accident insurance and discounts on rental cars and hotel rooms. Annual fees for Premier Card accounts were 10,000 escudos for the first card and 5,000 escudos for a second card (approximately $67 and $33, respectively). Interest rates and the terms and conditions for paying account balances were identical to those of the regular UNIBANCO card, but credit limits were considerably higher for the preferred gold-card customers.

THE COMPETITORS

When financial reforms finally allowed banks to issue their own credit cards in 1988, UNICRE faced the paradoxical situation of being forced into competition with its own stockholders. Realizing that this situation could lead to the eventual demise of the UNIBANCO card as banks pushed their own cards or to cutthroat competition for credit card customers among the member banks, Lancastre and his staff decided that rather than resist the competition, UNICRE would offer its expertise to banks that wanted to issue their own cards. Four options were devised and agreed to by the stockholder banks:

1. Banks could issue their own credit cards as principal members of an international credit card organization. UNICRE would offer assistance in making contacts and provide technical assistance. By 1991, three banks had become principal members of Visa. One of these was BPSM, which had been the first bank to issue a card before the revolution. In addition to regular cards, all three offered gold cards with features similar to UNIBANCO's but with higher annual fees.

2. A second option was for banks to continue to issue debit cards, a practice that had been permitted prior to credit card liberalization. These cards were used primarily as a convenience to replace the necessity of check writing, with charges automatically withdrawn from members' checking accounts. A number of banks had chosen this option and issued the cards as associate members of Visa, sponsored by UNICRE. Most debit cards were issued as gold cards, which, in addition to gold-card benefits, carried the extra attraction of prestige.

3. Banks could also issue regular credit cards as associate members of Visa sponsored by UNICRE. These cards carried the same rates and annual fees as the UNIBANCO card and could be issued as either standard cards or premier cards. Of the banks that had chosen this option, all had originally issued debit cards before the law was changed.

4. A final option was available for banks that chose not to enter the credit card business. The bank could offer a special UNIBANCO card that carried both the bank's logo and UNICRE's. The member bank received a fee from UNICRE for distributing the card. Also, banks that issued their own cards could offer UNIBANCO as a second card.

THE COMPETITIVE ENVIRONMENT

EXHIBIT 1 VALUE OF CREDIT CARD TRANSACTIONS IN PORTUGAL, 1987–1990 (IN MILLIONS OF ESCUDOS)

CREDIT CARD	1990	1989	1988	1987
UNIBANCO Visa card	46,210	29,963	21,110	14,046
Other Portuguese bank cards	34,881	14,234	5,162	1,376
Foreign bank cards[1]	43,373	31,200	21,765	15,717
Travel and entertainment cards[2]	15,186	14,244	12,118	10,330
Total	139,650	89,641	60,155	41,469

[1] Visa, MasterCard, and EuroCard.
[2] JCB, Carte Blanche, Diner's Club, American Express, and DKV.

Note: Figures are not adjusted for inflation. The consumer price inflation rate in Portugal was 13.5% in 1990, 11.8% in 1989, 9.6% in 1988, and 9.3% in 1987.

Source: UNICRE internal document.

Before 1991, most banks had not begun to compete directly with UNICRE for credit card customers, and those that issued cards offered only debit cards. That situation began to change, however. As the private banks grew and formerly state-owned banks were privatized, both began to seek out new sources of revenue offered by the credit card business. Although in 1991 there was still an implicit agreement among the banks not to compete on interest rates, the banks were beginning to compete on annual card fees, especially in the gold-card segment.

Compared to other European countries, credit card purchases as a percentage of all retail sales were quite low in Portugal. The country's economy was expanding rapidly, however, and credit purchases were rising along with it. Exhibit 1 details the total value of credit purchases by card type, and Exhibit 2 shows the number of transactions by type.

EXHIBIT 2 NUMBER OF CREDIT CARD TRANSACTIONS IN PORTUGAL, 1987–1990

CREDIT CARD	1990	1989	1988	1987
UNIBANCO Visa card	4,928,861	3,143,712	2,833,584	2,260,000
Other Portuguese bank cards	2,895,228	1,077,151	333,044	100,579
Foreign bank cards[1]	2,698,056	2,095,329	1,558,906	1,248,865
Travel and entertainment cards[2]	515,675	519,282	489,321	459,517
Total	11,037,820	6,835,474	5,214,855	4,068,961

[1] Visa, MasterCard, and EuroCard.
[2] JCB, Carte Blanche, Diner's Club, American Express, and DKV.

Source: UNICRE internal document.

REVENUES AND INDUSTRY DYNAMICS

REVENUES

Bank credit card companies such as UNICRE generate revenue from merchant discount fees, revolving credit charges, and cash advance fees.

Merchant Discount Fees. In return for processing credit card charges, UNICRE charged each participating merchant in the network a discount fee, regardless of the type of credit card used in the transaction or who issued the card that was used. The fee, determined by the type of business and the merchant's total annual volume, ranged from 2% to 5% of the total amount charged. Merchant fees were subtracted directly when credit charges were deposited in the merchant's bank. When banks began issuing their own cards in 1988, UNICRE adopted a plan for rebating portions of the merchant fees to them. For charges made using the UNIBANCO card, UNICRE continued to retain the entire discount. On charges made with independently issued cards, the issuing bank received 80% of the discount if it was a UNICRE stockholder, 50% if not. For charges made using cards issued by stockholder banks in association with UNICRE, the banks received 50% of the discount. Merchant discounts represented the largest portion of UNICRE's total revenues.

Exhibit 3 presents a financial and organizational summary of UNICRE. Exhibit 4 presents a breakdown of UNICRE's sources of revenue for the years 1988 through 1991. Note that the totals shown include the entire discount before rebates to the card-issuing banks.

Annual Fees. Annual card fees were paid by cardholders directly to the issuing bank. The revenues from annual fees shown in Exhibit 4 represent the fees collected by UNICRE for its regular and premiere UNIBANCO Visa cards.

Revolving Credit Charges. Interest payments are retained by the card-issuing bank, which collects payments from the cardholders on accounts. Totals shown in Exhibit 4 are the interest charges paid by UNIBANCO customers.

Cash Advance Fees. Cash advances were handled differently from regular merchandise charges. A cash advance fee of 3.33% was charged to the cardholder on the total amount of the advance. Before 1990, cash advances were simply passed on to Visa International. Starting in 1990, UNICRE retained the bulk of the fee, 3%, and the remaining 0.33% went directly to Visa International.

SEASONALITY

Transactions from foreign bank cards, which represent approximately 31% of all credit card purchases, are concentrated in the months of June, July, August, and September, the most active months for tourism in Portugal. This traditional seasonality has been offset somewhat in recent years by two de-

EXHIBIT 3 UNICRE—FINANCIAL AND ORGANIZATIONAL SUMMARY, 1987–1990

	1990	1989	1988	1987
FINANCIAL SUMMARY (VALUES IN 1,000 ESCUDOS)				
Total volume, inc. cash advances	139,650,000	89,641,000	60,155,000	41,469,000
Total revenue (all sources)	5,326,187	3,438,141	2,137,258	1,487,832
Distributions to stockholders	800,000	800,000	600,000	400,000
Net income (after taxes)	238,919	217,648	187,746	144,076
Dividends	100,000	80,000	75,000	70,000
Effective cash flow (including distributions to stockholders)	1,504,094	1,695,664	1,205,635	860,799
Reserve for contingencies:				
Additions	—	464,613	246,593	139,718
Balance	833,750	931,481	554,275	375,481
Depreciation/amortization	143,168	92,495	59,000	43,617
Bad debts:				
Additions	95,500	82,016	49,161	20,137
Balance	395,304	299,804	132,214	168,627
Leasehold payments	425,495	171,201	43,875	33,275
Provision for pension fund	125,000	80,000	120,000	100,000
Total personnel costs	1,362,244	919,233	723,292	565,120
Capital stock	1,000,00	500,000	500,000	500,000
Total stockholder's equity	1,559,612	916,318	769,601	601,335
NONFINANCIAL DATA				
Number of stockholders	18	13	12	10
Cards issued & in circulation	220,000	205,000	180,000	150,000
Merchants in network	19,500	16,214	13,736	11,638
Number of transactions processed	11,300,000	7,006,000	5,221,000	4,066,000
UNICRE employees	279	213	184	150

Note: Figures are not adjusted for inflation. The consumer price inflation rate in Portugal was 13.5% in 1990, 11.8% in 1989, 9.6% in 1988, and 9.3% in 1987.

Source: UNICRE internal document.

EXHIBIT 4 UNICRE REVENUES BY SOURCE, 1988–1991 (IN ESCUDOS)

SOURCE OF REVENUE	1991	1990	1989	1988
Merchant discounts	5,136,556	3,782,046	2,519,428	1,500,338
Annual card fees	604,689	396,659	265,172	167,032
Interest on card balances	1,595,832	988,119	653,541	469,888
Cash advance fees	269,876	159,363	—	—
Total revenues	7,606,953	5,326,187	3,438,141	2,137,258

Source: UNICRE internal document.

velopments. Winter tourism to the Algarve, Portugal's southern coast, has been increasing as the area's popularity with foreign visitors, particularly northern Europeans, has increased. Also, the increasing popularity of Formula 1 automobile racing in Portugal has increased tourism during its season in October.

Bank credit card activity from Portuguese-issued cards follows patterns similar to those in the United States, with December being by far the heaviest month because of Christmas buying. Domestic credit card activity also increases in the months of July, August, and September, which is the vacation season for Portuguese schools and businesses.

VISA INTERNATIONAL

Visa International, the world's largest credit card network, is operated through a nonprofit membership arrangement; Banks pay a membership fee to join and then pay fees for services and operations offered by the company. Any residual profits are redistributed to banks annually in proportion to their volumes of business. As of 1990, Visa International had over 265 million cards in circulation, generating an annual sales volume of more than $345 billion. Exhibit 5 lists the financial and organizational highlights of Visa International for the years 1987 to 1990. Exhibit 6 lists the number of cards and payment volumes in each of Visa's operating areas around the world for the same time period.

The fees UNICRE pays to Visa International are based on the number of cards in circulation and the total volume of credit business transacted. In 1991, the fees paid to Visa International totaled about $35,000 per quarter, plus cash advance fees and authorization fees. In return, Visa International operates its worldwide credit processing network and offers card membership services.

ORGANIZATION, MANAGEMENT, AND THE ENVIRONMENT

STOCKHOLDERS AND BOARD OF DIRECTORS

In 1991, three members, elected by the banks on a rotating basis, served on the company's board of directors. The board had a very close relationship with UNICRE, meeting every two weeks at UNICRE headquarters. Its relationship to management was an unusual one for Portugal, where strong boards normally dominate and managers act as administrators. Because of his experience and expertise in the industry, Lancastre's relationship to the board of directors was similar to that found in U.S. corporations. He was the chief strategist for the company, and the board usually supported his decisions.

Eighteen banks held stock in UNICRE, with ten of these holding over 90% of the capital stock. Banks may be added to the list of stockholders by approval

EXHIBIT 5 VISA INTERNATIONAL HIGHLIGHTS, 1987–1990 (U.S. DOLLARS IN THOUSANDS)

	1990	1989	1988	1987
Payment service volume (purchases and cash advances)	$345,557,150	$270,229,866	$212,048,010	$168,500,964
% change	27.9%	27.4%	25.8%	22.7%
Number of accounts	201,909,561	171,037,749	139,663,944	121,196,967
% change	18.0%	22.5%	15.2%	11.1%
Number of cards	256,744,000	220,558,000	186,568,000	163,798,000
% change	16.4%	18.2%	13.9%	10.4%
Number of member offices	332,843	278,981	249,070	215,584
% change	19.3%	12.0%	15.5%	11.1%
Total outstandings	$119,480,969	$98,616,094	$82,111,652	$68,085,947
% change	21.2%	20.1%	20.6%	17.7%
% of dollars delinquent	5.99%	4.86%	4.59%	4.48%
Net charge-offs as % of payment service volume:				
Credit	1.07%	1.14%	1.21%	1.34%
Fraud	.12%	.10%	.09%	.10%
Total	1.19%	1.24%	1.30%	1.44%

Source: Visa International Statistical Reports, 1990.

of the board of directors. In some cases, the existing banks simply sell a portion of their share holdings to the new member. In other cases, the amount of capital stock is increased to allow the new members to buy in. In 1990, five new banks joined UNICRE. This was the largest addition of bank members since the company's founding. UNICRE voted at that time to double its capital stock to 1 billion escudos. Exhibit 7 lists the member banks and their shares as of January 1991. The newest member bank was Banco Bilbao y Vizcaya (BBV), a Spanish bank that took over the Portuguese operations of Lloyd's Bank in June 1991, which had joined as one of the group of five in 1990. In 1991, two additional banks had applied for membership and were awaiting approval: Banco Fomento Exterior (BFE) and Barclay's Bank (BAR).

Membership in UNICRE was a profitable proposition for the banks. In 1990, 800 million escudos were distributed to the banks before taxes, and 100 million in dividends were paid (a total of approximately $6 million). Both types of distributions were made on the basis of the shares of stock held in the company.

EXHIBIT 6 VISA INTERNATIONAL CARDS IN CIRCULATION (IN MILLIONS) AND PAYMENT SERVICE VOLUME BY REGION (IN MILLIONS OF U.S. DOLLARS), 1987–1990

REGION	1990	1989	1988	1987
United States				
Cards in circulation	135.6	121.9	114.4	106.1
Card volume	$158,100	$134,000	$115,300	$97,400
Travelers checks	3,100	3,000	3,100	2,600
Total	$161,200	$137,000	$118,400	$100,000
Canada				
Cards in circulation	15.2	14.0	13.2	12.0
Card volume	$24,900	$21,800	$18,500	$16,000
Travelers checks	2,400	1,300	1,000	900
Total	$27,300	$23,100	$19,500	$16,900
Europe, Mideast, and Africa				
Cards in circulation	56.0	46.1	36.8	31.3
Card volume	$125,800	$90,900	$62,700	$43,900
Travelers checks	4,300	3,900	3,900	3,200
Total	$130,100	$94,800	$66,600	$47,100
Asia-Pacific				
Cards in circulation	39.2	29.0	15.2	9.5
Card volume	$28,400	$19,000	$13,000	$9,600
Travelers checks	4,300	3,100	2,300	1,700
Total	$32,700	$22,100	$15,300	$11,300
Latin America				
Cards in circulation	10.8	9.6	7.0	4.9
Card volume	$8,300	$4,500	$2,700	$1,400
Travelers checks	400	300	300	300
Total	$8,700	$4,800	$3,000	$1,700
Visa International (total)				
Cards in circulation	265.8	220.6	186.6	163.8
Card volume	$346,000	$270,000	$212,000	$168,000
Travelers checks	13,000	12,000	11,000	9,000
Total	$359,000	$282,000	$223,000	$177,000

Source: Visa International Statistical Reports, 1990.

ORGANIZATION AND MANAGEMENT

In 1991, UNICRE employees were divided into an administrative staff and eight functional divisions. Exhibit 8 contains UNICRE's organization chart. Operations, Data Processing, and Accounting & Finance were the responsibil-

EXHIBIT 7 MEMBER BANK STOCKHOLDERS OF UNICRE, 1991

MEMBER BANK (ABBREVIATION)	YEAR JOINED	LEGAL STATUS	CAPITAL STOCK (000 ESC)
Banco Totta & Acores (BTA)	founder	state owned	90,675
Banco Portugues do Atlantico (BPA)	founder	reprivatized	90,675
Banco Nacional Ultramarino (BNU)	founder	state owned	90,675
Banco Espirito Santo Comercial de Lisboa (BESCL)	founder	reprivatized	90,675
Banco Borges & Irmao (BBI)	founder	state owned	90,675
Banco Fonsecas & Burnay (BFB)	founder	state owned	90,675
Credito Predial Portugues (CPP)	1981	state owned	90,675
União de Bancos Portugues (UBP)	1983	state owned	90,675
Caixa Geral de Depositos (CGD)	1983	state owned*	90,675
Banco Pinto & Sotto Mayor (BPSM)	1984	reprivatized	90,675
Montepio Geral (MG)	1988	state owned	29,250
Banco Comercial Portugues (BCP)	1988	private**	29,250
Banco Internacional do Funchal (BANIF)	1989	state owned	9,750
Banco Comercial dos Acores (BCA)	1990	state owned	5,000
Banco Comercial de Macau (BCM)	1990	state owned	5,000
Banco Comercio de Industria (BCI)	1990	private**	5,000
Credit Lyonnais Portugal (CLP)	1990	private**	5,000
Banco Bilbao y Vizcaya (BBV) (formerly Lloyd's Bank)	1990	private**	5,000

*Exempt from eventual privatization.
**Established as a private bank after 1988 bank reforms.

Source: UNICRE internal document.

ity of director Amadeu Paiva, who was a recent addition to the UNICRE management team. Paiva, 37 years old, was a former executive of Banco Comercial dos Açores (BCA), one of the member bank stockholders of UNICRE. He was a graduate of the Technical University of Lisbon's Higher Institute of Economics and Management, one of the foremost business schools in Portugal. A growing part of Paiva's responsibilities was bank support services, which included UNICRE's assistance to member banks that were setting up and administering their own credit cards through the UNICRE system.

Operations was the largest division in the company, employing eighty-eight employees in four departments: Cardholder and Merchant Services, Foreign Operations, Invoicing (Proof), and Data Gathering (Capture). Managing the division was assistant director Ricardo Pimental, 47. Cardholder and Merchant Services, which employed thirty-four persons, handled requests and answered questions from clients and merchants in the UNICRE network. The department also was responsible for preparing reports from accounting data.

EXHIBIT 8 UNICRE–CARTÃO INTERNATIONAL DE CRÉDITO, S.A. ORGANIZATION CHART, 1991

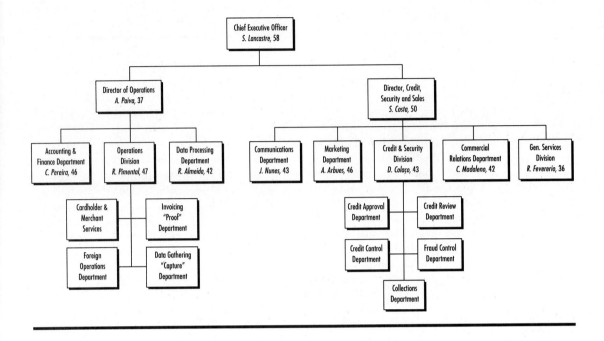

The Foreign Operations Department processed payments to and from foreign credit card operations, which resulted from foreign cards being used in Portugal and UNIBANCO cards being used in other countries.

The Invoicing, or "Proof," Department prepared batches of accounts from drafts received from merchants—the familiar carbon sets prepared by the merchant when a cardholder made a charge. It was also the responsibility of the ten employees in this department to check these drafts for errors and look for duplication of charges. They also looked for the prohibited "splitting" of orders, which merchants sometimes resorted to in an effort to avoid the necessity of calling UNICRE for credit authorization on charges exceeding 12,000 escudos.

The Data Gathering, or "Capture," Department, which employed thirty-four people, was responsible for entering each manually generated transaction into the computer. In 1991, approximately 61% of all credit card charges were still being handled by manual methods, although the number of point-of-sale (POS) transactions (those automatically entered by on-line computers in the store) was increasing each year.

The Foreign Operations Department had the responsibility for preparing and processing invoices for charges made in Portugal with foreign credit cards and processing payments to foreign countries for charges made by UNI-

BANCO cardholders traveling abroad. Ten employees were assigned to the department. The Accounting and Finance Department, which employed twelve, was headed by Costa Pereira, 46. The Data Processing Department, with twenty-eight employees, was headed by Antonio Almeida, 42.

Director Santos Costa had responsibility for the Credit and Security Division, Communications, Marketing, Merchant Relations, and General Services. Costa had more years of experience in the business than any member of the management team besides Lancastre. He was 50 years old and had been with UNICRE since 1974.

The Credit and Security Division, which was headed by Daniel Colaço, 43, was divided into five departments: Credit Approval, Credit Review, Credit Control, Fraud Control, and Collections. The Credit Approval Department, which employed twenty persons, was responsible for handling telephone calls for credit approval from merchants that used the manual system. Operators checked for card validity and the customer's credit limit via computer and issued verbal authorization for the charge. Credit Security also produced a card recovery bulletin for the merchants, which listed invalid card numbers.

The Credit Review Department, which employed four persons, reviewed applications for UNIBANCO card accounts, ran credit checks, and approved new accounts. Credit Control, with eight employees, was responsible for monitoring credit limits, changing the status of card accounts that were in arrears, and canceling cards. The department also handled requests for extension of credit limits. Fraud Control was responsible for preventing and controlling the unauthorized use of UNIBANCO cards. This department had the authority to cancel cards that had been fraudulently used or stolen. The Collections Department sent out letters and made telephone calls to account holders whose payments were in arrears, attempting to get the customer to make the account current. If they were unsuccessful, the accounts were turned over to legal authorities. Nine employees were assigned to the Fraud Department and four to Collections.

Communications and Marketing both were small departments. Communications, with only two employees, was responsible for handling public relations and published a magazine for cardholders that promoted the company's services. Marketing, with four employees, handled advertising and contacted prospective customers for the UNIBANCO gold card.

The Merchant Relations Department handled contacts with all merchants in the UNICRE network. This department was responsible for soliciting new merchants to join the network and for routine tasks such as seeing that merchants were stocked with forms and materials. The thirty-one members of the department were divided into regional groups serving Lisbon, Porto, and The Algarve and a headquarters staff that took care of the rest of the country. Merchant Services was headed up by Carlos Madaleno, 42. The General Services Division was responsible for general office functions, technical services, microfilm, mail, and records. It employed thirty people and was managed by Rui Fevereiro, 36.

According to Paiva, there were features of the organizational plan that sometimes caused confusion. For example, the Operations Division was traditionally considered "back office," but it had some responsibility for dealing directly with cardholders through its cardholder services department. Because the other offices that dealt directly with cardholders were located in the Credit and Security Division, cardholders were sometimes passed from one office to another when they contacted the company about their accounts. In addition, both the granting and the control of credit were vested in the same part of the organization, the Credit and Security Division. Although they were handled by different departments of the division, further separation of these functions could serve to increase credit security.

HUMAN RESOURCES MANAGEMENT

Human resources management at UNICRE was handled informally. Although employee records and payroll services were centralized, recruiting and selection were the responsibility of each department head. As position vacancies occurred, the department heads conducted their own internal and external searches, interviewed applicants, and hired new employees. For positions within the top four management levels, CEO Lancastre approved all promotions and new hires. For most positions, formal written job descriptions were not used, nor were formal training programs in place. As of 1991, UNICRE did not have a formal performance evaluation system for its 300 employees.

Pay and benefits for most administrative and secretarial positions within the company were kept equivalent to similar jobs in the banking industry. For specialized positions, management attempted to keep pay and benefits equal to or above other organizations, but UNICRE had lost a number of key technical employees to other companies. One source of competition for specialized technical skills had been the banks. When some of the banks started their own credit card operations following the 1988 relaxation of controls, they lured away key UNICRE employees with high salary offers.

Although managers at UNICRE were well paid in comparison to those in similar positions at the banks, they normally were given more responsibility and authority at an early age than were their banking counterparts. The growth of UNICRE over the years provided ample opportunity for managerial advancement, and vacancies in most positions had been filled from within the organization. An exception to that policy was the recent addition of Amadeu Paiva as director of operations. Paiva was hired from a member bank of UNICRE, Banco Comercial dos Açores (BCA).

OPERATIONS AND THE TECHNOLOGICAL ENVIRONMENT

For the 61% of all credit card transactions that were still being handled by manual methods, carbon copies of charge slips were the originating documents. These were delivered to UNICRE headquarters after being collected at the banks where they had been deposited by network merchants. At each bank, UNICRE maintained an account through which charges were cleared. When a merchant deposited his or her charge slips, his or her account was credited with the total immediately, and UNICRE's account was debited. This provided a means of eliminating long clearing times for the merchants. As UNICRE officials pointed out, this was a feature that was unique to their network system and could serve as a competitive advantage if a rival processing network ever came into being.

After arriving at the UNICRE operations center, batches of charge slips were cleaned and bunched. Operators then entered the information on the charge slips into the computer. Totals were prepared, by bank, for each day's charges. Because most of these operations were entered manually, they had to be checked often to ensure accuracy. Since the merchant had already been paid, time was money in this part of the business. In 1991, "float time," the length of time between a charge being incurred at the merchant and payment being received by UNICRE, averaged approximately thirty-five days for manual charges.

For charges that entered the system through point-of-sale (POS) computer terminals, all of these operations occurred automatically. The tedious "proof and capture" of each individual transaction by keyboard operators was circumvented, thereby saving many hours of labor and avoiding errors in the process. Another advantage of POS terminals was their ability to provide instantaneous checks for card validity, even on the smallest purchases. UNICRE officials estimated that POS charges averaged twelve to thirteen days less float time in the system than manual charges and this represented a substantial saving in short-term cash flow charges.

UNICRE was, for these reasons, interested in stepping up the adoption of POS equipment in Portugal. The larger merchants had their own POS equipment, which was often connected to bar-code scanning equipment for checkout speed and inventory control. Smaller merchants did not, and because of cost, had no plans for purchasing the equipment. Therefore, in 1990 UNICRE initiated a program of purchasing and installing POS equipment for members of its merchant network at no cost. As of 1991, 4,000 POS terminals had been installed, with another 2,000 slated for installation in 1991 and 1992. Each POS terminal, produced by Bull, Inc. of France, cost UNICRE 90,000 escudos (approximately $600). According to COO Paiva, "The POS terminals are a good investment for us because they reduce processing times substantially in the 'proof and capture' phase of the operation."

In 1991, most POS credit card charges made in large stores were handled through an integrated system run by Portugal's automatic teller machine (ATM) system, MultiBanco. The MultiBanco network, like UNICRE, was owned and operated by a consortium of major banks. The ATM system was linked to POS terminals in major chain stores so that customers could charge purchases directly to their checking account balances by using their ATM cards and entering a four-digit personal identification (PIN). Although it proved to be very efficient for the merchants, the system required that UNICRE's own POS equipment had to be tied into the MultiBanco system and that processing charges be paid to MultiBanco for system maintenance.

THE MERCHANT NETWORK

By virtue of the original noncompetitive agreement among the banks and legal protection until 1988, UNICRE had enjoyed a unique situation with respect to its merchant network. As of 1991, UNICRE still processed all credit card purchases made in the country, including those made with Visa and MasterCard and with T&E cards such as Diner's Club, Carte Blance, and American Express. Although under its virtual monopoly UNICRE could have adopted a "take-it-or-leave-it" attitude in its relationships with members of the network, it chose not do so. UNICRE management realized from the outset that a strong merchant network would be important for success in the credit card business and that for merchants to encourage the use of cards, UNICRE had to provide exceptional service. In addition to supplying all of the paper products needed to record charges, providing arrangements for immediate credit on deposits of card receipts, and purchasing POS terminals, UNICRE also offered direct consultation services to network merchants.

By 1991, growth in the merchant network had, for the previous five years, exceeded overall economic growth in Portugal. Travel and tourism, long an important industry for the country, grew rapidly. This growth in the tourism sector, while increasing overall credit card purchases, also added substantially to the merchant network. New businesses sprang up in tourist areas, and existing businesses adopted credit cards in order to capture more of the tourist trade. Recent growth in disposable incomes in Portugal also provided a major impetus to the expanded use of credit cards and thereby added to the growth of the merchant network. Exhibit 9 shows the number of merchants in the UNICRE network in 1989 and 1990, by merchant type and geographical area. Exhibit 10 lists the value of credit card purchases by merchant type and geographical area for the same two years.

FRAUD CONTROL

Losses from fraudulent use of credit cards, including unauthorized use of cards and charges made with stolen cards, were extremely low in Portugal. The total percentage of fraudulent transactions was just over 0.08% of all transactions in 1990 (see Exhibit 11). This represents a decrease from approximately 0.09% in the previous year. By comparison, Visa International reported fraud rates of approximately 0.12% worldwide.

Recent improvement in UNICRE's fraud rate was credited to the installation of the new POS machines, which afford an instantaneous validity check by on-line computer. According to CEO Lancastre, "Our consistently low rate of fraud is due to the efforts of a conscientious merchant network and also, in part, to the conservative card-issuing policy of UNICRE in the past." Also,

EXHIBIT 9 UNICRE MERCHANT NETWORK—NUMBER OF MERCHANTS BY TYPE AND GEOGRAPHIC AREA

	1990	1989
MERCHANT TYPES		
Hotels	989	895
Restaurants	3,259	2,599
Car rental agencies	425	384
Travel agencies	476	405
Retail stores and shops	12,286	10,324
Services	2,008	1,607
Total	19,443	16,214
GEOGRAPHIC AREA		
Lisbon and suburban area	7,624	6,611
Porto and surbuban area	3,320	2,630
Algarve	2,826	2,405
Northern provinces	1,598	1,261
Central and southern provinces	2,795	2,294
Madeira	826	690
The Azores	454	323
Total	19,443	16,214

Source: UNICRE internal document.

with fewer cards in circulation per capita than in, for example, the U.S., fewer were apt to be mislaid or not reported stolen.

Authentication of credit card validity is the responsibility of the merchant. Before accepting a card, the merchant is required to check the card's number against a list of invalid card numbers in the card recovery bulletin provided by UNICRE on a regular basis to all merchants in the network. On purchases of greater than 12,000 escudos, merchants are required to telephone UNICRE headquarters for specific credit approval. For POS terminal transactions, card validity and credit limits are checked automatically, regardless of the amount of the purchase.

Losses through fraudulent use are borne primarily by the institution that issued the card. If merchants fail to follow the required procedures to authenticate a card's validity, either by neglecting to call UNICRE or by failing to check the card recovery bulletin, they may also be liable for fraudulent charges.

FINANCIAL PERFORMANCE

UNICRE's growth rate over the period 1987 to 1990 was exceptional. Total volume of charges processed more than tripled during that time, and the number of UNIBANCO cards rose by nearly 50%. The merchant network, which

EXHIBIT 10 UNICRE MERCHANT NETWORK—VALUE OF TRANSACTIONS BY MERCHANT TYPE AND GEOGRAPHIC AREA (IN MILLIONS OF ESCUDOS)

	1990	1989
MERCHANT TYPE		
Hotels	26,659	20,932
Restaurants	21,195	13,424
Car rental agencies	4,575	3,722
Travel agencies	5,558	3,100
Retail stores and shops	48,335	27,894
Services	16,037	8,985
Total	122,359	78,057
GEOGRAPHIC AREA		
Lisbon and suburban area	70,488	43,875
Porto and suburban area	16,634	9,416
Algarve	17,917	13,582
Northern provinces	3,754	2,235
Central and southern provinces	7,587	4,711
Madeira	4,894	3,616
The Azores	1,085	622
Total	122,359	78,057

Note: Figures are not adjusted for inflation. The inflation rate in Portugal was 13.5% in 1990 and 11.8% in 1989.

Source: UNICRE internal document.

EXHIBIT 11 FRAUDULENT BANK CREDIT CARD TRANSACTIONS IN PORTUGAL, 1990

CARD TYPE	NUMBER OF TRANSACTIONS	VALUE (000 ESC.)	UNICRE LOSS (000 ESC.)
UNIBANCO Visa card	996	20,694	8,965
Other Portuguese bank cards	865	26,279	520
Foreign cards:			
Visa	3,401	40,917	1,393
MasterCard	2,761	35,549	1,258
Travel & entertainment cards	108	1,825	8
Total	8,131	125,264	12,144

Source: UNICRE internal document.

UNICRE officials feel is the key to expanded volume, also grew rapidly. Net income also rose over the period, even after increases were made in the levels of distributions to stockholders and of dividends.

UNICRE AND THE FUTURE

MARKET EXPANSION

The Portuguese economy is expected to continue to grow rapidly throughout the 1990s. UNICRE officials expect credit expansion to keep pace with this growth. According to COO Paiva, "The credit granting policies of the banks will probably be relaxed, and competition over rates and annual fees will be likely." In 1991, credit sales as a proportion of total retail sales were still quite low. UNICRE officials looked for lower inflation and interest rates to spur credit sales in Portugal and to encourage more cardholders to use their credit cards for large purchases.

MERCHANT NETWORK RELATIONS

In summer 1991, a debate was going on in the European Community over the types of merchant network arrangements that would be permitted under economic consolidation. "American-style" systems of payment, such as that employed by UNICRE, were the norm. In these, banks owned the system, took risks against nonpayment of accounts, and made profits, while merchant discounts provided the revenues. Other arrangements, such as merchant-controlled networks ("European" systems) were favored in a few countries. In Great Britain, there was a movement pushing for abolishing merchant discounts entirely. The contention was that, since the banks profited from the system, they should bear all of the costs. According to UNICRE officials, some accommodation might have to be made eventually, especially if the tide in EC regulatory bodies turned toward merchant-based systems. One alternative mentioned was the adoption of a system like that of Finland, where the country's single network was owned by a cooperative association of both merchants and banks.

Of more immediate concern to UNICRE's management was the increased militancy among Portuguese merchants. In a meeting held in July 1991, the Confederation of Independent Merchants declared that UNICRE's sliding scale of merchant discounts based on volume was discriminatory and demanded that it be replaced by a single discount rate for all. Contributing to this upsurge in merchant militancy was the rapid growth of large "hypermarket" chain stores throughout the country. Government agencies estimated that the hypermarkets, most of which were owned and controlled by foreign interests, would eventually displace up to 45,000 small merchants. Because of their large volumes, hypermarkets qualified for UNICRE's lowest discount rate of 2%. Countering the merchants' demands, UNICRE officials pointed out that there were increased costs associated with serving small accounts, most of whom still used manual charge forms, and thus higher discount rates were justified. Here, as in the debate over the EC network options, UNICRE management anticipated that some accommodation might have to be made eventually.

Following the 1988 reforms, UNICRE no longer enjoyed immunity from competition for its merchant network, which generated, through merchant discount payments, the majority of the company's revenues. The probability of a bank or group of banks starting a rival network, however, was considered to be remote at best. Potential returns for a second network in a country the size of Portugal would probably be quite low, especially in what could be expected to be a long start-up period. Besides, under the agreements that were in force in 1991, banks that had their own independent credit cards already received 80% of the merchant discounts generated with those cards through rebates from UNICRE. Moreover, must of UNICRE's profits were being returned to the banks. Thus, there was little incentive to justify the huge fixed cost investment required for a new merchant network.

Despite these seemingly poor potential returns, however, one company, American Express, which ran its own networks in other European countries, was considering the establishment of a separate network in Portugal. Total charges by American Express cardholders in Portugal were approximately 200 million escudos annually ($1.35 million).

CURRENCY CONSOLIDATION IN THE EUROPEAN COMMUNITY

One component of the income on foreign card sales is exchange revenues. For example, when an English tourist uses a Visa card in Portugal, UNICRE charges the cardholder's issuing company for the purchase in British pounds Sterling. By "bunching" all charges involving British cards in a single payment through Visa International, UNICRE receives very favorable exchange rate treatment, as do all members of the Visa network in similar cases.

The first steps toward currency consolidation in the European Community were being taken in 1991. Although the problems of consolidating the twelve currencies were considerable, EC officials hoped to have a single monetary system by the year 2000. When Europe goes to a single currency, the exchange rate revenues described above will disappear on all international purchases within the EC, and UNICRE will lose this source of revenue.

STOCKHOLDER RELATIONS

Since 1975, UNICRE has been, essentially, the subsidiary of a group of national banks. As privatization of the country's major banks began in 1991, UNICRE suddenly became the subsidiary of a mixture of private and public institutions. As could be expected, the orientation of its privatized stockholders is very different from that of its public bank members, and the managers of the privates, under pressure from their own stockholders to show profits, began to question a number of the company's policies.

A dispute over the handling of UNICRE's expansion and the distribution of earnings to stockholders was beginning to surface in mid-1991, which, in the opinion of some UNICRE managers, could eventually require the company to rethink its membership and capital structure. Membership expansion of UNICRE had been handled in two ways in the past—through adjusting existing members' shares or by increasing total capitalization. In either case, the shares and, inevitably, the earnings of existing members were diluted. Prior to 1991, when all of the banks were state owned, earnings dilution posed few problems since bank performance was not evaluated in profit-and-loss terms. With privatization pending for most of the larger banks, they had begun to question the process, since their UNICRE earnings distributions were adversely affected every time a new member was admitted. Private banks favored a change that would recognize the potential earnings being acquired by the new members and, conversely, earnings lost by existing members. UNICRE management felt that an open-market exchange of shares was not the answer, however, since that would make capital expansion more difficult.

A few of the members also had begun to question the policy of distributing earnings to member banks solely on the basis of their shares. They pointed out that some banks, primarily those that had large numbers of active cards in circulation and serviced large numbers of merchant accounts, actually contributed much more to the earnings of UNICRE than did some of the others. Caixa Geral de Depositos (the state savings bank), for instance, was one of the largest members but originated little of that type of income-generating activity. The banks that were questioning the policy pointed out that this policy might make sense for dividend distribution, but before-tax distributions, which had been 800 million escudos in 1990 ($5.3 million), should be made on some more equitable basis.

DEFINING THE BUSINESS

According to CEO Lancastre,

> We are not in one business, but four. First, there is the business of representing international credit card associations in Portugal. Second, there is the business of operating the country's merchant network and processing credit card charges. Third is the business of granting credit, issuing Visa cards under the UNIBANCO name, and collecting payments from customers. The fourth business is offering services to our member banks.

Prior to the financial reforms that were instituted beginning in 1988, UNICRE enjoyed protection under the law from competition in the first three of these business. The fourth business did not exist before the reform, but arose as a response to the new situation. In the context of the changes that were going on in Portugal and throughout Europe in 1991, each of the four businesses was being redefined.

Concerning the first of these four, UNICRE was no longer the sole representative of international credit card operations in Portugal. Three of its own bank members had recently become principal members of Visa International in order to issue their own independent cards, and one other was making preparations to join MasterCard/Eurocard. Other independent relationships were expected to develop under deregulation.

UNICRE's second business was, in most respects, its most profitable. Any threat to its dominance in the merchant business would have to be taken very seriously. According to COO Paiva, the merchant network seemed safe at least for the next five years. If the economy continued to grow, increased economies of scale might favor a new entry at some point. Even if that happened, Paiva felt that UNICRE could compete very effectively on the basis of service to merchants. A greater threat was the possible loss of revenues if a European-style payment system was forced on the company under EC consolidation or if the small merchants' demand for a single rate on discounts was enacted into law.

UNICRE's own credit card business was still strong. The company had the number-one credit card in the country, its UNIBANCO card. Competition for new credit card customers was increasing among all card-issuing institutions, however, including UNICRE's own member banks. UNICRE planned to continue to promote both its regular and gold cards in their respective target markets. Another strategy was to encourage banks to offer the UNIBANCO card as a second card, along with their own cards. Despite the inevitability of increasing competition in the market, UNICRE officials remained optimistic about the future of the UNIBANCO card. The possibility remained, however, that at some point UNICRE's stockholders could insist that it phase out its credit card business.

The fourth and newest business, banking services, was still in its infancy. The present focus of assisting members in starting and managing their own credit card operations was seen by some, including Paiva, as only a beginning. With its expertise in data processing and POS technology, its credibility and respect among members of the merchant community, and its contacts with a wide range of international organizations, UNICRE had a wealth of opportunities that could be exploited within the bank services industry. A strategic decision to push this business had not been made by 1991, however. To do so would first require the approval of its member stockholder banks and then increased investments for developing the organizational framework to emphasize that side of the business.

Overall, the company's businesses were undergoing very fundamental changes as new competitive forces were brought to bear on this previously protected industry. There was a feeling of optimism in the company about its chances of prospering in the new climate and an eagerness to take on the new challenges. As CEO Lancastre stated, "Now we must compete with our own shareholders, but there is room enough for all."

APPENDIX A

A Profile of Portugal

OFFICIAL NAME: REPUBLIC OF PORTUGAL

GEOGRAPHY

Area: 94,276 sq. km. (36,390 sq. mi), including the Azores and Madeira Islands; about the size of Indiana. **Cities:** *Capital*—Lisbon (pop. 2.1 million in the metropolitan district). *Other city*—Oporto (1.7 million in metropolitan district). **Terrain:** Mountainous in the north; rolling in central south. **Climate:** Maritime temperate.

PEOPLE

Nationality: *Noun and adjective*—Portuguese (sing. and pl.). **Population** (1989): 10.3 million. **Annual growth rate** (1989): 3%. **Ethnic groups:** Homogeneous Mediterranean stock with small black African minority. **Religion:** Roman Catholic 97%. **Language:** Portuguese. **Education:** *Years compulsory*—6. *Attendance*—60% Literacy (1985)—83.3%. **Health:** *Infant mortality rate* (1987)—14.2/1,000. *Life expectancy* (1985)—73 yrs. **Work force** (4.7 million, 1989): *Agriculture*—19%. *Industry*—35%. *Government, commerce, and services*—46%.

GOVERNMENT

Type: Parliamentary democracy. **Constitution:** Entered into effect April 25, 1976; revised October 30, 1982, and June 1, 1989.
Branches: *Executive*—president (chief of state), Council of State (presidential advisory body), prime minister (head of government), Council of Ministers. *Legislative*—unicameral Assembly of the Republic (between 230 and 235

Source: Background Notes, Portugal. United States Department of State, Bureau of Public Affairs. May, 1990.

deputies). *Judicial*—Supreme Court, district courts, appeals courts, Constitutional Tribunal.

Major political parties: Social Democratic Party (PSD), Socialist Party (PS), Portuguese Communist Party (PCP), Center Social Democratic Party (CDS), Democratic Renewal Party (PRD), Popular Monarchist Party (PPM). **Suffrage:** Universal over 18.

Subdivisions: 18 districts, 2 autonomous regions, and 1 dependency.

Central government budget (1990): $23.2 billion (expenditures).

Defense (1990): 2.2% of GDP.

Flag: A vertically divided field—one-third green along the staff, two-thirds red; centered on the dividing line is the Portuguese coat of arms encircled in gold.

ECONOMY

GDP (1989): $45 billion. **Annual growth rate** (1989): 5.4% **Per capita GDP** (1989): $4,363. **Avg. inflation rate** (1989): 12.6%.

Natural resources: Fish, cork, tungsten, iron, copper, tin, and uranium ores.

Production (percentages of 1988 total gross value added): Agriculture, forestry, fisheries (7%).

Industry (44% of GDP): *Types*—textiles, clothing, footwear (9%); construction (7%); food, beverages, tobacco (6%).

Services (49%): *Main branches*—commerce (20%), government and non-marketable services (15%), housing and other marketable services (10%), banking and finance (8%).

Trade (1989): *Exports*—$12.7 billion: clothing, footware, electrical machinery and appliances, automobiles. *Imports*—$18.9 billion: electrical and nonelectrical machinery, automobiles, fuel, appliances. *Partners*—European Community, US, European Free Trade Association (EFTA).

Official exchange rate (May 1990): 149 escudos = US$1.

MEMBERSHIP IN INTERNATIONAL ORGANIZATIONS

UN and its specialized agencies, Council of Europe, North Atlantic Treaty Organization (NATO), European Community (EC), Western European Union (WEU), Organization for Economic Cooperation and Development (OECD), International Energy Agency (IEA), INTELSAT, African Development Bank (ADB), African Development Fund (ADF), Coordinating Committee for Multi-Lateral Export Controls (COCOM).

CASE 19

YEAST WEST BAKERY

CORAL R. SNODGRASS
AND GERALD S.
ROSENFELDER

While talking in the quiet back booth in a dimly lit local cafe one day in the summer of 1989, Josh Ingram was asked why her bakery was in business. She thought about it for just a moment and then stated with simple sincerity, "To make a good loaf of bread." Josh is one of four collective owners (hereafter referred to as "the members") of a whole grain bakery, called the Yeast West Bakery, located in the previously run-down and recently fashionable Elmwood section of downtown Buffalo, NY.

The Yeast West Bakery (YWB) was started in 1976 to make both a political statement and a good loaf of bread while providing an environment in which people who were uncomfortable in a traditional corporate structure could earn a decent living. Through the years, it had enjoyed a fair amount of success on all counts and had endured some minor structural changes. Today, the members of the bakery are at a crossroads. Growing awareness of the dangers of environmental pollution and a growing concern with health issues have made the pure products of YWB very popular with a wide spectrum of consumers. The bakery is now faced with the possibility of substantial growth. However, the very concept of such growth may pose a challenge to the members' fundamental values for a cooperative, flexible workplace. In addition, the value system of the members is such that they have generally used excess profits to improve the benefits for their workers, not to support growth. Although the collective members do not believe a decision must be made immediately, there is a sense that the bakery is "riding the crest" of society's new concern for the environment, and the members need to define for themselves how they want to be a part of this.

Source: This case was prepared by the authors as a basis for classroom discussion and not to illustrate either effective or ineffective handling of managerial situations. © 1990, Coral R. Snodgrass.

FOUNDING: PREDECESSORS TO YWB

After two false starts, YWB was incorporated in January 1977. The bakery was a part of the dreams of a number of people in the Buffalo area who wanted to start a cooperative network. The network started with three storefront food co-ops and a vegetarian restaurant called the Greenfield Street Restaurant. The hopes were to expand the network to include a car mechanic co-op and a recycling co-op. When the food co-ops first started, they obtained all their natural baked goods from a bakery in Rochester, NY (about 50 miles away). However, members of the co-op community in Buffalo wanted to create more jobs, so they started their own bakery. The Maya Bakery was really a group of individuals who worked all through the night in the Greenfield Street Restaurant baking goods for the food co-ops. They were able to develop some good recipes, and they did make money. However, the people who worked at the Maya Bakery all had other full-time jobs and did not get paid to work at the bakery. In addition, no one wanted to apply for the required permits to do business. Consequently, the Maya Bakery closed, but the people involved left $800 in a bank account for anyone who wanted to try again.

A second group of people became interested in starting a bakery with the money left over from Maya. They planned to open on Fillmore Avenue in Buffalo and called themselves the "Fillmore Yeast." However, the rental deal for the building fell through, and the landlord confiscated their deposit money and their equipment, leaving them with nothing. The local co-op community of Buffalo threw a benefit and raised $500. With that money the group purchased a large, old oven, moved to the west side of town, changed the name to Yeast West, and started supplying the co-ops with baked goods.

EARLY DEVELOPMENT OF YWB

When YWB opened, the co-ops were the main outlets, accounting for 98% of sales. The bakery sold to a few health food stores, as well. At that time YWB consciously did not sell to supermarkets. To the members, such markets were the embodiment of a corrupt food system that exploited the relationships between the consumer, the employee, and the environment. It was precisely from such a system that YWB wanted to break away. The members' values were for a cooperative, interactive relationship that integrated quality supplies, participative decision making, concern for the environment, and the provision of pure foods at a reasonable price. The product line at that time was fairly simple. It consisted mainly of organic whole wheat bread with some cookies, muffins, and specialty items.

The ideals of the collective members of the bakery were the foundation of the organization's structures and systems and its relationship with the environment. The bakery started with six members who shared equally in the tasks, decisions, and responsibilities of the business. The goal was to establish a workplace based on mutual respect. The members wanted to provide good, affordable food and satisfying jobs. At first they paid themselves $25 per week, an amount they believed to be enough to live on given the supportive infrastructure of the co-op community, which provided inexpensive food and housing.

From the beginning, operations at YWB were informal, and everything was done as simply as possible. The dough was kneaded by hand, the food was packaged in simple wrappers, and deliveries were made from the back of a station wagon. The members never budgeted for advertising; they relied on word-of-mouth advertising with the co-ops. It was true that economics dictated that YWB not spend lavishly, but it was also true that the members' value systems would have called for such simplicity in any event. Their values for the bakery and its product line were part of the "politics of food." As a political statement, they wanted to make nutritional food with as few chemicals and pollutants as possible. Furthermore, they would not engage in behaviors that they believed to be inappropriate—advertising and merchandising, for example. The members kneaded the dough by hand not just because a dough mixer was expensive but because kneading by hand gave them a spiritual connection with their products.

TRANSITION FROM THE IDEAL TO THE REAL

The value system of the members of YWB established an ideal state. In this state, there is a consistent supply of organic goods at a reasonable price; all workers are fully participating owners who are both financially and emotionally invested in the bakery; the process of baking is an intimate, personal experience in which the individual is not alienated from the end product, and customers are provided with a product that not only tastes good but is good for them. However, such a value system often comes into conflict with the realities of doing business. Whenever a conflict has arisen, the members have responded by doing whatever is necessary to keep going without straying too far from their ideal state. (See Appendix A for the bakery's bylaws.)

Almost from the beginning, the members have understood the need to be flexible in order to ensure the survival of the bakery. For example, very early on they had problems with the consistency of both the quality and the quantity of the supply of the organic flour. In addition to the problem of a consistent supply is the problem of cost: Organic flour is very expensive. Consequently, even though YWB was never 100% organic, the members switched to 100% nonorganic flour. As members have dealt with these problems; they have modified their product line. They have now established a product line that is about half organic and half nonorganic. However, they use only whole grain flour.

The structure of six people (three female and three male) working together informally and equally also underwent some changes. The composition of the collective changed as individuals came and went. There have been twenty owners over the bakery's history. Leaving was voluntary in all but two cases. Two collective members were fired (the by-laws explain the process for "firing" an owner). The firing was not done lightly. The other members even appealed to an outside mediator in one case. But, in the final analysis, the firings were determined to be in the best interests of the bakery.

Since 1985 the bakery has hired nonmember employees who work at the bakery but do not have any ownership rights. This is not because the members do not want more members of the collective; in fact, they would like more. However, they require a steady, reliable work force, and a number of good people were happy to work for them without the responsibilities of ownership. The decision to have employees was a difficult one for the collective members to make, but they were happy to be able to provide good jobs to good people. At present there are four collective members, six employees, and a computer analyst. Of the four members, three have been there five years and one has been there eleven years.

THE PRESENT

PRODUCT LINE

The bakery has undergone many changes, most of which have been positive. The members have settled on a product line that is about half organic and half nonorganic. Although the goal is to be 100% organic, the costs are just too high to allow for a reasonable market price. In order to cover such costs, prices would have to be much higher than they already are. The product line has expanded to include approximately forty-seven different items, although eight products account for 75% of sales volume by dollars (see Exhibit 1). The staple of the product line is and always has been whole wheat bread, which constitutes 20% of sales volume. This bread is made with nonorganic flour. Another 6% of sales comes from organic whole wheat bread.

Changes to the product line come from experimentation at the bakery, recipes acquired through a nationwide cooperative network, and suggestions from customers. YWB produces a selection of products that are free of eggs, dairy products, salt, yeast, and wheat (see Exhibit 2). Any changes to the prod-

EXHIBIT 1 YEAST WEST BAKERY'S TOP EIGHT PRODUCTS BY DOLLARS OF SALES VOLUME

PRODUCT NAME	% OF SALES DOLLARS
Whole wheat bread	20%
Oatmeal raisin cookies	12
Three seed bread	11
Oat bran muffins	8
Granola	7
Organic whole wheat bread	6
Oat sunflower cookies	6
Bran muffins	4

EXHIBIT 2   CONTENTS OF YEAST WEST BAKERY PRODUCTS

BREADS
Whole wheat
Oatmeal bread[a]
Three seed[a]
Totally rye[a]
Pumpernickel[a]
Essene[a c]
Irish soda[a]
Organic whole wheat[a]
Lemon-sesame-date[a]
Salt-free[d]
Swedish rye
Cinnamon with raisins
Sourdough whole wheat[a c]

All breads are eggless and dairyless except for the salt-free and Irish soda breads.

[a]Made with organic flour
[b]Wheat free
[c]No yeast
[d]No added salt
[e]Eggless
[f]Dairyless

COOKIES
Oatmeal-raisin[e f]
Mint-carob chip[a d e]
Oat-sunflower[d e f]
Applesauce[d e f]
Macaroons[d]
Ginger
Auntie-Nuke
  (oatmeal Tollhouse)[a d e]

OTHER
Gingerbread[a f]
Carrot cake [a f]
Pizza[e]
Granola[b d e f]
Assorted muffins
Date-nut bread[a f]
Rebel bran muffins[a e f]
Halvah[b e]
Cinnamon swirls[a]
Veggie swirls[a]
Wheatless waffle mix[b]

uct line must fit into the members' value system, which is not always easy. For example, in 1989 there was a great deal of national media attention (some might call it hype) given to oat bran because of studies showing the beneficial effects of oat bran on cholesterol levels. Consequently, a great demand developed for oat bran in various forms. Because of the bakery's production flexibility and the fact that members already had been doing some experimentation, YWB was in a position to begin production of oat bran muffins very quickly. Such an opportunity might seem to be a marketer's dream—a product that has been shown to be healthful, is in demand, and could quickly be brought into production. Why shouldn't the bakery launch into production and take advantage of the trend? But the members of YWB were concerned that introducing oat bran muffins might be exploiting a media event. They took the time to explore the ramifications of their decisions and to determine the appropriateness of their actions. As it turns out, YWB did begin production of oat bran muffins, but only after the members were sure that the decision was in congruence with their value system. They produced oat bran muffins because one of their values is to be especially responsive to the dietary needs of their customers.

CUSTOMER BASE AND PRODUCT DEMAND

The customer base of YWB has grown over the years and covers a wide variety of people who are attracted to the bakery for a number of reasons. Some customers have allergies or other health problems and are seeking foods that will not harm them. Some are athletes who are seeking high-carbohydrate, sugar-free, no cholesterol foods. Some are senior citizens who are concerned about their health, and many of the customers are students. Some customers are "food political," such as some vegetarians, and some come for the "fad" value. The members of the bakery do not have a profile of their "typical customer" except to say that this customer is a health conscious, "mainstream" person who wants a healthful product and is willing to pay for it.

YWB products typically cost 50% more than similar supermarket foods (see Exhibit 3). For instance, four oat bran muffins from YWB cost $1.89. A package of six store-brand muffins (complete with chemicals and preservatives) costs $1.69. The two packages sit side by side on the shelf, and customers buy out the YWB goods daily. In April 1989, after increased costs prompted YWB to raise prices as much as 50% on some products, there was no immediate decrease in demand. The demand and the customer base appear to be not only sustainable but capable of growth. And even though the products are considerably more expensive than the supermarket brands, they compare quite favorably with premium national brands, especially when the contents are considered (see Exhibit 4). In addition, YWB compares favorably with

EXHIBIT 3 SELECTED COMPARATIVE PRICE LIST, 1990

PRODUCT	SUPERMARKET BRAND RETAIL	YWB RETAIL
Bran muffins	$1.69/6	$1.55/4
Oat bran muffins	$1.69/6	$1.89/4
Whole wheat bread	$0.59	$1.39
Oatmeal raisin cookies	$1.69/12	$0.90/2
Salt-free bread	$1.39 (low sodium)	$1.95
Swedish rye bread	$0.79	$1.50
Cinnamon swirls	$1.19/8	$1.50/2
Ginger cookies	$1.79/6	$0.70/2
Cinnamon raisin bread	$0.99	$1.55
Applesauce cookies	$1.69/12	$0.80/2
Pumpernickel bread	$0.99	$1.55
Sourdough bread	$0.79	$1.65
Chocolate chip cookies	$1.69/12	$.90/2
Fruitcake	$3.99	$5.50
Pecan pie	$2.69	$8.30
Pumpkin pie	$2.39	$8.30
Whole wheat rolls	$1.49/12	$1.65/6

EXHIBIT 4   COMPARISON OF SELECT PRODUCTS BY CONTENT, SIZE, AND PRICE.

PRODUCT	CONTENTS	WEIGHT	PRICE
WHOLE WHEAT BREAD			
YWB	whole wheat flour, water, raw honey, pure safflower oil, salt, yeast	1 lb., 2 oz.	$1.39
Pepperidge Farm	whole wheat flour, water, nonfat milk, unsulphured molasses, partially hydrogenated soybean oil, corn syrup, wheat gluten, yeast, salt, butter, calcium propionate, honey, mono- and diglycerides, soy lecithin	1 lb.	$1.55
OATMEAL RAISIN COOKIES			
YWB	rolled oats, whole wheat flour, honey, raisins, pure safflower oil, molasses, water, flax seed, vanilla, almond extract, salt, baking soda	4 oz.	$.90
Entenmann's	sugar, flour, rolled oats, nonfat milk, raisins, molasses, egg whites, baking powder, maltodextrin, salt, natural flavors, oat fiber, dextrose, spice, lecithin, xanthan gum, polysorbate 60, guar gum, artificial color	12 oz.	$2.49
OAT BRAN MUFFINS			
YWB	oat bran, oats, organic whole wheat flour, honey, wheat bran, raisins, safflower oil, poppy seeds, baking powder, vanilla, salt, spices	9 oz.	$1.89
Sara Lee	oat bran, egg whites, sugar, corn syrup, enriched flour, raisins, partially hydrogenated soybean and/or cottonseed oils, apples, vegetable fiber, baking powder, pyrophosphate, baking soda, corn starch, monocalcium phosphate, vanilla, lemon juice, salt, egg white solids, lecithin, oranges, spices, xanthan gum	10 oz.	$1.99

other bakeries. For example, YWB produces both a pecan and a pumpkin pie, each selling for $8.30. Two other local bakeries also make pecan and pumpkin pies and also claim to use pure ingredients. One bakery charges $9.50 for the pecan pie and $7.50 for the pumpkin pie. The other bakery charges $8.95 for a large pie and $6.95 for a small pie.

There is no doubt that the product line the bakery offers is quite popular. The bakery has seen constant increases in sales even though the members do not advertise and do no marketing (see Exhibits 5 and 6). One of the reasons the bakery has seen no decline in demand is the fact that it has no direct competition. Few bakeries offer organic products. Nonorganic bakeries that use processed sugar and flour are not perceived as direct competition. The customer who buys from YWB is not looking for just any loaf of bread. The niche that YWB enjoys in the market is not a particularly profitable one. In addition, at the present scale of operations, the existing cost structure is not expected to change. Consequently, new competitors are not expected to move in.

DISTRIBUTION CHANNELS

As the customer base has been growing steadily, the distribution channels have been changing. Whereas the co-ops used to be the main outlets, now they account for only 26% of sales. The other 75% comes from supermarkets and convenience stores. Very little retail business is done at the bakery itself. YWB now has forty-three outlets. However, five stores account for 32% of sales, and two food co-ops account for another 26% (see Exhibit 7).

The supermarkets and convenience stores initially approached the bakery for its products. These stores all are located in the central and northern districts of Buffalo. The growing and prosperous South Towns of Buffalo represent a market YWB has not even begun to serve. The members believe they could sell more products if they had them to sell.

IMPACT OF SUPERMARKET SALES

The change to the supermarkets and convenience stores prompted some changes at the bakery in terms of both personnel and the development of new recipes. The change in personnel came about because of the way large stores do business. Such stores pay by check and pay on longer time schedules. Consequently, the bakery had to have a way to keep good records. In addition, the bakery needed to have some control over its finances. All of the financial decisions are made by the collective members together, but the increases in sales have made control of the relevant financial data more difficult. Consequently, the members purchased a personal computer and hired a computer analyst to computerize their financial statements.

The shift to the supermarkets also forced the bakery to formalize its product line. Because supermarkets have their own product lines and prices computerized, they require a stable supply of products. They also require at least

EXHIBIT 5   YEAST WEST BAKERY INCOME STATEMENT, 1977-1982

	1977	1978	1979	1980	1981	1982
SALES						
wholesale	43,771	47,794	69,811	92,819	96,675	105,717
retail	2,304	2,515	3,916	2,678	4,950	3,968
other						1,431
Total Sales	46,075	50,309	73,727	95,497	101,625	111,116
average/week	886	967	1,418	1,836	1,954	2,137
− COST OF GOODS SOLD						
food	15,984	18,984	25,796	34,887	38,048	36,995
packaging	1,058	1,256	1,500	3,649	3,749	4,422
other						
Cost of Goods Sold	17,042	20,240	27,296	38,536	41,797	41,417
= GROSS OPERATING INCOME	29,033	30,069	46,431	56,961	59,828	69,699
Other Income	13	0	212	0	75	308
GROSS INCOME	29,046	30,069	46,643	56,961	59,903	70,007
− EXPENSES						
Net Salary	11,213	18,011	24,926	24,247	28,524	33,065
Fed & FICA witholding	931	1,065	1,892	4,958	6,611	7,070
EMPLOYEE BENEFITS	1,517	2,559	3,539	4,498	6,640	9,218
UTILITIES	717	1,410	2,900	3,804	3,395	3,870
EQUIPMENT						
truck repairs	905	905	793	269	772	970
insurance	479	779	1,051	2,066	1,327	1,959
tickets	85	44	97	86	71	101
gas & tolls	300	312	375	600	1,014	845
interest	0	32	482	468	290	
depreciation	360	1,182	1,800	2,194	1,796	1,083
repairs, other equip.	214	163	77	364	1,553	942
OTHER EXPENSES						
rent	1,958	2,090	2,310	3,010	3,557	5,550
total tax	45	250	250	468	0	1,464
advertising	356	48	0	35	395	194
miscellaneous	5,615	2,115	3,475	4,056	2,685	4,507
TOTAL EXPENSES	24,695	30,965	43,968	51,123	58,630	70,838
= NET INCOME	4,351	−896	2,675	5,838	1,273	−831

NOTE: TOTAL SALES − COST OF GOODS SOLD = GROSS OPERATING INCOME
GROSS OPERATING INCOME + OTHER INCOME − EXPENSES = NET INCOME

three weeks to put a new product into their computer. Once it is in there, they do not want to have to change it. They also require UPC bar codes. The stabilization of the product line has not been a welcomed change for the bakery because it has limited the amount of experimentation the members can

EXHIBIT 6 YEAST WEST BAKERY INCOME STATEMENT, 1983–1987

	1983	1984	1985	1986	1987
SALES					
wholesale	107,241	124,454	130,001	133,711	155,591
retail	2,642	2,953	3,098	2,676	3,302
farmer's market	2,217	3,311	3,619	4,287	2,116
merchandise			253	0	0
other					
Total Sales	112,100	130,718	136,971	140,674	161,009
average/week	2,156	2,514	2,634	2,705	3,096
− COST OF GOODS SOLD					
food	38,048	49,765	48,545	53,488	61,105
packaging	3,108	6,662	4,916	4,886	6,425
merchandise			125	0	0
Cost of Goods Sold	41,156	56,427	53,586	58,374	67,530
= GROSS OPERATING INCOME	70,944	74,291	83,385	82,300	93,479
+ OTHER INCOME					
dividends					
interest	197	69	161	247	84
sublet rents	275		501	225	225
other		750		456	
Other Income	472	819	662	928	309
GROSS INCOME	71,416	75,110	80,047	83,228	93,788
− EXPENSES					
TOTAL WAGES	42,838	41,613	48,577	47,703	57,537
net salary	X35,771	X34,511	X41,162	X39,371	X46,141
Fed & FICA witholding	X6,387	X6,055	X6,447	X6,700	X7,697
NYS witholding	X681	X1,047	X969	X871	X939
IRA, Life Ins. etc				X761	X613
EMPLOYEE BENEFITS					
FICA-Employer	2,737	2,913	3,408	3,421	3,959
NYS unemployment	1,976	1,528	1,363	1,023	596
Fed unemployment	329	390	353	341	340
health insurance	2,374	2,093	1,760	1,667	2,014
disability insurance	296	360	384	272	546
worker's compensation	2,534	1,737	2,786	3,353	2,681
UTILITIES	4,642	4,084			
gas			2,491	2,303	2,025
electric			1,519	1,408	1,866
NY telephone			810	699	620
US Sprint				150	35
other					

EXHIBIT 6 (Continued)

	1983	1984	1985	1986	1987
EQUIPMENT					
truck expenses	X4,116	X4,136	X6,849	55	25
truck repairs	1,777	2,222	3,487	1,253	668
insurance	1,371	1,390	1,675	1,792	1,347
tickets	147	139	42	125	105
gas & tolls	821	1,775	1,645	1,019	1,268
interest		58		203	710
depreciation	868	609	350	2,680	3,959
repairs–other equipment	90	564	196	402	602
OTHER EXPENSES					
rent	5,526	5,793	6,060	6,140	6,540
NYS franchise tax	250	250	315	342	250
NYS sales tax		27	3	0	
federal income tax	0	0	0	0	
contributions	399	549	320	351	222
advertising	0		25	0	35
professional services	150		468	115	50
cugea expenses	100	134	145	69	0
licenses & fees	285	202	169	384	614
liability insurance	249	347	304	360	852
petty cash				417	
linen	797	673	885	822	873
misc. supplies	3,574	714	1,629	1,202	1,454
TOTAL EXPENSES	74,130	70,164	81,169	80,071	91,793
= NET INCOME	−2,714	4,946	2,878	3,157	1,995

NOTE: TOTAL SALES − COST OF GOODS SOLD = GROSS OPERATING INCOME
GROSS OPERATING INCOME + OTHER INCOME − EXPENSES = NET INCOME
X BEFORE A NUMBER INDICATES THAT THE NUMBER IS NOT COUNTED IN TOTALS

EXHIBIT 7 YEAST WEST BAKERY'S TOP SEVEN RETAIL OUTLETS BY DOLLAR OF SALES VOLUME

STORE NUMBER	PERCENTAGE
Lexington Avenue Co-op	16%
North Buffalo Co-op	10
81—Wegmans on Alberta	8
516—Bells on Elmwood	7
229–Tops on Delaware	7
83—Wegmans on Sheridan	6
42—Tops at University Plaza	4

do. Furthermore, the products they do develop must be more carefully chosen. The members still do some experimentation and use the co-ops as outlets for the new products. In addition, the national co-op network holds summer conferences where recipes are exchanged. But in many ways the change to using the supermarkets has heavily constrained the members' freedom to experiment.

OPERATIONS

There have also been changes at the bakery in terms of machinery. Although the members felt very strongly that they did not want to become alienated from their products, they recognized that some things had to become mechanized. Kneading the dough by hand is difficult and exhausting work, so shortly after YWB opened the members purchased a dough mixer for $300. Some other steps in the production process are tedious and unfulfilling. One such step is wrapping the products. Although this is not now done by machine, the members believe that acquiring a packaging machine would be an appropriate use of resources.

The work at the bakery is a full and exhausting day's work. The day starts at 5:30 AM when the dough mixer and the muffin maker for the day start their dough. They work until 1:30 PM. Two other persons come in at 7:00 AM and work until 3:00 PM. A fifth person does a solo shift. The two ovens are used only until 1:30 PM making the main product line. Between 1:30 PM and 6:00 PM, the ovens can be used for special products and for experimentation. The bakery makes one delivery run each day. Everything ends by 6:00 PM.

The members mix and bake ten to fourteen doughs in eight hours. They believe they could push this a bit and add another one or two doughs with an extra hour of work. However, the delivery shift is at its limit. Delivery is constrained not only by the large number of outlets that must be served each day but also by the fact that many supermarkets have designated delivery hours. If the members did get another truck, they believe their present equipment would be sufficient to handle the increased demand (see Exhibit 8).

This is not to say the members would not like to acquire some new equip-

EXHIBIT 8 YEAST WEST BAKERY EQUIPMENT

Dough mixer
Two ovens
Sheeter
Two bread slicers
Dough divider
Food processor
Air conditioner
Assorted bowls, spoons, measuring devices

ment. They are concerned about their dough mixer and would like to replace it. However, new mixers cost between $5,000 and $10,000. In addition, they would like to add the packaging machine. But they are not now at a point in production volume that would make such a purchase cost effective. The members do not know what the break-even point would be for such a purchase. They also have a dough molder on their wish list.

YWB's capacity is somewhat constrained by the size of the ovens and the size of the facilities. The members could not add another oven because there is not enough room. They would have to replace the ovens, but they believe that if they were to do this, they should take the opportunity to move into a larger facility.

PERSONNEL

One of the real constraints on expansion is personnel. The owners and employees are almost at their physical limits now. If expansion occurs, it would likely come in the natural, incremental way it has in the past: The members will push themselves a bit harder. If the demand is sustained, they will expand by hiring some new workers. They are firmly opposed to an approach of hiring people and firing them if things do not work out.

All of the collective owners work full time. They work eight hours per day, four days per week. In addition, they all attend a weekly meeting that deals with day to day operations of the bakery. At these meetings, they discuss ways of improving the production process, efficiency, the quality of the supplies and any personal information. Long-term goals are discussed at monthly planning meetings.

The employees are all more or less part-time workers. They do not attend the weekly and monthly meetings. The members are at present considering ways to get the employees involved in meetings. The most appealing alternative is to have the employees meet with the members on paid time. Given the members' value system, it is important to them to have the employees and the members all participate in the decision-making process.

The decision making at YWB is not cost driven; it is worker driven. One of the founding values of the bakery that has not changed is the goal of providing people with a decent living in an atmosphere of openness and mutual respect. Consequently, job scheduling takes into account individuals' needs such as day care. The jobs rotate from day to day. And even though some individuals, through skills and experience, have begun to specialize in certain tasks, people can still do whatever task they want. One developing exception to this has emerged in the area of sales; one individual has become the predominant salesperson. This change has come about because of the nature of the market and the need to deal with that market in a uniform fashion. In general, however, titles are merely nominal and the structure is egalitarian. Power is shared along with responsibility. For the members of YWB, the value for the growth of the individuals is as important as the bread.

Because individual growth and support are so important, growth in sales has been used to support increased wages and benefits for the members and the employees. As the needs of the members changed, so did the benefits. Now there is support for child care and for health insurance. There are paid vacations in addition to the unpaid ones they always had. In order to be sure that the bakery and the people are growing together, they have frequent meetings. At weekly meetings they discuss general issues that people have put on the agenda. There are meetings away from the bakery for discussing long-term goals. They also have social gatherings. Because this personal interaction is so important, screening new members is vital. Anyone who wants to be a member of the collective must first go through an apprenticeship. During this period, he or she attends all the meetings but has no voting rights. After this probationary period, the members vote on admission into the collective. Such care about the interactions of the members and employees has helped sustain the bakery through all of its years of operation.

THE FUTURE

Growth for YWB has always been slow and natural. As the bakery has grown, change has been absorbed gradually. Until now, the informal, egalitarian structure has not been threatened by change.

There is a sense now that change may come more quickly and be more dramatic. Given the popularity of products such as YWB's and the changing relationship with the environment, competition may become a more important element in the members' decision making. Of course, the future can be whatever the collective members want it to be. Some would like to see the bakery in its own building with more delivery runs and more shifts. However, growth requires financing, and the bakery's financial situation does not inspire the confidence of loan officers. The greatest asset of YWB is the dedication of its members—but that can't be capitalized for a balance sheet. The members recently were turned down for a loan that would have allowed them to move into their own building a few blocks from their present location.

The dedication of the members may also be the greatest liability for the future. Baking is physically demanding, and the total involvement of the members is emotionally draining. They need something to give them energy for the future. And they need to decide what that future will be.

APPENDIX A

COOPERATIVE CORPORATION BY LAWS

Article 1. Purpose
A. Producing Outstanding Baked Goods
B. Providing Good Jobs

Article 2. Governance
A. Power
B. Decision Making Process
   1. The Use of Consensus
   2. Quorum
   3. Amending Bylaws and Articles of Incorporation
   4. Proxy
C. Membership Meetings
   1. Annual Meeting
   2. Special Meetings
   3. Business Meetings
D. Board of Directors
   1. Elections
   2. Duties and Powers
   3. Meetings
   4. Vacancies
   5. Removal
E. Officers

Article 3. Ownership
A. Shares
   1. Voting
   2. Capital Accounts
B. Distribution of Profit and Loss
   1. Yearly
   2. Cashing In
C. Equity
   1. Investments
   2. Liquidation or Sale
   3. Interest
   4. Record Keeping

Article 4. Membership
A. Hiring
   1. Training
   2. The Decision
   3. Initiation
B. Non-Member Employees
C. Withdrawal and Firing of Cooperative Members
   1. Withdrawal
   2. Firing
   3. Grounds for Immediate Firing
D. Conflict Resolution
   1. Outside Parties
   2. If Unavailable

ARTICLE 1. PURPOSE

A. PRODUCING OUTSTANDING BAKED GOODS

The first concern of the Yeast-West Bakery Inc. is to produce high-quality baked goods and other food products for the public. The health and well-being of our customers is the cornerstone of our business. The following policies flow from this concern:

1. We will use only whole grains in our products. Refined flours such as white flour and gluten flour will not be used because we believe them unnatural and harmful to the health of consumers when consumed regularly.
2. We will not use white sugar. Its negative effect on the human body has been widely documented.
3. We will not use chemical or artificial additives and preservatives.
4. We will be honest and open about our products and will not attempt to manipulate our customers.
5. We will operate in a way that supports our environment. For example, we will try to use organically grown ingredients whenever they are economically feasible.

B. PROVIDING GOOD JOBS

The Yeast-West Bakery Inc. will be operated democratically as a worker cooperative striving for the fulfillment of all the workers—in body, mind, and spirit.

419

ARTICLE 2. GOVERNANCE

A. POWER

As a worker cooperative, power will reside with the members of the cooperative. A member is a full- or part-time worker employed by the cooperative who has been accepted into the cooperative and has been issued a share by the cooperative. Only current members will be allowed to hold a voting share in the Yeast-West Bakery Inc.

B. DECISION MAKING PROCESS

1. *The Use of Consensus:* The operating decision making process on all levels of the YWB will be consensus. This is a process during which all members' concerns are synthesized into a decision which is acceptable enough to each member that each agrees to support the group in choosing it. When a member disagrees with a decision she has the power to block consensus at which time the group will continue to work toward another, more acceptable solution. However, to prevent a tyranny by a minority of members, a two-thirds majority of members present may vote to suspend consensus as a method of decision making and replace it with majority rule in order to decide a particular issue. When majority rule is in effect, secret ballot will be used if it is requested by one or more members.
2. *Quorum:* A two-thirds majority is required to conduct business at all levels of the YWB.
3. *Amending Bylaws and Articles of Incorporation:* Any of the Articles of Incorporation or Bylaws of the YWB may be amended by the members at the annual meeting or at a special meeting. All members must be notified at least a week in advance and not more than three weeks in advance, and must be given a written copy of the proposed amendments during that same time period.
4. *Proxy:* A member may participate in meetings either in person or by proxy appointed by an instrument in writing subscribed by the member or by her duly authorized attorney.

C. MEMBERSHIP MEETINGS

1. *Annual Meeting:* The annual meeting of the members of the YWB will take place on the third Tuesday of January at 5:00 P.M. While it is expected that members will meet frequently during the year to conduct the business of the YWB, only the annual meeting or a special meeting will be required to post their minutes in the corporate book and only these meetings have the power to amend the bylaws or Articles of Incorporation of the YWB, to elect officers or directors, or to issue stock to new members.
    a. Purpose—The annual meeting will be for the purpose of electing officers and directors and for the transaction of such business as may be brought before it.
    b. Place—The annual meeting will take place in the headquarters of the YWB.
    c. Notice—Notice of the annual meeting will be given personally or mailed to each member at least one week and not more than three weeks before the meeting.
2. *Special Meetings:* Special membership meetings must be called at the request in writing of a one-third minority of members. These meetings will require the same notice as the annual meeting, and the notice must include a written copy of proposals to be made at the meeting.
3. *Business Meetings:* Business meetings of the members of the YWB will be held on a regular basis as determined by members. The current rotation is two regular business meetings and one pot luck with a focused discussion each month. When a decision is made at a business meeting involving an expenditure of more than $500, all members must either be present or must have been notified of the item a week in advance of the meeting.

D. BOARD OF DIRECTORS

   1. *Elections:* The Board of Directors of the YWB will consist of the members of the YWB unless the members determine that such a Board is too unwieldy or decides that it would like to elect directors from outside the membership. In either of these cases, the members will come to a decision as to the number of directors needed and will formulate an election at an annual or special meeting.
      a. Term—If and when election becomes the method of choosing directors, they will be regularly chosen at the annual meeting of the members.
   2. *Duties and Powers:* The Board will have control and general management of the YWB between membership meetings.
   3. *Meetings:* Once the Board becomes an elected one, it will meet annually after the annual membership meeting and regularly at least three other times a year. Special meetings of the Board must be called upon the written request of two directors. The Board will adopt its own procedures and bylaws but must use the decision making process laid out in Article 2. Section B. of these bylaws.
   4. *Vacancies:* Vacancies in the Board of Directors may be filled for the unexpired portion of the term by a consensus of the remaining directors.
   5. *Removal:* Any or all of the directors may be removed, either with or without cause, at any time, by a majority vote of the members at a special meeting.

E. OFFICERS

The Officers of the YWB will consist of a president, vice-president, a secretary and a treasurer. The president will be the general manager and chief executive officer of the YWB with responsibility for general supervision, direction and control of the affairs of the YWB. The secretary and treasurer will have such authority and responsibility as are customary to those offices. All officers will be designated at the annual meeting and will serve an annual term without limitation on succession and can be removed at any time by a special meeting of the members.

ARTICLE 3. OWNERSHIP

A. SHARES

   1. *Voting:* A certificate, under the seal of the corporation, will be issued to each YWB worker when that worker is accepted for membership into the cooperative. The price of this share will be $1 and this fee will be placed in the worker's capital account. The certificate represents one voting share on all membership matters and entitles the member to a share in the profits and losses of the cooperative as enumerated in Article 3. Section B.

      When a member leaves the cooperative, their old certificate becomes invalid and should be turned in. They will then be issued a statement of the balance of their capital account.
   2. *Capital Accounts:* With the exception of outside investments (see C.1. below) the capital of the YWB will consist of retained earnings which will be distributed to the capital accounts. A capital account is an accounting device which divides up the capital of the cooperative on the basis of the amount of labor a worker contributes to the cooperative.

      In effect, the retained earnings of the YWB are distributed to the workers, who then deposit the money with the Bakery. This money is then "on loan" to the Bakery. Physically there is no pile of money put aside for each worker. The worth of the capital account is embedded in the worth of the YWB—in its equipment, inventory, bank accounts and other assets. A worker may recoup her "loan" according to the terms set out in section B.2. below.

B. DISTRIBUTION OF PROFIT AND LOSS

1. *Yearly:*
   a. Profit—At the end of each year, as part of the process of reconciling the bookkeeping, after interest is paid out on the capital accounts and after taxes are paid, the retained profit earned by the YWB will be allocated as follows. 20% will go into a collective reserve capital account which will serve to insure the individual capital accounts in the face of losses or an unfavorable end to the YWB. The remaining 80% will be distributed to the capital accounts of the current members of the YWB on the basis of their hours worked in that year. The 80%-20% ratio may be changed for a given year at a membership meeting within six months of the end of the year in question.
   b. Written notice of allocation—In any proportion determined by the members, the retained earnings which are distributed to the individual capital accounts can be paid in cash, in non-qualified written notices of allocation, and/or in qualified written notices of allocation. Unless approved by the members, written notices of allocation will be non-transferable. In the absence of such board approval any transfer of allocation notices, whether voluntary or involuntary, will be of no effect against the corporation and will not entitle the transferee to receive payment from the corporation.
   c. Loss—If there is a loss in a given year, it will be absorbed by up to 50% of the collective capital account, with the rest divided among the current members' capital accounts equally unless a member started working after the beginning of the year in which case they will not share in the loss.
2. *Cashing In:* When a member retires or otherwise leaves the YWB she becomes eligible to redeem the money in her capital account.

   Current members may also draw on their capital accounts upon the unanimous approval of the other members in a special or annual meeting.

   The amount of money available yearly to pay out to the capital accounts will be 1% of the average sales of the previous three years. This amount will be paid out to all those who are eligible who have put in a written claim for it by the last membership meeting. The payments will be made monthly and will be divided equally among those who have applied for them.

   When a member has been paid the full amount of her capital account, the capital account payouts will be redivided among those who are left who have made written requests at the last membership meeting.

C. EQUITY

1. *Investments:* Contributions of capital (cash or property) to the YWB will in all cases be subject to a specific agreement between the members and the investor concerning the value of the contribution, interest, and the disposition of the investment.
2. *Liquidation or Sale:* Upon liquidation or sale of the YWB, net proceeds will be divided pro-rata among the individual capital accounts and the collective capital account. The membership will decide the disposition of the collective capital account.
3. *Interest:* The individual capital accounts will be paid interest at the same rate paid by the BC3FCU Credit Union out of the profits of the business before they are distributed to the current years' members capital accounts.
4. *Record Keeping:*
   a. The YWB will be responsible for notifying all equity shareholders of any change in the YWB's address or legal status.
   b. All shareholders are responsible for notifying the YWB and keeping the YWB informed of their names and addresses.
   c. Before the March 15th tax deadline each year, the YWB will update its records concerning the division of its capital. By April 15, a current statement of the status of all capital accounts will be given to each person who has one.

ARTICLE 4. MEMBERSHIP

A. HIRING

1. *Training:* The cooperative may hire employees as needed. An employee is free to remain as an employee at the YWB as long as it is mutually acceptable to her and the YWB members. However, after 416 hours of work (13 weeks @ 4 days @ 8 hours = 416 hours = approximately 3 months) an employee can apply to become a member of the YWB. If the employee is accepted unanimously, during the next 416 hours of work she will be essentially training to become a member. She will be expected to attend business and other meetings and to help form and enact policies and decisions. During this period the goals of the employee and cooperative members will be: to assess their compatibility; to build trust; and to increase the relevant experience, responsibility and commitment of the potential member.
2. *The Decision:* 416 hours after an employee applies for membership, a decision can be made on accepting them. If they are not unanimously accepted either in applying after their first 416 hours or after training for 416 hours, they have the option of staying on as an employee if that is mutually acceptable to the employee and the membership.
3. *Initiation:* If the employee is unanimously accepted she becomes a member of the YWB. A membership meeting must be convened within two weeks at which time a voting share will be given to the new member and the member will be shown the YWB's list of chosen arbitrators. If the member objects to one or more of the arbitrators, the meeting will choose replacements by consensus.

   The new member's share of the year's profits will begin at the point she becomes a member. Her capital account will commence with the next adjustment of the capital accounts as provided in 3-5-c. The member will continue to be paid wages which will be independent of her capital account.

B. NON-MEMBER EMPLOYEES

Policies regarding employees will be set out in the YWB handbook and will include the following points:

1. Employees are not responsible or liable for management of the business and may not represent themselves to outside agents as a member of the YWB.
2. Employees are expected to uphold the policies and decisions of the members. They may petition the members, at any members' business meeting to change policies.
3. Employees are asked for 30 days notice before leaving employment.
4. Employees may be fired by unanimous consent of the members. They may appeal the firing at a members' business meeting which is required of the members within one week of such a request. Unanimous consent after the appeal makes the firing final.
5. Fired employees are given two weeks' notice of termination of employment, except when the members agree there are grounds for immediate termination.

C. WITHDRAWAL AND FIRING OF COOPERATIVE MEMBERS

1. *Withdrawal:* Members may voluntarily withdraw from the cooperative with three months' notice required. An effort should be made to coordinate one's leaving so as not to impose too much hardship on those who remain. If the remaining members unanimously agree that such an effort was not made, a penalty of 20% can be assessed against that member's capital account. If a member leaves to start or aid a competitor of the YWB, a penalty of up to 100% can be assessed against that member's capital account by a unanimous decision of the members.
2. *Firing:* Only one member may be fired at a time, and there must be six weeks between firings, unless there are grounds for immediate firing as set forth in point 3 of this Section. As early as possible in the process leading to a firing, other means of working out problems such as using an outside mediator should be explored.

a. The firing process:
   1. Any member may propose firing a specific member on the agenda for the next business meeting. This meeting must be between 3 and 14 days from the date the proposal is added to the agenda and notice must be given to all members.
   2. The proposal is discussed at the business meeting and an evaluation is scheduled for the person in question. The evaluation must be between three and twelve days from the date of this meeting.
   3. If the member in question refuses to participate in the evaluation, this is grounds for immediate firing.
   4. At the evaluation, if there is a consensus of all other members, the person in question is given at least one week's notice of termination.
3. *Grounds for Immediate Firing:*
   a. Refusal to participate in one's own evaluation after being given at least two days notice.
   b. Threatened or actual use of violence.
   c. Embezzlement or other willful misuse of YWB assets.
   d. Refusal to abide by the decision of an arbitrator. As many people as these grounds apply to may be fired simultaneously, when the rest of the members unanimously agree that such action occurred.

D. CONFLICT RESOLUTION

An arbitrator will be called in to help settle a dispute when a consensus is developed that such action is needed.

1. *Outside Parties:* The members will always have on hand the names of three outside parties willing to help settle conflicts. The group must review these names once each year or whenever a new member is added. These parties will always be the first resort unless the entire membership agrees on using another party. If the members cannot agree on which of the three to use when more than one is available, and cannot agree on any other outside party, then among those available, one shall be chosen by a form of chance (coin flip, etc.)
2. *If Unavailable:* If none of the parties on the list of three is available, and the members can't agree on an outside party, then the members will use an artibrator at random from a list provided by the American Arbitration Association.

CASE 20

POLAROID CORPORATION/ INNER CITY, INC.

JOHN A. SEEGER
AND MARIE ROCK

Bill Skelley, manager of Polaroid Corporation's Inner City subsidiary, gazed intently across his circular conference table, emphasizing his concerns with the company's future:

> We are a forty million dollar company, just as responsible for its operations as any other profit-center firm. We assemble parts for Polaroid's cameras . . . we package film . . . we do silk screen printing. At the same time, we help people who have never before succeeded at work to develop the skills they need, to hold a job anywhere. When we finish training somebody to be productive, we place them in a mainstream job with some other employer, to make room for a new trainee here.
>
> We're held responsible for the bottom line. Since 1978, we've returned more than our budgeted contribution to Polaroid headquarters. [Exhibit 1 shows Inner City's financial statements for 1985 and 1986.]
>
> Now, though, the whole economy is changing, with serious implications for us. Our history and skills lie in the manufacturing area, but all the economic growth is in the service sector: that's where the entry-level jobs are. To give our graduates a chance, we have to change the work we train them to do. We have to decide what work Inner City should take on—what new business we should go into.
>
> And the low unemployment rate here in Massachusetts makes it hard to attract new trainees. Our waiting list for employment used to have a thousand to fifteen hundred names; now there is virtually no waiting list at all. A skeptic might say our whole reason for existing is obsolete.

Source: Prepared by Professor John A. Seeger and Marie Rock, Bentley College, as a basis for class discussion. Distributed by the North American Case Research Association. © John A. Seeger, 1988.

POLAROID CORPORATION

Polaroid Corporation was founded in 1937 by Edwin H. Land, who continued to lead the firm until his retirement in 1980. Through those years the company was based entirely on the products of Dr. Land's inventive genius—polarized filters and instant photography. Polaroid experienced rapid growth in sales, employment, and profitability until 1978, when sales grew 30 percent over the previous year, reaching $1.4 billion with a return on equity of 13.8 percent. In 1979, however, several factors—including Kodak's penetration of the instant photography market, the failure of Polaroid's instant motion picture system, and an oil-starved economic recession—put an end to the growth. (Exhibit 2 on page 816 shows ten years' operating results for Polaroid.)

From its inception, Polaroid Corporation reflected the values of its founder. The company was an innovator in participative management systems and responsiveness to community needs. In the late 1960s, autonomous worker teams were introduced in Polaroid's film manufacturing plant. When public criticism in 1970 focused on the use of instant photography in South Africa's apartheid identification pass program, Polaroid sent an employee team to investigate; supporting that group's analysis, the company refused to

EXHIBIT 1 INNER CITY, INC. STATEMENT OF OPERATIONS

	YEAR ENDING DECEMBER 31,			
	1985		1986	
	Budget	*Actual*	*Budget*	*Actual*
Sales	$44,576	$38,457	$30,407	$35,401
Cost of Sales				
Direct Material	42,078	35,857	27,666	32,595
Direct Labor	490	610	536	621
	42,568	36,467	28,202	33,216
Gross Margin	2008	1,990	2,205	2,185
Other Direct Costs	0	0	113	154
Other Income	0	16	0	2
Subtotal	2,008	2,006	2,092	2,033
Operating Costs				
Indirect Labor[1]	646	655	860	693
Staff Labor[2]	798	793	840	746
Overhead	564	499	392	496
Subtotal	2008	1,947	2,092	1,935
Surplus from Operations[3]	$ 0	$ 59	$ 0	$ 98

EXHIBIT 1 (continued)

STATEMENT OF FINANCIAL CONDITION

	DECEMBER 31,	
	1985	*1986*
ASSETS		
Cash	$ 6	$ 44
Accounts Receivable		
Polaroid	558	480
Trade-Net	64	36
Other	3	5
Inventories	544	904
Prepaid Expenses	4	1
Total Current Assets	1,179	1,470
Plant and Equipment, Net	99	98
Total Assets	$1,278	$1,568
LIABILITIES AND OWNERS' EQUITY		
Accounts Payable	$ 7	$ 30
Accrued Expenses	16	42
Total Current Liabilities	23	72
Advance from Parent, Net	2,778	3,019
Total Liabilities	2,801	3,091
Capital Stock	1	1
Paid in Surplus	24	24
Retained Earnings (Deficit)	(1,548)	(1,548)
Total Liabilities and Owner's Equity	$1,278	$1,568

Note: Amounts given in thousands.
[1] Inner City, Inc. staff.
[2] Polaroid Corporation staff.
[3] Redistributed to Parent Corporation.

supply film to the government there. In 1978, Polaroid discontinued *all* sales in South Africa.

Richard Lawson, director of corporate materials management and services for Polaroid and president of Inner City, Inc., commented:

> Dr. Land believed in helping people to grow and attain their limits. He created the Polaroid philosophy, recognizing that it takes people to produce a quality product and that everyone, even the sweeper, had good ideas. Here, the sweeper has a chance to become a lab technician.

EXHIBIT 2 POLAROID CORPORATION AND SUBSIDIARY COMPANIES—TEN-YEAR FINANCIAL SUMMARY

	1986	1985	1984	1983	1982	1981	1980	1979	1978	1977
CONSOLIDATED STATEMENT OF EARNINGS										
Net sales										
United States	$964.3	$779.3	$743.5	$730.1	$752.5	$817.8	$791.8	$757.2	$817.4	$645.8
International	664.9	515.9	528.0	524.4	541.4	601.8	659.0	604.3	559.2	416.1
Total Net Sales	1629.2	1295.2	1271.5	1254.5	1293.9	1419.6	1450.8	1361.5	1376.6	1061.9
Cost of Goods Sold	921.7	756.0	735.2	698.3	769.6	855.4	831.1	876.8	778.3	575.7
Marketing, Research, Engineering and Administrative Expense	571.8	505.6	492.6	462.1	472.6	520.8	483.9	449.4	418.2	337.3
Total Costs	1493.5	1261.6	1227.8	1160.4	1242.2	1376.2	1315.0	1326.2	1196.5	913.0
Profit from Operations	135.7	33.6	43.7	94.1	51.7	43.4	135.8	35.3	180.1	148.9
Other Income	18.1	28.9	39.5	32.5	45.5	49.2	25.4	13.3	20.3	19.0
Interest Expense	18.6	22.3	20.9	26.5	35.5	29.9	17.0	12.8	5.9	6.4
Earnings Before Income Taxes	135.2	40.2	62.3	100.1	61.7	62.7	144.2	35.8	194.5	161.5
Federal, State, Foreign Income Taxes	31.7	3.3	36.6	50.4	38.2	31.6	58.8	(3)	76.1	69.2
Net Earnings	$103.5	$36.9	$25.7	$49.7	$23.5	$31.1	$85.4	$36.1	$118.4	$92.3
Earnings Per Share	3.34	1.19	.83	1.61	.73	.95	2.60	1.10	3.60	2.81
Cash Dividends Per Share	1.00	1.00	1.00	1.00	1.00	1.00	1.00	1.00	.90	.65
SELECTED BALANCE SHEET INFORMATION										
Working Capital	$637.0	$697.8	$734.2	$769.0	$745.4	$749.5	$721.9	$525.9	$609.5	$589.6
Net Property, Plant and Equipment	357.7	349.0	306.6	227.0	281.8	332.9	362.2	371.6	294.8	225.9
Total Assets	1479.2	1384.7	1346.0	1319.1	1323.6	1434.7	1404.0	1253.7	1276.0	1076.7
Long-Term Debt	—	124.6	124.5	124.4	124.3	124.2	124.1	—	—	—
Stockholders' Equity	994.7	922.2	916.3	921.6	902.9	958.2	960.0	907.5	904.3	815.5
OTHER STATISTICAL DATA										
Additions to Property, Plant and Equipment	$82.9	$104.5	$82.7	$51.8	$31.5	$42.5	$68.1	$134.6	$115.0	$68.7
Number of Employees	14,765	12,932	13,402	13,871	14,540	16,784	17,454	18,416	20,884	16,394
Return on Stockholders' Equity	10.8%	4.0%	2.0%	5.4%	2.5%	3.2%	9.1%	4.0%	13.8%	11.8%

Note: Unaudited. Years ended December 31. Dollars in millions, except per-share data.

> Our first goal is to build a company that makes a quality product we can all feel proud of. Hand in hand with this is a belief that we have to be good community members.

INNER CITY, INC.

Inner City, Inc. was a subcontract manufacturing firm, processing materials or assembling parts for Polaroid or other companies. Bill Skelley described his operation:

> We tell prospective customers, "We'd like to work for you. Send us your raw materials inventory. We'll process it and send it back to you. We're located on Columbus Avenue in Roxbury, and our work force is 95 percent minority."
>
> If we had to tell the whole story, we might add, "Most of our people are unskilled. They've been with us, on average, only a couple of months. Most have no previous work history, or they've had problems at earlier jobs. Some have served time. We hire from the bottom of the labor force; our incoming trainees don't attach any importance to timeclocks or absenteeism or discipline or dress. Most just don't know what real work is, or how an employer expects them to behave."
>
> When you ask prospective customers to send their work into Roxbury, all sorts of perceptions start running through their minds. But when they come to visit, they find our trainees obviously working hard, and they're surprised. They say, "Wow, you guys have a very efficient, neat, well-organized and clean operation! How do you do it?" We say, "That's what we expect. You can't run a place like this unless that's the order of business."

THE ENVIRONMENT

Inner City occupied the top four floors of a freshly painted, six-story brick and concrete building in Roxbury, a poor, predominantly black neighborhood of Boston. The building was flanked on two sides by vacant lots awaiting urban redevelopment; behind it were nineteenth century brick row houses, deteriorated by time and characteristic of much of historical Boston. Many houses were boarded up and abandoned, symbolizing the area's chronic unemployment—three times higher than that of surrounding neighborhoods. Across the street, bustling, dusty construction work continued on a new rapid transit line, spearhead of a major redevelopment program. According to plans for urban development, the area surrounding Inner City would eventually boast of cobblestone streets, brick walkways, and new housing.

When Inner City was incorporated in 1968 as a subsidiary of Polaroid Corporation, the city of Boston, along with the rest of the nation, was experiencing great social unrest. Only four years earlier, the first federal civil rights laws had been enacted. Equal employment opportunity had not yet been legislated; discrimination was commonplace in employment, housing, voting, education, transportation, and in the daily lives of many Americans. Organizations which had represented the black community since 1910 were joined by college students to protest social injustices. Often, demonstrations intended to be non-violent broke into rioting and destruction—sometimes initiated by law enforcement personnel, sometimes by extremists among the protesters. Press and television coverage brought the violent encounters into public consciousness.

Reacting to spreading social unrest and violence, President Johnson launched a number of projects, including the War on Poverty in 1964, designed to derail the accelerating problems of the nation's youth and unemployed. Antipoverty programs, including training programs conducted by public agencies and private corporations, sprang up around the country. Still, social upheaval continued. In the mid- to late 1960s, several civil rights leaders and activists were assassinated, sparking even more social dissension across the country. Protesters against racism, against the Vietnam War, and against "the Establishment" marched through city streets and across college campuses, including those in Boston.

Riots erupted in major U.S. cities. Large areas of Rochester burned, as did Washington's black neighborhood. In Los Angeles, the vast area called Watts burned for days as snipers prevented fire fighters from entering and looters vandalized those stores still standing; 35 died in the riot, as 833 others were injured and 3,600 more were arrested. In May of 1970, National Guard troops opened fire on students at Kent State University, killing 4 and wounding 10. Across the country, colleges closed until the following September, in sympathy with the slain students and to prevent further violence on their own campuses. Nervous civic leaders in Boston eyed the Roxbury ghetto, anticipating the worst.

THE FOUNDING OF INNER CITY, INC.

Governments, businesses, and civic minded groups of minorities and whites attempted to cope at the local level with the nationwide illnesses of racism and unemployment. At Polaroid Corporation, black employees and the Management Executive Committee focused on the issues. Richard Lawson, a member of the original planning team, recalled its formation:

> We had formed a "Volunteer Committee," where we shared ideas related to company business. At first we met on our own time. Then Polaroid let us meet on company time, and allowed us to do more and more. As the Volunteer Committee grew in size, its running became a full time job held by elected officials who represented to management Polaroid's black employee viewpoint.
>
> At this same time a movement was taking place in Washington which called for private enterprise to respond to the problem of hard-core unemployment in the nation's inner cities. We came up with the idea of establishing a small manufacturing plant in Boston's inner city, that would be a stepping stone for people coming to work at Polaroid or elsewhere.
>
> I worked at Inner City during its first year, and then went back to Polaroid. From there I went to the Harvard Business School. About a year after I returned to Polaroid, Inner City was in financial turmoil. Community leaders

felt the troubles resulted from mismanagement, and because I was a recent Harvard graduate, I was made manager of Inner City in 1973. Nowadays, assignments to Inner City are voluntary. Mine in '73, was not.

Inner City was losing $700,000 to $800,000 a year with no apparent end in sight, and turning out only about fifty graduates a year. It was costing us $9,000 to train a single graduate, far more than it would cost to send them to college. Inner City's operating systems duplicated all the overhead of the parent corporation; by simplifying things, I got the average cost down to $3,000 per graduate.

For the life of me, I couldn't run a business to see it lose money. And I didn't think it was right for a successful business to carry a losing business. Now we run Inner City like any business in the United States. It makes money. If it doesn't, it had better answer why. Inner City now has to answer questions like, "What did you do?," and "What do you plan to do?" [Exhibit 3 summarizes operating results for ten years, ending in 1986.]

ORGANIZATION

In 1987, Richard Lawson served as president and chairman of the board of directors of Inner City, Inc. Twelve other Polaroid executives, four of them

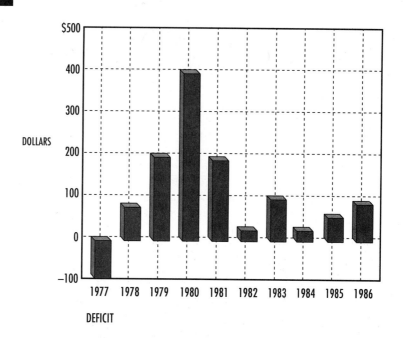

EXHIBIT 3 SURPLUS (DEFICIT) FROM OPERATIONS

members of the firm's executive committee, served as members of the Inner City board.

Inner City's own staff numbered about thirty, of whom seventeen were Polaroid employees on loan to the subsidiary. The balance were specialists in counseling, training, and placement areas, where skills were more plentiful in the open employment market than in Polaroid's staff. Some of these "Inner City staff" members were graduate students or interns from local universities.

Although small, the organization provided room for advancement for its people. One production supervisor had recently become a company planner, and several positions were held by former trainees. (Exhibit 4 shows the 1987 organization chart.)

MANUFACTURING OPERATIONS

Inner City's various material products included film and camera products, silk screen and offset printing products, and special products. Typically, Inner City purchased raw materials from its customer, processed them, and then sold the finished product back to the customer. According to Bill Skelley,

> Polaroid was reluctant at first to give us some of their work, as you can imagine, but we proved that we could package film worth many millions of dollars. Some of the products we manufacture are essential to Polaroid. If we couldn't make the production and delivery schedule, whole divisions could be shut down or wouldn't be able to build their final products. Camera drive trains are an example.

Inner City's manufacturing operations occupied the top four floors of the Roxbury building, receiving raw materials by truck from Polaroid locations in Needham, Norwood, and Waltham. The work day began at 7 A.M. and continued until 3:30 P.M., with trainees allowed one-half hour for lunch. Primary demand for Polaroid's products determined the number of trainees, which varied between 70 and 130 people. Bill Skelley had attempted to develop work from sources other than the parent company, but the jobs had not provided the kind of challenging work he felt was appropriate for the trainees.

Film packing operations were located on the sixth floor and occupied some 25 to 50 workers (of a total work force numbering 100 people.) Packs of film for the Sun 600 camera and the Spectra line arrived by pallet loads, totaling 30,000 to 80,000 packs per day, depending on the schedule. Inner City's people packaged this film into groups of two, three, four, and five packs. The work involved little skill and could be expanded quickly as demand changed.

On the fifth floor, another ten to fifteen trainees worked at assembling a portion of the "hard body" for the Sun camera, applying the lens panel, trim button and retainer, and decorative stripe. Approximately 7 to 10,000 bodies per day were shipped to the Norwood plant. Photocopying and silk screening operations—the only department to serve a significant number of outside customers—employed eight trainees on the fourth floor.

EXHIBIT 4 THE INNER CITY ORGANIZATION: POLAROID STAFF MEMBERS

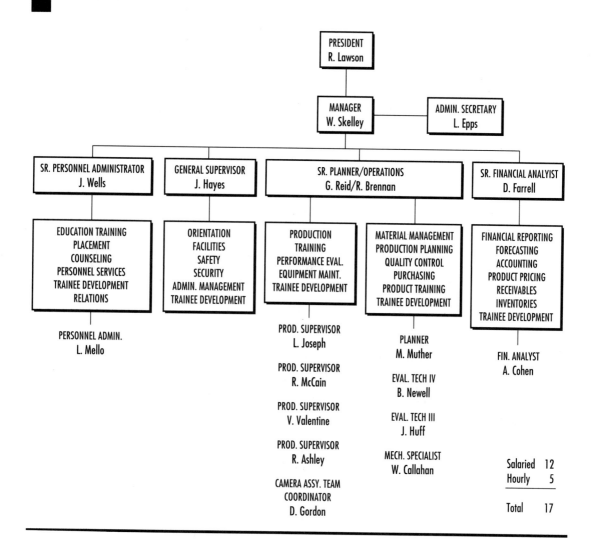

The most complex jobs in the Inner City involved the drive assembly for the Sun camera. Some thirty-five to forty trainees on the third floor worked at the task, handling twenty-six intricate parts to build the drives. Five to six of these people, two of whom were Polaroid staff members, worked on quality control. Drive production remained relatively constant at 3,600 per day; the long learning times involved made it difficult to scale up operations quickly. Bill Skelley discussed quality control:

We can't afford to have the slightest quality control problem. People will quickly take the work away from us. The standards that are applied to an operation like this versus the standards that are applied in the mainstream are really different. If you have 2 percent rejection, somehow the 2 percent looks like 25 perent because you are going to be held to a higher standard.

COMPETITION

Competition for Inner City existed in both training and manufacturing. In training, government manpower development programs attempted similar goals but rarely achieved them; the "hard-core unemployed" were considered beyond reach. In manufacturing, the chief competition was with Polaroid's own internal production operations. Bill Skelley commented:

> I don't think there is anyone that quite does what we do, but we do have competitors. I have to convince managers within Polaroid to allow us to quote on increasing our subcontracting load. If we can't competitively quote and produce scheduled quality work, then we won't get that product. We have lost a number of lines because our quotes weren't competitive with internal costs. However, in some cases we run a more efficient shop than Polaroid.
>
> There's also the offshore competition that the whole country is going through now. A lot of the type of work we do here, which is basic light hand assembly, is what America is sending offshore.
>
> If you're looking from the training point of view, I guess our competition comes from those companies that offer entry level employment at low wages and with no future, like some segments of the fast-food industry. They take people off the street and employ them a while. It takes people some time to realize that they're not going anywhere.
>
> And there are competitors in the manufacturing arena such as small subcontractors that still tend to run on a sweatshop mentality, pay slightly above minimum wages with no benefits packages, offer people somewhat steady employment, yet no opportunity for career advancement.

At one time, Inner City competed with workshop-training programs contracted by various charities and state rehabilitation commissions. According to Bill Skelley, Inner City had moved away from that sort of work:

> Workshops are no longer competitors of ours and I think that's a significant transition. Years ago we did the same kind of work—basic stuffing, putting components into a package. I think we've taken a significant step up: now we are focused on more intricate assembly, which is stepping into the high-tech arena, but requires much more in the way of quality control.

MANPOWER DEVELOPMENT OPERATIONS

In the 1960s, the federal government encouraged private industry to set up manpower training programs by paying companies to hire and train otherwise unqualified people. Jim Wells, senior personnel administrator, commented:

It was the thing to do, to take federal money and set up a nice program. But we didn't want bureaucrats coming in saying, "Hey, Jim Wells, tomorrow we want you to do this." The next year they take half your budget and say, "Well, sorry, but we need to put the money somewhere else!"

To our conscious knowledge, we did not borrow any program ideas from anyone. The program evolved. We didn't have a blueprint; we just built some things and they worked, so we expanded on them.

There has always been a tremendous difference between how the people were treated here, versus how they were dealt with in the federally funded city and state programs. I think it's the expectation levels we have here. Things are accepted in other programs that we just don't accept here.

PROGRAM DESIGN

The program began with a four- to eight-hour orientation session where applicants heard in detail what would be expected of them. Those who decided to go ahead were hired into the first of the program's three phases, as the minimum wage of $3.55/hour.

During their first week of Phase I, trainees were introduced to the program, the staff, and all the products which were manufactured at Inner City. Trainees were moved through different tasks to find the area that best suited their skills. Here they were told the quality and production standards that would be expected. Prominently displayed on the factory walls were easy-to-read charts tracking each trainee's attendance record and hourly production (for individuals) or daily output for groups.

After a month's demonstration of a cooperative attitude, good attendance, and work record, trainees were promoted to Phase II. Their pay was increased to $3.80 per hour. Trainees also attended required seminars on job performance, health and hygiene, and job seeking skills. (Exhibit 5 shows the content of these seminars and lists the other seminars available.)

Each month, Inner City selected one of its trainees for the "Employee of the Month" award. Eligible people were at least six weeks into Phase II, had perfect attendance records, and had demonstrated an ability to get along with others. Supervisors recommended trainees to a rotating committee of staff members who picked the monthly winners. "Recruiters from other companies love to pick up our Employees of the Month," said Bill Skelley.

Production workers at Inner City were permitted to develop their own preferred methods of accomplishing the work. Millie Muther, production supervisor, commented:

> We'll show them how to run a machine, but if they have a better way of doing it, and if the quality is as good, then they can do it their own way. There's no set way that a trainee must work.
>
> I'm a firm believer: the person that's building the product, really knows how to do it better than anyone else. They'll try to get the most done. They're being paid for it.

EXHIBIT 5   INNER CITY SEMINARS

SEMINAR SUBJECTS
1. Health and Hygiene
2. Job Performance
3. Transition Group
4. Financial Literacy
5. Educational and Vocational Choices for Adults
6. Planned Parenthood
7. Nutrition and Budgeting
8. Child Development
9. The Job Entry Phase
10. Emotions and Behavior
11. Preparing your taxes
12. Understanding the Judicial System
13. Jobs for the 80's
14. The Black Contribution
15. Consumer Education
16. Orientation to Computers
17. Polaroid Photography
18. Jobs in the Service Industry
19. Housing Resources

MANDATORY SEMINAR: JOB PERFORMANCE
8 hours total (4 hours Inner City time)
- Why People Work
- Components of Good Job Performance
- Importance of Quality
- Value of Performance Evaluations
- Criteria for Evaluating Performance
- Hierarchical Structure of Companies
- Jobs for the 80s
- How to be Successful on the Job
- Communicating Effectively with Supervisors
- Understanding the Supervisor's Job
- Job Benefits
- Job Postings
- Upward Mobility
- Resignations

MANDATORY SEMINAR: HEALTH AND HYGIENE
6 hours total (3 hours Inner City time)
- Proper Nutrition
- Preventive Medicine
- Care of the Body
- Hair Care
- Skin Care
- Nail Care
- Dental Care
- Health Clinics
- Patients' Rights
- The Physical Exam
- Birth Control
- Venereal Disease
- Sickle Cell Trait
- Hypertension

MANDATORY SEMINAR: TRANSITION GROUP, JOB-SEEKING SKILLS
26 hours total (14 hours Inner City time)
- Self-Assessment
- Motivation
- Getting What You Want
- Job Applications
- Resume Preparation
- Interviewing Techniques
- Role Play Interviews
- In-House Interviews
- Off-Site Interviews
- Stress Management
- Fitting In
- Adjustments to a New Job

TRAINEES

Although trainees joined the program in small groups, they completed it individually, depending on whether and when they were ready to work elsewhere. That decision was made by a group of Inner City staff, usually at the suggestion of the trainee's immediate supervisor. A trainee could be placed in an outside job in as little as four months or as long as nine months.

Other than a minimum age of eighteen, there were no eligibility requirements for Inner City trainees. Anyone could apply. Selection was on a first-come, first-served basis. Most trainees were in their early twenties. The oldest recruit was a man in his sixties; on occasion, the parent of a graduate became a trainee. Word-of-mouth communication was the program's only advertising up until 1985, when the thriving economy of Massachusetts had reduced the overall unemployment rate to just over 3 percent. At that time, Inner City began to use radio advertising to attract trainees.

Bill Skelley summed up the plight of many trainees:

> We have a lot of people in here who are really very bright, very sharp. But when it comes to work, they've had problems. Maybe because of social factors, maybe because of not knowing how to go about getting a job or maybe because the places they apply to have certain criteria that exclude them because of color or some other factor. In any event, they have less than desirable work histories.
>
> We take a couple of approaches to you as a trainee: we make you feel good about yourself initially; we tell you we expect an awful lot out of you; and we're not going to accept anything less. We say, "That's what you've got to do to be successful; now we'll help you with it. Are you willing to pay the price? That's the key question; if you are, you will be successful. If you're not, you'll probably wind up being terminated."

Trainee Gene Lang straddled a chair and chomped on a candy bar, hungry after working a full shift at Inner City, Inc.:

> Before I came to Inner City, I only got jobs for one thing: quick cold cash, then I'd split. But this place really turned my head around. This is a place that wants you to work, to be on time and to learn. They said to me, "You'll learn about holding on to a job by being here on time, by following the rules and by taking pride in yourself and your work." Well, that sounded like so much crap to me. But you get here, man, and you see the other trainees. They been here a few weeks and so you see that they really work together. And that's the key, it's family. I mean, you might have some family scraps once in a while, but everyone starts to care about each other.
>
> We all start to believe in each other, that we can make it through the program and graduate so that we can work in a permanent job someplace else. There *are* exceptions, the ones who don't want to be family; they usually goof off and get canned.
>
> And it's tough here. They want you to know that you can make it through the program, but it's up to you to show your supervisor that you're serious about it, 'cause they sure as hell are.

PLACEMENT

Inner City placed approximately 100 trainees per year in a variety of manufacturing and service settings. Since 1968 over 1,600 program graduates had been placed in 53 Boston-area companies, ranging from high technology to education to service. For the first ten years, the firm's trainees were placed with the parent company when their skills were sufficiently developed. In the business downturn of 1978, Polaroid's hiring policy changed; after that time, all graduates were placed with other Boston-area employers.

An important pre-placement activity was the "mock interview," with Inner City staff members playing the role of the potential employer. Millie Muther described the trainee's view of this experience:

> One of my people had his first mock interview just today; that's his suit hanging there in the corner. He worked until 1:00, then changed into his suit and tie in the men's room. He says, "Are you sure I look all right?" Well, his collar was folded up, so he let me fix it. He says, "Can you see me shaking? Do you know how nervous I am? Is he going to say hello first or do I say it first to him?" He just got caught up, and so nervous. They're very proud to be all dressed up and going for their first interview. Even if it's only a mock interview, it's very important to them. He went downstairs and did a super job.

Brian Stebbins, a college senior in a management internship program, served as an assistant supervisor to Millie Muther and described the progress of a former trainee who had experienced a successful placement.

> You hear from former trainees every once in a while. I'm thinking of one who came back here to visit; he had had a really tough life before he came here and he had a tough beginning here, too. He was finally placed after a while. When he came back, he showed us his new bank book to show us his savings, and he wanted us to look out the window to see the car he just bought. But I remember that he had some very tough problems while he was here. We just kept telling him: "Willie, if you just keep working and do well here, you'll get a good job and you'll see a big turnaround." He came into our office one day and just broke down and started crying. He's over forty, but he broke down trying to tell us that he was a man and he wanted a job. That was heartbreaking. We kept encouraging him. We said there would be a change, but I don't think that he believed us completely until he went out and got the job.

Bill Skelley pointed out another placement potential for some trainees—promotion to Inner City staff positions:

> One trainee was just made a supervisor. We found after she came here, she had graduated from college in North Carolina; she's done very well. Another former trainee handles our whole payroll system; she's taking college courses at Northeastern now. Another former trainee is doing a fine job as a crew chief on the production floor. It really helps to see someone who works beside you go up the ladder. These people are excellent role models.

RETENTION

Typically, about one-quarter of the trainees entering Inner City's program graduated to "regular" full-time employment. Some 30 percent—referred to as "negative results" by the staff—were either fired or quit in the face of termination. Another large group left after a few months' training, to take other, higher-paying jobs. Non-graduates, Bill Skelley pointed out, benefited from their training while employed in the program, even though they chose not to finish it. By year, the numbers of people hired and placed are shown in the first part of Exhibit 6.

Retention rates for Inner City graduates in their first jobs were tracked from 1982 to 1984 and indicated a substantial success during the graduates' first several months at work. The second part of Exhibit 6 shows that, of the total of 183 graduates covered by surveys, 158 or 85 percent stayed with their original employers for at least ninety days after placement. By the six-month point, retention had dropped only slightly to 140 or 77 percent. By year of placement, retention rates were measured as shown in Exhibit 6.

TRAINING POLICIES

Inner City emphasized its commitment to preparing people for long-term employment by implementing policies that might be considered stringent in many businesses.

SUSPENSIONS

Unruly and disruptive behavior or refusal to work was controlled through the use of suspensions. Millie Muther described handling a trainee's refusal to cooperate—a situation which might warrant a suspension:

> You say to yourself, "Why is that person doing that today? He is usually pretty good and has never refused to do a job." So you talk to that person and you

EXHIBIT 6 INDIVIDUALS HIRED AND PLACED

	1982	1983	1984	1985	1986
Number hired	248	426	479	511	460
Number placed	62	94	130	106	102

RETENTION RATES: 1984 STUDY GROUP

		EMPLOYEES STILL ON THE JOB AT			
YEAR PLACED	SURVEY TOTAL	3 Mo.	6 Mo.	12 Mo.	18 Mo.
1982	57	50 (88%)	44 (77%)	42 (74%)	38 (67%)
1983	85	75 (90%)	68 (82%)	43 (52%)	17 (21%)
1984	41*	33 (80%)	28 (68%)	*	*

*Small sample: first quarter placements only; this group not on job long enough to measure beyond six months.

get to the core of the problem and you solve it. It's usually a misunderstanding with someone else or a problem at home. But, if something like that continues, or is done more than once, we usually suspend them for three days because you can't refuse to do a job. You may not like to do it, but you can't refuse.

An example might be a trainee—Eddie—who has just been placed. He started out really well—had no problems at all. Then all at once he changed. He came in one day with a certain attitude; it just wasn't him. He still came in on time, but he wouldn't communicate. You can't place people with an attitude like that. We talked about his behavior to get at the source of his problem.

We had put up bars on all the sixth floor windows—kids were breaking in from the roof to steal film. The first day of the bars was when we saw the change in Eddie. It hadn't occurred to me that the bars would affect anyone. But Eddie had spent time in jail, and the bars had a special meaning for him. Knowing the problem helped me work with him. It made me feel pretty good when he finally did get a job—and it's a job he wants.

There are different ways to deal with problems. I've had people refuse to do a job, and when I've talked to them, it's because they've had this back problem, or they've had this operation, and they can't help it. If they don't speak up or communicate in the correct manner, they could wind up getting terminated. So it's another lesson for them.

TERMINATIONS

Continued disruptive behavior is usually a way of testing the supervisor and can lead to termination early in the program. Millie Muther described some of the tactics used by trainees, and their results:

They're brand new, so naturally they're going to put me through the test first. If there is a change in supervision, then they're going to put the new supervisor through the test to see if they can get away with more.

They test you by coming back from lunch or breaks late. They're supposed to punch in for morning, at lunch, at when they leave for the day, but not for breaks. So if they are late from break, the first time I usually ignore it, but after that I'll talk to them. And I'll say, "I saw you the other day when you were late. I didn't say anything because I was hoping it was just a mistake on your part."

I try to put the ownership back on them, and to make sure they realize that I'm not out to get them, that I want to help them. After that, they'll go on warning and then they could be terminated if their behavior doesn't improve. You stress to them that no matter where they work, they have to come back on time, not one or two minutes late, or they're not going to keep their job. They learn eventually.

We terminated a man on the spot, a couple of weeks ago. He put four packs of film underneath his hat. A lot of people saw that, so you can't let him get away with it. At first, we were going to wait—to catch him red-handed leaving the floor. But we've tried that before; you get interrupted for a few seconds, and the thief is gone. So we talked it over and said he's got it under his hat, and it shouldn't be there, so let's get rid of him now. A legal department in some big company would say the film doesn't cost you much; a lawsuit would cost a lot. But this is a training program. It's different. And even this guy has a right to appeal.

Trainees know up front that I'm not here to fire them. I don't fire people; I never have. I've signed the termination papers, but they've done the firing to themselves. They'll say, "I don't know why you fired me, I don't know what I did." And so you show them the record, and point out that they didn't learn by going on warning or by being talked to. There are only so many breaks I can give them.

There was no specific rule at Inner City regarding the number of warnings prior to termination from the program. Rules were well defined, however, regarding processes for reinstatement of trainees.

APPEALS BOARD

Not all terminations were permanent; Inner City gave its trainees a second chance. The terminated trainee received an appeals letter with his or her final check. The letter stated an appeal date, typically two weeks from the termination date, and a meeting time of 3:30 P.M. According to Millie Muther, punctuality was considered to be an important indicator of a trainee's willingness to continue with the program.

> They have to be prompt and be here by 3:30. If they're a minute late, we don't see them because it proves that they really don't want their job. Ninety-nine percent of them are here before 3:30. Right now, I have twenty-eight people on my floor; six of them have gone through the appeal process. When they come back, many of them seem to be okay for a while. Then all of a sudden some of them slip back again, and they end up being terminated. In the second termination, there is no appeal.

MEETING A CHANGING ENVIRONMENT

Long-term corporate commitment by Polaroid was essential to Inner City's ability to meet the challenges of an ever-changing environment.

CORPORATE COMMITMENT

The commitment of Polaroid to Inner City's survival had been evident since its inception. Bill Skelley addressed this issue:

> When the parent company experiences difficult times—which we have gone through—it is forced to look at all facets of the company. Look at Inner City. Is it a cost or a drain on the company? If we lost a million dollars, there would be a lot of people sitting in Polaroid headquarters questioning the validity of this program. That could happen very quickly. Unemployment is 3.7 percent in this state; the lowest since sliced bread came on the board. Jobs are going begging; you have to bus people in from Timbuktu.

It would be easy to ask. "Why do you need Inner City any more?" The people who make those decisions must have an in-depth understanding of what is happening in the real world. Polaroid went through a 30 percent reduction in personnel beginning in '78 or '79. Today the company is down to about 9,000 employees, domestically—some 14,000 worldwide. It really tested the corporate commitment to have products built by temporary people at Inner City, while full-time Polaroid employees were losing their jobs.

Now the corporation is staying lean. Like most big companies, it hires *only* temporary people for entry-level manufacturing work. Last year they hired over 2,000 temps, and many of them came right out of Inner City's ranks. Say you were working here at $3.50 an hour, and you got a note saying, "Come to work at Polaroid and you can make $7 an hour." You'd say, "When do I report?" We told our people those were only temporary jobs; they'd be let go in three to six months, and they couldn't come back here if they left. Some held on there longer than we'd expected; others were back on the streets within three weeks. But such is life.

CURRENT PROBLEMS AND ALTERNATIVES

Bill Skelley summarized some of the current problems and alternatives for Inner City:

For the first time in our history, the people we hire have options in their lives. Virtually *anyone* can get a job. Historically, our people had only us as a viable option.

How do we motivate people to go through training when they can go out and get a job on their own, even though it's a dead-ended job? That's what we're struggling with—trying to convince younger people today to do some long-range planning. Long-range career planning for many of them is based on next Saturday night's party. Planning for six to nine months, never mind the next couple of years, is difficult.

Do we have to pay them more? Then, how do we price our products competitively? And if we pay more, we create another problem: people won't want to leave here. This is an environment geared to making them feel good about themselves, and we're also convenient to their homes. So, if we raise their pay by "X" cents per hour, whatever that may be, we reduce their incentive for leaving.

Also, for the first time in our history, the majority of our 1986 placements were in the service sector. Now "service sector" means a lot of things. For us, it *doesn't* mean flipping hamburgers—because we won't do that. But it *could* mean working in a bank as a teller. It could mean working in a hotel as a telephone operator or a receptionist or a bell captain or a housekeeper.

The skill levels needed for service sector jobs are higher than for entry-level manufacturing jobs. Which means that our people have to be better prepared. To go and sit on the production line at an electronics firm as an entry-level manufacturing person is pretty basic—it's just putting the piece parts together. To go and do a comparable job in a hotel requires a lot more from you. For instance, one of our women in a housekeeping function at a major hotel has to interface with a computer five or six times a day. She's got to go to the computer and punch numbers in to find out where her next assignment is, how many towels and bars of soap she needs. And this is in an entry-level job. We have to do a better job of preparing our people.

We're finding a population more in need at the same time that the jobs are more demanding. There's a widening gap. The schools are at an all-time low on preparing people for the world of work. There's a 47 percent noncompletion rate in the city's schools, and even those that *do* complete aren't prepared to get a job on their own.

We're trying now to tailor our training program to the service sector. I think 56 percent of our graduates last year went into service sector jobs; two years ago it was 14 percent. The advantage of service sector jobs is that they are mostly in Boston; we don't run into the transportation problem we normally have. See, our people don't drive; 99 percent of them don't own a car. And if you get jobs out on Route 128 or in some distant suburb, you are limited by a transportation problem.

We're trying to expand our silk screening business with a new machine that more than quadruples our capacity. It teaches a specific skill. Hopefully we can place somebody in that type of business.

We have to look at other service-related alternatives. For example, the fulfillment business is a multi-billion dollar industry. Let's say that you buy five six-packs of a soft drink and send the labels in and you get a free digital watch. Who sends you the watch? Companies don't do it themselves. We tried to do it once, but we got out of it because we weren't doing it right. Now we're looking at doing it again.

We're also looking at data entry. What if we set up a data entry business here? That sounds good but changes the way we approach things: it would require a higher skilled person. It means that we would have to keep people longer. Rather than turning people over in six months it means that they're going to be here for two or three years. And if that happens, then you've got to pay them a competitive market wage. You've got to add a benefits package and you can't serve as many people. Our costs skyrocket. How do you offset those costs?

Another idea is an "externship" kind of program, where we place our temporary employees in a Polaroid production operation and we supervise them there. Hopefully it will be a good training tool for us. We're doing it now on a limited basis. We provide the supervisors, so we've got to make money at it.

We're still doing camera assembly, but some of it may be automated through robotics over the next few years, so I'm looking at products we can bring in for 1989. What happens if some of that gets automated? Then we switch to the service sector.

We've gone through our period of rapid growth. We're plateauing now, and looking at a redirection; new growth will come out of that. Redirection could mean that we'll be out of this building in a few years; I believe we'll have a new place to reside. There's going to be a *change* in direction. The world is changing around us. If we don't change with it, we limit what we can do.

CASE **21**

GM ALLISON JAPAN LTD.

RICHARD T. DAILEY

The decision by the Allison Division of General Motors Corporation (GM) to name James D. Swaim president of GM Allison Japan Ltd. (GMAJ) in June 1987 was a significant departure from the way Allison had been dealing with its Japanese joint venture. Swaim, who arrived at GMAJ in October 1984, was not only the first American selected to run the company, but also the first employee sent to GMAJ from Allison on a long-term assignment. Even though GMAJ had been in operation since 1972, the business had not performed up to Allison's expectations. By the early 1980s some problems, particularly warranty problems, had become serious, and Allison's management realized that something had to be changed.

On his arrival in Tokyo, Swaim said his first goal was "to help try to fix the problems at GMAJ and learn if we also had product problems that were aggravating the basic issues." After his appointment as GMAJ's president he reflected on the need to change the way the Japanese company had been doing business. One of his primary concerns, he commented, "was how to make sure that Allison's Japanese customers understood that Allison was indeed committed to the Japanese market for the long term."

ALLISON DIVISION

In the early 1970s, the Allison Division of General Motors Corporation and Isuzu Motors established GM Allison Japan Ltd. as a joint venture company for the purpose of selling heavy-duty transmissions to Japanese truck manufacturers. Although General Motors Corporation had established a marketing organization to sell automobiles in Japan in the late 1920s, this was its first effort at selling components to Japanese original equipment manufacturers (OEMs).

Source: This case was prepared by the author as a basis for classroom discussion and not to illustrate either effective or ineffective handling of managerial situations. The generous cooperation of GM Allison Japan Ltd. is gratefully acknowledged. © 1991, Richard T. Dailey.

Allison was a well-known U.S. manufacturer of gas turbine engines for fixed-wing aircraft and helicopters and of heavy-duty transmissions for trucks and buses, mining and construction equipment, and industrial applications. In 1970, a major change took place in the transmission side of the business when the company began manufacturing a family of new automatic transmissions for trucks, buses, and certain types of off-highway construction and mining equipment. The initial members of this family of transmissions were designed primarily for use in highway vehicles equipped with gasoline engines.

The company manufactured transmissions in a variety of sizes for school buses, the largest intercity buses, small city delivery trucks, and the largest over-the-road tractors. This new line of transmissions represented a major shift in both product line and product development, and this shift would require extensive marketing efforts to gain acceptance by end users.

In September 1970, General Motors merged its Detroit Diesel and Allison divisions, which gave Allison full access to the Detroit Diesel worldwide distribution system. The new Detroit Diesel Allison Division permitted a smoother integration of the new line of transmissions into GM's Detroit Diesel products.

ESTABLISHING THE JOINT VENTURE COMPANY

In early 1970, General Motors Corporation began discussions with Isuzu Motors, an OEM of automobiles, trucks, and buses, regarding the feasibility of GM assuming an equity position in Isuzu. Although Isuzu is not a major automobile manufacturer in Japan (its market share is about 3 percent), it is a major manufacturer of commercial vehicles, with a market share of around 16 percent (see Exhibits 1 and 2). The idea of an automatic transmission for trucks intrigued Isuzu's management and was an incentive for them to join GM in the joint venture. The Japanese partners envisioned local manufacture when sales volume reached sustainable levels.

An equity position in Isuzu, GM executives reasoned, would provide GM with a foothold in the growing Japanese motor vehicle market, which grew at an average annual rate of 3.7 percent between 1973 and 1988 (see Exhibit 3) and which GM, as well as other U.S. manufacturers, had been unsuccessful in entering. Other U.S. motor vehicle manufacturers were developing relationships with Japanese auto and truck manufacturers. Of necessity, the talks between Isuzu and GM were kept very quiet, because if word leaked out that a corporation the size of GM was negotiating with a company of Isuzu's size, the rumor would have a major impact on the price of Isuzu shares on the Tokyo stock exchange.

JAPANESE INDUSTRIAL ORGANIZATION

In order to smooth the development and operation of the new joint venture, GM needed to link up with one of Japan's industrial groups known as *keiretsu*. A *keiretsu* consists of about twenty major companies, one in each industrial

EXHIBIT 1 TRUCK SALES IN JAPAN 1984–1988 INDUSTRY VOLUME AND ISUZU VOLUME

	MODEL YEAR				
	1984	*1985*	*1986*	*1987*	*1988*
Heavy Duty					
Industry	116,236	111,374	109,243	126,925	165,419
Isuzu	30,214	28,492	28,215	33,055	42,460
10 Ton					
Industry	39,647	37,227	36,958	44,624	58,375
Isuzu	9,768	8,471	8,487	10,641	13,644
4 Ton					
Industry	65,237	63,767	62,749	72,256	93,729
Isuzu	17,965	17,781	17,514	20,278	26,193
Light Duty					
Industry	701,783	706,683	728,097	784,682	927,786
Isuzu	87,617	88,451	82,171	84,813	102,408
2–3 Ton					
Industry	154,876	158,869	160,835	170,112	207,551
Isuzu	49,120	50,798	48,576	53,310	65,260
1–1½ Ton					
Industry	206,077	209,825	208,602	228,103	272,053
Isuzu	32,761	33,004	29,585	27,727	30,286

Source: Company records.

sector. The typical *keiretsu* contains a bank, a trading company, an insurance company, and a company in one of the basic industries such as steel or motor vehicle manufacturing. Nearly all of the equity of the individual companies in the group is held by other members of the *keiretsu,* one of the characteristics of Japanese business culture that makes it difficult for outsiders to obtain a controlling ownership in a Japanese firm. A major purpose of the *keiretsu* is to help members of the group raise investment funds. General Motors chose to become associated with the *keiretsu* headed by Dai-Ichi Kangyo Bank (DKB) because GM had worked with DKB on previous occasions.

C. Itoh Trading Company. To ease any problems that GM might encounter in importing components to Japan, the company followed a suggestion that a Japanese trading company become a partner in the joint venture. GM chose C. Itoh, one of Japan's largest trading companies and a member of the DKB *keiretsu,* for this purpose. Isuzu Motors is also a member of this group of companies.

Kawasaki Heavy Industries. Kawasaki Heavy Industries (KHI), another member of the DKB group, became part of the joint venture because it manufactured manual transmissions for Isuzu. In addition, KHI was interested in the vehicular gas turbine engine Allison was developing. Kawasaki Heavy Industry

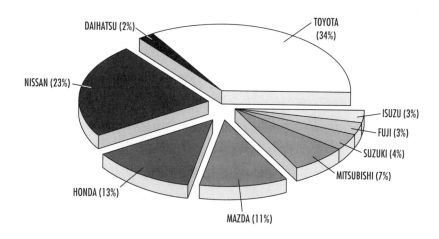

EXHIBIT 2 JAPANESE AUTOMOBILE PRODUCTION SHARE BY AUTOMAKER IN 1987

1987 AUTO PRODUCTION = 7.9 MILLION AUTOS

Source: Japan Automobile Manufacturer Association.

executives thought the engine might have applications in Japanese heavy-duty trucks and construction equipment.

EQUITY SHARES IN THE JOINT VENTURE

By 1972, the negotiations were completed and General Motors Allison Japan Ltd. became a reality. It was formed as a joint venture company with General Motors holding 50 percent of the shares, Isuzu 20 percent, Kawasaki 20 percent, and C. Itoh the remaining 10 percent. The new company was capitalized at ¥90 million. General Motors Corporation, meanwhile, had purchased a 38-percent equity position in Isuzu Motors, which represented an infusion of new capital for Isuzu.

Unfortunately, a Detroit Diesel Allison distributor in Japan who had been buying transmissions from Allison and selling them to Japanese truck manufacturers lost his marketing rights as a result of the new joint venture.

STAFFING THE NEW COMPANY

The agreement for staffing the new organization called for the president of the company to represent the Japanese partners of the joint venture and for the vice-president to represent the GM side of the business. Accordingly,

EXHIBIT 3 MOTOR VEHICLE SALES IN JAPAN

	CARS				TRUCKS				BUSES				Grand total
	Large	Small	Mini	Total	Large	Small	Mini	Total	Large	Small	Mini		
1973	489,273		97,014	586,287	70,499	592,558	410,775	1,073,832	14,843		14,843		1,674,962
1974	9,064	1,652,855	713,170	2,379,137	164,086	986,672	538,743	1,693,502	10,256	17,572	27,828		4,100,467
1975	45,125	2,531,396	157,120	2,737,641	121,118	999,155	431,181	1,551,454	8,818	11,018	19,836		4,308,931
1976	46,592	2,224,783	178,054	2,449,429	128,501	1,043,467	459,395	1,631,363	9,415	13,044	23,259		4,104,051
1977	53,069	2,277,934	165,072	2,500,095	132,041	1,031,804	587,393	1,671,238	9,327	13,509	22,916		4,194,249
1978	64,428	2,620,069	172,213	2,056,710	156,764	1,094,590	549,022	1,800,376	10,496	14,281	24,777		4,681,063
1979	84,721	2,781,889	170,263	3,036,873	185,732	1,220,668	686,494	2,092,894	9,589	14,396	23,985		5,153,752
1980	74,931	2,608,215	174,038	2,854,176	154,472	1,144,167	839,308	2,137,947	9,414	13,973	23,381		5,015,518
1981	78,221	2,522,936	165,538	2,866,695	126,731	1,045,420	1,064,253	2,237,404	9,358	13,539	22,897		5,126,996
1982	63,697	2,794,789	179,786	3,038,272	113,136	933,321	1,154,909	2,201,366	8,705	13,088	21,793		5,261,431
1983	80,210	2,857,490	197,911	3,135,611	111,314	910,529	1,204,553	2,226,396	7,947	12,363	20,310		5,382,317
1984	82,068	2,019,540	193,546	3,095,554	120,717	935,031	1,265,190	2,320,938	7,688	12,579	20,267		5,436,759
1985	73,539	2,069,527	161,013	3,104,083	110,009	945,484	1,367,685	2,431,172	8,798	12,775	21,513		5,556,834
1986	81,178	2,926,590	138,255	3,146,823	109,676	954,918	1,475,580	2,540,174	8,826	12,791	21,617		5,793,014
1987	111,415	3,036,517	126,868	3,274,880	132,114	1,042,219	1,547,247	2,721,581	8,786	13,232	22,018		6,010,399
1988	166,054	3,397,628	153,677	3,717,359	169,036	1,214,847	1,596,220	2,900,103	9,177	14,365	23,542		6,721,004

Source: Japan Automobile Manufacturers' Association

GMAJ's first president was Japanese and came from Kawasaki Heavy Industries. The GM vice-president was an American who was also vice-president of GM Overseas Corporation—Japan Branch. His office was in Tokyo but was some distance from GMAJ's offices. All other members of the joint venture company were Japanese.

SOURCE OF EMPLOYEES FOR GMAJ

Some employees of GMAJ were "seconded" employees from other companies participating in the joint venture. It is common practice among the Japanese *keiretsu* for one company in the group, especially one of the lead companies, to provide employees to another company in the group. These employees may be lent on a short-term basis to work on technical problems or may be sent to the company for an indefinite period of time.

Employees seconded to a company for the long term are likely to be near retirement age with no possibility of advancing any further in their organization. Often they are moved to make room for younger employees, or they may be sent as a favor to a manager of one of the participating companies. Several employees seconded to GMAJ were in these two categories.

Isuzu had high hopes for the success of the joint venture and seconded some of its best people to the new company. For example, an engineer who was seconded was considered one of Isuzu's best transmission designers for manual transmissions. Allison executives in Indianapolis reasoned that since the Japanese knew the truck market in Japan better than they did, it would not take long for GMAJ to become a profitable company.

In 1974, GMAJ's first president returned to Kawasaki Heavy Industries, and Toshihiko Tamura of Isuzu Motors became GMAJ's second president. He remained in that position until 1987. Mr. Tamura was trained as an electrical engineer, and although he had extensive experience in the marine engine business, he had none in the transmission business.

STAFF TRAINING AND SUPPORT

GMAJ's product engineers and certain technical support people were sent to Allison's manufacturing headquarters in Indianapolis for two- to four-week training sessions. They were provided with the latest technical information about Allison's automatic transmissions and had sessions on troubleshooting, the types of vehicles that were best suited for an automatic transmission, and the associated manuals and documentation that would assist them in answering their questions after they had returned to Japan. All technical manuals and other documentation provided to the GMAJ engineers were in English.

Periodically engineers from Indianapolis visited GMAJ to provide on-site technical support and service. Typically, these people visited Japan three or four times each year and stayed for two to three weeks.

A final support mechanism was provided by the Detroit Diesel Allison regional marketing organization headquartered in Singapore. Every four to six weeks, a Singapore-based sales representative, not necessarily an engineer, would visit GMAJ and spend one or two days providing whatever assistance he could to solve problems that could not be handled by the Japanese staff.

PRODUCT MARKETING

GM Allison Japan was established as a Japanese company to sell truck and bus transmissions initially to Isuzu Motors and subsequently to other Japanese vehicle manufacturers. Although a U.S. firm owned 50 percent of GMAJ, it conducted business as a Japanese firm. James Swaim pointed out that

> as a "child" company or captive firm, it serves at the pleasure of its owners, all of whom are represented on the board of directors. Japanese tradition for component suppliers required them to work only with the OEMs and leave all end user contact to the OEMs. Most U.S. component manufacturers and distributors work with the end users of their products, encouraging them to specify their equipment from the vehicle manufacturers. In this kind of relationship the component manufacturers quite often become complementary engineering organizations to the end users, as well as marketing partners to the OEMs.
>
> In Japan, however, the situation is much different. Sales representatives of the component manufacturers do not call on the end users. Rather they work primarily with the OEMs and, to a limited extent, the dealers, when selling their products. Thus, the executives of GMAJ never established the type of relationships with the end users that would result in their specifying Allison transmissions.

THE JAPANESE TRUCK MARKET

Over 95 percent of Japanese trucks are equipped with diesel engines, which tend to be more fuel efficient than gasoline engines. By comparison, approximately 45 percent of the U.S. trucks in the medium-duty class had diesel engines in 1984. (By 1990, however, that figure was expected to approach 90 percent.) Another aspect of the Japanese market that makes it different from its U.S. counterpart is that Japanese trucks are much smaller on average than those in the United States.

MARKETING STRATEGY

The marketing strategy Isuzu implemented at the outset of the joint venture was traditional for a Japanese company. It offered low option prices, special deals for fleet operators, and special programs to get the Allison product into the marketplace. Because of the relatively weak yen at that time (see Exhibit 4), import prices for the transmissions were rather high. Isuzu, however, ab-

EXHIBIT 4 ANNUAL AVERAGE RATE OF JAPANESE YEN PER U.S. DOLLAR 1971–1989

YEAR	¥/$
1971	347.48
1972	303.08
1973	270.89
1974	291.53
1975	296.69
1976	296.38
1977	267.80
1978	208.42
1979	218.18
1980	226.63
1981	220.63
1982	249.06
1983	237.55
1984	237.45
1985	238.47
1986	168.35
1987	144.60
1988	128.17
1989	138.07

Source: Federal Reserve Bulletin.

sorbed the higher costs internally in order to price the Allison product competitively.

PRICE INCREASES

Japanese captive companies such as GMAJ are unable to increase the product prices they charge to their parent firms solely on the basis of higher costs they may experience for labor, raw materials, energy, and the like. Instead, they are expected to improve productivity and manufacturing efficiency at least enough to hold the line on prices. They are expected to improve their production methods enough to reduce prices to their customers. If the captive firm is unable to develop programs that will reduce costs and thus prices, the parent firm will usually provide assistance by lending personnel, acquiring new technology, or whatever it may take to achieve productivity improvements. A price increase is considered a last resort.

Allison's costs were escalating due to a rapidly increasing rate of inflation in the U.S. during the late 1970s and early 1980s, and it was passing these costs on in the form of higher prices to its joint venture partner. In spite of these price increases, however, GMAJ was expected to do business in the Japanese manner. That meant minimal price increases to its customers. Even several years' losses were to be accepted as a normal part of doing business. (Exhibits 5, 6, and 7 show the company's financial position in the mid- to late 1980s.)

PRODUCT AVAILABILITY

Isuzu was so anxious to get Allison automatic transmissions into the marketplace that it sold one to anybody who requested it. This approach led to some technical difficulties because dealers often failed to select the proper options necessary for successful operation in certain applications and difficult operating conditions. For example, inner-city delivery trucks need transmissions that will stand up to stop-and-go conditions. Isuzu worked hard to overcome these initial growing pains and eventually was able to surmount most of the technical problems.

MARKET DEVELOPMENT

GM Allison Japan was established for the primary purpose of working with Isuzu Motors. Any programs with the other three truck manufacturers—Hino, Mitsubishi, and Nissan Diesel—would be secondary after the Isuzu market was established. By the end of 1973, the first transmissions were being tested under actual highway and other working conditions. The program was about ready to launch on a commercial scale, and with growing confidence in the product, Isuzu began an active marketing campaign.

THE 1978–1979 OIL SHOCK

Just about when the market for the automatic transmission began to show significant growth (see Exhibit 8), the Organization of Petroleum Exporting Countries' (OPEC's) oil embargo stunned the world's industrialized nations. This second oil shock of the decade was to send oil prices as high as $47 per barrel, thus increasing energy costs substantially on a worldwide basis.

Extremely high oil prices in Japan resulted in a significant recession and an annual rate of inflation that reached 18 percent. Commercial vehicle sales, as a result, declined to extremely low levels for the next several years (see Exhibit 3), and fuel efficiency became of paramount importance. The drop in truck and bus sales in Japan led to lower sales for automatic transmissions. Another factor discouraging automatic transmission sales at this time was the perception among some end users that automatics were less fuel efficient than manual transmissions.

In spite of rapidly rising prices for raw materials and energy products, it was impossible for GMAJ to raise transmission prices because captive companies must find ways to reduce costs rather than to raise prices. Thus, GMAJ's president, Toshihiko Tamura, was forced to implement a cost-cutting drive that included greatly reduced funds for travel and telephone expenses. For

EXHIBIT 5 INCOME STATEMENT (UNIT: YEN)

	APRIL 1, 1985 TO MARCH 31, 1986	APRIL 1, 1986 TO MARCH 31, 1987
Sales	632,687,169	318,832,286
Cost of sales	499,902,770	277,039,435
SELLING PROFIT	132,784,399	41,792,851
Selling, General & Admin. Expenses:		
Salaries and bonus	45,635,054	61,913,065
Legal welfare expenses	8,106,522	16,986,979
Rent	13,338,798	18,421,354
Advertisement	727,249	5,680,796
Claim expenses	4,676,082	5,906,500
Travel expenses	2,185,202	1,349,040
Depreciation	2,465,829	7,525,619
Other expenses	16,123,811	19,261,665
TOTAL EXPENSES	93,258,547	137,045,018
OPERATING PROFIT (LOSS)	39,525,852	(95,252,167)
Non-Operating Profit:		
Interest income	2,719,680	2,177,422
Miscellaneous income	12,951,823	123,085,022
TOTAL NON-OPERATING PROFIT	15,671,503	125,262,444
GROSS PROFIT (LOSS) FOR THE TERM	55,197,355	30,010,277
Non-Operating Loss:		
Interest paid	9,202,363	8,474,853
Tax for interest on deposit	465,311	403,635
Miscellaneous loss	15,239,486	15,210,587
TOTAL NON-OPERATING LOSS	24,907,160	24,089,075
Recurring profit (loss)	30,290,195	5,921,202
Income tax	10,915,660	*5,700,000
Net profit (loss) after taxes	19,374,535	221,202
Profit (loss) brought forward	(16,730,732)	2,643,803
Unappropriated profit	2,643,803	2,865,005
*Remarks:		
Corporate Income Tax	4,540,000	
Municipal Inhabitant Tax	1,160,000	
TOTAL INCOME TAX	5,700,000	
DISPOSITION OF PROFIT		
Unappropriated profit	2,865,005 Yen	
(Including profit for the term)	221,202 Yen	
We would like to dispose the above amount as follows:		
Profit carried forward	2,865,005 Yen	

EXHIBIT 6 BALANCE SHEET (UNIT: YEN)

	MARCH 31, 1986	MARCH 31, 1987
ASSETS		
Current:		
Cash, banks	94,982,382	81,304,533
Notes receivable	92,145,502	65,110,802[a]
A/C receivable	99,182,586	56,476,327
Inventory	89,034,191	94,361,413
Other current	84,701,978	112,277,592[b]
Allowance for doubtful A/C	(2,900,000)	(2,750,000)
TOTAL CURRENT ASSETS	457,146,639	406,780,667
Fixed:		
Buildings/structures	6,173,000	8,729,390
Machinery & equipment	11,124,742	11,274,742
Vehicles	5,874,450	8,320,000
Tools & office equipment	13,518,655	28,697,833
Telephone right	399,793	618,193
Telex right	25,938	—0—
Guarantee money	12,912,360	22,376,640
Accumulated depreciation	(28,655,767)	(32,428,476)
TOTAL FIXED ASSETS	21,373,171	47,588,322
TOTAL ASSETS	478,519,810	454,368,989

(*continued*)

example, GMAJ salesmen could not call on customers who were demanding on-site assistance.

TECHNICAL PROBLEMS

As a Japanese company, GMAJ was obliged to provide after-sales service to its end-user customers on a continuing basis. Allison provided the same warranty for its products to the Japanese original equipment manufacturers as it did for its U.S. customers; a two-year warranty on parts and labor. The OEMs, in turn, provided a one-year warranty as their standard vehicle warranty. However, Japanese vehicle manufacturers are accustomed to providing generous coverage on power train components to their customers regardless of the published warranty provisions.

ESCALATING WARRANTY COSTS

In 1979 Allison began experiencing serious technical problems with its automatic transmissions, nearly all of which had been installed in on-highway trucks and buses. The problems (and in many cases the complete failure of a unit) resulted in escalating warranty costs for the company. These problems

EXHIBIT 6 (Continued)

	MARCH 31, 1986	MARCH 31, 1987
LIABILITY & EQUITY		
Current:		
S/T borrowings	155,000,000	155,000,000
Notes payable	120,738,452	124,857,421
Accounts payable trade	74,284,562	39,920,661
Accounts payable others, due within one year	3,741,888	2,549,810
Tax payable for business tax	3,120,000	150,000
Other current	780,136	7,170,129
TOTAL CURRENT LIABILITIES	357,665,038	329,648,021
Reserve:		
Reserve for corporation tax	11,021,960	—0—
Reserve for bonus	1,930,000	4,670,105
Reserve for retirement allowance	13,799,009	25,725,858[c]
TOTAL RESERVE	26,750,969	30,395,963
TOTAL LIABILITIES & RESERVE	384,416,007	360,043,984
Equity:		
Common stock, ¥10,000 par value: authorized 36,000 shares, issues 9,000 shares	90,000,000	90,000,000
Profit (loss) brought forward	(16,730,732)	2,643,803
Profit (loss) for term	19,374,535	221,202
General contingency	1,460,000	1,460,000
TOTAL SHAREHOLDERS' EQUITY	94,103,803	94,325,005
TOTAL LIABILITY & SHAREHOLDER'S EQUITY	478,519,810	454,368,989

Notes: [a] Balance of notes discounted—none.

[b] Outstanding accounts receivable others in U.S. dollar denomination, U.S. $691,931.94, is included in Other Current Assets. Conversion into yen with exchange rate as of fiscal year end results in ¥100,226,341; accordingly exchange loss of ¥9,211,176 has been incurred.

[c] Reserve for director's retirement allowance (based on commercial law article (287-2) ¥15,225,858 has been included in Reserve for Retirement Allowance.

Remarks: Important Accounting Principles
1. Inventories are stated at Cost Standard by FIFO.
2. Depreciation of fixed assets—declining balance method.
3. Provisions and Reserves

    Reserve for Bonus is reserved on tax regulation basis (matching to payment terms).

    Reserve for Retirement Allowance is provided on tax regulation basis. 40% of retirement allowance at the end of the term.

    Standard of Provision for Uncollectible Accounts is provided on tax regulation basis.
4. Conversion of accounts receivable and payable on foreign currency basis into Japanese yen is rated by exchange rate at the time we received credit memorandum—received basis.

EXHIBIT 7 INCOME STATEMENT (UNIT: YEN)

	APRIL 1, 1986 TO MARCH 31, 1987	APRIL 1, 1987 TO MARCH 31, 1988
ORDINARY P/L		
Operating P/L:		
Sales	318,832,286	533,131,443
Cost of sales	277,039,435	464,796,986
Selling & admin. expenses	137,045,018	164,232,507
OPERATING LOSS	(95,252,167)	(95,898,050)
Non-Operating Income:		
Interest	2,177,422	1,219,775
Others, including Marketing Assistance	123,085,022	128,120,766
Non-Operating Expenses		
Interest	8,474,853	8,655,362
Others	15,614,222	24,526,493
ORDINARY PROFIT (LOSS)	5,921,202	250,636
EXTRA-ORDINARY P/L		
Profit		
Retirement reserve for director reverted	–0–	15,225,858
Loss		
Retirement gratuity paid	–0–	15,150,000
NET PROFIT BEFORE TAXES	5,921,202	326,494
INCOME TAX & RESIDENT TAX (CREDIT)	5,700,000	(3,330,380)
NET PROFIT AFTER TAXES	221,202	3,656,874
PROFIT BROUGHT FORWARD	2,643,803	2,865,005
UNAPPROPRIATED LOSS THIS TERM	2,865,005	6,521,879

Remarks: Tax details (refund for the taxes paid for the previous term):
  Income Tax   (3,004,730)
  Resident Tax   (325,650)

were also experienced by GMAJ and were far more serious in the Japanese market than in the U.S. Product quality and service are integral parts of the Japanese way of doing business. The goal is to establish long-term relationships between customers and suppliers. For example, contracts, if used, are usually written in a very broad manner with an opening date and automatic renewal. The principal concept of most agreements is to work together to resolve any conflicts in a mutually satisfactory manner.

TECHNICAL SPECIFICATION MISUNDERSTANDINGS

GM Allison Japan was caught in the position of receiving a product with a fixed set of technical specifications and requirements from Allison in the United States and then representing those specifications to a third party, an

EXHIBIT 8 GMAJ SALES OF ALLISON AUTOMATIC TRANSMISSIONS

FISCAL YEAR	UNITS
1973	10
1974	26
1975	114
1976	81
1977	299
1978	724
1979	1138
1980	977
1981	643
1982	481
1983	378
1984	445
1985	467
1986	600
1987	1034
1988	1050
1989	2753

Source: Company records.

OEM. In several instances, Japanese truck manufacturers wanted changes made in the transmission specifications to meet what they considered special Japanese operating conditions. Allison, however, was unwilling to agree to any changes in the technical specifications that GMAJ's engineers suggested or requested. Allison's marketing department took the position that since its transmissions were sold in several other countries without design changes, none were necessary for Japan. Furthermore, in the opinion of Allison's management, the Japanese market was not big enough to justify costly design changes.

As a result of the technical problems Allison was experiencing at this time, the Japanese OEMs were forced to deal with both application problems and product problems without recourse to technical improvements in the product. This left the Japanese manufacturers with the impression that Allison, a nonresident company attempting to sell automatic transmissions in Japan, was not interested in them. In short, they felt the Japanese market was not important to Allison.

Although GMAJ sales volume in its early years pointed toward a successful joint venture, more recent events placed the company in an unprofitable position. Managers at Allison's headquarters in Indiana, meanwhile, paid little attention to Japan. They recognized that sales in the Japanese market had become sluggish, but they were preoccupied with technical problems and the escalating warranty costs occurring in the U.S. market.

INCREASING INDUSTRY COMPETITION

The worldwide automotive industry was becoming increasingly competitive in the 1980s, particularly in the United States. For a variety of reasons including exchange rates, productivity, quality, service, and marketing, U.S. manufacturers of automotive products faced their stiffest competition from Japan.

In early 1984, Allison noted a shift developing in the U.S. market for medium-duty trucks. U.S. truck manufacturers had fallen behind their Japanese and European counterparts in the development and design of low-cab-forward or stub-nose trucks. In these vehicles the engine is behind or underneath the cab. Such trucks form the backbone of many inner-city delivery systems. Companies that needed fuel-efficient and maneuverable trucks were turning to Japanese and European models because of their superior designs and advanced dieselization.

Japan's entry into the U.S. medium-duty truck market was of primary importance. Allison had a 25-percent penetration in this market segment, and to maintain its market share it needed to make its transmissions broadly available in Japanese imports. This realization prompted Allison's senior management to conclude that to protect the home market, Allison through GMAJ must battle the Japanese on their home turf.

THE EARLY 1980s AT GMAJ

Allison's technical problems with its automatic transmissions in the United States had an additional ramification in the Japanese market. There, GMAJ's engineers discovered, the automatic transmission was still not technically correct for vehicles equipped with diesel engines. Additionally, Tamura's cost-cutting drive only added to GMAJ's problems because its salesmen could not provide adequate customer service. Recognizing the need to solve the company's continuing warranty problems, Allison's management formed a special interdisciplinary team to address those issues in 1981. Team members were relieved of their regular responsibilities and given a six-month assignment to study and provide solutions for the whole range of problems Allison was having with its transmissions. Among the disciplines represented were engineering, service, marketing, warranty, manufacturing, finance, and reliability. The team was headed by the director of quality control at Allison's aircraft engine operation, and James Swaim represented the sales and service side of the business.

SWAIM'S BACKGROUND

After earning a degree in engineering from the General Motors Institute, Swaim joined Allison's aircraft service department. From there he moved through several other departments at Allison. His work included an assignment as a field service representative in Okinawa from 1964 to 1966. As a manager in the transmission service department, Swaim created an after-sales service infrastructure that permitted a smooth integration of the transmission line into the Detroit Diesel Allison distribution system. From that position he was named manager of the service operations organization in the transmission service department. His responsibilities included technical support for the field organization and manufacturers, customer contact, product liability, and product liability litigation. In addition, he was worldwide technical coordinator for Allison's transmission products, a position that required him to interact with all of the various disciplines in the transmission operation.

ALLISON'S DECISION TO ASSIGN AN ENGINEER TO GMAJ

By the early part of 1984, Allison's senior executives had reached the conclusion that someone from the United States should be in Tokyo on a permanent basis. Considerable thought went into Allison's decision regarding the type of individual who should be sent to Japan. Swaim was selected on the basis of his previous experience in Okinawa, his knowledge of Allison's product line, the wide range of positions he had held with the company, and the fact that he and his wife could adapt to the Japanese culture.

THE SITUATION IN 1984

When Swaim arrived in Tokyo in October 1984, his assignment was to provide technical and engineering support to the GMAJ staff. He reported to Allison's headquarters in Indianapolis rather than to anyone in Japan.

Swaim learned after his arrival in Tokyo that because GMAJ acted as a traditional Japanese company, no one from GMAJ was contacting the end-user customers. In that culture, only the manufacturers and dealers have direct customer contact. Although Allison managers had been urging GMAJ's president to make direct customer contact in order to convince them of the advantages of automatic transmissions, Tamura did not feel that was his responsibility. Japanese component manufacturers don't usually deal directly with end users except to handle technical questions. Allison's managers in Indianapolis did not fully appreciate the rigidity of these Japanese business practices. Thus, they were unable to understand fully the extent of the problems at their joint venture operation in Tokyo. Likewise, the managers at GMAJ had very little knowledge of how to work with U.S. vendors or suppliers.

Swaim also learned that some GMAJ salesmen had little technical understanding of Allison's products. Furthermore, the joint venture OEM engineering groups often operated with insufficient technical data and on some occasions obsolete data. GMAJ management had decided to forego supplying comprehensive technical data to some of its non-Isuzu Japanese manufacturers. Since GMAJ considered the data to be proprietary in nature, there was concern about it falling into the hands of "Isuzu competitors." In the vendor-subservient role required of Japanese component suppliers, GMAJ found it difficult to implement the new technical specifications developed by the task force in Indianapolis to correct the product problems.

BUILDING RELATIONSHIPS

Until Swaim's arrival, no American from Allison had stayed at GMAJ longer than six weeks. Swaim, therefore, set out to reassure the Japanese that "he was an Allison employee and that his company was committed to the Japanese market; that he was now resident in Japan and here to help GMAJ and its OEM customers solve their technical problems. Of primary importance was convincing the Japanese that he would indeed be in Japan for an extended period of time." Japanese managers strive to build long-term business relationships with suppliers, manufacturers, wholesalers, customers, and any others who may be a part of the distribution chain. Therefore, Swaim's long-term commitment was an essential factor in building trust.

TRANSMISSION SERVICE NETWORK

GMAJ sold Allison transmissions directly to the OEMs and thus acted as both wholesaler and distributor. It did not, however, provide company-owned, after-sales service to either the manufacturers or the end users. Instead, by contracting with an Isuzu dealer and an Isuzu dealer-related organization, GMAJ developed a service support network for Allison transmissions. Since the owner of a Nissan Diesel, for example, would be unwilling to take his truck to an Isuzu dealer for service, GMAJ arranged for an independent diesel repair shop to service Allison transmissions for end users who did not own Isuzu trucks.

PRICING

GMAJ purchased Allison transmissions for resale to its four OEM customers at a special discounted price from the Allison factory. GMAJ charged the OEMs prices ranging from ¥500,000 to ¥600,000 with no fixed, recognizable pricing policy. Because of the special relationship between GMAJ and Isuzu, however, GMAJ was able to charge Isuzu slightly higher prices than it charged the other three OEMs. To increase the sales volume of its child company, Isuzu elected to sell Allison transmissions in the marketplace as an option for ¥200,000 and absorb the cost difference. The other OEMs' option prices were ¥800,000. Because of this large disparity, the other OEMs concluded that GMAJ, with its close Isuzu relationship, offered preferential pricing to Isuzu.

THE GMAJ STAFF IN 1984

When Swaim arrived in Tokyo, the staff at GMAJ consisted of two engineers, a bookkeeper, a sales manager, and three salesmen, all of whom were seconded employees from Isuzu. The engineering manager, though a competent engineer, had little management experience. The sales manager had been in the sales promotion side of the business at Isuzu, was without technical ability, and had no experience in selling trucks or truck components. The group also included an employee seconded from C. Itoh. Most of these people were near retirement age and came to GMAJ expecting to be there three or four years. In addition, two young employees had been hired from outside the participant companies. None of GMAJ's 1984 employees had been there when the company was started in 1972.

A NEW PRESIDENT

Swaim had been in Japan for nearly three years when he was named president of GMAJ, and he realized that he must move the company in a new direction. He understood the need to develop a strategy that would expand Allison's share of the Japanese transmission market. He also was aware of the importance of developing the Japanese market in order to protect Allison's market share in the U.S.

CASE 22

THE SWATCH

ARIEH A. ULLMANN

THE SWISS WATCH INDUSTRY IN THE LATE 1970s

In 1978, when Dr. Ernst Thomke became managing director of ETA Industries after a 20-year leave of absence from the watch industry, the position of this Swiss flagship industry had changed dramatically. Just like other industries suffering from the competitive onslaught from the Far East, the Swiss watch industry faced the biggest challenge in its 400 years of existence. Once the undisputed leaders in technology and market share—a position the Swiss had gained thanks to breakthroughs in mechanizing the watch manufacturing process during the 19th century—the Swiss had fallen on hard times.

In 1980, Switzerland's share of the world market, which in 1952 stood at 56%, had fallen to a mere 20% of the finished watch segment while world production had grown from 61 million to 320 million pieces and movements annually. Even more troubling was the fact that the market share loss was more pronounced in finished watches compared to nonassembled movements (see Exhibit 1). Measured in dollars, the decline was not quite as evident, because the Swiss continued to dominate the luxury segment of the market while withdrawing from the budget price and middle segments.

The Swiss, once the industry's leaders in innovation, had fallen behind. Manufacturers in the United States, Japan, and Hong Kong had started to gain share, especially since the introduction of the electronic watch. Although in 1967 the Swiss were the first to introduce a model of an electronic wristwatch

---

Source: **This case was prepared by Arieh A. Ullmann, State University of New York at Binghamton, as a basis for class discussion rather than to illustrate either appropriate or inappropriate handling of an administrative situation. Distributed by the North American Case Research Association. © 1991, Arieh A. Ullmann and the North American Case Research Association.**

EXHIBIT 1 WORLD WATCH PRODUCTION AND MAJOR PRODUCING COUNTRIES (1980)

COUNTRY	PRODUCTION (MILLION PIECES)			MARKET SHARE (%)
	Electronic	Mechanic	Total	
Switzerland: watches	10.4	52.6	63.0	20
incl. nonassembled movements	13.0	83.0	96.0	30
Japan: watches	50.4	17.1	67.5	21
incl. nonassembled movements	53.8	34.1	87.9	28
United States: watches & movements	2.0	10.1[1]	12.1[1]	
Rest of Europe: watches & movements	4.5	57.2[1]	61.7[1]	42[2]
Rest of Asia: watches & movements	76.0	31.3[1]	113.0[1]	
Latin America: watches & movements	—	2.7[1]	2.7[1]	

[1] Includes unassembled movements.
[2] Without unassembled movements.
Source: Swiss Watchmanufacturers Federation (FH).

(at the Concours de Chronométrie of the Neuchâtel Observatory) smashing all accuracy records, they dismissed the new technology as a fad and continued to rely on their mechanical timepieces where most of their research efforts were concentrated. The Swiss dominated the watch segments based on older technologies, but their market shares were markedly lower for watches incorporating recently developed technologies (see Exhibit 2). Thus, when electronic watches gained widespread acceptance, the Swiss watch producers found themselves in a catch-up race against the Japanese, who held the technological edge (see Exhibit 3).

The situation of this industry, which exported more than 90% of its production, was aggravated by adverse exchange rate movements relative to the U.S. dollar, making Swiss watches more expensive in the U.S.—then the most important export market. Until the early 1970s the exchange rate stood at

EXHIBIT 2 SWITZERLAND'S SHARE OF WORLD PRODUCTION BY TYPE OF TECHNOLOGY (1975)

TECHNOLOGY	YEAR OF INTRODUCTION	STAGE OF PRODUCT LIFE CYCLE	SWISS SHARE (%)
Simple mechanical	pre WWII	declining	35
Automatic	1948	mature	24
Electric	1953	declining	18
Quartz (high freq.)	1970	growing	10
Quartz (solid state)	1972	growing	3

Source: Swiss Watchmanufacturers Federation, Bulletin No. 13, Bienne, June 30, 1977.

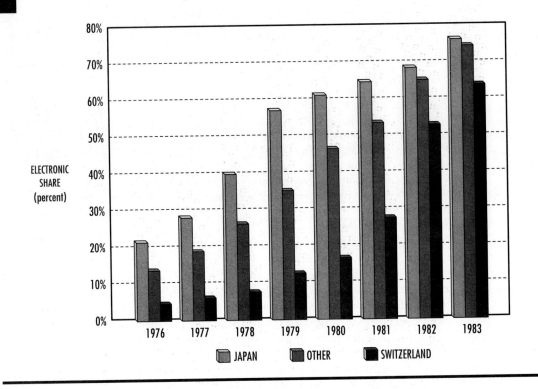

EXHIBIT 3 SHARE OF ELECTRONIC WATCHES OF ANNUAL OUTPUT

US$1 = SFr. 4.30; by the end of the decade it had dropped to about US$1 = SFr. 1.90.

STRUCTURAL CHANGE IN THE INDUSTRY

Throughout its history the Swiss watch industry was characterized by an extreme degree of fragmentation. Until the end of the 1970s, frequently up to 30 independent companies were involved in the production of a single watch. Skilled craftsmen called suppliers manufactured the many different parts of the watch in hundreds of tiny shops, each one specializing in a few parts. The movements were either sold in loose parts (*ébauche*) or assembled to *chablons* by *termineurs*, which in turn supplied the *établisseurs*, where the entire watch was put together. In 1975, 63,000 employees in 12,000 workshops and plants were involved in the manufacture of watches and parts. Each établisseur designed its own models and assembled the various pieces purchased from the many suppliers. Only a few vertically integrated manufacturers, which performed most of the production stages inhouse, existed (see Exhibit 4). The watches were either exported bearing the assembler's or manufacturer's brand name (factory label) through wholly owned distributors and independent importers or sold under the name of the customer (private label). By the late 1970s, private label sales constituted about 75% of Swiss exports of finished watches. In addition, the Swiss also exported movements and unassembled parts to foreign customers (see Exhibit 5).

This horizontally and vertically fragmented industry structure had developed over centuries around a locally concentrated infrastructure and depended entirely on highly skilled craftsmen. Watchmaking encompassed a large number of sophisticated techniques for producing the mechanical watches, and this complexity was exacerbated by the extremely large number of watch models. The industry was highly specialized around highly qualified labor, requiring flexibility, quality, and first-class styling at low cost.

This structure was, however, poorly suited to absorb the new electronic technology. Not only did electronics render obsolete many of the watchmaker's skills that had been cultivated over centuries, it also required large production volumes to take advantage of the significant scale and potential experience effects. The traditional Swiss manufacturing methods provided few benefits from mass production, and the extreme fragmentation from the suppliers to the distributors prevented even these. Furthermore, the critical stages in the value-added chain of the watch shifted from parts and assembly—where the Swiss had their stronghold—to distribution, where the Japanese concentrated their efforts. En-

EXHIBIT 4 TRADITIONAL STRUCTURE OF SWISS WATCH INDUSTRY

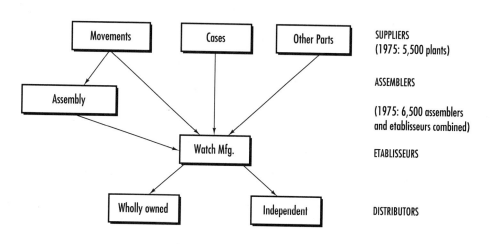

Source: Bernheim, 1981.

EXHIBIT 5 SWISS EXPORTS OF WATCHES, MOVEMENTS, AND PARTS 1960–1980

	FINISHED WATCHES		ASSEMBLED MOVEMENTS		UNASSEMBLED MOVEMENTS	
YEAR	Pieces[1]	Francs[2]	Pieces[1]	Francs[2]	Pieces[1]	Francs[2]
1960	16.7	767.2	8.2	192.7	n.a.	n.a.
1965	38.4	1334.4	14.8	282.7	n.a.	n.a.
1970	52.6	2033.8	18.8	329.5	n.a.	n.a.
1975	47.2	2391.2	18.6	329.1	5.4	44.0
1976	42.0	2262.4	20.0	343.0	8.0	54.2
1977	44.1	2474.5	21.9	381.3	15.8	94.8
1978	39.7	2520.0	20.6	380.3	18.7	103.5
1979	30.3	2355.6	18.6	371.1	20.2	121.0
1980	28.5	2505.8	22.5	411.8	32.7	189.2
1981	25.2	2880.2	19.9	382.5	27.5	160.5
1982	18.5	2754.6	12.7	256.4	14.5	81.0
1983	15.7	2676.6	14.6	247.1	12.7	76.8
1984	17.8	3063.9	14.5	235.0	14.6	98.5
1985	25.1	3444.1	13.4	220.4	18.8	138.9
1986	28.1	3391.0	13.3	213.4	19.4	133.3
1987	27.6	3568.0	11.1	179.4	20.9	122.8
1988	28.0	4128.8	12.2	202.8	31.9	162.1
1989	29.9	5080.0	12.6	217.7	28.4	136.3

[1] in millions
[2] in millions of current Swiss Francs

Source: Swiss Watchmanufacturers Federation.

casement, marketing, wholesale, and retail distribution, which the Japanese producers emphasized, represented over 80% of the value added.

Sales of mechanical watches in the budget and middle price segments dropped rapidly when electronic watches entered the market. Initially, these electronic watches were introduced by U.S. producers with electronic capability such as Texas Instruments, Inc.; National Semiconductor Corp.; Hughes Aircraft; Intel; and Time Computer. Due to rapidly rising production and sales volumes of electronic watches, unit prices dropped dramatically from $2,000 to $1,000 in 1970 to $40 in 1975 and less than $20 by the end of the 1970s. At this time most of the early American digital watch producers had started to withdraw from the watch business, and it was the cheap digital watch from Hong Kong that flooded the market. As an indication of the eroded market power of the Swiss, the sale of assembled and unassembled movements had started to rise while exports of finished watches declined (Exhibit 5)—a trend that negatively affected domestic employment.

The industry's misfortune caused large-scale layoffs, and bankruptcies started to increase steeply in the 1970s. Since the watch industry was concentrated around a few towns in the western part of Switzerland, the ensuing job losses led to regional unemployment rates unknown in Switzerland since the 1930s (see Exhibit 6).

ETA, where Dr. Thomke became managing director, was a subsidiary of Ebauches SA, which in turn was a subsidiary of ASUAG (General Corporation of Swiss Horological Industries Ltd.). ASUAG had been created in 1931 during the first consolidation period in the industry. It was Switzerland's largest watch corporation (total sales in 1979: SFr. 1,212 million) and combined a multitude of companies under its holding structure, including such famous brands as Certina, Eterna, Longines, and Rado. Ebauches, of which ETA was part, was the major producer of watch movements for ASUAG and most of the other Swiss établisseurs. The other large Swiss manufacturer was SSIH (Swiss Watch Industry Corporation Ltd.), which also was a creation of the same 1931 consolidation and whose flagships were Omega and Tissot. During the second half of the 1970s, ASUAG suffered from declining profitability and cash flow, poor liquidity, rising long-term debt, and dwindling financial reserves due to sluggish sales of outdated mechanical watches and movements, which made up about two-thirds of ASUAG's watch sales. Diversified businesses outside the watch segment contributed less than 5% of total sales.

EXHIBIT 6 SWISS WATCH INDUSTRY: COMPANIES AND EMPLOYMENT

YEAR	NUMBER OF COMPANIES	EMPLOYMENT
1960	2,167	65,127
1965	1,927	72,600
1970	1,618	76,045
1975	1,169	55,954
1976	1,083	49,991
1977	1,021	49,822
1978	979	48,305
1979	867	43,596
1980	861	44,173
1981	793	43,300
1982	727	36,808
1983	686	32,327
1984	634	30,978
1985	634	31,949
1986	592	32,688
1987	568	29,809
1988	562	30,122

Source: Swiss Watchmanufacturers Federation.

TURNAROUND AT ETA

ERNST THOMKE

Ernst Thomke grew up in Bienne, the Swiss capital of watchmaking. After an apprenticeship in watchmaking with ETA, he enrolled in the University of Berne, where he first studied physics and chemistry and later medicine. After his studies he joined Beechams, a large British pharmaceuticals and consumer products company, as a pharmaceutical salesman. In 1978, when his old boss at ETA asked him to return to his first love, he was managing director of Beecham's Swiss subsidiary and had just been promoted to Brussels. However, his family did not wish to move and so, after eighteen years, he was back in the watch business.

When he took over, morale at ETA was at an all-time low due to the prolonged period of market share losses and continued dismissals of personnel. ETA's engineers and managers no longer believed in their capabilities of beating the competition from Japan and Hong Kong. Although ETA as the prime supplier of watch movements did not consider itself directly responsible for the series of failures, it was equally affected by the weakened position of the Swiss watch manufacturers. When Thomke assumed his role as managing director of ETA, he clearly understood that for a successful turnaround his subordinates needed a success story to regain their self-confidence. But first a painful shrinking process had to be undertaken in order to bring costs under control. Production, which used to be distributed over a dozen factories, was concentrated in three centers and the number of movement models reduced from over 1,000 to about 250.

THE TURNAROUND PLAN

As a first step, a project called "Delirium" was formulated with the objective of creating the world's thinnest analog quartz movement—a record held by Seiko at that time. When Thomke revealed his idea to ETA's engineers, they were quick to nickname it "Delirium Tremens" because they considered it crazy. But Thomke insisted on the project despite his staff's doubts. To save even the tiniest fraction of a millimeter, some watch parts were for the first time bonded to the case instead of layered on top of the watch back. In addition, a new extra-thin battery was invented.

The first watch with the Delirium movement was launched in 1979, and ETA had its first success in a long tine. In that year, ASUAG sold more than 5,000 pieces at an average price of $4,700, with the top model retailing for $16,000.

The Delirium project not only helped boost the morale of ETA's employees, it also led to a significant change in strategy and philosophy with ETA's parent, Ebauches SA. No longer was Ebauches content with its role as the supplier of movement parts. In order to fulfill its responsibility as the primary supplier of technologically advanced quality movements at competitive prices to Switzerland's établisseurs, Ebauches argued, it was necessary to maintain a minimum sales volume that exceeded the reduced domestic demand. Therefore, in 1981 ETA expanded its movement sales beyond its then current customers in Switzerland, France, and Germany. This expansion meant sales to Japan, Hong Kong, and Brazil. Ebauches thus entered into direct international competition with Japanese, French, German, and Soviet manufacturers. In short, ETA claimed more control over its distribution channels and increased authority in formulating its strategy.

As a second step, ETA's organizational culture and structure were revamped to foster creativity and to encourage employees to express their ideas. Management layers were scrapped and red tape reduced to a minimum. Communication across departments and hierarchical levels was stressed, continued learning and long-term thinking encouraged, and playful trial-and-error and risk taking reinforced. The intention was to boost morale and create corporate heroes.

The third step consisted of defining a revolutionary product in the medium- or low-price category. By expanding even farther into the downstream activities, Thomke argued, ETA would control more than 50% instead of merely 10% of the total value added. Since 1970 the watch segments below SFr. 200 had experienced the highest growth rates (see Exhibit 7). These were the segments the Swiss had ceded to the competitors from Japan and Hong Kong. As a consequence, the average price of Swiss watch exports had steadily risen, whereas the competitors exported at declining prices. Given the overall objective to reverse the long-term trend of segment retreat, it was crucial to reenter one or both of the formerly abandoned segments. Thomke decided to focus on the low price segment. "We thought we'd leave the middle market for Seiko and Citizen. We would go for the top and the bottom to squeeze the Japanese in the sandwich." The new concept was summarized in four objectives:

1. Price: Quartz-analog watch, retailing for no more than SFr. 50.
2. Sales target: 10 million pieces during the first three years.
3. Manufacturing costs: Initially SFr. 15, less than those of any competitor. At a cumulative volume of 5 million pieces, learning and scale econ-

EXHIBIT 7 WORLD WATCH PRODUCTION BY PRICE CATEGORY, 1970 vs. 1980

PRICE CATEGORY	1970 SALES	1980 SALES	GROWTH%
	(Million pieces)		
less than 100 SFr.	110	290	264
100–200 SFr.	33	50	52
200–500 SFr.	20	20	0
more than 500 SFr.	7	10	43

Source: Thomke, Ernst, "In der Umsetzung von der Produktidee zur Marktreife liegtein entscheidender Erfolgsfaktor," io Management-Zeitschrift, no. 2 (1985), pp. 60–64.

omies would reduce costs to SFr. 10 or less. Continued expansion would yield long-term estimated costs per watch of less than SFr. 7.
4. Quality: High quality, waterproof, shock resistant, no repair possible, battery the only replaceable element, all parts standardized, free choice of material, model variations only in dial and hands.

The objectives were deliberately set so high that it was impossible to reach them by improving existing technologies; instead, they required novel approaches. When confronted with these parameters for a new watch, ETA's engineers responded with "That's impossible," "Absurd," "You're crazy." Many considered it typical of Thomke's occasionally autocratic management style, which had brought him the nickname "Ayatollah." After all, the unassembled parts of the cheapest existing Swiss watch at that time cost more than twice as much! Also, the largest Swiss watch assembler—ETA's parent ASUAG—sold 750,000 watches annually scattered over several hundred models.

In an interview with the *Sunday Times Magazine,* Thomke told the story: "A couple of kids, under 30, said they'd go away and look at the Delirium work and see if they could come up with anything. And they did. They mounted the moving parts directly on to a moulded case. It was very low cost. And it was new, and that is vital in marketing." The concept was the brainchild of two engineers. Elmar Mock, a qualified plastics engineer, had recommended earlier that ETA acquire an injection molding machine to investigate the possibilities of producing watch parts made of plastic. Jacques Muller was a horological engineer and specialist in watch movements. Their new idea was systematically evaluated and improved by interdisciplinary teams consisting of the inventors; product and manufacturing engineers; specialists from costing, marketing, and accounting; as well as outside members not involved in the watch industry.

The fourth step required that ETA develop its own marketing. In the 1970s and early 1980s it did not have a marketing department. Thomke turned to some independent consultants and people outside the watch industry with extensive marketing experience in apparel, shoes, and sporting goods to bring creative marketing to the project. Later, as sales of the Swatch (as the new watch was called) expanded worldwide, a new marketing team was built up to cover the growing marketing, communications, and distribution activities.

PRODUCT AND PROCESS TECHNOLOGY

A conventionally designed analog watch consisted of a case in which the movement was mounted. The case was closed with a glass or crystal. The movement included a frame onto which the wheels, the micromotor needed for analog display, other mechanical parts, and the electronic module were attached with screws. First the movement was assembled and then mechanically fixed in the case. Later the straps were attached to the case.

The Swatch differed with regard to both its construction and the manufacturing process.

Construction. First, the *case* not only was an outer shell but served as the mounting plate as well. The individual parts of the movement were mounted directly into the case—the Delirium technology was perfected. The case itself was produced by a new, very precise injection molding process that was developed specifically for this purpose. The case was made of extremely durable plastic, which created a super-light watch.

Second, the number of *components* was reduced significantly from 91 parts for a conventional analog quartz watch to 51 parts. Unlike conventional watch assembly, the individual parts of the movement—the electronic module and the motor module—were first assembled in subgroups before mounting and then placed in the case like a system of building blocks.

Third, the *method of construction* differed: The parts were no longer attached with screws. Components were riveted and welded together ultrasonically. This process eliminated screws and threads, reduced the number of parts, and made the product rugged and shock resistant. As the crystal was also welded to the case, the watch was guaranteed water-resistant up to 100 feet.

Fourth, the tear-proof *strap* was integrated into the case with a new, patented hinge system that improved wearing comfort.

Fifth, the *battery*—the only part with a limited life expectancy of about three years—was inserted into the bottom of the case and closed with a cover.

Production. First, as a special advantage the Swatch could be assembled from one side only.

Second, because of the one-sided assembly, it was possible to fully automate the watch-mounting process. Ordinary watches were assembled in two separate operations: the mounting of the movement and the finishing. The Swatch, however, was produced in one single operation. According to representatives of the Swiss watch manufacturers, this technology incorporated advanced CAD/CAM technology as well as extensive use of robotics and was the most advanced of its kind in the world.

Third, due to the new design the number of elements needed for the Swatch could be significantly reduced and the assembly process simplified. As a prerequisite for incorporating this new product technology, new materials had to be developed for the case, the glass, and the micromotor. A new assembly technology was designed and the pressure diecasting process perfected.

Fourth, quality requirements had to be tightened, because the watch could not be reopened and therefore, except for the battery, could not be repaired. Given these constraints, each step in the manufacturing process had to be carefully controlled including the parts, the preassembled modules, the assembly process itself, and the final product. This was especially important because in the past high reject rates of parts and casings indicated that many Swiss manufacturers had difficulties with quality control, which damaged their reputation.

Overall, the new product design and production technology reduced the costs significantly and raised product quality above watches in the same price category produced by conventional technology.

MARKETING

The new marketing team came up with an approach that was unheard of in this industry dominated by engineers.

Product Positioning. Contrary to conventional wisdom in the industry, it was not the product, its styling, and its technical value that were emphasized but its brand name. Quality attributes such as waterproofness, shock resistance, color, and preciseness were less important than the association of the brand name with positive emotions such as "fun," "vacation," and "joy of life." The watch was positioned as a high-fashion accessory for fashion-conscious people between ages 18 and 30. As it turned out, many people outside this age range started buying the Swatch. Jean Robert, a Zurich-based designer, was responsible for Swatch's innovative designs.

Pricing. The price was set at a level that allowed for spontaneous purchases yet provided the high margins needed for massive advertising.

Distribution. As a high-fashion item competing in the same price range as some Timex and Casio models, the Swatch was not sold through drugstores and mass retailers. Instead, department stores, chic boutiques, and jewelry shops were used as distribution channels. Attractive distributor margins and extensive training of the retailers' sales personnel combined with innovative advertising ensured the unique positioning of the product.

Brand name. In 1982, 20,000 prototypes of 25 Swatch models were pretested in the United States, which was viewed as the toughest market and the trendsetter for the rest of the world. The unisex models differed only in color of the cases and straps and the dial designs. It was during these pretests that Franz Sprecher, one of the outside consultants of the marketing team, came up with the name "Swatch" (Swiss + Watch = Swatch) during a brainstorming session with a New York–based advertising agency concerning the product's positioning and name. Up until then Sprecher's notes repeatedly mentioned the abbreviation "S'Watch." During this meeting Sprecher took the abbreviation one step further and created the final name.

THE SWATCH TEAM

Besides Thomke, three individuals were crucial for the successful launching of the Swatch: Franz Sprecher, Max Imgrueth, and Jacques Irniger.

Franz Sprecher obtained a masters in economics and business from the University of Basle. Following one year as a research assistant and doctoral student, he decided to abandon academia and to enter the international business world as a management trainee with Armour Foods in Chicago. After six months, he returned to Switzerland and joined Nestlé in international marketing. Two years later he became sales and marketing director of a small Swiss/Austrian food additives company. Later Sprecher moved to the positions of international marketing director of Rivella and then account group manager at the Dr. Dieter Jaeggi Advertising Agency in Basle. Sprecher took a sabbatical at this point in his career and planned to return to the international business world as a consultant within a year. Toward the end of this period, while thinking of accepting a position as a professor at the Hoehere Wirtschafts- and Verwaltungschochschule in Lucerne, he received a phone call from Dr. Thomke concerning the new watch. Thomke told Sprecher: "You've got too much time and not enough money, so why don't you come and work for me." Sprecher then took over the marketing of the as of yet unnamed product as a freelance consultant. Today, he continues to consult for Swatch as well as for other brands such as Tissot and Omega.

Another important person involved in the creation of the Swatch was Max Imgrueth. Imgrueth was born in Lucerne, Switzerland. Following graduation from high school in St. Maurice, a small town in the Valais surrounded by high mountains, he studied art history in Florence and fashion and leather design in Milan. After a brief stint in linguistics, he enrolled in business courses at the Regency Polytechnic in England and at New York University. In 1969 he left the United States because he had difficulties obtaining a work permit and started to work in a women's specialty store in Zurich, Switzerland. Two years later he switched to apparel manufacturing and became manager for product development and marketing. In 1976 he was recruited by SSIH, owners of the Omega and Tissot brands. From 1976 to 1981 he was in charge of product development and design at Omega's headquarters in Bienne. Conflicts with the banks—which at that time effectively owned SSIH due to continued losses—over Omega's strategy led him to resign from his job and to start a consulting business. One of his first clients was ETA, which was just getting ready to test-market the Swatch in San Antonio, Texas. He succeeded in convincing ETA that San Antonio was the wrong test market and that the Swatch as a new product required other than the traditional distributors. As a consequence, New York and Dallas were chosen as primary test sites and TV advertising and unconventional forms of public relations were tried out. While working on debugging the introduction of the Swatch he was offered the position of president of Swatch USA, a job that initially consisted of an office on Manhattan's Fifth Avenue and a secretary.

The third individual involved in the early phase of the Swatch was Jacques Irniger, who joined ETA in 1983 as vice-president of marketing and sales for both ETA and Swatch worldwide. In 1985 he was a board member of Swatch SA, vice-president of marketing-sales of ETA SA Fabriques d'Ebauches, and president of Omega Watch Corp., New York. Irniger received his doctorate in economics from the University of Fribourg, a small city located in the French-speaking part of Switzerland. After training positions in marketing research and management at Unilever and Nestlé, he became marketing manager at

Colgate Palmolive in Germany. After Colgate, he moved on to Beecham Germany as vice-president of marketing. Before joining ETA he was vice-president of marketing and sales for Bahksen International.

MARKET INTRODUCTION

The Swatch was officially introduced in Switzerland on March 1, 1983—the same year that ASUAG and SSIH merged after continued severe losses that necessitated a SFr. 1.2 billion bailout by the Swiss banks. During the first four months 25,000 Swatch pieces were sold, more than a third of the initial sales objective of 70,000 for the first 12 months. According to some distinguished jewelry stores located on Zurich's famous Bahnhofstrasse, where Switzerland's most prestigious and expensive watches were purchased by an endless stream of tourists from all over the world, the Swatch did not compete with the traditional models. On the contrary, some jewelers reported that the Swatch stimulated sales of their more expensive models. The success of the Swatch encouraged other Swiss manufacturers to develop similar models, which, however, incorporated conventional quartz technology.

Subsequent market introductions in other countries used high-powered promotion. In Germany, the launching of the Swatch was accompanied by a huge replica of a bright yellow Swatch that covered the entire facade of the black Commerzbank skyscraper in Frankfurt's business district. The same approach was used in Japan. On Christmas Eve in 1985, the front of a tall building in Tokyo was decorated with a huge Swatch that was 11 yards long and weighed more than 14,000 pounds. Japan, however, turned out to be a difficult market for the Swatch. The 7,000-yen Swatch competed with domestic plastic models half the price. Distribution was restricted to 11 department stores in Tokyo only and carried out without a Japanese partner. After six months it became obvious that the original sales target of SFr. 25 million for the first year could not be reached. The head of the Japanese Swatch operation, Harold Tune (an American), resigned. His successor was a Japanese.

In the United States, initial sales profited from the fact that many American tourists coming home from vacations in Switzerland helped in spreading the word about this fancy product, which quickly became as popular a souvenir as Swiss army knives. U.S. sales of this $30 colorful watch grew from 100,000 pieces in 1983 to 3.5 million pieces in 1985—a sign that Swatch USA, ETA's American subsidiary, was successful in changing the way timepieces were sold and worn. No longer were watches precious pieces given as presents on special occasions such as confirmations, bar mitzvahs, and marriages and meant to be worn for a lifetime. "Swatch yourself" meant wearing two or three watches simultaneously like plastic bracelets. Swatch managers traveling back and forth between the United States and Switzerland wore two watches, one showing EST time, the other Swiss time.

The initial success prompted the company to introduce a ladies' line one year after the initial introduction, thus leading to 12 models. New Swatch varieties were created about twice a year. In addition, special models were designed for the crucial Christmas season. In 1984 scented models were launched, and a year later a limited edition model with diamonds, called Limelight, sold for $100.

The Swatch was a very advertising-intensive line of business. For 1985, the advertising budget of Swatch USA alone was $8 million, with U.S. sales estimated at $45 million (1984 sales: $18 million). In 1985, Swatch USA sponsored MTV's New Year's Eve show; the year before it had sponsored a breakdancing festival offering $25,000 in prizes and the Fresh Festival '84 in Philadelphia.

Swatch managers were careful not to flood the market. They claimed that in 1984 an additional 2 million watches could have been sold in the United States. In England, 600,000 watches were sold in the first year, and the British distributor claimed he could have sold twice as many.

CONTINUED GROWTH

The marketing strategy called for complementing the $30 dollar timepiece with a range of Swatch accessories. The idea behind this strategy was to associate the product with a lifestyle and thereby create brand identity and distinction from the range of look-alikes that had entered the market and were copying the Swatch models with a delay of about three months. In late 1985 Swatch USA introduced an active apparel line called Funwear. T-shirts, umbrellas, and sunglasses followed in the hope of adding an extra $100 million in sales in 1986. Product introduction was accompanied by an expensive and elaborate publicity campaign including a four-month TV commercial series costing $2.5 million; an eight-page Swatch insert featuring a dozen Swatch accessories in *Glamour, GQ, Vogue,* and *Rolling Stone;* and a $2.25 million campaign on MTV. In January 1985 Swatch AG was spun off from ETA. The purpose of the new Swatch subsidiary was to design and distribute watches and related consumer goods such as shoes, leather and leather imitation accessories, clothes, jewelry and perfumes, toys, sports goods, glasses and accessories, pens, lighters, and cigarettes. Swatch production, however, remained with ETA. Furthermore, licenses were being considered for the distribution of the products. All of these products as well as the watches were designed in the United States, with subsequent adaptations for European markets.

This strategy of broadening the product line was, however, not without risks, because it could dilute the impact of the brand name. *Forbes* mentioned the examples of Nike, which failed miserably when it tried to expand from running wear to leisure wear, and Lewis, when it attempted to attach its brand recognition to more formal apparel. Yet Max Imgrueth was quick to point to other examples such as Terence Conran, a designer and furniture maker who succeeded in building a retail empire ranging from kitchen towels to desk lamps around his inexpensive, well-designed home furnishings aimed at the young.

ENSURING SUCCESS

At the end of 1985, 45,000 Swatch units were produced daily and annual sales were expected to reach 8 million pieces (1984: 3.7 million). The Swatch was so successful that by the end of 1984 Swatch profits after recovering all product-related investments and expenditures contributed significantly toward ETA's overhead. The Swatch represented 75% of SMH's unit sales of finished watches and made it SMH's number one brand in terms of unit sales and number two brand in terms of revenues, topping such prestige brands as Longines and Rado. (The Swiss Corporation for Microelectronics and Watchmaking Industries Ltd.—SMH—was the new name of the Swatch parent after the ASUAG-SSIH merger in 1983.) Thanks to the Swatch, SMH was able to increase its share of the world market (1985: 400 million units) from 1% to 3% within four years. The success also invigorated the Swiss industry at large (Exhibit 5).

Despite this success, the managers at Swatch continued to perfect and expand the Swatch line. In 1986, the Maxi-Swatch, which was ten times the size of the regular Swatch, was introduced. Before the start of the ski season during the same year, the Pop-Swatch, which could be combined with different-color wristbands, was launched. As a high-technology extravaganza, the Pop-Swatch could also be worn in combination with a "Recco-Reflector," which had been developed by another SMH subsidiary. The Recco reflected radar waves emitted from a system and thus helped locate skiers covered by avalanches.

In 1987 Swatch wall models and the Swatch Twinphone were introduced. The latter was not just colorful. It had a memory to facilitate dialing and, true to its origin, provided the unconventional service of a built-in "party line" so that two people could use it simultaneously.

1988 saw the successful introduction of the Twinphone in the USA, Japan, and the airport duty-free business as well as the expansion of the Pop-Swatch product line. The Swatch accessories line was discontinued due to unmet profit objectives and negative impact on the Swatch brand image.

In its 1989 annual report SMH reported cumulative sales of over 70 million Swatch pieces (see Exhibit 8). Over 450 models of the original concept had been introduced during the first seven years. In addition, the Swatch had become a collector's item. Limited-edition models designed by well-known artists brought auction prices of SFr. 1,600, SFr. 3,900, and SFr. 9,400—about 25 to 160 times the original price!

In 1990 the "Swatch-Chrono" was launched to take advantage of the chronometer fashion. Except for the basic concept—plastic encasement and battery as the only replaceable part—it had little in common with the original model and represented a much more complex instrument. It had four micromotors instead of only one due to the added functions and was somewhat larger in diameter. Despite the added complexity, it was claimed to be as exact

EXHIBIT 8   SWATCH SALES

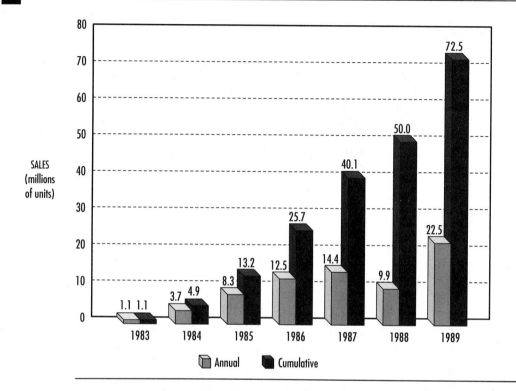

and robust as the original Swatch. As a special attraction the watch, which was available in six models, retailed for only SFr. 100. The company was also experimenting with a mechanical Swatch to be marketed in developing countries where battery replacement posed a problem. In this way the company hoped to boost sales in regions that represented only a minor export market for the Swiss.

The success of the Swatch at the market front was supported by a carefully structured organization. Just like the other major brands of SMH, the Swatch had its own organization in each major market responsible for marketing, sales, and communication. These regional offices where supported by SMH country organizations that handled services common to all brands such as logistics, finance, controlling, administration, EDP, and after-sales service.

The Swatch also meant a big boost for Dr. Thomke's career. He was appointed general manager of the entire watch business of the reorganized SMH and became one of the key decision makers of the new management team that took over in January 1985. The "Swatch Story" was instrumental in the turnaround of SMH, the result of the merger of two moribund companies. Only six years later, SMH showed a very healthy bottom line (see Exhibit 9).

EXHIBIT 9 SMH: FINANCIAL DATA (IN MILLION SFR.)

	1989	1988	1987	1986	1985	1984
A. Income Statement Data						
SALES REVENUES						
Gross Sales	2,146	1,847	1,787	1,895	1,896	1,665
COSTS						
of which: Materials	793	681	670	759	812	714
Personnel	646	580	577	593	556	541
External services	346	331	335	356	360	286
Depreciation	80	71	73	68	61	60
Total operating costs	1,865	1,663	1,655	1,776	1,789	1,758
Operating profit (loss)	236	142	117	103	66	51
Income before taxes	209	126	90	82	72	38
Net income	175	105	77	70	60	26
B. Balance Sheet Data						
ASSETS						
Current assets	1,194	1,065	1,103	1,080	1,070	1,049
of which: Inventories	602	562	528	568	513	524
Fixed assets	529	510	533	507	456	451
Total assets	1,723	1,575	1,636	1,587	1,526	1,500
LIABILITIES AND STOCKHOLDER'S EQUITY						
Short-term debt	367	384	442	503	524	501
Long-term debt	295	302	798	801	862	898
Total liabilities	662	686	1,240	1,304	1,386	1,399
Total shareholders equity	892	760	697	648	490	420
Total liabilities & shareholders equity	1,723	1,575	1,636	1,587	1,526	1,500
C. Other Data						
Personnel: in Switzerland	8,822	8,385	8,526	9,323	9,173	8,982
Personnel: abroad	2,963	2,893	2,597	2,611	2,353	2,311
Personnel: total	11,785	11,278	11,123	11,934	11,526	11,293
Stock price* high	560	395	490	700	410	**
low	378	178	150	375	127	

*Nominal value SFr./share.
**No shares publicly traded.

THE FUTURE

Despite the smashing success of the Swatch and its contribution to the reinvigoration of the Swiss watchmaking industry, future success was by no means guaranteed.

First, competition remained as fierce as ever. The 1980s were characterized by an oversupply of cheap watches because many manufacturers had built capacity ahead of demand. Prices dropped, especially for the cheapest digital watches, a segment that the Swiss avoided. However, several competitors switched to the more sophisticated analog models and thus created competition for the Swatch. Many look-alikes with names such as Action Watch, A-Watch, and so on flooded the market.

Second, the Swiss had to guard their brand recognition and not just because of the diversification of the Swatch line. It was not clear whether the Swatch brand name was strong enough to create a sustainable position against the imitations. In addition, the quality advantage of the Swatch was neither evident to the consumer nor a top priority in the purchasing decision.

A third issue was for how long the Swatch could maintain its technological advantage. By the late 1980s all imitations were welded together. In addition, many competitors, especially the Japanese, were larger than SMH and therefore able to support larger R&D budgets.

A fourth threat was market saturation. Although countries with a GDP per capita of over $5,000 made up only 17% of the world's population, they absorbed 87% of Swiss watch exports. The changes in watch technology and pricing during the previous 10 years had increased watch consumption. In England, consumption grew from 275 watches per 1,000 inhabitants in 1974 to 370 watches 10 years later. In the United States, the respective figures were 240 and 425 units, of which 90% comprised low-price electronic models. The average life of a watch was much shorter today and consumers had started to own several watches, but market saturation could not be ruled out. Given the trendy nature of the Swatch, it could fall out of fashion as quickly as it had conquered the market. For this situation SMH was not as well prepared as, say, Seiko or Casio, whose non-watch businesses were much stronger and contributed more in terms of overall sales and profits.

A fifth threat was the continued rapid development of technology, especially in the field of communications. Increasingly, time measurement was evolving into one of several features of an integrated communication system. Clocks were already integrated in a wide variety of products including household durables, computers, and telephones. Several SMH subsidiaries involved in microelectronics, electronic components, and telecommunications were busy developing products in this area and searching for applications in other markets as well. In the late 1980s SMH started to test prototypes of a combined watch/pager. In late 1990 Motorola introduced a combined watch/pager. It was not clear how SMH and its Swatch subsidiary would fare in this evolving area despite its high-technology sector, which, however, was smaller than that of its competitors (see Exhibit 10).

Finally, despite the success of the Swatch and of several mid-priced models under other brand names such as Tissot, the Swiss continued to experience higher than average unit prices for their watches. This was partially due to the success of their luxury mechanical watch pieces, which were frequently encased in precious metal and adorned with precious stones. However, executives of Swiss companies expressed concern about this trend.

EXHIBIT 10 SMH SUBSIDIARIES (1990)

SMH SWISS CORPORATION FOR MICRO-ELECTRONICS AND WATCHMAKING INDUSTRIES LTD NEUCHÂTEL	HOLDING COMPANY	
COMPANY NAME, REGISTERED OFFICES	FIELD OF ACTIVITY	SHAREHOLDING SMH DIRECT OR INDIRECT IN %
Omega SA, Bienne	Watches	100
Compagnie des montres Longines Francillon SA, Saint-Imier	Watches	100
—SA Longines pour la vente en Suisse, Saint-Imier	Distribution	100
—Columna SA, Lausanne	Distribution	100
—Longines (Singapore) PTE Ltd. Singapore (SIN)	Distribution	100
—Longines (Malaysia) Sdn. Kuala Lumpur (MAL)	Distribution	100
Montres Rado SA, Lengnau	Watches	100
Tissot SA, Le Locle	Watches	100
Certina, Kurth Frères SA, Grenchen	Watches	100
Mido G. Schaeren & Co SA, Bienne	Watches	100
—Mido Industria e Comercio de Relogios Ltda, Rio de Janeiro (BRA)	Distribution	100
Swatch SA, Bienne	Watches	100
ETA SA Fabriques d'Ebauches, Grenchen	Watches, movements, electronic components and systems	100
—ETA (Thailand) Co Ltd. Bangkok (THA)	Watches and movements	100
—Leader Watch Case Co. Ltd. Bangkok (THA)	Watch cases	100
Endura SA, Bienne	Watches	100
Lascor SpA, Sesto Calende (ITA)	Watch cases	100
Diantus Watch SA, Castel San Pietro	Watches and movements	100
Société Européenne de Fabrication d'Ebauches d'Annemasse (SEFEA) SA, Annemasse (FRA)	Watch components and electronic assembly	100
Ruedin George SA. Bassecourt	Watch cases	100
EM Microelectronic-Mann SA, Marin	Microelectronics	100
SMH Italia S.p.A. Rozzano (ITA)	Distribution (Omega, Rado, Tissot, Swatch, Flik Flak)	100
SMH (UK) Ltd. Eastleigh (GBR)	Distribution (Omega, Tissot)	100
SMH Australia Ltd. Prahran (AUS)	Distribution (Omega, Tissot, Swatch, Flik Flak)	100
SMH Belgium SA, Bruxelles (BEL)	Distribution (Omega, Tissot, Flik Flak)	100
SMH Ireland Ltd. Dublin (IRL)	Distribution (Omega)	100
SMH Sweden AB, Stockholm (SWE)	Distribution (Omega, Longines, Tissot, Certina, Swatch, Flik Flak)	100

EXHIBIT 10 (Continued)

SMH SWISS CORPORATION FOR MICRO-ELECTRONICS AND WATCHMAKING INDUSTRIES LTD NEUCHÂTEL	HOLDING COMPANY	
COMPANY NAME, REGISTERED OFFICES	FIELD OF ACTIVITY	SHAREHOLDING SMH DIRECT OR INDIRECT IN %
SMH Uhren und Mikroelektronik GmbH, Bad Soden (RFA)	Distribution (Omega, Longines, Rado, Tissot, Certina, Swatch, Flik Flak)	100
SMH France SA, Paris (FRA)	Distribution (Omega, Longines, Rado, Tissot, Certina, Swatch, Flik Flak)	100
SMH España SA, Madrid (ESP)	Distribution (Omega, Tissot, Swatch, Flik Flak)	100
SMH Japan KK, Tokyo (JPN)	Distribution (Longines, Tissot, Swatch)	100
SMH (HK) Ltd. Hong Kong (HKG)	Distribution (ETA, Longines, Swatch, Flik Flak)	100
SMH (US) Inc., Dover Del. (USA)	Holding company	100
—Hamilton Watch Co Inc., Lancaster Pa. (USA)	Distribution	100
—Omega Watch Corp., New York N.Y. (USA)	Distribution	100
—Rado Watch Co Inc., New York N.Y. (USA)	Distribution	100
—Swatch Watch U.S.A. Inc., New York N.Y. (USA)	Distribution (Swatch, Flik Flak)	100
—ETA Industries Inc., New York N.Y. (USA)	Distribution	100
—Unitime Industries Inc., Virgin Islands V.I. (USA)	Assembly	100
—Movomatic USA, Inc., Lancaster Pa. (USA)	Distribution (Movomatic, Farco)	100
—Tissot (US), Inc., New York N.Y. (USA)	Distribution	100
—Omega Electronics Equipment (US), Inc., Lancaster Pa. (USA)	Distribution	100
—SMH (US) Services, Inc., Lancaster Pa. (USA)	Service, watches	100
Technocorp Holding SA, Le Locle	Holding	100
—Renata SA, Itingen	Miniature batteries	100
—Oscilloquartz SA, Neuchâtel	High stability frequency sources	100
—OSA-France Sar. Boulogne-Billancourt (FRA)	Distribution	100
—Omega Electronics SA, Bienne	Sports timing equipment, score-board information systems	100
—Omega Elecronics Ltd. Eastleigh (GBR)	Distribution	100
—Lasag SA, Thun	Laser for industrial and medical application	100
—Lasag USA. Inc., Arlington Heights Ill. (USA)	Distribution	100
—Technica SA, Grenchen	Machine tools and tools	100

(*continued*)

EXHIBIT 10 (Continued)

SMH SWISS CORPORATION FOR MICRO-ELECTRONICS AND WATCHMAKING INDUSTRIES LTD NEUCHÂTEL

HOLDING COMPANY

COMPANY NAME, REGISTERED OFFICES	FIELD OF ACTIVITY	SHAREHOLDING SMH DIRECT OR INDIRECT IN %
—Meseltron SA, Corcelles	High precision length measurement (Cary) and automatic size control (Movomatic)	100
—Farco SA, Le Locle	Bonding equipment	100
—Comadur SA, La Chaux-de-Fonds	Products in hard materials	100
—Nivarox-FAR SA, Le Locle	Watch components and thin wires	100
—A. Michel SA, Grenchen	Industrial components and delay systems	100
—Régis Mainier SA, Bonnétage (FRA)	Precision and watch components	97.5
—Vuillemin Marc. Bonnétage (FRA)	Precision and watch components	70.1
Chronometrage Suisse SA (Swiss Timing), Bienne	Sports timing	100
Asulab SA, Bienne	Research and development	100
ICB Ingénieurs Conseils en Brevets SA, Bienne	Patents	100
SMH Marketing Services SA, Bienne	Services and licences	100

REFERENCES

Bernheim, Ronnie A. *Koordination in zersplitterten Maerkten.* Berne, 1981: Paul Haupt Publ.

ETA S.A. "SWATCH. The Revolutionary New Technology." Company brochure.

Federation de l'industrie horlogère Suisse (Swiss Watchmanufacturers Federation). *Annual Reports, 1983–1989.* Bienne.

Heller, Matthew. "Swatch Switches." *Forbes,* January 27, 1986, pp. 86–87.

Hieronymi, O., et al. *La diffusion de nouvelles technologies en Suisse.* Saint-Saphorin, 1983: Georgi.

Hill, Wilhelm, *Die Wettbewerbsstellung der schweizerischen Uhrenindustrie.* Report for the Swiss Federal Department of Economics. Mimeo. Basle, 1977.

Ludwig, Benoit D. "Innovation ist mehr als neue Produkte." *io Management-Zeitschrift,* no. 2 (1985), pp. 54–59.

Moynahan, Brian, and Andreas Heumann. "The Man Who Made the Cuckoo Sing." *Sunday Times Magazine,* August 18, 1985, pp. 23–25.

Mueller, Jacques, and Elmar Mock. "Swatch. Eine Revolution in der Uhrentechnik." *Neue Zuercher Zeitung,* Fernausgabe Nr. 50, March 2, 1983.

Neue Zuercher Zeitung, various issues 1980–1990.

SMH Swiss Corporation for Microelectronics and Watchmaking Industries Ltd. Annual Reports 1984–1989.

"Swatch-Chef in Japan hat den Hut genommen." *Swiss American Review,* July 2, 1986, p. 9.

Thomke, Ernst. "In der Umsetzung von der Produktidee zur Marktreife liegt ein entscheidender Erfolgsfaktor," *io Management-Zeitschrift,* no. 2 (1985), pp. 60–64.

Union Bank of Switzerland, *The Swiss Watchmaking Industry.* USB Publications on Business, Banking and Monetary Topics No. 100, Zurich, March 1986.

CASE 23

NEC CORPORATION'S ENTRY INTO EUROPEAN MICROCOMPUTERS

MICHAEL HERGERT
AND ROBIN HERGERT

In April 1985, nearly five years after the introduction of its first personal computer to the European market, NEC Corporation (formerly Nippon Electric Company, Ltd.) had not yet established a significant presence in Europe. Despite the vast commercial potential of microcomputers, and despite NEC's widely recognized technological leadership and considerable financial resources, the company had not transferred its phenomenal success in Japan, where it had captured 55 percent of the personal computer market, to Europe. The time had come for NEC to reevaluate its strategy for entry into the rapidly evolving European microcomputer market, to review its current position, and to consider its options for the future.

EVOLUTION OF NEC CORPORATION

From its modest beginnings in 1899 as an importer and then manufacturer of telephone equipment. NEC, with 1984 sales of $8 billion, and net income of nearly $200 million, had become a leading international force in telecommunications, the world's third largest vendor of microchips, and Japan's number two computer maker (behind Fujitsu). Expanding from a single plant in Tokyo, NEC became a multinational corporation, manufacturing 15,000 products in 71 plants scattered throughout Japan and 11 other countries, supplying these products to over 140 nations through its 21 marketing and service organizations in 13 countries, and employing 78,000 people worldwide. Expertise in the three major areas of the information industry—telecommunications, semiconductors, and computers—placed NEC in a unique and enviable posi-

---

Source: **Prepared by Professors Michael Hergert and Robin Hergert, San Diego State University, as a basis for classroom discussion.** © Michael Hergert and Robin Hergert, 1990.

tion to challenge its rivals both at home and abroad. Claimed Tadahiro Sekimoto, NEC's president, "IBM may be ahead in computers, AT&T has good capacity in communications, and Texas Instruments is strong in semiconductors. But no company has such a combination of businesses in all three areas."

Until only 25 years ago, however, NEC's primary line of business was making telecommunications equipment for the domestic market. Set up in 1899 by American Telephone and Telegraph's (AT&T) Western Electric subsidiary, NEC became Japan's first joint venture company. During these early years, Western Electric furnished all the product designs for its minority partner. In 1925 NEC passed into the hands of International Telephone and Telegraph (ITT), which sold off the last of its shares in 1978.

Natural disasters and human catastrophes played a major role in shaping the course of NEC's evolution. A major earthquake in 1923 destroyed a large proportion of Japan's wired communications system, prompting the Ministry of Communications not only to rebuild the network, but also to supplement it with a radio broadcasting system, which would not be as vulnerable to seismological activity. NEC thus moved into the field of radio, borrowing Western Electric technology to produce its first vacuum tubes in 1928. World War II precipitated the destruction of nearly 80 percent of the telephone installations in Japan. Japanese authorities once again sought desperately to replace the communications infrastructure, and this time it appeared that microwave technology would provide the answer. NEC thus entered the field of microwave communications. In 1985 it claimed world leadership in microwave, with over 30 percent of "uncommitted" (those that do not favor local suppliers) world markets. Ironically, NEC also licensed its technology for microwave devices made of gallium arsenide to its former joint venture partner, Western Electric.

The postwar years also witnessed the creation of a climate favorable to NEC's development in other directions. Reconstruction of the telecommunications system stimulated the demand for equipment, and the network was to be administered by the newly created Nippon Telegraph and Telephone Public Corporation (NTT). NEC, whose former president became first president of NTT, was NTT's largest supplier, although NTT had not been increasing investment levels and was beginning to bow to strong political pressure to purchase some equipment from the United States.

During the years immediately following the war, Japanese authorities eased restrictions on consumer radio use, thus accelerating the growth of a consumer segment. In response, NEC created a wholly owned subsidiary in 1953, New Nippon Electric, Ltd. (NNE), to take responsibility for the production and sales of electric household appliances. At one time NEC's second most important business after communications, accounting for 20 percent of NEC's sales, consumer products dwindled to 8 percent of sales in the early 1970s.

It was also during the postwar period that NEC began researching solid-state technology. In 1949 the company turned its investigative efforts toward semiconductors, a more reliable and higher-quality alternative to vacuum tubes. Soon after transistors became commercially available in the early 1950s. NEC launched an all-out campaign to catch up with the United States. It began volume production of transistors in 1958, and in 1964 its efforts were rewarded by a major contract in Australia. More recently, NEC's rapid growth in computer sales had provided a large in-house market for its semiconductor division. Rather than depend exclusively on its captive market, however, the company had spent heavily to expand into the merchant market, becoming Japan's largest chip maker in the process. NEC boasted that its Kumamoto plant on Kyushu—Japan's "silicon island"—was the largest factory in the world producing memory chips. According to an industry expert, "NEC is the leader because it was the first Japanese company to understand that semiconductors are big business in itself (sic)."

Although "buy domestic" policies currently represented an ever-increasing threat to NEC's penetration of American and European markets, protectionist attitudes at home during the 1930s provided the catalyst for research that would eventually lead NEC into such advanced technologies as fiber optics. At that time, most of the patents, parts, and materials for telecommunications equipment originated outside Japan, eliciting a wave of sentiment for domestic technology. The search began for an alternative to Bell Laboratories' "loaded" cable for long-distance transmission. The solution was found in 1937 with the completion of a "nonloaded" cable carrier transmission system. One of the engineers working on this all-Japanese project was Dr. Koji Kobayashi, NEC's chairman and chief executive officer. Short, stocky, and still domineering enough at the age of 78 to frighten his colleagues, Kobayashi had been the principal architect of NEC's success in the last 20 years. NEC's continued involvement in transmission technology led to the development of a system capable of carrying digital signals in 1962. Six years later, following investigation into the possibility of using light to transmit information, NEC produced SELFOC, its first optical fiber.

NEC's pioneering role in microwave transmission enabled the company to carve a distinctive international niche and to apply its expertise to the field of satellite communications. After watching the first television show to be relayed by Telestar 1, Dr. Kobayashi personally orchestrated NEC's entry into this emerging industry. Traveling to Hughes Aircraft Company headquarters in Los Angeles, he arranged a joint venture with Hughes to develop a synchronous communications satellite. The successful product of this collaborative effort was Relay I, whose first transmission was the shocking announcement of President John F. Kennedy's assassination. By 1985 NEC had established a dominant position in satellite communications and was the only company to supply the entire system, including the satellite itself.

It was also telecommunications research that provided NEC's springboard into data processing. Company engineers, seeking a faster way to design filters for transmission lines, developed the world's first solid-state computer. NEC licensed Honeywell technology from 1962 to 1979, and, following a suggestion from MITI in 1971, elected to produce mainframe computers that were not compatible with those of IBM. This decision contributed to NEC's limited presence in world data-processing markets; meanwhile archrivals Fujitsu and Hitachi, also under MITI's direction, built up a significant international business in the so-called IBM plug-compatible computers, designed to be plugged into IBM installations as replacements for IBM machines. Nevertheless, at home NEC had captured 16 percent of the thriving mainframe market, and it dominated the markets for printers, displays, and other peripherals. NEC's personal computers had raced to the front of the pack in Japan since their introduction in 1979.

To its competitors outside Japan, NEC was known and respected primarily as a supplier of microchips and telecommunications equipment. Although the company had been involved in several ventures in the Far East during the first 20 years of its existence, it was not until the early 1960s, an era of falling trade restrictions and resultant growth in world trade, that NEC emerged as a multinational corporation. Its first overseas manufacturing facility, a joint venture in telecommunications, was set up in Taiwan in 1958. Other plants followed in neighboring Asian countries, Latin America, and the United States, where NEC incorporated its first North American subsidiary, Nippon Electric New York, Inc., in 1963. Its first European plant, for assembly of microchips, was opened in Ireland in 1975. A second, bigger chip factory in Scotland became operational in late 1982. Representing only 10 percent of sales in 1965, international sales accounted for 35 percent of NEC's revenues in 1984. Over half of these overseas sales were attributable to communications, a market NEC had exploited particularly successfully in the United States and Brazil. The corporation supplied equipment to five of the seven regional Bell operating companies formed after the breakup of AT&T and held 80 percent of the Brazilian microwave market. NEC's stock is currently listed on the Amsterdam, Frankfurt, London, Basel, Zurich, and Geneva exchanges. Financial data for NEC appears in Exhibit 1.

PRODUCT AREAS

NEC is divided into four separate divisions for its main businesses: communications, computers and industrial electronic systems, electric components, and home electronics. Summaries of the company's performance by product area follow with analyses of the major factors that characterize the respective markets and a list of NEC's major products.

COMMUNICATIONS

Sales of communications systems and equipment in fiscal 1984 rose to $2.55 billion and had been growing at a compounded annual rate of 15.3 percent since 1980. NEC is the largest Japanese telecommunications company and has had considerable success in export markets, including selling its digital public telephone exchange in 28 countries. The company is also the world's largest supplier of satellite earth stations and microwave communications equipment,

EXHIBIT 1 NEC INCOME STATEMENT AND BALANCE SHEET DATA, 1984

	1984	PERCENT CHANGE 1983–1984
Income Statement Data (in thousands, except per share figures):		
Sales and other income	$8,017,862	23%
Net sales	7,830,489	22
Communications	2,546,031	9
Computers and industrial electronic systems	2,391,107	34
Electron devices	1,889,231	35
Home electronics	754,693	14
Other	249,427	1
Income before income taxes	384,578	36
Income taxes	213,671	29
Net income	170,907	35
Per share of common stock		
Net income	0.166	30
Cash dividends	0.034	19
Balance Sheet Data (in millions):		
Assets:		
Cash and securities	$1,894	
Accounts receivable	3,299	
Inventories	1,572	
Gross fixed assets	3,773	
Accumulated depreciation (loss)	(1,780)	
Other assets	485	
Total assets	$9,243	
Liabilities and net worth:		
Short-term debt	$2,091	
Accounts payable	2,010	
Other current liabilities	1,089	
Long-term debt	1,579	
Other long-term liabilities	657	
Stockholders' equity	1,171	
Retained earnings	646	
Total liabilities and net worth	$9,243	

Source: NEC annual report.

having captured 50 percent and 33 percent, respectively, of these world markets.

NEC's product offerings in this area are very broad. The major products are electronic telephone-switching systems, digital data-switching systems, telephone sets, teleconference systems, facsimile equipment, carrier-transmission equipment, submarine cable repeaters, fiber-optic communication systems, microwave and satellite communications systems, laser communications equipment, mobile radio equipment, pagers, broadcast equipment, satellites, radio application equipment, and defense electronic systems.

Although just under one third of NEC's sales are in communications, profit margins in this area have been squeezed as the company makes the transfer from analog to digital communications. International markets for telecommunications have become intensely competitive as companies struggle to maintain a presence in an overcrowded market. Sustained growth in computer sales has helped to reduce NEC's dependence on communications from 44 percent of sales in 1974 to 32 percent in 1984.

As the volume of NEC's business with its major customer, NNT, did not grow significantly in 1984, NEC is looking to the private sector and overseas markets for future growth. The company projects that the world telecommunications market will grow more rapidly in the latter half of the decade than it has over the past five years. NEC is keen to enter the newly liberalized U.K. market; it intends to build a plant in the United Kingdom and has recently won a major order to supply British Telecom and Securicor with mobile radios for their joint cellular radio mobile telephone network.

COMPUTERS AND INDUSTRIAL ELECTRONIC SYSTEMS

Computer and industrial electronic systems recorded sales of $2.39 billion in fiscal 1984, sustaining a compounded annual growth rate of 26.7 percent since 1980. The division has an extensive product list. The major products are super computers, general-purpose ACOS series computers, minicomputers, control computers, personal computers and software, data communications equipment and software, peripheral and terminal equipment, magnetic memory equipment, distributed data-processing systems, office-automation systems, word processors, industrial telemetering systems, postal automation systems, numerical control equipment, medical electronic equipment, speech recognizers, industrial and communications control systems, robots, and CAD/CAM systems.

Although within Japan, NEC still lags behind Fujitsu and IBM in overall computer sales, the company leads the Japanese market in sales of personal computers with a 55 percent share. It was also the only major computer maker between 1974 and 1981 to increase its share of the Japanese market, both in cumulative value and number of machines installed. As a result, computers now account for 31 percent of revenues, up from 20 percent in 1974. According to Takeshi Kawashi, head of radio communications, the major reason for this success lies in NEC's strength in semiconductors.

Although NEC is looking to overseas data-processing markets for growth, its penetration of international markets for computers is very limited. The Japanese company has garnered only a tiny share of the personal computer market in the United States, the single largest of NEC's foreign markets. The

16-bit Advanced Personal Computer (APC) made its marketing debut in Europe in fiscal 1984, following its introduction in Australia and the United States the year before. In March 1984, NEC entered into an agreement with the United States–based Honeywell Information Systems, Inc., granting Honeywell distribution and manufacturing rights for NEC's large computers. The link with Honeywell gives NEC a strong marketing arm and access to a customer base in the United States. It also gives Honeywell an extension to its range of computers it could not have afforded to develop itself. In years past NEC had licensed technology from Honeywell.

Industry analysts attribute NEC's lack of significant international presence in computers in foreign markets to the company's refusal to produce IBM-compatible mainframes. Observers note that IBM's more aggressive stance and its dominance of the mainframe market has made it very hard for other companies to succeed with different systems. NEC counters that companies that seek to poach IBM's customers by offering technically compatible machines expose themselves to the threat of crippling retaliation by IBM. Yukio Mizuno, senior vice president in charge of the computer division, intimates that the battle with the U.S. giant is undergoing a shift in emphasis: "IBM's profits will come increasingly from software, maintenance, and system communications rather than from the computer hardware itself. So we have to compete with IBM in software rather than hardware."

Though NEC is putting huge resources into improving the production of its software—it has 13 wholly owned software subsidiaries and employs some 8,500 programmers—senior vice president Tomihiro Matsumura believes that Japan's social and educational system may be a handicap. By emphasizing highly organized group activity, he thinks it discourages the individualism that often sparks off innovation. The company aims to fill the gap by tapping outside talent. It has already commissioned American software houses to write programs for it, notably for its personal computers. It plans to set up its own software centers in the United States and recruit American programmers to staff them.

Although NEC management predicts that demand for computers and industrial electronic systems will continue to rise as harsh conditions force companies to rationalize and upgrade their operations, it also admits that competition is certain to mount as computer manufacturers around the world move to capitalize on the wealth of opportunity at hand. Industry observers are less than completely enthusiastic about NEC's ability to capitalize on these international opportunities. Says Frederic G. Withington, vice president for information systems at Arthur D. Little, "While they've done fine with the Spinwriter [high-quality printer] and [semiconductor] components, in computers they aren't strong enough."

ELECTRONIC COMPONENTS

NEC's sales of electronic devices reached $1.89 billion in fiscal 1984 and had been growing at a compounded annual rate of 23.1 percent since 1980. The company leads the increasingly successful Japanese assault on the world's semiconductor markets, and it ranks among the globe's top four microchip suppliers, along with Texas Instruments, National Semiconductor, and Motorola of the United States. A sustained global shortage of memory and other devices has contributed heavily to this performance. NEC's chip business currently accounts for 24 percent of revenues, up from 16 percent in 1975, and it is the most profitable of its product lines.

The company produces a wide range of electronic devices. The major products are integrated circuits (ICs), circuits for large-scale integration (LSIs), circuits for very-large-scale integration (VLSIs), microprocessors, transistors, diodes, gallium arsenide field-effect transistors; gate arrays, electron tubes, color picture tubes, display tubes, plasma display panels, lasers, laser application devices, circuit components, rectifiers, bubble memories, and vacuum equipment.

While Texas Instruments, the world's biggest chip maker, is laying off workers in anticipation of a weaker semiconductor market, NEC is pressing ahead with the construction of new plants and the expansion of existing facilities, both at home and abroad. The Japanese multinational insists that demand for its chips still outstrips supply, and it is vying for top position in the chipmakers' league by year's end. According to preliminary estimates by the California market research firm Dataquest, NEC's semiconductor sales will grow by about 60 percent in 1985, allowing it to overtake Motorola and to close the gap on TI.

NEC can apparently withstand the slower market growth more easily than its American rivals because Japanese demand for chips has been less volatile than demand across the Pacific. The four top Japanese chip makers—NEC, Fujitsu, Hitachi, and Toshiba—are also four of the biggest chip consumers. This makes demand easier to forecast and moderates the industry's boom-bust cycles. There is thus no need for chip users to overbook to ensure deliveries when demand is rising.

Another factor in NEC's favor is its strength in both memory chips and microprocessors. Prices for the latter tend to be more stable than prices for memory chips. The firm has also invested heavily in the mass production of cheap memory chips. NEC's main microchip plant in Kumamoto, southern Japan, is the largest and most efficient in the world.

HOME ELECTRONICS

The fourth main area of NEC's business is home electronics. This division posted sales of $755 million in fiscal 1984 and has grown at a compounded annual rate of 11 percent since 1980. It is an area of NEC's activities that is easily overlooked because it only represents 10 percent of revenues, down from 14 percent in 1981, and is fairly insignificant alongside the leading producers of consumer electronics in Japan such as Matsushita, Sony, Sanyo, JVC, and Hitachi.

The NEC-brand product line is extensive, and the major products include television sets, video recorders, portable video cameras, television projectors, radio receivers, transceivers, tape recorders, hi-fi audio systems, compact disk digital audio systems, personal computers, lighting products, refrigerators, microwave ovens, kitchen appliances, and air conditioners. NEC does not manufacture the whole range, but concentrates on producing consumer electronic products while rebranding the nonelectronic appliances.

Despite the firm's modest showing in consumer electronics, NEC believes that the division, and particularly the personal computer, is potentially highly important. NEC's president explains, "In 10 or 20 years' time, consumer products will be the largest single part of [our strategy]."

NEC STRATEGY

NEC sees itself as a tree whose roots are firmly embedded in high technology. One product recently developed by the Tokyo-based company is an automatic software-development system that makes productivity 5 to 50 times more efficient than previous manual work. Known as SEA/I, the system is designed for automation of software development, which was chiefly a manual process until now. SEA/I is among the most advanced systems of its kind in the world. Yet management thinks it could do better, committing over 10 percent of consolidated sales to research, development, and engineering activities.

NEC's competitors are beginning to run out of adjectives to describe such relentless striving for higher performance. The Japanese multinational, however, harbors still bolder ambitions. It has set its sights on the twin goals of increasing sales at an annual pace of 18–20 percent for the rest of the decade and of becoming a world leader in the creation of the high-technology information society of tomorrow. To reach these overall growth objectives, NEC plans to raise overseas contribution to sales from 35 percent to 40 percent, half of it manufactured outside Japan.

If NEC's targets are bold, its operational style is even riskier. While archrivals Fujitsu Ltd. and Hitachi Ltd. have set up partnerships with computer manufacturers in the United States and Europe to assure a sizable penetration of the information-processing markets, NEC has generally shunned such shortcuts in favor of developing its brand name. Explains Dr. Kobayashi, NEC's chairman, "Our intention is simple: walking on our own feet." The company's president, Dr. Tadahiro Sekimoto, elaborates on this point: "We aim to establish real companies abroad that can design, make, and maintain the products that they sell on their own." He is convinced that this policy of decentralization is the most effective way to secure NEC's future in an increasingly volatile and treacherous business climate. Indeed, growing fears of a trade war with the United States and the European Economic Community (EEC) have heightened the sense of urgency.

As a result of this go-it-alone approach, coupled with the decision not to make computers that are compatible with those made by IBM, NEC's machines have not yet achieved significant penetration in the West. To compensate,

NEC has resorted to aggressive marketing and ruthless price cutting. "NEC uses its profits in other areas to allow it to cut prices in computers," says Tamizo Kimura, an analyst at Yamaichi Research Institute. A strategy based on price competition, however, is not totally without risk. In a suit brought by U.S. rivals Aydin Corporation and MCL, Inc., the Commerce Department in 1982 found Nippon Electric guilty of dumping $3 million worth of microwave communications components on the U.S. market.

As NEC has also discovered, establishing offshore manufacturing operations can cause other kinds of headaches as well. Neither Electronic Arrays, a small California chip maker bought in 1978, nor its telecommunications plant opened the same year in Dallas, Texas, was judged to be up to Japanese quality standards in 1982. Executives were appalled by the conditions they found when they took over Electronic Arrays. Workers at NEC's Kumamoto plant must change into special protective garments and pass through a forced-air "shower" before entering the ultra-clean section where the most delicate part of the chipmaking process is performed. "But in California, people were wandering in wearing street clothes," according to one NEC manager. A good deal of management effort has been devoted to bringing the plants up to snuff.

Although NEC departed from the firm's policy of developing largely through internal growth when it acquired Electronic Arrays, executives say there are no plans to bolster international marketing operations through the purchase of other companies with strong marketing organizations. However, Dr. Sekimoto does not rule out this possibility categorically. An enthusiast of American futurologist Alvin Toffler, the president quips, "After all, this is the Age of Drastic Change."

NEC's second driving ambition is symbolized in its slogan "C&C," standing for the convergence of computer and communications technologies that lies at the heart of the revolution in electronic information handling. Since Dr. Kobayashi first publicly coined the term at the International Telecommunications Exposition in Atlanta in 1977, NEC's patriarch has been actively promoting C&C within his entire organization. This theme dominates NEC management and activities to an almost obsessive degree. No document, no conversation—whether formal or informal—is complete without some reference to C&C.

This convergence of computer and communications technologies is, of course, widely recognized by electronics companies throughout the world, bringing computer companies such as IBM into telecommunications and communications companies such as AT&T into data processing. Few companies, however, have made this convergence into such a pervasive management theme, and fewer still actually straddle these worlds quite as comprehensively as NEC. The concept is made tangible in the so-called decision room at corporate headquarters in Tokyo, where top management regularly meets. An elegant wood-paneled chamber, it is equipped with a panoply of sophisticated systems permitting two-way video communications with distant offices and instantaneous retrieval and display of massive amounts of information.

Despite NEC's technical achievements and strongly held belief in the convergence of computers and communications, the company has a long way to go in coordinating its communications, computer, semiconductor, and consumer electronics divisions. Says Dr. Sekimoto, "I think they will remain separate forever. For instance, the communications business will always be there ... the telephone will never disappear. In the same way the stand-alone computer will never disappear. However, C&C will create new fields and will become very much bigger."

The enhance cooperation, the company has set up occasional project teams that span the different divisions, such as for automatic broadcasting equipment and some defense projects. In addition, the marketing and sales organization, which is separate from the manufacturing divisions, has a team devoted to the promotion of C&C products such as office and factory automation.

THE EUROPEAN MICROCOMPUTER INDUSTRY

In 1985 the microcomputer industry in Europe displayed many features typical of emerging markets. Great technological uncertainty, buyer confusion, and unclear market segments created an environment where strategy formulation was difficult at best. Current events left many industry observers puzzled; spectacular successes and failures were the norm, and some of the world's mightiest multinationals had proven unable to establish viable competitive positions. Among this group was NEC, whose European microcomputers had failed to capture a significant market share, even after five years of attempts.

In this market, even a precise product description is controversial. Microcomputers span the range from simple machines costing a few hundred dollars and primarily used for playing games to sophisticated desktop units capable of supporting several hundred users simultaneously. For the following discussion, the main emphasis is on products selling for $1,000 to $10,000 and designed for individual use. A typical microcomputer setup has the components described below.

SYSTEM UNIT

The system unit is the heart of a microcomputer. It contains the microprocessor, which is the semiconductor chip where numerical operations actually take place. The microprocessor size is an important determinant of the speed and power of the computer. First-generation microcomputers, such as the Apple II, relied on an 8-bit microprocessor, meaning that information is processed for computations in blocks of 8 units. An 8-bit microprocessor is quite adequate for many applications, and is still used in a large number of products.

IBM ushered in the second generation of microcomputers in August 1981 when it introduced the PC. The PC uses the Intel 8088 microprocessor, which processes 16 bits of information at a time. This permits the IBM PC and other second-generation products to run more powerful software and handle larger problems. It also creates the possibility of making the microcomputer a multitasking machine (i.e., capable of handling more than one job at a time) and a multiuser machine (i.e., capable of handling more than one user at a time).

More recently, even larger microprocessors have become common. The IBM AT, introduced in August 1984, is a 16–24 bit product, and the Apple Macintosh, also introduced in 1984, has a 32-bit processor. Although the technology of large microprocessors was well established by 1985, limited availability and high costs have made many microcomputer producers wary of committing to advanced technology.

In addition to a central processing unit, a microcomputer must have internal memory. Internal memory consists of RAM (Random Access Memory) and ROM (Read Only Memory). Both RAM and ROM are made up of memory chips installed inside the system unit. ROM consists of instructions permanently stored in the machine that cannot be modified by the user. ROM memory often contains essential software to control the operation of the machine and increasingly is used to provide applications packages, such as word processing or spreadsheet software. RAM memory is addressable by the user, meaning that he can write his own data and programs to memory for temporary storage and can modify the contents at will. The amount of internal memory in a microcomputer plays a large role in determining the size of the problem that can be handled. Memory is measured in kilobytes (K). Most microcomputers have at least 64K of RAM. Larger machines may be expanded to 640K or more.

EXTERNAL MEMORY

In addition to internal memory, microcomputers generally provide some form of external storage medium for permanent storage. Early microcomputers stored data on audio cassettes, but this proved to be slow and unreliable. In 1978 Apple began using floppy diskettes for external storage, which quickly became adopted as the standard system. Floppy diskettes are inexpensive disks of magnetic storage film that are capable of recording 160–2400K of data. Individual diskettes sell for under $2.50. The disk drive used to store data onto diskettes sells for $150 to $500, depending on size and storage capacity. A typical microcomputer system will have one or two disk drives, which can be mounted inside the system unit or in separate expansion cabinets. During 1984 and 1985, the use of hard disks as a storage medium increased dramatically. Hard disks, also known as Winchester disks or fixed disks, are similar in size to floppy disks, but are capable of holding far greater amounts of information. Hard disks for microcomputers typically hold 10–20 megabytes of data (1 megabyte = 1000 kilobytes), and are available up to 100 megabytes or more. Prices for hard disks have fallen drastically during the last two years, and they are now available for as little as $500. Exotic mass storage devices of even greater capacity should be available in the near future. In 1985, 3M announced a laser optical disk capable of holding 450 megabytes of information on a 5.25-inch disk. Industry analysts expect the disk drive to sell for under $1,500 within a few years.

VIDEO DISPLAY

Microcomputers display information on several forms of video devices. Early microcomputers were often hooked into television sets for display. Current computers typically have a dedicated cathode ray tube (CRT) device, which can display output in multiple colors and screen formats. In order to increase the portability of microcomputers, extensive research is being done on LCD, plasma, and other flat-screen technologies. In late 1984, Data General announced a notebook-sized computer with a fold-up, full-sized (25 lines by 80 characters) display.

PRINTERS

To create a physical record of microcomputer output, it is necessary to use some form of printing device. The most popular printer technology is the dot matrix. Dot-matrix printers are inexpensive ($200 and up) and relatively fast (as many as 400 characters per second). The main drawback of dot-matrix printers is that they are unable to provide high-quality output and are viewed by many people as unsuitable for business correspondence. For letter-quality printing, daisy wheel printers are more common. Daisy wheel printers work on the same principle as many office typewriters and are able to provide very high-quality output. A daisy wheel printer intended for office use will usually sell for at least $1,000.

New printing technologies are also emerging. In 1984 Hewlett Packard introduced its LaserJet printer, which is based on the xerographic process used in copier machines. Laser printers are fast, very high quality, capable of producing any form of graphics output (unlike daisy wheel printers), and are extremely quiet. Similar printers had been available previously from Xerox and others, but at prices of $25,000 to $400,000. The HP LaserJet sells for approximately $3,000.

MODEMS

Modems (or modulator-demodulators) are devices that allow a microcomputer to access another computer over telephone lines. This is very useful for accessing data provided by an outside information vendor, or for accessing data stored in a central location within a company. Modems also allow microcomputers to function as computer terminals for use with a larger computer to run jobs beyond the capability of the microcomputer. This linkage is viewed as an important first step in office automation.

SOFTWARE

Most microcomputer users view their machines as a black box capable of running specific applications. Software is the complementary product that makes this possible. The two main categories of software are operating system software and applications software.

Operating systems software does the housekeeping of a microcomputer. It manages files and controls the operations of other programs, such as applications software. Because this function is central to the operation of a microcomputer, the operating system determines the extent to which data and programs can be shared between two microcomputers. Generally, two microcomputers that share the same operating system are compatible, although different versions of the same system can lead to problems. Because the operating system controls the microprocessor, the software is somewhat specific to the chip and architecture of the individual product.

For the first generation of 8-bit microcomputers, CP/M, developed by Digital Research Corporation, was the most widely used operating system. However, since the advent of 16-bit microprocessors, the operating system used by IBM, MS DOS, has emerged as the de facto industry standard. The choice of which operating system to employ is a crucial one to the strategy of a firm. The choice of operating system will determine which applications programs will run on a given computer. If a firm chooses to follow IBM's lead and uses MS DOS, this provides the advantage of immediate access to a large number of software programs available in the market. Unfortunately, it also creates a stigma of copying IBM's product and being viewed as a "me-too" producer. Alternatively, a firm can choose to provide a proprietary operating system. This has the advantage of allowing a firm to differentiate itself and provide the only applications software capable of being used on the machine. It also creates the risk that the new operating system and software will not be viewed as sufficiently superior to the industry standard products to warrant switching systems. Apple has followed this latter approach in developing specialized software for its Macintosh line of products.

Applications software provides functional capability to a microcomputer. The main uses for applications software are word processing, spreadsheet analysis, database management, graphics, communications between computers, and games. In addition, language compilers, such as BASIC and FORTRAN, allow users to run specific programs written in those languages. Some of the most popular software packages and their prices are shown in Exhibit 2.

A cottage industry supplying software for microcomputers has emerged in the United States and Europe. For example, the DataPro Directory of Microcomputer Software lists over 1,000 firms in the United States in which PC software is included in their principal line of business. Early analysts of the microcomputer industry predicted that a typical user would spend at least as much on software as on hardware. Recent events have led these analysts to reconsider their positions. Many microcomputer producers have adopted the practice of bundling software with their hardware and pricing the package very aggressively. For example, in early 1985, the Sanyo MBC 555, an IBM-compatible microcomputer with 128K of RAM and two floppy disk drives, was available for under $1,000. This price included several popular software packages, such as MS DOS, Easywriter, Wordstar, Calcstar, Spellstar, Mailmerge, and Infostar, which if bought separately would cost over $1,000. For many users, this is all the software they would ever need.

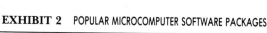

EXHIBIT 2 POPULAR MICROCOMPUTER SOFTWARE PACKAGES

PRODUCT	RETAIL PRICE	MAIL-ORDER PRICE	APPLICATION
dBase III	$695	$339	Database
Framework	695	339	Integrated multifunction
Multiplan	195	115	Spreadsheet
Sidekick	55	35	Utility
1-2-3	495	289	Integrated multifunction
Symphony	695	409	Integrated multifunction
Wordstar 2000	495	239	Word processing
VisiCalc 4	250	159	Spreadsheet
Volkswriter Deluxe	395	149	Word processing
rBase: 4000	495	269	Database
Microsoft Word	375	235	Word processing
TK Solver!	399	265	Modeling/simulation
SuperCalc III	395	245	Spreadsheet
Perfect Writer	349	179	Word processing
Crosstalk XVI	195	99	Communications
Prokey	130	79	Utility

Source: PC World, March 1985.

MARKET SIZE AND SEGMENTATION

The European microcomputer industry is not a unified market of standard products or users. Rather, it is composed of many national markets, each with different requirements, levels of sophistication, and distribution channels. As a result, it is dangerous to generalize about competitive requirements for success using the whole of Europe as a reference point.

Many industry observers believe that the evolution of the European market will parallel the development of the American market. In the 1970s, this seemed to be the case, as European markets were dominated by American multinationals exporting products they were already selling in the United States. A brief summary of key events in the evolution of the microcomputer industry appears in Exhibit 3.

The largest market in Europe is the United Kingdom, with approximately 24 percent of the $2 billion industry in 1983. As shown in Exhibit 4, Germany is a close second, and the four largest markets (United Kingdom, Germany, France, and Italy) account for 76 percent of European sales.

The major market segments are as follows:

- The home user/hobbyist whose demand is oriented toward smaller micros and leisure applications. This segment was especially well developed in England by Sinclair. A strong position in the home market is

EXHIBIT 3   EVOLUTION OF MICROCOMPUTER INDUSTRY

1974	Intel announces the 8080 microprocessor
	Motorola announces the 8600 microprocessor
1975	Early microcomputer kits appear on market
	Dick Heiser opens first retail computer store in Santa Monica
1976	Zilog announces Z80 microprocessor
	Steve Wozniak designs Apple 1; Apple founded by Wozniak and Steve Jobs
	Steve Leninger joins Radio Shack to design a computer
	100 companies active in field by year-end
	132 computer clubs in existence by year-end
1977	Apple II announced
	Radio Shack TRS-80 announced
	Microsoft begins to market BASIC and FORTRAN for microcomputers
	First Computerland franchise store opened in Morristown, New Jersey; 24 stores open by year-end
	Over 200 active manufacturers by year-end
1978	Atari announces the 400 and 800 computers
	Apple and Radio Shack begin using 5¼″ disk drives
	Dan Bricklin and Bob Frankston write VisiCalc
1979	Texas Instruments introduces 99/4 home computer
	Radio Shack announces Model II business computer
	Micropro announces Wordstar
	NEC demonstrates the 8000 computer at Hannover, West Germany, trade show
1980	Sinclair ZX80 introduces first computer under $200
	Apple introduces the Apple III
	Epson announces the MX-80 printer
	Microsoft agrees to work with IBM to design software
	Xerox, DEC, and Intel announce Ethernet Local Area Network
1981	Osborne introduces the first transportable computer
	IBM announces the PC
	Microsoft produces MS-DOS (PC-DOS) for IBM PC
1982	Commodore 64 announced
	DEC announces Rainbow 100
	Apple begins selling "user friendly" LISA in United States
	Franklin introduces Apple-compatible ACE 100
	NEC announces 16-bit Advanced Personal Computer
	NEC introduces the 8800 series in Europe
	Seven IBM-compatible computers appear on the market
1983	IBM introduces PCjr and PC XT
	Radio Shack announces Model 100 notebook computer; NEC announces 8201
	Timex introduces Timex/Sinclair 2000, but withdraws from market eight months later
	Texas Instruments withdraws 99/4A
	Osborne Computer files for bankruptcy

EXHIBIT 3 (continued)

1984
- NEC begins selling 8201 notebook computer in Europe
- IBM lookalikes flood the market
- Apple announces Macintosh, Apple IIc
- Hewlett-Packard introduces Model 110 notebook portable, similar in power to desktop machines
- Mattel, Timex, Specta-Video, Victor, Actrix, and Computer Devices leave market or sell out
- Warner sells Atari to Jack Tramiel after losses of $539 million
- NEC sells over 1 million personal computers in Japan
- First national TV advertising for software (Lotus Symphony and Ashton-Tate Framework); number of software manufacturers tops 500

Source: Creative Computing, November 1984.

EXHIBIT 4 EUROPEAN NATIONAL MARKETS, 1983

	REVENUES	PERCENTAGE OF EUROPEAN MARKET
United Kingdom	$480 million	24%
Germany	460	23
France	360	18
Italy	220	11
Scandinavia	160	8
Benelux countries	140	7
Spain/Portugal	100	5
Switzerland/Austria	80	4
Total (approximately 300,000 units)	$2 billion	100%

EUROPEAN USER SEGMENTS BY SIZE

	PERCENTAGE OF TOTAL MARKET	
	UNITS	VALUE
Home	61%	12%
Business	26	63
Education	7	3
Scientific	6	22

Source: International Data Corporation.

thought to provide a basis for creating customer loyalty that can be exploited in trade-ups to larger products.
- The educational institution that purchases microcomputers to teach computer literacy. This segment has not proven very lucrative for producers because government purchasers are price sensitive and may use their purchasing power to promote a national champion. This segment has been used as a loss leader by some manufacturers to create brand visibility and preferences. For example, Apple has created an educational consortium of major universities that receive Macintosh computers at deep discounts.
- The scientist who uses the microcomputer instead of a mainframe to perform very specific applications. Scientific applications typically require powerful microcomputers with specialized software.
- The business user who relies on a microcomputer for word processing, data analysis, terminal emulation, or a variety of other administrative tasks. As shown in Exhibit 4, this is the largest segment in Europe, accounting for nearly two thirds of all microcomputer revenues.

DISTRIBUTION

Microcomputers in Europe are sold through a variety of channels. Although distribution networks differ somewhat across countries, the following channels generally exist to some extent in all European nations. A summary of the distribution channels for Europe appears in Exhibit 5.

DIRECT SALES FORCE

For large accounts, direct sales calls are common. Companies with an existing position in a related field, such as telecommunications, large computers, or office products, are most likely to emphasize this channel. This provides the advantage of being able to sell a bundle of related products as a customized system to corporate clients. The ability to provide such systems is thought to be a crucial capability for future success in large accounts.

RETAIL STORES

Retail computer stores are the single most important channel of distribution, accounting for over one third of all sales in Europe, and as much as 45 percent in the United Kingdom. This category includes company-owned stores, such as those used by Tandy as its exclusive form of distribution, mass merchandisers who sell a wide variety of consumer products in addition to microcomputers, independent retailers, and franchise chains, of which Computerland and Entre are the largest. As of 1984, Computerland operated 791 stores worldwide and generated sales of $1.4 billion. Computer franchise stores, which originally appeared in the United States and are well established in

EXHIBIT 5 EUROPEAN DISTRIBUTION NETWORKS FOR MICROCOMPUTERS PRICED $1,000 AND ABOVE

	RETAIL OUTLETS	SYSTEM HOUSES	TOTAL NETWORK
United Kingdom	832	350	1,182
Germany	672	250	922
France	620	250	870
Italy	580	100	680
Belgium	144	100	244
Netherlands	145	70	215
Spain	130	70	200

DISTRIBUTION NETWORK BY TYPE OF OUTLET (PERCENTAGES BASED ON 1983 VOLUMES)

	MASS OUTLETS	COMPUTER STORES	OFFICE EQUIPMENT STORES	SYSTEM HOUSES	DIRECT SALES
United Kingdom	7–10%	42–45%	2–4%	23–25%	20–22%
Germany	3–4	26–29	22–24	24–26	20–22
France	<1	38–40	4–5	32–34	22–25
Italy	—	31–35	19–21	28–32	16–18
Spain	4–6	33–35	16–18	29–31	13–15
Belgium	3–5	38–40	8–10	24–28	21–23
Netherlands	2–4	33–35	12–14	18–20	30–32
USA	28	33	6	13	15

Source: Electronics Business and Electronics Intelligence.

that market, have yet to make a similar impact in Europe. Nonetheless, both Computerland and Entre have announced aggressive plans to expand their European networks.

PRODUCTION

Manufacturing microcomputers is a relatively easy task. Components and subassemblies are readily available on world markets, and many producers have adopted policies of purchasing nearly all inputs externally and simply assembling the product and attaching their brand name. Even IBM, with its great potential for vertical integration, has chosen to rely on outside vendors for nearly all of the components of the PC. As shown in Exhibit 6, approximately 73 percent of the manufacturing cost of the IBM PC comes from components purchased from Asian producers. Exhibit 7 summarizes the manufacturing strategies of several major microcomputer producers.

EXHIBIT 6 IBM PC MANUFACTURING SOURCES

ELEMENT	IBM	OTHER	
Video display	—	Korea	$ 85
Printer	—	Japan	160
Floppy disks	$ 25	Singapore	165
Keyboard	—	Japan	50
Semiconductors	105	Japan	105
Power supply	—	Japan	60
Case and final assembly	105		—
Total cost	$235		$625

Source: Business Week, March 11, 1985.

BASES FOR COMPETITIVE ADVANTAGE

In choosing a competitive strategy in microcomputers, there are numerous bases for competitive advantage. The strategies of many competitors are derived from their strategies in related markets. Because the microcomputer is at the intersection of several technologies, firms have been attracted to the industry from many directions. This pattern of gateways is summarized in Exhibit 8. For example, as producers of typewriters, such as Olivetti and Triumph-Adler, saw their products increasingly being replaced by word processors, they were induced into offering their own microcomputers. Similarly, as microcomputers became more powerful and better substitutes for larger computers, integrated computer companies were motivated to introduce their own products. On the technology side, the trend toward a convergence of data processing and telecommunications brought the entry of AT&T, ITT, and NEC. Similarly, consumer electronics companies (Panasonic, Sharp, Tandy), toy producers (Atari, Mattel, Coleco), and start-ups (Apple, Fortune) all entered the market with distinctive motivations, resources, and ways of doing business.

This variety of perspectives has manifested itself in different competitive postures. It is possible to strive for competitive advantage in any of the following (not necessarily mutually exclusive) ways.

COST LEADERSHIP

In its announcements and in its actions IBM has indicated that it intends to be the low-cost producer of microcomputers. It has even deviated substantially from corporate tradition to attain this goal. For example, despite its strong existing capabilities in many aspects of microcomputer technology, IBM has

EXHIBIT 7 MICROCOMPUTER MANUFACTURING STRATEGIES

COMPANY	MAJOR MODELS	MAIN UNIT	KEYBOARD	MONITOR	DISK DRIVE	PRINTER	SOFTWARE
Apple	IIe, Lisa	MF	OS	OS	OS	OS	MF
Atari	400, 800	MF	OS	N/A	OS	OS	MF
Commodore	VIC-20, 64	MF	OS	OS	OS	OS	MF
DEC	Rainbow	MF	MF	MF	MF	MF	OS/MF
Hewlett-Packard	75C, HP-86, 87, 150	MF	OS	MF	MF	MF	MF
IBM	PC, XT	OS/MF	OS	OS	OS	OS	OS/MF
Tandy	Model III, Model XVI, Color Computer	MF	OS	MF	OS	OS	MF
Texas Instruments	Professional	MF	MF	OS	MF	MF	MF

Abbreviations: MF = manufactured in-house; OS = bought from outside supplier

EXHIBIT 8 MICROCOMPUTER ENTRY GATEWAYS

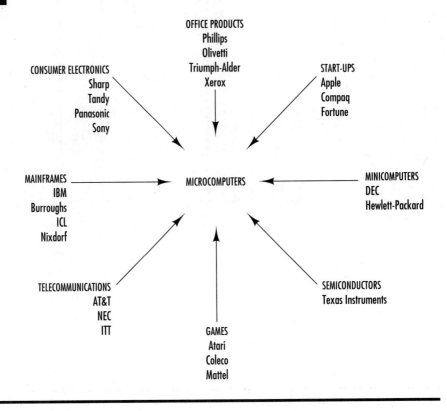

declined to vertically integrate for fear of increasing its costs. In the case of printers, which IBM purchases from Epson, the IBM printer-manufacturing division was invited to submit a bid for supplying dot-matrix printers. The bid was higher than Epson's, and thus was refused, despite tremendous internal politicking to push it through. IBM's large market share allows it to receive volume purchasing discounts and scale economies in assembly and marketing. Although it has yet to occur, industry analysts look to Asia for significant future challengers to IBM's cost position.

FULL-LINE COMPLEMENTARITY

Another strategic approach is to view the microcomputer not as a stand-alone product but as part of an office system. Producers who sell a full line of office products, such as PABXs, local area networks, telex machines, terminals, large computers, and word processors, can sell their microcomputers as part of an integrated system. This overcomes the problems of incompatibility between individual products supplied by different vendors. DEC and Xerox have been leaders in pursuing this strategy.

PROPRIETARY CLOSED SYSTEM

As an alternative to conforming to industry standards in hardware and software, a microcomputer producer may elect to introduce its own unique computer architecture and operating system. As mentioned earlier, the benefits of differentiation must be weighed against the risk of the market not accepting the new system.

Microcomputers exist in multiple configurations of processor speed, memory size, machine size, and other special features. It is possible for a manufacturer to specialize in one hardware segment of the market and attempt to build an image as the industry leader. For example, Compaq recorded the all-time largest volume of sales in the first year of operation for a company (over $100 million) by dominating the market for "transportable" microcomputers. These products weigh approximately 30 pounds and are self-contained for relatively easy movement.

"ME-TOO"

The single most common competitive strategy in microcomputers is to offer a clone or look-alike product that emulates the industry standard (generally IBM). There are currently hundreds of companies that produce microcomputers that are physical and electronic copies of IBM's PC. Such products generally sell for discounts of 15–40 percent off the IBM price. This strategy is not limited to small firms: ITT, Siemens, Ericsson, Olivetti, and Tandy have joined ranks with the many start-up firms that offer products with little or no enhancement to the basic IBM model. Indeed, this has led many observers to speculate that the microcomputer may be entering a stage of evolution resembling a commodity.

NATIONAL MARKET SEGMENTATION

European national markets for microcomputers demonstrate some differentiating characteristics that create the possibility of national market segmentation. Local governments have a long history of preferential purchasing of large computers, and this has continued into the realm of microcomputers as well. Different languages and cultures also create possible advantages for a local supplier. For example, no foreign producer has succeeded in capturing any significant share of the Japanese market. IBM failed to reach the company target of 120,000 PCs sold in Japan in 1984 despite a reorganization and new product design to push the microcomputer. Attempts by Sinclair, Tandy, Commodore, and Apple have been similarly frustrated. Early product offerings by all these companies were simply exports of existing machines and were unable to use kana and kanji characters. Today, NEC has over 50 percent of the Japanese microcomputer market, and its chief rivals are all Japanese firms.

TECHNOLOGICAL LEADERSHIP

Another method for strategic differentiation is to strive for leadership in the underlying technology of microcomputers. The current standard microcomputer, as exemplified by the IBM PC, is a modest machine relative to state-of-the-art possibilities. Faster microprocessors, higher density storage, more advanced memory chips, better fundamental architecture, and more sophisticated operating systems are all currently possible. However, packaging these components into a high-powered microcomputer creates significant risks: lack of software, high costs, risks of supply interruptions, and general lack of customer acceptance in the same way as a proprietary closed system.

COMPETITOR PROFILES

In 1985 the European microcomputer market was crowded with several hundred firms, ranging from small start-ups working out of a garage to some of the world's largest corporations. Exhibit 9 provides a financial overview of some of the most significant competitors. Strategic profiles appear in the following paragraphs.

IBM

IBM is the world leader in microcomputers. IBM began selling microcomputers in the United States in August 1981 and started exports to Europe in January 1983. Today, IBM dominates both markets. In 1984 it is estimated that IBM sold over 2 million PCs in the United States alone. IBM's market share is especially high in the corporate market. In early 1985 it was estimated that 76 percent of all desktop computers in Fortune 500 companies are made by IBM. To serve this market, IBM relies on its direct selling staff of 6,000 to 7,000 people, compared to 60 for Apple, the second largest supplier.

In the European market, IBM attained a market share of 16 percent in its first year. This figure would have been higher if not for chronic parts shortages at its Greenock, Scotland, plant. By 1984 IBM had captured over 30 percent of the market and seemed destined to replay its American success.

IBM's strategy was based on several key elements. As mentioned earlier, IBM is dedicated to low-cost production, even if this implies reliance on outside vendors. Low costs have been translated into aggressive pricing. As shown in Exhibit 10, IBM has cut the price of the PC by over 62 percent since its introduction. This has kept tremendous pressure on "me-too" producers to keep their prices low.

IBM has also blanketed the microcomputer market with a full line of products. At the low end, IBM introduced the PCjr in late 1983 at a price of $699.

EXHIBIT 9 COMPETITOR PROFILES

APPLE COMPUTER (1983)

Income statement data	(millions)	Sales by activity	
Net sales	$983	Microcomputers	100%
COGS	484		
Depreciation	22		
R&D	60	Sales by area	
Marketing	230	United States	78%
G&A	57	Europe	13
EBIT	130	Other	9
Net income	77		
Dividends	0		
Balance sheet data			
Cash	$143	Accounts payable	$ 53
Accounts receivable	136	Notes payable	0
Inventory	142	Other current liabilities	76
Other current assets	48	Long-term debt	0
Fixed assets	67	Other liabilities	50
Other noncurrent assets	21	Shareholders' equity	378
		Preferred stock	0

IBM (1983)

Income statement data	(millions)	Sales by activity	
Net sales	$23,274	Processors	23%
Other income	16,906	Peripherals	15
COGS	13,033	Office systems	14
Depreciation	3,362	Program products	6
R&D	2,514	Other sales	6
Engineering expense	1,068	Rentals	23
SG&A	10,614	Maintenance	11
Operating profit	9,589	Other services	2
Other income	741		
EBIT	10,330	Sales by area	
Net income	5,485	United States	58%
Dividends	2,251	Europe	27
		Americas/Far East	15
Balance sheet data			
Cash	$ 5,336	Accounts payable	$ 1,253
Accounts receivable	6,380	Notes payable	532
Inventory	4,381	Other current liabilities	7,722
Other current assets	973	Long-term debt	2,674
Net fixed assets	16,142	Other liabilities	1,843
Other noncurrent assets	3,831	Shareholders's equity	23,019
		Preferred stock	0

(*continued*)

EXHIBIT 9 (continued)

COMMODORE INTERNATIONAL (1983)

Income statement data	(millions)	Sales by activity	
Net sales	$681	Home computers	45%
COGS	346	Business and educational systems	23
Depreciation	14	Peripherals	19
R&D	37	Software	9
Marketing	139	Office equipment	4
SG&A	24		
EBIT	121	Sales by area	
Extraordinary item	4	United States	58%
Net income	92	Canada	16
Dividends	0	Europe	23
		Other	3
Balance sheet data			
Cash	$ 23	Accounts payable	$246
Accounts receivable	180	Notes payable	21
Inventory	327	Other current liabilities	61
Fixed assets	81	Long-term debt	92
Other noncurrent assets	4	Other liabilities	4
		Shareholders' equity	191
		Preferred stock	0

TANDY CORPORATION (1983)

Income statement data	(millions)	Sales by activity	
Net sales	$2,475	Microcomputers	35%
Other income	38	Stereos	18
COGS	1,008	Radios and TVs	14
Depreciation	39	Components	13
R&D	N/A	Calculators and toys	12
SG&A	930	Telephones	8
EBIT	536		
Net income	279	Sales by area	
Dividends	0	United States	84%
		Canada	8
		Europe	5
		Other	3
Balance sheet data			
Cash	$280	Accounts payable	$ 65
Accounts receivable	107	Notes payable	56
Inventory	844	Other current liabilities	165
Other current assets	32	Long-term debt	138
Fixed assets	258	Other liabilities	37
Other noncurrent assets	61	Shareholders' equity	1,121
		Preferred stock	0

EXHIBIT 9 (continued)

OLIVETTI (1983)

Income Statement data	(billions of lire)	Sales by activity	
Net sales	L3,736	Typewriters and word processors	23%
COGS	1,824	Terminals	24
Depreciation	226	Computers	21
R&D	187	Telecommunications	5
SG&A	1,031	Other office equipment	27
Operating profit	468		
Other expenses	173		
Net income	295	Sales by area	
Dividends	84	United States	7%
		Europe	76
		Latin America	5
		Other	12

Balance sheet data			
Cash	L1,381	Accounts payable	L 797
Accounts receivable	1,546	Notes payable	715
Inventory	808	Other current liabilities	603
Other current assets	105	Long-term debt	1,391
Fixed assets	1,034	Other liabilities	373
Other noncurrent assets	247	Shareholders' equity	1,242

HEWLETT PACKARD (1983)

Income statement data	(millions)	Sales by activity	
Net sales	$4,710	Computers	60%
COGS	2,195	Test equipment	26
R&D	493	Medical instruments	9
Marketing	771	Analytical	5
SG&A	523		
Net income	296	Sales by area	
Dividends	432	United States	59%
	0	Europe	29
		Other	12

Balance sheet data			
Cash	$ 880	Accounts payable	$ 351
Accounts receivable	951	Other current liabilities	569
Inventory	798	Long-term debt	71
Other current assets	151	Other liabilities	283
Fixed assets	1,431	Shareholders' equity	2,937

EXHIBIT 10 IBM PRICING STRATEGY FOR THE PC

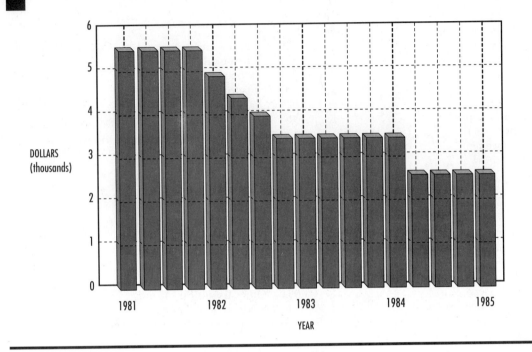

The PCjr was targeted at the home user and was capable of running much of the software written for the PC. IBM's first venture into the home market was backed up with extensive advertising. According to IBM sources, during the period from August 1 to December 31, 1984, 98 percent of the American public saw at least 30 PCjr advertising messages. At the high end, IBM announced the PC AT in August 1984 as the flagship of its microcomputer line. The AT is based on a sophisticated microprocessor that facilitates multitasking and multiuser systems. Along with the AT, IBM introduced a local area network capable of supporting up to 72 users simultaneously.

IBM's strategy has also capitalized on its strengths in related markets. As the world's largest computer maker, IBM has a worldwide distribution network and an unequaled reputation for service. In 1982 the U.S. Justice Department dropped a 13-year antitrust suit against IBM, and since that date IBM has moved aggressively into new markets and technologies. IBM has acquired Rolm Corporation, a leading producer of telecommunications products, and has purchased a minority interest in Intel, the supplier of microprocessors for the PC. IBM has also experienced antitrust problems in Europe. The European Commission of the European Economic Community filed suit against IBM in late 1980 accusing the company of abusing its leadership position and restricting competition. For IBM, the stakes in Europe are high. IBM operates 15 factories and nine research laboratories in Europe, employing over 100,000 people.

APPLE COMPUTER

Apple is one of the legends of microcomputing. In 1976 Steve Jobs and Steve Wozniak quit their jobs in Silicon Valley and began experimenting with the use of microprocessors. After designing a crude computer system, Jobs and Wozniak sold their van and calculator to raise $1,300 in seed money. The machine was an instant success, and Apple began to grow explosively. From these humble beginnings, Apple Computer grew to $1.9 billion in annual sales by 1985 and took its place in the Fortune 500.

Apple's early success was based on its ability to innovate and to make computers less threatening to large segments of the population, many of whom had never used a computer before. Apple's early leadership gave it extensive distribution in hobby and specialist shops and a large market share in small businesses and the home. Apple entered the European market in 1978 and proceeded to attain a very strong position. However, increased competition has led to an erosion in Apple's position in both the United States and Europe. In 1984 Apple pinned its hopes on the Macintosh, a machine designed to make computers as friendly and as easy to use as possible. Apple claimed that a new user could begin to perform productive work within 30 minutes of using the Macintosh for the first time. This is in stark contrast to the esoteric and complex languages associated with most microcomputer applications. Priced at $2,495, the Macintosh was placed in direct competition with IBM's PC.

TANDY

One of Apple's earliest competitors in microcomputers was Tandy Corporation. Tandy built a strong position in the early stages of market development on the basis of its strong retail store network. In 1985 Tandy sold computers out of approximately 1,350 Radio Shack stores worldwide. Until 1984 Tandy had maintained a proprietary operating system. However, more recent products are IBM compatible. Tandy is particularly strong in the "notebook" (under 10 pounds) segment, where it has the largest share of any producer.

COMMODORE

Commodore was another early entrant into the microcomputer business. In the United States, Commodore focused on the low end of the market and built a strong position in inexpensive machines used for game playing and computer literacy. Commodate entered the European market in 1977 and was somewhat more successful in penetrating the small-business segment. By 1983 Commodore had the largest installed base of microcomputers (in terms of units) of any manufacturer in Europe. In 1984 Commodore introduced a line of IBM-compatible machines targeted at the corporate market.

EUROPEAN COMPETITORS

The leading European producers of microcomputers were Oliveti of Italy, Triumph-Adler of Germany, Applied Computer Technologies of the United Kingdom, Bull-Micral and SMT-Goupil of France, and L. M. Ericsson of Sweden. Although each of these firms had captured roughly 10 percent of their home markets, none had succeeded in developing significant exports. In addition to the leading firms in each national market, many small companies had emerged. For example, in France alone, there were over 90 small firms offering 170 different machines. These small competitors were joined by nearly every large European firm that had previously sold large computers, telecommunications equipment, consumer electronics, office products, or other related goods. The list of competitors includes such firms as Rank Xerox, Siemens, Philips, ICL, Nixdorf, and Thomson. In 1984 AT&T bought 25 percent of Olivetti and began a program of reciprocal product distribution. This exchange was intended to strengthen Olivetti's position in telecommunications products and AT&T's position in small computers. Like most of the competitors mentioned, Olivetti's strategy was to offer an IBM compatible machine at a lower price.

JAPANESE COMPETITORS

Although often discussed, the Japanese threat in microcomputers had failed to materialize in either American or Europe. As shown in Exhibit 11, many Japanese firms exported their products. However, none had attained an overall share of 5 percent or more outside of Japan. The failure of the Japanese to penetrate the United States or Europe was attributed to the following factors:

Inadequate Distribution. The landslide of entrants into microcomputers left many firms scrambling for distribution. Japanese firms generally lacked established channels of their own and were slow to break into other means of distribution. The problem was particularly severe in Europe, where most dealers would handle only three brands at a time. This meant that available shelf space was often captured by IBM, Apple, and a local producer.

Poor Software. Early Japanese products were offered with little software for applications. The first generation of Japanese products were late to adopt the popular CP/M operating system, thus leaving users confused as to what software was available. More recently, the Japanese products have usually followed the IBM standard and have access to the large published base of programs. However, critics often complain that the Japanese products do not offer any advantages over the IBM machine or its look-alikes.

Poor Documentation. In the rush to bring products to the market, many user guides were translated quickly and were poorly produced. This gave the Japanese products a reputation for being hard to use.

EXHIBIT 11 JAPANESE MICROCOMPUTERS FOR EXPORT

COMPANY	PRODUCT	RAM	MICROPROCESSOR	FORMAT	SOFTWARE BUNDLE
Canon	X-07	8K–24K	8 bit	P	No
	AS-100	64K–512K	16 bit	D	No
Casio	FP-200	8K	8 bit	P	Yes
Epson	HX-20	16K–32K	8 bit	P	No
	QX-10	16K–256K	8 bit	D	Yes
Fujitsu	16s	128K–1Mb	8 bit	D	No
NEC	APC	128K–640K	16 bit	D	No
	APC III	128K–640K	16 bit	D	No
	PC-6000	16K–32K	8 bit	D	No
	PC-8800	128K	8 bit	D	No
	PC-8200	16K	8 bit	P	Yes
	PC-8401	64K	8 bit	P	Yes
Panasonic	Sr. Partner	128K–512K	16 bit	T	Yes
Ricoh (OEM)	Monroe 2000	128K–640K	16 bit	D	No
Sanyo MBC	550/555	128K–256K	16 bit	D	Yes
MBC	1100/1150	64K	8 bit	D	Yes
MBC	4000/4050	128K–512K	16 bit	D	Yes
Seiko	8600 XP	256K	16 bit	D	Yes
Sharp	PC-5000	128K–256K	16 bit	P	Yes
Sony	SMC-70	64K	8 bit	D	No
Sord	IS-11	32K–64K	8 bit	P	Yes
	M23P	128K	8 bit	D	Yes
	M68	256K–1Mb	16/32 bit	D	No
Toshiba	T300	192K–512K	16 bit	D	No

Abbreviations: P = portable; D = desk top; T = transportable.

Source: Creative Computing, August 1984.

Despite the poor start by Japanese firms, the presence of these companies gave many competitors cause for concern. Memories of the Japanese success in televisions, VCRs, stereo equipment, cameras, and other similar products were painfully fresh for microcomputer firms who had competed with the Japanese in these markets previously.

NEC'S ENTRY INTO THE EUROPEAN MICROCOMPUTER MARKET

In 1985 NEC was struggling to find a way to transfer its success in the Japanese microcomputer market to Europe. At home, NEC enjoyed a market share of over 55 percent in personal computers. In addition to systems, NEC offered a full line of peripherals such as printers, screens, and modems. NEC's position in the Japanese market was similar to the role of IBM in America and Europe. A majority of personal computer software developed in Japan was written for NEC machines.

NEC first tested the European market in 1979 when it displayed the PC 8000 at the annual industrial fair in Hannover, West Germany. The PC 8000 was an 8-bit machine with 32K of RAM, expandable to 64K. As a result of a mediocre response at Hannover, NEC delayed the entry of the PC 8000 until the following year. By 1981 NEC was selling microcomputers in Germany, The Netherlands, France, Spain, and Italy. Sales grew slowly, but steadily, and in late 1982 NEC launched the PC 8800, an upgraded machine with a 8-bit processor, 64K memory, and excellent color graphics. These two machines were the mainstays of NEC's product line for the next two years.

NEC continued to expand into both smaller and large machines. In 1983 NEC introduced the 8201, a notebook computer weighing only four pounds. Despite its small size, the 8201 featured an 8-bit processor and 16–64K of RAM, with three software packages built in. In 1985 the 8401 was introduced and offered more memory, a bigger screen, more software, and a built-in modem, all for under $1,000. As they have done in mainframes, NEC has declined to conform to the IBM standard in microcomputers.

During this period, NEC began to develop distribution channels throughout Europe. Some observers felt that this process was inhibited by NEC's complex organizational structure. Small computers were administered through two independent divisions: NEC Home Electronics, headquartered in Neuss, West Germany, and NEC Business Systems, headquartered in London, England. NEC Home Electronics was responsible for distributing 8-bit computers, such as the 8000 and 8800 series, and the supporting peripherals. NEC Business Systems handled 16-bit computers, such as the APC and APC III, introduced in 1984, as well as office-automation equipment. The two divisions operated independently and were responsible for developing their own marketing strategy and distribution channels. For most countries, NEC worked through an exclusive national distributor who specialized in NEC products and sought retail distributors. For example, in France, NEC worked through Omnium Promotion, who had secured retail distribution for NEC in 80 stores throughout France.

NEC was best known in Europe for its computer peripherals. Obtaining distribution for microcomputers was extremely difficult as a result of the practice of handling only three brands in each store. For peripherals, however, distribution was far easier for NEC to obtain. NEC's Spinwriter series of printers was extremely popular and in great demand by retail store operators. In France, the Spinwriters are sold through over 350 outlets. In addition, competition in peripherals was less intense. Although it was widely suspected that few microcomputer companies were making a profit on their computers, NEC acknowledged that the peripherals business was very lucrative.

NEC produced all of its microcomputers in Japan. The freight to Europe was approximately 10 percent of the product's cost, and an additional 5.4 percent duty was paid on entry. NEC stated that it would continue to produce exclusively in Japan as long as delivered costs were minimized. If volume in Europe became sufficient, or EEC policy dictated import penalties, NEC would consider local production.

RECENT EVENTS

As NEC contemplated its strategy for the European market in early 1985, recent events gave the company cause for concern. Persistent rumors of an imminent shake-out made NEC executives wonder if the time for a major commitment to this market had already passed. Several smaller firms, such as Osborne and Gavilan, had already gone bankrupt, and even the industry leaders were beginning to feel the pinch. In March 1985 IBM announced that the PCjr had not met expectations and would be discontinued. Similarly, Apple suffered a number of setbacks. Sales for the Macintosh dropped 45 percent in the first quarter of 1985, and Apple was forced to shut down four factories to work off unsold inventories. Continued sluggish sales of the higher-priced LISA finally led Apple to discontinue the product. Meanwhile, DEC stopped production of its Rainbow, and Xerox was rumored to be getting out of the microcomputer business entirely. NEC management felt that its outstanding technological skills in microcomputers and related markets and its competitive cost structure should provide the basis for success. However, making the concept of C&C a reality was proving far more elusive than NEC had anticipated.

CASE 24

MAYTAG CORPORATION

PETER P. SCHODERBEK
AND SATISH P.
DESHPANDE

In early 1988 Maytag CEO Daniel Krumm was in his office when he received word that Salomon Brothers, a New York investment banking firm, had found a potential merger candidate that would give Maytag an entry into the European market before the European Economic Community pact took effect in 1992. By the end of the year, Maytag had acquired the Chicago Pacific Corporation, owner of the Hoover Co., which had product lines in vacuum cleaners and household appliances. Hoover would serve as the basis for Maytag's expansion into Western Europe.

News of Maytag's acquisition brought mixed responses from Wall Street. Some financial analysts thought it was a necessary move for further growth, but others questioned whether Krumm had made the right decision.

MARKET SATURATION OF THE U.S.

Exhibit 1 shows the amount of saturation of the U.S. appliance market. Future sales are expected mainly from replacement demand and new housing. The saturation value noted in column two of Exhibit 1 shows the percentage of households in the U.S. who own the corresponding appliance. The high values show that the American market is filled, with 75% of sales going for replacement or upgrading. New housing starts account for most of the remaining appliance sales. For every new home built, four new appliances are sold. The industry outlook for appliances shows a fairly steady demand over the next several years.

Although growth prospects for appliances in the U.S. market for the 1990s appear to be good, there is little doubt that the industry has taken on the

Source: **This case was prepared by the authors as a basis for class discussion rather than to illustrate either appropriate or inappropriate handling of an administrative situation.** © 1991, Peter P. Schoderbek.

EXHIBIT 1 MARKET SHARE, MAJOR APPLIANCE MANUFACTURERS (1988)

MAJOR PRODUCERS (MARKET SHARE)		SATURATION
Refrigerators (7,227,000 unit sales)		99.9%
GE	34%	
Whirlpool	27%	
Electrolux/WCI	20%	
Maytag/Admiral	11%	
Raytheon/Amana	6%	
Others	2%	
Washers (6,190,400)		71.0%
Whirlpool	50%	
Maytag	18%	
GE	15%	
Electrolux/WCI	11%	
Raytheon/Speed Queen	4%	
Others	2%	
Dishwashers (3,907,400)		48.0%
GE	40%	
Whirlpool	29%	
Electrolux/WCI	21%	
Maytag	7%	
Thermador/Waste King	1%	
Others	2%	
Dryers (Electric) (3,303,900)		51.4%
Whirlpool	50%	
GE	15%	
Maytag	15%	
Electrolux/WCI	13%	
Raytheon/Speed Queen	4%	
Others	2%	
Dryers (Gas) (1,046,800)		na
Whirlpool	50%	
Maytag	16%	
GE	15%	
Electrolux/WCI	13%	
Raytheon/Speed Queen	4%	
Others	2%	
Ranges (Electric) (3,201,600)		62.0%
GE	41%	
Elecrolux/WCI	21%	
Whirlpool	15%	
Maytag (Magic Chef, Hardwick, Jenn-Air)	11%	
Raytheon/Caloric	6%	
Thermador/Waste King	1%	
Others	5%	

(*continued*)

EXHIBIT 1 (Continued)

MAJOR PRODUCERS (MARKET SHARE)		SATURATION
Ranges (Gas) (2,167,300)		42.0%
Maytag/Magic Chef		
Hardwick	32%	
Electrolux/WCI	28%	
Raytheon/Caloric	18%	
GE/Roper	15%	
Brown	3%	
Others	4%	
Microwave Ovens (10,810,000)		60.5%
Samsung	17%	
Goldstar	17%	
Sharp	15%	
Matsushita	12%	
Sanyo	12%	
Litton	6%	
Electrolux/Tappan	6%	
Raytheon/Amana	5%	
Maytag/Magic Chef	3%	
Toshiba	2%	
Whirlpool	1%	
Others	4%	
Freezers (1,348,800)		na
Whirlpool	33%	
Electrolux/WCI	33%	
Maytag/Admiral	23%	
Raytheon/Amana	6%	
Others	5%	
Disposers (3,907,400)		na
In-Sink Erator	60%	
Electrolux/Anaheim	30%	
Thermador/Waste King	5%	
Watertown/Metal Products	3%	
Maytag	1%	

na = not available

Source: Adapted from *Standard & Poor's Industry Surveys*, 1988; and *Appliance*, 1989, p. 71.

characteristics of maturity. The consolidation of firms, established market shares, and high levels of productivity all signal intense competition in the United States. Several of the major participants feel that opportunities for increased market shares must come from overseas operations.

HISTORY OF MAYTAG

The Maytag company was founded by F. L. Maytag and three other men in Newton, Iowa, in 1893. The company produced threshing machine band cutters and self-feeder attachments invented by one of the founders of the company. In the early 1900s the line was expanded to include a variety of farm products such as hay presses, hog waterers, and harvesting equipment. As a sideline to counteract the seasonal slump in the farm equipment line, the company produced a washing machine. About this time, F. L. Maytag became the sole owner of the firm.

During the next two decades the company made steady improvements and became a national leader in the new laundry appliance industry. The manufacture of farm implements was discontinued in the early 1920s, and exclusive attention was devoted to the laundry appliance industry. The company went public in 1925, and by 1927 Maytag had produced its millionth washer.

Despite the economic depression of the 1930s, the company remained financially sound. During World War II the company converted all its manufacturing to military purposes.

Clothes dryers were added to the company product line in 1953, and five years later the company expanded into the commercial laundry field. A line of ranges and refrigerators, manufactured under the Maytag name by other companies since 1946, was discontinued by 1960.

The company reentered the kitchen appliance field in 1960 with a portable dishwasher and in 1968 with a food-waste disposer.

MANAGEMENT AT MAYTAG

Daniel Krumm was appointed president in 1972 and in 1974 was named chief executive officer; in 1986 he became chairman of the board of directors of Maytag. Krumm, a Sioux City, Iowa, native, typifies Maytag's management, which is long on service and home bred. Krumm has been with Maytag for 36 years; Sterling Swanger, senior vice-president for manufacturing, 42 years (now retired); Robert Faust, vice-president, manufacturing, 34 years; Dean Ward, director of purchases, 35 years; Leonard Hadley, executive vice-president and president of the Appliance Group, 30 years; Ray Dahlman, chief manufacturing engineer, 31 years; Doug Ringger, manager, product testing, 36 years; G. H. Weaver, manager, quality control, 20 years; Fred Swank, supervisor, manufacturing engineering, 41 years; Jesse White, who has played the role of 'Ol Lonely, 23 years (now retired); Einar Larsen, director of advertising 38 years, (now retired). Maytag management believes that such lengthy service promotes teamwork, which is part of the organization's culture.

Although Wall Street does not tag Maytag as a glamor company, it does respect it as a well-run firm that sticks to basic manufacturing and marketing. Maytag prides itself on its conservatism which extends to most aspects of its business. Maytag stock is a favorite among widows, trust departments of banks, and pension funds. Appendix A contains financial highlights of the company for the period 1985 to 1989.

It may be said that Maytag's executives are a tight-knit group. Not only do they work together, but they socialize together, as well. The company strongly believes in promotion from within, a policy that fosters a fierce loyalty to the company. Nearly all the top managers started near the bottom of the organization. The company describes its employees, both management and workers, as "down to earth with virtually no distance between the president and the assembly-line worker." Under Krumm, Maytag has maintained its image as a "comfortable, old shoes type of company, a builder of dependable products." Krumm admits that prior to its expansion in 1986 Maytag had a reputation of growing by "plodding along." Top officers state that Maytag is "no master of rapid change" but moves only if quality can be assured.

Wall Street experts thought that Maytag's expansion in 1986 with the acquisition of Magic Chef was necessary because of consolidation in the industry; however, one industry analyst at that time worried whether Krumm had done enough to lead Maytag into the future.

Krumm stated in early 1987 that Maytag was "dedicated to remaining independent. We have taken every protection for a company that we could take."[1] Although the company adopted a "poison-pill" anti-takeover measure in the summer of 1986, rumors periodically circulated that the company was a target.

MAYTAG'S COMPANY CULTURE—QUALITY AND INVOLVEMENT

All Maytag managers and employees have the same commitment to quality. This philosophy has helped create a work force with a high degree of pride. As one Maytag manager stated:

> Quality is a religion here . . . we are brought up in an atmosphere of quality. Quality emanates from the top to the bottom and from the bottom to the top. Quality starts with design and doesn't end until the product is shipped out the door and even then it doesn't end because consumers must believe and know that they're getting a quality product. Our employees don't know anything other than quality since it's a philosophy here.[2]

The Maytag company has long practiced employee participation as a means of improving quality. Individual and team recognition and financial incentive programs are used extensively for improving productivity. For example, an Employees' Idea Plan pays the worker one-half of the net savings resulting from his or her idea during a six-month period up to a maxium of $7,500. In 1986, 95% of the production employees submitted suggestions to the plan that resulted in an average cost savings of $375 per employee. The average submission rate of suggestions was 3.2 per employee, with an installation rate of 1.5 ideas per worker. The Employees' Idea Plan is a consistent winner of the excellent performance award given by the National Association of Suggestions Systems. The company's financial incentive systems cover 95% of the direct-labor operations.[3]

Teamwork prevails throughout the company. Such things as quality circles aren't deemed necessary because employees constantly interact with their supervisors. Both new supervisors and new production employees go through a training program of work simplification aimed at cost-cutting measures.

Supervisors also participate in a cost-reduction program; they receive no financial awards but they do receive recognition awards. In 1986, the submission rate resulted in an installation of 9.5 ideas per supervisor and a cost reduction of $24,835 per supervisor.[4]

Maytag employs a variety of means to assure quality. Consumer focus groups are used to discuss product features, and quality reliablity testing is done based on market research that looks at average consumer usage. Test criteria are three times average consumer use. Many parts are tested for 20-year use equivalency.

PRICING STRATEGY OF THE MAYTAG COMPANY

Maytag Company's pricing strategy centers on premium quality. Maytag has chosen not to compete on price, even though other competitors have been known to cut prices in order to expand their markets. A cost leadership position dictates economies of scale and a large market share. Maytag has maintained its commitment to the high end of the market. Maytag has long recognized the importance of its brand name in developing and implementing its "pull" strategy, (that is, the customer is committed to the Maytag brand before entering the store). Quality and dependability have been the cornerstones of its strategy. In a "push" strategy, manufacturers give retailers higher profit margins and advertising allowances in an effort to switch customers to higher-priced models. People are encouraged to enter the store by highly advertised low-priced models before they are moved up to higher-priced models. Store personnel are financially motivated to "trade up" the customer.

Ol' Lonely, Maytag's lonely repairman who personifies the company's commitment to quality, has been around for over 20 years. His recoginition, according to Maytag, is about 90%. The advertising strategy, according to Ol' Lonely, is "based on positioning the company as a supplier of superior products.... Dependability, which means 'Built better and built to last longer' to us, is not quite as easy to dramatize as performance. This is what the character of Ol' Lonely does so well for us. He dramatizes the benefits of long life and dependability."[5]

DISTRIBUTION AT MAYTAG

Until 1982 Maytag utilized independent dealers, some of whom carried only the Maytag line while others carried a variety of lines. Maytag bypassed independent distributors who were used by other manufacturers. Some of the old-line dealers had exclusive dealerships in some communities. In 1982 Montgomery Ward was franchised as a dealer for laundry equipment. Some viewed this as an opportunity to broaden Maytag's selling base and as a way to reach more consumers through a national chain store that offered revolving credit. A survey showed that the availability of credit was the principal reason for purchasing a washer or dryer at Wards. In 1986 Montgomery Ward began selling Maytag dishwashers.

Because of the expanded line of products, in 1985 Maytag established a financing plan for dealers (floor planning) to allow them to carry larger inventories. More recently, Maytag products have been distributed through stores like Best Buy.

Because of its increased product line, in 1986 Maytag initiated an aggressive program to sell directly to the builder market. Up to this time Maytag had concentrated on sales at the retail level since sales of laundry appliances were a small market to home builders. However, with the addition of kitchen appliances to the Maytag line, the home builder market represented new territory for Maytag that would not detract from existing retail business. Some observers believe that with the trend to two-income families, consumers were becoming less price sensitive and more quality conscious. Builders were able to purchase Hardwick, Jenn-Air, or Maytag appliances directly from the company.

MARKETS

There are two major markets for appliances in the U.S.—retail and contract. Retailers include mass merchandisers, appliance dealers who carry many brands, discount stores such as K-Mart or Best Buy, and department stores. Mass merchandisers such as Sears carry their own brands manufactured according to their specifications. In 1989 Sears made the decision to carry a variety of competitor's products. Department store sales recently have slipped and seem to have been taken up by regionals that specialize in appliances.

The contract market consists of builders and contractors who often decide which appliances to put into new housing. Builders are typically cost conscious and usually buy appliances at the middle or lower end of the line. Since they can save on transportaion costs and can exact some price concessions because of quantity buying, all appliances are usually pruchased from one manufacturer. General Electric has long dominated the new housing market because of its solid relations with builders and its strong brand image.

MAYTAG IN THE 1980s—A PERIOD OF GROWTH

Although Maytag expected to share in the expected growth of the appliance industry in the 1980s, the company's officers felt that its participation was somewhat limited because of its short line of products. At the same time, the company had just completed a large modernization program. Capital needs were low and cash reserves were growing. Company personnel decided to seek out new opportunities, and the best alternative discovered was to purchase an existing product line rather than develop one of their own. The appliance industry at the time was consolidating, partly because of the economies of scale that could be acheived with larger volume and partly because of pressure by dealers for full product lines. Because most dealers are members of groups that may order hundreds of millions of dollars in products a year, their desire for full product lines carries weight with manufacturers.

Maytag purchased Hardwick Stove in 1981 and Jenn-Air Corporation in 1982. Hardwick was a leading producer of gas and electric stoves whose history dated back 103 years. Hardwick was purchased for $4.5 million and 968,250 shares of Maytag stock, which had a value of $23.6 million.

Jenn-Air was acquired for $20.7 million cash and a promissory note of $30 million. Jenn-Air manufactures and markets a line of built-in and free-standing electric and gas ranges that utilize down-draft venting. The company markets to the home construction and remodeling industries. Jenn Industries, a subsidiary of Jenn-Air that manufactured and marketed power ventilation equipment for institutional, commercial, and industrial buildings, was sold in 1988 because management felt that it did not serve markets significant to the corporation.

In the early 1980s Maytag decided to enter the cooking appliance market with a complete line. New products included several versions of a microwave oven and new models of a free-standing stove with a variety of options such as continuous cleaning, gas, electric, attached microwave, and so on. Wall ovens were also introduced as a companion feature to the Jenn-Air grill-range and featured both conventional and convection cooking.

In 1983, Maytag decided to suspend production of the wringer washer it had manufactured continuously for 76 years. Sales of this product totaled 11.7 million units.

In 1985 the company introduced a stacked pair of clothes dryers designed for use in commercial laundry stores or in coin-operated laundries in apartment buildings.

Nineteen eighty-six was considered a banner year for Maytag. The company issued 16,072,000 shares of stock for the acquisition of all of the outstanding stock of Magic Chef, Inc. and its full range of appliances. Magic Chef brought to Maytag the Admiral Company, which made refrigerators, freezers, and dehumidifiers. Magic Chef, Inc. also owned Norge, which manufactured washing machines and dryers, and Warwick, which produced compact refrigerators. CEO Dan Krumm stated that consolidation in the appliance industry, which has led to fewer, larger companies, increased concern about Maytag's long-range future in the industry. The purchase of Magic Chef tripled the number of employees from 5,000 to 15,000; sales increased from $700 million to about $1.8 billion; and factories from 6 to 21. Market share increased from 5% to 13%.

Maytag and Jenn-Air had traditionally been positioned at the high end of the market, but Magic Chef's target market was the broad middle range. Admiral and Norge, divisions of Magic Chef, also manufactured for the private label market. Maytag's officers felt that this merger allowed the company to serve more of the appliance market. As with Hardwick and Jenn-Air, each of the individual brands retained their own identities. As a full-line manufacturer,

Maytag ranked behind only G.E., Whirlpool, and Electrolux. These companies dominated the American market.

In 1986 Jenn-Air introduced a line of refrigerators and freezers manufactured by Admiral. Admiral also introduced a 40-bottle Wine Cellar, a temperature-controlled cooler. Toastmaster, a Magic Chef company, was sold because it did not strategically fit with major appliances. Heatube, a division of Toastmaster, was not included in the sale; the company manufactured heating elements used by Magic Chef as well as other appliance manufacturers. Other companies included in the Magic Chef merger were Dixie-Narco, which manufactured soft-drink vending machines; Warwick, whose compact refrigerators and freezers were sold under a variety of labels, including Magic Chef and Admiral; and Ardac, which manufactured electronic money changers. Magic Chef Air Conditioning (sold in 1988) produced a full line of residential and industrial heating and cooling equipment. Maycor was a new company formed to provide product service and repair parts distribution for all the appliances.

THE ACQUISITION OF CHICAGO PACIFIC CORPORATION

On October 27, 1988, Maytag made a cash tender offer under which it bought 6.4 million shares, or about 49%, of Chicago Pacific stock for $60 a share, or $384 million. The remainder of Chicago Pacific's shares were exchanged for Maytag stock at the rate of one share of Chicago Pacific for 2.72 shares of Maytag stock. Maytag Corporation issued 27.5 million new shares to complete the exchange. The total cost of the acquisition was in excess of $900 million. Maytag put more than $300 million of goodwill on its books.

Chicago Pacific Corporation, the successor of the Chicago, Rock Island and Pacific Railroad, had purchased the Hoover Co. in 1985 for $534 million. The Hoover Company, which had product lines in vacuum cleaners and household appliances, established bases in Britain and Australia. Its European operations included washers, dryers, dishwashers, refrigerators, and microwave ovens.

Exhibit 2 depicts an organization chart for the Maytag Corporation after the Chicago Pacific/Hoover acquisition.

Hoover had 14 manufacturing facilities in 8 countries and approximately 15,100 employees. Net sales of Hoover in 1988 were $1.5 billion. The market for major appliances in Australia is $250 million.

With the acquisition of Chicago Pacific Corporation, Maytag also acquired six furniture businesses, which were sold in late 1989.

At the time of the acquisition, Maytag, with its low debt and large asset base, was a prime target for a takeover, according to many Wall Street rumormongers. Analysts said that it was simply a question of "eat or be eaten."[6] In fall 1988 Maytag's stock experienced a brief rise as a result of the rumors. This change signaled officials of Maytag that they needed to firm up company strategy to go international. Company officers claimed to have already been committed to the globalization of Maytag because of (1) the changes that

EXHIBIT 2 ORGANIZATION CHART OF THE MAYTAG CORPORATION

APPLIANCE GROUP	HOOVER GROUP	DIVERSIFIED PRODUCTS GROUP
Admiral Company	Hoover North America	Dixie-Narco, Inc.
Heatube Company	Hoover United Kingdom	Warwick
Jenn-Air Company	Hoover Trading	
Maycor Appliance Parts & Service Co.	Hoover Australia	
Magic Chef Company	Domicor, Inc.	
Maytag Company		

would be brought about by the European Economic Community in 1992, (2) market saturation in the U.S., and (3) the trend toward internationalization of markets and strategies by other appliance firms.

EUROPEAN ECONOMIC COMMUNITY

The European Economic Community pact that was expected to go into effect in 1992 would provide a market of 350 million people with a gross national product of about $4.5 trillion—a population about 40% greater than that of the United States. In 1988, households numbered about 130 million in Europe, compared to about 91 million in the U.S. Because of a rising standard of living, Europeans were enjoying a significant increase in purchasing power and were expected to have almost as much money as the consumers of the U.S. and Japan combined. Gross domestic product per capita in about half of the Western European countries exceeded that of the United States.

The potential of this tariff-free market was causing firms throughout the world to relocate, merge, or acquire European firms to give them access to the market. Krumm felt that "it is absolutely essential that we have a presence established in Europe prior to 1992.... As an American company, if you're not there by 1992, you're not going to participate at all."[7]

THE INTERNATIONALIZATION AND CONSOLIDATION OF APPLIANCE COMPANIES

As of 1989, some appliance firms had already made a commitment to globalization. A. B. Electrolux, for example, had acquired White Consolidated, which owned seven appliance companies including Westinghouse and Frigidaire. Electrolux also acquired appliance manufacturers in Italy and the United Kingdom. (See Exhibit 3 for further consolidations in the appliance industry.)

Whirlpool established a joint venture with the Dutch giant N. V. Philips,

EXHIBIT 3 CONSOLIDATION IN THE APPLIANCE INDUSTRY

1970	1980	1988	1989
GE	GE	GE	GE/GEC (England)
Roper	Roper		
Whirlpool	Whirlpool		
KitchenAid	Dart & Kraft	Whirlpool	Whirlpool/Philips
Chambers			
Roper	Roper		
Thermador/Waste King	Thermador/Waste King	Masco	Masco
Magic Chef			
Johnson Corp			
Gafters & Sattler	Magic Chef		
Admiral		Maytag	Maytag Hoover
Norge			
Revco			
Warwick (Philco)	Warwick		
Maytag	Maytag		
Hardwick	Jenn-Air		
Amana			
Caloric			
Glenwood Range	Raytheon	Raytheon	Raytheon
Modern Maid			
Speed Queen			
Matsushita	Matsushita	Matsushita	Matsushita
AB Electrolux	AB Electrolux		
Arthur-Martin	Corpero		
Husqvarna	Zanussi		
Vest-Frost	Thorn		
Zanker	Domar		
Gibson			
Franklin			
Hamilton		AB Electrolux	AB Electrolux
Kelvinator	WCI		
Athens Stove			
Westinghouse			
Frigidaire			
D & M	D & M		
Tappan	ABE		
Eureka			
Philips	Philips		
Ignis	Baukecht	Philips	
Sanyo	Sanyo	Sanyo	Sanyo
	Samsung	Samsung	Samsung
Bosch	Bosch-Siemens		
Siemens	Constructa	Bosch-Siemens	Bosch-Siemens
	Neff		Balay
Merioni	Merioni	Merioni/INdesit	Merioni
Candy	Candy	Candy Rosieres	Candy

in which it had a 53% stake. It also had joint ventures in India and Mexico; owned 70% of Inglis, Canada's second largest appliance company; and had a 65% interest in an Italian company. It was the second largest appliance maker in Europe, after Electrolux.

In 1989, recent consolidations in Europe had significantly altered market shares of both major and minor players. Strong competition existed at both ends of the market. Firms such as Bosch-Siemens, which dominated Germany, competed aggressively in the high-quality segment of the market, and the Italian firms were strong competitors at the low-price end. Many of the large firms had a significant presence in Europe. France was dominated by Thomson-Brandt, which had a 40+% share of the refrigerator and washing machine market. The company marketed a full price range of appliances. Sweden and Holland, countries with well-developed markets, were dominated respectively by Electrolux and Philips.

Hoover, Maytag's recent acquisition, did not rank among the top ten producers in the U.K., although British consumers accounted for about 75% of Hoover's $600 million European market. Hoover was a very small player in the European market.

THE TREND TOWARD STANDARDIZATION

Managers at Electrolux and Whirlpool believed that appliances worldwide would become standardized, allowing for economies of scale and worldwide distribution. For example, custom tariffs already had been waived among most countries, and an international agreement had been instituted for standards of aperture size for built-in appliances.

Many industry observers maintained that even with differentiation in the various countries, economies of scale persisted because flexible factories allowed for differentiated production batches. Some standardization of parts had already come about for individual companies. Most analysts agreed that consolidation would occur as Europe became one market, and the companies that survived would be either the low-cost producers or niche marketers.

Krumm, CEO of Maytag, expressed confidence in this standardization as far back as 1982. He stated:

> Up until now many of the products we make have not been seriously challenged from abroad. Foreign makers have not been inclined to produce and export the full-size major appliances that the American market requires, without a viable domestic market of their own. But as we in the United States edge closer to what is being manufactured abroad, to perhaps produce a "world appliance"—one that can be sold throughout the United States, Europe, and Japan—the possibility of greater competition may grow. The potential would grow for vast new markets for U.S manufacturers, but it also may well invite increased foreign competition within the United States.[8]

The benefits of standardization, however, may be some time in coming, some experts said. Loyalties die hard. For example, Frank Vaughn, head of

Chicago Pacific's appliance group, stated that although their front-loading washing machines are accepted in Britain, "you can't give them away in France. The French are a top-loading nation."[9]

THE DECISION TO COMPETE ABROAD

Although the European market was somewhat different because its appliances had fewer features and it was somewhat smaller in size, Maytag officials felt that Maytag definitely could compete overseas, not by producing for export but through an overseas acquisition. They expressed the thought that the overseas market would simply be a natural extension of their business. Albert Turner, an analyst with Duff & Phelps, Inc., did not think the task would be as easy as that. He stated, "Maytag will essentially be introducing new products into new markets."[10] Others thought that Maytag faced a real struggle since Europeans were fiercely loyal to domestic brands. Some European companies looked to the United States as a potential source of sales.

An official of Thomson-Brandt, the French appliance producer, stated:

> Our domestic market is Europe, and it is saturated; demand is on the decline. . . . Therefore, it is only logical that any company that can afford to invest in other markets should do so. . . . I believe the U.S., Canada, and Japan all offer an opportunity for our products. But at this stage, we are only evaluating the feasibility.[11]

Maytag's strategy to penetrate the European market appeared to be a turn-around position for the company that previous stated, ". . . there is little advantage in moving into international markets."[12] According to one Maytag official, "times change and companies must constantly review their markets." While Krumm admitted publicly that the deal was partly an exercise in raider-proofing, he also said his overriding strategy was to grab some growth overseas.[13] Appendixes B and C reflect Maytag's attitude toward and awareness of internationalization. Appendix D gives a general overview of the European appliance market in 1988.

Typically, U.S. manufacturers who venture into Europe find intense competition. Some skeptics flatly stated that it may be Maytag salesman rather than the repairman who gets lonely in Europe.[14] Maytag officials stated that they had no intention to sell the Maytag brand in Europe but planned to throw their expertise behind the well-known Hoover name, which was expected to contribute about one-third of Maytag's sales.

Maytag's entry into the European market was not its first. Krumm was sent to Belgium in 1962 to manage European distribution of coin-operated washers and dryers. When the president of a jointly owned facility in Germany died, Krumm was put in charge. After being clobbered in the marketplace by Italian-made appliances for two years, Krumm sold the plant and returned to Iowa.

As of 1989, other U.S. appliance manufacturers, were content to stay at home in the belief that uniformity of appliances in Europe would not be achieved in the near future. Standardization, tried in the past by European companies with both washers and stoves, failed miserably. National preferences for certain features and cultural barriers so far have precluded the acceptance of uniform products. The exceptions to this rule appeared to be room air conditioners and microwave ovens.

ENDNOTES

1. *Des Moines Register,* January 25, 1987, 15W.
2. Maytag manager, company interview, November 1, 1989.
3. "Design for Mechanization," *Appliance Manufacturer,* November 1987, 41, 44.
4. Ibid.
5. "Ol' Lonely: Heart and Soul of Maytag Brand," *Appliance Manufacturer,* November 1987, 58, 60.
6. Brian Bremmer, "Can Maytag Clean Up the World?" *Business Week,* January 30, 1989, 86.
7. "Maytag: Pursuing a Global Market," *Cedar Rapids (Iowa) Gazette,* February 12, 1989.
8. "AHAM (Associated Home Appliances Manufacturers) Execs Wrestle with Tough Problem," *Mart,* June 1982.
9. Bremmer, "Can Maytag Clean Up the World?" 87.
10. Ibid.
11. Jules Arbose, *Appliance Management,* April 1983.
12. *Standard & Poor's Industry Surveys,* September 8, 1988, vol. 2, p. T100.
13. Bremmer, "Can Maytag Clean Up the World?" 86.
14. Ibid.

ADDITIONAL REFERENCES

Elbert, David. "Iowa Firms Await Knock of Opportunity in Europe in '92." *Des Moines Sunday Register,* March 26, 1989, 1A, 5A.

"Holders Approve a Merger with Chicago Pacific Corp." *Wall Street Journal,* December 8, 1988, B10.

"Home Appliance Industry." *Value Line Investment Survey,* March 24, 1989, 130.

"Household Goods." *Forbes,* January 2, 1985.

"Low-key Krumm is Key to Maytag Success." *Des Moines Register,* January 25, 1987.

Maytag Annual Reports, 1985, 1986, 1987, 1988.

"Maytag Corp." *New York Times,* December 28, 1988, D4.

Maytag Corporation company publications.

"Maytag Merger is Completed." *New York Times,* January 27, 1989, D4.

"Maytag to Spend Millions." *Repository* (Canton, Ohio), March 22, 1989, B11.

"Maytag's First Step in Chicago Pacific Takeover Under Way." *Wall Street Journal,* December 8, 1988, C16.

"Maytag's New Girth Will Test Its Marketing Muscle." *Business Week,* January 16, 1987, 68–69.

Moody's Industrial Manual, 1988, vol. 1.

"On the Verge of a World War in White Goods." *Business Week,* November 2, 1987.

Standard & Poor's Industry Surveys, September 8, 1988, vol. 2, pp. T98–T100.

APPENDIX A

Maytag Corporation Financial Highlights

SELECTED FINANCIAL DATA (THOUSANDS OF DOLLARS EXCEPT PER SHARE DATA)

	1989*	1988	1987	1986	1985
Net sales	$3,088,753	$1,885,641	$1,822,106	$1,632,924	$1,571,032
Cost of sales	2,312,645	1,413,627	1,318,122	1,183,377	1,141,119
Income taxes	75,500	79,700	105,300	97,500	99,300
Income from continuing operations	131,472	135,522	147,678	114,739	119,318
Percent of income from continuing operations of net sales	4.3%	7.2%	8.1%	7.0%	7.6%
Income from continuing operations per share	$ 1.27	$ 1.77	$ 1.84	$ 1.32	$ 1.38
Dividends paid per share	0.950	0.950	0.950	0.850	0.825
Average shares outstanding (in thousands)	103,694	76,563	80,151	86,619	86,502
Working capital	$ 650,905	$ 317,145	$ 286,124	$ 330,116	$ 393,967
Depreciation of property, plant and equipment	68,077	34,454	35,277	32,659	33,765
Additions to property, plant and equipment	127,838	101,756	42,564	45,619	41,066
Total assets	2,436,319	1,330,069	854,925	882,576	893,608
Long-term debt	876,836	518,165	140,765	46,189	98,570
Total debt to capitalization	50.6%	51.5%	28.1%	11.0%	16.9%
Shareowners' equity per share	$ 8.89	$ 6.55	$ 5.43	$ 6.53	$ 6.48

*These amounts reflect the acquisition of Hoover on January 26, 1989.

APPENDIX B

Some Questions Directed to Maytag CEO Dan Krumm at the 1988 Annual Meeting

Q. What are the basic elements of Maytag's corporate strategy?

A. Our business plan is to broaden market shares of premium-priced appliances, increase penetration with multiple brands in the mid-range market, and expand in the growing international markets. Implicit in this plan are our objectives of improving profitability and achieving long-term growth in both sales and earnings.

Q. Some people viewed the merger with Chicago Pacific as an anti-takeover move on the part of Maytag. Was it?

A. Clearly not. It was a strategic business move on our part to include international markets in Maytag's long-range plan for growth. Hoover's major appliance business is very strong in the United Kingdom and Australia, and it is growing on the European continent. This was just the type of entry into the overseas appliance market that we were looking for. Any defensive characteristics are incidental to our objective of providing long-term growth.

APPENDIX C

On Consolidation and Globalization (from the Maytag 1988 Annual Report)

For a number of years, consolidation has been the dominant trend in the U.S. appliance industry, and 1988 was no exception. Whirlpool and General Electric each made a bid for Roper Corp., a manufacturer of gas and electric ranges and outdoor power equipment. Both firms sought Roper's gas range production capabilities plus the company's strong ties with Sears.

GE ended up acquiring Roper's factories and assets, but Whirlpool received the Roper brand name and an agreement from GE to supply Roper brand cooking appliances for two years. Whirlpool plans to market a full line of Roper brand major appliances in the low to middle price range. Meanwhile, GE announced it would activate the RCA brand name and use it on a complete line of major appliances.

In another move, Whirlpool's KitchenAid division acquired the dishwasher and trash compactor business of Emerson Electric Company.

Added to the continuing consolidation trend in 1988 was an increased interest in global appliance markets. In many parts of the world, the saturation levels of major appliances are much lower than they are in the mature U.S. market, so the potential for growth is greater.

Whirlpool implemented a joint venture by announcing its plans to acquire a 53 percent ownership in the major appliance division of N.V. Philips, which is based in the Netherlands. According to Whirlpool, the combination makes it the world's largest producer of major appliances, surpassing A. B. Electrolux of Sweden. At the end of three years, Whirlpool has the option to acquire the balance of Philips' appliance division.

A. B. Electrolux, which owns some 10 companies in the U.S. including White Consolidated Industries, continued its long-running acquisition program in 1988 by buying Roper's outdoor power equipment division from GE.

Electrolux now owns over 400 companies and has about 135,000 employees throughout the world.

Early in 1989, General Electric entered the overseas appliance business by teaming up with General Electric Company GEC, an unrelated British firm. In this joint venture, GE acquired 50 percent of GEC's European household appliance business.

APPENDIX D

European Market 1988*

MARKET OVERVIEW

In 1988, European appliance manufacturers sold approximately 50 million units of large kitchen appliances, compared to approximately 40 million units sold in the United States. Table 1 provides a summary of European sales for the period 1984 to 1988.

TABLE 1 SUMMARY OF MAJOR APPLIANCE SALES IN EUROPE, 1984–1988[a]

MARKET	SHARE OF TOTAL (UNITS IN THOUSANDS)					
	1984	1985	1986	1987	1988[b]	
France	6,375	6,498	7,291	8,472	9,579E	18.8%
Germany	7,825	7,925	8,625	9,475	10,190	20.0
Italy	4,769	5,333	5,698	5,811	6,350E	12.5
United Kingdom	8,610	8,926	9,334	9,643	10,268E	20.2
Big Four Total	27,579	29,682	30,948	33,401	36,387	71.6
European Total	38,038	39,673	42,582	46,405	50,825	100.0
U.S. factory sales	33,216	35,718	39,178	40,814	39,511	

[a]Major appliances include refrigerators, freezers, ranges, microwave ovens, washers, dryers, and dishwashers.
[b]Estimated.

Source: Euromonitor Publications, Association of Appliance Manufacturers, Salomon Brothers, Inc.

*All of the information included in this section was drawn from Russell L. Leavitt, Peter Knox, and Daniel Perla, *Consumer Electrical Products: The White Goods Industry—Focus on Europe*, Stock Research Report, Salomon Brothers, September 1989.

EUROPEAN SATURATION RATES OF APPLIANCES

Saturation rates in Europe generally were lower than in the United States for all large kitchen appliances except washing machines; the saturation rate for freezers was the same in Europe as in the U.S. Table 2 displays the 1987 saturation rates of appliances in Europe and the United States.

TABLE 2   HOUSEHOLD SATURATION RATES OF LARGE KITCHEN APPLIANCES, 1987

	WASHING MACHINES	TUMBLE DRYERS	DISH-WASHERS	REFRIGERATORS	FREEZERS	ELECTRIC RANGES	MICROWAVE OVENS
Austria	89%	5%	28%	94%	57%	67%	8%
Belgium	83	28	21	98	58	34	6
Denmark	88	32	24	100	71	76	5
Finland	86	2	23	85	58	90	13
France	86	5	26	98	44	6	9
W. Germany	91	17	32	96	56	74	11
Greece	69	na	3	73	24	74	na
Italy	96	na	22	99	22	4	3
Netherlands	95	15	9	98	42	16	3
Norway	92	na	25	96	na	95	na
Portugal	43	na	9	83	12	na	na
Spain	92	4	10	98	5	3	2
Sweden	93	28	38	96	73	na	12
Switzerland	96	19	36	99	63	na	10
U. Kingdom	87	31	10	97	45	34	33
Europe	85%	15%	22%	95%	41%	50%	18%
U.S.A	70%	42%	48%	100%	41%	59%	66%

na = not available

Source: Euromonitor Publications and Salomon Brothers, Inc.

The largest growth in appliances was in microwave ovens, where the Japanese manufacturers dominate. Of the eight firms that dominated this market, six were Japanese. Japanese manufacturers, however, had not been able to penetrate the other sectors of the European white goods market.

In the period 1983–1988, average growth in appliance sales, (excluding microwaves) was 4.4%. Growth rates in the major countries were as follows:

- United Kingdom   3.6%
- West Germany   1.4
- France   4.9
- Italy   6.0

MARKET SHARES OF EUROPEAN MAJOR COUNTRIES

Table 3 depicts the ranking of market shares in Europe in 1980 and 1988; the large increases are accounted for mainly by acquisitions. The table shows that four firms had over 50% of the market and 10 firms controlled 80% of the market.

TABLE 3 MAJOR EUROPEAN APPLIANCE MANUFACTURERS AND RESPECTIVE MARKET SHARES, 1980 AND 1988

COMPANY	1980	1988
Electrolux	8.0%	20.5%
Whirlpool International (Philips)	8.0	11.5
Bosch-Siemens	7.5	11.0
Merioni	2.0	10.0
Candy	2.5	5.5
Thomson	5.0	5.0
GEC Hotpoint	2.0	5.0
AEG	6.0	5.0
Miele	3.5	4.0
Ocean	0.5	2.5
Total	45.0%	80.0%

DISTRIBUTION IN EUROPE

Although, in 1988, the distribution of appliances in Europe varied significantly, the majority of them (52%) were sold through electrical chain stores; another 14% were sold through independent electrical retail outlets and 12% through co-op/department stores. Kitchen design specialists accounted for 5% and builders another 5%.

CASE 25

CATERPILLAR, INC., IN LATIN AMERICA

ROBERT P. VICHAS
AND TOMASZ
MROCZKOWSKI

Although Caterpillar's presence in Latin America dated to 1914, when the U.S.-based multinational corporation opened its first dealership in Panama, manufacturing in Latin America did not commence until 1960, when the company initiated assembly operations in Brazil, its fourth largest national market.

A giant in the global construction equipment industry, Caterpillar was challenged in the early 1980s by Komatsu Ltd., a Japanese multinational corporation. Having grown from a weak rival one-tenth the size of Caterpillar in 1961 to the world's second largest supplier of construction equipment, Komatsu confronted Caterpillar on the latter's home turf in the U.S. as Caterpillar had done 20 years earlier in Japan.

In 1988 Komatsu renewed its assault by forming a strategic alliance with Dresser Industries of Dallas, Texas. The Komatsu-Dresser joint venture presented the latest threat to Caterpillar's Latin American markets. Although Caterpillar, with a strategy of competitive renewal and its "plant with a future," had successfully defended itself from Komatsu's strategic thrusts in the 1980s, the U.S. MNC would face a new set of challenges in the 1990s.

CATERPILLAR, INC.

A U.S. multinational corporation headquartered in Peoria, Illinois, Caterpillar could trace its origins to two inventors who, in the late 1800s, independently had developed leading-edge technology of that era. Their inventions led to automation of agricultural production in the state of California. Subsequently the two formed the Caterpillar Tractor Co.

Source: Prepared by Professor Robert P. Vichas, Florida Atlantic University, and Professor Tomasz Mroczkowski, American University, as a basis for classroom discussion and not to illustrate either effective or ineffective handling of administrative situations. © Robert P. Vichas, 1990.

Although the company for years had exported its products from the United States, globalization began in 1950 when the firm announced formation of its first foreign subsidiary in the United Kingdom. By the end of the 1950s, it had established manufacturing subsidiaries in the United Kingdom, Australia, and Brazil. Before the end of the 1960s, the MNC had expanded operations into France, Belgium, South Africa, and Mexico with sales subsidiaries in Europe and the Far East to service those dealerships.

Historically, Caterpillar had led the global construction equipment industry with a strategy of broad and deep market penetration within two main categories of heavy equipment: (1) earthmoving, construction, and materials handling machinery, and (2) engines. Several subsidiaries serviced the Latin American markets.

CATERPILLAR AMERICAS CO.

To support its 34 dealers who sold Caterpillar machines, engines, lift trucks, paving products, parts, and repair service in Latin America and the Caribbean, Caterpillar Americas Co. (also headquartered in Peoria, Illinois) controlled four district offices.

Two of these district offices were located in Plantation, Florida. The Northern District Office supported dealers in Colombia (1985), Ecuador (1925), French Guiana (1973), Guyana (1975), Netherland Antilles (1987), Suriname (1941), and Venezuela (1927). (Numbers in parentheses represent year dealership was established.) The Caribbean/Central America District Office serviced 16 dealers, the first of whom was appointed in Panama (1914), the most recent in Jamaica (1987).

In Santiago, Chile, a third district office served dealers in Argentina (1971), Bolivia (1969), Chile (1940), Paraguay (1951), Peru (1942), and Uruguay (1927). Located in Houston, Texas, the fourth district office assisted customers and dealers in Mexico.

CATERPILLAR AMERICAS EXPORTING COMPANY (CAMEC)

Yet another subsidiary, CAMEC, called Florida home. The Miami Lakes operation exported Caterpillar parts on behalf of its Latin American and Caribbean dealers. These replacement parts and components might have been manufactured in Latin America, shipped to the United States, and then reexported to still another Latin American country.

CATERPILLAR WORLD TRADING CORPORATION

Another subsidiary, Caterpillar World Trading Corporation, arranged for the acquisition of Caterpillar products through countertrade or barter for a variety of products. This type of trade permitted Caterpillar to penetrate markets where inconvertibility of foreign currency remained a problem.

Of its 15 manufacturing plants outside of the United States, both Brazilian and Mexican subsidiaries were wholly owned. The only other Latin American manufacturing plant, an independent manufacturer in Argentina, produced under a licensing agreement with Caterpillar. Altogether, the MNC marketed over 100 models of earthmoving, construction, and materials-handling machines; 40 paving/compaction products; 80 lift truck models; and 25 basic engine models.

Brazil. Caterpillar Brasil S.A. (CBSA) opened a parts distribution center in 1954 in Santo Amaro. To support Brazilian exports, it initiated assembly operations in 1960. Inaugurated in 1976 in Piracicaba, a second plant manufactured tracktype tractors, motor graders, wheel loaders, and scrapers. Brazil represented the MNC's fourth largest national market.[1]

To maintain market dominance, Caterpillar Brasil strengthened its manufacturing presence during the latter 1970s in response to competitive challenges of Komatsu, Dresser Industries, Case, Fiatallis, VME, and TEREX. Caterpillar expanded both manufacturing capacity and product lines. In 1973, it had purchased nearly 1,000 acres of land, about one-half of the new industrial park, Unidade Industrial Unileste, north of Piracicaba, which was the largest land acquisition Caterpillar had ever made outside of the United States.

By 1989, the firm had enlarged the Piracicaba operation to almost 1 million square feet with ambitions nearly to double the physical size again by 1992, at which time it planned to close the Santo Amaro plant. Altogether the two facilities in Brazil employed about 5,000 persons.[2]

Not only had CBSA management to cope with the competitive thrusts of Komatsu and Dresser but also with various constraints imposed by Brazilian government policies and regulations, such as local content laws. In order to obtain more duty- and tax-free import privileges, which benefits its competitors were already receiving, CBSA signed an accord with the government in 1980. CBSA agreed to export $2.0 billion worth of equipment between 1980 and 1990. (Note: All monetary values are stated in U.S. dollars.) The commitment was predicated on projections that domestic and export demand for the 1980s would at least be equal to or better than the 1970s,

However, demand declined. CBSA project manager Bill Cook said that the world market for construction equipment collapsed after Caterpillar had entered into the agreement. "Both the export market and the domestic market declined. So we couldn't export what we said we would, nor did we need to import what we thought."

Of the 1980 export pact, CBSA vice president Don Coonan said, "There was a very real threat there. We had a contractual agreement that we weren't meeting. In fact, it looked like we would only get about 40 percent of that amount. We agreed we ought to have a strategy for CBSA."

Facing a potential penalty of $335 million for not meeting the export target, management had to reevaluate its goals and strategy. Of its several short and long term goals, the following ranked highest:

1. Become more cost effective.
2. Increase management effectiveness.
3. Emphasize quality in the production processes.
4. Develop a more export driven organization.
5. Comply with local content laws.
6. Meet aggressive market challenges of Komatsu and Dresser.

Several task forces were created. Coonan headed an export task force. Its objective was to increase exports from Brazil. Another group focused on a new strategy for CBSA. They found that CBSA had noncurrent product, volatile demand, complex operations, deteriorating manufacturing facilities, and excess costs.

During the mid-1980s, corporate headquarters had compiled an in-depth study and evaluation of Komatsu. Management reevaluated its Latin American presence. Caterpillar had realized a 16-percent gain for all of Latin America during 1986; much of that headway was attributable to the Brazilian operations. In 1987, corporate headquarters opted to strengthen its commitment in Brazil and support changes required by CBSA.

The new strategy embraced several significant elements. First, the new strategy called for renegotiation of the contract with the Brazilian government. CBSA management succeeded in renegotiating export requirements from $2 billion down to $816 million.

Second, to meet the goal of making CBSA a more export driven organization, Brazil would become the new world source for scraper bowls (except elevating scrapers). A new motor grader series, as well as the D4H along with a newer model of the track-type tractor, would be dual-sourced with Brazil designated as one of two manufacturing sites. Also, CBSA would manufacture the 3116 engine and countershaft transmission for use in Brazilian-built machines. Over the long term CBSA wanted its exports to account for 35 percent of total sales.

Third, modernization to achieve better cost and quality control became part of the manufacturing plan. Consolidation included expansion of the Piracicaba plant to accommodate increased production. Chuck Gladson, technical director, said, "We upgraded and simplified our processes through use of technology and layout."

Factories were reorganized to improve materials handling. Cook said, "We positioned ourselves with new manufacturing philosophies."

Fourth, because cost effectiveness was essential to remain competitive, CBSA planned to reduce the number of different models it built. At that time CBSA built two distinct versions of each model: one for the domestic market that complied with local content requirements, another version for export.

Fifth, in order to increase the allowable volume of products for domestic sale, CBSA intended to improve supplier capabilities in Brazil. Cook said, "We explained to our suppliers that we're looking at things from a world class perspective—that means higher volumes, lower costs and high expectations for quality and reliability from them." Reaching its local content goal would permit CBSA to expand Brazilian sales. Without greater domestic sales, CBSA's earning power would be considerably restricted.

Sixth, to meet efficiency goals, CBSA management reorganized its reporting structure in 1988 to implement consolidation of the two-plant operations. The departments of manufacturing, industrial relations, quality control, and materials at each plant were merged under one department head, who held simultaneous responsibility for the departments in both plants. Management created the new organizational structure in Exhibit 1 to improve accountability and efficiency.

Implementation of the new strategy, consolidation, modernization, and new product programs were scheduled over a five-year period. However, CBSA faced a number of environmental challenges:

1. A volatile Brazilian market.
2. Inflation of 1,000 percent a year.
3. Price controls that limited prices of final outputs but not necessarily the cost of raw material inputs and labor.
4. Government-owned and protected industries.
5. Brazilian debt crisis that restricted availability of foreign exchange for imports and profit repatriation.
6. Local content regulations.
7. A massive governmental bureaucracy.
8. Political uncertainty and capital flight.
9. An aggressive foreign competitor, Komatsu.

On the positive side, Brazil, the world's seventh largest economy with abundant natural resources, offered potential opportunities in mining, agri-

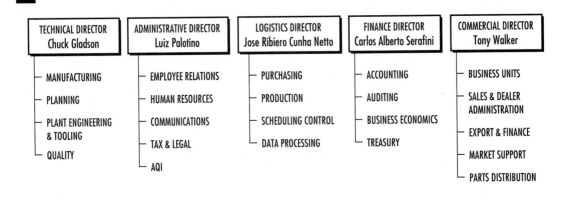

EXHIBIT 1 PARTIAL ORGANIZATION CHART OF CBSA, 1988

cultural, and construction markets, as well as growing infrastructure needs. Brazil had the highest developed industrial structure in South America; many MNCs considered it a potentially attractive investment; and should Brazil resolve its political and fiscal problems, established companies would have first crack at newly emerging opportunities. However, even from a perspective of late 1988, realization of market projections were subject to considerable variance. Since uncertainties continued into 1989 for Brazil, Mexico seemed to offer greater promise.

Mexico. During the early part of the decade of the 1980s, the U.S. MNC suffered a precipitous decline in Mexican sales due in part to lower oil prices. (Mexico was a net exporter of petroleum, an important generator of foreign exchange.) Caterpillar blamed a challenging economic environment, high foreign debt, and high interest rates in the U.S. for its problems in Latin America.

Despite operating losses, Caterpillar preserved a strong relationship with its Mexican dealers in Chihuahua (1945), Monterrey (1981), Ciudad Obregon (1929), Mexico City (1926), and Guadalajara (1974). This established dealership network was costly to sustain. Caterpillar typically turned around requests for parts within 48 hours—an important consideration in the purchase of heavy equipment—and service that competitors could not always match. In addition to its dealerships, the firm maintained manufacturing facilities in Monterrey.

Of Caterpillar's seven wholly owned foreign subsidiaries, two of them were located in Latin America: one in Brazil, the other, Conek SA de CV, in Mexico. For the first time in company history Caterpillar had accepted a minority interest of 49 percent in a joint venture formed in 1981 with the Mexican chemical producer, CYDSA, which owned the other 51 percent of Conek. The name, Conek, derived from the two words: construction plus equipment. Caterpillar believed that a partnership with CYDSA was a good match; CYDSA had operations throughout Mexico, and Mexican law required a local partner.

Caterpillar had decided to locate the plant in Monterrey, Nuevo Leon, for several reasons.

1. CYDSA recommended the location.
2. Monterrey was the second largest industrial city in Mexico.
3. It was near raw material sources: natural gas, steel, and trained labor and technical people educated at Monterrey Institute of Technology.
4. There was stability of state and local governments.
5. Fewer labor problems arose here than in some border areas where organized labor had disrupted work.
6. The work ethic and business philosophy seemed more akin to the U.S.

With the crash of the Mexican economy in 1982, CYDSA found itself under financial constraints due to its U.S. dollar-denominated debts and wanted to divest its interest in Conek. Caterpillar searched for a new Mexican partner. Partners which Caterpillar preferred had insufficient capital; those who came forward with sufficient capital Caterpillar did not want. Consequently, in December 1983, Caterpillar requested exemption from Mexican law and permission from the government for 100 percent ownership of the subsidiary. (Note: Current Mexican law allows 100 percent foreign ownership; however for foreign investments exceeding $100 million, the foreign investor must have a Mexican partner.)

In August 1984 the government gave its permission for the company to assume 100 percent ownership of its Mexican subsidiary. In November 1984 Caterpillar completed the transaction and acquired CYDSA's interest in Conek; in that month Conek became a wholly owned subsidiary of Caterpillar, Inc. in Peoria, Illinois. Until that point in time, Conek's operations had been essentially an assembly plant. Beginning in early 1985, the subsidiary began full-scale manufacturing to produce components and parts primarily for sale to the United States.

Conek shipped its output to corporate headquarters in Illinois or to other Caterpillar sales companies in the United States for reexport. By mid-1989, export production at Conek was about 40 percent finished products and 40 percent components and replacement parts; the remaining 20 percent of manufacture was destined for production of lift trucks and parts for the Mexican market. Local content varied according to the product; heavy manufactures requiring substantial steel usage might have 99 percent local content.

Products were transported by truck to Texas. Ing. Adan J. Peña Guerrero, treasury manager at Conek, said that by clearing customs in Monterrey prior to shipment, the paperwork required about 24 hours versus three days at the Texas border. He also said that with anticipated construction of the Colombia Bridge between Nuevo Leon and Texas, built exclusively for the expedient movement of exports and imports, the new 10-mile bridge near Laredo would save the firm considerable time and money. Currently, strong labor unions required expensive and delaying off-loading and reloading to cross the border. Additionally, the Mexican government sought private investors to construct a 15-mile toll highway direct to the bridge to bypass Nuevo Laredo.

Caterpillar maintained three industrial locations near Monterrey. Nearly 3.3 million square feet, the main manufacturing plant sat on 272 acres of industrial land. A second location, used for parts warehousing and some electronics manufacture, comprised almost 100 acres, plus a third site at Santa Catarina about half that size.

With a 1989 total of 1,700 office and plant workers (whose average age was 23 years) on a three-shift schedule, Conek operated at full capacity. Ing. Peña Guerrero proudly pointed out that office workers followed the American system of 8:00 to 5:00 with a 30-minute lunch break in the plant cafeteria. He said, "Most office employees usually arrive 15 or 20 minutes before 8 and do not leave until 10 or 15 minutes after 5." This contrasted sharply with Mexico City where the work day traditionally might begin at 9:00, with a two-hour mid-afternoon lunch, and end at 7:00 P.M.

Although Ing. Peña Guerrero was born in Monterrey, he preferred the efficiency of a U.S.-styled system. He had earned his M.S. degree in engineering at the Monterrey Institute of Technology (ITSEM), a private university, and an M.B.A. from the University of Wisconsin at Milwaukee. At age 31, he managed five supervisors and a total of 42 employees over whom he kept a watchful eye. He reported directly to another Mexican, Juan Gamez, finance manager, who, in turn, reported to the general manager, Jim Palmer.

Conek paid plant workers slightly above market rates and generated employee loyalty and cooperation by:

1. using a complaint and suggestion book to which management usually reacted within one week;
2. publishing a monthly employee newsletter, titled "Conexion";
3. holding periodic one-hour plant-wide meetings to inform employees of news, progress, and events;
4. maintaining close supervision over all employees;
5. creating an intense training program to improve quality and productivity;
6. offering free bus service to employees from the city to the plant.

Because the manufacturing facility was some distance from urban Monterrey, a daily bus picked up employees at designated points and times. Several advantages derived from this program:

1. Employee costs for transportation were reduced.
2. People arrived at work on time.
3. Riders could either rest or develop friendships during the ride.
4. Employees were less likely to talk casually with unionized workers from other plants.

The training program helped achieve corporate goals of greater productivity (lower costs of production) and higher quality. For example, welders must be adept at using a technique not employed in typical manufacturing. Conek required a six-week intense training course. Peña said that Conek had sent some employees to Texas for special welding training. After two weeks the welding school had sent them back to Mexico, because Conek had already trained them better for specific tasks than the school could. Peña added, "Conek also pays employees for college courses and for M.B.A. degrees."

Conek used Just-in-Time (JIT) inventory control and Duran Quality Control techniques. To resolve minor problems at the shop level, small quality control (QC) circles were activated. For larger problems Conek employed an annual quality improvement program (QIP), which, according to Peña, excelled over QC. Functioning like a task force, QIP focused on specific problems and on how to save money. All of this effort had paid off for the manufacturer. Peña said, "Conek has had no delivery or quality problems [since 1986]."

In Mexico, Caterpillar's chief competitor, Komatsu, was number two in the construction equipment market. Clark Equipment ranked as an unimportant third-place competitor; and all remaining competitors together represented only a minor threat to Caterpillar.

Conek and its parent had many strengths: It was well established in the market. It maintained a costly dealership network. It had built an international reputation. Its trademark, CAT, and the distinct yellow color of its equipment were instantly recognizable. Conek, as one of several sourcing points for components in a world-wide network, was assured of continued demand for its manufactures. Additionally, in its manufacture of finished products and components, Conek:

1. used a high grade heavy steel, from a Mexican source, not readily available everywhere;
2. maintained very good relations with its local steel supplier and had experienced no sourcing problems;
3. manufactured high quality products which required less refabrication, and, therefore, lowered overall costs;
4. tested all equipment thoroughly at the plant site and before shipment;
5. maintained careful quality control in its highly integrated operations;
6. insisted upon quality workmanship (e.g., welding) not necessarily found in all competing products;
7. achieved good cost control and continued to strive for higher productivity to maintain price competitiveness.

Financially the operation had not achieved payback of investment due to large start-up costs. A typical payback period in this industry would be on the order of 10 to 15 years. CYDSA, Conek's former partner, used payback projections of 18 years. By taking advantage of its experience curve, training employees for quality and productivity, and achieving a careful mix of exports and imports, Caterpillar expected to shorten the payback period of its Mexican subsidiary.

To test possibilities of diversification, Conek modestly invested in a small plant to assemble tractor electronics. The project had not been financially successful, due, in part, to sourcing problems for electronic chips. Its foreign source provided chips only twice yearly, which generated an inventory problem between overinvesting in inventory or a stock-out which would shut down the production line. The chip manufacturer needed longer production runs to bring down its costs. Since Conek was not a major purchaser, it had little influence on the supplier.

Peter Donis, president of Caterpillar, in early 1989, had said that profitability was constrained by higher material costs, higher start-up costs incurred by the factory modernization program, and higher-than-expected short term interest rates to finance working capital needs.

Nevertheless, with a turnaround expected by 1990 in the Mexican economy, Caterpillar anticipated an increase in sales of construction machinery. The new president of Mexico seemed to have considerable popular support for his economic development strategy, which was to: (a) open the economy to foreign competition, (b) privatize most public enterprises, (c) move toward creating a market economy, (d) encourage foreign direct investment, and (e) *inter alia*. Despite Caterpillar's aggressive stance, Komatsu's yellow (in imitation of CAT products) bulldozers could be seen excavating sites for construction of new commercial buildings in the heart of Monterrey, not many miles from Caterpillar's production facilities.

KOMATSU, LTD.

Caterpillar's chief competitor was the Japanese multinational corporation, Komatsu Ltd. Within most Latin American markets, Caterpillar and Komatsu's other competitors were frequently a distant number three or four in a particular country, often market spoilers; but altogether they did account for a respectable volume of business. Not only had Komatsu to concern itself with Caterpillar but also with those competitors whose presence in individual markets was most threatening to the Japanese firm.

Originating as the Takeuchi Mining Factory in 1894, Komatsu Ltd. manufactured and marketed a full line of construction equipment, industrial presses, and machinery such as robots and laser machines to customers in over 150 countries. The parent organization of the Komatsu Group, comprised of 60 affiliated companies, Komatsu Ltd., maintained world headquarters in Tokyo, Japan.

Komatsu had faced a major crisis in 1961 when Caterpillar announced a joint venture in Japan with Mitsubushi Heavy Industries Ltd. With one-tenth the sales of Caterpillar, Komatsu recognized that survival was problematic unless prices and quality of its products were competitive. Komatsu signed a license agreement with Cummins Engine, Inc. (U.S.) to manufacture and sell diesel engines, and subsequently entered into several other joint venture agreements with U.S. firms (which were later terminated).

Nevertheless, Komatsu did not establish its first foreign subsidiary until 1967: N.V. Komatsu Europe S.A. in Belgium. Global expansion began in earnest with creation of Komatsu America Corp. and the establishment of Brazilian and German subsidiaries. Bulldozer production commenced at Komatsu do Brasil in 1975, at Dina Komatsu Nacional S.A. in Mexico in 1976, and at P.T. Komatsu Indonesia in 1983.

BRAZIL

Formed in 1970 in São Paulo, Komatsu do Brasil initialized the first overseas bulldozer production in 1975. In those early years the Brazilian operation neither figured prominently in Komatsu's corporate global plans nor had it been successful financially. Because corporate net income in 1983 had declined about 20 percent from 1982, management blamed the Brazilian subsidiary for a significant share of those corporate losses and attributed them to unfavorable economic conditions in Brazil.

Of Third World countries, Shoji Nogawa (president of Komatsu) wrote: "Developing countries, also important markets for the industry, generally experienced economic difficulties, with their burdens of extensive debt further aggravated by the high level of U.S. interest rates."[3] (The Middle East had been Komatsu's most important foreign market.)

Corporate management said, in 1985, "Internationalization for Komatsu means not only establishing more efficient corporate management in overseas marketplaces but, more importantly, pursuing more effective customer-focused operations as the Company continues to expand its worldwide customer portfolio."[4] Despite management's stated commitment to globalization, the firm continued to manufacture principally in Japan for export to its foreign markets. Even as late as 1986, foreign manufacturing represented only 5 percent of company total, while 95 percent of manufacturing was still done in Japan.

Then, in 1987, under leadership of Komatsu's new corporate president, Masao Tanaka, the company sped up globalization of its operations. Setting a new target, management wanted foreign manufacturing to account for 35 percent of total production and pushed to integrate its manufacturing bases in Brazil, Mexico, and Indonesia into a framework of strategically defined roles.

MEXICO

Komatsu's Mexican subsidiary, Dina Komatsu Nacional, S.A. de C.V., also experienced a change during 1987 when the Japanese MNC's share in this joint venture rose from 40 to 68 percent ownership.[5] Dina Komatsu Nacional, a joint venture with Nacional Financiera, the government-owned Mexican development bank, began to manufacture bulldozers in 1976; but it produced no profit in its nearly 13-year history. The Mexican government, under President Salinas de Gotari, had been trying to privatize much of the public sector and divest itself of unprofitable joint ventures. Although the government's investment in Komatsu had been on the sale block since early 1988, potential private investors showed little interest in the offer.

Primarily, Komatsu's global strategy had been one of export development. The Mexican venture figured in a defensive move to counter Caterpillar in Mexico. Perceiving the Mexican market as a subunit of the larger North and South American market, Komatsu chose to do battle on U.S. soil and in 1988 sought to strengthen its presence in the Americas' market with a joint venture (JV).

THE UNITED STATES

Management of the world's second largest integrated maker of construction machinery stated that competitive strength "lies in its versatile technological base and its tradition of quality first."[6] Entry into the U.S. construction equipment market was a cornerstone in Komatsu's global market penetration strategy.[7]

When Komatsu opened its manufacturing facility in Chattanooga, Tennessee in 1985, it had an 8-percent share of the U.S. market, which it had hoped to double. Nobuo Murai, president of Komatsu America Corp., said, "Our goal is a market share of 15 percent in the near term and 20 to 25 percent in the long term."[8] Komatsu faced increasing obstacles in its exports to the United States due to the depreciated value of the dollar coupled with trade conflict issues between the U.S. and Japan.

Masao Tanaka (corporate president) in 1988 wrote: "Strategically, we are committed to establish a competitive operational system on a global scale, by setting up a worldwide manufacturing/sales network capable of flexibly and effectively responding to changes in the economic climate."[9]

To strengthen its competitive position in both North and South America, Komatsu and Texas-based Dresser Industries, Inc. announced in February 1988 the formation of a strategic alliance in which the two companies would combine their construction equipment manufacturing and engineering facilities in the U.S., Canada, and Latin America. Operationalized September 1, 1988, the 50-50 joint venture, Komatsu Dresser Company, constituted an initial capitalization of $200 million for machinery and automation plus $50 million to refurbish manufacturing plants. Sales for 1989 were projected at $1.5 billion. The strategic alliance also called for the creation of Komatsu Dresser Finance Division to finance sales both to wholesale and retail customers.[10]

Essential elements of the agreement were: Komatsu and Dresser would share equally in the management of Komatsu Dresser, which had exclusive manufacturing and marketing rights for North, Central, and South America. The joint venture also would distribute replacement parts, engage in engineering, and establish training and test centers as well as sales and administrative offices.[11]

The new alliance also required consolidation of three foreign subsidiaries—Komatsu America Corp., Komatsu America Manufacturing Corp., and Komatsu do Brasil—together with Dresser's Construction Equipment and Haulpak divisions and Dresser's manufacturing subsidiary in Brazil. Of this 1988 joint venture, Komatsu management wrote:

> The venture clearly symbolizes one successful outcome of Komatsu's internationalization strategy to establish the three-core comprehensive operations in Japan, the U.S. and Europe. It also advances Komatsu's commitment to further promote international cooperation with other firms for mutual business expansion as an equal partner.[12]

Based in Libertyville, Illinois, a Chicago suburb, Komatsu Dresser Company began operations in late 1988 with 5,000 workers employed at eight plants in the United States, Canada, and Brazil. It had more than 3.5 million square feet of factory space. One of these plants, the Haulpak Division (which produced mining trucks), was only 22 blocks down Adams Street from Caterpillar's Peoria, Illinois, corporate headquarters.

The new strategic alliance allowed Komatsu to shift much final assembly from Japan to the Americas and fight the battle for Brazil and the rest of Latin America right in Illinois. The new company would become number two in the Americas in the construction equipment industry.

FIGHTING FOR MARKET DOMINANCE

When battle lines between the two firms were drawn in 1961, Komatsu developed Total Quality Control (TQC) to become competitive in price and quality, broadened its product offerings to match Caterpillar's, reduced manufacturing costs, increased exports, and, by 1980, became recognized as the world's second largest manufacturer of construction machinery. It dominated the Japanese market with a 60 percent share.

Generally, in every country-market the Japanese had entered in recent decades, they applied a market-share pricing strategy, which meant using a low entry price to build market share and, in the long run, dominate the targeted market. However, shifts in exchange rates and the debt-laden economies of Brazil and Mexico dampened that success pattern for Komatsu.

Komatsu's exports to the U.S. had doubled in 1983. Its world market share rose to around 20 percent; and its U.S. market share had been expanded to 8 percent by the mid-1980s. The Japanese firm had managed to boost volume by 40 percent with very little escalation in employment by the heavy application of robotics. Management was spending $80 million a year alone on automation while continuing to diversify products in order to become a major producer of automated production systems and robots. By 1985, the firm had erected three large R & D laboratories, established five foreign production facilities—including a plant in the United States and in the United Kingdom—and added plastics, electronics, robots, metal presses, and other products to its line.

Prior to 1985 a high dollar exchange rate and price-cutting strategy gave Komatsu a 40 percent price advantage over Caterpillar. Its export ratio was 64 percent. But environmental factors swung against Komatsu. The dollar-yen relationship turned in favor of the dollar. Due to the strong yen, export-oriented Komatsu had to raise prices by 18 percent in 1986, while Caterpillar raised their prices an average 3 percent, the first increase since 1984; Komatsu lost 2 percent market share to Caterpillar. Komatsu's 1986 profits plummeted by 33 percent, exports fell nearly 5 percent, and in 1987 its president, Shoji Nogawa, resigned in the midst of unfavorable rumors. Komatsu's battle cry had been *MARU 'C'* (or "encircle CAT") to put Caterpillar in a defensive position.

However, Caterpillar maintained a solid financial position, held significant leadership in many areas of construction equipment technology, and by its size and global network was well positioned to take an offensive, rather than a defensive, position. Management initiated a strategic analysis.

Asked to assess strengths and weaknesses of Caterpillar and Komatsu, middle managers from various functional activities developed a comparative competitive analysis between Japan and the U.S. By rating the two firms on a seven-point scale, they developed comparative analysis on 17 factors. Professors Tomasz Mroczkowski and Marek Wermus tabulated the summary of responses appearing in Exhibit 2. On the seven-point scale, a rating of 1 was most favorable to Komatsu, a rating of 7 most favorable to Caterpillar. The

EXHIBIT 2 KOMATSU VS. CATERPILLAR: COMPETITIVE ADVANTAGES AS PERCEIVED BY U.S. EXECUTIVES (SUMMARY OF RESPONSES)

AREA	ADVANTAGE/SAMPLE MEAN							ADDITIONAL STATS		
	KOMATSU				CATERPILLAR					
	1	2	3	4	5	6	7	$S_{\bar{x}}$	Mc	Mo
1. Cooperative labor-management relations	1.52							.16	1.25	1.00 (18)
2. Cooperative business-government relations	1.59							.15	1.34	1.00 (16)
3. Labor costs	1.82							.26	1.34	1.00 (16)
4. Workforce trained in stat & quality control		2.07						.17	2.05	2.00 (10)
5. Strong organizational culture		2.22						.25	1.02	1.00 (11)
6. Pressure of management for short-term profit		2.64						.26	2.43	2.00 (7)
7. Better trained blue-collar			2.92					.32	3.69	4.00 (8)
8. Capital charges			3.32					.27	3.68	4.00 (11)
9. Responses to international markets			3.65					.29	3.79	4.00 (7)
10. Better trained white-collar			3.67					.32	3.60	4.00 (8)
11. Overall management				4.04				.25	4.06	4.00 (8)
12. Superior marketing intelligence				4.52				.36	4.63	4.00 (6)
13. Modern equipment & machinery				4.78				.21	4.71	4.00 (7)
14. Advanced manufacturing technology					5.15			.28	5.64	6.00 (17)
15. Product research & development					5.78			.19	5.94	6.00 (17)
16. Technologically more advanced products						5.96		.16	6.03	6.00 (16)
17. Superior design & product development capabilities						6.00		.21	6.13	6.00 (12)

Source: Tomasz Mroczkowski and Marek Wermus, "Improving Competitiveness Survey."

arithmetic mean represented the management group's averages. Additional statistics are included in the table.

Caterpillar's managers perceived Komatsu as operating in a lower labor cost environment and enjoying access to lower cost capital, a cooperative industry-government relationship, a cooperative labor force that had extensive skills in statistical process control, and that Komatsu's managers were not under pressures to produce short term profits.

Caterpillar's managers saw their own superiority in design and product development, R&D, technological level of products, and a world-wide reputation for quality products supported by a dealer network.

To counteract Komatsu's drive, Caterpillar reduced production capacity 25 percent, cut inventories 37 percent, slimmed down its labor force, and closed plants. With plant closures Caterpillar was no longer a vertically integrated company. It defended market share with deep price discounts, and offered smaller machines to smaller sized contractors. The heart of the turnaround decision was to (a) cut operating costs by 22 percent, (b) give more price authority to local managers, and (c) diversify into other product areas.

PLANT WITH A FUTURE

In October 1986, Caterpillar president Peter Donis said:

> Although we've reduced costs by more than 20 percent, we're not stopping there. We've returned to profitability, but we expect cost and price pressures to continue. Our costs are still 15 to 20 percent higher than our foreign competitor's, and in spite of the dollar weakening, transaction prices for our products are about the same now that they were in 1981. So, Caterpillar's long-term profitability will not be secure until we do, in fact, become the industry's low cost producer. We've developed a strategy for achieving the additional cost reduction. We call it our Plant with a Future.[13]

For Caterpillar, the Plant with a Future (PWAF) concept portrayed in Exhibit 3 embraced all elements of manufacturing as well as product design, supplier relationships, and logistics. Although this new manufacturing strategy went beyond simple cost cutting, its implementation and integration of facilities would continue for the rest of this century. At the heart of PWAF was automation, new factory layouts, and continuous work flow. Caterpillar executive vice president, Pierre Gueridon, said, "We believe computer-integrated manufacturing is our supreme weapon for cost reduction. It's the area where we have the largest long term advantage over the Japanese."

Based on a cell manufacturing concept, plants and equipment were arranged to process families of components from start to finish. For example, machining, welding, heat treating, and painting might all be functions within a single cell. Work flow was continuous. Since all cells fed the assembly line just-in-time, it required JIT delivery to the cells. Immediate objectives were to simplify and integrate.

EXHIBIT 3 PWAF AND ITS THREE BASIC COMPONENTS

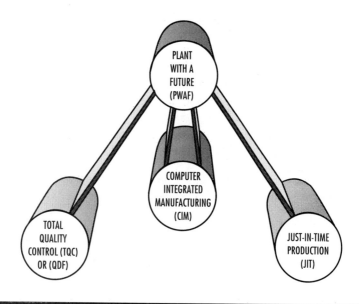

Computer integrated manufacturing (CIM) linked self-contained manufacturing cells (i.e., independent islands of automation) to a material, tooling, and information network to allow for electronic communication between engineering, logistics, and the factory floor. By the next decade, interplant communication would be routine through a corporate information center coupled with global marketing and financial data bases. With complete implementation of the strategy and integration of operations, all systems, from the plant's host computer to personal computers on the shop floor, could communicate to result in unprecedented coordination and optimization of all manufacturing functions: supplier delivery, scheduling of equipment, tooling, quality control, maintenance, and troubleshooting.

Gueridon said, "At our Gosselies [Belgium] plant, for example, we expect PWAF changes to result in a 22 percent reduction in material costs and a 31 percent reduction in labor costs by 1990."

Conek, the Mexican subsidiary, exemplified successful execution of this new strategy. Management implemented JIT and Duran quality control techniques, small QC circles at the shop level, and an annual QIP to resolve bigger challenges. Critical to success at Monterrey were cost and quality control.

On the other hand, CBSA, the Brazilian subsidiary, best reflected "gradualism": Caterpillar's chief approach to automation and implementation of the PWAF. PWAF automation was conceived as a self-financing program with highest priorities for capital investments. Funds generated from reduced inventories and improvement in efficiencies would finance these investments. Caterpillar management expected its manufacturing plants to migrate from present systems to a hybrid system and to end up with PWAF, a purely customer-driven manufacturing philosophy.

RETURN TO PROFITABILITY AND A NEW CHALLENGE

The Japanese invader was not invincible. Komatsu's exports decreased because most were dollar denominated; and the dollar was overpriced in terms of yen. Its profits fell by a third in 1986.

On the other hand, Caterpillar's competitive position sharply improved. Profits in 1986 were $76 million ($0.77 per share), and, in 1987, $350 million ($3.51 per share). Sales were up; employment at Caterpillar increased by 732 persons in 1987; and market share rose. Exhibit 4 depicts global market shares in 1987.

Caterpillar still had the most recognizable and respected name in the construction equipment industry. Its products commanded a price premium. It had a world-wide dealership and parts distribution network. Project teams were working on quality improvement projects. A massive program of statistical process control training had been successfully launched to transfer the responsibility for quality control to employees. The PWAF strategy, now in

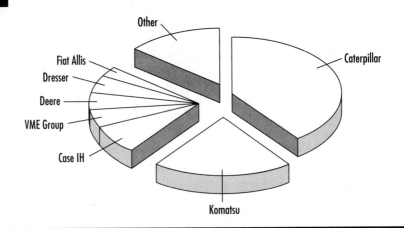

EXHIBIT 4 SHARES OF WORLD CONSTRUCTION MACHINERY SALES, 1987

Source: Robert S. Eckley, "Caterpillar's Ordeal: Foreign Competition in Capitol Goods," *Business Horizons*, vol.32(2) (March/April, 1989): 80–86.

place, seemed to function well. Certainly 1988 would be a good and trouble-free year.

A banner year, 1988, not only witnessed a 25 percent rise in revenue but also a 76 percent leap in profits. (See Exhibit 5 for summary financial data and other statistics.) Alexander Blanton, of Merrill Lynch, said, "I estimate the company's earnings power at between $8 and $10 per share by 1990." Exhibit 6 graphically illustrates quarterly changes in net income during the decade.

Komatsu had not been especially successful in Latin America. Its Mexican joint venture had never produced a profit. Brazilian losses severely affected corporate profitability. It did not have the dealership network that Caterpillar had long ago established throughout Central and South America as well as the Caribbean.

Nevertheless, the Komatsu-Dresser strategic alliance presented a serious challenge to Caterpillar in Latin America. With both Komatsu and Dresser, along with Caterpillar, having a strong manufacturing presence in Brazil, this market might become the strategic battleground for Latin America. Although all companies had older, less efficient manufacturing facilities, Caterpillar had already initiated its program of modernization to cut costs, improve quality, and consolidate product line—the PWAF strategy.

In its 1988 JV agreement, Komatsu would give up to $300 million to Dresser to upgrade factories, which, prior to the agreement had been running at 50 percent capacity. Although both Komatsu and Dresser continued to introduce new products, they maintained separate, yet competing, dealerships.

By July 1989, Caterpillar had registered strong gains in sales outside of the U.S.; approximately 52 percent of business now derived from foreign sources. (See data in Exhibit 7 for foreign versus domestic sales, 1984–1988.) Global revenues of $5.7 billion marked a 15 percent increase over the comparable six-month period in 1988. Net income for the first half on 1989 of $282 million resulted in $2.78 profit per share of common stock compared to $2.60 per share the first six months of 1988. Employment rose to 60,881.[14]

Early 1989 recorded no further major changes in the Latin American environments for either MNC. Considerable uncertainty reined in most key Latin American markets. Argentina experienced yet another economic crisis as a new president was about to assume office. Peru's hyperinflation and communist terrorism produced a chaotic situation as the country entered a campaign year for the presidency. Brazil's economic condition continued to deteriorate; national elections were scheduled for late 1989. The most stable economies appeared to be Chile, which had successfully implemented a program partially consistent with free market philosophy, and Mexico, which was trying to move toward a market economy. Chile would elect a new president by year's end; and Mexico's president was still in the first half of his term.

Caterpillar had parried Komatsu's strategic thrust but not without difficulties. For instance, for the three-year 1986–1988 period, decreases in production costs fell short of the targeted 5-percent annual rate of reduction. Part of the problem could be attributed to translation losses due to unfavorable swings in foreign exchange rates. During 1989 the PWAF program experi-

EXHIBIT 5 CATERPILLAR, INC.: CONSOLIDATED FINANCIAL POSITION AT DECEMBER 31, 19___

	1980	1981	1982	1983	1984	1985	1986	1987	1988
Current assets	2933	3544	3433	3383	2915	2982	3363	4006	5317
Intangible assets	—	147	117	99	96	77	60	47	71
Other fixed assets	3165	3594	3651	3486	3212	2957	2865	3578	4298
TOTAL ASSETS	6098	7285	7201	6968	6223	6016	6288	7631	9686
Current liabilities	1711	2369	1197	1576	1939	1742	2180	2758	3435
Long term debt	955	1059	2508	2055	1432	1206	959	1308	2138
Equity	3432	3857	3496	3337	2852	3068	3149	3565	4113
TOTAL DEBT/EQUITY	6098	7285	7201	6968	6223	6016	6288	7631	9686

CONSOLIDATED INCOME STATEMENT AT DECEMBER 31, 19___

	1980	1981	1982	1983	1984	1985	1986	1987	1988
Revenue	8598	9154	6469	5424	6576	6725	7321	8180	10255
Operating profit	831	903	(253)	(310)	(339)	233	137	498	924
Net profit (loss)	565	579	(180)	(345)	(428)	198	76	350	616
Dividends per share of common stock ($)	2,325	2.40	2.40	1.50	1.25	0.50	0.50	0.50	0.75
Average number of employees	86,350	83,455	73,249	58,402	61,624	53,616	53,731	54,463	60,558

Note: Figures given in millions of U.S. dollars.

Sources: Figures derived from annual reports.

EXHIBIT 6 CATERPILLAR QUARTERLY NET INCOME

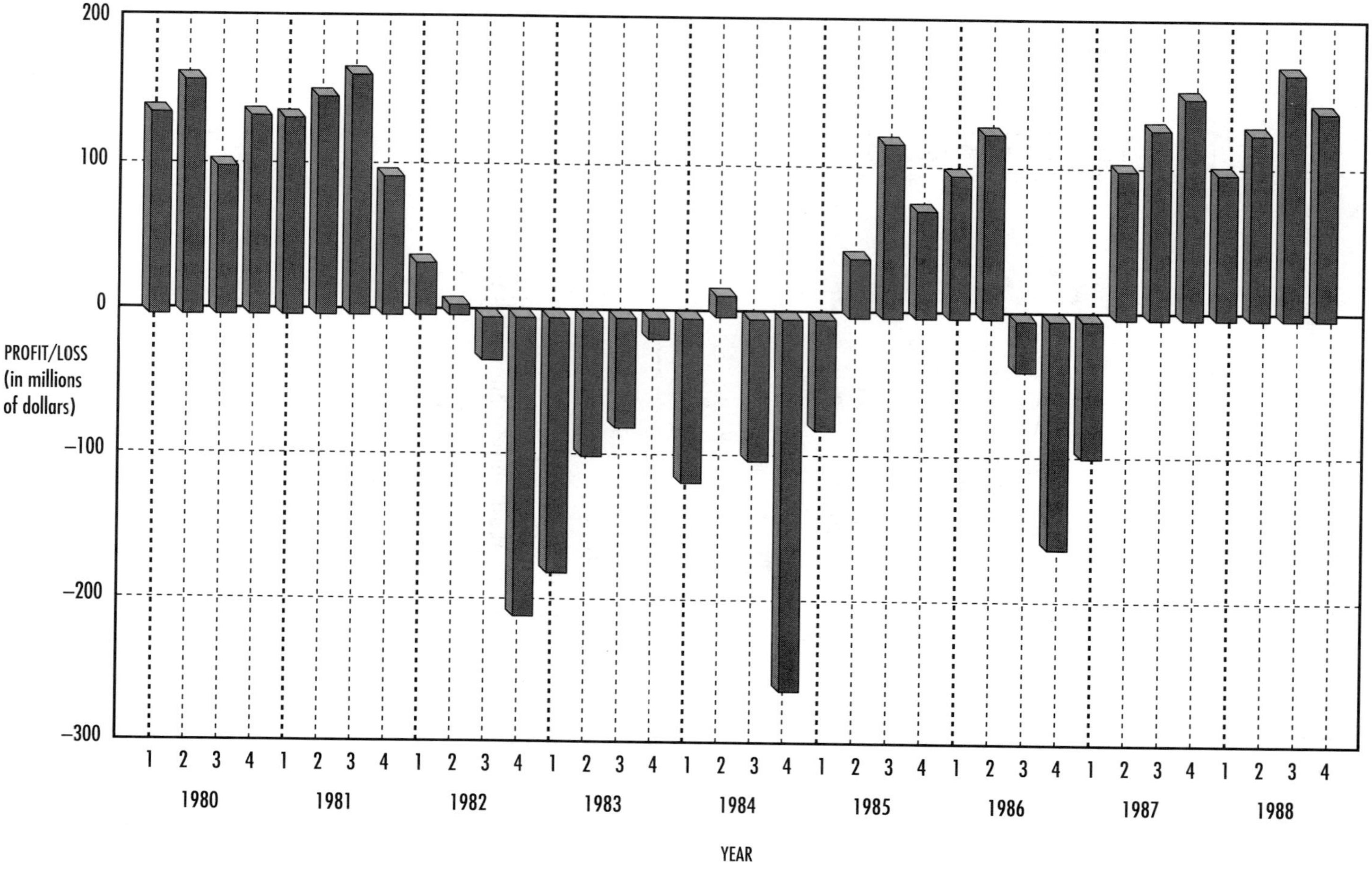

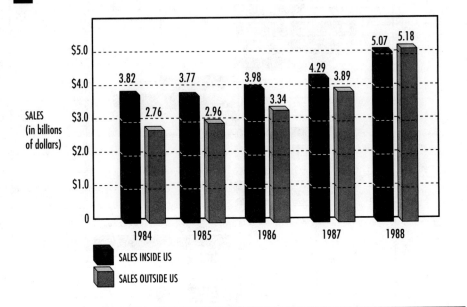

EXHIBIT 7 CATERPILLAR, INC.: FOREIGN AND DOMESTIC SALES

enced cost overruns exceeding $300 million. Uncertainty still characterized Latin American markets. A new competitor, Komatsu Dresser Company, was in training for yet another round. In early 1989, the Strategic Planning Committee, comprised of senior managers from various functional areas, was charged with the task of evaluating strategic options for the 1990s. The challenge to Caterpillar continued.

ENDNOTES

1. "A Letter for Caterpillar Management," April 1989 (internal document):4.

2. "Cat Unit Merges Brazilian Facilities," *Journal Star* (Peoria, Ill.), (December 10, 1988): 2.

3. Komatsu, *1983 Annual Report*, p. 3.

4. Komatsu, *1984 Annual Report*, p. 10.

5. "Komatsu Raises Stake in Mexico Venture," *Japanese Economic Journal,* 25 (August 29, 1987): 13.

6. "A Letter for Caterpillar Management," cover.

7. "Komatsu Digs Deeper into the U.S.," *Business Week* (October 1, 1984): 53.

8. Farnsworth, Clyde, "Chattanooga Reviving Itself with Foreign Capital," *Chattanooga Times* (October 10, 1985).

9. Komatsu, *[Quarterly] Financial Report* (March 31, 1988): 2.

10. *Wall Street Journal* (August 17, 1988): 32.

11. "Dresser, Komatsu Form Joint Venture," *Pit & Quarry* (March 1988): 12.

12. Komatsu, *1987 Annual Report* p. 8.

13. Speech by Peter Donis at the General Electric/Northwestern University Executive Dialog Series, October 14, 1986.

14. Caterpillar 1989 quarterly financial reports.

APPENDIX

fisCAL Software

INTRODUCTION

Accompanying *Strategic Management Cases* is the financial analysis software package fisCAL, a product of the Halcyon Group. The most comprehensive microcomputer-based program of its type available, fisCAL is widely used by financial analysts, investors, and strategic decision makers. fisCAL provides an interactive financial decision-making environment, producing a wide variety of analyses and reports and is capable of multi-period analysis. Using its data base of industry statistics, fisCAL generates comparisons between the firm and competitors in its industry. The following list contains reports generated by fisCAL.

- Breakeven analysis
- Financial ratio analysis
- Industry comparisons by dollar value
- Industry comparisons by percentage
- Operating capital analysis
- Cash market value analysis (5 methods)
- Trends analysis, including z-score bankruptcy predictor
- Cash flow analysis
- Operating ratio analysis
- Dupont strategic profit model
- Index of sustainable growth model
- Gross margin return on inventory investment model
- Statistical anlysis
- Pro forma income statements, 5 years
- Pro forma balance sheets, 5 years
- Projected cash flow analysis, 5 years

Despite its sophistication, fisCAL is easy to use. All instructions may be selected from easy-to-understand menus, and the reports generated by fisCAL are clear and easy to read. To guide the user through the analyses and to avoid "information overload," each investigation is accompanied by a report summary written in both a quantitative and a narrative format.

Eight cases from *Strategic Management Cases* have been prepared for use with fisCAL. They range in complexity from single period break-even analysis in the Pizza Delights case to sophisticated considerations of financial expansion and merger in the Eastman Kodak case. Table 1 contains a listing of the fisCAL cases along with the strategic financial factors addressed in each case.

Using the order of cases suggested here, the student is gradually introduced to increasingly more complex financial analyses. Starting with single-period analysis and simple financial procedures such as breakeven analysis in the first fisCAL case, students can work at their own speed to discover how the program works. By the fifth case, Sonoco Products Company, students will be able to utilize multiperiod data to compare statements and financial ratios with data from industry competitors, analyze trends in balance sheet and income statement accounts, interpret Dupont strategic profit models, generate

TABLE 1 fisCAL CASES

CASE NUMBER	CASE	STRATEGIC FINANCIAL FACTORS
3	Pizza Delights	Growth Profit sustainability
23	NEC Corporation's Entry into European Microcomputers	Industry Comparisons Downside Risk
12	Toys "R" Us, 1989	Expansion in Slow-Growth Industry Multiyear Analysis
13	Delta Air Lines	Downside Risk Price Wars Expansion
8	Sonoco Products Company	High Growth Rate Heavy Debt Risk Factors
10	Lincoln Electric Company, 1989	Controlled Expansion Controlled Costs Stock Value
25	Caterpillar, Inc., in Latin America	Market Competition Profitability Cost Reduction
9	Eastman Kodak Co.	Expansion Merger Cost of Capital

pro forma statements, do "what-if" analysis, and use a wide range of other procedures and models available with fisCAL. Students who have had previous experience with advanced financial analysis concepts may opt to start with one of the later cases.

The following is a case-by-case summary of the strategic financial issues and applicable reports generated by fisCAL. Instructions for installing and starting the program on your computer are contained in the fisCAL package.

Case 3: PIZZA DELIGHTS

Financial considerations in the Pizza Delights case center around profitability concerns and the future growth of the enterprise. Reports are for single-period analysis only, making this a good case to use as an introduction to fisCAL.

The following reports are applicable to the investigation of the strategic financial issues in the Pizza Delights case: breakeven analysis, comparison of financial statement accounts to industry norms, and financial ratios comparisons. These reports will reveal a number of areas of concern to Pizza Delights management, including the necessity to engage in cost cutting. Since cost containment is a primary consideration in the case, special attention also should be given to the firm's breakeven analysis report.

If the student is just beginning to use fisCAL, more advanced analyses might best be omitted for now. Growth considerations, however, are an important topic in the case. Therefore the fisCAL index of sustainable growth report, which compares profits, dividends, and payout ratios to industry norms, might prove interesting. Although several additional reports are also generated by fisCAL for Pizza Delights (including operating capital analysis, cash market value analysis, and Dupont strategic profit model) these should be studied only to get an idea of their utility, since these analyses do not bear directly on the issues in the case.

Case 23: NEC CORPORATION'S ENTRY INTO EUROPEAN MICROCOMPUTERS

The NEC case is an excellent one for the introduction of multiple-firm analysis using fisCAL. In addition to the 1984 results for NEC, financial data for six competitors has also been coded. Included are the 1983 figures for Apple Computer, Commodore International, Hewlett-Packard, IBM, Olivetti, and Tandy. To standardize the data, figures for Olivetti were converted to dollars at the rate of 1,000 Italian lira per dollar and entered as millions of dollars. All analyses are for single period results only. Therefore, trends analysis and pro forma results are not applicable in the NEC case.

Breakeven analysis, industry comparison of balance sheet and income statement items, financial ratio analysis, and operating capital analysis are all relevant in the NEC case. Given the availability of these reports for all seven

TABLE 2 APPLICABLE REPORTS BY CASE

	PIZZA	NEC (1)	TOYS	DELTA	SONOCO	LINCOLN	CATERPILLAR	EASTMAN
Single Period								
Summary	X	X	X	X	X	X	X	X
Breakeven	X	X	X	X	X	X		
Industry comparisons	X	X						
Financial ratios	X	X		X	X			X
Operating capital		X		X	X			X
Cash market value						X (2)		X
Trends								
Analysis		X	X	X	X		X	
Cash flow			X	X	X			X
Operating ratios			X	X	X			X
samSON								
Dupont model		X		X	X	X	X	X
Index of sustainable growth	X	X	X		X	X		
Growth model ROII								
proFOR								
Statistical analysis (3)	X					X	X	X
Future position			X		X	X	X	X

Notes:

(1) For the NEC case, reports listed are also available for six competitors: Apple Computer, Commodore, Hewlett-Packard, IBM, Olivetti, and Tandy.

(2) In the Lincoln case, students should convert cash market value to per share stock value manually.

(3) To obtain statistical analysis of past trends, students should <PRINT SCREEN> when the statistical analysis is shown in proFOR.

firms, students should be able to obtain a clear picture of the dynamics of competition in the European microcomputer industry.

Recent events described at the end of the case pose the direct threat of market deterioration. Therefore, downside risk considerations should be a primary concern in the financial analysis of NEC and its competitors. NEC's Dupont strategic growth model and its index of sustainable growth should provide some insight into the likelihood of NEC surviving in case of restricted market conditions. Comparing these anlayses with those of the six other competitors might also lend some insight into predicting the outcome of a market shakeout.

Case 12: TOYS "R" US, 1989

The Toys "R" Us case provides the first opportunity to do multiple-year analysis. Data for 1987 and 1988 are coded for fisCAL analysis. The principal financial strategic issue for this industry-leading company is maintaining its expansion program in a slow-growth industry.

Trends, cash flow, and operating ratio analyses should be carefully studied. Although the comparisons are based on only two years of data, significant tendencies are highlighted. Given the company's strategy of rapid growth, the index of sustainable growth report also should be interpreted carefully.

Given the size and dominance of Toys "R" Us, industry comparisons generated by fisCAL should be taken lightly and should not be a primary focus of study. Considering TRU's high fixed costs and expansion plans, however, breakeven analysis is important.

Pro forma statements are available in the Toys "R" Us case. These are especially helpful in analyzing potential problems associated with the company's ambitious growth strategy.

Case 13: DELTA AIR LINES

The principal strategic financial issues in the Delta Air Lines case are

(1) Effects of the industry-wide price wars on the firm's profitability
(2) Provision of the financial resources for the company's planned expansion
(3) Downside risk associated with predictions of decreased industry profits in the future

fisCAL analysis may be used to address each of these issues, either one at a time or simultaneously.

Relevant single-period fisCAL reports in the Delta case are breakeven analysis, financial ratio analysis, and operating capital analysis. Since the passenger airline industry is undergoing a severe but temporary "shock wave," industry comparisons should be interpreted cautiously. A cash market value analysis may also generated for Delta, but as there are no merger, acquisition, or divestiture issues in the case, it is not relevant for decision-making purposes.

Trends analyses generated by fisCAL are helpful in the Delta case. Two years of data, 1986 and 1987, have been coded for analysis. Trends analysis reports, cash flow analysis, and operating ratios should all be studied for relevant decision issues. Given the questions surrounding future profitability and planned expansion, the Dupont analysis of the composition of net profits and the five-year projected statements generated by the proFOR routine are very useful in assisting strategic decision making in the case.

Case 8: SONOCO PRODUCTS, INC.

Sonoco is a high growth rate company that has recently acquired a sizable new subsidiary by financing the acquisition with debt. Strategic financial issues therefore revolve around the effects of this acquisition and the accompanying debt load on future profitability and subsequent growth of the enterprise. Two years of financial data, 1987 and 1988, have been coded for analysis.

Breakeven analysis, financial ratio comparisons, and an analysis of operating capital are all relevant in the Sonoco case, since each of these can shed light on the effects of the acquisition. fisCAL multi-year analyses are also relevant. Trends in balance sheet and income statement accounts and in ratios are essential to understanding the strategic financial situation in which the company has placed itself. Cash flow analysis, which highlights cash flows from operations versus investing and financing activities, should be studied in light of the recent merger.

Considering Sonoco's stated policy of sustained rapid growth, both the Dupont analysis of the composition of net profit margin and the index of sustainable growth analysis should be considered relevant to decision makers. Pro forma statements should also be studied.

Case 10: LINCOLN ELECTRIC COMPANY, 1989

Lincoln Electric, in contrast to Sonoco, is a firm with the stated policy of internal growth through the retention of earnings and stock purchases of employees rather than through the use of debt. fisCAL financial analysis should therefore center on whether Lincoln's policies of slow, controlled expansion, close control over costs, and managing for enhanced stock value are adequate to provide for the company's capital needs.

Relevant single period fisCAL analyses for the Lincoln Electric case are the breakeven analysis, which highlights cost factors, and the cash market value analysis, which indicates how the employee/owners' investments are performing. (Note that the cash market value analysis must be manually converted to per share data to be relevant to that issue.)

Nine years of historical data provide the basis for trends analysis. Although most balance sheet and income statement trends are not significant, trends in ratios, most of which are positive, lend support to the company's very careful financial management policies. Cash flow analysis is not relevant in this case but the Dupont strategic profit model is. Given Lincoln Electric's policy of using very little financial leverage, the index of sustainable growth model should be studied in terms of the options that the policy foregoes.

Case 25: CATERPILLAR, INC., IN LATIN AMERICA

Strategic financial factors in the Caterpillar case include intense market competition, profitability, and cost reduction. Caterpillar faces a severe challenge to its Latin American markets from Komatsu, supported by a powerful Komatsu-Dresser joint venture in the United States. The company has recently adopted a new competitive strategy that includes significant improvements in cost effectiveness and a large-scale plant modernization program. fisCAL analysis should therefore focus on projections of long-run performance in light of these goals.

Since much of the detail for individual balance sheet and income statement accounts is omitted in this case, in-depth industry comparisons and financial ratio analysis are not available. Summary data have been coded for nine years, however, and these provide a good basis for establishing trends. The fisCAL trend analysis report reveals that, while the company is correct in choosing cost effectiveness as one of its major objectives, its recent performance—cost trend vs. revenue—can certainly be improved.

Although the company's most immediate concerns are controlling costs and meeting the Komatsu challenge in Latin America, long-run growth goals should also be assessed. Both the Dupont strategic profit model and the index of sustainable growth analysis are therefore relevant.

Pro forma analysis is perhaps the most important area for analyzing the Caterpillar case. The five-year financial statement projections and cash flow analysis, which can be altered by changing the assumptions to fit various competitive scenarios, should be thoroughly studied.

Case 9: EASTMAN KODAK COMPANY: THE STERLING DRUG ACQUISITION

The Eastman Kodak case provides an opportunity for more sophisticated financial analysis. Strategic issues in the case that may be analyzed with fisCAL are the effects of a large recent merger and future expansion plans of the company.

Eastman is facing possible obsolescence of its main product lines and has recently embarked on a program of diversification. The recent acquisition of Sterling Drug Company, which dramatically increased the company's revenues, has also created a significant increase in its debt position. Eight years of data have been coded for fisCAL analysis.

Relevant single period analyses include industry comparisons, financial ratio analysis, and cash market value analysis. Note that 1988 data are for the newly merged entity and should therefore be critical in assessing Eastman's ability to assimilate its acquisition of Sterling Drug.

Trends in financial statement accounts and ratios as compared to industry standards reveal a number of strong and weak points in the case that should be noted. Multi-year cash flow analysis is useful for separating the cash flow from operations from the effects of financing the Sterling merger. The Dupont strategic profit model, which analyzes the sources of Eastman's high rates of returns, should also be studied. The index of sustainable growth, which shows a very high growth rate for the company, should be used as well.

fisCAL pro forma statistical analysis and five-year projections for Eastman are perhaps the most important reports in this case. Assumptions about sales growth rates and costs should be altered and "what-if" analysis run. The company's program of expansion will require significant earnings in the future, so the analysis should try to determine the company's sensitivity to downturns in revenue and possible increases in both fixed and variable costs.